D1688333

Gutenberg-Jahrbuch 2023

98. Jahrgang
Begründet 1926 von Aloys Ruppel

Gutenberg-Jahrbuch 2023

Im Auftrag der Gutenberg-Gesellschaft herausgegeben
von Philip Ajouri, Julia Bangert, Gerhard Lauer
und Nikolaus Weichselbaumer

Vorwort

Jahrbücher wechseln zwar regelmäßig ihre Jahreszahlen, seltener dagegen ihre Herausgeber. Mit dem Gutenberg-Jahrbuch 2023 gibt es einen solchen Wechsel in der Herausgeberschaft. Stephan Füssel, der das Jahrbuch seit 1994 herausgegeben hat, hat die Herausgeberschaft an seinen Nachfolger auf dem Gutenberg-Lehrstuhl der Universität Mainz, Gerhard Lauer, übergeben. Das ist nach fast dreißig Jahren ein Wechsel. Mit Gerhard Lauer treten in die Herausgeberschaft auch die Buchwissenschaftler Philip Ajouri, Julia Bangert und Nikolaus Weichselbaumer ein. Sie geben zusammen die nächsten Bände des Gutenberg-Jahrbuchs heraus. An dieser Stelle danken die neuen Herausgeber Stephan Füssel herzlich für seine Arbeit in den letzten drei Dekaden. Großer Dank gebührt auch Ralf de Jong, der seit 2003 die herausragende Gestaltung des Jahrbuchs verantwortet hat. Mit dem vorliegenden Band übernimmt Dan Reynolds diese Aufgabe. Er hatte schon einmal indirekt das Gutenberg-Jahrbuch geprägt: der Band 2010 war aus Reynolds *Malabar* gesetzt.

Zugleich wechselte Michael Ebling im Oktober 2022 vom Amt des Oberbürgermeisters der Stadt Mainz in das des Innenministers des Landes Rheinland-Pfalz. Damit schied er zugleich aus dem Amt des Präsidenten der Gutenberg-Gesellschaft aus, ein Amt, das er mehr als zehn Jahre innehatte. Auch ihm danken die Herausgeber mit Nachdruck für seine Arbeit.

Am 17. Dezember 2022 verstarb Eckehart SchumacherGebler, Drucker, Schriftsetzer und Bewahrer vieler Bestände der Druckerei-Geschichte und auch Träger des Gutenberg-Preises 2022. Sein Aufsatz über den *Einfluss Bodonis und anderer ausländischer Schriftschneider auf die Entstehung klassizistischer Druckschriften in Deutschland* im Gutenberg-Jahrbuch von 1993 hat den Lesern des Jahrbuchs schon damals einen Eindruck seiner stupenden technikhistorischen Kenntnisse gegeben. Zusammen mit Eckehart SchumacherGebler erhielt der amerikanische Kunsthistoriker Jeffrey Hamburger den Gutenberg-Preis des Jahres 2022.

Das Gutenberg-Jahrbuch 2023 bringt eine Reihe von Beiträgen von der Frühgeschichte des Drucks bis zur Typografiegeschichte des 20. Jahrhunderts. Don Skemer sichtet die erstaunlich vielen, bis heute erhaltenen Manuskripte des *Philobiblon, sive, De amore librorum* (1345) des Durhamer Bischofs Richard de Bury und diskutiert die Funktion dieses Buchs über die Bücherliebe für die Schreiber, Leser, Besitzer und Bibliotheken in England und den deutschen Ländern des 15. Jahrhunderts. Das Verhältnis von Papier und Buchdruck im Spätmittelalter und die Frage der angemessenen, auch der statistisch-messenden Erfassung des

Wandels von der Papierherstellung und -nutzung im Übergang zum Druckzeitalter sind das Thema des Beitrags von Paul Schweitzer-Martin.

Harald Berger geht der Frage nach dem Verfasser der wiederholt in Basel durch Nikolaus Kessler und in Hagenau durch Heinrich Gran Ende des 15. Jahrhunderts gedruckten logischen Werke nach, die das Lehrbuch des Petrus Hispanus zur Vorlage haben, das *Commentum in primum tractatum Petri Hispani*. Eine verwandte Frage nach dem Verfasser analysiert Louis Pitschmann und argumentiert, dass die *Küchenmeisterei* und andere, ihr vorausgehende volkssprachliche Inkunabeln nicht einem unbekannten Koch oder Mediziner zuzuschreiben sind, sondern wahrscheinlicher dem Augsburger Druckerverleger Johann Bämler. Vinicius de Freitas Morais untersucht die Bild- und Erzählereignisse in den antijüdischen Inkunabeln zu der angeblichen Hostienschändung zu Sternberg 1492. Einen bisher unbekannten Prospekt des Nürnberger Druckers Anton Koberger hat Randall Herz in der Universitätsbibliothek Erlangen-Nürnberg gefunden. Er enthält eine Ermahnung an die Priester zur geistlichen Reinheit während der Hl. Messe und ist typografiegeschichtlich von Interesse, da er mit derselben Type gedruckt wurde wie die lateinische Edition der Schedelschen Weltchronik von 1493. Schließlich stellt Danielle Gurnelli den Karriereweg und das Werk des florentinischen Buchmalers Bartolomeo Varnucci vor.

An die nur wenigen bekannte Tradition des hebräischen Buchdrucks in den jüdischen Gemeinden des 17. und 18. Jahrhunderts in Novy Oleksiniec nahe Brody (Ukraine) in der damaligen polnisch-litauischen Königlichen Republik erinnert Marvin Heller. Hansjörg Rabanser geht den kaum bekannten druckenden und verlegenden Gesellen, Buchbindern und Buchhändlern des 17. und 18. Jahrhunderts in Innsbruck nach, die nicht unwesentlich zur Produktion der Bücher damals beigetragen haben. Die Fälschungen und illegitimen Nachdrucke des philosophischen Romans *Bélisaire* des französischen Enzyklopädisten Jean-François Marmontel betrachtet der Beitrag von Muriel Collart, Daniel Droixhe und Alice Piette am Beispiel des Nachdrucks durch Jean-François Bassompierre aus dem Jahr 1767.

Jade Samara Piaia und Priscila Lena Farias beschreiben den regen Handel mit beweglichen Lettern zwischen Deutschland und Brasilien um die Jahrhundertwende zum 20. Jahrhundert. Laudationes, Nachrufe und der Bericht der Gutenberg-Gesellschaft runden den Band ab.

Wir danken allen Beiträgerinnen und Beiträgern des Jahrbuchs, dem Typografen Dan Reynolds und dem Verlagsleiter des Harrassowitz Verlags Stephan Specht, dann auch Julia Kammerzelt und Olga Lemmerich für die Unterstützung bei den Korrekturgängen für dieses Jahrbuch. Nun kann es seine Leser finden.

Mainz, im Frühjahr 2023

Philip Ajouri | Julia Bangert | Gerhard Lauer | Nikolaus Weichselbaumer

Inhaltsverzeichnis

Vorwort **5**

Susanne Zippel **9**
Laudatio auf Eckehart SchumacherGebler

Falk Eisermann **14**
Laudatio auf Jeffrey Hamburger

Don C. Skemer **17**
Philobiblon and Its Medieval Readers

Paul Schweitzer-Martin **48**
Zum Verhältnis von Papier und Buchdruck im Spätmittelalter

Daniele Guernelli **58**
Bartolomeo Varnucci imprenditore del libro: ulteriori aggiornamenti

Louis A. Pitschmann **71**
Johann Bämler and the Making of *Küchenmeisterei*

Vinicius de Freitas Morais **87**
Das Blut Christi und die blutenden Hostien in den Inkunabeln zum Sternberger Fall (1492): Überlegungen zu ihren Bildern, den Normen ihrer antijüdischen Andachtstypen und zur Genese der Endfassung der Erzählereignisse

Randall Herz **117**
O Vos Sacerdotes Dei: A New Broadside from Anton Koberger's Nuremberg Press. With notes on the content, audience, and transmission, including an analysis of the typographical relation to the Latin edition of the *Liber chronicarum* and its family of types

Harald Berger **140**
Wer könnte der Verfasser der logischen Werke in den Drucken Basel 1487 sowie Hagenau 1495 und 1503 sein?

Hansjörg Rabanser **150**
Buchhändler, verlegende Buchbinder und druckende Gesellen des 17. und 18. Jahrhunderts in Innsbruck

Marvin J. Heller **174**
Hebrew printing in Novy Oleksiniec: A Rose in the desert: a Brief, Barely Remembered Hebrew Press

Muriel Collart, Daniel Droixhe et Alice Piette **185**
« Je suis à la troisième édition de *Bélisaire* ». Une contrefaçon du *Bélisaire* de Marmontel par le Liégeois Jean-François Bassompierre (1767)

Jade Samara Piaia and Priscila Lena Farias **199**
Movable metal type trade between Germany and Brazil at the turn of the 19th to the 20th century

Falk Eisermann **206**
Neue Publikationen zur Inkunabelforschung: das Jahr 2022. Mit Nachträgen zu den Jahren 2020 und 2021

Stephan Füssel und Julia Bangert **237**
Nachruf auf Eckehart SchumacherGebler

Jahresbericht der internationalen Gutenberg-Gesellschaft für 2022 **238**

Abkürzungsverzeichnis **245**

Ehrentafel **252**

Impressum **256**

Susanne Zippel

Laudatio auf Eckehart SchumacherGebler,
gehalten in Mainz am 25. Juni 2022

Lieber Professor Eckehart SchumacherGebler,
sehr geehrte Anwesende,

Gut Ding will Weile haben – und jetzt ist es gut, denn endlich kommt er, der verdiente Ritterschlag, der seit langem schon verdient worden war. So sehr verdient, dass ich in den zugestandenen Redeminuten gar nicht erst versuchen werde, den Leistungskatalog des Preisträgers komplett aufzulisten. Die hier anwesenden Gäste, größtenteils allein für dich heute von weither angereist, wissen darum und sind längst deine Groupies, lieber Eckehart SchumacherGebler. Oder sage ich besser ESG – das Akronym, das in der Fach- und Freundeswelt geradezu mit Ehr-Furcht ausgesprochen wird?

Kennengelernt habe ich ESG 2004 auf den Leipziger Typotagen, ein von ihm aus der Taufe gehobenes *gehobenes* Symposium, das bis heute Bestand hat! Ich erinnere mich lebhaft an Sprecher wie den unvergessenen Kurt Weidemann, an das »Maschinengewehr der Typografie« Günter Gerhard Lange, an Hans Eduard Meier und Hildegard Korger oder an – den heute auch unter uns sitzenden – Martin Majoor. Das kann er, der ESG – die Großen, die er alle kennt, versammeln, um sie den Kleinen vorzustellen, damit sie mit ihnen groß werden können.

Doch woher kommt dieses Vermögen? Überfliegen wir in gebotener Kürze den tonnenschweren Katalog des Überfliegers:

Begonnen hatte alles ohne den Big Bang für einen jungen Menschen, der sich – vom Elternhaus abgenabelt – auf den Weg in die große weite Welt macht, um seine Träume zu erfüllen. Eckehart wurde in eine Druckerfamilie hineingeboren und irgendwann hieß es: »Der Junge übernimmt die Firma.« – Der Junge kam also zum Thema nicht wie die Jungfrau zum Kinde, sondern die Mutter übergab dem Jungen die Druckerei in der Münchner Goethestraße, nachdem dieser bereits willig eine Lehre zum Drucker absolviert hatte; auch Setzer wäre eine Option gewesen, doch mit dem Drucken war angeblich schneller mehr Geld zu verdienen.

Selbstverständlich wurde er später auch Setzer. Drucker und Setzer in Personalunion; Sie alle kennen den anerkennenden Begriff aus dem Fachjargon dafür. Nach den handwerklichen Ausbildungen folgte noch das Fachstudium an der Akademie für das Graphische Gewerbe München. Und dann: die Übernahme des Familienbetriebes.

Schnell entwickelt der junge Mann Passion bis hin zur Besessenheit für die Zunft, doch von Beginn an immer auch das Unternehmerkalkül. Diese Tugendpaarung wird ihn später auf die Weltbühne des Schwarzen Handwerks heben.

Der unternehmerische Start war alles andere als einfach. Zum einen fehlte ein schlüssiges Firmenkonzept, bis dato druckte man querbeet, was eben so verlangt wurde. Und: Der Schriftbestand war nicht sensationell. Man investierte damals weniger in neue Schriften als in vermeintlich effizientere Druckmaschinen.

Genau das machte insbesondere den Schriftgießereien zu schaffen. Sie entwickelten die raffinierte Strategie, ihre neuesten Kreationen nicht mehr Druckereien anzubieten, sondern den Werbeagenturen. Und fand denn ein Art-Director Gefallen an der Ausdruckskraft einer neuen Schrift, war die betreuende Druckerei gezwungen, sich diese zuzulegen. Auf diese Weise entstanden neue Spezialbetriebe, die sogenannten Layoutsetzereien, die sich schnell ausbreiteten, indes – in München fehlte solch ein Angebot.

Es schlägt die Stunde für SchumacherGebler. Er gründet neben der Druckerei – die weiter bestehen bleibt – eine Layoutsetzerei, ausgestattet mit den wesentlichsten Schriften seiner Zeit. So entsteht das Typostudio SchumacherGebler, das sich bald bis über die Tore der Stadt hinaus einen Namen macht. Wir sind im Jahr 1961.

Beeindruckend – nicht ganz uneitel – wird in den Schriftmusterbüchern, den Specimen der Setzerei, ab sofort ein Buchstabe aus dem Alphabet gestrichen, nämlich das große F, an dessen Stelle das große S gesetzt wird: A B C D *E S G* … Die Initialen des Hausherren werden zum Manifest (der buchstäblich initialzündende F-S-Tausch ist übrigens Kurt Weidemann zu verdanken) und stehen bis heute nicht nur für einen Namen, sondern gleichermaßen für ein einzigartiges Qualitätsprogramm.

Der Laden läuft und wächst in jeder Hinsicht. Das Typostudio entwickelt sich zu dem Qualitätsbetrieb schlechthin: »Mehr Qualität ist in München nicht möglich gewesen, mehr konnte man gar nicht erwarten«, berichtet Rudolf Paulus Gorbach als ehemaliger Kunde. In der Branche ist klar: »SchumacherGebler ist nicht der Billigste. Aber der Beste.«

Der Umstand, dass inzwischen der Fotosatz auf leisen Sohlen, aber mit Lichtgeschwindigkeit Einzug hält, führte zu der Frage: »Was geschieht mit den Monotype-Matrizen?« ESG nutzt die Situation für einen weiteren Geniestreich: Gerade die Großbetriebe stellen von Hand- auf Fotosatz um, wollen ihren Matrizenbestand loswerden und verscherbeln ihn. SG macht sich daran, sämtliche Monotype-Matrizen dieser Welt zusammenzutragen – der leidenschaftliche Sammler ist in seinem Element! Matrizen, Matrizen, Matrizen wandern in die Goethestraße, darunter von Schnitten, die noch nie oder höchst selten in Deutschland zum Einsatz gekommen waren, wie die Barbou, Bell, Perpetua, Van Dijck und, und, und …

Mit den Matrizen kommen die Monotype-Maschinen, die man sonst verschrottet hätte. ESG avanciert zum Monotype-Magnaten schlechthin und besitzt zeitweise 25 Maschinen – wohlgemerkt alle funktionstüchtig. Ich musste lächeln bei der Anekdote des damals blutjungen Neuangestellten im Typostudio, Michi Bundscherer: »Als ich ihm mal sagte, dass da ja interessante Pressen 'rumstehen, korrigierte er mich sofort: ›Die stehen da nicht herum, die stehen da.‹«

Legendär wird auch die Büchersammlung, die ESG zusammenträgt, eine Fachbibliothek, die ihresgleichen sucht und nicht finden wird, und in ihrer unfassbaren Dimension an Quantität und Qualität inzwischen über verschiedene Standorte verteilt ist.

Das hier angehäufte enzyklopädische Wissen scheint er selbst tief inhaliert zu haben. Der Typo-Ästhet ist ein wandelndes Lexikon, das sich freizügig vor jedem Interessierten aufblättert. Jeder, der auch nur einmal das Vergnügen hatte, mit ihm über Bücher, Schriften, Maschinen oder Biografien ins Gespräch zu kommen, weiß, wovon hier die Rede ist. Eckehart SchumacherGebler spricht nachdrücklich, beeindruckend, druckreif!

Nach der Wende wird er von der unternehmerischen Gründungswelle der Neunziger ergriffen: Von der Treuhand erwirbt er nach schwierigen Verhandlungen den Hochdruckbetrieb der Leipziger Traditionsdruckerei Haag-Drugulin, in Ostdeutschland seit 1954 als Offizin Andersen Nexö firmierend, unter der Auflage, alle 18 Mitarbeiter zu übernehmen und ihnen für zwei Jahre eine Anstellung zu garantieren. – Der westdeutsche Unternehmer rettet alte Maschinen vor der Verschrottung, die neuen Bundesbürger vor dem Kapitalismus.

Der gesamte Bestand an Bleisatz sowie an Hochdrucktechnik wurde bereits zu DDR-Zeiten am Standort Nonnenstraße zusammengefasst – für uns ein klingender Name, weiß doch jeder hier, dass sich dort das Museum für Druckkunst befindet. Und ja, *(zu ESG schauen!)* es war Eckehart SchumacherGebler, der es 1994 gründete.

Das Museum wurde in eine Stiftung bürgerlichen Rechts überführt. SchumacherGebler hat an sie sein wertvolles Ensemble an Druckpressen, Schriften und Gerätschaften aller Art, kurz: seine Sammlung in ihrer ganzen Reichhaltigkeit der Allgemeinheit abgetreten. Wir reden hier von einer im Grunde voll funktionierenden druckgraphischen Werkstatt. Fast alle Maschinen in sämtlichen nur denkbaren Facetten, wären sofort betriebsbereit, – wenn sie denn jemand bedienen könnte.

Nun, wo aber ist der Nachwuchs, ohne den kein Erbe weitergetragen werden kann? SchumacherGebler trommelt ihn zusammen und initiiert 2013 den Verein zur Förderung der Schwarzen Kunst mit 160 Gründungsmitgliedern und – Stand heute – 137 aktiven Mitgliedern aus ganz Deutschland, den Niederlanden, der Schweiz, aus Österreich, Spanien, Italien und Frankreich! Was für stolze Zahlen für eine Zunft, die ständig totgesagt wird und doch gerade ihr Revival erlebt – *(cool down, nicht heulen!)* der menschlichen Sinnessehnsucht, der Sinn-lichkeit, auch Idealismus und Hartnäckigkeit eines Eckehart SchumacherGebler sei Dank! Seiner Leidenschaft und seiner Weitsicht ist es zu verdanken, dass nationales Kulturgut erfassbar, anfassbar und bedienbar bleibt, dass sich die Zunft dichter vernetzt hat, dass das traditionelle Drucker-Handwerk von den Alten an eine wieder wachsende Schar junger, begeisterter Leute weitergegeben wird – die ihn verehrt als die graue Eminenz der Schwarzen Kunst!

In welchen Zwischenräumen hat dieser Mensch, recht nebenbei auch Großfamilienvater, nur die Zeit und Kraft gefunden, die eigene, die legendäre Bibliothek SG aufzubauen, deren Bände mehrfach als schönste Bücher Deutschlands gekürt und zu Kostbarkeiten für bibliophile Sammler wurden? Der schöne Druck zu weltliterarischem Inhalt immer auch ergänzt durch einen genüsslich zu lesenden Essay über die verwendete Satzschrift aus der Feder des Meisters himself.

Als Herausgeber, Redakteur, Autor, Gestalter und Drucker zeichnet er Werke – visuelle und haptische Kleinode – verantwortlich, wie:

– Die Jahreskalender *26 Lettern*. So viele Buchstaben hat unser Alphabet, klar. Wie aber bringt man den Leuten nahe, dass es unterschiedliche Schriften gibt? Über 52 Wochen verteilt! – Zwei Wochen auf eine Schrift schauen, auf die Gestalter, überhaupt auf die sonst völlig unbemerkte Leistung, eine zeitlos erlesene Schrift zu erschaffen, und dies in großen Lettern unterhaltsam beschreiben. So genial wie simpel, man muss nur darauf kommen!

– Oder *Grundsetzliches* (-setzliches mit *e* !) in sechs Bändchen, ein profunder Exkurs in die Schriftgeschichte.

– Oder die *Typothek*, bleigesetzte Einzelblätter, die das Vergleichen von essentiellen Schriften möglich machte, als wir noch weit entfernt waren vom schnellen Nachschlagen im Internet. Gleiches Anliegen, andere Zielgruppe, Fachmenschen, die schon viel wissen, aber mit quasi Kriminalgeschichten auch mehr über die Hintergründe der Schriftentstehungen erfahren. Ich selbst habe in meinem typolastigen Umfeld mit dem Wiedergeben dieser Geschichten enorme Boni eingefahren.

– Und dann die *Satzinnovationen*. Sowas von tiefgestapelt, so kennen wir ihn; aus Innovationen besteht bereits die gesamte verlesene Leistungsliste. Die Broschüre *Satzinnovationen* wurde auf der IBA, der Internationalen Buchkunst-Ausstellung, in Leipzig 1989 mit einer Silbermedaille ausgezeichnet. Eine Silbermedaille auf der IBA, die heute vergoldet wird. Mehr geht nicht?

– Doch, da ist noch der Schneidler, *F. H. Ernst Schneidler*, das 3-Kilo-Mammut-Werk in Kollaboration mit Max Caflisch, Hans Peter Willberg, auch Albert Kapr und Antonia Weiß; letzere beide Novizen eines der größten Schriftentwerfer, Kalligraphen und Lehrer des 20. Jahrhunderts. Allein dieses Buch stellte ein Lebenswerk dar. (*Luft holen …*)

Aktiv, rastlos geradezu ist ESG bis zur unmittelbaren Gegenwart. (*Fragend an ESG:*) Wirst du, lieber Eckehart, der du in wenigen Wochen den 88. Geburtstag begehst, nachher noch deine bibliophilen Juwelen in den Kofferraum packen und zur nächsten Messe weiterziehen? Oder nimmst du gleich einen Telefontermin mit Südkorea wahr, wo du seit 2016 die Gründung eines weltweiten Dachverbandes für Druckmuseen unterstützt? Ganz sicher aber fährst du morgen gleich wieder nach Dresden, wohin du nach deiner Leipziger Zeit mit der Druckerei gezogen bist (*zu Eckehart schauen, er wird nicken??!* :), wo dich ganz aktuell ein Kellerausbau in Atem hält, um die von dir zusammengetragenen Schätze – ich sage nur: Schriften, Schriften, Schriften – für die Nachwelt sicher unter Dach und Fach zu bringen, da das jetzige Archiv nicht mehr zur Verfügung steht. Ich hoffe inständig, dass du zwischendurch Luft findest, das nächste Schriftenfest vorzubereiten – eine Event-Institution, ein weiteres jährliches Must-go-Symposium seit 2013 Jahren für alle schriftverwendenden und -interessierten Typen. Oder ...

(*Blick auf die Uhr*)

Ich danke der Gutenberg-Gesellschaft und der Stadt Mainz für die Wahl zum diesjährigen Preisträger, die nicht nur ehrt im stillen Kämmerlein, sondern durch sie auch das Anliegen und das Werk von Professor Eckehart SchumacherGebler einer noch größeren Öffentlichkeit vorgestellt werden wird und wünsche mir nun, dass die Wellen dieses bewegendes Momentes im Moment bis nach Leipzig schlagen, dem Ort, an dem er uns, der Nachwelt und sich bereits ein Museum gesetzt hat.

(*Phew, ich bin exakt in der Zeit geblieben – allein für den langen Familiennamen hätte mir eine Minute mehr Redezeit zugestanden.*)

So möchte ich schließlich schließen mit Albert Camus: »Wenn die Welt klar wäre, bräuchte es keine Kunst.« Menschen, wie Eckehart SchumacherGebler, malen nicht, sondern setzen schwarz – auf weiß. Und er weiß, dass gut Gesetztes in Stein gemeißelt ist.

Gott grüß die Kunst – und ihre(n) Jünger!

Natürlich folgen jetzt standing ovations, aber dann wieder – *Setzen bitte*!

Falk Eisermann

Laudatio auf Jeffrey Hamburger,
gehalten in Mainz am 25. Juni 2022

Es war eine möglicherweise für Manche überraschende, in jedem Fall aber kluge Entscheidung, Jeffrey Hamburger den Gutenbergpreis 2022 zu verleihen. Ich weiß, dass es selbst für einen seit langem etablierten und international anerkannten Harvard-Kunsthistoriker gar nicht so einfach ist, seine fachlichen Interessen gegenüber der eigenen akademischen Community zu behaupten und zu verteidigen. Denn mehr noch als in Europa gilt in den USA die Maxime, dass eine wissenschaftliche Karriere als Kunsthistoriker:in sich vor allem aus der Beschäftigung mit der sogenannten »Höhenkammkunst« erbauen lässt, weil mediävistische Untersuchungsgebiete vorzugsweise in Frankreich, Italien, den burgundischen Niederlanden liegen sollten. Lehrstühle für »German Art und Culture«, wie Hamburger ihn innehat, gibt es nicht allzu viele; und die Wahl seiner Lebensthemen – zusammengefasst: »Frauen – Kloster – Kunst«, also die Geschichte der Buchillustration und die Kultur der Frauenklöster im Mittelalter – dürfte durch manche amerikanische Brille als durchaus exotisch erscheinen.[1] Daher ist es von enormer Bedeutung, dass seine Forschungen von ihrem Zielpublikum, den Menschen im deutschen Sprachraum, wissenschaftlich anerkannt und gesellschaftlich honoriert werden. Dies geschieht in mustergültiger Weise mit der Zuerkennung des Gutenbergpreises, der 2022 erstmals an einen Kunsthistoriker vergeben wurde, auch wenn Hamburger von seinem Profil her nicht als typischer Preisträger erscheinen mag.

Aber was heißt schon typisch bei einer so bunten wie illustren Reihe? Mit vielen vorherigen Preisträger:innen hat er doch eins gemeinsam: Zeitlebens vermittelt er die Geschichte des abendländischen Buchs nicht nur an das Fachpublikum, sondern auch an die weitere Öffentlichkeit. So heißt es auf der Website der Gutenberg-Gesellschaft zur Begründung: »Er schließt (...) eine (...) wissenschaftliche Lücke der Kunst- und der Buchforschung und es gelingt ihm in besonderer Weise, mittelalterliche und moderne visuelle Kultur im Dialog zu erklären«.[2] Ich hänge ihm also noch ein weiteres ehrenvoll gemeintes Attribut um und nenne ihn: den beharrlichen Brückenbauer. Er ist ein Brückenbauer zunächst zwischen der Kunstgeschichte und ihren Nachbardisziplinen, vor allem Germanistik, Geschichte und Kirchengeschichte. Seine legendäre Kooperation mit dem jüngst verstorbenen Oxforder Germanisten Nigel Palmer gipfelte nach fünfzehn Jahren in dem 2015 erschienenen, multidisziplinären Mammutwerk »The Prayer Book of Ursula Begerin«,

---

[1] Exemplarisch: *Frauen – Kloster – Kunst. Neue Forschungen zur Kulturgeschichte des Mittelalters. Beiträge zum Internationalen Kolloquium vom 13. bis 16. Mai 2005 anlässlich der Ausstellung »Krone und Schleier«*. Hrsg. von JEFFREY F. HAMBURGER u. a. Turnhout 2007.

[2] gutenberg-gesellschaft.de/gutenbergpreis/ [15.12.2022].

zu dem eine der vielen positiven Rezensionen bemerkte: »Eine ebenso gelehrte wie gründliche Bearbeitung wünscht man sich für jede illuminierte mittelalterliche Handschrift«.³ Ein umfassenderes Lob ist kaum vorstellbar. Dem Wunsch der Rezensentin nachgekommen ist Hamburger erneut in seiner jüngsten Monographie »Color in Cusanus«, die in starker Verdichtung die kunsthistorischen, theologie- und philosophiegeschichtlichen Implikationen des Gebrauchs der Farbe in Handschriften und Drucken der Werke des Nikolaus von Kues analysiert und dabei anhand seines aktuellen Kernthemas – Geschichte und Ikonographie des Diagramms in der mittelalterlichen (Buch-)Kunst – erneut die außergewöhnliche Expertise ihres Autors über alle Fächergrenzen hinweg unter Beweis stellt.⁴

Ein Brückenbauer eigener Prägung ist Hamburger auch in seiner erfolgreichen musealen Vermittlungsarbeit, die sich in der Konzeption zahlreicher, oft spektakulärer und enorm öffentlichkeitswirksamer Ausstellungen auf beiden Seiten des Atlantiks artikuliert. Die von der Bundesregierung geförderte Schau »Krone und Schleier« von 2005 etwa wurde weithin als einer der ersten Ausstellungshöhepunkte des neuen Jahrtausends gefeiert, wirkt mit ihren Begleitpublikationen bis heute weit in die Forschung hinein und hat in vielerlei Hinsicht Maßstäbe gesetzt.⁵ Ganz neu ist der – wie vieles von ihm – auf Englisch und Deutsch erhältliche Band »Kaiserliche Pracht. Deutsche Buchkunst von 800 bis 1500«, der neben Handschriften auch zentrale Zeugnisse illustrierter Inkunabeln und Frühdrucke in magistralem Zugriff einbezieht. Das Werk erschien anlässlich der Ausstellung »Imperial Splendor«, die im Winter 2021/22 in der Pierpont Morgan Library in New York stattfand, und verweist auf eine weitere brückenbauerische Eigenschaft Hamburgers: als Vermittler deutscher Kunstgeschichte, insbesondere der Erzeugnisse der Manuskript- und Druckkunst, in die US-amerikanische Kultur und Gesellschaft hinein.⁶

Auch sonst baut Hamburger in seinem wissenschaftlichen Werk und ebenso im persönlichen Bereich Brücken von der Kunstgeschichte zu den Buch- und Bibliothekswissenschaften. Auch hierfür mögen einige weitere Buchtitel Zeugnis ablegen: Phänomenale Wirkung zeitigte der von ihm herausgegebene Tagungsband »Unter Druck« von 2018, der die, wie man im Bild bleibend sagen könnte, »Brückentechnologie« der Buchillumination des 15. Jahrhunderts in umfassendem Zugriff beschreibt; »Script as Image« aus dem Jahr 2014 legt dar, wie das geschriebene Wort im Mittelalter weit mehr war als ein Informationsträger, sondern an bestimmten medialen Schnittstellen auch selbst zum Bild, zum Kunstwerk wurde.⁷ Von dem materialreichen Aufsatz zu »Frauen und Schriftlichkeit in der Schweiz im Mittelalter«, der einen minutiös aus den Quellen gearbeiteten Einblick in die Vielfalt des weiblichen Buchgebrauchs und in die Reichtümer der Frauenklösterbibliotheken im 15. und 16. Jahrhundert vermittelt, bin ich auch 20 Jahre nach dem Erscheinen noch beeindruckt.⁸ Als ein weiterer Lektüretipp sei ein grundlegender Aufsatz mit dem bewusst provozierenden Titel »Am Anfang war das Bild« aus dem Jahr 2004 genannt.⁹

---

3 JEFFREY F. HAMBURGER und NIGEL F. PALMER, *The Prayer Book of Ursula Begerin.* 2 Bde. Dietikon-Zürich 2015; Rezension von GIA TOUSSAINT. In: *Das Mittelalter.* 21 (2016) S. 469–470, hier S. 470.

4 JEFFREY F. HAMBURGER: *Color in Cusanus.* Stuttgart 2021.

5 *Krone und Schleier. Kunst aus mittelalterlichen Frauenklöstern. Ausstellungskatalog Essen/Bonn 18. März bis 19. Juli 2005.* Hrsg. von JEFFREY HAMBURGER u. v. a. München 2005.

6 JEFFREY F. HAMBURGER und JOSHUA O'DRISCOLL: *Kaiserliche Pracht. Deutsche Buchkunst von 800 bis 1500. Ausstellungskatalog, The Morgan Library and Museum, 15. Oktober 2021 bis 23. Januar 2022.* Luzern 2021. Englischer Originaltitel: *Imperial Splendor. The Art of the Book in the Holy Roman Empire, 800–1500.* New York, Lewes (UK) 2021.

7 *Unter Druck. Mitteleuropäische Buchmalerei im 15. Jahrhundert. Tagungsband zum internationalen Kolloquium in Wien, Österreichische Akademie der Wissenschaften, 13.–17. Januar 2016.* Hrsg. von JEFFREY F. HAMBURGER und MARIA THEISEN. Petersberg 2018 (Buchmalerei des 15. Jahrhunderts in Mitteleuropa. 15); JEFFREY F. HAMBURGER: *Script as Image.* Leuven, Paris 2014 (Corpus of Illuminated Manuscripts. 21).

8 In: *Bibliotheken bauen: Tradition und Vision – Building for Books: Traditions and Visions.* Hrsg. von SUSANNE BIERI und WALTER FUCHS. Basel, Boston, Berlin 2001, S. 71–163.

9 JEFFREY F. HAMBURGER: Am Anfang war das Bild. Kunst und Frauenspiritualität im Spätmittelalter. In: *Studien und Texte zur literarischen und materiellen Kultur der Frauenklöster im späten Mittelalter. Ergebnisse eines Arbeitsgesprächs in der Herzog August Bibliothek Wolfenbüttel, 24.–26. Febr. 1999.* Hrsg. von FALK EISERMANN, EVA SCHLOTHEUBER und VOLKER HONEMANN. Leiden, Boston 2004 (Studies in Medieval and Reformation Thought. 99), S. 1–43.

Zuletzt empfehle ich, das vorjährige Gutenberg-Jahrbuch zu konsultieren, für das er einen grundlegenden Beitrag zu einem sehr merkwürdigen und bislang missverstandenen – oder unbeachteten – Großfragment eines »Spiegels der menschlichen Erlösung« (»Speculum humanae salvationis«, GW M43016) von 1476 beigesteuert hat.[10] Die Art und Weise, wie Handschrift und Buchdruck, Text und Bild, Deutsch und Latein in diesem hybriden Zeugnis verschmelzen, ohne zu einem Buch im eigentlichen Sinn zu werden, stellt ein singuläres Phänomen in der Inkunabelzeit dar. Doch zeigt Hamburgers neuer Erklärungsansatz, dass es historisch gesehen vielleicht gar nicht so singulär ist, dass indes die großen Überlieferungslücken und unser bei weitem nicht vollständiges Wissen über die künstlerischen Aspekte bei der Produktion früher Drucke uns bislang daran gehindert haben, den besonderen Wert und die Funktion dieses unikalen Artefakts zu erkennen. Dieser und viele andere Beiträge aus seiner Feder können dazu beitragen, die oft eher unverbunden einander gegenüberliegenden Ufer der traditionellen Handschriftenforschung und der historisch ausgerichteten Buchwissenschaft zu einer neuen Mediengeschichte des Mittelalters und der frühen Neuzeit zu verbinden – wie es Auftrag und Passion des Brückenbauers Jeffrey Hamburger entsprechen.

---

10 JEFFREY F. HAMBURGER: Between Basel and Lyon: Bernhard Richel, Martin Huss, and a Possible Printer's Vade Mecum (The Morgan Library & Museum, MS M. 158). In: *GJ* 97 (2022), S. 16–37.

Don C. Skemer

Philobiblon and Its Medieval Readers

Richard de Bury (1287–1345), bishop of Durham, has enjoyed an honored place in book history because of his treatise *Philobiblon, sive, De amore librorum* (1345). Scholarly attention has focused on his public life, book collecting, and the authorship of *Philobiblon*. But efforts to establish an authoritative text have tended to privilege earlier manuscript copies of English origin over the larger number of copies from the Continent. *Philobiblon*'s modern bibliophilic appeal has tended to obscure its early readership, 1350–1500. This article attempts to redress this situation with a new census of manuscripts and attention to their scribes, readers, owners, annotators, library holders, and works bound with them in multi-text manuscripts. Sixty-five manuscripts are listed in the Appendix. This is about twenty more than identified and located in previous surveys. Early library catalogues, printing history, and provenance research offer additional evidence. The census shows that twice as many *Philobiblon* manuscripts, including fragments and lost copies, were produced in German-speaking lands rather than England. Many of these date from the second half of the fifteenth century, when two incunable editions were also printed (1473, 1483) in Germany and a third was proposed (1484). A comparative approach to *Philobiblon* manuscripts suggests significant differences in early readership and reception. English readers, including bibliophile bishops and administrators, were often interested in *Philobiblon* because of its wide learning and value as a textual model for Latin prose composition, rhetoric, and letter-writing. German readers, including Pre-Reformation theologians, university masters, preachers, and members of religious orders influenced by the *Devotio Moderna*, embraced *Philobiblon*'s reformist emphasis on improved monastic education and the centrality of books in a Christian ministry to serve God.

Richard de Bury (1287–1345) and his treatise *Philobiblon, sive, De amore librorum* (1345), have long enjoyed an honored place in book history because of the author's love of books as cherished physical objects, as well as conveyors of learning. Born Richard Aungerville, near the cathedral town of Bury St. Edmunds, Suffolk, he was among the university-educated royal clerks who rose through the ranks of English central government during the reign of King Edward II (r. 1307–27). He came to hold the posts of Lord Privy Seal, Lord Chancellor, and Treasurer under Edward III (r. 1327–77), and he was elevated to bishop of Durham (r. 1333–45), exercising broad powers over the surrounding County Palatine.[1] Richard de Bury purchased or commissioned manuscripts from booksellers, and he acquired others by gift, purchase, and borrowing from

[1] NOËL DENHOLM-YOUNG: Richard de Bury (1287–1345). In: *Transactions of the Royal Historical Society*. 4th series. 20 (1937), pp. 135–68. JOSEPH DE GHELLINCK: Un évêque bibliophile au XIVe siècle. Richard d'Aungerville (1345). Contribution à l'histoire de la littérature et des bibliothèques médiévales. In: *Revue de histoire ecclésiastique*. 18 (1922), pp. 271–312, 482–508; 19 (1923), pp. 157–200. CHRISTOPHER R. CHENEY: Richard de Bury, Borrower of Books. In: *Speculum*. 48 (1973) 2, pp. 325–28. EMILY STEINER: Collecting, Violence, Literature: Richard de Bury's *Philobiblon* and the Forms of Literary History. In: *The Medieval Literary: Beyond Form*. Ed. ROBERT J. MEYER-LEE and CATHERINE SANOK. Woodbridge, Suffolk 2018, pp. 243–66.

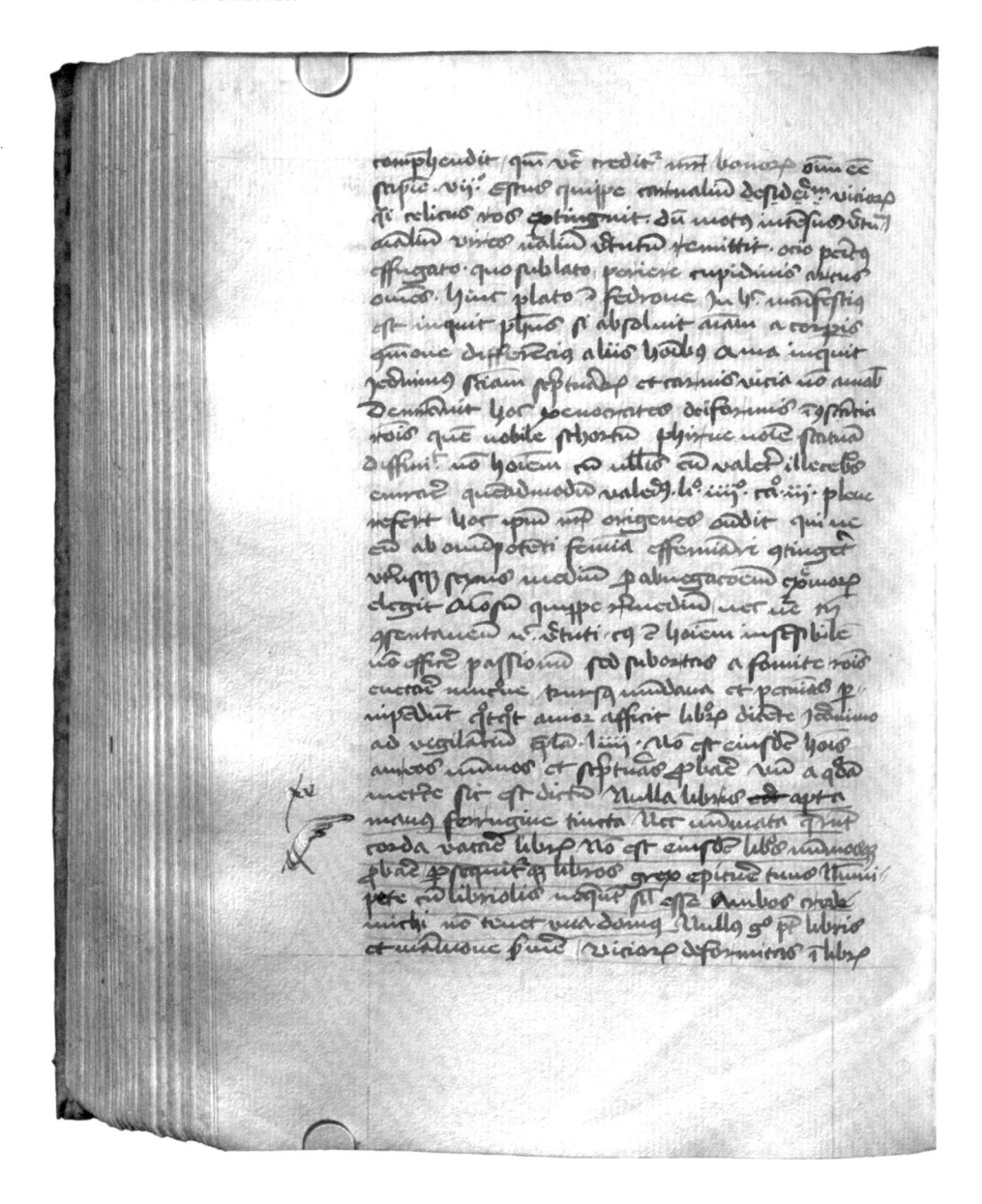

Erlangen-Nürnberg, Universitätsbibliothek, Ms. 542, fol. 242v. An early reader of *Philobiblon* in a German manuscript miscellany of 1450–75 added a *nota bene* mark pointing to a passage in chapter xv about serving God through the love of books. Digital link to Ms. 542: urn:nbn:de:bvb:29-bv042580123-1

monasteries. He is thought to have collected fifteen-hundred volumes or more for a new library at Durham College, Oxford. *Philobiblon* concludes with an exhortation to its future students at Oxford to beseech Christ to have mercy upon the bishop and the hall's other benefactors, but his executors had to sell his library to pay debts. Richard de Bury lived on through *Philobiblon* and by the nineteenth century was celebrated as the premier medieval British book collector and a forerunner of modern bibliomania.[2] *Philobiblon* has remained in print for centuries and has been translated into many languages. Richard de Bury's invented Greek title word has been used as an evocation of all things bookish and applied to learned societies, bibliophile clubs, academic journals, and an electronic database. Modern bibliophilic appeal has tended to obscure *Philobiblon*'s early readership, 1350–1500. This article attempts to redress this with an up-to-date census of *Philobiblon* manuscripts (including extracts and incomplete copies) and attention to their scribes, readers, owners, annotators, library holders, and works bound with *Philobiblon* in multi-text manuscripts. Sixty-five manuscript copies of British and Continental origin are listed in the Appendix. Most newly identified copies are from lands once part of the Holy Roman Empire. Other copies have been identified in medieval library catalogues.

Extant manuscripts of *Philobiblon* have been surveyed to establish an authoritative text and resolve authorship questions. Thomas James (1572/3–1629), librarian to Thomas Bodley (1545–1613), collated at least six manuscripts at Oxford and Cambridge for his *Philobiblon* edition (1599), and viewed Richard de Bury as a medieval precursor of Bodley.[3] These were among the English manuscript copies that Edward Bernard (1638–97) described almost a century later with the help of Humfrey Wanley (1672–1726).[4] In 1843, the Dresden bibliographer E. G. Vogel identified nineteen *Philobiblon* manuscripts.[5] Surveys of *Philobiblon* manuscripts were undertaken for various editions and translations published between 1854 and 1954: Hippolyte Cocheris, Samuel Hand, Ernest C. Thomas, Andrew F. West, Marco Besso, Axel Nelson, and Antonio Altamura, whose survey was the most complete, identifying forty-three manuscripts and listing others in *siglae codicum* and among *manoscritti perduti*. In 1960, Michael Maclagan listed and examined thirty-five manuscripts, and added brief notes about manuscripts not cited or located by Thomas and Altamura.[6] Modern scholarship generally assigns Richard de Bury authorship. However, there is no holograph or original manuscript of *Philobiblon*. The text was not completed until 24 January 1345 at Auckland Castle, a few months before the death of Richard de Bury, who had been ailing for some time and probably needed the aid of the English Dominican theologian Robert Holcot (c. 1291–1349), his chaplain and household member.[7] Holcot's role is characterized in several

---

2 The British writer F. Somner Merryweather (1827–1900) observed that modern bibliophiles, in their devotion to the "sweet madness called bibliomania," can admire Richard de Bury as a "bibliomaniac of the first order." F. SOMNER MERRYWEATHER: *Bibliomania in the Middle Ages...* London 1849, pp. 71, 75.

3 THOMAS JAMES (Ed.): *Philobiblon Richardi Dunelmensis sive De amore librorum, et institutione bibliothecae, tractatus pulcherrimus ex collatione cum variis manuscriptis editio jam secunda: cui accessit appendix de manuscriptis Oxoniensibus...* Oxford 1599, unpaginated "Appendix de manuscriptis Oxoniensibus".

4 EDWARD BERNARD: *Catalogi librorum manuscriptorum Angliae et Hiberniae in unum collecti, cum indice alphabetico.* Oxford 1697. Vol. 1, pp. 41, 44, 53, 59, 103; Vol. 2, p. 81.

5 E. G. VOGEL: Die Philobiblon Richards. In: *Serapeum: Zeitschrift für Bibliothekwissenschaft, Handschriftenkunde und ältere Litteratur.* 4 (1843), pp. 138–41, 154–60, here pp. 140–41.

6 HIPPOLYTE COCHERIS (Ed.): *Philobiblon. Excellent traité sur l'amour des livres par Richard de Bury, Évêque de Durham.* Paris 1854, pp. xix–xxii. SAMUEL HAND: *Philobiblon: A Treatise on the Love of Books by Richard de Bury, Bishop of Durham and Lord Chancellor of England.* Albany, N.Y. 1861, pp. 13–16. ERNEST C. THOMAS: *The Philobiblon of Richard de Bury, Bishop of Durham, Treasurer and Chancellor of Edward III.* London 1888, pp. lxv–lxxvii. ANDREW F. WEST (Ed.): *The Philobiblon of Richard De Bury.* New York 1889, pp. 59–94. MARCO BESSO: Il 'Philobiblon' di Riccardo de Bury. Rome 1914, pp. xlix–li. AXEL NELSON (Ed.): *Philobiblon eller om kärleken till böckerna, af Richard de Bury ... met inledning, latinsk text och anmärkningar utgifven och öfversatt af Axel Nelson.* Stockholm 1922. AXEL NELSON: Intorno al 'Philobiblon' di Riccardo de Bury e ad alcuni nuovi codici di quell' opera. In: *Nordisk tidskrift för bok-och biblioteksväsen.* XVI (1929), pp. 104–112. ANTONIO ALTAMURA (Ed.): *Riccardo da Bury, Philobiblon.* Naples 1954, pp. 19–39. ERNEST C. THOMAS (Ed.): *Philobiblon of Richard de Bury ... Edited with a Foreword by Michael Maclagan.* Oxford 1960, pp. lv–lxxiii. Maclagan incorrectly identifies two *Philobiblon* manuscripts: Oxford, Balliol Coll. Ms. 243; and Trier, StB Ms. 685/247. Richard Sharpe cited Thomas and Altamura, without ennumerating manuscripts. RICHARD SHARPE: *A Handlist of Latin Writers of Great Britain and Ireland before 1540.* Turnhout 1997 (Publications of the Journal of Medieval Latin. 1), pp. 463, 556. Stella Maris Fernández republished Altamura's list. STELLA MARIS FERNÁNDEZ: *Bibliofilía y Philobiblon de Richard de Bury.* Buenos Aires 2002, pp. 135–54.

7 According to the *Continuatio Historiae Dunelmensis*, attributed to William de Chambre, the bishop had been in failing health for a considerable time ("longa infirmitate decoctus"). JAMES RAINE (Ed.): *Historiae Dunelmensis scriptores tres, Gaufridus de Coldingham, Robertus de Graystanes, et Williemus de Chambre.* London, Edinburgh 1839 (Publications of the Surtees Society. 9), p. 130.

manuscripts by the Latin word *editus*, which could signify authorship, but also publishing (*publicare*), in the sense of bringing forth or producing a text or document in its final written form and making it publicly available.[8] In the absence of an *Urtext*, *Philobiblon* editors have emphasized earlier English and French copies, such as the British Library, Ms. Royal 8 F xiv; Oxford, Bodleian Library, Ms. Digby 147; Cambridge, Corpus Christi College, Ms. 456; and Paris, Bibliothèque Nationale de France, Ms. 15168. Andrew F. West noted, "As I have shown that the true text lies in manuscripts of the English tradition, and that the received printed text comes from corrupt German copies, I have discarded the latter almost entirely.... [T]he English tradition preserves the true text in twenty-three MSS ranging in date from 1370 to 1450 or later." West aimed to provide "a representation of the *Philobiblon* as it left its writer's hands"[9] Unfortunately, this quest for textual purity discouraged interest in later German copies.

Ernest C. Thomas mentions a *Philobiblon* manuscript that Dr. Thomas Caius (d. 1572) claimed Richard de Bury had given to Durham College and which Caius consulted at Oxford late in the reign of Henry VIII (r. 1509–47).[10] No such manuscript can be found. The only copy in Durham today is a mid fifteenth-century miscellany (Cosin V.v.2 A), acquired in the time of Bishop John Cosin (r. 1660–72) of Durham by his chaplain George Davenport (d. 1677), Rector of Houghton-le-Spring, a Durham bibliophile who bought manuscripts from London booksellers and other sources, then donated many of them to the Cosin library. The Cosin *Philobiblon* was owned in c. 1500 by "R. Langley," possibly Ralph Langley, who was either a Westminster monk or a Cambridge-educated vicar of Prestwich.[11] James G. Clark has stated in error that the Durham monk Thomas Swalwell (c. 1463–1539) owned a miscellany with *Philobiblon*.[12] Beyond Durham, the earliest *Philobiblon* manuscripts were in large monastic libraries, which benefited from its chapters on effective library management, preservation, and access. But *Philobiblon* could also support the academic and administrative interests of university-educated abbots and priors, and the education and spiritual reading of novices and monks.[13] Broader subject interests are evident at an early date in multi-text volumes including *Philobiblon*, such as Cambridge, Corpus Christi College, Parker Library, Ms. 456. It is the sixth of seventh items in this composite manuscript of 1375–1400, which also includes Johannes Sacro Bosco, *De sphera mundi*; Alexander de Villa Dei, *Algorismus*; and the Pseudo-Aristotle, *Secretum secretorum*.[14] Other early copies include British Library, Ms. Royal 8 F xiv. Henry of Kirkstede (c. 1314–after 1378), librarian of the Benedictine Abbey of Bury St. Edmund's, Suffolk (1338–61), acquired this manuscript for the abbey and listed it in his *Catalogus de libris autenticis et apocrifis* (a guide to 674 known authors and 3900 works), which he compiled in the 1340s and 1350s before becoming prior in 1361. This copy of *Philobiblon* was bound with works of Hugh of Saint Victor

---

8 WILLIAM SOMNER: *Dictionarium Saxonico-Latino-Anglicum...* Oxford 1659, unpaginated (under the Old English word *Acennan*, meaning to produce or make known). J. F. NIERMEYER: *Mediae Latinitis lexicon minus*. Leiden 1976, p. 366. D. R. HOWLETT: *Dictionary of Medieval Latin from British Sources, Fascicule XIII: Pro-Reg*. London 2010, pp. 260–61.

9 WEST, pp. vii, 10, 99.

10 THOMAS, p. lxxvii.

11 BRENDA M. PASK and MARGARET M. HARVEY (Ed.): *The Letters of George Davenport, 1651–1677*. Woodbridge, Suffolk 2011 (Publications of the Surtees Society. 215), pp. 25–26, 260–61 (no. 51). A. I. DOYLE: The Cosin Manuscripts and George Davenport. In: *The Book Collector*. 53 (2004) 1, pp. 32–45. RALPH GAMESON: *Literature and Devotion in Later Medieval England: A Selection of Manuscripts from Durham University Library*. Durham 2021, pp. 27–28: "Pertinet R. Langley (possible candidates of the right period include Ralph Langley, a monk of Westminster from 1465/6–1501, and a man of the same name who studied canon law at Cambridge in 1488 and is recorded as vicar at Prestwich, Lancashire, in 1493)." Concerning the latter, Ralph Langley (c. 1469–98), see *A Cambridge Alumni Database* (available on www.venn.lib/cam.ac.uk, [20.1.2023]).

12 Concerning BL, Ms. Add. 28805, James G. Clark states, "Thomas Swalwell, a Durham monk who studied theology at Oxford in the 1470s, compiled an anthology that included Thomas Merke's *Liber de modis dictamine* and Geoffrey of Vinsauf's *Poetria nova*, together with Richard Bury's *Philobiblon*." JAMES G. CLARK: University Monks in Late Medieval England. In: *Medieval Monastic Education*. Ed. GEORGE FERZOCO and CAROLYN MUESSIG. London 2001, pp. 56–71, here pp. 66, 70 (n. 43). *Philobiblon* is not in the entry for Ms. Add. 28805 in BL. *Manuscripts and Archives*: searcharchives.bl.uk [20.1.2023].

13 MARTIN HEALE: *The Abbots and Priors of Late Medieval and Reformation England*. Oxford 2016, pp. 84–91. JAMES G. CLARK: An Abbot and his Books in Late Medieval and Pre-Reformation England. In: *The Prelate in England and Europe, 1300–1560*. Ed. MARTIN HEALE. Woodbridge, Suffolk 2014, pp. 101–26.

14 M. R. JAMES: *A Descriptive Catalogue of the Manuscripts in the Library of Corpus Christi College Library Cambridge*. Cambridge 1912, part VI (vol. II, part III, nos. 451–538), pp. 379–80, no. 456.

and monastic rules.[15] Abbots and priors who owned *Philobiblon* manuscripts often donated or bequeathed them to monastic libraries. One of five manuscripts that Abbot William Welde (r. 1387–1405) gave to St. Augustine's Benedictine Abbey, Canterbury, is a miscellany including *Philobiblon*, as well as Alain de Lille (c. 1128–1202), *De planctu naturae*, and John of Limoges (fl. 1255–60), *Morale somnium Pharaonis* (British Library, Ms. Harley 3224).[16]

Philobiblon was a slim *libellum* in twenty essay-like chapters and was most often bound with texts that copyists, readers, donors, and libraries considered complementary. Substantive reader's notes are rare, relative to corrector's marks and keywords in the margins. Some readers marked passages of personal interest. For example, a fifteenth-century reader of a copy of *Philobiblon* in a composite manuscript of French origin marked the margins of chap. xvii with brackets and the word "nota" next to passages about careless young readers mishandling, marking, and damaging manuscripts (Vatican City, Bibliotheca Apostolica Vaticana, Ottoboni lat. 259, fols. 61v–65v).[17] Original ownership and physical context are most often the best indicators of intended readership and possible uses. Most of the sixteen British extant manuscripts are in miscellanies and composite volumes containing five to ten other texts, though in one case thirty-four (Bodley, Ms. Digby 147). Today only one of the extant English copies is separately bound (Cambridge, Sidney Sussex College, Ms. 38). A similar situation prevailed on the Continent. A separately bound *Philobiblon* manuscript of c. 1480 in the Morgan Library and Museum (Ms. M 448), possibly removed from a larger volume in the past, has been identified as English, though its *Hybrida* script and textual variants suggest origins in Germany or the Netherlands.[18] Particular copies began as booklets; that is, self-contained textual units in one or more quires, which could be brought together and bound with other booklets of similar page size and layout, often with a contents list added. For example, *Philobiblon* is in Booklet C in a composite parchment manuscript of unknown English monastic origin, made from four booklets bound together in the 1600s (Cambridge, Trinity College, Ms. R. 9. 17).[19] Book owners and libraries might move their *Philobiblon* manuscripts, like a 1400–25 copy now bound with a thirteenth-century manuscript of John of Salisbury's *Polycraticus* in a volume formerly in Salisbury Cathedral (Oxford, Corpus Christi College, Ms. 222).[20] Clearly, *Philobiblon* manuscripts in personal and institutional libraries could serve different readers over time.

---

[15] RICHARD H. ROUSE and MARY A. ROUSE (Ed.): *Henry of Kirkestede, Catalogus de libris autenticis et apocrifis*. London 2004 (Corpus of British Medieval Library Catalogues. 11), p. 446, K527: "Richardus de Bury, episcopus Dunelm[ensis] florit A. Ch. 1342 et scripsit Librum qui dicitur Philobiblon, id est amor librorum." SHARPE: *Handlist*, p. 172, no. 462.

[16] M. R. JAMES: *The Ancient Libraries of Canterbury and Dover*. Cambridge 1903, pp. lxxiii, 299, no. 964, duplicated as no. 965. Other Welde manuscripts are described on p. 354 (nos. 1323, 1324); p. 355 (nos. 1337, 1338). M. R. James mentions Welde's "partiality for Canon law". The BL manuscript's flyleaf ownership inscription is datable to the first years of the century (fol. 1v: "Liber de acquisicione Williami Welde Abbatis"). B. C. BARKER-BENFIELD (Ed.): *St Augustine's Abbey, Canterbury*. London 2008 (Corpus of British Medieval Library Catalogues. 13). Vol. 2, pp. 989–90 ("Epistolaria, BA: 964"; "philobiblon Ricardi Episcopi dunelmensis").

[17] Vatican City, B Apostolica Vaticana, Ottoboni lat. 259, fols. 61v–65v. *Bibliotheca Laureshamensis*: https://www.bibliotheca-laureshamensis-digital.de, [last consulted, January 22, 2023]. *Philobiblon* is in the second fascicule, which was possibly from the Benedictine Abbey of Saint-Benoît-sur-Loire, Fleury at the end of the fourteenth century.

[18] The Morgan manuscript came to light in the antiquarian book trade during the nineteenth century. West examined it by 1889, when it was owned by the Birmingham antiquarian Samuel Timmins (1826–1902). West (p. 95) said the text was a "German variant" and probably of Flemish origin. Much of the Timmins collection was auctioned in London by Sotheby, Wilkinson, & Hodge (1899). The manuscript passed to the collection of Robert Hoe (1839–1909). It was sold at a sale beginning on April 24, 1911: *No. 905. Catalogue of the Library of Robert Hoe of New York. Part I – A to K*. New York 1911, p. 352, no. 2120. The Morgan's *Medieval & Renaissance Manuscripts* gives England as the place of origin: https://www.themorgan.org/manuscript/112335, [last consulted, January 22, 2023]. However, the Morgan Library's older "Curatorial Description" suggests Flanders: https://corsair.morganlibrary.org/BBM0448a.pdf, [last consulted, January 22, 2023].

[19] ELAINE TREHARNE: Cambridge. Trinity College R. 9.17 (819). In: *Medieval and Renaissance Texts and Studies*. 343 (2008), pp. 35–42; *The Production and Use of English Manuscripts 1060 to 1220* (available on www.le.ac.uk [20.1.2023]).

[20] *Philobiblon* comprises the first twenty-eight folios of Oxford, Corpus Christi Coll. Ms. 222, removed from what is now Corpus Christi Coll. Ms. 167, before Patrick Young (1584–1652) catalogued the manuscripts of Salisbury Cathedral in 1622. A table of contents on fol. 57r of Ms. 222 lists four texts, but only *Philobiblon* is present: (1) *Philobiblon*; (2) *Tractatus de decimus*; (3) Giles of Rome, *De peccato originali egidii de roma*; and (4) *Tabula super legendam auream*. N. R. KER: Salisbury Cathedral Manuscripts and Patrick Young's Catalogue. In: *Wiltshire Archaeology and Natural History Magazine*. 53 (1950), pp. 153–83. N. R. KER: *Medieval Libraries of Great Britain: A List of Surviving Books*. 2nd edition. London 1964, p. 172.

In the fifteenth century, various copies were owned by university-educated bishops like Richard de Bury, with broad academic interests. Henry of Chichele (c. 1364–1443), archbishop of Canterbury (r. 1414–43), donated a parchment miscellany in which *Philobiblon* is the sixth of seven texts, including history and science, to the University of Oxford for the chained theological library of All Souls College (Oxford, All Souls College, Ms. 31), which he founded in 1438. Born to a family of London grocers, Chichele studied at Oxford (1387–92) and worked as a canon lawyer and royal diplomat before and after his elevation to archbishop of Canterbury.[21] Another such donor was William Gray [Grey] (d. 1478), who served as chancellor of Oxford (1440–42), bishop of Ely (r. 1454–78), and Lord High Treasurer (1469–70). Born to an aristocratic family, Gray studied theology at Oxford (D.D., 1445). He also traveled on the Continent and studied in Cologne, where he could have acquired his miscellany with *Philobiblon* (Balliol College, Ms. 166A). He also lived and studied in several Italian cities. Between the 1440s and 1470s, Gray purchased or commissioned many manuscripts from Oxford stationers and Italian booksellers. He thus formed one of the major personal libraries in England. He had a special interest in works of classical authors and early and contemporary Italian humanists. Balliol College, Ms. 166A is one of as many as two hundred manuscripts that he donated to the college, three-quarters of which remain.[22]

Broad subject interests beyond theology can be seen with other *Philobiblon* manuscripts. *Frater* William Charite (1422–c. 1502), a canon regular of Augustinian Abbey of St. Mary de Pratis in Leicester, East Midlands, copied *Philobiblon* ("Philabiblon[!] d[omi]ni Ricardi de Buri per fr. W. Charite") as the first of eight texts in a multi-text volume (no. 470), no longer extant, listed in the abbey's catalogue, completed by Charite, of its 941-volume library. The volume is the second of several "Volumina de diuersis materiis". The next volume (no. 471) includes Ranulf Higden (c. 1260–1364), *Ars componendi sermones*, a manual on the art of preaching, copied by Charite; and Alain de Lille, *De planctu naturae*.[23] Charite's contemporary, Johannes Gisborne (d. 1502), canon regular, cellarer, and prior (1488) at the Augustinian Priory of St. Mary of Merton, Surrey, owned a composite manuscript including *Philobiblon*; Alain de Lille, *De planctu naturae*; the Latin translation of Walter of Henley's *Husbandry* (c. 1280), and texts or extracts on medicine, alchemy, astronomy, prognostication, and mathematics (Oxford, Digby Ms. 147). Gisborne studied at Oxford (1456) and was a donor to Merton Priory.[24] *Frater* Walter Hotham (c. 1451–d. after 1495), a monk of the Benedictine Abbey of St. Mary, York, who received a B.D. at Cambridge (1472/73) and in 1478 was licensed to preach in his diocese, was largely responsible for copying *Philobiblon* and other texts in his miscellany, including Alain de Lille, *De planctu naturae*; Thomas Merke (d. 1409), *Formula moderni et usitati dictaminis*; and *Quamvis* on the art of preaching (British Library, Ms. Add. 24361). In 1484 and 1492, Hotham was also prior of the Benedictine Priory of Rumburgh, Suffolk, a dependency of St. Mary's, Sussex.

---

[21] HENRY O. COXE: *Catalogus Codicum Mss. qui in Collegiis Aulisque Oxoniensibus hodie adservantur*. Oxford 1852. Vol. 2, pp. 8–9. STEPHEN J. WILLIAMS: *The Secret of Secrets: The Scholarly Career of a Pseudo-Aristotelian Text in the Latin Middle Ages*. Ann Arbor 2003, p. 210, n. 104. N. R. KER: *Records of All Souls College Library, 1437–1600*. Oxford 1971, list II, no. 52.

[22] ROBERTO WEISS: *Humanism in England during the Fifteenth Century*. Oxford 1941, pp. 86–96. JOHN A. F. THOMSON: *The Transformation of Medieval England, 1370–1529*. London 1983, p. 352.

[23] TERESA WEBBER and ANDREW G. WATSON (Ed.): *The Libraries of the Augustinian Canons* (Corpus of British Medieval Library Catalogues. 6). London 1998, p. 270. M. R. JAMES: Catalogue of the Library of Leicester Abbey. Section I (continued). In: *Transactions of the Leicestershire Archaeological Society*. 19 (1937), pp. 377–440, here pp. 428–29. DAVID N. BELL: Monastic Libraries: 1400–1557. In: *The Cambridge History of the Book in Britain*. Ed. LOTTE HELLINGA and J. B. TRAPP. Cambridge 1999, pp. 229–54, here p. 242. Charite's subject interests included astronomy and astrology. He also donated another miscellany with nine texts (no. 472) and three astronomical instruments. HILARY M. CAREY: *Courting Disaster: Astrology at the English Court and University in the Later Middle Ages*. London 1992, pp. 41–42. JONATHAN HUGHES: William Charite (1422–ca. 1502), Compiler of Monastic Records and Prior of Leicester. In: *Oxford Dictionary of National Biography*. Vol. 61. https://DOI: 10.1093/ref:odnb/5140 [last consulted, January 23, 2023].

[24] R. W. HUNT and A. G. WATSON: *Bodleian Library Quarto Catalogues. IX: Digby Manuscripts*. Oxford 1999, pp. 65–66, 170, cols. 144–146. ALFRED HEALES AND MILL STEPHENSON: *The Records of Merton Priory in the County of Surrey, Chiefly from Early and Unpublished Documents*. London 1898, pp. 303–5, 309, 358. N. R. KER: *Medieval Libraries of Great Britain: A List of Surviving Books*. 2nd edition. London 1964, p. 282.

He entrusted this manuscript to William Covyrdaill (Coverdale), a monk at St. Mary's, who retained it until c. 1520.[25]

Several other *Philobiblon* manuscripts can be traced to mendicant preachers and parish priests. *Magister* John Martyll (born c. 1381), a Dominican in West Yorkshire, owned one (Oxford, Bodleian Library, Magdalen College, Ms. Lat. 6). He served as a deacon of the Archdeaconry of Richmond and was later a fellow of Oriel College, Oxford. A gift inscription expresses Martyll's hope that future holders of the manuscript should be priests, who will preach and pray for his soul and those of his parishioners.[26] A similar inscription was used for *Magister* John Alwart (d. 1457/8), who owned a miscellany including *Philobiblon* and Bernard de Gordon (d. 1330), *Lilium medicinae* (Oxford, St. John's College, Ms. 172). He was rector of the parish church of Stoke Bruerne in a Northamptonshire village near Towcester. On fol. 322v (back flyleaf) are inscriptions relating to Alwart's bequest to Oxford, seeking prayers for his soul, family, and parishioners.[27] A later owner was William Pratt (d. 1701/2), who was a native of County Durham and ordained Anglican priest (Cambridge, Sidney Sussex College, Ms. 38).[28] Two *Philobiblon* manuscripts, not extant, were in the Bridgettine Abbey of Syon (1415), a dual monastery of nuns and monks, founded by King Henry V (r. 1413–22) at Isleworth, Middlesex County, in devotion to St. Bridget of Sweden. The *Registrum* of Syon Abbey's Library of the Brethren (Cambridge, Corpus Christi College Library, Ms. 441), completed by Thomas Betson (d. 1516) after 1500, lists the *Philobiblon* manuscripts with authorship attributed to Robert Holcot. *Philobiblon* was the third of seven texts (fols. 74–86) in a miscellany (A.18) of texts on rhetoric, letter-writing, and poetics; and a separately bound copy (A.19).[29] Donors are not listed, but we know that newly professed Brethren donated about three-quarters of the more than 900 miscellanies and other books to the library during its rapid growth period (1459–1520s). Syon Abbey library served the needs of the Brethren, many of whom were university-educated, for sermon preparation, preaching, and providing spiritual guidance to the nuns. Syon's holdings could be supplemented by those of the Carthusian Priory of Sheen, founded by Henry V in what is now the London Borough of Richmond upon Thames (1414). Sheen Priory had formal ties with Syon Abbey.[30]

Richard de Bury's proposed Oxford library supported efforts to improve education for English monks who were attending universities in growing numbers to help prepare for careers in ecclesiastical administration and royal government.[31] Academic degrees in canon and civil law helped launch careers in cathedral chapters and higher-level diocesan

---

25 BL, Ms. Add. 24361, fol. 89v, "Explicit Biblia versificata per libros et capitula quod Walterus Hothom Monachus"; fol. 1v, "Liber monasterii beate Marie Eboraci attinens Fratri Wuillelmo Couyrdaill ex dono Fratris Walteri Hothome ambobus eiusdem Cenobii accoliis ac concenobitis." *A Cambridge Alumni Database* (available on www.venn.lib/cam.ac.uk, [20.1.2023]). He also owned an Ovid manuscript (BL, Ms. Burney 220). KER: *Medieval Libraries of Great Britain*, pp. 217, 321. STACY GEE: 'At the Sygne of the Cardynalles Hat': The Book Trade and the Market for Books in Yorkshire, c. 1450–1550. Diss. phil. York 1999, p. 46.

26 The note is beneath the *tabula capitulorum* on fol. 2r-v for the Dominican Peter de Limoges's *Tractatus moralis de oculo*. Oriel Coll. Ms. 43 was also from Martyll. GEORGE C. RICHARDS and CHARLES L. SHADWELL: *The Provosts and Fellows of Oriel College, Oxford*. Oxford 1922, p. 19. RICHARD NEWHAUSER: Der ‚Tractatus moralis de oculo' des Petrus von Limoges und seine *exempla*. In: *Fortuna vitrea: Arbeiten zur literarischen Tradition zwischen 13. und 16. Jahrhundert*. Ed. WALTER HAUG and BURGHART WACHINGER. Tübingen 1991, pp. 95–136, here pp. 128–29.

27 RALPH HANNA: *A Descriptive Catalogue of the Western Medieval Manuscripts of St John's College, Oxford*. Oxford 2002, p. 240. Inscription reads, "Istum librum legavit magister [Johannes] Alwart, Ad orandum pro anima eius et animabus parentis et parochialibus eius […]" WILLIAM DUNN MACRAY: *Annals of the Bodleian Library Oxford*. 2nd edition. Oxford 1890, p. 11. ALBINIA DE LA MARE and STANLEY GILLAM: *Duke Humphrey's Library and the Divinity School, 1488–1988: An Exhibition at the Bodleian Library June-August 1988*. Oxford 1988, p. 58.

28 Pratt had a B.A. (1666/7) and M.A. (1670), Cambridge, and served as vicar of Bossall, 1673–1701, a parish church in the village of Bossall, North Riding, Yorkshire. *A Cambridge Alumni Database* (available on www.vennlib/cam.ac.uk, [20.1.2023]). M. R. JAMES: *A Descriptive Catalogue of the Manuscripts in the Library of Sidney Sussex College, Cambridge*. Cambridge 1895, pp. 25–26, no. 38.

29 VINCENT GILLESPIE (Ed.): *Syon Abbey, with the Libraries of the Carthusians*, edited by A. I. Doyle. London 2001 (Corpus of British Medieval Library Catalogues. 9), p. 11, 442, 540. Registrum SS 2.9c [A18]; SS 2.10 [A 19]: "Holcote ordinis praedicatorum in suo pilobiblion de commendacione, amore et pia tractabilitate librorum, fo. 74." MARY BATESON: *Catalogue of the Library of Syon Monastery, Isleworth*. Cambridge 1898, pp. xxix, 227.

30 GILLESPIE: *Syon Abbey*, pp. xxxvi–lxvi. E. A. JONES and ALEXANDRA WALSHAM (Ed.): *Syon Abbey and its Books: Reading, Writing, and Religion, c. 1400–1700*. Woodbridge, Suffolk 2010, pp. 57–59, 100–101, 113.

31 NICHOLAS ORME: *Medieval Schools from Roman Britain to Renaissance England*. New Haven 2006, pp. 266–71; JOAN GREATREX: Monk Students from Norwich Cathedral Priory at Oxford and Cambridge, c. 1300 to 1530. In: *English Historical Review*. 106 (1991) 420, pp. 555–83.

governance. *Ars dictaminis* or *dictamen*, long taught at the University of Bologna in connection with legal education, was a branch of rhetoric that emphasized the composition and style of expression of official letters and to a lesser extent legal documents. As such, it was an asset to clerical and monastic career advancement and mobility. Some English university students, particularly at Oxford, acquired or copied miscellanies of such texts during their studies and returned with them to their monasteries. *Philobiblon* circulated along with other texts and manuals that praised learning, and in time, even if written for other reasons, came to be models for teaching Latin prose composition and rhetoric. Martin Camargo has identified Philobiblon and Alain de Lille's *De planctu naturae* as two of four such texts that often circulated together.[32] Indeed, ten of sixteen *Philobiblon* manuscripts of English origin (62.5 percent) are bound with *De planctu naturae* (Appendix, nos. 11, 13, 19, 28, 29, 31, 32, 34, 49, 54). *De planctu naturae* was also bound with one of two *Philobiblon* manuscripts in the Syon Abbey catalogue, as previously noted. This text circulated widely, more in German-speaking lands than in England. Robert Holcot praised Alain de Lille's text, which offered moral guidance and condemned unnatural sex and human vice. It was also written in a distinctive rhetorical style, for which reason many copies were used to teach rhetoric and Latin prose style.[33] The *Philobiblon* manuscript in Canterbury, St. Augustine's Abbey (British Library, Ms. Harley 3224), is no. 964 in the abbey's library catalogue, listed under "Epistolaria."[34] One of ten extant English manuscripts including *Philobiblon* and *De planctu naturae* also includes Alain de Lille's *Anticlaudianus* (Durham, Bishop Cosin's Library, Cosin V.v.2).

Martin Camargo discusses two other texts circulating with *Philobiblon* and *De planctu naturae* as models of Latin prose style: John of Limoges, *Morale somnium Pharaonis* (1255–60), an epistolary text; and Guido della Colonne, *Historia de bello troico* (1287), a prose retelling of Homer. Three of the sixteen extant English manuscripts of *Philobiblon* are bound with one of these two texts (British Library, Ms. Harley 3224; Oxford, Balliol College, Ms. 263; Oxford, St. John's College, Ms. 172), as well as one on the Continent (Basel, Universitätsbibliothek. Ms. A. X. 143). Other treatises and model texts include Geoffrey de Vinsauf (fl. c. 1208–13), *Poetria nova*, an intermediate-level school text on *ars poetica*, used in teaching rhetoric and prose composition at Oxford. Two extant *Philobiblon* manuscripts were bound with *Poetria nova* (Durham, Bishop Cosin's Library, Cosin V.v.2; Oxford, Balliol College, Ms. 166A).[35] Thomas Merke, a monk of Westminster Abbey and later bishop of Carlisle, used *Poetria nova* to compile *Formula moderni et usitati dictaminis* (c. 1390), a textbook on prose composition and that strove to classicize *dictamen*. Two of eleven extant manuscripts of Merke's textbook are bound with *Philobiblon* (British Library, Ms. Add. 24361; Oxford, Balliol, Ms. 263).[36] Italian and French treatises are also found in miscellanies with *Philobiblon*. One copy is in a miscellany of the mid fifteenth century, beginning with five texts by the Bolognese rhetorician Guido Faba (1190–1243) on *ars dictaminis* (fols. 2r–58r) and including a commonplace book

---

[32] MARTIN CAMARGO: Beyond the *Libri Catoniani* Models of Latin Prose Style at Oxford University ca. 1400. In: *Mediaeval Studies*. 56 (1994) 1, pp. 165–87.

[33] NIKOLAUS M. HARING: Alain of Lille, *De Planctu naturae*. In: *Studi medievali*, ser. 3, 19 (1978) 2, pp. 797–870, here p. 805. FRANÇOISE HUDRY: Prologus Alani "De Planctu nature". In: *Archives d'histoire doctrinale et littéraire du Moyen Age*. 55 (1988), pp. 169–85. GUY RAYNAUD DE LAGE: *Alain de Lille, poète du XIIe siècle*. Montréal 1951, pp. 182–83. The latter lists thirty manuscripts of *De planctu naturae* in German and Austrian libraries, and twenty-three in England.

[34] BARKER-BENFIELD: *St Augustine's Abbey, Canterbury*. Vol. 2, pp. 989–90.

[35] IAN CORNELIUS: The Rhetoric of Advancement: *Ars dictaminis, Cursus,* and Clerical Careerism in Late Medieval England. In: *New Medieval Literatures*. 12 (2010), pp. 287–328. MARJORIE CURRY WOODS: Using the *Poetria nova* to Teach *Dictamen* in Italy and Central Europe. In: *Atti dei Convegno Internationale 'Dictamen, Poetria and Cicero: Conference and Diversification, Bologna, 10–11 Maggio 2002*. Ed. LUCIA CALBOLI MONTEFUSCO. Rome 2003 (Università degli Studi di Bologna, Departmento di Filologia Classica e Medioevale. 7. Papers on Rhetoric. 5), pp. 261–79. *MARJORIE CURRY WOODS*: Classroom Commentaries: Teaching the Poetria nova across Medieval and Renaissance Europe. Columbus, Ohio 2010, pp. 227–33. MALCOLM RICHARDSON: The *Dictamen* and its Influence on Fifteenth-Century English Prose. In: *Rhetorica: A Journal of the History of Rhetoric*. 2 (1984) 3, pp. 207–26. MICHEL NICOLAS: Diffusion et réception du *Somnium morale Pharaonis* de Jean de Limoges: pour une meilleure connaissance des pratiques dictaminales. In: *Archivum Latinitatis Medii Aevi*. 74 (2016), pp. 127–74.

[36] SHARPE: *Handlist*, pp. 668–69, no. 1791. MARTIN CAMARGO: *Medieval Rhetorics of Prose Composition: Five English Artes Dictandi and their Tradition*. Binghamton, N.Y. 1994, pp. 105–47. JAMES G. CLARK: *A Monastic Renaissance at St Albans: Thomas Walsingham and his Circle c. 1350–1440*. Oxford 2004, pp. 216–27.

of letters (*Provinciale*) transcribed from the register of Cardinal Annibale (d. 1350?), bishop of Toscolano, Lombardy, probably to serve as an epistolary model (British Library, Ms. Cotton, Appendix IV).[37] Another is in a manuscript that includes Matthew of Vendôme (1100–85), *De arte versificatoria* (Oxford, Balliol College, Ms. 263). Also useful for pedagogical purposes were discussions in *Philobiblon* of classical authors and texts, whose mastery improved one's Latinity and understanding of pagan errors (chap. ix–xi, xiii).[38] A late fourteenth-century miscellany with *Philobiblon* includes *Ovid Moralisée* (c. 1316–28), an Old French translation of *Metamorphoses* (British Library, Ms. Royal 8 F xiv). One miscellany includes three letters from Seneca's *Epistulae morales ad Lucilium* and other texts relating to Seneca (Cambridge, St. John's College, Ms. 115). Such texts appealed to Oxford's classicizing friars for use in biblical exegesis and in making sermons more appealing for preaching.[39]

Richard de Bury described his own elegant Latin prose style as being modern and light. This was perhaps true, as Martin Camargo suggests, by comparison with *De planctu naturae*.[40] As Noël Denholm-Young explained, *Philobiblon* was "couched in the form of a letter or manifesto," written in accordance with the rules of the *Cursus Curiae Romanae* as practiced in the Papal Chancery. In Denholm-Young's view, the frequency of types and sub-types of *clausulae* in *Philobiblon*'s prose rhythms supports Richard de Bury's authorship.[41] Royal clerks composing official letters needed to master refined Latin prose expression, which was desirable for foreign letters penned by royal officials. From his early career in royal bureaucracy, Richard de Bury valued *ars dictaminis* manuals and papal chancery practices of rhythmic prose as guides to Latin expression. His interest is evident in *Liber Epistolaris* (c. 1324), his commonplace book or formulary of some 1500 model letters and other items that he selected and transcribed in a volume, along with papal bulls and letters, formularies of Italian and French origin, and a treatise on eloquence.[42] Such compilations were reference books for epistolary forms and precedents.

Philobiblon also interested administrators and lay clerks in Greater London. A late fourteenth-century miscellany including *Philobiblon* and other texts (British Library, Ms. Royal 15 C xvi) was owned by Henry Spicer [de Harleston] (d. 1437), a canon of St. George's Chapel, Windsor Castle, and long associated with Chichester Cathedral as a canon and prebendary of Gates, 1402–37. The miscellany also included Alain de Lille, *De planctu naturae*; and Petrus Berchorius (1290–1362), *Ovidius moralizatus* (1340).[43] Among other duties, each of the thirteen canons of St. George's Chapel supervised a priest-vicar or minor canon responsible for saying the daily offices, and some were book owners and involved

---

[37] *Catalogue of the Manuscripts in the Cottonian Library, Deposited in the British Museum.* London 1802, p. 614. ("Provinciale catholicorum Cristianorum vivorum; sumptum de registro D. Hanibaldi Episc[opi] Tusculanensis, cardinalis, A.D. 1343").

[38] CLARK: *Monastic Renaissance at St Albans*, pp. 216–17.

[39] BERYL SMALLEY: *English Friars and Antiquity in the Early Fourteenth Century.* Oxford 1960, p. 44. JOHN T. SLOTEMAKER and JEFFERY C. WITT: *Robert Holcot.* Oxford 2016, pp. 130–31. SIEGFRIED WENZEL: The Classics in Late-Medieval Preaching. In: *Medieval Antiquity.* Ed. ANDRIES WELKHUYSEN, HERMAN BRAET, and WERNER VERBEKE. Leuven 1995, pp. 127–43, here pp. 127–28. CLARK: University Monks in Late Medieval England, pp. 56–70.

[40] ALTAMURA, p. 73 (*Prologus*: "...parvulinum tractatum edidimus stilo quidem levissimo modernorum..."). ANDREW F. WEST: Lexicographical Gleanings from the *Philobiblon* of Richard de Bury. In: *Transactions of the American Philological Association.* 22 (1891), pp. 93–104, here p. 93. CAMARGO: Beyond the *Libri Catoniani* Models of Latin Prose Style, p. 180.

[41] NOËL DENHOLM-YOUNG: Richard de Bury (1287–1345) and the *Liber Epistolaris*. In: *Collected Papers of N. Denholm-Young.* 1969, pp. 1–41, here pp. 34–35. NOËL DENHOLM-YOUNG: The *Cursus* in England. In: ibid., pp. 42–73. NOËL DENHOLM-YOUNG: Review of Gudrun Lindholm: *Studien zum mittellateinischen Prosarhythmus: Seine Entwicklung und sein Abklingen in der Briefliteratur Italiens.* Stockholm 1963. In: *Medium Aevum.* 32 (January 1963), p. 170. See also CHARLES CHRISTOPHER MIEROW: Mediaeval Latin Vocabulary, Usage, and Style: As Illustrated by the *Philobiblon* (1345) of Richard de Bury. In: *Classical Philology.* 25 (1930) 4, pp. 343–57.

[42] The Abbey of Bury St. Edmunds acquired Richard de Bury's manuscript after his death and the dispersal of his L. The original manuscript is at Aberystwyth, The NL of Wales, Brogyntyn Ms. II.7 (Porkington 21). Description at www.archifau.llyfrgell.cymru, [20.1.2023]. About 500 letters are published in NOËL DENHOLM-YOUNG (Ed.): *The Liber Epistolaris of Richard de Bury.* Oxford 1950 (Roxburghe Club. 212).

[43] BL. *Manuscripts and Archives*: www.searcharchives.bl.uk, [20.1.2023]. Dieter Blume and Christel Meier-Staubach (Ed.): *Petrus Berchorius und der antike Mythos in 14. Jahrhundert.* Berlin 2021. Vol. 1, pp. 45–46.

in the royal civil service at Westminster.⁴⁴ He donated the miscellany to the Hospital of St. Thomas of Acre [Acon], a London collegiate church, then under the leadership of John Neel, Master of the Hospital (r. 1420–63). Neel later pledged the miscellany to the Austin Canons of Ashridge Priory, Hertfordshire. N. R. Ker lists James Butler (1496–1546), ninth earl of Ormond, whose family were Hospital patrons and manuscript owners, as the donor of this miscellany and three other manuscripts to the Hospital.⁴⁵ Neel played a major role in efforts to increase the Hospital's endowment and support its school to provide education for young men and boys and improve liturgy in the Hospital. He was also involved with efforts to expand London schools and increase the number of schoolmasters and choristers. These efforts perhaps encouraged the Hospital's benefactors to donate manuscripts, including four volumes of theology and sermons now in the British Library and a copy of Ranulf Higden's *Polychronicon*.⁴⁶

Lay clerks were among private owners of *Philobiblon* manuscripts. The most prominent was John Carpenter (c. 1372–1442), Town Clerk of London (1417–38) and a member of Parliament for the City of London (1436–39), who owned a copy that is no longer extant. As Town Clerk, he was responsible for keeping the minutes of council and committee meetings. He also compiled the *Liber Albus* (1419) on London history, law, customs, and governance; and he played a role in creating the Guildhall Library (1425) under the will of former Lord Mayor Richard Whittington (c. 1354–1423), who was involved in the same educational efforts as John Neel. Carpenter's own will (1442) lists twenty-six Latin and Anglo-Norman manuscripts, including devotional reading and technical manuals, some received as gifts. He bequeathed his books to particular clerics and town clerks.⁴⁷ His miscellany with *Philobiblon* was left to Richard Delafield (1400–83), who in the mid-1440s was one of King Henry VI's royal clerks and married Eleanor Waldern, daughter of William Waldern (d. 1424), former Mayor of London.⁴⁸ The miscellany also included Alain de Lille, *De planctu naturae; Tractatus dictaminis*, possibly referring to Thomas Merke, *Formula moderni et usitati dictaminis*; and the pseudo-Ovidian moralistic poem *De vetula*, which Richard de Bury quoted in *Philobiblon* to decry the decline in clerical learning and to recommend the comfort of books and virtuous diversions.⁴⁹ Carpenter owned a second copy of *De planctu naturae* and one of *Anticlaudianus*; as well as Pseudo-Aristotle, *Secretum secretorum*; and manuals on documents and record-keeping under Common Law and London customs. Carpenter consigned these for life to city clerk Robert Blount, an attorney and possibly a member of Gray's Inn, reverting thereafter to the Guildhall of London "for the information of the clerks there." George Shuffleton suggests that Carpenter's career and books show "how lay clerks appropriated a Latinate intellectual inheritance that formerly belonged to elite ecclesiastical administrators and monks. As they assumed priestly roles in the service of secular institutions, lay clerks buttressed their work with the books of their ecclesiastical predecessors."[50]

Now let us turn from England to the Continent and its forty-nine *Philobiblon* manuscripts (75.4 percent of total). *Philobiblon* was being copied in France from the late fourteenth century, though few French copies survive (Appendix, nos. 56, 57, 62). In Paris, Jehan La Masse (d. 1458), a canon regular and later prior of the Augustinian Abbey of Saint Victor (r. 1448–58), was responsible for commissioning or purchasing more than a hundred manuscripts on theology and other subjects for the abbey's library. Among his acquisitions was an older composite volume, probably purchased second-hand, containing *Philobiblon* and theological works of Bernard of Clairvaux, Hugh of Saint Victor, and William of Auxerre (Paris, Bibliothèque Nationale de France, Ms. 15168).[51] The Avignon library under Benedict XIII (r. 1394–1423) had a miscellany including a copy of *Philobiblon* (Paris, Bibliothèque Nationale de France, Ms. 3352C), with authorship attributed to Robert Holcot ("Philobiblon Olchoti Anglici"). The manuscript corresponds to no. 956 in medieval library inventories.[52] Avignon's library holdings began to expand under Pope John XXII (r. 1316–34), when Richard de Bury was on two diplomatic missions for King Edward III to the papal court (1330, 1333) and met Petrarch. The library expanded rapidly under Pope Clement VI (r. 1342–52), who sought Petrarch's aid finding manuscripts of Cicero and other classical authors. It came to hold more than 2000 volumes acquired by gift, purchase, scribal commissions, and inheritance from prelates in the curia.[53]

The largest number of extant *Philobiblon* manuscripts on the Continent are from German-speaking areas (including former parts of Germania), where monastic and ecclesiastical libraries remained intact until being secularized centuries later and with far fewer losses than the British Isles, where the Dissolution of the Monasteries (1536–40) took a terrible toll on manuscripts. Smaller numbers of *Philobiblon* copies originated in France, Spain, and Italy (beyond the Tyrol). In contrast to the sixteen extant *Philobiblon* manuscripts of English origin (24.6 percent), there are thirty-two manuscripts from Germania (50.8 percent); and six others that are either from German- or Netherlandic-speaking (Dutch or Flemish) areas (9.2 percent). Michael Maclagan noted without explanation, "Richard de Bury's lively work was more appreciated overseas, especially perhaps in Germany, than it was in his own land."[54] Research on dated scribal colophons tends to show sizable increases in production of *Philobiblon* manuscripts in the second quarter and especially the third quarter of the fifteenth century, coinciding with the advent of printing, followed by a sharp fall.[55] *Philobiblon* manuscripts from German- and Netherlandic-

---

[50] GEORGE SHUFFLETON, JOHN CARPENTER, and LAY CLERK: *The Chaucer Review*. 48 (2014) 4, pp. 34–56. LYNN STALEY: *Following Chaucer: Offices of the Active Life*. Ann Arbor 2020, pp. 102–4. SYLVIA L. THRUPP: *The Merchant Class of Medieval London, 1300–1500*. Ann Arbor 1976, pp. 248–49. PENNY TUCKER: *Law Courts and Lawyers in the City of London, 1300–1500*. Cambridge 2007, pp. 311–12.

[51] BNF Ms. 15168. LÉOPOLD DELISLE: *Inventaire des manuscrits de l'Abbaye de Saint-Victor conservés à la Bibliothèque Impériale, sous les numéros 14232–15175 de fonts latin*. Paris 1869, p. 78 (fol. 45r: "Hunc librum acquisiuit monasterio sancti victoris prope parisius frater Johannes lamasse dum esset prior eiusdem ecclesie."). Other manuscripts have evidence of previous ownership. In 1417, for example, La Masse purchased a manuscript (BNF Ms. 14557) from executors for the estate of Germanus Famuli de Rungiaco, a cleric in the diocese of Paris, who held a licentiate (1400) and doctorate in theology (1403) from the U of Paris. THOMAS SULLIVAN: *Parisian Licentiates in Theology, A.D. 1373–1500: A Biographical Register. Vol. II. The Secular Clergy*. Leiden 2011, p. 489. LÉOPOLD DELISLE: *Le cabinet des manuscrits de la Bibliothèque Nationale*. Paris 1874. Vol. 2, p. 217.

[52] MARIE-HENRIETTE JULLIEN DE POMMEROL and JACQUES MONFRIN (Ed.): *La Bibliothèque Pontificale à Avignon et à Peñiscola pendant le Grand Schisme d'Occident et sa dispersion. Inventaires et concordances*. Rome 1910 (Publications de l'École Française de Rome, Année 1991. 141). Vol. 1, pp. 243 (537), 327 (171), 671 (313). MAURICE FAUCON: *La librairie des papes d'Avignon: Sa formation, sa composition, ses catalogues*. Paris 1887 (Bibliothèque des Écoles Françaises d'Athènes et de Rome. 50). Vol. 2, p. 38 ("Item Philobibl[i]on Olchoti Anglici in quaternis ligatis cum folio in papiro"). Later the manuscript was in the L of Cardinal Pierre de Foix, le vieux (1386–1464), archbishop of Arles; and the French statesman Jean-Baptiste Colbert (1619–83), no. 2167.

[53] NOËL DENHOLM-YOUNG: Richard de Bury (1287–1345) and the *Liber Epistolaris*. In: *Noël Denholm-Young, Collected Papers of N. Denholm-Young*. Cardiff 1969, pp. 1–41, here pp. 27–28. CAROLYN P. COLLETTE: Richard de Bury, Petrarch and Avignon. In: *Anglo-Italian Cultural Relations in the Later Middle Ages*. Ed. MICHELE CAMPOPIANO and HELEN FULTON. Woodbridge, Suffolk 2018, pp. 40–51. JOËLLE ROLLO-KOSTER: *Avignon and its Papacy, 1309–1417: Popes, Institutions, and Society*. Lanham 2015, pp. 48, 65–69.

[54] MACLAGAN, p. lxxiii.

[55] ELTJO BURINGH: *Medieval Manuscript Production in the Latin West: Exploration with a Global Database*. Leiden 2011, p. 267 (Table 5.8: "Production Estimates for Germany, Italy, France, and Britain, eleventh to fifteenth centuries").

speaking areas tend to date from the second half of the fifteenth century (60.0 percent of total), including eleven dated and datable copies between the 1450s and 1480s (Appendix, nos. 1, 3, 5, 6, 8, 14, 23, 37, 43, 50, 58), compared with only three in the 1420s and 1430s (nos. 16, 39, 59). English copies tend to be earlier but are rarely dated. Twelve of the sixteen in England are estimated to date from 1375–1425 (Appendix, nos. 10, 13, 29, 31, 32, 33, 34, 47, 49, 51, 52, 53).

The circulation of *Philobiblon* manuscripts and printed books in late medieval Germany and the Netherlands is related in large measure to the efforts of several religious orders and changes in spiritual life. The Carthusians in particular encouraged copying and sharing of Latin and vernacular or bilingual books, most often written on paper in common book scripts, such as *Hybrida formata* and *Cursiva currens*.[56] They surely appreciated *Philobiblon*'s assertion that monks exercised an office of sacred piety (*sacratae pietatis officium*) in relation to production, dissemination, and keeping of books; and its appeals to monks and mendicants for the exercise of religion based on deeper knowledge of scripture.[57] Late medieval Cologne and its diocese was at the center of the mystical tradition associated with Dominican philosophers and theologians, such as Meister Eckhart (c. 1260–c. 1328), Johannes Taler (c. 1300–61), and Heinrich Suso (1295–1366), who emphasized a personal relationship between the individual and God. From the 1370s, the *Devotio Moderna* spread in the Netherlands and Germany, advocating religious reform. Its lay devotional communes embraced the contemplative life and forms of piety, meditation, and inner spirituality exemplified by Thomas à Kempis, *De imitatione Christi*. The *Devotio Moderna* influenced the Brethren of the Common Life, founded in Deventer by the Dutch preacher and mystic Geert Groote (1340–84), who focused on seeking God through an inner conversion and an abhorrence of worldly things; Canons Regular of the Order of the Holy Cross (Crosiers); and the Augustinian Canons Regular of the Congregation of Windesheim, which his disciples founded at Windesheim (near Zwolle), Overijssel. Scripture, service books, sermons, and treatises were copied and read to spread the word of God at the Congregation's more than two dozen German priories.[58]

This background helps explain why particular religious orders are so well represented among producers, owners, and readers of *Philobiblon*. Six manuscripts with *Philobiblon* were from Carthusian monasteries (nos. 14, 18, 25, 26, 36, 48). Five manuscripts also contain Jean Gerson (1363–1429), *De laude scriptorum* (Appendix, nos. 14, 15, 16, 48, 50). The two texts were also paired in a lost manuscript once in the Charterhouse of St. Barbara, Cologne, which was influenced by the *Devotio Moderna*.[59] Gerson was the best-represented medieval author in the Charterhouse library. *De laude scriptorum* was valued because it praised Carthusian scribal copying for the benefit of the faithful, not only for the personal salvation of monks. The text was in the tradition of Cassiodorus (c. 490–c. 585), who praised scribal copying as a form of "preaching with the hands".[60] Charterhouses also allowed manuscripts to be borrowed by scribes and

---

[56] GEERT WARNER: Prelude: Northern Circulation of Fourteenth-Century Mystical Texts. In: *A Companion to Mysticism and Devotion in the Late Middle Ages*. Ed. ELIZABETH ANDERSEN, HENRIKE LAHNEMANN, and ANNE SIMON. Leiden 2014, pp. 159–78, here pp. 159–61. HENRIKE LÄHNEMANN: Bilingual Devotion in Northern Germany: Prayer Books from the Lüneburg Convents. In: *Ibid.*, pp. 317–41, here p. 317.

[57] ALTAMURA, p. 84 (chap. iv): "...et quid per libros recipitis fideliter computetis, et invenietis libros totius nobilis status vestri quodam modo creatores..." p. 125 (chap. xvii): "Non solum Deo prestamus obsequium novorum librorum preparando volumina, sed sacrate pietatis exercemus officium, si eosdem nunc illese tractemus, nunc locis idoneis redditos illibate custodie commendemus, ut gaudeant puritate..." p. 91 (chap. v): "Patres igitur reverendi, patrum vestrorum dignemini reminisci et librorum propensius indulgete studio, sine quibus quelibet vacillabit religio, sine quibus ut testa virtus devocionis arescet, sine quibus nullum lumen poteritis mundo prebere." p. 93 (chap. vi): "Sacra scriptura non exponitur, sed omnino seponitur, quasi trita per vicos et omnibus divulgata supponitur..."

[58] JOHN VAN ENGEN: *Sisters and Brothers of the Common Life: The Devotio Moderna and the World of the Later Middle Ages*. Philadelphia 2008, pp. 1, 4–6. FRANCIS OAKLEY: *The Western Church in the Later Middle Ages*. Ithaca 1979, pp. 102, 233. On the Windesheim Congregation and manuscripts, see R. R. POST: *The Modern Devotion: Confrontation with Reformation and Humanism*. Leiden 1968, pp. 293–313. WOLFGANG OESER: Die Brüder des gemeinsamen Lebens in Münster als Bücherschreiber. In: *Archiv für Geschichte des Buchwesens*. 5 (1964), pp. 197–398.

[59] RICHARD B. MARKS: *The Medieval Manuscript Library of the Charterhouse of St. Barbara in Cologne*. Salzburg 1974 (Analecta Cartusiana). Vol. 2, p. 432. Cited in a seventeenth-century shelf-list.

[60] MARKS: *The Medieval Manuscript Library of the Charterhouse*. Vol. 1, p. 141–42. FELIX HEINZER: Preaching with the Hands: Notes on Cassiodorus' Praise of Handwriting and its Medieval Reception. In: *Exploring Written Artefacts: Objects, Methods, and Concepts*. Ed. JÖRG B. QUENZER. Berlin 2021, pp. 947–63.

printers.⁶¹ At least six *Philobiblon* manuscripts were associated with religious communities influenced by the *Devotio Moderna* (Appendix, nos. 4, 14, 16, 23, 24, 60). In addition, there are copies of *Philobiblon* in theological miscellanies that provided general reference for ordained monks and secular clergy serving as cathedral preachers, to spread the word of God and combat heresy.⁶² Indeed, *Philobiblon* has been described as "a sermon in itself, a sermon about books."⁶³ It also appealed to the *Ordo Praedicatorum*. Six miscellanies including *Philobiblon* had a connection with Dominican houses in German-speaking lands (Appendix, nos. 1, 4, 5, 6, 44, 59); and another was listed in the library catalogue of the Dominican Monastery of Vienna (1513).⁶⁴ Scholars have suggested that Dominicans may have ascribed authorship or editorship to Robert Holcot because he was a member of their order.⁶⁵

From the late fourteenth century, various theologians and masters retained copies of *Philobiblon* in theological miscellanies within their personal libraries, which supported theological inquiry and provided manuals, florilegia, and sermons useful for preachers. Among the earliest theological miscellanies with *Philobiblon* was Erfurt, Universitäts- und Forschungsbibliothek, Dep. Erf. 4° 123, which originally contained twenty-five items, including eight theological texts and seventeen sermons or homilies. *Philobiblon* was the final text ("a Roberto Holkoth scriptus et Richardo dedicatus"), probably beginning on fol. 268r. The copy of *Philobiblon* was later removed from the volume and is now considered lost. The manuscript's copyist and owner was the theologian Paulus de Gelria (1353–1404), also known as Paul von Geldern, whose surname suggests Netherlandish origins in the Duchy of Guelders.⁶⁶ He studied and taught at the universities of Paris (1375–82), Prague (1382–83), Vienna (1383–97), and Cologne (1397–1404). In 1396, Gelria became *doctor theologiae* and dean of the theology faculty at Vienna. He wrote on theology and scriptural commentary, and he was in the circle of Heinrich von Langenstein and Heinrich Totting von Oyta until their deaths in 1397.⁶⁷ The miscellany was one of about twenty Gelria manuscripts later in the Biblioteca Amploniana, founded by Amplonius Rating de Berka (c. 1363/64–1435), professor of medicine and rector at the universities of Erfurt and Cologne. It is cited in Berka's 1410 library catalogue. In 1412, Berka donated 633 manuscripts, including *Philobiblon* and others purchased in Cologne after Gelria's death, to the *Collegium Porta Caeli* (or *Amplonianum*) that he founded in Erfurt. Berka collected beyond theology and

---

61 DENNIS MARTIN: *Fifteenth-Century Carthusian Reform: The World of Nicholas Kempf*. Leiden 1992, pp. 230–33. Other texts could also provide bibliographic guidance to improve holdings in the interest of serving God. For example, a German theological miscellany (UB Augsburg, Cod II 1.2° 160) contains the following extracts: fols. 173r–175r, GUILELMUS PERALDUS (c. 1190–1271): *De eruditione religiosorum*; fols. 175r–183v, *Opusculum libros et lectionem commendans*. HARDO HILG: *Die Handschriften der Universitätsbibliothek Augsburg. Zweiter Band. Lateinische mittelalterliche Handschriften in folio. Cod. II. 1.2° 91–226*. Wiesbaden 1999, p. 227. Hilg notes in connection with the anonymous second (Benedictine) text: »Anfangsteil von Kap. 1 weitgehend übereinstimmend mit Richardus de Bury, *Philobiblon*, Kap. 1.«

62 RICHARD H. ROUSE and MARY A. ROUSE: *Preachers, Florilegia and Sermons: Studies on the Manipulus florum of Thomas of Ireland*. Toronto 1979, pp. 43–64. JAMES HOGG: Early Fifteenth-Century Chapterhouse Sermons at the Charterhouse of Mainz. In: *Medieval Monastic Preaching*. Ed. CAROLYN MUESSIG. Leiden 1998, pp. 53–72. MATTHEW WRANOVIX: *Priests and their Books in Late Medieval Eichstätt*. Lanham, Md 2017, pp. 275–82 (Appendix A: "Texts Appearing in Books Owned and/or Produced by Priests in the Diocese of Eichstätt"). R. W. SCRIBNER: *Religion and Culture in Germany (1400–1800)*. Ed. LYNDAL ROPER. Leiden 2001, pp. 248–49.

63 W. M. DICKIE: Richard de Bury and the Philobiblon. In: *Proceedings of the Leeds Philosophical and Literary Society*. Literary and Historical Section. 6 (1944) 3, pp. 148–62, here p. 155.

64 THEODOR GOTTLIEB (Ed.): *Mittelalterliche Bibliothekskataloge Österreichs*. Vienna 1915. Vol. 1, p. 345 (shelfmark, G 57).

65 Thomas suggested this possibility, pp. xliii–xliv. Three English manuscripts (Appendix, nos. 45, 51, 52) and one Italian (no. 63) also had a connection with the Dominicans.

66 WILHELM SCHUM: *Beschreibenes Verzeichniss der amplonianisches Handschriften-Sammlung zu Erfurt*. Berlin 1887, pp. 380–383; at p. 383. *Manuscripta Mediaevalia* (available on http://www.manuscripta-mediaevalia.de, [20.1.2023]). He added scribal colophons to some manuscripts copied in Cologne, such as "Hic liber est scriptus per manus Pauli Fabri de Gelria Wyenne in collegio domini ducis a. D. millesimo CCC° 87°" (Erfurt, Dep. Erf. 4° 79, fol. 167r).

67 BRIGITTE PFEIL: Das 'Matrjoschka-Prinzip': Büchersammlungen von Gelehrten und Universitätslehrern des 14. Jahrhundert im Bestand der Erfurter 'Bibliotheca Amploniana'. In: *Mitteldeutsches Jahrbuch für Kultur und Geschichte*. 19 (2012), pp. 31–47, here pp. 32, 38–40, 44–46. FRIDERICUS STEGMÜLLER (Ed.): *Repertorium biblicum medii aevi*. Madrid 1989, p. 198, nos. 6332, 6333. EGBERT BOS and STEPHEN READ (Ed.): *Concepts: The Treatises of Thomas of Cleves and Paul of Gelria: An Edition of the Texts with a Systematic Introduction*. Louvain-la-Neuve 2001, pp. 18–21. JOSEPH ASCHBACH: *Geschichte der Wiener Universität im ersten Jahrhunderte ihres Bestehens*. Vienna 1865, pp. 44, 125, 153, 419n. ALBERT ZIMMERMANN: *Die Kölner Universität im Mittelalter: geistige Wurzeln und soziale Wirklichkeit*. Berlin 1969, pp. 437, 534.

had broad interests in philosophy, medicine, grammar, rhetoric, classical texts, and law.⁶⁸

Peter Rode (d. 1483), a native of Lüneburg, Lower Saxony, had a paper miscellany including twelve folios of *Philobiblon* (chap. i–xvi) and seven other texts and extracts copied for his own use in Leipzig and Magdeburg, 1462–69 (Berlin, Staatsbibliothek zu Berlin, Preußischer Kulturbesitz, Ms. Magdeburgica 32). Rode had a substantial library of theology and canon law (chiefly penitentials), most personally copied and often annotated in the late 1450s and 1460s. The longest text in the miscellany with *Philobiblon* is *Flores operum*, a florilegium of writings by St. Bernard of Clairvaux (1090–1153).⁶⁹ Rode had studied at the Universität Leipzig (1441–62) and earned the degrees of B.A., M.A., and *licentiatus theologiae*. He taught theology at the Universität Leipzig and served as Dean of the Art Faculty (1459) and Rector (1461). In 1464, he became a canon (*Domherr*) of the Domstift St. Moritz of Magdeburg Cathedral and was cathedral preacher (*Domprediger*; *lector primarius*), 1464–83.⁷⁰ Rode bequeathed the miscellany and thirty-three other bound manuscripts and nineteen incunables dating from 1473 to 1482 to the library of the Dominican Monastery of St. Moritz, Magdeburg. Rode also gave at least three manuscripts to the library of Magdeburg Cathedral.⁷¹

The personal library of the Carthusian theologian Jakob von Jüterbog (1381–1465) included a miscellany including *Philobiblon* (Göttingen, Niedersächsische Universitätsbibliothek, Theol. Ms. 119). He was born Benedict Stolzenhagen, near Potsdam, but known by other names, such as Jacobus de Clusa, Jacobus de Erfordia, and Jakob von Paradies. The miscellany dates from c. 1452–55, when he was lecturing on theology and canon law at the Universität Erfurt, becoming rector in 1455. *Philobiblon* is the first of twenty-two texts, including at least ten theological works by Jüterbog himself. He was a monk (1403–41) and abbot (1432–41) of the Cistercian Abbey of Paradies, formerly in Meseritz, Prussia (now in Poland). Jüterbog matriculated at the University of Cracow (Jagiellonian) in 1420 and was promoted to *magisterium theologiae* in 1432. He studied and taught at Cracow until 1441, when he joined the Carthusians and entered the Charterhouse of St. Salvatorberg, Erfurt, Thuringia.⁷² Jüterbog was a leading Erfurt theologian and the best-known member of the community at the time. His theology was primarily Scholastic, but he contributed to mystical theology by his *De mystica theologia*, heavily influenced by Jean Gerson. He influenced Pre-Reformation theology by his writings, including about 185 treatises, sermons, a confessional, and a tract on indulgences. His works circulated in manuscript and were in monastic libraries across the German-speaking world, including the Erfurt and Cologne charterhouses, and some texts were being printed posthumously from c. 1472. He advocated monastic reform in *Petitiones religiosorum pro reformatione sui status* and supported Conciliarism and addressed a petition to Pope Nicholas V (r. 1447–55), *Avisamentum ad papam pro*

68 WILHELM SCHUM: *Beschreibendes Verzeichnis der amplonianischen Handschriften-Sammlung zu Erfurt*. Berlin 1887. Vol. 2, pp. 346, 380–83. EDUARD JACOBS: Amplonius von Berka. In: *Allgemeine Deutsche Biographie*. Leipzig 1900. Vol. 45, pp. 772–74.

69 URSULA WINTER: *Die Manuscripta Magdeburgica der Staatsbibliothek zu Berlin Preussischer Kulturbesitz. Teil I: Ms. Magdeb. 1–75*. Wiesbaden 2001, pp. 114–16 (at p. 115).

70 *Die Matrikel der Universität Leipzig*. Vol. 3, p. 712. In *Codex Diplomaticus Saxoniae Regiae* (available on www.codex.isgv.de, [20.1.2023]).

71 GOTTFRIED WENTZ and BERENT SCHWINEKÖPER: *Das Erzbistum Magdeburg, Das Domstift St. Moritz in Magdeburg*. Berlin 1972 (Germania sacra: Historisch-Statistiche Beschreibung der Kirche des alten Reiches). Vol. 1, part 1, pp. 541–45 (*Philobiblon* cited on p. 543). WINTER: *Die Manuscripta Magdeburgica, passim*. ANJA FRECKMANN: *Die Bibliothek des Kloster Bursfelde im Spätmittelalter*. Göttingen 2006, pp. 318–20. HEINRICH HALLER and ERIKA BAUER (Ed.): *Iacobus de Paradiso: ‚Passio Christi'*. Vol. 136. Salzburg 2005 (Analecta Cartusiana), p. 35. RENATE SCHIPKE and KURT HEYDECK: *Handschriftencensus der kleineren Sammlungen in den Östlichen Bundesländern Deutschlands*. Wiesbaden 2000, pp. 122–23, nos. 181, 182, 183.

72 WILHELM MEYER: *Die Handschriften in Göttingen*. Berlin 1893. Vol. 2 (Universitätsbibliothek), pp. 360–64.

reformatione ecclesiae.⁷³ Jüterbog's *Philobiblon* miscellany appears to have been in a monastic library after his death, to judge from verses added on fol. 31v after the *subscriptio of Philobiblon*. Versions of these verses, which addressed monks reading library manuscripts to handle them with care, are found in German monastic manuscripts, c. 1440–1505. Jüterbog's miscellany is not recorded in library catalogues of the Charterhouse of Erfurt. At the end of the fifteenth century, the charterhouse library had a *Sammelband* that included handwritten *Philobiblon* extracts and printed texts of 1475–81.⁷⁴

Among other theologians who owned copies of *Philobiblon* was Theoderich von Oestinghausen (d. post 1480), a Dominican whose surname refers to a village and parish north of Soest, North Rhine-Westphalia. He had a copy of *Philobiblon* dating from c. 1420 in a paper miscellany of eight texts copied by different scribes, 1373–1470 (Soest, Stadtbibliothek, Cod. 22). Oestinghausen became a *doctor theologiae* and served as a lecturer in theology (1454) and prior (1456) of the Dominican Monastery of Soest. The miscellany was his gift or bequest to the abbey library.⁷⁵ Another such miscellany was in the library of Conrad Wagner von Nürnberg (d. 1461), also known as Konrad Mülner and Conradus de Sancto Gallo. *Philobiblon* was copied by Scribe B in 1451, and another part by Johannes Steinhauser, *vicarius* in St. Sebalduskirche, Nürnberg, 1453. Much of the volume was copied for Wagner, who bequeathed it to the Benedictine Abbey of Melk, Lower Austria, as recorded in 1464 (Bodley, Ms. Lyell 63). In addition to *Philobiblon*, the volume includes works of Heinrich von Langenstein and Hermann Zoestius von Münster (d. c. 1445), a monk of Kloster Marienfeld. Wagner was *doctor theologiae* from the University of Vienna and served as dean of its arts faculty (1444). Melk listed the miscellany in its library catalogue (1483).⁷⁶ Wagner authored vernacular devotional texts, such as *Traktat vom schauenden Menschen*. He copied and bequeathed manuscripts to other libraries, including the Benedictine Abbey of St. Mang in Füssen, Diocese of

---

73 LUDGER MEIER: *Die Werke des Erfurter Kartäusers Jakob von Jüterbog in ihrer handschriftlichen Überlieferung*. Münster 1955 (Beiträge zur Geschichte der Philosophie und Theologie des Mittelalters. Band 37, Heft 5), pp. 8–92. Göttingen holds other manuscripts with Jüterbog's writings, including Theol. 129, 130, 131, 132, 133, 134; and Lüneburg, 32, 36 (Kloster St. Michael in Lüneburg). MEYER: *Die Handschriften in Göttingen*. Vol. 2, pp. 369–73, 512, 515–16. Jüterbog's miscellany was later "Tomus III" in the L of the German theologian and philologist Jacob Friedrich Reimmann (1668–1743). *Bibliotheca Historiae Literariae critica, eaque generalis, hoc est, Catalogi Bibliothecae Reimmannianae...* Hildesheim 1739. Vol. 2, pp. 796–805 (at pp. 796–97). STEPHEN M. METZGER: How to Use a Well-Stocked Library: Erfurt Carthusians on the *Industriae* of Mystical Theology. In: *Die Bibliothek—The Library—La Bibliothèque: Denkräume und Wissensordnungen*. Ed. ANDREAS SPEER and LARS REUKE. Berlin 2020 (Miscellanea Mediaevalia: Veröffentlichungen des Thomas-Instituts der Universität zu Köln. 41), pp. 656–75. BERNHARD STASIEWSKI: Jakob von Jüterbog. In: *Neue Deutsche Biographie*. Berlin 1974. Vol. 10, pp. 318–19.

74 The *Sammelband* was listed in the *Registrum librarie fratrum Carthusiensium apud Erffordiam* at the end of the fifteenth century. PAUL LEHMANN (Ed.): *Mittelalterliche Bibliothekskataloge Deutschlands und der Schweiz. Zweiter Band. Bistum Mainz, Erfurt*. Munich 1928, p. 233. The verses in the Erfurt manuscript: "In liberariis scribantur. Hac sunt in cella doctorum grata libella ... Pro dei laude libros lege, postea claude." Versions can be found in manuscripts at Kloster Niederwerth of the Augustinian Canons Regular of the Congregation of Windesheim, Rhineland-Palatinate (U- und LandesB Bonn, S 732, fol. 4r); Benedictine Abbey of Bursfelde, Lower Saxony (UB Marburg, Mscr. 75, fol. 383r); Salem Cistercian Abbey, Baden-Württemberg (Cod. Sal. VII 99, fol. 1v; Cod. Sal. VIII 41, fol. 133v); and possibly Kloster St. Wipert, Quedlinburg, Sachsen-Anhalt (Stifts- und GymnasialB Quedlinburg in Halle, Qu. Cod. 102, fols. 1v–2r). JÜRGEN GEISS: *Katalog der mittelalterlichen Handschriften der Universitäts- und Landesbibliothek Bonn*. Berlin 2016, pp. 252–53. SIRKA HEYNE: *Die mittelalterlichen Handschriften der Universitätsbibliothek Marburg*. Wiesbaden 2002, p. 231. WILFRIED WERNER: *Die mittelalterlichen nichtliturgischen Handschriften des Zisterzienserkloster Salem*. Wiesbaden 2000, pp. 53, 129. JUTTA FLIEGE: *Die Handschriften der ehemaligen Stifts- und Gymnasialbibliothek in Halle*. Halle 1982, p. 129. See also WILHELM WATTENBACH: *Das Schriftwesen im Mittelalter*. 2nd edition. Leipzig 1875, pp. 497–98. HANS WALTHER: *Initia carminum ac versuum Medii Aevi posterioris Latinorum*. Göttingen 1969 (Carmina Medii Aevi Posterioris Latina. 1), p. 374 (no. 7437); p. 382 (no. 7593).

75 BERNDT MICHAEL and TILO BRANDIS: *Die mittelalterlichen Handschriften der Wissenschaftlichen Stadtbibliothek Soest*. Wiesbaden 1990, pp. 38, 144–48 (at p. 147). ULYSSE CHEVALIER: *Répertoire des sources historiques du moyen age*. Paris 1907. Vol. 1, pt. 2, 1907, col. 1465. Chevalier adds that Oestinghausen was a "théologien à Avignon" and gives 1484 as his year of death.

76 ALBINIA DE LA MARE: *Catalogue of the Collection of Medieval Manuscripts Bequeathed to the Bodleian Library by James P. R. Lyell*. Oxford 1971, pp. 191–99 (at p. 94). ANDREW G. WATSON: *Catalogue of Dated and Datable Manuscripts, c. 435–1600, in Oxford Libraries*. Oxford 1984. Vol. 1, p. 106, no. 642. GOTTLIEB: *Mittelalterliche Bibliothekskataloge Österreichs*. Vol. 1, p. 234. In 1937, British collector James P. R. Lyell (1871–1948) acquired the manuscript from the bookseller E. P. Goldschmidt (1887–1954), [Catalogue no. 44] *Twenty Manuscripts and a Selection of Rare Old Books Mostly Illustrated with Woodcuts* (1937), no. 17A.

Augsburg, Bavaria.⁷⁷ The Carmelite *Frater* Matthias Farinator (d. 1505) owned a miscellany with *Philobiblon*, copied for his own use at the Universität Erfurt, 1472–75. The miscellany also includes Thomas à Kempis (1380–1471), *De imitatione Christi*; and Heinrich von Langenstein, *Speculum animae* (Munich, Bayerische Staatsbibliothek, Clm 3586). Farinator lectured at Carmelite houses in Bamberg and Vienna, and he was *Socius des Provinzial der Oberdeutschen Provinz* (1475–78) in Augsburg.⁷⁸

The Pre-Reformation mystical theologian Gabriel Biel (1420–95) owned a miscellany including *Philobiblon* (Giessen, Universitätsbibliothek, Hs. 792). He was the author, scribe, and corrector of sermons and other texts in the miscellany (fols. 195r–284v), which included several works of St. Bernardino of Siena and Heinrich von Langenstein.⁷⁹ Watermark evidence suggests that much of the manuscript was written in 1452–60, when Biel was preaching in Erfurt, Cologne, and Mainz. Among influences on his theology was the Carthusian Jakob von Jüterbog, who also taught at the Universität Erfurt.⁸⁰ Biel later donated or bequeathed the miscellany to the *Fraterherrenstift* St. Markus in Butzbach, Hesse, founded in 1468 with Biel as its first prior. He was from the Speyer area and associated with the Brethren and Congregation of Windesheim. Biel played a role in the spread of *Fraterherren* houses in the 1460s. Adolf II of Nassau (1422–75), elector-archbishop of Mainz (r. 1461–75), founded the *Kugelherrenstift* at Marienthal and other houses, including St. Marien at Königstein im Taunus, Hesse.⁸¹ Biel was a proponent of the *via moderna* of William of Ockham (c. 1287–1347) and Nominalism, providing a new approach to the study of theology and philosophy, beyond the *via antiqua* of St. Thomas Aquinas (1225–74) and Scholasticism. Two German miscellanies with *Philobiblon* also include texts by William of Ockham (Appendix, nos. 18, 64). Biel's *via moderna* approach had an indirect influence on the theology of Martin Luther through the latter's studies at the Universität Erfurt (1501–5), Luther's theology was critical of Biel's.⁸² From 1484 to 1489, Biel was a professor of theology at the Universität Tübingen and twice served as rector. He authored many theological treatises and sermons, including *Lectura super canone misse in alma universitate Tuwingensi ordinarie lecta* ([Reutlingen: Johann Otmar], 1488).⁸³

The German preacher Johannes Veghe (c. 1430–1504), a native of Münster, owned a miscellany (c. 1450–75) with *Philobiblon* and texts by the Cistercians John of Limoges, *Morale somnium pharaonis*; and Hermann

---

77 KARIN SCHNEIDER: Konrad Wagner. In: *Die deutsche Literatur des Mittelalters Verfasserlexikon*. Berlin 2010. Vol. 10, cols. 570–71. PAUL UIBLEIN (Ed.): *Die Akten der theologischen Fakultät der Universität Wien (1396–1508)*. Vienna 1978. Vol. 1, p. 634. Concerning other manuscripts, see GÜNTER HÄGELE: *Lateinische mittelalterliche Handschriften in Folio der Universitätsbibliothek Augsburg. Die Signaturengruppe Cod. 1. 2. 2° und Cod. H. 1. 2° 1–90*. Wiesbaden 1996, pp. 143–44. CHRISTOPH ROTH: *Literatur und Klosterreform: Die Bibliothek der Benediktiner von St. Mang zu Füssen im 15. Jahrhundert*. Berlin 1999, p. 95. KARL HEINZ KELLER: *Katalog der lateinischen Handschriften der Staatlichen Bibliothek (Schlossbibliothek) Ansbach. Band I: Ms. Lat. 1–Ms. Lat. 93*. Wiesbaden 1994, pp. 156–57 (Ms. Lat. 50).

78 In Augsburg, he prepared the 1477 first edition and subsequent editions through 1482 of Bérenger de Landore (1260–1300), *Lumen animae*, a Dominican florilegium of *exempla* for priests preparing sermons. ERWIN RAUNER: *Katalog der lateinischen Handschriften der Bayerischen Staatsbibliothek Munchen. Die Handschriften aus Augsburger Bibliotheken*. Wiesbaden 2007. Vol. 1, pp. 378–95 (at p. 379).

79 JOACHIM OTT: *Die Handschriften des ehemaligen Fraterherrenstifts St. Markus zu Butzbach in der Universitätsbibliothek Gießen*. Gießen 2004, part 2, pp. 174–79 (at p. 176).

80 DETLEF METZ: *Gabriel Biel und die Mystik*. Stuttgart 2001 (Contubernium: Tübinger Beiträge zur Universitäts- und Wissenschaftsgeschichte. 55), pp. 71–73.

81 GERHARD FAIX: *Gabriel Biel und die Brüder vom Gemeinsamen Leben: Quellen und Untersuchungen zu Verfassung und Selbstverständnis des Oberdeutschen Generalkapitels*. Tübingen 1999, pp. 36–38.

82 HEIKO A. OBERMAN: *The Dawn of the Reformation: Essays in Late Medieval and Early Reformation Thought*. Grand Rapids, Michigan 1992, p. 101. LAWRENCE F. MURPHY: Gabriel Biel as Transmitter of Aquinas to Luther. In: *Renaissance and Reformation*. New series. 7 (1983) 1, pp. 26–41. PEKKA KÄRKKÄINEN: Nominalism and the *Via Moderna* in Luther's Theological Work. In: *Oxford Research Encyclopedia of Religion* (available on www.oxfordindex.oup, [20.1.2023]).

83 WILLIAM H. LANDEEN: Gabriel Biel and the Brethren of the Common Life in Germany. In: *Church History*. 20 (1951) 1, pp. 23–36. PAUL VAN GEEST: Gabriel Biel: Brother of the Common Life and Alter Augustinus? Aim and Meaning of his *Tractatus de communi vita clericorum*. In: *Augustiniana*. 58 (2008) 3–4, pp. 305–57. Biel's theology discussed in HEIKO A. OBERMAN: *The Harvest of Medieval Theology: Gabriel Biel and Late Medieval Nominalism*. Cambridge 1963. POST: *The Modern Devotion*, pp. 486–89.

Zoestius von Münster, *Phaselexis* (Basel, Universitätsbibliothek. MS. A. X. 143 [olim B. VIII. 11]).⁸⁴ Other German manuscripts include these texts. A composite manuscript, possibly from the Cistercian Abbey of St. Maria, Heilsbronn, Franconia, includes *Philobiblon* (attributed to Robert Holcot) and Hermann Zoestius, *Phaselexis* (Erlangen-Nürnberg, Universitätsbibliothek, Ms. 542).⁸⁵ These texts are in manuscript miscellanies listed in the 1497 and 1510 library catalogues for the Universität Erfurt.⁸⁶ Veghe gave the Basel miscellany to *Dominus* Johannes Durr, described as *beneficiatus* of Basel Cathedral, probably indicating a bishop's prebendary with administrative duties. The manuscript was later in the Dominican Convent of Basel. Veghe matriculated at the University of Cologne (1450), where his name was recorded as "Johann ten Loe alias Veghe, clericus Monasteriensis." The surname *ten Loe* was probably a variant of the Dutch *ten Loo*. Veghe joined the Brethren of the Common Life in Münster (1451), served as rector of the Brethren in Rostock (1469–71) and Münster (1475–81), and finally was confessor to the Sisters of Niesink in Münster (1481–1504), sister house of the Münster Brethren. He authored many religious texts and sermons in Low German.⁸⁷

Theological miscellanies including *Philobiblon* were occasional charitable gifts to monastic libraries in Cologne and other places in support of spiritual and intellectual life. For example, *Magister* Johannes de Stummel of Cologne (d. 1455) donated such a miscellany to the Charterhouse of St. Barbara, Cologne (Cambridge, University Library, Ms. Add. 3145). In addition to *Philobiblon*, the miscellany also contains Jean Gerson, *De laude scriptorum*, and texts of Heinrich von Langenstein and St. Bernard of Clairvaux.⁸⁸ Cologne had one of Germany's foremost Carthusian libraries until a major fire in 1451. Priors of the Charterhouse rebuilt the library by 1453 and replaced lost manuscripts by gift and purchase, scribal copying in its own scriptorium, and aid from local religious houses. Certain manuscript acquisitions show the Charterhouse's devotion to ecclesiastical reform. In rebuilding its holdings after 1451, Richard B. Marks suggested that "most of the books were the ones that the monks desired for their reading interests." The lay brothers generally read in their cells.⁸⁹ Stummel was a prominent local cleric and donor. He had studied at the University of Cologne and had a long church career in Cologne, becoming protonotary of Cologne (1417), parish priest of St. Columba (1440), and canon and finally dean of the Basilica of the Holy Apostles (1423, 1449).⁹⁰ The gift inscription in the miscellany records that Stummel had donated it "ad usum fratrum prefate domus".

---

84 GUSTAV MEYER and MAX BURCKHARDT: *Die mittelalterlichen Handschriften der Universitätsbibliothek Basel. Beschreibendes Verzeichnis. Abteilung B: Theologische Pergamenthandschriften. Zweiter Band: Signaturen B VIII 11 – B XI 26*. Basel 1966, p. 1. MARTIN STEINMANN: *Die Handschriften der Universitätsbibliothek Basel: Register zu den Abteilungen A1–AXI und O*. Basel 1982, p. 524. Gift inscription (fol. 38v): "Iste libellus presentabitur domino Ioanni Durr beneficiato in ecclesia Basiliensi quem mittit ei Ioannes Veghe presbyter Monasteriensis."

85 HANS FISCHER: *Die lateinischen Papierhandschriften der Universitätsbibliothek Erlangen*. Wiesbaden 1971, pp. 171–76 (at pp. 173–74). EBERHARD LUTZKE: *Die Bilderhandschriften der Universitätsbibliothek Erlangen*. Wiesbaden 1971, pp. 97–98. Erlangen-Nürnberg Ms. 542 came from the U Aldorf. Texts related to calendar reform at the Council of Basel (1431–49) suggest a connection with Heilsbronn Abbey at the time of Prior Nikolaus von Heilsbronn (Nicolaus de Fontissalutis). But the manuscript could also have been from Nürnberg.

86 LEHMANN: *Mittelalterliche Bibliothekskataloge Deutschlands und der Schweiz. Zweiter Band. Bistum Mainz, Erfurt*, pp. 145, 188.

87 FRANZ JOSTEN: *Johannes Veghe: Ein deutscher Prediger des XV. Jahrhunderts*. Halle 1882, pp. 15–21. HERMANN KEUSSEN and WILHELM SCHMITZ: *Die Matrikel der Universität Köln, 1389 bis 1559. Erster Band, 1389–1466*. Bonn 1892. Vol. 1, p. 406. ALOYS BÖMER: *Das literarische Leben in Münster bis zur endgültigen Rezeption des Humanismus*. Münster 1906, pp. 55–63.

88 JAYNE S. RINGROSE: *Summary Catalogue of the Additional Medieval Manuscripts in the Cambridge University Library*. Woodbridge, Suffolk 2009, pp. 74–75. The ownership inscription (fol. 1v) reads, "Liber domus beate Barbare in Colonia ordinis Carthusiensis quem, pro suis memoria [...] dominus magister Johannes de Stummel decanus ecclesie sanctorum apostolorum in Colonia ad usum fratrum prefate domus dedit." The Edinburgh collector David Laing (1793–1878) acquired it indirectly from Rotterdam bookseller J. L. C. Jacob in 1839 and later donated it to Cambridge. HAROLD L. PINK: Unpublished Description by H. L. Pink of Cambridge, University Library, MS Add. 3145... (available on www.repository.cam.ac.uk, [20.1.2023]).

89 MARKS: *The Medieval Manuscript Library of the Charterhouse of St. Barbara*. Vol. 1, pp. vi–vii (quotation), 8–15.

90 KEUSSEN: *Die Matrikel der Universität Köln*. Vol. 1, pp. 80, 172. JOSEPH HANSEN: *Westfalen und Rheinland im 15. Jahrhundert*. Leipzig 1888, pp. 421, 427. RICHARD KNIPPING (Ed.): *Die Kolner Stadtrechnungen des Mittelalters mit einer Darstellung der Finanzverwaltung*. Bonn 1897. Vol. 1, p. 93. EDUARD FIRMENICH-RICHARTZ: *Die Brüder Boisserée*. Jena 1916. Vol. 1, pp. 497–98.

Stummel probably gave it after the 1451 fire in the hope of prayers being said in his memory, as he expressed in another manuscript.⁹¹

Philobiblon is found in other theological miscellanies in western Germany. One was copied in 1436 by *Frater* Abbo de Middelburg (d. 1459/60), a Canon Regular of the Holy Cross, Cologne. He was from the city of Middelburg, province of Zeeland, and relocated to Cologne like several other Netherlandish copyists. *Philobiblon* is the first text in the volume, which also includes Jean Gerson, *De laude scriptorum* (1423); a table of contents for Johannes Balbus (d. c. 1298), *Catholicon; Mystice acceptationes terminorum secundum ordinem alphabeti* (Cologne, Historisches Archiv der Stadt Köln, Best. 7004 [Handschriften, GB quart. 215; Gymnasialbibliothek, Ms. G.B. 4° 215]).⁹² The miscellany also includes Thomas of Ireland (c. 1265–c. 1329), *Manipulus florum* (1306), a florilegium of about 6000 extracts from classical, patristic, and medieval works, organized under 266 alphabetical headings. Nearly 200 manuscripts survive, many once owned by preachers.⁹³ Another miscellany with *Philobiblon* was from the *Kreuzherren* of Hohenbusch, North Rhine-Westphalia, and includes Jean Gerson, *De laude scriptorum*, and Heinrich von Friemar (c. 1245–1340), *De decem praeceptis*, a commentary on the Ten Commandments (Cologne, Erzbischöfliche Diözesan- und Dombibliothek, Cod. 1073).⁹⁴ *Philobiblon* survives in a paper miscellany from the Kloster Eberhardsklausen, Rhineland-Palatinate, founded in 1456 by the Congregation of Windesheim. *Philobiblon* is bound with sermons by Paulus van Zomeren (d. 1503), prior of the Augustinian Canons Regular of Windesheim in Eindhoven, North Brabant (r. 1460–75), and by other Canons Regular of Windesheim (Trier, Stadtbibliothek, Ms. 305).⁹⁵ Finally, a copy of *Philobiblon* is in a miscellany of c. 1503–10 on parchment and paper in the Bibliotheca Domus Presbyterorum Gaesdonck, Goch, North Rhine-Westphalia (Goch, Collegium Augustinianum, 12 [Ms. 33]). The library was in a convent founded in c. 1400 by the Congregation of Windesheim, with a scriptorium and bindery. The miscellany including *Philobiblon* was copied under Prior Johann Meisters (r. 1482–1513) and includes twenty-three other Latin texts and many

---

91 Stummel expressed this wish in a manuscript containing Jean Gerson, *De consolatione theologiae* (1418), donated in 1436 to the Charterhouse (Münster UB, N. R. 1551). Stummel had purchased N. R. 1551 in 1450 from Johannes Veghe, the Elder, of Münster, *magister artium* from the U of Paris, who matriculated at the U of Cologne (1430). He is not the previously mentioned Johannes Veghe (c. 1430–1504), possibly his son. Veghe had probably copied this manuscript in Münster for his own use from a 1424 exemplar, and he sold it to Stummel on 3 November 1450. MARKS: *The Medieval Manuscript Library of the Charterhouse of St. Barbara*. Vol. 2, pp. 380–81. E. A. OVERGAAUW: *Die mittelalterlichen Handschriften der Universitäts- und Landesbibliothek Münster*. Wiesbaden 1996, pp. 188–89. E. A. OVERGAAUW: Zekerheden, twijfels en vermoedens over het Veghe-handschrift van 1436 in de Universitäts- und Landesbibliothek Münster. In: *Jaarboek voor Nederlandse boekgeschiedenis*. 7 (2000), pp. 97–107. The manuscript records Stummel's gift (fol. 1v): "…dedit eis dominus Johannes Stummel. Oretur pro eo." Later owned by Leander van Eß (1772–1847) and Sir Thomas Phillipps (1792–1872).

92 JOACHIM VENNEBUSCH: *Die theologischen Handschriften des Stadtbibliothek Köln. T. II: Die Quart-Handschriften des Stadtarchivs der Gymnasialbibliothek*. Cologne, Vienna 1980, p. 271: fol. 1r: "Incipit prologus in librum De amore librorum qui Philobiblion dicitur. MCCCCXXXVI circa Exaltacionem s. crucis". fol. 124r: "Explicit etc. per manus fr. Abbonis de Middelburch Zelandie anno d[omini] M°CCCC°XXXVI° circa Exaltacionem". See also ROUSE and ROUSE: *Preachers, Florilegia and Sermons*, pp. 218, 346. JOSEPH THEELE: Aus der Bibliothek des Kölner Kreuzbrüderklosters. In: *Mittelalterliche Handschriften … Festgabe zum 60. Geburtstage von Hermann Degering*. Ed. ALOIS BÖMER. Leipzig 1926, pp. 256–57. ALBERT DEROLEZ's review of Vennebusch in *Bulletin codicologique*. *Scriptorium*. 38 (1984) 1, p. 58, no. 290.

93 Richard and Mary Rouse note that such multi-text volumes were popular in fifteenth-century Germany for reference use and describe the Cologne miscellany as a "bibliographic corpus." MARY A. ROUSE and RICHARD H. ROUSE: Backgrounds to Print: Aspects of the Manuscript Book in Northern Europe of the Fifteenth Century. In: ROUSE and ROUSE: *Authentic Witnesses: Approaches to Medieval Texts and Manuscripts*. Notre Dame, Indiana 1991, p. 455. ROUSE and ROUSE: *Preachers, Florilegia and Sermons*, p. 218.

94 Erzbischöfliche Diözesan- und DomB Köln, Digitale Sammlungen: www.digital.dombibliothek-koeln.de, [20.1.2023]. MANFRED THALLER and TORSTEN SCHASSAN: *Mittelalterliche Handschriften im Internet: CEEC Codices Electronici Ecclesiae Colonienis*: www.webdoc.gwdg.de, [20.1.2023]. HARALD HORST: *Wissensraum am Niederrhein: Rekonstruktion der Bibliothek des Kreuzherrensklosters Hohenbusch in kulturhistorischer Perspektive*. Diss. phil. Berlin 2017, pp. 114–15, 216: www.d-nb.info, [last consulted, January 21, 2023].

95 MAX KEUFFER: *Beschreibendes Verzeichnis der Handschriften der Stadtbibliothek zu Trier. Erstes Heft*. Trier 1888, pp. 118–121. This is one of approximately 200 Eberhardsklausen manuscripts in the SB Trier. Concerning Eberhardsklausen manuscripts, see KURT HEYDECK und GIULIANO STACCIOLI: *Die lateinischen Handschriften aus dem Augustiner-Chorherrenstift Eberhardsklausen der Stadtbibliothek Trier: Teil I*. Wiesbaden 2007. BETTY C. BUSHEY: *Die deutschen und niederländischen Handschriften der Stadtbibliothek Trier bis 1600*. Wiesbaden 1996.

extracts in various hands, chiefly works by Thomas à Kempis, which were most likely copied from an early printed edition.[96]

Several later paper miscellanies including *Philobiblon* were copied by scribes connected with parish churches or monasteries in which ordained monks performed priestly duties. In 1454, Wolfgang Klammer, chaplain to the parish priest in Gmund am Tegernsee, located about 45 kilometers south of Munich, copied *Philobiblon* along with works of St. Augustine and Heinrich von Langenstein, and concludes with Matthew of Cracow (1345–1410), *Sermo in synodi Pragensi a. 1386* (Munich, Bayerische Staatsbibliothek, Ms. 4705A). In the 1450s and 1460s, Klammer copied several German vernacular manuscripts for the nearby Benedictine Abbey of St. Quirinus, Tegernsee, which was known for its interest in humanism and vernacular translations of Latin texts. The Klammer manuscript was part of the substantial library holdings of Tegernsee Abbey, which numbered some two thousand volumes when the abbey was secularized in 1803. The manuscript is listed in *Pater* Ambrosius Schwerzenbeck's catalogue (1483/84).[97] In 1493, Klammer's copy of *Philobiblon* was used as the exemplar for a second reading copy of *Philobiblon* (Teg. 1742) at Tegernsee Abbey (Munich, Bayerische Staatsbibliothek, Ms. 19742).[98] Another miscellany with *Philobiblon* was in the Premonstratensian Abbey of Schäftlarn, Bavaria (Munich, Bayerische Staatsbibliothek, Ms. 17292). It was bound with works on celebrating mass and giving penance, along with Johannes de Auerbach (d. 1469), *Directorium curatorum*, which is found in manuscripts of 1450–1500 intended for Bavarian parish clergy and ordained monks.[99]

Possibly copied for use by canons or priests is a Netherlandish paper miscellany of c. 1479–90, including a *Philobiblon* extract ("parvum manuale extractum ex Philobiblio") that corresponds to chap. xviii, in which Richard de Bury explains that his library would be available to all Oxford students for reading and study (Brussels, Bibliothèque Royale de Belgique, Ms. 3716–30 [1292]). The miscellany includes theological works by St. Bonaventure, St. Thomas Aquinas, and Jean Gerson, as well as sermons. A note in the manuscript indicates that the manuscript was commissioned by Baldwin, styled "Domnus" (probably meaning "lord"), son of Anthony, in connection with Nieuwerkerk, in Duiveland, Diocese of Utrecht.[100] The volume might have been intended for use at a new religious establishments in Zeeland, possibly one of those founded by Anne of Burgundy (1435–1503) and her brother Baldwin of Burgundy (1446–1508), illegitimate children of Duke Philip III the Good of Burgundy (r. 1419–67). In 1490, Anne of Burgundy founded Johanneskerk in Nieuwerkerk, now in the municipality of Schouwen-Duiveland, Zeeland. It was a collegiate church with a chapter of canons and could appoint priests. In 1492, probably with her brother Baldwin, she founded a cloister under the Canons Regular of the Holy Cross

---

[96] HEINZ FINGER, MARIANNE RIETHMÜLLER, et al.: *Handschriftencensus Rheinland*. Wiesbaden 1993 (Schriften der Universitäts- und Landesbibliothek Düsseldorf. 18), p. 538, no. 912. GREGOR HÖVELMANN: Die Handschriften der Klosterbibliothek Gaesdonck: Ein Versuch den ursprünglichen Bestand zu rekonstruieren: mit einem Anhang über die Schreibtätigkeit des Gaesdoncker Konvents. In: *Gaesdoncker Blätter*. 21 (1968), pp. 44–75. ROBERT SCHOLTEN: *Gaesdonck: Geschichte des Klosters der regulierten Chorherren des Hülfspriesterseminars oder Priesterhauses und des Collegium Augustinianum bis 1873*. Munster 1906, pp. 111–12. *Opera: Sermones, epistolae et alia opuscula*. Nürnberg 1494. ISTC identifies in 179 holding institutions for the 1494 edition.

[97] The manuscript came to Munich from the Benedictine Abbey of Benediktbeuern (Ms. 205). *Catalogus codicum manu scriptorum Bibliothecae Regiae Monacensis, Tomi III Pars II*. Munich 1894, p. 231. KARIN SCHNEIDER: *Die deutschen Handschriften der Bayerischen Staatsbibliothek München. Cgm 201–350*. Wiesbaden 1970, pp. 210, 211. HELMUT WECK: *Die "Rechtsumme" der Bruder Bertholds: Eine deutsche abecedarische Bearbeitung der "Summa Confessorum" des Johannes von Freiburg: Die handschriftliche Überlieferung*. Tübingen 1982, pp. 159–160, 229, 325. HERMANN KNAUS: *Mittelalterliche Bibliothekskataloge Deutschlands und der Schweiz*. Munich 1979. Vol. 4, pt. 2, p. 836 (shelfmark "b 54"). DENNIS D. MARTIN: Popular and Monastic Pastoral Issues in the Later Middle Ages. In: *Church History*. 56 (1987) 3, pp. 320–32, here p. 320, n. 3. Tegernsee, Benediktinerabtei St. Quirinus. In: *Marburger Repertorium zur Übersetzungsliteratur im deutschen Frühhumanismus* (available on www.mrfh.de, [20.1.2023]).

[98] *Catalogus codicum manu scriptorum Bibliothecae Regiae Monacensis. Tomi IV Pars III*. Munich 1878, p. 271.

[99] MATTHEW WRANOVIX: *Priests and their Books in Late Medieval Eichstätt*. Lanham 2017, pp. 16, 31, 49, 69, 70, 79, 134, 184.

[100] JOSEPH VAN DEN GREYN: *Catalogue des manuscrits de la Bibliothèque Royale de Belgique*. Brussels 1904. Vol. 4, pp. 260–61, no. 1292. Two explicits at the end of texts by Pope Gregory the Great provide completion dates: fol. 56r, June 1, 1479, for *Liber dialogorum*; and fol. 98v, March 18, 1490, for *Liber regulae pastoralis*. Fol. 98v: "… completus et finitus expensis domni Baldewini filii Anthonii de nova ecclesia Duvelandie Traiectensis dyocesis."

in Sint-Annaland, located about ten kilometers to the southeast.[101] Another *Philobiblon* copy (Princeton University Library, Taylor Ms. 15) was from a German or Netherlandish miscellany of c. 1480. In the original manuscript, *Philobiblon* (fols. 1r–27v) was followed by eight other texts, including Petrarch's *Dialogus de vanitate et sapientia, Dialogus Salomonis et Marcolfi*, and a work on the Fall of Constantinople (1453). The New York bookseller H. P. Kraus probably acquired the full manuscript from London bookseller Bernard Quaritch and removed *Philobiblon* after 1943 for separate sale.[102] Quaritch interpreted the abbreviated name in the scribal colophon as a priest named Johannes Vansarem ("per manus Io. Vsare presbyteri"). However, the surname could also be read as *von Sarn* or *von Saren*, suggesting origins near the city of Duisburg, North Rhine-Westphalia.[103]

In the 1470s and 1480s, demand for copies of *Philobiblon* was sufficient for two printers in North Rhine-Westphalia and Rhineland-Palatinate to accept the financial risks of printed editions: Cologne: [Printer of St. Augustine's *De fide*, possibly Johann Schilling], 1473; and Speyer: [Johann and Conrad Hist], 1483). While incunable press runs are rarely well documented, one can estimate that the two *Philobiblon* editions were probably in the range of 300–500 copies each. The *ISTC* reports thirty-four and twenty-three extant copies respectively. They appear to have served a similar readership as manuscript copies and could be bound in *Sammelbänder*. For example, the Brethren of the Common Life of St. Marien at Königstein im Taunus, Hesse, founded in 1465, owned a *Sammelband* (c. 1469–73) of eight manuscripts and three printed texts, including the Cologne *editio princeps* of *Philobiblon* (Hofbibliothek und Stiftsbibliothek Aschaffenenburg, Ms. Pap. 29, fols. 172r–219v).[104] The *Sammelband* was from the time of Heinrich Kroesen von Zülpich [de Tulpelo] (d. c. 1490), who came from Cologne to Königstein in 1467 to be its first rector and had dealings with Gabriel Biel in Butzbach because their houses were part of the Colloquium of Münster.[105] Printed copies were added to the libraries of two reformist Benedictine houses: the Cologne edition in Bursfelde Abbey, Lower Saxony, influenced by the *Devotio Moderna* (The Hague, Museum Meermanno-Westreenianum, 144 K 003); and the Speyer edition in the Abbey of St. Emmeram, Regensburg, Bavaria (Oxford, Bodleian Library, Auct. 6Q 6.46).[106]

---

101 AUBERTUS MIRAEUS: *De collegiis canonicorum per Germaniam, Belgium, Galliam, Hispaniam, Italiam, aliasque orbis Christiani Provincias, Liber singularis*. Cologne 1615, pp. 190–91. J. B. KRÜGER: *Potamo-Chorographie, of Naauwkeurige navorschingen over de Schelde ... met een beknopt historisch verhaal van Zeeland...* Bergen-op-Zoom 1854. Vol. 2, p. 168. ABRAHAM JACOB VAN DER AA: *Aardrijkskundig Woordenboek der Nederlanden ... Zevende Deel*. Gorinchem 1846, p. 142. [ISAAC TELTING]: *Rapport over de Vicariegoederen, in hun verband met de andere geestelijke goederen in Zeeland* (n. p.: n. d., 1885), pp. 100–102. JAN KUYS. *Repertorium van collegiale kapittels in het middeleeuwse bisdom Utrecht*. Hilversum 2014, pp. 222–24. Anthony, Bastard of Burgundy (1421–1504), was also an illegitimate child of Philip the Good, but not Baldwin's father.

102 Robert H. Taylor (1908–85) acquired the manuscript for his collection, bequeathed to the Princeton UL. The back pastedown has an unnamed German bookseller's notes: »M. Ms. I.1 1956« and »Schrift- & Buchkunde G1.29 Bibliophilie MS. Bury, Richard de. Philobiblon. Papier-MS: Deutschland ca. 1480 BG/23.« It appears to be the same *Philobiblon* manuscript (Germania, c. 1480), 27 folios, offered in 1952 by the New York bookseller H. P. Kraus (No 60: *Fifty Select Books, Manuscripts and Autographs*, no. 11). Kraus offered *Philobiblon* separately in 1948 (*New Acquisitions: Fifty Outstanding Books and Manuscripts*, no. 10). He had acquired the complete manuscript from London bookseller Bernard Quaritch, which had offered it in at least six catalogues: 1931 (No. 446), 1934 (No. 484), 1938 (No. 551–561), 1939 (No. 562), 1940 (No. 582), and 1943 (No. 613). Kraus probably sold *Philobiblon* to a German bookseller, who in turn sold it to Robert H. Taylor. DON C. SKEMER: *Medieval and Renaissance Manuscripts in the Princeton University Library*. Princeton 2013. Vol. 1, pp. 435–36. It is not known if the remainder of the original miscellany survives.

103 Quaritch's speculation about the scribe was followed in *Colophons de manuscrits occidentaux des origines au XVI siècle*. Vol. 3. Fribourg 1973, p. 103, no. 8250. There is no record of a priest named Johann von Sarn in this period. But Peter von Sarn (1674–1735), of Duisburg, was a preacher (*Prediger*) active in the cities of Moers and Krefeld, North Rhine-Palatinate, as well an author of theology, history, and poetry. JOHANN ARNOLD VON RECHLINGHAUSEN: *Reformations-Geschichte der Länder Jülich, Berg, Cleve und Meurs*. Ed. C. H. E. VON OVEN. Solingen, Gummersbach 1837. Vol. 3, pp. 299–300, 302.

104 LUDWIG K. WALTER: *Katalog der Wiegendrucke der Stiftsbibliothek zu Aschaffenburg*. Würzburg 1999, pp. 166, 296–97, 320. LUDWIG K. WALTER: Zur Spiritualität der Brüder vom gemeinsamen Leben: Handschriften und Inkunabeln des Fraterherrenhauses Königstein im Taunus in der Stiftsbibliothek Aschaffenburg. In: *Würzburger Diözesangeschichtsblätter*. 58 (1996), pp. 109–40. *Hofbibliothek Aschaffenburg Online-Katalog* (available on www.fgwstp20.bib-bvb.de, [20.1.2023]). *Philobiblon* has an ownership inscription on the first folio: "Liber Capituli sancte marie in konicksteyn." The other two printed texts are THOMAS AQUINAS: *De beatitudine aeternitatis*. Cologne not after 1472; and JEAN GERSON: *De laude scriptorum* (Cologne c. 1473). On incunable press runs after 1480, see FALK EISERMANN: Fifty Thousand Veronicas. Press Runs of Broadsheets in the Fifteenth and Early Sixteenth Centuries. In: *Single-sheet Publishing in the First Age of Print*. Ed. ANDREW PETTEGREE. Leiden 2017, pp. 76–113, here p. 78.

105 FAIX: *Gabriel Biel*, pp. 83–84.

106 ISTC: *Material Evidence in Incunabula* (*MEI*) (available on www.data.cerl.org, [20.1.2023]). ANJA FRECKMANN: *Die Bibliothek des Klosters Bursfelde im Spätmittelalter*. Hannover 2006, pp. 15, 18–19, 373.

One manuscript offers interesting evidence about early printing (Bamberg, Staatsbibliothek, Msc. Patr. 89). Johannes Kaufmann (c. 1430–89) of Würzburg, abbot of Ebrach Cistercian Abbey (r. 1474–89), located thirty-five kilometers west of Bamberg, Franconia, owned a composite volume including *Philobiblon*, copied by *Frater* Johannes Hilpurchausen (possibly the place name Hildburghausen, Thuringia), a monk at the abbey. At the University of Vienna, Kaufmann earned the degree of *doctor sacrae theologiae* and then taught theology (1466–84), while also serving as confessor to the future Holy Roman Emperor Maximilian I (r. 1508–19). On 17 September 1484, as recorded in Msc. Patr. 89 (fol. 267v), Kaufmann drafted a letter about the Speyer edition (1483) of *Philobiblon* to Friedrich Creussner, a Nürnberg printer of Latin and German, active 1472–99. The abbot had read *Philobiblon* as a student in Vienna and considered it a remarkable short work ("opusculum hoc insigne"), valuable as meditational and recreational reading for monks ("libellus meditatione recreatrioneque dignus"). He examined and collated the Speyer edition with the Ebrach manuscript, probably aided by his monks, and concluded that the edition was filled with textual errors ("false, triviatim atque corrupte") that made it incomprehensible in places and doing violence to its author's text ("tum ipsius opificis Domini Praesulis gravi injuria"). Kaufmann had the text corrected, with marginal notes and clarifications, which he offered to Creussner in the hope he would undertake printing a new edition.[107] Kaufmann may have known Creussner because the abbey maintained a *Klosterhof* in Nürnberg to manage agricultural lands and interests.[108] Nürnberg-area monasteries offered a ready market for copies.[109] We do not know if Creussner received or considered the abbot's proposal. There would be no new printing until the Jodocus Bodius edition (Paris: Gaspard Philippe, for Jean Petit, 1 Mar. 1500/1).

On the Continent, printed copies of *Philobiblon* occasionally served as exemplars for scribal copying. Curt F. Bühler once observed, "every manuscript ascribed to the second half of the fifteenth century is potentially (and often without question) a copy of some incunable."[110] Forty-eight of the manuscripts in the library of Raphael de Marcatellis (1437–1508), abbot of the Benedictine Abbey of St. Bavon, Ghent (r. 1478–1507), were copied from printed editions. Included was a parchment miscellany with *Philobiblon*, probably copied from the 1473 edition (Ghent, Universiteitsbibliotheek, Ms. 67). He had studied theology at the Sorbonne and became a monk of St. Peter's Benedictine Abbey, Ghent. Professional book artisans in his native Bruges were probably responsible for many of the fifty-seven manuscripts that he commissioned for St. Bavon, many illuminated on parchment and finely bound. Marcatellis's *Philobiblon* opens with full border decoration and an illuminated initial (fol. 1r). His love for deluxe manuscripts, including classical and humanistic texts, was inspired by the aristocratic book culture of his father, Duke Philip III the Good of Burgundy, not by the spiritual needs of monks.[111] The *Philobiblon* volume also includes a transcription of the *editio princeps* of Johannes Trithemius (1462–1516), *De scriptoribus*

---

107 FRIEDRICH LEITSCHUH: *Katalog der Handschriften der Königlichen Bibliothek zu Bamberg*. Bamberg 1895. Vol. 1, pp. 467–68. Kaufmann's letter transcribed in HEINRICH JOACHIM JAECK: Nachtrag zu 'Richardi de Buri Philobiblon' in No. 9 des Serapeum. In: *Serapeum: Zeitschrift für Bibliothekwissenschaft, Handschriftenkunde und ältere Litteratur*. 4 (1843), pp. 191–92.

108 HILDEGARD WEISS: *Die Zisterzienserabtei Ebrach: Eine Untersuchung zur Grundherrschaft, Gerichtsherrschaft und Dorfgemeinde in fränkischen Raum*. Stuttgart 1962, pp. 20–21. JOHANNES JAEGER: *Die Cisterziener-Abtei Ebrach zur Zeit der Reformation*. Erlangen 1895, pp. 10–11. JOSEPH DE GHELLINCK: Un évêque bibliophile au XIVe siècle, p. 289, assumes that Creussner declined despite the abbot's recommendation.

109 There is a copy of *Philobiblon* in a theological miscellany from the Nürnberg Dominican Monastery (Nürnberg, SB, Cent. II 10). KARIN SCHNEIDER: *Die Handschriften der Stadtbibliothek, Nürnberg. Band II: Die lateinischen mittelalterlichen Handschriften. Teil I: Theologische Handschriften*. Wiesbaden 1967. Vol. 2, pp. 137–40 (at p. 138). Another is cited in the L catalogue of the Benedictine (Schotten) Abbey of St. Egidien, Nürnberg. PAUL RUF (Ed.): *Mittelalterliche Bibliothekskataloge Deutschlands und der Schweiz*. Munich 1939. Vol. 3, part 3, pp. 470, 551 (shelfmark: D 27).

110 CURT F. BÜHLER: *The Fifteenth-Century Book: The Scribes, the Printers, the Decorators*. Philadephia 1960, pp. 16 (quotation), 37, 117, 118, 156.

111 JULES DE SAINT-GENOIS: *Catalogue méthodique et raisonné des manuscrits de la Bibliothèque de la Ville de Gand*. Ghent 1849. Vol. 1, pp. 378–79, no. 538. ALBERT DEROLEZ: *The Library of Raphaël de Marcatellis, Abbot of St. Bavon's, Ghent, 1437–1508*. Ghent 1979, pp. 195, 304 (no. 35). ALBERT DEROLEZ: Early Humanism in Flanders: New Data and Observations on the Library of Abbot Raphaël de Marcatellis (†1508). In: *Les humanistes et leur bibliotheques: Actes du colloque internationale / Humanists and their Libraries: Proceedings of the International Conference: Bruxelles, 26–28 août 1999*. Ed. RUDOLF DE SMET. Leuven 2002, pp. 37–57. ALBERT DEROLEZ: The Copying of Printed Books for Humanistic Bibliophiles in the Fifteenth Century. In: *From Script to Book: Proceedings of the 7th International Symposium Organized by the Centre for the Study of Vernacular Literature in the Middle Ages, Held in Odense University on 15–16 November, 1982*. Ed. HANS BEKKER-NIELSEN et al. Odense 1986, pp. 140–60. Digitized by the UB (available on www.lib.ugent.de, [20.1.2023]).

ecclesiasticis, a bibliographical reference book on church authors through Thomas à Kempis, Heinrich Totting von Oyta, and Heinrich Langenstein, whose works are found in some miscellanies with *Philobiblon*. Trithemius's entry for Richard de Bury is quoted in prefatory matter for the Paris edition (1500/1). He was a library builder as abbot of the Benedictine Abbey of Sponheim, Rhineland-Palatinate (r. 1483–1506), and of Schottenkloster, Würzburg, Franconia (r. 1506–16).[112]

After 1500, most collectors of *Philobiblon* manuscripts had an antiquarian, bibliophilic, or scholarly interest in preserving the medieval textual heritage. Tudor manuscript researchers and collectors sought to rescue medieval English authors and their textual heritage from oblivion.[113] John Leland (c. 1502–52) listed several *Philobiblon* copies in his *De rebus Britannicis collectanea* (c. 1535), including a manuscript then at Cambridge, Clare College.[114] Archbishop Matthew Parker of Canterbury (r. 1559–75) owned a miscellany that included *Philobiblon*, dating from 1375–1400 (Cambridge, Corpus Christi College, Parker Library, Ms. 456).[115] His eldest son, Sir John Parker (d. c. 1618) owned a miscellany including *Philobiblon*, c. 1400 (Cambridge, Trinity College, Ms. R. 9. 17 [819]).[116] Manuscripts remained available through the English book trade.[117] On the Continent, antiquarians and humanists acquired *Philobiblon* as part of large collections of medieval manuscripts and early printed books. For example, there was a copy among the 300 Codices Rehdigerani that Breslau humanist Thomas Rehdiger (1541–76) collected during travels across Europe (Wrocław, Biblioteka Uniwersytecka; Stadtbibliothek, Breslau, Cod. 130). He studied with Philip Melanchthon at Wittenberg and devoted his life to collecting manuscripts, which were preserved in the Breslau Stadtbibliothek after his death.[118] The German classicist and bibliophile Marquard Gude (1635–89) owned a separately bound *Philobiblon* manuscript (Copenhagen, Det Kongelige Bibliotek, Ms. Fabricius 21, 2°). Gude was the librarian of Duke Christian Albert of Holstein-Gottorp (r. 1659–95) and later counsellor (*Hofrath*) in Kiel to the Duchy of Holstein. He acquired Latin and Greek manuscripts in his native Schleswig-Holstein and in Münster, North Rhine-Westphalia.[119] In later centuries, humanists, antiquarians, and aristocratic bibliophiles were the principal collectors of the medieval manuscripts, and the collecting of *Philobiblon* continued through the nineteenth and twentieth centuries.

---

112 JOHANNES TRITHEMIUS: *Liber de scriptoribus ecclesiasticis*, edited by Johann Heynlein. Basel 1494, fol. 89v. BARBARA C. HALPORN: *The Correspondence of Johann Amerbach: Early Printing in its Social Context*. Ann Arbor 2000, pp. 65–69.

113 SEYMOUR DE RICCI: *English Collectors of Books and Manuscripts (1530–1930) and their Marks of Ownership: Sandars Lectures, 1929–1930*. Cambridge 1930, p. 14.

114 THOMAS HEARNE (Ed.): *Joannis Lelandi antiquarii de rebus Britannicis collectanea cum Thomae Hearnii praefatione notis et indice ad editionem primam. Editio altera*. Vol. 3. London 1774, p. 385 ("E libro Richardi de Bury alias Augervile, episcopi Dunelmensis, cui titulus Philobiblon"). M. R. JAMES: *A Descriptive Catalogue of the Western Manuscripts in the Library of Clare College Cambridge*. Cambridge 1905, p. vii (Coll. iv. 19: «Philobiblon, autore Angravyle»). PETER D. CLARKE (Ed.): *The University and College Libraries of Cambridge*. London 2002 (Corpus of British Medieval Library Catalogues. 10), p. 155, no. 29.

115 Bishop Parker's source has not been identified for Ms. 456. M. R. JAMES: *The Sources of Archbishop Parker's Collection of MSS at Corpus Christi College, Cambridge with a Reprint of the Catalogue of Thomas Markaunt's Library*. Cambridge 1899. ANTHONY GRAFTON: Matthew Parker: The Book as Archive. In: *History of Humanities*. 2 (2017) 1, pp. 15–50.

116 ELAINE TREHARNE: Cambridge. Trinity College R. 9.17 (819). In: *Medieval and Renaissance Texts and Studies*. 343 (2008), pp. 35–42; *The Production and Use of English Manuscripts 1060 to 1220* (available on www.le.ac.uk, [20.1.2023]). Treharne notes that the composite manuscript belonged to John Parker (d. c. 1618), eldest son of Archbishop Matthew Parker (1504–1575) of Canterbury, and was listed in the latter's memorandum book (London, Lambeth Palace, MS. 737), which documents his collecting. SHEILA STRONGMAN: John Parker's Manuscripts: An Edition of the Lists in Lambeth Palace MS 737. In: *Transactions of the Cambridge Bibliographical Society*. 7 (1977) 1, pp. 1–27.

117 In 1626, for example, Sir Simonds D'Ewes (1602–50) paid only two shillings for a manuscript including *Philobiblon* (BL, Ms. Harley 492), and Thomas Wriothesley (1607–67), earl of Southampton, paid twenty-two shillings and six pence (fol. 1r: "pretium xxii^s vi^d") for the manuscript he donated to Cambridge in the 1630s (Cambridge, St. John's c, Ms. 115). BL. *Manuscripts and Archives* (available on www.searcharchives.bl.uk, [20.1.2023]). M. R. JAMES: *A Descriptive Catalogue of the Manuscripts in the Library of St. John's College, Cambridge*. Cambridge 1913, pp. 148–49.

118 ALBRECHT W. J. WACHLER: *Thomas Rehdiger und seine Büchersammlung in Breslau: Ein biographisch-literarischer Versuch*. Breslau 1828, p. 56 (description of Cod. 130). KONRAD ZIEGLER: *Catalogus codicum latinorum classicorum qui in Bibliotheca Urbica Wratislaviensi adservantum*. Wrocław 1915; reprint edition, Hildesheim 1975, pp. 103–5. The manuscript is described in older catalogues, but was probably lost during World War II, according to Maclagan (p. lxxi), and is not listed in *PINAX: Inventarium manuscriptorum Bibliothecae Universitatis Wratislaviensis*: www.pinax.bu.uni.wroc.pl, [20.1.2023].

119 Most of Gude's collection is at HAB because of a 1710 purchase by its librarian, Gottfried Wilhelm Leibnitz (1646–1718). Briefly listed in Gude's *Bibliotheca exquisitissimis libris ... a viro illustri domino Marquardo Gudio ...* Kiel 1706, p. 575, no. 359. Johann Albert Fabricius mentions the *Philobiblon* manuscript in *Bibliotheca latina mediae et infimae aetatis cum supplemento Christiani Schoettgenii...* Padua 1754. Vol. 1, p. 508. FRANZ KOEHLER and GUSTAV MILCHSACK: *Die Gudischen Handschriften*. Wolfenbüttel 1913, p. xvii. HAB now holds 476 manuscripts from Gude's collection, including 361 in Latin.

In conclusion, the English historical context and manuscript tradition of *Philobiblon* have long enjoyed a privileged place in scholarship, even though a national orientation in book history can prevent a fuller appreciation of texts circulating outside modern political borders.[120] An up-to-date census underscores *Philobiblon*'s wider medieval readership and bifurcated reception. The earliest *Philobiblon* manuscripts were indeed English monastic copies acquired by bookish prelates—university-educated men with broad subject interests, including scientific and humanistic texts. *Philobiblon* provided guidance for library management and preservation. English copies were often bound with manuals and models for Latin rhetoric, prose expression, and letter-writing, which were essential skills for ambitious clerics and monks hoping to pursue professional careers in church or royal administration. Yet twice as many *Philobiblon* manuscripts survive from German-speaking areas, chiefly after 1450, supplemented by two incunable editions. Many manuscripts were in libraries associated with the Carthusians and religious orders influenced by the *Devotio Moderna*. German theologians, religious writers, and preachers who read *Philobiblon* valued its reformist emphasis on improved monastic education and the centrality of books in a Christian ministry to serve God. We see this with annotations by an early reader of *Philobiblon*, which is a booklet in a composite manuscript of 1450–75, possibly from a Cistercian abbey in Heilsbronn (Erlangen-Nürnberg, Universitätsbibliothek, Ms. 542). An anonymous reader added a *nota bene* mark in chap. xv. A manicule points to a significant passage (fol. 242v), reproduced on p. 18, in which *Philobiblon* explains that the love of books serves God, helps battle the Devil, and precludes devotion to Mammon and human greed. The reader underlined the passage and then copied it on the first blank page in the booklet after the text (fol. 250v).[121] Many other readers in Pre-Reformation Germany must have shared these sentiments, which helps explain why *Philobiblon* so often circulated with texts that supported theological study, sermon-writing, and preaching, and why it was recommended as meditative and recreational reading for members of religious orders.

Appendix

Philobiblon Manuscripts: Provenance information is provided in the Appendix when not discussed in the article's text and notes. The term *Germania* indicates that the manuscript is from a German-speaking area. Altamura's description is cited when appropriate.

[1] Bamberg, Staatsbibliothek, Msc. Patr. 89, fols. 267v–318r. Germania, c. 1484. FRIEDRICH LEITSCHUH: *Katalog der Handschriften der Königlichen Bibliothek zu Bamberg*. Bamberg 1895. Vol. 1, pp. 467–68. Altamura, pp. 25–26.

---

[120] *Philobiblon* is certainly not the only Anglo-Latin text with many manuscripts copied and preserved on the Continent. German and other Continental L held manuscripts of Robert Holcot, Walter Burley, and Thomas Bradwardine, who were members of Richard de Bury's circle in the period 1333–45. SHARPE: *Handlist*, pp. 553–58, 642–44, 709–29. Another author with manuscripts in Germania was the English mystic Richard Rolle of Hampole (1300–49). MICHAEL VAN DUSSEN: Richard Rolle's Latin Psalter in Central European Manuscripts. In: *Medium aevum*. 87 (2018) 1, pp. 41–71. On comparative book history, see ROBERT DARNTON: Histoire du livre. Geschichte des Buchwesens. An Agenda for Comparative History. In: *Publishing History*. 22 (1987), pp. 33–41.

[121] Erlangen-Nürnberg, UB, Ms. 542, fol. 250v: "Nulla libris apta manus ferrugine tincta / Nec nummata queunt corda vacare libris / Non est eiusdem libros nummosque probare / persequiturque libros grex epicure tuus / Nummipete cum libricolis nequeunt simul esse / Ambos crede mihi non tenet una domus." The *Philobiblon* passage was derived from John of Salisbury (c. 1115–1180), *Entheticus major* (c. 1154–56), which could serve as introductory verses to his *Polycraticus*. Altamura, p. 120. THOMAS: p. 138. J. A. GILES (Ed.): *Joannis Saresberiensis postea Episcopi Carnotensis opera omnia nunc primum in unum collegit et cum codicibus manuscriptis*. Oxford 1848. Vol. 3, p. 9. CARY J. NEDERMAN (Ed.): *John of Salisbury: Policraticus of the Frivolities of Courtiers and the Footprints of Philosophers*. Cambridge 1990, pp. xvii–xviii. Trithemius's *De laude scriptorum manualium*, originally a 1492 letter to Gerlach von Breitbach, abbot of Deutz, Cologne, offers advice similar to Richard de Bury's. JOANNES BUSAEUS (Ed.): *Ioannis Trithemii Spanhemensis primum, deinde D. Iacobi in suburbano Herbipolensi, abbatis eruditissimi. Opera pia et spiritualia...* Mainz 1604, p. 763 (chap. xvi).

[2] Barcelona, Biblioteca de Catalunya, Ms. 635, fols. 8r–55r. Spain (?), c. 1450–1500. *Philobiblon* is the only text in Ms. 635. Provenance unknown before the Biblioteca Dalmases, Barcelona, 1699–1916, founded by Pau Ignasi de Damases i Ros, Marqués de Vilallonga (1670–1718). *Catàlegs. Biblioteca de Catalunya*: https://explora.bnc.cat/discovery, [last consulted, January 21, 2023]. Altamura, p. 37.

[3] Basel, Universitätsbibliothek, MS. A. VI. 34, fols. 226r–252r. Germania, c. 1470. MARTIN STEINMANN: *Die Handschriften der Universitätsbibliothek Basel: Register zu den Abteilungen A1–AXI und O*. Basel 1982, p. 247. Altamura, p. 24.

[4] Basel, Universitätsbibliothek. Ms. A. X. 143 [olim B. VIII. 11], fols. 1r–38v. Germania, 1450–75. MARTIN STEINMANN: *Die Handschriften der Universitätsbibliothek Basel: Register zu den Abteilungen A1–AXI und O*. Basel 1982, p. 524. Altamura, pp. 24–25.

[5] Basel, Universitätsbibliothek, Ms. F. IX 15 (a. 1454), fols. 82r–105r. Germania, 1454. *Philobiblon* (attributed to Robert Holcot) is the second text in this paper miscellany, which also contains a text by Joan Bolons (fl. 1433–49) on the logic of Ramon Llull (1232–1316). Owned by the Dominicans of Basel (*Predigerkirche*) in the second half of the fifteenth century and later by Konrad Pfister (1576–1638). BEAT MATTHIAS VON SCARPATETTI: *Katalog der datierten Handschriften in der Schweiz in lateinischer Schrift vom Anfang des Mittelalters bis 1550: Bd. 1*. Zurich 1977, p. 215, no. 595. MARTA M. M. ROMANO: Il primo lullismo in Italia: tradizione manoscritta e contesto della *Lectura* di Joan Bolons. In: *Studia Lulliana* (2007). 47, pp. 71–115, here p. 81. Online descriptions in *swisscollections*: http://ubunibass.ch, [last consulted, January 25, 2023]; and *Mirabile: Archivio Digitale della Cultura Medievale*, http://www.mirabileweb.it, [last consulted, January 25, 2023].

[6] Berlin, Staatsbibliothek zu Berlin, Preußischer Kulturbesitz, Ms. Magdeburgica 32, fols. 210r–222v. Germania, 1462–69. URSULA WINTER: *Die Manuscripta Magdeburgica der Staatsbibliothek zu Berlin Preussischer Kulturbesitz. Teil I. Ms. Magdeb. 1–75*. Wiesbaden 2001, pp. 114–15.

[7] Brussels, Bibliothèque Royale de Belgique, Ms. 738, fols. 129v–141v. Low Countries, s. XV. Paper miscellany from the library of the Augustinian Canons Regular of the Priorij van Sint-Maartensdal, Leuven. JOSEPH VAN DEN GREYN: *Catalogue des manuscrits de la Bibliothèque Royale de Belgique*. Brussels 1905. Vol. 3, pp. 101–2, no. 1709.

[8] Brussels, Bibliothèque Royale de Belgique, 3716–30 [1292], fols. 191v–194r. Low Countries, 1479–90. JOSEPH VAN DEN GREYN: *Catalogue des manuscrits de la Bibliothèque Royale de Belgique*. Brussels 1904. Vol. 4, pp. 260–61, no. 1292. Altamura, pp. 19–20.

[9] Brussels, Bibliothèque Royale de Belgique, Ms. 11465, fols. 1r–48r. Low Countries, s. XV. *Philobiblon* is the main text in a paper manuscript

from the library of the Premonstratensian Canons Regular of the Abdij van Park, in Heverlee, near Leuven. JOSEPH VAN DEN GREYN: *Catalogue des manuscrits de la Bibliothèque Royale de Belgique*. Brussels 1901. Vol. 1, p. 93, no. 206. Altamura, p. 20.

[10] Cambridge, Corpus Christi College, Parker Library, Ms. 456, pp. 127–202. England, 1375–1400. M. R. JAMES: *A Descriptive Catalogue of the Manuscripts in the Library of Corpus Christi College Library Cambridge*. Cambridge 1912. Part VI (vol. II, part III), nos. 451–538), pp. 379–80, no. 456. Described and digitized in *Parker Library on the Web*: https://parker.stanford.edu/parker, [last consulted, January 21, 2023]. Altamura, p. 33.

[11] Cambridge, St. John's College, Ms. 115 (E.12), fols. 57r–87r. England, 1425–50. M. R. JAMES: *A Descriptive Catalogue of the Manuscripts in the Library of St. John's College, Cambridge*. Cambridge 1913, pp. 148–49. Altamura, pp. 32–33.

[12] Cambridge, Sidney Sussex College, Ms. 38. (A.2.16. [C.M.A. 706]), fols. 1r–44r. England, s. XVex. M. R. JAMES: *A Descriptive Catalogue of the Manuscripts in the Library of Sidney Sussex College, Cambridge*. Cambridge 1895, pp. 25–26, no. 38. Altamura, p. 34.

[13] Cambridge, Trinity College, Ms. R. 9. 17 (819), fols. 48r–66r. England, s. XIV/XV. M. R. JAMES: *The Western Manuscripts in the Library of Trinity College, Cambridge: A Descriptive Catalogue*. Cambridge 1901. Vol. 2, pp. 256–58, no. 518. Altamura, p. 33.

[14] Cambridge, University Library, Ms. Add. 3145, fols. 9r–59r. Germania, 1450s. JAYNE S. RINGROSE: *Summary Catalogue of the Additional Medieval Manuscripts in the Cambridge University Library*. Woodbridge 2009, pp. 74–75. Altamura, p. 35.

[15] Cologne, Erzbischöfliche Diözesan- und Dombibliothek, Cod. 1073, fols. 112r–161r. Germania, s. XV. MANFRED THALLER and TORSTEN SCHASSAN: *Mittelalterliche Handschriften im Internet: CEEC Codices Electronici Ecclesiae Colonienis*: www.webdoc.gwdg.de, [last consulted, January 21, 2023]. Described and digitized in *Erzbischöfliche Diözesan- und Dombibliothek Köln, Digitale Sammlungen*: https://digital.dombibliothek-koeln.de/hs/content/titleinfo/315498, [last consulted, January 22, 2023].

[16] Cologne, Historisches Archiv der Stadt Köln, Best. 7004 (Handschriften, GB quart. 215) [Gymnasialbibliothek, Ms. G.B. 4° 215], fols. 1r–30r. Germania, 1436. JOACHIM VENNEBUSCH: *Die theologischen Handschriften des Stadtbibliothek Köln. T. II: Die Quart-Handschriften des Stadtarchivs der Gymnasialbibliothek*. Cologne, Vienna 1980, p. 271.

[17] Copenhagen, Det Kongelige Bibliotek, Ms. Fabricius 21, 2°. fols. 1r–33r. Germania, 1375–1400. Description and digital images available in *Det Kongelige Bibliotek. e-manuskripter*: http://www5.kb.dk/permalink/2006/manus/72/eng/, [last consulted, January 22, 2023]. Altamura, pp. 20–21.

[18] Darmstadt, Universitäts- und Landesbibliothek, Hs. 797, fols. 148r–174v. Germania, 1400–25. KURT HANS STAUB AND HERMANN KNAUS: *Die Handschriften der Hessischen Landes- und Hochschulbibliothek Darmstadt*. Wiesbaden 1979. Vol. 4, pp. 204–5.

[19] Durham University Library, Bishop Cosin's Library, Cosin V.v.2, fols. 161r–208r. England, s. XVmed. BERIAH BOTFIELD (Ed.): *Catalogi veteres librorum Ecclesiae Cathedralis Dunelm...* London 1838. Appendix, pp. 177–78. Altamura, p. 34.

[20] Erfurt, Universitäts- und Forschungsbibliothek, Dep. Erf. 4° 123, Biblioteca Amploniana. MS q123. Germania, s. XIVex. WILHELM SCHUM: *Beschreibenes Verzeichniss der amplonianisches Handschriften-Sammlung zu Erfurt*. Berlin 1887, pp. 380–83 (at p. 383). Altamura, p. 38.

[21] Erlangen-Nürnberg, Universitätsbibliothek, Ms. 542, fols. 216r–50r. Germania, 1450–75. HANS FISCHER: *Die lateinischen Papierhandschriften der Universitätsbibliothek Erlangen*. Wiesbaden 1971, pp. 171–76 (at pp. 173–74). Described and digitized: https://nbn-resolving.org/urn:nbn:de:bvb:29-bv042580123-1, [last consulted, January 22, 2023].

[22] Ghent, Universiteitsbibliotheek, MS. 67, fols. 1r–18v. Low Countries, post-1494. Albert Derolez: *The Library of Raphaël de Marcatellis, Abbot of St. Bavon's, Ghent, 1437–1508*. Ghent 1979, pp. 195, 304 (no. 35). Digitized by the Universiteitsbibiotheek and available on www.lib.ugent.de, [last consulted, January 21, 2023].

[23] Giessen, Universitätsbibliothek, Hs. 792, fols. 139r–59r. Germania, c. 1452–60. JOACHIM OTT: *Die Handschriften des emaligen Fraterherrenstifts St. Markus zu Butzbach in der Universitätsbibliothek Giessen*. Giessen 2004. Part 2, pp. 174–79 (at p. 176).

[24] Goch, Collegium Augustinianum, Bibliotheca domus presbyterorum Gaesdonck, 12 (Ms. 33), fols. 238r–258v. HEINZ FINGER, MARIANNE RIETHMÜLLER, et al.: *Handschriftencensus Rheinland*. Wiesbaden 1993 (Schriften der Universitäts- und Landesbibliothek Düsseldorf, 18), p. 538, no. 912.

[25] Göttingen, Niedersächsische Universitätsbibliothek, Theol. Ms. 119, fols. 12r–31v. Germania, s. XVmed. WILHELM MEYER: *Die Handschriften in Göttingen Universitäts-Bibliothek*. Berlin 1893. Vol. 2, pp. 360–64. Altamura, pp. 26–27.

[26] Innsbruck, Universitäts- und Landesbibliothek, Cod. 144, fols. 128r–142v. Germania, c. 1425. *Philobiblon* is the second part of a paper manuscript from the Charterhouse of Allerengelsberg, Schnalstal, in the South Tyrol. WALTER NEUHAUSER: *Katalog der Handschriften der Universitätsbibliothek, Innsbruck. Teil 2: Cod. 101–200*. Vienna 1991 (Denkschriften der phil.-hist. Klasse, 214), pp. 115–16.

[27] Leiden, Universiteitbibliotheek, ms BPL 31, fols. 59r–59v, 121v. Germania, *s*. XVmed. *Philobiblon* (extracts) from chap. v–vi (fols. 59r–

59v) and chap. vii, xvi, xx (fol. 121v). PHILIPP CHRISTIAAN MOL-HUYSEN: *Codices bibliothecae publicae latini*. Leiden 1912, pp. 18–19 (at p. 19).

[28] London, British Library, Ms. Add. 24361, fols. 4v–21r. England, c. 1470s–80s. *Catalogue of Additions to the Manuscripts of the British Museum in the Years MCCCCLIV–MDCCCLXXV*. London 1877. Vol. 2, p. 59. Altamura, p. 29.

[29] London, British Library, Ms. Arundel 335, fols. 58r–101v. England, 1400–25. Manuscript of Cistercian origin, according to C. H. TALBOT: "A List of Cistercian Manuscripts in Great Britain," *Traditio: Studies in Ancient and Medieval History, Thought and Religion*. 8 (1952), pp. 402–18, here p. 404. Formerly in the libraries of Henry Howard Norfolk (1628–84), duke of Norfolk and earl of Arundel; and in the Bibliotheca Norfolciana, Ms. 3224: 25 (Gresham College, London). Acquired by the British Library in 1831 and described in *Catalogue of Manuscripts in The British Museum, New Series*. London 1834. Vol. I, part 1: T*he Arundel Manuscripts*, p. 100. Altamura, p. 29.

[30] London, British Library, Ms. Cotton, Appendix IV, fols. 103r–119v. England, mid-fifteenth century. *Catalogue of the Manuscripts in the Cottonian Library, Deposited in the British Museum*. London 1802, p. 614. This manuscript must correspond to one that Bernard de Montfaucon (1655–1741) listed at the end of Cotton Faustina (P. 158). BERNARD DE MONTFAUCON: *Bibliotheca bibliothecarum manuscriptorum nova*. Paris 1739. Vol. 1, p. 640. Altamura, p. 29.

[31] London, British Library, Ms. Harley 492, fols. 55r–95r. England, 1400–25. *A Catalogue of the Harleian Manuscripts in the British Museum*. London 1808. Vol. 1, p. 327. Altamura, p. 28.

[32] London, British Library, Ms. Harley 3224, fols 67r–109v. England, 1400–25. *A Catalogue of the Harleian Manuscripts in the British Museum*. London 1808. Vol. 3, p. 10. Altamura, p. 28.

[33] London, British Library, Ms. Royal 8 F xiv, fols. 76r–89v. England, c. 1380–1400. GEORGE F. WARNER and JULIUS P. GILSON: *Catalogue of Western Manuscripts in the Old Royal and King's Collections*. London 1921. Vol. 1, p. 271. Altamura, pp. 27–28.

[35] London, British Library, Ms. Royal 15 C xvi, fols. 59r–71r. England, s. XIVex. BL. Manuscripts and Archives: https://searcharchives.bl.uk, [last consulted, January 22, 2023]. Altamura, p. 28.

[35] Madrid, Real Biblioteca del Monasterio de San Lorenzo de El Escorial, MS. J. II. 25, fols. 157r–185r. Spain(?), c. 1440? GUILLERMO ANTOLÍN: *Catálogo de los Códices Latins de la Real Biblioteca del Escorial*. Madrid 1911. Vol. 2, pp. 488–90 (at p. 489). WILHELM VON HÄRTEL: Bibliotheca patrum latinorum Hispaniensis. Vienna 1887. Vol. 1, pp. 85–86 (at p. 86). Altamura, p. 37.

[36] Mainz, Wissenschaftliche Stadtbibliothek, Hs. I, 172, fols. 159r–193v. Germania, 1400–50. GERHARD LIST: *Die Handschriften der Stadtbibliothek Mainz. Band II: Hs. I 151–Hs. I 250.* Wiesbaden 1998, pp. 108–11 (at p. 109). Described and digitized in *Bibliotheca Cartusiana Moguntina—digital*: https://digi.ub.uni-heidelberg.de/diglit/mzstb_hs_i_172, [last consulted, January 23, 2023].

[37] Munich, Bayerische Staatsbibliothek, Clm. 3586, fols. 1r–23v. Germania, 1472–75. ERWIN RAUNER: *Katalog der lateinischen Handschriften der Bayerischen Staatsbibliothek Munchen. Die Handschriften aus Augsburger Bibliotheken.* Wiesbaden 2007. Vol. 1, pp. 378–95 (at p. 379). *Catalogus codicum manu scriptorum Bibliothecae Regiae Monacensis, Tomi III Pars II*. Munich 1894, pp. 112–13. Formerly in the Staats-, Kreis-, und Stadtbibliothek, Augsburg. Altamura, p. 22.

[38] Munich, Bayerische Staatsbibliothek, Ms. 4705, fols. 147v–170r. Germania, s. XV med. KARIN SCHNEIDER: *Die deutschen Handschrifen der Bayerischen Staatsbibliothek München. Cgm 201–350*. Wiesbaden 1970, pp. 210–11. Altamura, p. 25.

[39] Munich, Bayerische Staatsbibliothek, Ms. 5829, fols. 305v–329r. Germania, 1426. *Philobiblon* in the final text in a paper manuscript miscellany (Ms. 29) from the library of the Benedictine Abbey of Eversberg, Bavaria. In 1426, the manuscript was written in Gries, Diocese of Trent (now Gries am Brenner, South Tyrol, Italy). *Catalogus codicum manu scriptorum Bibliothecae Regiae Monacensis, Tomi III Pars III*. Munich 1873, p. 43. Altamura, p. 25.

[40] Munich, Bayerische Staatsbibliothek, Ms. 17292, fols. 139r–150r. Germania, *s.* XV. *Catalogus codicum manu scriptorum Bibliothecae Regiae Monacensis. Tomi IV Pars III*. Munich 1878, p. 94. Altamura, p. 23.

[41] Munich, Bayerische Staatsbibliothek, Ms. 19742, fols. 1r–16v. Germania, 1493. *Catalogus codicum manu scriptorum Bibliothecae Regiae Monacensis. Tomi IV Pars III*. Munich 1878, p. 271. Altamura, pp. 23–24.

[42] Munich, Bayerische Staatsbibliothek, Ms. 23952 [ZZ 952], fols. 19r–40r. 1493. *Catalogus codicum manu scriptorum Bibliothecae Regiae Monacensis. Tomi II Pars IV*. Munich 1881, p. 111. Altamura, p. 24.

[43] New York, The Morgan Library and Museum, Ms. M 448, fols. 1r–45v. Germania or Low Countries(?), c. 1480. *Medieval & Renaissance Manuscripts*: https://www.themorgan.org/manuscript/112335, [last consulted, January 22, 2023]. Altamura, p. 35.

[44] Nürnberg, Stadtbibliothek, Cent. II 10, fols. 240v–249v. Nürnberg, 1400–50. KARIN SCHNEIDER: *Die Handschriften der Stadtbibliothek, Nürnberg. Band II: Die lateinischen mittelalterlichen Handschriften. Teil I: Theologische Handschriften*. Wiesbaden 1967. Vol. 2, pp. 137–40 (at p. 138).

[45] Oxford, University of Oxford, All Souls College, Ms. 31, fols. 236v–254v. England, 1400–50. ANDREW G. WATSON: *Descriptive Catalogue of the Medieval Manuscripts of All Souls College, Oxford*. Oxford 1997, pp. 61–63. HENRY O. COXE: Catalogue of Manuscripts in the Library of All Souls College. Oxford 1842, p. 9. Altamura, pp. 31–32.

[46] Oxford, University of Oxford, Balliol College, Ms. 166A, pp. 791–816. Germania(?), s. XVmed. R.A.B. MYNORS: *Catalogue of the Manuscripts of Balliol College, Oxford*. Oxford 1963, pp. 170–72. Altamura, pp. 30-31.

[47] Oxford, University of Oxford, Balliol College, Ms. 263, fols. 124v–137r. England, s. XIV/XV. R.A.B. MYNORS: *Catalogue of the Manuscripts of Balliol College, Oxford*. Oxford 1963, pp. 281–83. Altamura, p. 31.

[48] Oxford, University of Oxford, Bodley, Add. MS. C. 108, fols. 20v–39r. Germania, 1450–1500. R. W. HUNT, FALCONER MADAN, et al.: *A Summary Catalogue of Western Manuscripts in the Bodleian Library at Oxford*. Oxford 1895. Vol. 5, pp. 530–31, no. 28940. Described in *Medieval Manuscripts in Oxford Libraries*: https://medieval.bodleian.ox.ac.uk, [last consulted, January 22, 2023]. Digitized in *Digital Bodleian*: https://digital.bodleian.ox.ac.uk, [last consulted, January 22, 2023]. Altamura, p. 30.

[49] Oxford, University of Oxford, Bodley, Ms. Digby 147, fols. 9r–28r. England, 1375–1400. R. W. HUNT and A. G. WATSON: *Bodleian Library Quarto Catalogues. IX: Digby Manuscripts*. Oxford 1999, pp. 65–66, 170, cols. 144–46. Altamura, pp. 29–30.

[50] Oxford, University of Oxford, Bodley, Ms. Lyell 63, fols. 181r–201r. Germania, c. 1451–53. ALBINIA DE LA MARE: *Catalogue of the Collection of Medieval Manuscripts Bequeathed to the Bodleian Library by James P. R. Lyell*. Oxford 1971, pp. 191–99 (at p. 94). Altamura, pp. 34–35.

[51] Oxford, University of Oxford, Lincoln College, Lat. 81, fols. 80r–94r. England, c. 1420. Binding of the Elizabethan courtier Sir Philip Sidney (1554–86). HENRY O. COXE: *Catalogus Codicum Mss. qui in Collegiis Aulisque Oxoniensibus hodie adservantur*. Oxford 1852. Vol. 1, pp. 41–42. Altamura, p. 31.

[52] Oxford, Bodley, Magdalen College, Ms. Lat. 6, fols. 164r–187r. England, 1400–25. HENRY O. COXE: *Catalogus Codicum Mss. qui in Collegiis Aulisque Oxoniensibus hodie adservantur*. Oxford 1852. Vol. 2, pp. 9–10. Altamura, p. 31.

[53] Oxford, Corpus Christi College, Ms. 222, fols. 57r–84r. England, 1400–25. HENRY O. COXE: *Catalogus Codicum Mss. qui in Collegiis Aulisque Oxoniensibus hodie adservantur*. Oxford 1852. Vol. 2, p. 88. Altamura, p. 32.

[54] Oxford, St. John's College, Ms. 172, fols 1r–30r. England, 1425–50. RALPH HANNA: *A Descriptive Catalogue of the Western Medieval*

Manuscripts of St John's College, Oxford. Oxford 2002, pp. 237–40. Altamura, pp. 32–33.

[55] Paris, Bibliothèque Nationale de France, Ms. 2454, fols. 169r–185r. Germania, s. XVmed. PHILIPPE LAUER: *Catalogue général des manuscrits latins. Tome II (Nos. 1439–2692).* Paris 1940, pp. 466–67. Altamura, p. 21.

[56] Paris, Bibliothèque Nationale de France, Ms. 3352C, fols. 89r–103v. France, s. XIVex. *Catalogue général des manuscrits latins: Nos. 3278 à 3535.* Paris 1966. Vol. 5, pp. 267–68. Altamura, p. 21.

[57] Paris, Bibliothèque Nationale de France, Ms. 15168, fols. 1r–45r. France, c. 1380–1400. LÉOPOLD DELISLE: *Inventaire des manuscrits de l'Abbaye de Saint-Victor conservés à la Bibliothèque Impériale, sous les numéros 14232–15175 de fonts latin.* Paris 1869, p. 78. Altamura, pp. 21–22.

[58] Princeton, University Library, Taylor Ms. 15, fols. 1r–27v. Germania or Low Countries (?), c. 1480. DON C. SKEMER: *Medieval and Renaissance Manuscripts in the Princeton University Library.* Princeton 2013. Vol. 1, pp. 435–36.

[59] Soest, Stadtbibliothek, Cod. 22, fols. 320r–337r. Germania, c. 1420. BERNDT MICHAEL and TILO BRANDIS: *Die mittelalterlichen Handschriften der Wissenschaftlichen Stadtbibliothek Soest.* Wiesbaden 1990, pp. 144–48 (at p. 147).

[60] Trier, Stadtbibliothek, Ms. 305, fols. 219r–265r. Germania, Low Countries, c. 1450–1500. MAX KEUFFER: *Beschreibendes Verzeichnis der Handschriften der Stadtbibliothek zu Trier. Erstes Heft.* Trier 1888, pp. 118–21 (at p. 121). Altamura, p. 26.

[61] Tübingen, Universitätsbibliothek. Abteilung Berliner Handschriften, Cod. Lat. Fol. 588, fols. 1r–26v(?). Italy(?). c. 1470. Sir Thomas Phillipps (1792–1872) listed no 16416 among "Miscellaneous MSS." (16416–16456). *Catalogus librorum manuscriptorum in Bibliotheca D. Thomae Phillipps, Bart. A.D. 1837.* Middehill 1837, p. 318. The manuscript remained in the Phillipps Collection and was sold in 1897 by Sotheby's Wilkinson & Hodge, London: *Further Portion of the Famous Collection of Classical, Historical, Genealogical and Other Manuscripts and Autograph Letters of the Late Sir Thomas Phillipps, Pt. 60* (17 May 1897), no. 60. From 1897, the manuscript was in Berlin, Deutsche Staatsbibliothek as Cod. Lat. 588. After World War II, this and other Berlin manuscripts were housed in Tübingen (Abteilung Berliner Handschriften). PAUL OSKAR KRISTELLER *Iter italicum: A Finding Aid of Uncatalogued or Incompletely Catalogued Humanistic Manuscripts of the Renaissance in Italian and Other Libraries. London, Leiden 1983. Volume III (Alia Itinera I) Australia to Germany,* p. 483. Altamura, p. 25.

[62] Vatican City, Bibliotheca Apostolica Vaticana, Ottoboni lat. 259, fols. 30v–66v. France, s. XIVex. *Philobiblon* is in a composite parchment

manuscript with two separate parts of independent origin: fascicle I, Carolingian, Lorsch Abbey, 800–850; fascicle II, including *Philobiblon*, possibly from the Benedictine Abbey of Saint-Benoît-sur-Loire, Fleury, s. XIVex. Possibly removed from the abbey's library by the French bibliophile and jurist Pierre Daniel [d'Orléans] (1531–1604), whose library was acquired after his death by Paul Petau (1568–1614). The manuscript was later in the antiquarian collections of Queen Christina of Sweden (1626–1689; r. 1632–1654), and Cardinal Pietro Ottoboni (1667–1740). *Recensio manuscriptorum codicum qui ex universa Bibliotheca Vaticana...* Leipzig 1803, p. 124, no. 475. Described and digitized in the *Bibliotheca Lauresbamensis*: https://www.bibliotheca-lauresbamensis-digital.de, [last consulted, January 22, 2023]. Altamura, pp. 36–37.

[63] Venice, Biblioteca Marciana, Cod. 111 (L 1, Cod. XLI), fols. 35r–55r. Italy, s. XIVex. Parchment composite manuscript came to the Marciana in 1789 from the Dominican Basilica dei Santi Giovanni e Paolo (San Zanipolo), Venice (no. 13). JOSEPH VALENTINELLI: *Bibliotheca manuscripta ad S. Marci Venetiarum: Codices MSS. Latini*. Venice 1868. Vol. 1, pp. 257–58. Altamura, p. 36.

[64] Wrocław, Biblioteka Uniwersytecka (olim Biblioteca Urbica Wratislaviensi; Stadtbibliothek, Breslau), Cod. 130, fols. 171v–185v. Germania(?) 1375–1400. ALBRECHT W. J. WACHLER: *Thomas Rehdiger und seine Büchersammlumng in Breslau: Ein biographisch-literarischer Versuch*. Breslau 1828, p. 56. KONRAD ZIEGLER: *Catalogus codicum latinorum classicorum qui in Bibliotheca Urbica Wratislaviensi adservantum*. Wrocław 1915, pp. 103–5.

[65] Copenhagen, Det Kongelige Bibliotek, Gl. Kgl. S. 3401, fols. 1016r–1017v. *Philobiblon*, ch. xvii (extract De custodia librorum here attributed to Robert Holcot), in a miscellany from the Benedictine Abbey of St. John the Baptist at Cisnar, near Grömitz, Schleswig-Holstein. Germania, c. 1500. Manuscript later in the Bibliotheca Gottorpiensis, Duchy of Schleswig-Holstein. ELLEN JØRGENSEN: *Catalogus codicum latinorum medii aevi Bibliothecae Regiae Hafniensis. Fasciculus I*. Copenhagen 1923, p. 138. AXEL NELSON: Richard de Bury och Thomas a Kempis. In: *Bok- och biblioteks-historiska studier tillägnade Isak Collijn på hans 50-årsdag*. Ed. Axel Nelson. Uppsala 1925, pp. 59–70 (at p. 59, n. 2).

Paul Schweitzer-Martin

Zum Verhältnis von Papier und Buchdruck im Spätmittelalter[1]

In the first decades after Gutenberg's *invention*, a large number of printing presses had been established throughout Europe and millions of books produced. The vast majority of these incunabula were printed on paper. This impressively high number of books implies an even higher figure of paper sheets needed to produce them. Within only a few years, printers had become a new group of bigtime buyers on the paper market. How can the apparent increase in the demand for paper be identified today? Is it possible for statistical approaches to be combined with the analysis of medieval paper manuscripts and prints to establish the quantity of paper needed for production? If so, would the results correlate with our knowledge about the increase in paper mills in the 15th century? Based on these questions, this article studies if paper for print differed to that for writing and how the type of paper required by printers changed the production, quality, character and format of paper. By undertaking a systematic search for information referring to paper in various recent publications this study will evaluate the relevant data to establish what sources and methods are most promising to track late medieval paper and the changes effected with the introduction of movable type. A key question thereby is what the materiality of medieval paper can tell us and what methods are fruitful to examine these papers.

Trotz rapider Digitalisierung ist auch in der dritten Dekade des 21. Jahrhunderts immer wieder das Phänomen des Papiermangels zu beobachten. Dieser schlägt sich auf unterschiedliche Weise nieder, aber nicht zuletzt darin, dass Publikationen sich verzögern oder in der Produktion deutlich teurer geworden sind als noch in den Jahren zuvor. Der aktuelle Mangel an Papier in der Buchherstellung und die damit einhergehenden Probleme verweisen auf die engen Verbindungen zwischen dem Bedruckstoff Papier und der Buchproduktion in der heutigen Zeit. Diese Verbindung lässt sich auch für die früheste Zeit des Buchdrucks mit beweglichen Lettern beobachten, auch wenn sich durchaus auf anderen Materialien drucken lässt und dies auch von der frühsten Zeit an praktiziert wurde. Bekanntermaßen wurden von der Gutenberg-Bibel sowohl Exemplare auf Papier als auch auf Pergament hergestellt.[2] Nicht nur bei Bibeln, sondern vor allem bei liturgischen Drucken und Ablassbriefen war dies im 15. Jahrhundert eine gängige Praxis.[3] Auf die Masse der Drucke gesehen muss man dennoch dem Benediktinerabt Johannes Trithemius in seinem Diktum von 1493 folgen, dass es sich bei gedruckten Büchern um eine *res papirea*, eine papierene Sache also, handelt.[4]

---

[1] Dieser Beitrag beruht auf Ergebnissen, die im Rahmen der Tätigkeit im Heidelberger Sonderforschungsbereich 933 »Materiale Textkulturen. Materialität und Präsenz des Geschriebenen in non-typographischen Gesellschaften« (Teilprojekt A06 »Die papierene Umwälzung«) gewonnen wurden. Der SFB 933 (2011–2023) wurde durch die Deutsche Forschungsgemeinschaft finanziert. Dieser Beitrag greift zudem teilweise auf Überlegungen aus dem gemeinsamen Vortrag »Late Medieval Paper and Print« mit Carla Meyer-Schlenkrich (Münster) aus dem Jahr 2018 bei der Tagung »Paper-Stuff: Materiality, Technology and Invention« am Cambridge Centre for Material Texts zurück. Für das Projekt sei verwiesen auf: BERND SCHNEIDMÜLLER und PAUL SCHWEITZER-MARTIN: Massenkommunikation als Motor einer neuen Zeit. In: *Ruperto Carola Forschungsmagazin*. 16 (2020), S. 137–43.

[2] Zu den Exemplaren der Gutenberg-Bibel vgl. ERIC MARSHALL WHITE: *Editio princeps. A History of the Gutenberg Bible*. London/Turnhout 2017 (Studies in Medieval and Early Renaissance Art History).

[3] Vgl. PAUL SCHWEITZER-MARTIN: Material und Format liturgischer Inkunabeldrucke. Eine Fallstudie zur Offizin Johannes Sensenschmidt. In: *Wissen und Buchgestalt*. Hrsg. von PHILIPP HEGEL und MICHAEL KREWET. Wiesbaden 2022 (Episteme. 26), S. 301–21. ERNST DANIEL GOLDSCHMIDT: *Der Brevierdruck des XV. Jahrhunderts*. Berlin 1935 (Beiträge zur Inkunabelkunde. 7). FALK EISERMANN: The Indulgence as a Media Event: Developments in Communication through Broadsides in the Fifteenth Century. In: *Promissory Notes on the Treasury of Merits. Indulgences in Late Medieval Europe*. Hrsg. von ROBERT. N. SWANSON. Leiden 2006 (Brill's Companion to the Christian Tradition. 5), S. 309–30.

[4] JOHANNES TRITHEMIUS: *De laude scriptorum*. Hrsg. und übers. von KLAUS ARNOLD. Würzburg 1973, S. 62.

Dieser Aufsatz untersucht das Verhältnis von Papier und Buchdruck im Spätmittelalter mit einem besonderen Augenmerk auf die Materialität des Bedruckstoffs Papier. Dabei wird besonders der Zusammenhang von mittelalterlicher Papierherstellung und Inkunabelproduktion näher beleuchtet. Dafür werden aktuelle Forschungsergebnisse aufgezeigt und es wird diskutiert, unter welchen Gesichtspunkten mittelalterliches Papier untersucht werden kann, sowie, welche Rückschlüsse sich dadurch für die Druckgeschichte ergeben. Der weniger intensiv genutzte Bedruckstoff Pergament soll an dieser Stelle außen vor bleiben.[5]

Papiermühlen in der Inkunabelzeit

Für die Inkunabelzeit sind die Druckereien und deren Produktion inzwischen gut erschlossen.[6] Eine vergleichbare Erschließung der mittelalterlichen Papiermühlen gibt es nicht und ist aus verschiedenen Gründen wohl auch nicht zu erwarten. Dank der Studie *Papierherstellung im deutschen Südwesten* von Sandra Schultz liegen aber zumindest zu den Erstbelegen von Papiermühlen für das Reich nördlich der Alpen zuverlässige Zahlen vor.[7] In der Studie findet sich eine Auflistung aller Papiermühlen in diesen Territorien anhand der bekannten Quellen unter Verweis auf die entsprechenden Erstbelege.[8] Betrachtet man diese Liste nach Jahrzehnten [siehe Abb. 1], so wird deutlich, dass ab den 1460er Jahren ein deutlicher Anstieg der Zahl der Erstbelege für Papiermühlen zu verzeichnen ist. Dieser Anstieg fällt zeitlich mit der Durchsetzung des Buchdrucks mit beweglichen Lettern zusammen, lässt sich aber sicherlich nicht alleine durch diesen erklären. Neben dem Buchdruck ist auch auf die wachsende handschriftliche Buchproduktion und auf zunehmende Schriftlichkeit zumindest im urbanen Raum des ausgehenden Mittelalters zu verweisen.[9]

Für andere Länder und Regionen, insbesondere für Italien, die Wiege der Papierherstellung im lateinischen Europa, müssen entsprechende Daten aus einer Vielzahl von Studien zusammengetragen werden.[10] Schließlich sind auch die verfügbaren Zahlen nicht in allen Fällen belastbar: Oftmals fehlen den Studien sowie insbesondere auch den

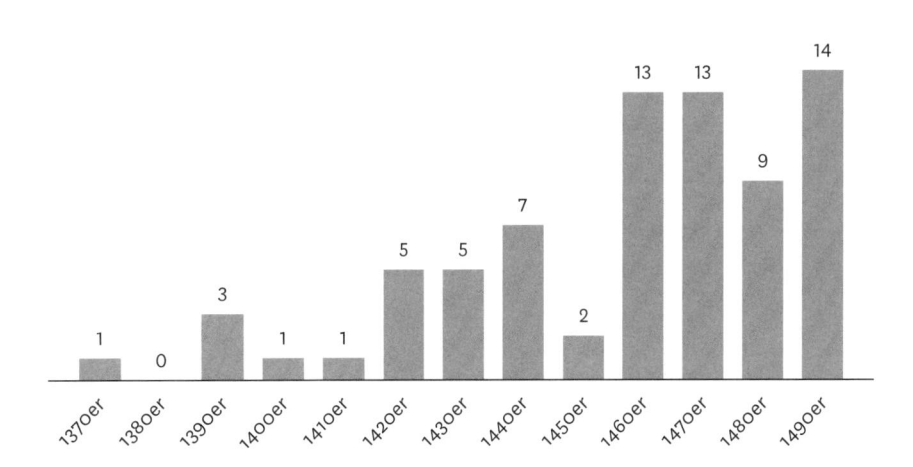

---

5 Zum Druck auf Pergament siehe exemplarisch: ROBIN C. ALSTON und BRAD S. HILL: *Books Printed on Vellum in the Collections of the British Library*. London 1996. PAUL NEEDHAM: Book Production on Paper and Vellum in the fourteenth and fifteenth Centuries. In: *Papier im mittelalterlichen Europa. Herstellung und Gebrauch*. Hrsg. von CARLA MEYER, SANDRA SCHULTZ und BERND SCHNEIDMÜLLER. Berlin, Boston 2015 (Materiale Textkulturen. 7), S. 247–74.

6 Exemplarisch und grundlegend: ISTC. Geldner. GW.

7 Vgl. SANDRA SCHULTZ: *Papierherstellung im deutschen Südwesten. Ein neues Gewerbe im späten Mittelalter*. Berlin, Boston 2018 (Materiale Textkulturen. 18). Eine Zusammenfassung findet sich bei CARLA MEYER-SCHLENKRICH und PAUL SCHWEITZER-MARTIN: How does a New Trade Rise? The Case of Paper Production. In: *Methods in Premodern Economic History. Case Studies from the Holy Roman Empire, c. 1300–c. 1600*. Hrsg. von JULIA BRUCH, ULLA KYPTA und TANJA SKAMBRAKS. Basingstoke 2019, S. 225–8.

8 Vgl. SCHULTZ (s. Anm. 7), S. 508–10.

9 Vgl. NEEDHAM (s. Anm. 5), S. 269–71. CLAUDIA BRINKER-VON DER HEYDE: *Die literarische Welt des Mittelalters*. Darmstadt 2007, S. 15–6.

10 Exemplarisch zur italienischen Papierherstellung: SYLVIA R. ALBRO: *Fabriano. City of Medieval and Renaissance papermaking*. New Castle (Delaware) 2016. Zu den Niederen Landen: INGE VAN WEGENS: Paper consumption and the foundation of the first paper mills in the Low Countries, 13th–15th century. A status quaestionis. In: *Papier im mittelalterlichen Europa* (s. Anm. 5), S. 71–91.

Abb. 1 Anzahl der Erstbelege für Papiermühlen im Reich bis 1500 (außer Reichsitalien) auf Grundlage der Studie von Sandra Schultz

Karten, die mittelalterliche Papiermühlen visualisieren, die konkreten Belege, auf denen die Ergebnisse beruhen.[11] Dies ist ein erhebliches Problem, da viele dieser Mühlen nicht sehr gut bezeugt sind. Die frühesten Nachweise sind meist Papiere mit einem Wasserzeichen, das einer Mühle zugeschrieben wird, oder Kaufbelege. In schriftlichen Quellen finden sich scheinbar immer wieder Nennungen der Herkunft von Papieren, es bleibt bei näherer Untersuchung aber oft unklar, ob es sich bei solchen Nennungen tatsächlich um den Herstellungsort oder nur die Herkunft des Verkäufers handelt. Exemplarisch wird dieses Phänomen an den Papiermühlen in Ravensburg und Schopfheim sichtbar, deren Existenz teils schon für das frühe 14. Jahrhundert vermutet wurde, was sich jedoch in der neueren Forschung nicht erhärten ließ.[12]

Das skizzierte Problem ist zudem eng mit der Frage verwoben, wie viele Jahre die jeweiligen Mühlen betrieben wurden und wie dies methodisch erfasst werden kann. Diese Einschränkung ist wichtig, denn Sandra Schultz konnte zeigen, dass die Produktionszeitspanne von Papiermühlen von Jahrhunderten bis hin zu nur wenigen Jahren reichen konnte.[13] Dies bedeutet, dass in den meisten Fällen nicht mit Sicherheit gesagt werden kann, zu welchem Zeitpunkt wie viele Mühlen aktiv waren, was in den Karten selten berücksichtigt wird und auch nur sehr schwer dargestellt werden kann. Bei den Erstbelegen muss also mitgedacht werden, dass sie keine unmittelbare Auskunft über die Einrichtung einer Mühle oder deren Laufzeit geben. Dennoch handelt es sich um eine der wenigen Möglichkeiten, überhaupt belastbare und als Vergleichsgrundlage geeignete Aussagen über mittelalterliche Papiermühlen zu treffen.

Neben der Verdichtung der Erstbelege für Papiermühlen ist im 14. und 15. Jahrhundert auch eine deutliche Zunahme der Buchherstellung zu beobachten.[14] Nicht nur die Zahl produzierter Bücher stieg, sondern auch das Verhältnis von Pergament- zu Papierbüchern verschob sich zusehends. Spätestens ab dem Ende des 14. Jahrhunderts wurden Bücher mehrheitlich auf Papier produziert.[15] Hinzu kommen noch hohe Quantitäten an Archivgut sowie eine Vielzahl an papierenen Dokumenten, die sehr verstreut überliefert und daher kaum zu quantifizieren sind.

Ähnlich wie beim Buchdruck hat sich die Forschung mit der Frage nach dem Technologietransfer und der Wechselwirkung zwischen Asien und Europa im Mittelalter beschäftigt. Während beim Buchdruck bis heute unklar ist, ob und inwiefern die asiatischen Vorläufer Gutenberg und sein Umfeld beeinflussten,[16] gibt es für das Papier eindeutigere Befunde. Das Wissen um das Verfahren zur Papierherstellung kam im Hochmittelalter aus Asien über das islamische Einflussgebiet nach Italien und auf die Iberische Halbinsel.[17] Rund um das oberitalienische Fabriano wurde die Technik weiterentwickelt und verbreitete sich von dort aus auch nördlich der Alpen.[18]

Zwei wichtige Entwicklungen in Oberitalien betrafen die Schöpfsiebe und die Leimung der Bögen. Für die Siebe wurden bei der Herstellung Drähte eingesetzt, die durch technische Neuerungen zunehmend dünner gezogen werden konnten und somit feinere Strukturen erlaubten.[19] Diese Innovation ermöglichte dann auch die Herstellung dünnerer

11 Exemplarisch die an sich gelungene Visualisierung in The Atlas of Early Printing (verfügbar auf www.atlas.lib.uiowa.edu, [19.10.2022]).

12 Vgl. FRIEDER SCHMIDT: *Von der Mühle zur Fabrik. Die Geschichte der Papierherstellung in der württembergischen und badischen Frühindustrialisierung*. Ubstadt-Weiher 1994 (Technik + Arbeit. 6), S. 41. SCHULTZ (s. Anm. 7), S. 1–2.

13 Vgl. SCHULTZ (s. Anm. 7), S. 485–7.

14 Vgl. ELTJO BURINGH und JAN LUITEN VAN ZANDEN: Charting the 'Rise of the West': Manuscripts and Printed Books in Europe, A Long-Term Perspective from the Sixth through Eighteenth Centuries. In: *The Journal of Economic History*. 69/2 (2009), S. 409–45, hier S. 416–7.

15 Vgl. NEEDHAM (s. Anm. 5), S. 269.

16 Vgl. u.a. WOLFGANG STROMER VON REICHENBACH: *Gutenbergs Geheimnis. Von Turfan zum Karlstein – die Seidenstraße als Mittler der Druckverfahren von Zentralasien nach Mitteleuropa*. Hrsg. von DIRK REITZ. Genf 2000.

17 Vgl. CARLA MEYER und REBECCA SAUER: Papier. In: *Materiale Textkulturen. Konzepte – Materialien – Praktiken*. Hrsg. von THOMAS MEIER, MICHAEL R. OTT und REBECCA SAUER. Berlin, Boston 2015 (Materiale Textkulturen. 1), S. 355–70, hier S. 357–9.

18 Vgl. MEYER und SAUER (s. Anm. 17), S. 360–3. RICHARD L. HILL: Early Italian Papermaking. A Crucial Technical Revolution. In: *Jahrbuch für Papiergeschichte*. 9 (1992), S. 37–46.

19 Vgl. SCHULTZ (s. Anm. 7), S. 105–7.

Bögen. Um Papierbögen nach dem Schöpfen tintenfest zu machen, müssen diese geleimt werden.[20] In der arabischen Welt war eine Paste verwendet worden, die auf Weizenstärke basierte. Um die Wende vom 13. zum 14. Jahrhundert wurde in Italien dann eine Tauchleimung entwickelt. Für diese wurde ein Glutinleim eingesetzt, der durch das Auskochen tierischer Knochen oder Haut gewonnen wurde. Im Unterschied zur arabischen Leimungspraxis konnten mehrere Bögen gleichzeitig eingetaucht werden, was den Herstellungsprozess beschleunigte. Zudem verbesserte sich dadurch die Stabilität und Haltbarkeit der Blätter.[21]

Tinte und Druckerschwärze unterscheiden sich in ihrer Zusammensetzung und erfordern daher für optimale Ergebnisse einen unterschiedlichen Grad der Leimung. Ab welchem Zeitpunkt Schreib- und Druckpapiere in der Produktion differenziert wurden, ist nicht geklärt.[22] Laboruntersuchungen von Timothy Barrett und seinem Team konnten jedoch zeigen, dass sich um die Wende des 15. zum 16. Jahrhunderts der Gelatineanteil in Papieren mehr als halbierte.[23] Diese Veränderung ist mit Sicherheit auf die Leimung zurückzuführen und veränderte zweifellos auch den Druckprozess, zum Beispiel im Hinblick darauf, wie stark Bögen befeuchtet werden mussten. Genauere Untersuchungen zum Verhältnis von Druck- und Schreibpapieren in dieser Zeit sind derzeit noch ein Desiderat der Forschung und vertiefende Studien wären wünschenswert.

Labortechnische Untersuchungen vormoderner Papiere sind bisher eher selten, was mit den Kosten, der Verfügbarkeit entsprechender Instrumente in Bibliotheken und ähnlichen Institutionen, aber auch der Tatsache zusammenhängt, dass nicht alle technischen Untersuchungsverfahren zerstörungsfrei anwendbar sind. Gleichwohl sie großes Erkenntnispotential mit sich bringen, zeichnet sich daher derzeit mittelfristig kein breiter Einsatz dieser Methoden ab.

Die Überlegungen verdeutlichen, wie kleinteilig der gesamte Produktionsprozess war und wie viele Schritte berücksichtigt werden müssen. Da der Prozess der Papierproduktion an anderer Stelle schon ausführlich dargelegt wurde, soll er hier nicht nochmals ausgeführt werden.[24] Die Vergegenwärtigung und der praktische Nachvollzug der Herstellungsschritte ist jedoch bei einer intensiveren Auseinandersetzung mit dem Beschreib- und Bedruckstoff unerlässlich.

Die Erforschung mittelalterlicher Papiere

In manchen Fachkreisen, insbesondere unter Bibliothekarinnen und Bibliothekaren sowie Restauratorinnen und Restauratoren, besteht schon länger ein wissenschaftliches Interesse an Papier. In den letzten Jahren ist jedoch auch ein verstärktes Interesse sowohl der breiteren Mittelalter- als auch der Frühneuzeitforschung zu beobachten.[25] Teils sind dabei die Themen Papier und Buchdruck eng miteinander verzahnt, teils wird auch das Papier unabhängig vom Buchdruck untersucht. Allen Forschungsbeiträgen gemeinsam ist jedoch wohl, dass die aktuelle

---

20 Vgl. SCHULTZ (s. Anm. 7), S. 143–5.

21 Vgl. SCHULTZ (s. Anm. 7), S. 143–62. Siehe dazu auch CARLA MEYER-SCHLENKRICH: *Wann beginnt die Papierzeit? Zur Wissensgeschichte eines hoch- und spätmittelalterlichen Beschreibstoffs*. Habilitationsschrift Heidelberg 2018 (in Druckvorbereitung), S. 117–9.

22 Vgl. PAUL SCHWEITZER-MARTIN: *Kooperation und Innovation im Speyerer Buchdruck des ausgehenden Mittelalters*. Berlin, Boston 2022 (Materiale Textkulturen. 37), S. 156–7.

23 Vgl. TIMOTHY D. BARRETT: Parchment, Paper and Artisanal Research Techniques. In: *Scraped, Stroked, and Bound. Materially Engaged Readings of Medieval Manuscripts*. Hrsg. von JONATHAN WILCOX. Turnhout 2013, S. 115–27, hier S. 124. TIMOTHY BARRETT, MARK ORMSBY und JOSEPH B. LANG: Non-Destructive Analysis of 14th–19th Century European Handmade Papers. In: *Restaurator. International Journal for the Preservation of Library and Archival Material*. 37/2 (2016), S. 93–135, hier besonders S. 106.

24 Als Überblick zur Herstellung empfehlen sich: SANDRA SCHULTZ: Ein neues Handwerk. Die ersten Papiermühlen im deutschen Südwesten und ihre Papiermacher. In: *Werkstatt Geschichte*. 86/2 (2022), S. 15–31. TIMOTHY D. BARRETT: *European Hand Papermaking. Traditions, Tools and Techniques*. Ann Arbor 2018.

25 Vgl. PAUL M. DOVER: *The Information Revolution in Early Modern Europe*. Cambridge 2021 (New Approaches to European History). DANIEL BELLINGRADT: *Vernetzte Papiermärkte. Einblicke in den Amsterdamer Handel mit Papier im 18. Jahrhundert*. Köln 2020. ORIETTA DA ROLD: *Paper in Medieval England: From Pulp to Fictions*. Cambridge 2020 (Cambridge Studies in Medieval Literature 112). SILVIA HUFNAGEL, ÞÓRUNN SIGURÐARDÓTTIR und DAVÍÐ ÓLAFSSON (Hg.): *Paper Stories: Paper and Book History in Post-Medieval Europe*. Berlin, Boston 2023 (Materiale Textkulturen 39) (im Druck). Ein bibliographischer Überblick findet sich bei SANDRA ZAWREL: Papierhandel im Europa der Frühen Neuzeit. Ein Forschungsbericht. In: *Jahrbuch für Kommunikationsgeschichte*. 19 (2017), S. 98–120.

Forschungsperspektive durch den Wandel zum digitalen Zeitalter geprägt und gleichzeitig geschärft ist.²⁶

Im Mittelalter wurde Papier für ganz unterschiedliche Dinge genutzt, etwa als Verpackungs- oder Dämmmaterial.²⁷ Ganz selbstverständlich war es jedoch ein Beschreib- und Bedruckstoff. Da Bücher gegenüber anderen mittelalterlichen Papierartefakten eine besonders hohe Überlieferungschance haben und durch die Katalogisierungsprojekte der letzten Jahre gut erschlossen sind, bieten sich diese besonders für die Untersuchung des Papiers an.²⁸ Ferner verdienen Druckereien als Fallbeispiele massenhaften Papiergebrauchs besonderes Interesse.²⁹

Die Frage nach der Herkunft der von Druckereien genutzten Papiere wurde vor allem auf Grundlage der Wasserzeichen bearbeitet. Grundlegend sind für die breitere Wasserzeichenforschung Charles M. Briquet und Gerhard Piccard zu nennen, in deren Nachfolge zahlreiche Forscherinnen und Forscher wichtige Erschließungs- und Grundlagenarbeit geleistet haben, von der besonders die Handschriften- und Frühdruckforschung profitieren konnten.³⁰ Spezifisch bezüglich des frühen Buchdrucks wurde etwa nach den in den Gutenberg-Bibeln verwendeten Papieren gefragt.³¹ Darüber hinaus wurden in einzelnen anderen Studien die Herkunft der in Offizinen verwendeten Papiere und deren Handelsströme untersucht.³² Es sei zudem auf das derzeit laufende Forschungsprojekt »Werck der Bücher‹ – Transitions, experimentation, and collaboration in reprographic technologies, 1440–1470« verwiesen, das unter anderem Wasserzeichen in den frühsten Drucken untersucht.³³

Die Untersuchung der Wasserzeichen gehört zu den wohl etabliertesten Methoden. Welche Möglichkeiten gibt es jedoch jenseits dieses Forschungszweiges? Generell ist die Frage nach der Materialität in den Geschichts- wie auch in den Buchwissenschaften in den letzten Jahren wieder stärker ins Zentrum gerückt, wovon unter anderem der Sammelband *Materielle Aspekte in der Inkunabelforschung* zeugt.³⁴ Neben einem Beitrag zu Wasserzeichen³⁵ hat Frieder Schmidt in Bezug auf Inkunabeln *Spätmittelalterliches Papier als dingliches Artefakt*³⁶ auf theoretischer Ebene betrachtet. Dabei hat er verschiedene relevante Parameter identifiziert. Zudem diskutiert Paul Needham die Bogengrößen und Formate der Inkunabelpapiere.³⁷ Besonders dieser Aspekt wird im Folgenden noch näher betrachtet werden.

Bei der konkreten Untersuchung mittelalterlicher Papiere muss grundsätzlich zwischen unterschiedlich aufwändigen Verfahren differenziert werden, die zudem teils technisch so voraussetzungsreich sind, dass

---

26 Vgl. SCHULTZ (s. Anm. 24), S. 15.

27 Vgl. MARIA ZAAR-GÖRGENS: *Champagne – Bar – Lothringen. Papierproduktion und Papierabsatz vom 14. bis zum Ende des 16. Jahrhunderts*. Trier 2004 (Beiträge zur Landes- und Kulturgeschichte 3), S. 188–92. BIRGIT KATA: Papier und Pappe im archäologischen Fundspektrum – Bemerkungen zu einer unterschätzten Quellengattung für die Alltagsgeschichte des Mittelalters und der Frühen Neuzeit. In: *Papier im mittelalterlichen Europa* (s. Anm. 5), S. 275–306.

28 Grundlegend zur Überlieferung: ARNOLD ESCH: Überlieferungs-Chance und Überlieferungs-Zufall als methodisches Problem des Historikers. In: *Historische Zeitschrift*. 240 (1985), S. 529–70.

29 Vgl. SCHWEITZER-MARTIN (s. Anm. 22), S. 151.

30 Vgl. HERMANN BANNASCH: Von der Malkunst zur Wasserzeichenkunde. Zu Weg und Werk des Wasserzeichenforschers Gerhard Piccard (1909–1989). In: *Archivalische Zeitschrift*. 86 (2004), S. 287–322. HANS B. KÄLIN: Briquet, Charles-Moïse. In: LGB². 1 (1987), Stuttgart, S. 550. Siehe zu den aktuellen Perspektiven: ERWIN FRAUENKNECHT, GERALD MAIER und PETER RÜCKERT (Hg.): *Das Wasserzeicheninformationssystem (WZIS). Bilanz und Perspektiven*. Stuttgart 2017 (Sonderveröffentlichungen des Landesarchivs Baden-Württemberg).

31 Vgl. PAUL NEEDHAM: The Paper Supply of the Gutenberg Bible. In: *The Papers of the Bibliographical Society of America*. 79/3 (1985), S. 303–74.

32 Vgl. exemplarisch RENAUD ADAM: The Paper Supply of a Printing House as a Mirror of the Paper Trade in the Early Modern Low Countries: The Case of Dirk Martens' Workshop. In: *The Paper Trade in Early Modern Europe. Practices, Materials, Networks*. Hrsg. von DANIEL BELLINGRADT und ANNA REYNOLDS. Leiden 2021 (Library of the Written Word 89/The Handpress World 70), S. 90–105.

33 Vgl. zum Projekt die Beschreibung der DFG ›Werck der Bücher‹ – Transitions, experimentation, and collaboration in reprographic technologies, 1440–1470: (verfügbar auf www.gepris.dfg.de, [6.11.2022]).

34 Vgl. CHRISTOPH RESKE und WOLFGANG SCHMITZ (Hg.): *Materielle Aspekte in der Inkunabelforschung*. Wiesbaden 2017 (Wolfenbütteler Schriften zur Geschichte des Buchwesens. 49).

35 Vgl. PETER RÜCKERT: Wasserzeichen in Inkunabeln. Neue Forschungsperspektiven in digitalem Format. In: *Materielle Aspekte in der Inkunabelforschung* (s. Anm. 34), S. 121–32.

36 Vgl. FRIEDER SCHMIDT: Spätmittelalterliches Papier als dingliches Artefakt. In: *Materielle Aspekte in der Inkunabelforschung* (s. Anm. 34), S. 109–20.

37 Vgl. PAUL NEEDHAM: Format and Paper Size in Fifteenth-Century Printing. In: *Materielle Aspekte in der Inkunabelforschung* (s. Anm. 34), S. 59–107.

sie nicht an jedem Artefakt durchgeführt werden können.³⁸ Auf Grund der schieren Masse an Inkunabeln ist die vollumfängliche Erschließung aller Parameter weder durchführbar noch geboten. Jedoch kann abhängig von der Fragestellung die Untersuchung weiterer Eigenschaften des Bedruckstoffs Papier sehr ergiebig sein, wie im Folgenden aufgezeigt werden soll. Fast durchweg ist die Untersuchung der relevanten Parameter nur an den Originalen oder mit Hilfe spezieller Aufnahmen möglich.

Format und Bogengröße

Bei Inkunabeln wird in allen gängigen Verzeichnissen und Katalogen das bibliographische Format angegeben. Die Angaben (Folio, Quarto, Octavo, etc.) beziehen sich auf die Faltung der Bögen und beinhalten damit nur implizit eine Aussage zur Größe der jeweiligen Drucke. Diese hängt zunächst von der Ausgangsgröße der verwendeten Papierbögen und zudem vom Beschnitt durch die Buchbinder ab.³⁹

Um die verwendeten Papiere besser vergleichen zu können, lohnt es sich daher, neben der Formatangabe, die essenziell ist, auch die tatsächliche Blattgröße zu erfassen, die sich wiederum auf den gesamten Bogen hochrechnen lässt. Einzelne Kataloge haben diese Praxis inzwischen aufgenommen. Der Vorschlag, die Maße der Exemplare flächendeckend zu verzeichnen, blieb aber bisher weitestgehend ungehört.⁴⁰

Unabhängig von der Einführung des Buchdrucks etablierten sich feste Bogengrößen mit eigenen Namen.⁴¹ Aufgrund der dünnen Quellenlage lässt sich nicht genau nachvollziehen, welche Begrifflichkeiten wo verwendet wurden. Aus einzelnen Regionen sind jedoch Regularien bekannt. Die wohl bekannteste Dokumentation der Regeln zur Papierherstellung und der Größe der Bögen sind die Statuten aus Bologna aus dem 14. Jahrhundert, die Bogengrößen mit spezifischen Namen verknüpfen.⁴² Auch spätere Papiermacherordnungen verdeutlichen, dass gezielt bestimmte Papierbogengrößen hergestellt wurden.⁴³ Diese Standardisierung hatte bei der Weiterverarbeitung der Papiere, etwa durch den Buchdruck, erhebliche Vorteile.⁴⁴

Die systematische Verzeichnung der in einzelnen Inkunabeln verwendeten Papierbogengrößen würde erlauben, den Papiergebrauch und möglicherweise auch -bezug verschiedener Offizinen miteinander zu vergleichen. Weiterhin ließen sich regionale Trends und Unterschiede untersuchen. Zudem könnte über die Inkunabelzeit hinweg danach gefragt werden, ob sich Konventionen für die Größe von Büchern durchsetzten. Es ist beispielsweise für bestimmte Regionen bekannt, dass im Lauf der Zeit zunehmend Quart- und Octavausgaben produziert wurden.⁴⁵ Welche Größenänderung der Bücher das aber konkret mit sich brachte, ist nicht erforscht. Dabei wäre nicht nur der Papierbogen, sondern auch das Verhältnis zum Schriftspiegel zu berücksichtigen.

Meine eigenen Untersuchungen zu den Inkunabeldruckern in Speyer konnten zeigen, dass die vier Druckereien dort auf Papierbestände unterschiedlicher Ausgangsgrößen zurückgriffen. Insbesondere

---

38 Siehe exemplarisch für die große Zahl an möglichen Untersuchungsparametern und -möglichkeiten SCHULTZ (s. Anm. 7), S. 517–52.

39 Zu den Grundlagen der Herstellung mittelalterlicher Bücher sei verwiesen auf MATHIAS KLUGE (Hg.): *Handschriften des Mittelalters. Grundwissen Kodikologie und Paläographie.* Ostfildern 2014.

40 Vgl. NEEDHAM (s. Anm. 37), S. 64–5.

41 Vgl. PAUL NEEDHAM: Res papirea: Sizes and Formats of the Late Medieval Book. In: *Rationalisierung der Buchherstellung im Mittelalter und in der frühen Neuzeit.* Hrsg. von PETER RÜCK und MARTIN BOGHARDT. Marburg a. d. Lahn 1994 (elementa diplomatica 2), S. 123–45.

42 Vgl. ZAAR-GÖRGENS (s. Anm. 27), S. 94–5. SCHULTZ (s. Anm. 7), S. 46–7.

43 Vgl. NEEDHAM (s. Anm. 41), S. 125–6.

44 Vgl. SCHWEITZER-MARTIN (s. Anm. 22), S. 159.

45 Vgl. GORAN PROOT: The Transformation of the Typical Page in the Handpress Era in the Southern Netherlands, 1473–c.1800. In: *Impagination – Layout and Materiality of Writing and Publication. Interdisciplinary Approaches from East and West.* Hrsg. von KU-MING (KEVIN) CHANG, ANTHONY GRAFTON und GLENN WARREN MOST. Berlin, Boston 2021, S. 237–72, hier S. 242–4.

die Druckerei Drach benutzte für ausgewählte Werke deutlich größere Bögen als die übrigen Offizinen, was ihr unter anderem erlaubte, andere Gattungen zu produzieren und damit ein breiteres sowie differenzierteres Repertoire an Druckwerken aufzuweisen als die übrigen Werkstätten in Speyer.[46]

Die Verzeichnung der Papierbogengröße ist auf Ebene des GW oder des ISTC nicht sinnvoll, da es sich um eine exemplarspezifische Eigenschaft handelt. Der Vergleich mehrerer Exemplare einer Inkunabel zeigt, dass die Größe aufgrund des Beschnitts durch den Buchbinder teils um mehrere Zentimeter abweichen kann.[47] Die Erfassung dieser Information auf Ebene der Exemplarbeschreibungen in den Katalogen ist daher umso wichtiger und kann vor allem ohne größeren Aufwand und zerstörungsfrei durchgeführt werden.

Papierdicke

Gelegentlich findet die Papierdicke von Inkunabeln in Veröffentlichungen Erwähnung. Bisher gibt es jedoch nur wenige Studien, die sich eingehend mit diesem Phänomen befassen und genauere Beschreibungen liefern als die, dass das Papier *dick* oder *dünn* sei. Oftmals bleibt auch vage, wie diese Feststellung getroffen wurde oder was genau unter *dick* und *dünn* verstanden wird.[48]

Da das Gewicht und die Dicke eines Papierbogens korrelieren, ist das Abwiegen und Messen eines Papierbogens ein guter Weg, um zuverlässige Werte zu erheben.[49] In den meisten Fällen kann diese Methode jedoch nicht auf gebundene Bücher angewendet werden, da man das Gewicht des Einbandes nicht herausrechnen kann. In der Forschung wurden daher verschiedene Ansätze erprobt und entwickelt, die auf Papierdickenmessgeräte zurückgreifen. Da handgeschöpfte Papiere auch bei hervorragender Qualität keine ganz gleichmäßige Stärke bzw. Dicke aufweisen, hat sich eingebürgert, an mehreren Stellen auf einem Bogen zu messen.[50]

Eine der größeren Untersuchungen, die zeitlich auch über das Mittelalter hinausgeht, stammt vom schon erwähnten Timothy Barrett und seinem Team. Diese haben im Laufe der Jahre handgeschöpfte Büttenpapiere aus verschiedenen Regionen und Epochen untersucht. In einer 2016 veröffentlichten Zusammenfassung der Arbeit des Teams zeigen sie, dass die durchschnittliche Dicke der Blätter im Verlauf des Mittelalters abnahm. Für ihre Studien wurde ein Handmikrometer (Dickenmessgerät) verwendet und jeweils ein Stapel von zehn Blättern gemessen.[51] Die Ergebnisse zeigen, dass die Papierdicke bis etwa zum 17. Jahrhundert zurückging.[52] Diese Studie verweist auch auf die gewöhnliche Schwankung der Papierdicke innerhalb desselben Buches, bietet aber keine detaillierte Erklärung für diese Schwankung.[53]

In jüngster Zeit hat Joran Proot aufwendige Feldforschungen und Messungen an frühen gedruckten Büchern aus den südlichen Niederlanden durchgeführt. Er hat Layout, Formate, Blattgrößen und die Dicke

---

[46] Vgl. SCHWEITZER-MARTIN (s. Anm. 22), S. 163–6.

[47] Vgl. SCHWEITZER-MARTIN (s. Anm. 22), S. 160–2.

[48] Ein Forschungsüberblick findet sich bei: JORAN PROOT (unter Mitwirkung von PAUL SCHWEITZER-MARTIN und WOLFGANG JACQUET): Papier bij Colard Mansion. Een methodologische verkenning van de papierdikte bij de incunabel Controversie de la noblesse (Brugge, 1476). In: *Boeken uit Brugge. Studies over Brugse boekgeschiedenis.* Hrsg. von Renaud Adam. Brugge 2021, S. 22–37, hier S. 23–5. SCHWEITZER-MARTIN (s. Anm. 22), S. 166–71.

[49] Vgl. CARLA MEYER und THOMAS KLINKE: Geknickt, zerrissen, abgegriffen. Gebrauchsspuren auf historischen Papieren und ihr kulturhistorischer Aussagewert. In: *Papier im mittelalterlichen Europa* (s. Anm. 5), S. 135–78, hier S. 142–3. In einigen Fällen kann eine Röntgenaufnahme verwendet werden, die die genaueste Methode darstellt. Einzelne Blätter werden in einem Röntgengerät analysiert, um die Struktur des Blattes ohne Einschränkungen hinsichtlich der Tinte oder anderer Substanzen auf der Oberfläche zu erkennen. Vgl. hierzu den unveröffentlichten Vortrag von D. Steven Keller »Investigation of watermarks in paper structure using soft x (grenz) and β-radiographic imaging with non-contact profilometry« am 8. Juni 2021 in Washington D.C. im Rahmen des 35. Kongresses der International Association of Paper Historians.

[50] Vgl. PROOT (s. Anm 48.), S. 30–2. SCHULTZ (s. Anm. 7), S. 545–6. EZIO ORNATO, PAOLA BUSONERO, PAOLA F. MUNAFÒ und MARIA SPERANZA STORACE: *La carta occidentale nel tardo medioevo. Prefazione di Carlo Federici.* Bd. 1: *Problemi metodologici e aspetti qualitativi.* Rom 2001, S. 44. BARRETT, ORMSBY und LANG (s. Anm. 23), S. 102–5.

[51] Vgl. BARRETT, ORMSBY und LANG (s. Anm. 23), S. 103.

[52] Vgl. BARRETT, ORMSBY und LANG (s. Anm. 23), S. 107–8.

[53] Vgl. BARRETT, ORMSBY und LANG (s. Anm. 23), S. 103. Zu den Schwankungen siehe PROOT (s. Anm. 48), 29–34.

des Papiers, letztere ebenfalls mit einem Handmikrometer, untersucht. Seine Fallstudie zeigt deutlich, wie sich die durchschnittliche Papierdicke zwischen den 1470er Jahren und 1540 verändert hat.[54]

Auch meine eigene Studie zu Speyer gelangte im Bereich der Papierdicke zu ähnlichen Ergebnissen. Für den Zeitraum zwischen 1471 und 1500 lässt sich eine kontinuierliche Abnahme der Dicke der in Speyer für den Druck verwendeten Papiere beobachten. Gleichzeitig wurde deutlich, dass im Hinblick auf die Stärke unterschiedliche Papiere genutzt wurden. Eindeutig ist jedoch, dass die Durchschnittswerte vor 1480 bei mindestens 2mm für je zehn Blätter lagen, während der Durchschnitt nach 1480 darunter lag.[55]

Forschungsperspektivisch wäre es wichtig, darüber einzukommen, wie die Dicke handgeschöpfter Papiere standardisiert gemessen werden soll, damit diese Werte reproduzierbar und vergleichbar sind.[56] Zudem wären breiter angelegte Studien wünschenswert, um die Entwicklungen überregional besser zu verstehen und vergleichen zu können. Es ist anzunehmen, dass die Veränderungen in der Beschaffenheit der Papiere in Wechselwirkung zu Veränderungen und Entwicklungen in der Druckgeschichte stehen. Da bisher die Erforschung der Papierdicke jenseits eher allgemeiner Beobachtungen noch in ihren Anfängen begriffen ist, sind solche Überlegungen meist eher spekulativ. Jedoch scheint gerade die Zeit um das Jahr 1480 eine wichtige Zäsur im frühen Buchdruck darzustellen. Gerhard Piccard vermutete, dass ab dieser Zeit Papiere auch anders geleimt wurden,[57] und nicht zuletzt nahm gleichzeitig die Zahl der Offizinen stark zu.[58] Ein erhöhter und veränderter Papierbedarf der Druckereien könnte also in unmittelbarem Zusammenhang mit der Veränderung der Papierdicke stehen. Dünneres Papier erlaubt beispielsweise, mit der gleichen Menge an Fasern eine größere Zahl an Bögen herzustellen, um nur eine konkrete Implikation zu verdeutlichen.

Weitere Merkmale handgeschöpfter Papiere

Obwohl handgeschöpfte Papierbögen aus derselben Mühle einander sehr ähnlich sind und von der hohen Kunstfertigkeit der Papiermacher zeugen, gleichen sie einander als manuell hergestellte Produkte niemals vollkommen. Kleinere Veränderungen am Schöpfsieb oder der Verschleiß der Drahtfiguren, durch die die Wasserzeichen entstanden, sind mit dem bloßen Auge kaum zu erkennen. Schöpffehler hingegen sind auch ohne Hilfsmittel oftmals leicht zu identifizieren. Auf einige der typischen Herstellungsspuren in handgeschöpftem Papier soll hier aufmerksam gemacht werden.[59]

Die Qualität und Farbe handgeschöpfter Papiere hängt in großen Teilen von den verwendeten Rohstoffen und deren Aufbereitung ab. Um einen sauberen Bogen Papier zu erhalten, ist es wichtig, die Fasern sorgfältig aufzubereiten. In der Regel wurde im Mittelalter auf Lumpen zurückgegriffen, die aus Leinen und Hanf bestanden.[60] Wenn der Faserbrei verunreinigt war oder einzelne Fasern nicht korrekt zerkleinert wurden,

---

[54] Vgl. PROOT (s. Anm. 45), S. 237–272.

[55] Vgl. SCHWEITZER-MARTIN (s. Anm. 22), S. 169–71.

[56] Vgl. PROOT (s. Anm. 48), S. 30–5.

[57] Vgl. GERHARD PICCARD: Einleitung. In: *Die Wasserzeichenkartei Piccard im Hauptstaatsarchiv Stuttgart. Findbuch II: Die Ochsenkopf-Wasserzeichen*, 1. Teil. Bearb. von GERHARD PICCARD. Stuttgart 1966 (Veröffentlichungen der Staatlichen Archivverwaltung Baden-Württemberg. Sonderreihe), S. 1–40, hier S. 7–11.

[58] URSULA RAUTENBERG: Von Mainz in die Welt. Buchdruck und Buchhandel in der Inkunabelzeit. In: *Gutenberg. Aventur und Kunst. Vom Geheimunternehmen zur ersten Medienrevolution*. Hrsg. von der Stadt Mainz. Mainz 2000, S. 236–47.

[59] Ausführlicher zu diesem Thema: SANDRA SCHULTZ und JOHANNES FOLLMER: Von Brillen, Knoten und Wassertropfen. Auf der Suche nach Herstellungsspuren in historischen Papieren am Beispiel von Archivalien des Stadtarchivs Ravensburg. In: *Papier im mittelalterlichen Europa* (s. Anm. 5), S. 11–46. Zum Herstellungsprozess handgeschöpfter Papiere siehe Anmerkung 24.

[60] Vgl. SCHMIDT (s. Anm. 36), S. 113–15.

ist dies im Papierbogen unmittelbar als dunkle Stelle oder Verdickung sichtbar.[61]

Zwei Hinweise auf schnelles Arbeiten an der Bütte sind Wassertropfen und sogenanntes wolkiges Papier. Tropfen entstehen, wenn Wasser auf die noch feuchten Papierbögen fällt, und sind als kleine Kreise sichtbar. An dieser Stelle ist das Papier auch etwas dünner, da die Fasern durch den Wassertropfen verdrängt werden. Wolkiges Papier entsteht, wenn der Faserbrei ungleich verteilt wird.[62]

Nach dem Schöpfen mussten die Papiere durch sogenanntes *gautschen* von den Sieben abgenommen werden. Auch hier konnte es durch Unachtsamkeit zu zahlreichen Fehlern kommen. Besonders sichtbar sind sogenannte *Brillen*, die bei den ersten Bögen eines neuen Papierstapels (*Pauscht*) durch Luftblasen entstehen können. Hier ist wohl von unerfahrenen Gautschern auszugehen.[63]

Auf den Produktionsprozess von Inkunabeln haben diese Herstellungsspuren und Fehler keinen unmittelbaren Einfluss. Der Druck und später auch die Bindung der Bücher wird nicht beeinträchtigt. In einigen Fällen kann jedoch das Druckbild beeinträchtigt sein, insbesondere wenn viele dunkle Einsprengsel oder auch Faserverunreinigungen auf der jeweiligen Seite zu sehen sind. Die gedruckte Seite kann dann unordentlich wirken und die ästhetische Qualität eines Buches leiden. Bei Inkunabeln ist dies jedoch nur sehr selten zu beobachten, was darauf hindeutet, dass in den Druckereien auf die Verwendung hochwertiger Papiere geachtet wurde. Fehlerhafte Papiere können zudem durch dünne Stellen auch leichter reißen, was ein weiterer Grund sein könnte, warum sie in der Regel nicht für Inkunabeln genutzt wurden.

Es lässt sich durchaus untersuchen, wie die für den Buchdruck verwendeten Papiere beschaffen sind und ob fehlerhafte Bögen überhaupt genutzt wurden. Eine Vielzahl an Papierbögen mit Schöpffehlern oder eine geringe Zahl solcher Bögen können darauf hinweisen, dass jedes verfügbare Blatt eingesetzt wurde oder aber nur ausgewählte Papiere. Beide Befunde sind natürlich nur Deutungen, können aber mit anderen Indizien, wie dem Zustand der verwendeten Typen und Holzschnitte sowie weiteren Quellen zur Offizin, zu belastbaren Interpretationen führen. Nur in seltenen Fällen ist das Papier alleine als historische Quelle aussagekräftig, jedoch kann es durchaus als ein wichtiger Baustein bei der Untersuchung dienen.

Ausblick

Abschließend bleibt als Auffälligkeit hervorzuheben, dass, während die Zeitgenossen den Buchdruck vielfach positiv wie negativ kommentierten,[64] sie gleichzeitig das Papier und dessen massenhaften Gebrauch im Buchdruck weitestgehend unkommentiert ließen.[65] Fast schon analog spielte das Papier lange Zeit auch in der Forschung, wenn überhaupt, eine ungeordnete Rolle. Beinahe kann man den Eindruck gewinnen, dass das Papier sowohl im Mittelalter als auch in der Gegenwart mehr oder

61 Vgl. exemplarisch SCHULTZ (s. Anm. 7), S. 92.

62 Vgl. SCHULTZ und FOLLMER (s. Anm. 59), S. 28–32.

63 Vgl. SCHULTZ und FOLLMER (s. Anm. 59), S. 32–3.

64 Exemplarisch HANS WIDMANN: *Vom Nutzen und Nachteil der Erfindung des Buchdrucks – aus der Sicht der Zeitgenossen des Erfinders*. Mainz 1973 (Kleiner Druck der Gutenberg-Gesellschaft. 92).

65 Vgl. MEYER-SCHLENKRICH (s. Anm. 21).

weniger als gegeben hingenommen wurde, sofern nicht gerade Mangel daran herrscht.[66]

Tatsächlich war Papier für die Erfindung des Buchdrucks mit beweglichen Lettern keine Notwendigkeit, sehr wohl allerdings für dessen zweifelsohne schnelle Durchsetzung. Denn Pergament hätte den immensen Bedarf an Bedruckstoff wohl kaum gedeckt.[67] Man kann also durchaus sagen, dass sich die Durchsetzung des Papiers und die Durchsetzung des Buchdrucks mit beweglichen Lettern positiv bedingt und auch beschleunigt haben.

Dieser sich positiv bedingende Zusammenhang von Buchdruck und Papier war in der bisherigen Forschung durchaus bekannt. Dennoch lag und liegt der Fokus meist auf der Drucktechnik sowie den Druckerzeugnissen und weniger auf dem Bedruckstoff. Dies wird daran deutlich, dass bei Drucken das Material, wenn es Papier ist, meist gar nicht erst in Katalogen verzeichnet wird. Dies ist einerseits pragmatisch und spiegelt andererseits dessen Selbstverständlichkeit. Zudem werden nur in den seltensten Fällen die Maße angegeben.

Die für Inkunabeln, aber auch spätere Drucke verwendeten Papiere bergen ein hohes analytisches Potential. Dieses erhöht sich zudem, wenn es mit den Inhalten und der Gestaltung der einzelnen Drucke sowie deren Verbreitung und den Gebrauchsspuren verknüpft wird. Im günstigsten Fall lässt sich auf der Grundlage dieser Zugänge sagen, wo das Papier für eine Inkunabel hergestellt wurde und wo es bedruckt wurde. Oftmals sind schon dies zwei unterschiedliche Orte. Hinzu kommt in vielen Fällen noch ein zeitgenössischer Verkaufs- und Aufbewahrungsort. Wenn man diese Transaktionen und Orte verzeichnet, lassen sich so Handelsnetzwerke und -routen des Spätmittelalters genauer nachvollziehen, was für die Wirtschaftsgeschichte dienlich ist.[68]

Der differenzierte Blick auf das Artefakt Papier erlaubt Rückschlüsse auf die Praktiken der Offizinen und ist damit auch für die Druckgeschichte von Bedeutung. So können die Eigenschaften der Bögen wie Wasserzeichen oder Maße beispielsweise Rückschlüsse darauf erlauben, ob Offizinen auf ähnliche oder unterschiedliche Papierbestände zurückgreifen.

Das Papier in den Drucken bietet also eine Vielzahl an Untersuchungs- und auch Erkenntnismöglichkeiten. Dieser Beitrag ist daher auch als Plädoyer dafür zu verstehen, Inkunabeln und deren Papier als materiale Objekte zu begreifen, die als solche physisch untersucht werden müssen, um die Entwicklungen der Inkunabelzeit besser zu verstehen.

---

[66] Vgl. JOHN BIDWELL: *Paper and Type. Bibliographical Essays.* Charlottesville 2019, S. 3.

[67] Vgl. WOLFGANG SCHMITZ: *Grundriss der Inkunabelkunde. Das gedruckte Buch im Zeitalter des Medienwandels.* Stuttgart 2018 (Bibliothek des Buchwesens 27), S. 71. SCHMIDT (s. Anm. 36), S. 110.

[68] Vgl. exemplarisch SCHWEITZER-MARTIN (s. Anm. 22), S. 199–252.

Daniele Guernelli

Bartolomeo Varnucci imprenditore del libro: ulteriori aggiornamenti

The article provides an overview of the career of Bartolomeo Varnucci as a 'cartolaio' and illuminator, adding new attributions to and considerations about his work. Varnucci lived in Florence between the II and III quarter of the xvth Century, and kept a cartolaio workshop in piazza San Firenze, near the Palazzo del Podestà, for about forty years. In his activity he was helped by his brothers Giovanni and Chimenti, illuminator and cartolaio the former, and cartolaio the latter (also illuminator?), who continued the workshop activity after Bartolomeo's death. Varnucci's shop was located near that of Vespasiano da Bisticci's, and supposedly there was competition between the two. Vespasiano was particularly knowledgeable in texts and philology, therefore attracting humanists, meanwhile Bartolomeo used the art of illumination as a special skill to attract business. To his activity as illuminator it is possible to add a couple of manuscripts, both held by the Biblioteca Apostolica Vaticana. One is a copy of Cicero Orationes (ms. Pal. Lat. 1486), which has an owner's note by Giannozzo Manetti; the other one is a Breviary (ms. Vat. lat. 4761), to which the coat of arms of pope Giulio II della Rovere was added later in time. Bartolomeo's education remains unclear, even if it is quite probable that he spent his early years in a cartolaio shop (Calderino di Francesco? Lorenzo di Bindo?), being influenced by artists like Battista di Biagio Sanguigni, Giovanni Toscani, Master of Sherman predella, and greater artists like Masolino da Panicale and Beato Angelico.

Nella Firenze del XV secolo il luogo in cui si concentrarono le maestranze legate alla produzione del libro fu nei pressi dell'area che sta tra il convento della Badia Fiorentina e il Palazzo del Podestà, ora Museo del Bargello.[1] In questi pochi metri, chiamati via dei librai, si raggrupparono molte botteghe, che furono presidi capitali per lo sviluppo dello stesso umanesimo fiorentino, e della sua diffusione. Come si può vedere ancora in una incisione settecentesca di Giuseppe Zocchi,[2] molte di queste erano collocate lungo il perimetro della Badia,[3] che ne era proprietaria, ma ancora altre erano situate oltre il Palazzo del Podestà [fig. 1]. Al loro interno, spesso fatto di due ambienti, i cartolai che le dirigevano svolgevano diversi compiti, che il mercato moderno ha poi separato. Vendevano al dettaglio materie prime come carta e pergamena, vendevano libri usati e ne rilegavano dei nuovi. Ma accanto a questo fungevano anche da stazionari, come nelle università dei secoli precedenti, occupandosi di coordinare il lavoro di procacciamento della pergamena, della copia, della decorazione e della rilegatura di opere a loro commissionate, o che potevano essere ragionevolmente realizzate *ex ante* una

---

[1] Sul tema si veda ALBINIA DE LA MARE: New Research on Humanistic Scribes in Florence. In: *Miniatura fiorentina del Rinascimento, 1440–1525. Un primo censimento.* Ed. ANNAROSA GARZELLI. Firenze 1985, pp. 398–415; ANNA MELOGRANI: The illuminated manuscript as a commodity: production, consumption and the cartolaio's role in fifteenth-century Italy. In: *The Material Renaissance.* Ed. MICHELLE O'MALLEY e EVELYN WELCH. Manchester 2007, pp. 197–221; EADEM: Manuscript materials: cost and the market for parchment in Renaissance Italy. In: *Trade in artists' materials. Markets and commerce in Europe to 1700.* Ed. JO KIRBY, SUSIE NASH e JOANNA CANNON. Londra 2010, pp. 199–219; JONATHAN J. G. ALEXANDER: *The Painted Book in Renaissance Italy. 1450–1600.* New Haven/Londra 2016, pp. 199–206. Per una breve sintesi sul tema, CLAUDIO SORRENTINO: Una bottega fiorentina di cartolai del secolo XV. In: *I beni culturali.* 10, 6 (2012), pp. 1–4.

[2] Sull'artista si veda da ultimo *Giuseppe Zocchi. Vedute di Firenze nel '700: l'Arno, le piazze, le chiese, i palazzi nella prima serie di incisioni della città granducale.* Ed. MARIA FRANCESCA BONETTI e GAETANO CAMBIAGI. Roma 2014; BOŻENA ANNA KOWALCZYK: Bellotto e Zocchi tra Venezia, Firenze e Roma. In: *Venezia Settecento. Studi in memoria di Alessandro Bettagno.* Ed. BOŻENA ANNA KOWALCZYK. Cinisello Balsamo 2015, pp. 75–83; GIANCARLO SESTIERI: Giuseppe Zocchi sulle orme di Gian Paolo Panini. In: *Originali, repliche, copie, uno sguardo diverso sui grandi maestri.* Ed. PIETRO DI LORETO e GIULIA MARTINA WESTON. Roma 2018, pp. 265–271.

[3] ALESSANFRO GUIDOTTI: *La Badia Fiorentina.* Firenze 1982; IDEM: Vicende storico-artistiche della Badia Fiorentina. In: *La Badia Fiorentina.* Ed. ERNESTO SESTAN, MAURILIO ADRIANI e ALESSANDRO GUIDOTTI. Firenze 1982, pp. 47–224; ANNA LEADER: *The Badia of Florence: Art and Observance in a Renaissance Monastery.* Bloomington 2012.

Fig. 1 Giuseppe Zocchi, *Veduta di Firenze*, 1744

4 ALESSANDRO GUIDOTTI: Nuovi documenti su Vespasiano da Bisticci, la sua bottega e la sua famiglia. In: *Federico da Montefeltro. Lo stato, le arti, la cultura*. Ed. GIORGIO CERBONI BAIARDI, GIORGIO CHITTOLINI e PIERO FLORIANI. Roma 1986, vol. 3, pp. 97–111; ALBINIA DE LA MARE: Vespasiano da Bisticci as Producer of Classical Manuscripts in Fifteenth-Century Florence. In: *Medieval Manuscripts of the Latin Classics: Production and use, Proceedings of the Seminar in the History of the Book to 1500* (Leida, 1993). Ed. CLAUDINE A. CHAVANNES-MAZEL e MARGARET M. SMITH. Los Altos Hills/Londra 1996, pp. 167–207; LUCA BOSCHETTO: Letteratura e politica nella Firenze del Quattrocento. La collaborazione tra Vespasiano e Manetti per l'Oratio funebris di Giannozzo Pandolfini. In: *Palaeography, Manuscript Illumination and Humanism in Renaissance Italy. Studies in Memory of A. C. de la Mare*. Ed. ROBERT CLACK, JILL KRAVE e LAURA NUVOLONI. Londra 2016, pp. 23–37; WI-SEON KIM: Vespasiano da Bisticci: un cartolaio dissenziente nella Firenze del Quattrocento. In: *ibidem*, pp. 39–52; ANGELA DILLON BUSSI: Albinia C. de la Mare, Vespasiano da Bisticci e la miniatura: il caso di Bartolomeo Varnucci. In: *ibidem*, pp. 323–332; ROSS KING: *The Bookseller of Florence. Vespasiano da Bisticci and the Manuscripts that Illuminated the Renaissance*. Londra 2021; CHRISTOPHER DE HAMEL, *The Posthumous Papers of the Manuscripts Club*. Londra 2022, pp. 93–129.

5 DE LA MARE (vedi nota 1), p. 406, nota 71; MARY A. E RICHARD H. ROUSE: *Cartolai, Illuminators, and Printers in Fifteenth-Century Italy. The Evidence of the Ripoli Press*. Los Angeles 1988, pp. 20–21.

6 Per un profilo sull'artista si veda da ultimo DANIELE GUERNELLI: Aggiornamenti su Bartolomeo Varnucci. In: *Zeitschrift für Kunstgeschichte*. 3 (2021), pp. 325–364, con letteratura precedente.

7 ALESSANDRO GUIDOTTI: Indagini su botteghe di cartolai e miniatori a Firenze nel XV secolo. In: *La miniatura italiana tra Gotico e Rinascimento*. Ed. EMANUELA SESTI. Firenze 1985, vol. 2, pp. 473–507, pp. 479, 481, 484.

loro commercializzazione sul libero mercato. Ed ancora, potevano essere i punti di riferimento editoriale per la pubblicazione di nuovi testi, composti dai letterati del loro tempo, che pagavano per la realizzazione di copie di dedica. Ovviamente il personaggio più significativo fra loro fu senza dubbio Vespasiano da Bisticci, che oltre ad aver rappresentato il principale terminale del patrocinio librario mediceo, e dei più importanti committenti dell'epoca, scrisse un fondamentale testo contenente ben centotre vite di bibliofili della sua epoca, che rappresenta una fonte storico-biografica fondamentale.[4] Tuttavia, Vespasiano non fu il solo, tanto che sappiamo che i cartolai alla Badia furono dodici negli anni quaranta, diciotto negli anni cinquanta, diciassette negli anni sessanta, una ventina nel decennio successivo, fino a superare i trenta a fine secolo.[5]

A pochi passi dalla bottega di Vespasiano, infatti, vi fu un'altra bottega, questa volta a conduzione familiare, dei fratelli Varnucci, il cui membro più importante, Bartolomeo, è ad oggi noto per essere stato miniatore. Bartolomeo era figlio di Antonio di Luca di Jacopo Varnucci, che possedeva una bottega di guainaio in Ponte Vecchio.[6] Lui e la moglie Benedetta inizialmente vivevano in via Santa Maria, nel popolo di San Pier Maggiore, ma nel 1446 si spostarono in via Ghibellina, nel popolo di Sant'Ambrogio, mentre nel 1451 risiedevano in via Pietrapiana. La coppia ebbe cinque figli: Bartolomeo, Giovanni, Bernardo, Giuliana e Chimenti. Nonostante il mestiere del padre, ben tre dei quattro figli maschi intrapresero la professione di cartolaio. Infatti, già dal 1441 Bartolomeo e Giovanni presero in affitto una bottega che era stata di Calderino di Francesco cartolaio.[7] Non è impossibile che fosse proprio sotto di lui che i due avessero fatto i primi passi nel mondo del libro. Come che sia, Bartolomeo è testimoniato come cartolaio nel 1448, nel 1450, e in due documenti del 1448 e del 1451 lui e il fratello Giovanni risultano titolari di una delle botteghe della Badia Fiorentina, all'attuale numero 6

Incipit liber sermonū bti leonis pape urbis rome. Sermo pm̅us de ordinatione sua.

Gaudem̅ do-
loquař eg me-
um. ī nomē
sc̅m eius a̅ia
mea: ne s̅p̅ i ca-
ro: lingua mā
benedicat. z
Q̅ia non uerecunde. sz ingrate mentis uitiū e. beneficia tacere diuina. ı satis dignum est a sacri ficijs d̅nice laudis. obsequiū cō secrati pontificis inchoare. O̅ła i̅n humilitate n̅ra memor fuit n̅rı dominus. z b̅ndi̅xit nobis. Q̅uia fecit m̅ mirabilia mag̅s solus. ut p̅sentē me cerneret uire s̅c̅itatis affectio. quē fecerat ne cessitas longe peregrinatis. ab sente. E̅go igitur deo n̅ro gr̅as i semp. acturus sum pro o̅ibus que retribuit m̅. N̅ı quoq̅ fa uoris arbitrū. debita gr̅ar ac tōe celebro. euidenter intelli gens. quantū m̅ posiut reuerē

tie amoris ı fidei. studia uire di lectionis impendere. animarū uı̅ar̅ salute. pastorali sollicitu dine cupienti. qui tā sc̅m de me nullis a̅o modū p̅cedentibus me ritis iudicium p̅tulistis. Obsecro igitur p̅ m̅ias d̅ni. muuate uotis que desiderijs expetistis. ut s̅p̅ gr̅e maneat in me. ı iudicia uı̅a non fluctuet. S̅z estet in o̅m̅ue omnibus nobis. pacis bonū. qui uobis unanimitatis studia in fudit. ut omnibus diebus uite mee in o̅ipotentis dei fruciū. ı ad uı̅a paratus obsequia. cū fiducia possi d̅nm deprecari. Pater sc̅e osua eg̅o in noie tuo quog̅ dedisti m̅. sep̅q̅ proficientibus uobis ad salutē magnificet a̅ia mea d̅nm. ı in fu turi retributiōe iudicij. uel m̅ apud iustū iudicē sacdotij met ro subsistat. ut uos m̅ plena opa uī sitis gaudiū. uos corona. qui bona uoluntate sincerū p̅ sc̅is uīe testimoniū p̅stitistis. I̅o no n̅abile igit m̅ dilectissimi hodie̅nū diem fecit d̅nī ı a

Fig. 2 Frontespizio con iniziale 'L' abitata da un putto. In: Leone Magno, *Sermones*. Firenze, B Medicea Laurenziana, ms. Ashburnham 875, c. 1r

8 MIRELLA LEVI D'ANCONA: *Miniatura e miniatori a Firenze dal XIV al XVI secolo*. Firenze 1962, pp. 33–37; GUIDOTTI (vedi nota 7), p. 484. Sulla collocazione delle botteghe degli artisti a Firenze nella prima metà del XV secolo si vedano le mappe pubblicate da WERNER JACOBSEN: *Die Maler von Florenz zu Beginn der Renaissance*. Berlino 2001.

9 LEVI D'ANCONA (vedi nota 8), pp. 33–34.

10 LEVI D'ANCONA (vedi nota 8), p. 35.

11 LEVI D'ANCONA (vedi nota 8), pp. 34–37.

12 LEVI D'ANCONA (vedi nota 8), p. 34. L'unico tentativo fatto per rilevare la specifica identità stilistica di Giovanni si è rivelato fallace, dato che il nucleo di opere a lui precedentemente riferito è stato incluso nel catalogo di Battista di Niccolò da Padova, ANGELA DILLON BUSSI: Battista di Niccolò da Padova e Giovanni Varnucci: lo scambio delle parti? (e alcune note su Riccardo di Nanni). In: *Rivista di Storia della Miniatura* 3, 1998, pp. 105–114; EADEM: Battista di Niccolò da Padova. In: *Dizionario biografico dei miniatori italiani, secoli IX–XVI*. Ed. MILVIA BOLLATI. Cinisello Balsamo 2004, pp. 72–74.

13 LEVI D'ANCONA (vedi nota 8), pp. 33–34.

14 LEVI D'ANCONA (vedi nota 8), p. 37.

15 GIUSEPPE SERGIO MARTINI: *La bottega di un cartolaio fiorentino della seconda metà del Quattrocento. Nuovi contributi biografici intorno a Gherardo e Monte di Giovanni*. Firenze 1956, pp. 15, 27; LEVI D'ANCONA (vedi nota 8), pp. 127–137, 199–211; DIEGO GALIZZI: Gherardo di Giovanni e Monte di Giovanni. In: *Dizionario biografico dei miniatori italiani* (vedi nota 12), pp. 258–262, 798–801.

16 FRANÇOIS AVRIL: *Dix siècles d'enluminure italienne (VIe–XVIe siècles)*, catalogo della mostra (Parigi, BNF, Galerie Mazarine). Parigi 1984, pp. 116–117, cat. 99.

di piazza San Firenze, di fronte all'oggi distrutta chiesa di Sant'Apollinare, ora sostituita con quella di San Filippo Neri.8 Nel 1453 i due fratelli, definiti «miniatori», affittano due botteghe sotto il dormitorio della Badia, affitto che venne rinnovato in due contratti separati, ma è supponibile per ambienti adiacenti, il 21 ottobre 1454, momento in cui Bartolomeo «miniatore» prende a pigione una bottega, ed il 15 novembre 1454, quando Giovanni «miniatore» fece la stessa cosa.9 Ancora nel 1455 Giovanni è detto «cartolaio», mentre un altro documento testimonia che «el banco de Medici, cioè Cosimo e de compagni, deono dare ai 19 di dicembre fiorini 238 i quali ebbono per noi da Bartolomeo d'Antonio e frategli cartolai i quali furono per nostro pagamento d'un podere».10

In sostanza, la professione ‹principale› di cartolai veniva trainata dalla specializzazione dei due fratelli nella decorazione miniata, affiancata – verosimilmente tramite collaboratori – dalle altre dovute competenze. I pagamenti documentati parlano chiaro: il 21 novembre 1440 Bartolomeo per la decorazione di un *Messale*, il 28 gennaio 1443 Bartolomeo e Giovanni per la miniatura e legatura di una *Regola* di San Benedetto, il 27 novembre 1449 Bartolomeo per la miniatura e la legatura di un codice, il 30 agosto 1453 Bartolomeo e Giovanni per legatura e miniatura di un *Breviario* scritto da don Zaccheria, mentre il 21 ottobre 1454 per la miniatura di due libri e per legatura e miniatura di un libro «vocato la carità di Frate Giovanni Dominici».11 Tuttavia, questa collaborazione familiare terminò, poiché nel 1456 Giovanni morì.12 È verosimile che dopo questo lutto Bartolomeo rimase il solo responsabile della bottega. Tuttavia, da un documento del 25 febbraio dell'anno successivo si scopre che l'ultimogenito della famiglia, Chimenti, abitava in casa di Bartolomeo in via Ghibellina. Non stupisce quindi che un atto del 2 maggio 1463 definisca Bartolomeo e Chimenti «cartolai e miniatori», i quali in quell'occasione prendono a pigione una bottega nel popolo di S. Ambrogio.13 I due rinnovarono l'affitto della bottega da cartolaio in via del Garbo (1465–68), prospicente alla Badia, mentre nel 1475 vengono definiti «cartolai» del popolo di Sant'Ambrogio, «che tennero a pigione la nostra bottegha nel popolo di Sanpulinari e nella via del Garbo».14 A queste date Bartolomeo doveva avere una consolidata esperienza, come conferma un atto del 4 settembre 1476, in cui lui, e Bartolomeo di Angelo Tucci e Jacopo di Bartolomeo di Francesco cartolai, vennero chiamati a dirimere la controversia scoppiata tra i fratelli Bartolomeo, Gherardo e Monte del Fora, che avevano pure bottega alla Badia, i quali anche loro avevano fatto dalla professione del miniatore quella trainante nella loro bottega da cartolai.15

Dunque, i fratelli Varnucci furono concorrenti di Vespasiano e non deve stupire che si conosca un unico caso di collaborazione tra loro, rappresentata da un codice, la *Vitae atque sententiae philosophorum* di Diogene Laerzio della Bibliothèque Nationale de France di Parigi (ms. lat. 6069 B), nel cui piatto posteriore si trova un'iscrizione che ne attesta la realizzazione nella bottega di Vespasiano.16 Evidentemente il da Bisticci, avendo assunto impegni al di là delle possibilità lavorative dei suoi usuali collaboratori, passò a Bartolomeo Varnucci la decorazione del codice.

17 ALBERT DEROLEZ: *Archaeology of the Manuscript Book of the Italian Renaissance*. Roma 2018, pp. 99, 114–115, 125–126, 155–157.

18 Da ultimo si veda BOSCHETTO (vedi nota 4); KIM (vedi nota 4).

19 GUERNELLI (vedi nota 6), pp. 329–331.

20 ALBINIA DE LA MARE: Florentine Manuscripts of Livy in the Fifteenth Century. In: *Livy*. Ed. THOMAS A. DOREY. Londra 1971, pp. 177–199, 181; EADEM: Further Italian Illuminated Manuscripts in the Bodleian Library. In: *La miniatura italiana tra Gotico e Rinascimento*. Ed. EMANUELA SESTI. Firenze 1985, vol. 2, pp. 127–154, in particolare pp. 132–133; FRANCIS AMES-LEWIS: *The Library and Manuscripts of Piero di Cosimo de Medici*, New York/Londra 1984, p. 322, cat. 76; ALBINIA DE LA MARE: Cosimo and His Books. In: *Cosimo «il Vecchio» de' Medici, 1389–1464. Essays in Commemoration of the 600th Anniversary of Cosimo de' Medici's Birth, including the Papers delivered at the Society for Renaissance Studies*. Ed. FRANCIS AMES-LEWIS. Oxford 1992, pp. 115–156, in particolare p. 147, cat. 143; MELANIA CECCANTI: cat. 288. In: *Seneca, una vicenda testuale. Mostra di manoscritti ed edizioni*, catalogo della mostra (Firenze, B Medicea Laurenziana). Ed. TERESA DE ROBERTI e GIANVITO RESTA. Firenze 2004, pp. 277–278. Sul copista si veda da ultimo DEROLEZ (vedi nota 17), pp. 114–115, 125–126, 155–157.

21 DE LA MARE (vedi nota 1), p. 398, n. 17.

22 Sul tema si veda CHARLES DEMPSEY: *Inventing the Renaissance Putto*. Chapel Hill/Londra 2001. In realtà, come notato da ALEXANDER (vedi nota 1), p. 287 n. 9, putti simili erano già presenti in opere tardogotiche, come quelle del Maestro delle Iniziali di Bruxelles. Sul tema si veda anche ANNE RITZ-GUILBERT: *Des drôleries gothiques au bestiaire de Pisanello. Le Bréviaire de Marie de Savoie*. Chambéry 2010, 211–225.

23 DE LA MARE (vedi nota 4), p. 169.

24 GUERNELLI (vedi nota 6), pp. 329–331.

Per quanto riguarda i copisti, invece, le due botteghe utilizzavano non di rado figure comuni (ad esempio Antonio di Mario).[17] O meglio, Vespasiano dovette appoggiarsi a personalità che probabilmente Bartolomeo già conosceva ed utilizzava. Perché è bene non dimenticare che tra i due vi era una differenza di quasi una decina di anni. Vespasiano era nato all'inizio degli anni venti (1422 c.),[18] mentre la nascita di Bartolomeo è da collocarsi tra 1412 e 1415, più verosimilmente tra 1412–1413.[19] Non è noto presso quale bottega Bartolomeo ebbe la sua educazione artistica, ma è ovvio che iniziò a frequentare i cartolai di via dei librai molto presto, e fu in questo periodo che licenziò come miniatore alcuni codici che rappresentano i suoi primi numeri del suo catalogo: una copia delle *Opere* di Seneca (Firenze, Biblioteca Laurenziana, ms. Plut. 76.35), scritta nel 1426 da Antonio di Mario per Cosimo de' Medici,[20] una delle *Lettere* dello stesso autore (Città del Vaticano, Biblioteca Apostolica Vaticana, ms. Vat. Lat. 2208), scritta a Roma da un copista francese prima del 23 ottobre 1426 per Poggio Bracciolini, e una delle *Opere filosofiche* di Cicerone (Bav, ms. Pal. Lat. 1516), terminata il 10 maggio dello stesso anno.[21] Questi manoscritti mostrano un apparato decorativo presentante piccoli interventi, con letterine a bianchi girari e *spiritelli* galleggianti su nuvolette accanto al testo, che Albinia de la Mare ritenne potessero essere i primi esempi del libro rinascimentale.[22] Sebbene la studiosa abbia poi espresso dubbi sulla possibile attribuzione di tali interventi ad un tredicenne,[23] sono dell'opinione che al contrario si tratti precisamente del tipo di incarico da attribuire ad un ragazzo di bottega ancora inesperto, e non pronto per le grandi illustrazioni dei cicli di corali.[24]

Quello che è certo è che da quel momento Bartolomeo non si fermò più, e che la sua produzione identificabile, di cui mi sono occupato di recente, continua a crescere tanto da esercitare una certa influenza sull'ambiente fiorentino, come mostra una copia dei *Sermones* di Leone Magno della Biblioteca Medicea Laurenziana di Firenze (ms. Ashburnham 875) segnalatami da Stephen Oakley, che seppur non attribuibile alla sua mano pare discenderne direttamente [fig. 2]. I primi anni della carriera del nostro, quelli nei quali non risulta ancora essere cartolaio, perlomeno a livello documentario, sono densi di interventi nell'ambito del nuovo libro umanistico fiorentino, che come detto in quel tempo si caratterizza per la tipica decorazione a bianchi girari, costituita da tralci intrecciati realizzati a biacca che derivano da quelli della tradizione romanica toscana, a loro volta lontani figli della decorazione anglosassone

Fig. 3 Frontespizio con iniziale 'E' e putti. In: Cicerone, *Orationes*. Città del Vaticano, B Apostolica Vaticana, ms. Pal. Lat. 1486, c. 1r

25 Sui bianchi-girari si veda OTTO PÄCHT: Notes and Observations on the Origin of Humanistic Book-Decoration. In: *Fritz Saxl 1890–1948. A Volume of Memorial Essays from His Friends in England*. Ed. DONALD J. GORDON. Edimburgo 1957, pp. 184–194; FEDERICA TONIOLO: Marco dell'Avogaro e la decorazione all'antica. In: *Le Muse e il Principe. Arte di corte nel Rinascimento padano*, catalogo della mostra (Milano, M Poldi Pezzoli). Ed. ALESSANDRA MOTTOLA MOLFINO e MAURO NATALE. Modena 1991, pp. 132–140; EADEM: Decorazione all'antica nei manoscritti per Malatesta Novello. In: *Libraria Domini. I manoscritti della Biblioteca Malatestiana: decorazioni e testi*. Ed. FABRIZIO LOLLINI, PIERO LUCCHI. Bologna 1995, pp. 143–153; MELANIA CECCANTI: Proposte per la storia dei primi codici umanistici a bianchi girari. In: *Miniatura*. 5–6 (1993–1996), pp. 11–16; FABRIZIO CRIVELLO: «Vetustioris litere maiestas». Un manoscritto di sant'Agostino del Petrarca, gli umanisti e qualche osservazione sulle iniziali a «bianchi girari». In: *Italia Medievale e Umanistica*. 44 (2003), pp. 227–234; DANIELE GUERNELLI: Note per una tipologia decorativa umanistica bolognese. In: *Schede umanistiche*. 1 (2006), pp. 21–42; PIER LUIGI MULAS: ‹Bianchi girari› mantouans dans un incunable de Cristoforo (et Baldassarre). In: *Le manuscrit enluminé. Études réunies en hommage à Patricia Stirnemann*. Ed. CLAUDIA RABEL. Parigi 2014, pp. 257–271; FABRIZIO LOLLINI: Minime considerazioni sui bianchi girari cesenati. In: *Hortus in bibliotheca. Un itinerario nel giardino della miniatura*, atti del convegno (Cesena, 5-6 ottobre 2018). Ed. MARINO MENGOZZI. Cesena 2020, pp. 137–162.

26 GIUSEPPE M. CAGNI: I codici Vaticani Palatino-Latini appartenuti alla Biblioteca di Giannozzo Manetti. In: *La Bibliofilia*. 62 (1960), pp. 1–43, qui p. 26; MICHAEL D. REEVE: Before and After Poggio. Some Manuscripts of Cicero's Speeches. In: *Rivista di filologia e di istruzione classica*. 112 (1984), pp. 266–284, qui p. 272; PAUL BOTLEY: Giannozzo Manetti, Alfonso of Aragon and Pompey the Great: a Crusading Document of 1455. In: *Journal of the Warburg and Courtald Institutes*. 67 (2004), pp. 129–156, qui p. 140.

altomedievale.[25] Il Varnucci fu un punto di riferimento fondamentale per questa produzione umanistica e di tradizione testuale classica. Si tratta di caratteristiche che si ritrovano anche in un codice finora sfuggito alle attenzioni della critica, una copia delle *Orationes* di Cicerone della Biblioteca Apostolica Vaticana (ms. Pal. Lat. 1486). Il manoscritto presenta a carta 2v la nota di possesso di Giannozzo Manetti, il quale non riempì lo spazio per l'araldica in *bas de page* del frontespizio, segno che molto probabilmente l'opera venne confezionata per il mercato.[26] Decorato con una serie di iniziali a bianchi girari a marcare ogni orazione [fig. 3], il codice mostra un incipit con uno spiritello appeso al tralcio dell'iniziale sorretto da nuvolette, soluzione tipica già presente nelle sue opere degli anni trenta, come ad esempio nelle *Epistolae ad Familiares* della Schoyen

Fig. 4 Frontespizio con iniziale 'B' e putti. In: San Basilio, *De divinitate Filii et Spiritus Sancti adversus Eunomium*. Parigi, BNF, ms. Lat. 1703, c. 1r

27 GUERNELLI (vedi nota 6), p. 332 (disponibile su www.schoyencollection.com, [20/01/2023]).

28 TAMMARO DE MARINIS: *La biblioteca napoletana dei re d'Aragona*, Milano 1947, vol. 1, p. 176, vol. 2, pp. 25, 201–204; vol. 5, Verona 1969, p. 10 n. 4; MARIE-PIERRE LAFITTE: Une acquisition de la Bibliothèque du roi au XVIIe. Les manuscrits de la familie Hurault. In: *Bulletin du Bibliophile*. 1 (2008), pp. 42–98; GENNARO TOSCANO: cat. 56. In: *Une Renaissance en Normandie. Le cardinal Georges d'Amboise bibliophile et mécène*, catalogo della mostra (Évreux, Musée d'Art, Histoire et Archéologie), Ed. FLORENCE CALAME-LEVERT, MAXENCE HERMAN e GENNARO TOSCANO. Parigi 2017, pp. 180–181. Sul copista si veda DEROLEZ (vedi nota 17), pp. 118, 159.

29 AVRIL (vedi nota 16), pp. 115–116, cat. 98; MARIE-PIERRE LAFITTE: cat. 4. In: *Sigismundus rex et imperator. Art et culture à l'époque de Sigismond de Luxembourg, 1387–1437*, catalogo della mostra (Budapest, Szépművészeti Múzeum; Lussemburgo, Musée national d'Histoire et d'Art). Ed. IMRE TAKÁCS. Magonza 2006, p. 394; CHARLOTTE DENOEL: cat. 16. In: *Mattia Corvino e Firenze. Arte e umanesimo alla corte del re di Ungheria*, catalogo della mostra (Firenze, M di San Marco). Ed. PÉTER FARBAKY. Firenze 2013, pp. 88–89; GIOVANNA MURANO: Un codice di dedica del Monarchia con interventi autografi di Antonio Roselli (ms. Paris, BNF, lat. 4237). In: *Honos alit artes. Studi per il settantesimo compleanno di Mario Ascheri, III. Il cammino delle idee dal Medioevo all'antico regime. Diritto e cultura nell'esperienza europea*. Ed. PAOLA MAFFEI e GIAN MARIA VARANINI. Firenze 2014, pp. 83–91.

30 PATRICIA STIRNEMANN: cat. 4. In: *La Biblioteca Reial de Nàpols, d'Alfons el Magnànim al Duc de Calàbria*, catalogo della mostra (València, Biblioteca Valenciana, Antic Monestir de Sant Miquel dels Reis). Ed. MARIA CRUZ CABEZA SÀNCHEZ-ALBORNOZ e GENNARO TOSCANO. Valencia 1999, pp. 48–51.

31 MIKLOS BOSKOVITS: Un nuovo strumento per la conoscenza della miniatura fiorentina del Rinascimento. In: *Arte Cristiana*. 74 (1986), pp. 277–280.

32 GUERNELLI (vedi nota 6), p. 332.

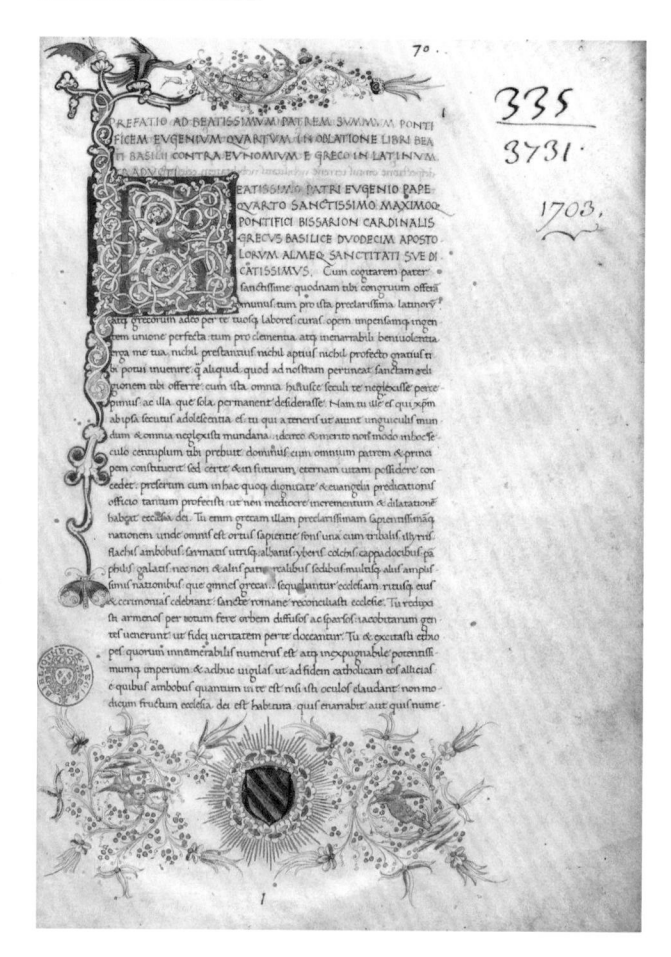

Collection di Oslo (ms. 612).[27] Tuttavia, nel margine inferiore i puttini reggi stemma sono affiancati da una serie di tralci filigranati a penna con foglioline dorate che ricordano esempi quali quelli nel frontespizio del *De divinitate Filii et Spiritus Sancti adversus Eunomium* di San Basilio nella traduzione di Giorgio Trapezunzio (Parigi, Bibliothèque Nationale de France, ms. Lat. 1703), copiato da Pietro di Benedetto Strozzi [fig. 4].[28] Il manoscritto palatino andrà dunque datato verso i primi anni quaranta, epoca nella quale il miniatore aveva iniziato ad essere attratto da soluzioni più propriamente di gotico cortese, come dimostrano il *Monarchia, sive tractatus de potestate imperatoris et papae* di Antonio Roselli della Bibliothèque Nationale de France di Parigi (ms. lat. 4237), compiuto verso il 1437,[29] o gli *Stratagemata* di Frontino della stessa collezione (ms. lat. 7245), scritti nel 1438 da Ser Giovanni di Pietro da Stia [fig. 5].[30]

Quale sia stata la ragione di questa svolta non è dato sapere. La critica ha finora individuato una certa vicinanza con l'arte di Battista di Biagio Sanguigni o di Giovanni Toscani, ma non pare di poter inferire qualcosa di più di tangenze.[31] Accanto a questi, mi sembra che possano individuarsi ragioni di vicinanza con il Paolo Uccello degli anni trenta e col Maestro della Predella Sherman.[32] Tuttavia, come detto, è nel mondo dei cartolai che verosimilmente Bartolomeo ebbe modo di affermarsi e di crescere professionalmente. Forse nella bottega di Calderino di Francesco, come più sopra ipoteticamente indicato. Accanto a quest'ipotesi

Fig. 5 Frontespizio con ritratto di Frotino. In: Frontino, *Stratagemata*. Parigi, BNF, ms. lat. 7245, c. 1r

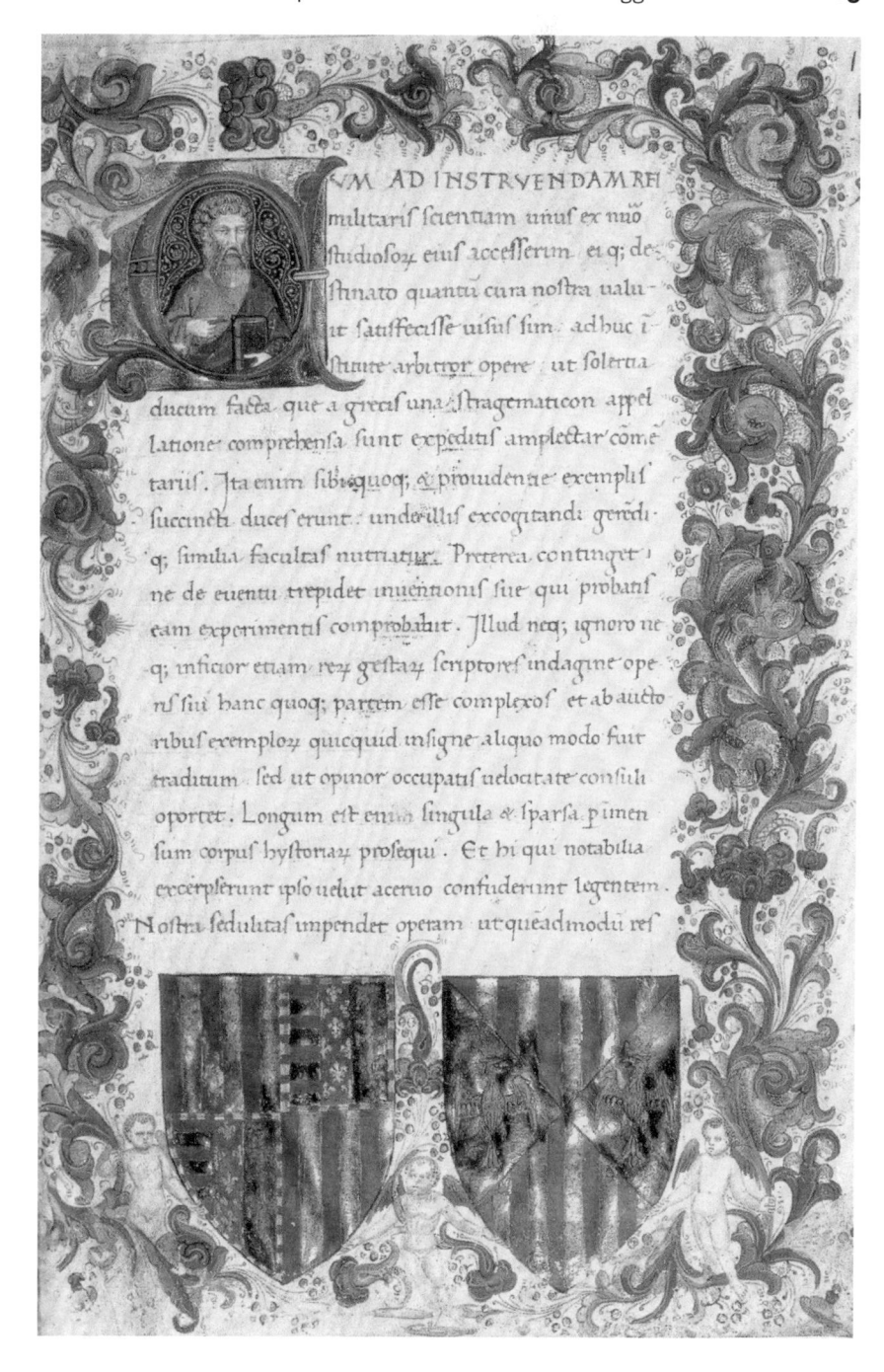

33 MARIA GRAZIA CIARDI DUPRÈ DAL POGGETTO: *Codici liturgici miniati dei Benedettini in Toscana, catalogo della mostra (Firenze, Certosa)*. Firenze 1982, pp. 292–301, 404–418, 432–446, 447–453 (schede di GIULIANA TONINI), 390–402 (schede di GIULIANA CHESNE DAUPHINÉ GRIFFO), 454–468, 469–488, 493–502 (schede di MARIA DATA MAZZONI).

34 ANNA DE FLORIANI: Per Bartolomeo Varnucci. Un Messale e alcune precisazioni. In: *Miniatura*, 5-6 (1996), pp. 49–60, qui p. 57.

esiste un ulteriore possibile indizio della formazione di Bartolomeo. Lo fornisce una recente proposta relativa ai corali di Santa Maria di Monte Oliveto Maggiore, vicino Siena, oggi conservati al Museo Diocesano di Arte Sacra di Chiusi. La serie venne miniata tra il 1459 ed il 1479 da un *pool* di illustri artisti provenienti da diverse aree geografiche, tra cui Liberale da Verona, Girolamo da Cremona, Venturino Mercati e Sano di Pietro, una molteplicità evidentemente frutto della rete dei contatti olivetani nel centro-nord della penisola.[33] Accanto a questi la critica ha ascritto alla mano di Bartolomeo Varnucci interventi in diversi di questi tomi, in particolare i corali D, O, P, T, U, V, X.[34]

35 HANS JOACHIM EBERHARDT: *Liberale da Verona*. In: *Dizionario biografico dei miniatori italiani* (vedi nota 12), p. 380.

36 GIORDANA MARIANI CANOVA e MAURO TAGLIABUE: I corali miniati di Santa Maria di Monte Oliveto: nuovi documenti e nuove considerazioni, in Bernardo Tolomei e le origini di Monte Oliveto. In: *Atti del convegno di Studi per il VII centenario di fondazione dell'abbazia* (Monte Oliveto Maggiore, 9–10 maggio 2019). Ed. GIANCARLO ANDENNA e MAURO TAGLIABUE. Cesena 2020, pp. 323–396, qui pp. 368, 370–371.

37 MARIANI CANOVA, TAGLIABUE (vedi nota 36), pp. 336–339, 341–342, 346, 395.

38 Il primo datato 1446, l'ultimo 4 febbraio 1448 (1449 *more fiorentino*). ANGELA DILLON BUSSI: La miniatura quattrocentesca per il Duomo di Firenze. Prime indagini e alcune novità. In: *I libri del Duomo di Firenze. Codici liturgici e Biblioteca di Santa Maria del Fiore, catalogo della mostra (Firenze, Biblioteca Medicea Laurenziana)*. Ed. LORENZO FABBRI e MARIA TACCONI. Firenze 1997, pp. 79–96, in particolare pp. 79, 92, 95.

39 MARIA GRAZIA CIARDI DUPRÈ DAL POGGETTO: Un ‹Offiziolo› casereccio ed altre cose di Bartolomeo Varnucci. In: *Antichità viva*. 10, 5 (1971), pp. 39–48, in particolare pp. 39–41; ANGELA DILLON BUSSI: cat. I.51. In: *Miniatura del '400 a San Marco. Dalle suggestioni avignonesi all'ambient dell'Angelico* (catalogo della mostra, Firenze, M di San Marco). Ed. MAGNOLIA SCUDIERI e GIOVANNA ROSARIO. Firenze 2003, p. 195.

40 ADA LABRIOLA: *I manoscritti miniati del Museo di San Marco a Firenze: Corali francescani (1440-1530)*. Firenze 2020, pp. 19–27.

41 JONATHAN J. G. ALEXANDER, ALBINIA DE LA MARE: *The Italian Manuscripts in the Library of Major J. R. Abbey*. Londra 1969, pp. 32–35; CIARDI DUPRÈ DAL POGGETTO (vedi nota 39), p. 42; *Illuminated Manuscripts from The Celebrated Library of Major J. R. Abbey*, Londra, Sotheby's, 19 giugno 1989, lotto 3020.

42 LEVI D'ANCONA (vedi nota 8), pp. 169–171; JACOBSEN (vedi nota 8), p. 589.

43 Da ultimo, ANNA MELOGRANI: *Quanto costa la magnificenza?: il caso della «bibia bella» di Borso d'Este*. In: *Bollettino d'Arte*, 6, 93, 2008 (2009), 144, pp. 7–24, con bibliografia precedente.

44 MARIANI CANOVA, TAGLIABUE (vedi nota 36), p. 338.

In un recente contributo Giordana Mariani Canova ha ripreso l'idea, già suggerita da Hans Joachim Eberhardt,[35] riguardante la possibile attribuzione di queste miniature di stile fiorentino a Lorenzo da Firenze, per cui i documenti rimastici relativi alla serie attestano pagamenti nel 1458, 1460 e 1461.[36] Il confronto proposto dalla studiosa è quello con le opere certe e documentate del Varnucci,[37] quelle che hanno fornito un punto di appiglio per la ricostruzione della sua personalità artistica, ovvero il *Lezionario* realizzato per il Duomo di Firenze, realizzato con la collaborazione del fratello minore Giovanni e di Battista di Niccolò da Padova (Firenze, Biblioteca Medicea Laurenziana, mss. Edili 144, 147),[38] per cui esistono pagamenti da lui ricevuti tra 1447 e 1450 per la decorazione del primo e del quarto volume, ed i due *Messali* sempre per il Duomo (mss. Edili 103-104), pagati tra 1456 e 1458.[39] Effettivamente, i codici laurenziani sono di qualità più alta degli interventi chiusini, ma questo non ha impedito alla critica di andare a ricostruire un vasto catalogo che paga inevitabilmente una certa variabilità di risultati, come è normale che sia per durata di carriera e uso di assistenti di bottega (probabilmente i fratelli stessi). Per quanto mi riguarda, nel merito dei corali chiusini, i principali minii del codice O sono esempi cristallini dell'arte del Varnucci, come diversi altri nei manoscritti della serie olivetana. Ad esempio, si confrontino la *Vergine che adora il Bambino* di carta 39v o la *Nascita di Cristo* di c. 47v [fig. 6] con gli interventi di Bartolomeo negli Antifonari 575 o 583 del Museo di San Marco a Firenze,[40] o il *Gesù in gloria* di c. 83r del cod. S con il frontespizio delle *Regole della Schuola di Sancto Giovanni Evangelista* di collezione privata, del 1451.[41]

Quello che è interessante però, è che l'unico Lorenzo miniatore conosciuto dalle fonti fiorentine dell'epoca è Lorenzo di Bindo di Lippo Rosselli. Questo artista risulta aver ricevuto pagamenti nel 1451 e nel 1456, ma soprattutto, risulta essere stato cartolaio già dal gennaio del 1422.[42] Dunque, se si trattasse veramente della stessa persona citata dai documenti chiusini, in nessun modo potrebbe essere considerato un assistente della bottega del Varnucci, che nel 1422 doveva avere sui dieci anni, mentre è inferibile che Lorenzo di Bindo fosse maggiorenne, quindi di almeno 25 anni. Semmai fosse, dunque, non è del tutto impossibile che si tratti proprio del contrario, e cioè che la bottega di cartolaio di Lorenzo di Bindo possa essere stata il primo luogo di apprendistato di Bartolomeo, a cui il più attempato maestro si sarebbe appoggiato per la commissione olivetana, di cui riscosse il compenso nella stessa maniera in cui Taddeo Crivelli e Franco dei Russi vennero pagati per la *Bibbia* di Borso d'Este (ms. Lat. 422-423), da loro per parte importante subappaltata ad altri artisti.[43] Si tratta ovviamente solo di un'ipotesi, poiché come giustamente nota la Mariani Canova, potrebbe semplicemente essere che i libri di pagamento al Varnucci per i corali olivetani siano andati perduti,[44] senza contare che all'epoca Bartolomeo sembra essere stato di lunga più importante di Lorenzo, e dunque capace di attirare commissioni da fuori. Tuttavia, a fronte della mancanza di altri indizi, val la pena di tenerla in campo, nonostante sia tutta da dimostrare.

Fig. 6 Natività. In: *Graduale*. Chiusi, M Diocesano di Arte Sacra, codice O, c. 47v

Come che sia, la carriera di Bartolomeo evolvette verso uno stile indubbiamente più toccato da umori tardogotici, forse anche in ragione del contatto con opere come il *Pontificale Calderini* (Houghton Library, Harvard University, ms. Typ 1), che avevo mancato di citare nel mio recente contributo sul miniatore. Il completamento del manoscritto, iniziato in precedenza da artisti del *coté* romano e aquilano, è stato correttamente ascritto al Varnucci da Avril,[45] attribuzione confermata di recente dalla critica, che giustamente scorge nel suo intervento rimandi all'arte di Masolino da Panicale e Beato Angelico.[46] Altri codici da aggiungere al catalogo del miniatore [fig. 7] sono la copia delle *Moralia in Job* di Gregorio Magno della Biblioteca Augusta di Perugia (ms. F 47), già correttamente ascritto al Varnucci nella scheda dedicata all'opera in Internet culturale,[47] la *Miscellanea* di lettere umanistiche (di Petrarca, Stefano Porcari, Leonardo Bruni, Francesco Filelfo, Giannozzo Manetti e Piero Buonaccorsi), passata da H. P. Kraus nel 2003,[48] e un foglio di *Graduale* con *La chiamata di Pietro e Andrea* della Free Library of Philadelphia (Lewis E M 74:15).[49]

---

45 FRANÇOIS AVRIL: *Stephanus de Aquila*. In: *Illuminare l'Abruzzo: codici miniati tra Medioevo e Rinascimento*, catalogo della mostra (Chieti, Palazzo De'Mayo). Ed. GAETANO CURZI. Pescara 2012, pp. 51–57, qui p. 54.

46 FRANCESCA MANZARI: cat. 220. In: *Beyond Words. Illuminated Manuscripts in Boston Collections*, catalogo della mostra (Cambridge, Houghton L; Boston, McMullen M of Art e Isabella Stewart Gardner M). Ed. JEFFREY HAMBURGER et alii. Boston 2016, pp. 274–276; CRISTIANA PASQUALETTI: Novità sul Pontificale Calderini e sulle vicende della miniatura fra l'Aquila e l'Urbe negli anni del Grande Scisma (con una traccia su Zaccaria da Teramo «scriptore et miniatore»). In: *Prospettiva*. 165–166 (2017), pp. 32-59; FRANCESCA MANZARI: Illuminating in Rome and L'Aquila during the Schism and in Florence during the Council. Artists and Patrons of the Calderini Pontifical (Harvard, Houghton L, MS. Typ 1). In: *Beyond Words. New research on manuscripts in Boston collections*. Ed. JEFFREY HAMBURGER et alii. Toronto 2021, pp. 153–176.

47 Disponibile su www.internetculturale.il, [20/01/2023].

48 *The inventory of H. P. Kraus*, New York, 4–5 dicembre 2003, p. 393, lotto 491, dove è correttamente ascritto a bottega dell'artista.

49 Disponibile su https://libwww.freelibrary.org/digital [20/01/2023].

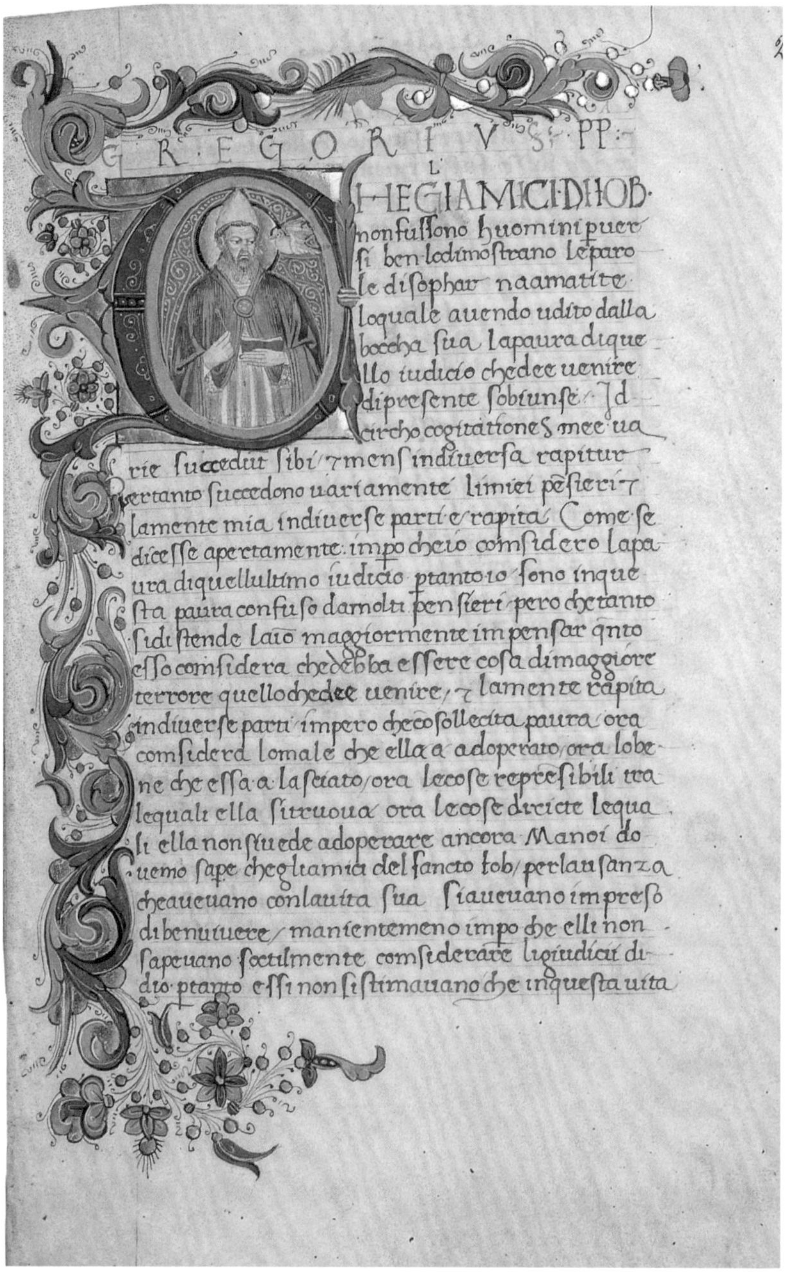

Fig. 7 Frontespizio con ritratto di Gregorio Magno. In: Gregorio Magno, *Moralia in Job*. Perugia, B Augusta, ms. F 47, c. 2r

50 Disponibile su www.digi.vatlib.it, [20/01/2023].

51 ALBERTO SERAFINI: Ricerche sulla miniatura umbra (secoli XIV–XVI). In: *L'Arte. Rivista di storia dell'arte medioevale e moderna*. 15 (1912), pp. 417–439, qui p. 428.

52 CECILIA O'BRIAN: Renaissance Book and Raphael's Disputa: Contextualizing the Image. In: *Medieval Texts and Images. Studies of Manuscripts from the Middle Ages*. Ed. MARGARET M. MANION e BERNARD J. MUIR. Chur 1991, pp. 71–89, qui pp. 77, 81; GIACOMO BAROFFIO: Kalendaria Italica. Inventario. In: *Aevum. Rassegna di scienze storiche, linguistiche e filologiche*. 77 (2003), pp. 449–472, p. 470.

53 JESUS DOMINGUEZ BORDONA: *Manuscritos con pinturas. Nota para un inventario de los conservados en colecciones pública y particulares de España*. Madrid 1938, vol. 1, p. 399 n. 951; GARZELLI (vedi nota 1), p. 31.

Infine, al catalogo del Varnucci sarà necessario restituire il ms. Vat. lat. 4761 della Biblioteca Apostolica Vaticana, un *Breviario* a cui venne aggiunto a carta 7v lo stemma della Rovere all'epoca di Giulio II.[50] Il manoscritto, dopo un primo momento in cui fu etichettato come umbro,[51] è stato correttamente identificato come di origine toscana e fiorentina.[52] Tuttavia, finora la critica ha mancato di legare le sue 42 iniziali miniate alla mano del Varnucci tardo. Basti posare l'occhio sull'unica scena racchiusa da un riquadro del codice, che si aggiunge alle iniziali abitate, quella del *Beatus Vir* di c. 185r, in cui si ritrova la stessa scena che rappresenta *Davide davanti alle mura di Gerusalemme* presente a carta 2r del ms. Vitr/22/10 della Biblioteca Nacional di Madrid, databile agli anni cinquanta [fig. 8].[53] Il codice vaticano colloca il gruppo più lontano dalla

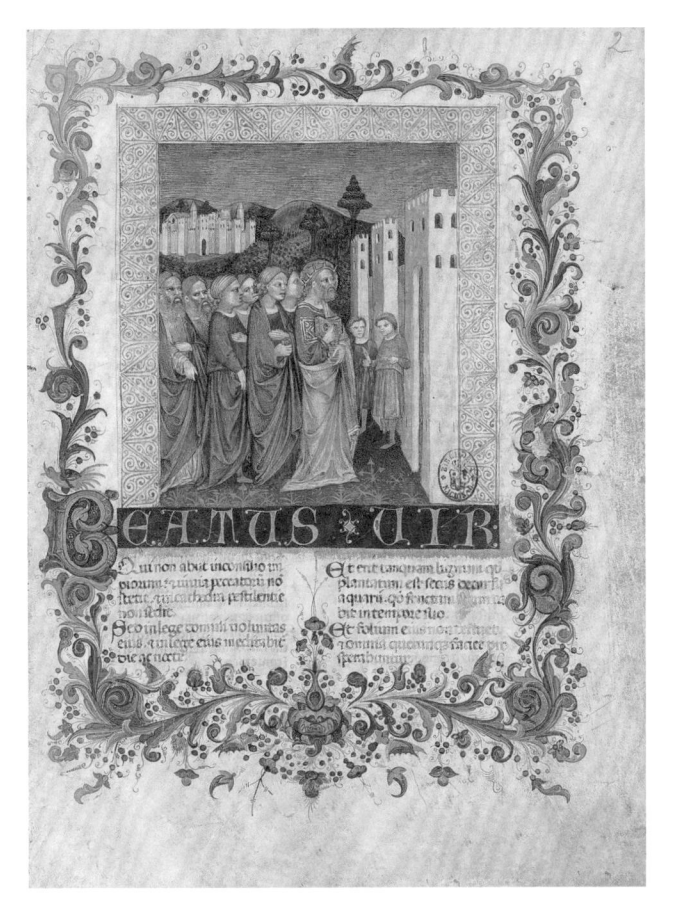

Figg. 8–9 Davide davanti alle mura di Gerusalemme. In: *Salterio*, Madrid, BN, ms. Vitr/22/10, c. 2r (sinistra); I tre vivi e i tre morti. In: *Libro d'Ore*. Toledo, B Capitular, ms. 43-19, c. 158v (giusto)

54 JAVIER DOCAMPO e JOSEFINA PLANAS: *Horae. El poder de la imagen. Libros de horas en bibliotecas españolas*. Madrid 2016, pp. 335–340, cat. 41; GUERNELLI (vedi nota 6), p. 352.

55 PAOLO D'ANCONA: *La miniatura fiorentina, secoli 11.–16.* Firenze 1914, vol. 2, pp. 517–518; venne attribuito a Varnucci da GARZELLI (vedi nota 1), p. 31; MARIA PRUNAI FALCIANI: cat. 50. In: *Pregare nel segreto. Libri d'Ore e testi di spiritualità nella tradizione cristiana*, catalogo della mostra (Roma, B Vallicelliana). Ed. GUGLIELMO CAVALLO. Roma 1994, pp. 64–65.

56 DE FLORIANI (vedi nota 34), pp. 59–60; ADRIANA DI DOMENICO: L'Offiziolo riconsiderato. Antonio di Niccolò allievo di Bartolomeo Varnucci? In: *Rara Volumina*. 2 (1997), pp. 19–28; MILVIA BOLLATI: *Antonio di Niccolò di Lorenzo di Domenico*. In: *Dizionario biografico dei miniatori italiani* (vedi nota 12), pp. 34–35.

città, che viene rappresentata sullo sfondo, ma importa con qualche variante la sequenza del corteo che segue il re ebreo. Ritornano il prato fogliaceo, il cielo realizzato con tratti orizzontali bianchi e azzurri, e gli alberelli, che vengono questa volta ravvivati nel repertorio. Che si tratti di un'opera dell'ultimo momento della carriera di Bartolomeo lo dimostra il confronto con l'ultima produzione del nostro, si pensi ad esempio al *Libro d'Ore* della Biblioteca Capitular di Toledo (ms. 43-19), un tempo di Francisco Javier Zelada y Rodríguez [fig. 9],[54] o a quello della Biblioteca Riccardiana di Firenze (ms. 458),[55] realizzato in collaborazione con Antonio di Niccolò di Domenico,[56] opere ormai nell'ottavo decennio del secolo che mostrano uno sfrangiamento della pennellata ed una diminuzione qualitativa, chissà se dovuta all'intervento del fratello Chimenti. Non si dimentichi che nel 1470 Bartolomeo licenziò un *Breviario* per Monna Tommasa de Gianfigliazzi, che tra 1470–71 ne miniò uno 'camereccio' (portatile) fatto fare dalla suddetta Monna Tommasa per Marietta e Perpetua, «sue figliole monache nelle Murate», e che sempre nel 1471 (tra primo febbraio e 2 novembre) realizzò un altro *Breviario* per Don Antonio, monaco della Badia.

Come che sia, secondo i documenti sopra menzionati, negli anni settanta la bottega dei Varnucci fu senza dubbio un punto di riferimento nel panorama librario fiorentino. E questo lo fu anche dopo la morte di Bartolomeo, databile tra 1480 e 1481, dato che un atto dell'8 giugno 1481 testimonia Chimenti ricevere pagamenti per miniature e legature eseguite dal fratello tra il 21 agosto 1477 al 21 novembre 1479. In quell'anno (1481) Chimenti d'Antonio di Luca Varnucci «cartolaio» risulta abitare nel popolo di S. Pier Maggiore, dove ebbe in affitto una bottega dai frati della Badia fino ad almeno il 1483.[57] Il giovane Varnucci ebbe modo anche di essere citato accanto ad altri ventisette cartolai nel famoso *Diario* (scritto intorno al 1476-84) della stamperia Rispoli, con cui pure collaborò legando alcuni incunaboli.[58] Dunque la bottega familiare impostata da Bartolomeo Varnucci trovò modo di continuare dopo la sua morte, anche se la sensazione è che fu privata della sua precipua specificità. Infatti, in tutto il secolo Bartolomeo fu uno dei pochi miniatori che le fonti dichiarano come tale attivo nei locali della Badia, e oltre lui e i fratelli si possono contare solo Antonio di Bindo, Bastiano di Niccolò di Monte, don Niccolò di Rossello, Mariano del Buono, Felice di Michele e Monte di Giovanni di Miniato.[59] Senza dubbio fu una specializzazione che venne tenuta da conto, e che fece la fortuna della sua bottega di cartolaio, la quale però non poté davvero mai confrontarsi – per importanza, prestigio, e mole produttiva – con l'attività di chi, come Vespasiano da Bisticci, poteva contare su specifiche competenze testuali tali da potersi interconnettere con gli intellettuali dell'epoca. Molto probabilmente, parlando con Bartolomeo uno di questi illustri letterati non avrebbe sentito quella preparazione e quella saldezza di conoscenze, di merito e di contenuti, che avrebbe certo sentito in Vespasiano, e che probabilmente fu la vera ragione del successo di quest'ultimo.

---

57 LEVI D'ANCONA (vedi nota 8), pp. 34-37.

58 ROUSE (vedi nota 5), pp. 34, 40-41, 50-51.

59 GUIDOTTI (vedi nota 7), pp. 481-482.

Louis A. Pitschmann

Johann Bämler and the Making of *Küchenmeisterei*

This article explores key questions regarding the authorship of *Küchenmeisterei*, the oldest known printed collection of German culinary recipes. Unlike previous investigations of this text, which have relied primarily on its various fifteenth-century editions, this article bases its findings not only on an assessment of the text's content and possible sources but more broadly on a comparison of specific terminology imbedded in the text that is also found in other 15th-century German-language incunabula. This comparative assessment moves *Küchenmeisterei* beyond the narrow focus of a cookbook and places it in the larger context of 15th-century instructional manuals and handbooks. This broader context reveals how closely specific editorial features found in *Küchenmeisterei* and other instructional texts resemble similar, at times identical, features present in works printed, written, and/or edited by Augsburg printer Johann Bämler. Relying on these textual similarities and on what is known about Bämler's business endeavors, this article demonstrates why Bämler, whether working alone or in close collaboration with others, was in all probability the intellectual force behind the creation and earliest printing of *Küchenmeisterei*.

Introduction

Peter Wagner issued the earliest dated edition of *Küchenmeisterei* in Nuremberg on November 10, 1485 (ISTC ik00039100, GW M16467). That edition and all subsequent editions appeared without attribution. Attempts to identify the author have, for the most part, not ventured beyond ascribing authorship to an unnamed cook in a monastic kitchen or in the home of a noble or patrician family. Looking beyond its culinary content, scholars have more recently acknowledged that dietary advice and regimens for specific health problems in the text required the author to possess some degree of medical knowledge. Relying on a comparative bibliographic assessment of *Küchenmeisterei* and other German vernacular incunables which predate it, this article presents a series of justifications for attributing authorship not to a cook or a medical expert but to the Augsburg printer-publisher Johann Bämler.[1]

Possibly the earliest description of *Küchenmeisterei* is that recorded by Gotthold Ephraim Lessing while serving as librarian of the Herzog August Library in Wolfenbüttel, Germany. Concerning the copy in his possession, he wrote that he owned an old German cookbook, which from all appearances he believed was the first of its kind. In addition to providing the title and collation, he noted that the book included neither

---

[1] The terms *author* and *authorship* are used throughout this article in the broadest sense. They are not intended to imply sole responsibility for the intellectual content found in *Küchenmeisterei* but rather to convey the degree of intellectual creativity required to compile, edit, and organize content from a variety of sources to produce an entirely new, albeit derivative, work.

the printer's name nor the place of publication and lacked pagination and catch words.[2] Bibliographers have since identified Lessing's copy as one from Peter Wagner's edition of ca. 1490 (ISTC ik00039400, GW M16470). By 1501, *Küchenmeisterei* had become a bestseller, appearing in no fewer than 15 editions[3] with many more editions and printings appearing well into the sixteenth century.

Scholarly analysis of the text's content began in the last quarter of the 19th century when the philologist Anton Birlinger turned his attention to the text's culinary terminology.[4] A more comprehensive assessment of the text did not appear until Hans Wegener's 1939 facsimile of Lessing's copy,[5] which was followed by Rolf Ehnert's facsimile edition of Johann Petri's Passau edition from ca. 1486 (ISTC ik00039250, GW M16471).[6] It was, however, Trude Ehlert's studies of *Küchenmeisterei* that fostered ongoing scholarly investigations which earlier studies had failed to engender. Research by Ehlert and her colleagues has been extensive in its breadth and depth and has yielded critically important findings relating to *Küchenmeisterei*'s culinary and dietary content, linguistic features, and textual variants among the editions, points which Wegener had only touched on. As for the identity of the *Küchenmeisterei*'s anonymous author, Ehlert has concluded the text's content reveals a person with medical and dietary knowledge, but she offers no specific names of who that might have been.[7]

Regarding *Küchenmeisterei*'s origins more broadly, Ehlert has shown that two manuscripts containing some of the recipes found in *Küchenmeisterei* and initially appearing to hold possible answers to the text's origins are in fact merely copies made from one or more printed editions of the text.[8] Efforts by others to locate the source(s) of *Küchenmeisterei*'s culinary recipes, and ideally its author, have only underscored the text's potentially unique content, as researchers have not found verbatim examples of its recipes in any of the more than 50 German-language culinary recipe collections preserved in 14th and 15th-century manuscripts.[9] The similarities *Küchenmeisterei* shares with some of those recipes are vague, making it unclear whether they simply indicate how widespread and popular the dishes themselves were or whether they were derived from a common source. Further, rather than translating or merely copying recipes from his sources, *Küchenmeisterei*'s creator summarized, paraphrased, and possibly even conflated content from multiple sources to prepare an entirely new work, a work not intended to serve as his own resource but as a text intended for publication. Such summarizing and paraphrasing of texts was not an uncommon practice in early modern times. Examples can be found in various texts, including some attributed to Johann Bämler, and would explain why Thomas Gloning's research to identify the source of the instructions on making and preserving wines and vinegars has proven only partially successful.[10]

Gloning bases critical questions regarding the sources used to create *Küchenmeisterei* on the premise that the Nuremberg printer Peter Wagner was its creator. He dismisses other printers from consideration by asking why the idea of publishing *Küchenmeisterei* had not occurred to

---

[2] GOTTHOLD EPHRAIM LESSING: *Lessings Werke*. Versehen v. Julius Petersen und Waldemar von Olshausen, and Julius Petersen in Verbindung mit Karl Borinski. Berlin 1926, p. 183. Cited in *Küchenmeisterei in Nürnberg von Peter Wagner um 1490 gedruckt: Faksimile nach dem Exemplar der Herzog-August-Bibliothek in Wolfenbüttel*. Eingeleitet von Hans Wegener. Leipzig 1939 (VGT Reihe B. Seltene Frühdrucke in Nachbildungen. III), p. 6 note 1.

[3] Included in this count is the undated edition which both ISTC ik00040800 and GW M16465 dated as "after 1500?".

[4] ANTON BIRLINGER: Älteres Küchen- und Kellerdeutsch. In: *Alemannia*. 18 (1890), pp. 244–267.

[5] HANS WEGENER: *Küchenmeisterei, in Nürnberg von Peter Wagner um 1490 gedruckt: Faksimile nach dem Exemplar der Herzog-August-Bibliothek in Wolfenbüttel* (see note 2).

[6] ROLF EHNERT: *Kuchenmeysterey: (Passau: Johann Petri, um 1486)*. Göppingen 1981 (Litterae. Göppinger Beiträge zur Textgeschichte. 71).

[7] TRUDE EHLERT: Wissensvermittlung in deutschsprachiger Fachliteratur des Mittelalters, oder Wie kam die Diätik in die Kochbücher? In: *Würzburger medizinhistorische Mitteilungen*. 10 (1990), pp. 137–159, here p. 140.

[8] TRUDE EHLERT: *Küchenmeisterei: Edition, Übersetzung und Kommentar zweier Kochbuch-Handschriften des 15. Jahrhunderts*. Frankfurt a. M. 2010. (Kultur, Wissenschaft, Literatur: Beiträge zur Mittelalterforschung. 21), p. 389.

[9] TRUDE EHLERT: Handschriftliche Vorläufer der 'Küchenmeisterei' und ihr Verhältnis zu den Drucken: der Codex S 490 der Zentralbibliothek Solothurn und die Handschrift G. B. 4° 27 des Stadtarchivs Köln. In: *De consolatione philogiae: Studies in Honor of Evelyn S. Firchow*. Ed. by Heinrich Beck, Anna Grotans, and Anton Schwob. Göppingen 2000, pp. 41–65, here p. 49.

[10] THOMAS GLONING: Die 'Küchenmeisterei' (1485ff.): Überlegungen zu Möglichkeiten und Grenzen der Beschreibung lokaler Gebrauchstextwelten. In: *Zeitschrift für deutsche Philologie*. 134 (Sonderheft 2015), pp. 89–110, here pp. 105–108.

the leading printers in Nuremberg or even their competitors in Augsburg, many of whom were noted for their vernacular guides and manuals. He singles out Johann Bämler in particular for not seizing the opportunity to be the first printer associated with *Küchenmeisterei*.[11] Accepting the premise that Wagner's edition of November 10, 1485 is the *editio princeps* and that Wagner was, therefore, the first person to arrive at the idea of publishing *Küchenmeisterei*, however, precludes a broader context in which to seek a more comprehensive understanding of *Küchenmeisterei*'s origins: its author, his sources, and potentially earlier editions. To be sure, Wagner's role in the history of the text as we know it cannot be ignored, nor can one ignore the much larger genre of German-language advice books and instructional manuals of which *Küchenmeisterei* is just one example.

Küchenmeisterei in the Context of German-Vernacular Texts

The earliest printed editions of German-language texts pre-date *Küchenmeisterei* by roughly thirty years, and by the time Peter Wagner printed the presumed first edition in November 1485, slightly more than one thousand editions and reprints of German-language texts had appeared, three quarters of which had appeared in Augsburg, Strassburg, Nuremberg, Ulm, Mainz, and Speyer.[12] By the close of 1485, an estimated 123 vernacular texts had been printed in Strassburg, and the five cities where the earliest editions of *Küchenmeisterei* appeared accounted for a combined total of only 254 vernacular titles on various topics: Nuremberg (115), Ulm (83), Mainz (26), Speyer (24), and Passau (6). As early as 1480, Augsburg had become known as the center of German vernacular printing, a reputation it retained throughout the remainder of the 15th century. When compared to other printing centers, Augsburg's printers had produced no fewer than 380 German-language texts by the close of 1485, nearly a quarter of which had been produced by Johann Bämler alone.

Like *Küchenmeisterei*, many of the German-language texts which Bämler and others produced were instructional in nature – advising how to achieve a good life, whether a good life was to be obtained by knowing how to select a wife, care for a child, follow a healthful regimen, or prepare spiritually for a good death. Still, other guides of the period instructed the reader how to master specific skills such as making, preserving, and flavoring wines; distilling spirits that were both pleasant to the taste and beneficial to one's health; selecting and caring for one's horse; or mastering the art of falconry.

Placing *Küchenmeisterei* in the context of instructional guides and manuals reveals a number of lexical and editorial similarities which are striking in their uniformity and placement within the texts. One finds in their incipits and prefatory matter, as well as in a limited number of cases in explicits and colophons,[13] repeated occurrences of a relatively small number of specific words and phrases employed to assure the reader

---

[11] GLONING (see note 10), pp. 100 and 104.

[12] ISTC includes some 1,050 records of such texts printed prior to 1486. More than half of these appeared in three cities: Augsburg, Strassburg, and Nuremberg. Counts shown here are based on ISTC records by using an advanced search string consisting of place of printing AND language German AND date before 1486. The variant spellings Nuremberg and Nürnberg yielded only slightly different results, 115 and 110 records respectively.

[13] See, for example, the closing lines in BÄMLER'S 1479 edition of *De vinis* (ISTC ia01081000, GW 2538): Here ends the praiseworthy pamphlet on the preparation of wine (»Hie enndet sich das loblich büchlin von bereyttung der wein...«).

of a text's importance. When considered within the context of an individual title, they might go unnoticed or simply be attributed to the author's efforts to promote his work. When viewed across multiple texts, they appear instead to be the words of the printer or publisher to entice buyers, much like today's use of dustjacket blurbs, as the texts are frequently described as "little books" (*büchlein*) or "praiseworthy" (*löblich*) which readers will find "useful" (*nüczlich, nuczber*), some even "entertaining" (*kurczweilich*). Many are described as containing "instructions" (*vnderweisungen*), albeit in some cases "brief instructions" (*kurcze vnderweisungen*), of value to "many people" (*vil menschen*), who are not infrequently identified as "everyone" or "anyone" (*ein yeglicher mensch*). As for the sources from which these texts are derived, prefatory matter often explains that the text is based on information from "authorities" on the subject (*maister*) or on "authoritative books," written in Latin, the content of which has been compiled and summarized and rendered into German for the sake of the reader's convenience as is stated in Bämler's ca. 1473 edition of *Andechs: Von dem Ursprung und Anfang des heiligen Bergs zu Andechs* (ISTC ia00573950, GW 1639).

In the case of *Küchenmeisterei*, one need only peruse the foreword (*Vorred*), a brief page and a half, to find where the book's similarities with other fifteenth-century instructional guides become at once apparent. It is here that the words and phrases assuring readers of the books' qualitative as well as authoritative content appear with the highest frequency and in closest proximity to one another. The opening line of the *Vorred* to *Küchenmeisterei* informs readers that many people are inclined to consume natural and appealing food (»Vil menschen sein...geneigt czu natürlicher vnd lustiger speisse....«). It continues by pointing out to perspective buyers that "this little book" (büchlein), called *Küchenmeisterei*, is written in a rather short and useful manner and is provided with practical and well-composed instructions for many dishes (»gar kurcz auch nüczlich begriffen vnd angezeiget mit hübscher warhafftiger vnterweysunge von mangerley speyßse«). The *Vorred* further explains how the dishes are to be prepared and then served to princes and lords, be they clergy or nobility, and even served to the common man (»fürsten und herren geistlichen oder weltlichen auch dem gemainen man...«). Reading further, one is assured that *Küchenmeisterei* includes instructions on the use of herbs, spices, and other ingredients for a broad range of meats, fowl, game, fish, crabs, eggs, soups and vegetables. For a proper cook who makes well-prepared dishes is nowadays the best doctor (»...ein ordentlicher koch mit wol bereitter natürlicher speiß ist hie in disser zeit der best artzt«).

The foreword further alerts the reader that Part Five of "this little book" includes short, natural, and useful instructions on how its readers should conduct themselves by following a proper regimen of food and drink as well as in other aspects of life (»Mitsampt einer kurczen natürlichen vnd nuczbern vnderweisungen, wie sich ein yeczlich mensch in seynem regiment mit essen vnd trincken auch andern sachen wesenlich vnd gebürlich halten sol.«) The *Vorred* then concludes with assurance to its readers that following the regimen regarding food and drink found in the text will ensure the readers' good health more productively and fruitfully (»nüczer vnd fruchtberlicher«) than all currently available medicine (»den[n] alle zeitliche erczney«).

Not all vernacular texts contain these or similar words of assurance. Some authors and printers used them only inconsistently, others not at all. The earliest printers of *Küchenmeisterei* were similarly inconsistent in providing readers with assurances of the quality of other titles they printed. Prior to printing *Küchenmeisterei* in March of 1487, Peter Drach had printed barely a dozen German texts, and those were primarily almanacs and bilingual vocabularies which contain no references to the texts' quality. Peter Wagner and Johann Petri had printed even fewer German texts before issuing *Küchenmeisterei*. An online search of the ISTC retrieved only two vernacular titles, from a total of 13 texts which Petri had printed in Passau about the same time he issued *Küchenmeisterei*, ca. 1486: an almanac for the year 1485, printed as a broadside at the close of 1484 or the start of 1485 (ISTC ia00506800, GW 1393), and the six-leaf German pamphlet on the election of Maximilian I (ISTC im00385200 GW M22081), neither of which provided prospective buyers any assurance of its quality or importance.

Wagner's press by late 1485 had produced chiefly Latin texts. Notwithstanding the still-debated question whether Konrad Zeninger or Wagner printed the German translation of Johannes Jacobi's *Regimen contra pestilentiam* (ISTC ij00014480, GW M1048610),[14] Wagner's earliest example of a vernacular instructional manual emanating from his printing office is presumably Schrick's *Von den ausgebrannten Wassern* of 1483 (ISTC is00329300, GW M36499). The *incipit* on leaf A1 recto advises the reader that the text contains information that is useful to know (*nuczlich zuwissen*), and leaf A2 recto further assures the reader of the text's importance by stating that useful content (*nuczlich materi*) about spirits and how to use them for one's health follows and then implies the importance and validity of the text by stating that Dr. Michael Schrick had compiled the pamphlet (*puchlin*) from other books. These assuring words regarding the content of this text, however, are not Wagner's words; they are Bämler's words which appeared in his edition of the text no later than October 1477, and which he continued to use in his editions of June 1478, May 1479, and July 1482.[15]

Konrad Dinckmut and Peter Schoeffer on the other hand had printed a number of vernacular texts before turning to *Küchenmeisterei*. In his earliest German edition of *Regimen sanitatis: Die Ordnung der Gesundheit* of October 5, 1482 (ISTC ir00051000, GW M37288), Dinckmut opened the text proper with the statement »Hie nach volget ain nützlich regimentt wer sich dar nach haltet der mag seinn leben lang inn gesundtheitt behaltenn.« (Hereafter follows a useful regimen; whoever follows it may maintain his good health throughout his life.) A short two weeks later on October 19, 1482, he advised readers on leaf 1 recto of his edition of *Von den ausgebrannten Wassern* (ISTC is00329000, GW M36507) that the content which followed was both very good and useful to know

14 FRIEDER SCHANZE: 'Pestregiment Herrn Kamits' eine unbekannte deutsche Inkunabel. In: *GJ* 65 (1993), pp 88–90.

15 Although Wagner's use of the word *besunder* (special) in the phrase »*durch liebe vnd besunder gebe*« suggests that his reprint was derived from Schönsperger's reprint of 1482 (ISTC is00327000, GW M36484), his reassuring words on A1r and A2r are precisely those found in Bämler's edition of 27.10.1477 (ISTC is00325000, GW M136474) as well as in Bämler's subsequent editions and multiple reprints by other printers including Dinckmut in Ulm.

(»...*gar gůt vnd nützlich ze wissen*«), and on leaf 2 recto he further reassured the reader that what followed was useful material (»*ain nutzliche materi*«). It should not go unnoted that these two examples from Dinckmut's press were essentially reprints of earlier editions printed by Bämler and retained Bämler's assurances to prospective buyers. It should also be pointed out that Dinckmut failed to express similar assurances that the reader would find practical information or useful material in his edition of *Gart der Gesundheit* of March 31, 1487 (ISTC ig00103000 GW M09746), a text that Bämler appears to have never printed.

Prior to printing *Küchenmeisterei* in March of 1487 (ISTC ik00039270, GW M16466), Schoeffer's vernacular texts were for the most part Church-related, such as indulgences and papal bulls. These were not texts that the reader would need to be assured of their quality; their religious nature alone would have implied such assurances. Like Dinckmut's edition of *Gart der Gesundheit*, Schoeffer's edition of that title on March 28, 1485 (ISTC ig00097000, GW M09766) lacks the formulaic praise and assurances of usefulness he included in his edition of *Küchenmeisterei* only two years later.

Looking beyond *Küchenmeisterei*, one finds similar inconsistencies in the use of qualitative assurances in a number of other vernacular texts. As early as the 1470s or possibly somewhat earlier, printers such as Günther Zainer, Friedrich Creussner, Anton Koberger, Anton Sorg, and Konrad Fyner provided readers with no qualitative assurances of their editions of Albertus von Eyb's *Ehebüchlein*, Ortolf von Baierland's *Arzneibuch*, Meister Albrecht's *Arzneibuch der Rosse*, and Johannes von Cuba's *Gart der Gesundheit*. Yet during this same period, Anton Sorg and others frequently promoted their publications with the same or synonymous terms of praise and quality assurance as those found in *Küchenmeisterei*, most frequently when reprinting titles which Bämler had previously issued. Johann Zainer, when reprinting *Die vierundzwanzig goldenen Harfen* in 1476 (ISTC in00224000, GW M26865), repeated the very words Bämler had used in the incipit to the first edition of the text no later than 1470 (ISTC in00222000, GW M26853), »Hie hebt sich an das allernüczlichest bůch, genant die viervndzweinczig gulden harpffen« (Here begins the most useful book called *The Twenty-Four Golden Harps*). Zainer's orthography is somewhat modified, but he retained Bämler's exact wording. The same wording appears in a subsequent printing by Sorg on 21 June, 1484 (ISTC in00224200, GW M26860), and nearly a decade later Martin Schott on August 3, 1493 (ISTC in00225000, GW M26863) continued to use Bämler's wording.[16]

A review of these and other texts, reveals that Bämler used laudatory and assuring descriptors earlier and far more frequently than did other printers, a practice he began not later than 1470 in his edition of *Die vierundzwanzig goldenen Harfen* (ISTC in00222000, GW M26853).[17] This was followed on April 22, 1472 by *Lehre und Unterweisung*, (ISTC il00126000, GW M17713), a compendium of seven texts, in which Bämler provided the commendatory terminology not only in the table of contents but again in the incipits and introductory statements preceding six of the

[16] Among other examples which illustrate the extent to which printers used these terms and phrases one finds *Die fünf Anfechtungen, die ein jeder Mensch erstehen muss in seinen letzten Zeiten* (ISTC il00126000 GW M17713); Conrad von Megenberg's *Buch der Natur* (ISTC ic00842000, GW M16426); Arnoldus de Villa Nova's *De vinis: Von Bewahrung und Bereitung der Weine* (ISTC ia01081000, GW 2538); *Auslegung der heiligen Messe* (ISTC ia01396000, GW 3086).

[17] A note in the ISTC record states, "A copy in Munich BSB has a rubricator's date 1470." (available on www.data.cerl.org [9.11.2022]).

seven texts. Only the edition of Steinhöwel's *Historia Griseldis* is without the customary words of quality assurance which one might expect.[18]

Bämler's assurances of quality continued to appear in various forms in his later publications. In his 1481 edition of Conrad von Megenberg's *Buch der Natur* (ISTC ic00844000, GW M16430), which he first published in 1475 (ISTC ic00842000, GW M16426), he stated on leaf 4a, »Vnd [es] ist gar eyn nüczliche kürczweylige materi, darinnen eyn yegklicher mensch vil selczsamer sachen vnterrichtet mag warden.« The following year in 1482 in his reprint of Schrick's *Von den ausgebrannten Wassern* (ISTC is00328000, GW M36477), he repeated the same assurances he had used in his printing of October 27, 1477 (ISTC is00325000, GW M36474). In the incipit on leaf 1a he informs the reader that the content »...ist gar gut vnd nüczlich zu wissen...« and again on leaf 2a he states, »Hie nach vollget ein nüczliche materi von manigerley ausz gepranten wassern, wie man die nüczen vnd prauchen sol zu gesuntheit der menschen.«

Even in a text of a devotional nature, his *Auslegung der heiligen Messe* in 1484 (ISTC ia01396000, GW 03086), Bämler found it appropriate to assure readers of its usefulness (*nucz*) by stating on leaf 2a, »Hyenach volget gar ein lobliche heylsame auszlegung der heyligen messe gar gůt vnd fruchtber geystlichen vnd weltlichen menschen zůlesen, darausz einem yegklichen menschen grosser nucz vnd fruchtberkeit wol entspringen mag.«

When placing German-language incunables, especially instructional manuals, into either of two groups, (a) those in which readers are assured of a book's quality and usefulness or (b) those in which such assurances are lacking, titles with the assuring terms and phrases were most frequently first printed by Bämler and later reprinted by others. In the case of Bämler's editions without the laudatory or reassuring descriptors, either he did not print the first edition, or the author of the text is clearly named in prefatory matter. For example, even though Bämler produced the first two editions of Berchtold's German translation of Johannes Friburgensis' *Summa confessorum* on Sept 25, 1472 (ISTC ij00317000, GW M13592) and again on June 20, 1478 (ISTC ij00318000; GW M13596), he used none of the assuring terms and phrases. In both editions, however, Bämler names Bruder Berchtold as the translator in the explicit, »Hie endet sich Summa Johannis...in tewtsch gemacht durch ein hochgelerten man Bruder Berchtold prediger ordens....« (Here ends *Summa Johannis*...translated into German by a highly educated man, Brother Berchtold, Order of Preachers....) In a sense, Bämler provided in this case a double assurance of the importance of the text proper and the quality of the translation by not only naming the author of the Latin source but also by naming the translator and describing him as highly educated. Further qualitative assurances were unnecessary.

Bämler also omitted his usual assurances in his 1472 edition of Eyb's *Ehebüchlein* (ISTC ie00182000, GW 9523) which had been preceded by Koberger's edition of 1472 (ISTC ie00179000, GW 9520), two additional printings by Creussner that same year (ISTC ie00179500,

---

18 (a) *Lehre und Unterweisung wie ein junger mensch...* In the table of contents the reader learns: »...das ist ein hübsche materi darinne ein yegclich mensch lernen mag wie er sich in erberkeyt vnd in guten syten gegen got vnd den menschen halten sol« and in the prefatory statement to the text on leaf 1a »Hienach volgent gůt nüczlich lere vnd vnderweysung in teütsch beschriben ausz den parabolen vnd beyssprüchen Salomonis..., Darinne ain junger mensch vnderricht würt, wie er sich in erberkeyt vnd gůten syten gegen got vnd dem menschen halten sol.« (b) *Lehre und Predigt wie sich zwei menschen in dem sacrament der heiligen ehe halten soll*. In the incipit on leaf 3a, Bämler assures the reader, »Hie nach volgt ain nüczliche lere vnd predig...« (c) *Menschenspiegel*. In the table of contents, Bämler states »...ein nüczliche geystliche vnderweisung...« and rephrases that assurance in the incipit on leaf 39a with »Hienach volgent ein hailsame nüczliche ler....« (d) *Historia Griseldis* is without any qualitative assessment or assurance. (5) *Die fünf Anfechtungen...* Here the incipit on leaf 46a reads »Hienach volgent die fünff anfächtigung die ein yedlich mensch ersteen můsz...mit...gepeten die offt vnd nuczlich zesprechen sint mit andacht.« (6) *Regimen sanitatis* [German] *Von Ordnung der Gesundheit*. Bämler's assurances concerning this title, especially those in the incipit, would appear to anticipate the nearly identical guarantees of a healthy long life promised in the *Vorred* to *Küchenmeisterei*. The table of contents assures the reader the text includes additional useful material (»...mit sampt vil anderen nüczlichen materien...«); and in the incipit on leaf 59a, he reassures that what follows is a useful regimen; whoever follows it may maintain good health throughout his life (»Hie nach volgt ein nüczlich regiment, wer sich darnach haltet der mag sein leben lang in gesuntheit behalten.«) (7) *Die Zehn Gebote* leaf 109a »Hienach volgent die zehen gepot gottess mit einer nuczlichen außlegung....«.

GW 0952010N; and ISTC ie00180000, GW 9521), and Günther Zainer's edition, ca. 1473 (ISTC ie00181000, GW 9522). Bämler's decision not to use his usual store of assurances and qualitative assessments may have been for one of two reasons. Either he knew the marketability of *Ehebüchlein*, or he believed that the author's name and academic training which are clearly stated in the opening lines of the text substantiated the book's importance and the validity of its content.

Bämler's much more consistent use of these words in incipits and other prefatory matter is telling and allows one to deduce that their use in the *Vorred* to *Küchenmeisterei* points to Bämler as having played a key role in creating *Küchenmeisterei*. Its earliest printers, Wagner, Petri, Drach and Schoeffer,[19] like several of their contemporaries, merely repeated Bämler's words found in the original printer's copy or an earlier now lost edition. However, as important as these lexical and stylistic similarities may be in suggesting Bämler as the author of *Küchenmeisterei*, they merely provide the foundation for such a premise. More substantive and conclusive evidence supporting Bämler's role is found in answers to the following questions:

- What is the probability that Bämler printed an earlier but now lost edition of *Küchenmeisterei*?
- Could Bämler have authored the text but commissioned Wagner or others to print it?
- What evidence would confirm or suggest he possessed the requisite skills to author *Küchenmeisterei*?
- What might his possible sources have been and how might he have gained access to them?

Possible Lost Bämler Editions

It is not inappropriate to propose that one or more editions of *Küchenmeisterei* may have originated from Bämler's press but are no longer extant. Wegener stated with certainty that over the course of time some 15th-century editions of *Küchenmeisterei* had been lost, but he did not opine who their printers may have been or whether such editions may have preceded Wagner's printing of 1485.[20] One might argue against Bämler's role as printer on the grounds that none of his broadsides advertising books for sale mention *Küchenmeisterei* by title or by any generic descriptive term or phrase. That is indeed true, but as Jürgen Vorderstemann has shown, Bämler's surviving broadsides announcing titles for sale did not list all titles he had previously published.[21] In addition, in her observations of damage and loss among both Latin and vernacular incunables, Inge Leipold has pointed out that vernacular texts experienced greater wear and greater loss than did Latin texts.[22] More recent studies based on statistical analyses suggest the probability of high rates of loss of entire editions across all formats and languages in which incunables appeared.[23]

---

[19] Dinckmut's edition of ca. 1487 (ISTC ik00039260, GW M1647410) is not referenced here, as the surviving fragments do not include the *Vorred*.

[20] WEGENER (see note 5), p. 9.

[21] JÜRGEN VORDERSTEMANN: Augsburger Bücheranzeigen des 15. Jahrhunderts. In: *Augsburger Buchdruck und Verlagswesen von den Anfängen bis zur Gegenwart*. Ed. HELMUT GIER und JOHANNES JANOTA. Wiesbaden 1997, pp. 55–71, here p. 60.

[22] INGE LEIPOLD: Das Verlagsprogramm des Augsburger Druckers Johann Bämler: zum Funktionstyp "Frühe deutschsprachige Druckprosa". In: *Bibliotheksforum Bayern*. 4 (1976). pp 236–252, here pp. 238 and 240.

[23] JONATHAN GREEN, FRANK MCINTYRE and PAUL NEEDHAM: The Shape of Incunable Survival and Statistical Estimation of Lost Editions. In: *The Papers of the Bibliographical Society of America*. 105 (June 2011). pp. 141–175.

The condition and small number of surviving copies of *Küchenmeisterei* make it a prime example of such loss and damage. Of the 15 pre-1501 extant editions of *Küchenmeisterei*, the ISTC and the GW have located only 36 copies and fragments. A single copy exists of the presumed *editio princeps* issued by Wagner on November 10, 1485 (ISTC ik00039100, GW M16467); a mere three double leaves have survived from Dinckmut's edition, ca. 1487 (ISTC ik00039260, GW 1647010); and only defective copies survive of some other editions (*e.g.*, ISTC ik00040700, GW M16464). Haebler's often cited estimate that printers would have only rarely printed a modest one hundred or even fewer copies[24] would mean that the pre-1501 editions of *Küchenmeisterei* would have had a combined total of no fewer than 1,500 copies, of which only 36 are extant, a number which represents a loss of more than 97% of the estimated total copies. The rate of loss would be considerably greater if any of the extant editions had larger print runs than Haebler's relatively low estimate. This high rate of loss among extant editions supports Wegener's belief that entire editions of *Küchenmeisterei* may not have survived.

That so few copies have survived is not surprising. *Küchenmeisterei* was issued in what today would be described as a pamphlet format. The earliest editions consisted of only 32 leaves with some editions consisting of as few as four quires. Once purchased, the permanent home of "this little book" would have been most appropriately in a kitchen or a cook's apron pocket – in either place, not an ideal environment for long-term preservation. Oily fingers, loose ingredients, and spills would have contributed to the loss of certain pages or entire copies. Even careful but repeated use would have worn and tattered the pages. If placed too close to the cook's fire, damage or loss was inevitable. As has always been the case of any good cookbook, copies of *Küchenmeisterei* were used to tatters; and copies that survived to be passed through the hands of two or more generations of cooks would have eventually been discarded when their recipes and remedies were no longer in vogue.

Did Bämler Commission the Printing of *Küchenmeisterei*?

Bämler had moved away from primarily printing texts by the early 1480s and had become more involved in supporting their publication, distribution, and sale. A review of ISTC and GW records reveals that Bämler's annual output of publications declined around 1483 or 1484, but tax records confirm that his tax liabilities did not. Indeed, when *Küchenmeisterei* was first appearing in Nuremberg, Passau, Ulm, Mainz, and Speyer, his tax obligations were significantly greater than in previous years.[25] The decrease in output from his press and the increase in his tax obligations are directly attributable to his significantly expanded commercial interests in other endeavors. For example, to mitigate an ongoing paper shortage in 1485, Bämler purchased the Augsburg papermill known as the *Untere Papiermühle am Pfannenstiel an der Sinkel* which he managed from 1485 to 1487, the very years when the earliest editions of *Küchenmeisterei* under review in this article appeared.[26]

24 KONRAD HAEBLER: *Handbuch der Inkunabelkunde*. Leipzig 1925, p. 142.

25 HANS-JÖRG KÜNAST: *Getruckt zu Augsburg: Buchdruck und Buchhandel in Augsburg zwischen 1468 und 1555*. Tübingen 1997, pp. 35–37.

26 FRIEDER SCHMIDT: Papierherstellung in Augsburg bis zur Frühindustrialisierung. In: *Augsburger Buchdruck und Verlagswesen von den Anfängen bis zur Gegenwart*. Ed. HELMUT GIER and JOHANNES JANOTA. Wiesbaden 1997, pp. 73–95, here pp. 76 and 91.

The 1480s also witnessed Bämler's increased emphasis on bookselling, not merely his own titles but also those of others. This endeavor was no modest undertaking. In addition to selling in Augsburg where he was assisted by his wife, Bämler relied on itinerate booksellers to sell his stock in other towns and cities, and he relied heavily on the Nördlinger fair, which proved to be a lucrative venue for the sale of pamphlets and broadsides.[27] Further evidence of Bämler's activities as a bookseller can be found in broadsides announcing books available for sale. Although few in number, surviving book lists document the emphasis printers and booksellers placed on advertising available titles. In Bämler's case, one such list in his font, which included not only titles he had printed but also titles issued by Sorg, Schönsperger and others, illustrates the ever greater emphasis he placed on the sale of printed materials over their production.[28]

This particular list warrants close consideration for two reasons. For it not only dates to the precise years when the earliest extant copies of *Küchenmeisterei* were appearing in Nuremberg, Passau, Ulm, Mainz, and Speyer, but it also corresponds to the years when Bämler is known to have placed decreased emphasis on printing, the very years in which he would have had time to devote to writing or overseeing the creation of *Küchenmeisterei*. At a minimum, Bämler's emphasis on the production of paper and the sale of books in the 1480s rather than the printing of books provides further reason why no copies of *Küchenmeisterei* are known to have been printed on Bämler's own press but instead were produced by other printers.

By the 1480s, it was not uncommon for printers to produce some titles on commission. Such outsourcing would further explain why Bämler is not known to have printed *Küchenmeisterei*. That possibility is not easily dismissed when one considers that two of the men who printed early editions of *Küchenmeisterei*, Peter Schoeffer and Peter Drach, are among those known to have printed texts on commission.[29] Potential collaborations between Bämler and Drach become even more probable when one considers that Bämler's brother-in-law, Caspar Traut, had established himself as a bookseller early on and was serving as Drach's agent by 1485 when the earliest dated edition of *Küchenmeisterei* appeared.[30]

Business dealings with Wagner in Nuremberg may have originated through Bämler's step-son Johann Schönsperger d. Ä. When first established in his own printing office, Schönsperger accepted a commission to print for the wealthy Nuremberger Hans Tucher his guide to the Holy Land, *Reise in das gelobte Land* (ISTC it00490000, GW M47728), which appeared before February 23, 1482.[31] Dissatisfied with Schönsperger's work, Tucher turned only weeks later to Konrad Zeninger in Nuremberg to print a revised edition, which appeared no later than July 12, 1482 and possibly as early as late March of that year.[32] Not to be outshone by Zeninger's improved edition and undoubtedly to restore his reputation with Tucher and his circle of influence, Schönsperger that same year reprinted Zeninger's edition containing Tucher's revisions.

---

27 KÜNAST (see note 25), p. 153.

28 JÜRGEN VORDERSTEMANN: Eine neue Augsburger Bücheranzeige aus der Mitte der achtziger Jahre des 15. Jahrhunderts. In: *GJ* 65 (1980). pp. 44–50.

29 HEINRICH GRIMM: Die Buchführer des deutschen Kulturbereichs und ihre Niederlassungsorte in der Zeitspanne 1490 bis um 1550. In: *Archiv für Geschichte des Buchwesens*. 7 (1966), col. 1154–1771, here col. 1204.

30 Drach's *Rechenbuch* records ongoing business dealings between Drach and Traut over several years in the 1480s. As Drach's agent, Traut's sales and services not only confirm an extended business relationship between the two men but also confirm a volume of sales that accounted for large sums paid to Traut for his work. See FERDINAND GELDNER: Das Rechnungsbuch des Speyrer Druckherrn, Verlegers und Grossbuchhändlers Peter Drach. In: *Archiv für die Geschichte des Buchwesens*. 5 (1964), col. 1–195, here col. 80 and 95.

31 RANDALL HERZ: *Studien zur Drucküberlieferung der "Reise ins gelobte Land" Hans Tuchers des Älteren*. Nürnberg 2005, p. 107.

32 HERZ (see note 31), p. 121.

This Schönsperger-Tucher-Zeninger association is not insignificant in the study of early editions of *Küchenmeisterei*, as Zeninger ceased printing in Nuremberg shortly after his revised edition of Tucher's guide to the Holy Land had appeared, and his fonts were acquired very soon thereafter by Peter Wagner. This acquisition would not have gone unnoticed by Bämler and others in Augsburg. One of the first books Wagner printed after acquiring Zeninger's fonts was *Von den ausgebrannten Wassern* (ISTC is00329300, GW M36499) in 1483, a title Bämler had issued several times earlier beginning in 1476.[33] It is possible that Bämler or another member of the Schönsperger network or a bookseller (*e.g.*, Bämler's brother-in-law, Caspar Traut) had contracted with Wagner to produce *Von den ausgebrannten Wassern* and not long thereafter commissioned him to print one or more of the three earliest extant editions of *Küchenmeisterei*, the first dated November 10, 1485, followed by the edition of March 4, 1486, and a third ca. 1486.

Schönsperger may also be the link between Bämler and Dinckmut in Ulm, another early printer of *Küchenmeisterei*. It is known that Dinckmut used Schönsperger's font to print two editions of *Der Seelenwurzgarten* in 1483, approximately four years before his earliest known edition of *Küchenmeisterei* appeared (ISTC ik00039260, GW M1647410). Unfortunately, as Peter Amelung has pointed out, there is no surviving documentation regarding why Dinckmut used Schönsperger's font and under what conditions the font was returned to Schönsperger for his edition of *Der Seelenwurzgarten* less than a year later in August 1484.[34]

Although no direct evidence has been found in the course of researching this paper to confirm that Bämler commissioned any one of *Küchenmeisterei*'s earliest printers to prepare an edition at his expense, their direct and indirect ties to Bämler when considered in the context of his expanded business endeavors in the 1480s cannot rule out the probability that he collaborated to some degree with one or more of them in publishing *Küchenmeisterei*.

That probability notwithstanding, regional fairs, such as those in Nördlingen, and the much larger Frankfurt fair, which by the 1480s had become a major market for printers and publishers, afforded Bämler additional opportunities to establish ties with printers located in various cities. Bämler's wife's business transactions conducted at the Frankfurt fair in 1484 and 1485 are well documented.[35] Her presence and that of other members of the Bämler-Schönsperger family at Frankfurt fairs in those years would imply that they attended the fair an unknown number of times both before and after the years referenced in the fair's records. In addition to the fairs in Nördlingen and Frankfurt, the Leipzig fair assured Bämler and the larger Schönsperger network professional dealings with printers and booksellers from Basel, Ulm, and Strassburg.[36] Still further, the printers Bernhard Richel in Basel and Adolf Rusch in Strassburg were among several printers and booksellers from outside Augsburg known to visit their printer and bookseller counterparts in Augsburg.[37] Bämler's professional contacts with printers were extensive and long-standing and would have afforded him many opportunities to

---

33 See note 15.

34 PETER AMELUNG: *Der Frühdruck im deutschen Südwesten, 1473-1500: eine Ausstellung der Württembergischen Landesbibliothek Stuttgart*. Stuttgart 1979, pp. 164 and 182.

35 KÜNAST (see note 25), p. 92. See also WALTER KARL ZÜLCH and GUSTAV MORI (Ed.): *Frankfurter Urkundenbuch zur Frühgeschichte des Buchdrucks*. Frankfurt am Main 1920, p. 32. Fair records document complaints Barbara Bämler levied with the fair's officials against the Strassburg bookseller Jakob Ebert for lack for payment for books he had acquired from her. The nature of her complaint suggests that Ebert's obligations to her arose from their transactions at an earlier fair.

36 KÜNAST (see note 25), p. 95.

37 KÜNAST (see note 25), pp. 140–141.

commission the services of another printer to produce *Küchenmeisterei* at his expense, examples of which may no longer be extant.

Bämler as Author and Editor

It is perhaps the three works which scholars have attributed to Bämler that provide some of the most persuasive evidence of his probable role in creating *Küchenmeisterei*. The earliest of these texts is his *Menschenspiegel* edition of April 1472 (ISTC il00126000, GW M17713). In her 1991 monograph, *Sündenspiegel im 15. Jahrhundert*, Gunhild Roth opines that Bämler may have drawn the content of this text from various Latin sources that would have been available to him. She based her belief in part on the absence of evidence that *Menschenspiegel* grew out of a manuscript tradition predating the appearance of Bämler's printed text.[38] She further supported her opinion by citing Ferdinand Geldner's statement that he, too, suspected Bämler's hand in the creation of certain texts when he called for a closer examination of Bämler's activities as a redactor of texts.[39]

Four years after *Menschenspiegel* appeared, Bämler produced the first edition of *Von den ausgebrannten Wassern* (ISTC is00324500, GW M36472). Originally issued without attribution, he credited the Viennese physician Michael Puff von Schrick as the author in his edition of 1477 (ISTC is00325000, GW M36474). A significant portion of the content is in fact derived from Puff's *Tractatus de virtutibus aquarum*, but because certain other content was derived from other sources, scholars consider the printed text a compilation assembled by Bämler or a person in his employ.[40]

A third example of Bämler's role as editor and compiler appeared in October 1476. After printing Jacob Twinger von Königshofen's *Chronik von allen Kaisern und Königen seit Christi Geburt* (ISTC ik00038000, GW M48346), Bämler issued his own significantly redacted edition of the text under a slightly revised title, *Chronik von allen Kaisern, Königen und Päpsten*. (ISTC ib00008000, GW 3163) and without attribution. For this new text, Bämler used only chapters 2 and 30 of Twinger's text while incorporating additional content borrowed from Stainhöwel's *Deutsche Chronik* (ISTC is00765000, GW 10075), which Johann Zainer had printed in Ulm on February 10, 1473. The expanded chronicle of popes up to Sixtus IV is considered Bämler's own work.[41] Reflective of his business acumen, Bämler omitted portions of Twinger's text that were specific to the history of Strassburg when creating his *Chronik*, subject matter which he apparently believed would be of less interest to his intended buyers in Augsburg.[42]

Like *Menschenspiegel*, *Chronik von allen Kaisern, Königen und Päpsten*, and the first printing of *Von den ausgebrannten Wassern*, *Küchenmeisterei* appeared without attribution, and just as he had done in creating the first three texts, Bämler created *Küchenmeisterei* by merging and melding related content from various sources, which he at times so heavily

---

38 GUNHILD ROTH: *Sündenspiegel im 15. Jahrhundert: Untersuchungen zum pseudo-augustinischen 'Speculum peccatoris' in deutscher Überlieferung*. Bern 1991 (Deutsche Literatur von den Anfängen bis 1700. 12), pp. 105–6, 141–2.

39 FERDINAND GELDNER: Ein Probesatz des "Buches der Kunst, dadurch der weltliche Mensch mag geistlich werden" (Augsburg, Johann Bämler 1476). In: *GJ* 1970, pp. 108–113, here p. 113.

40 HELMUT WALTER and GUNDOLF KEIL: Puff, Michael, aus Schrick. In: *VL²*. Vol. 7, col. 909–910.

41 KURT OHLY: Bämler, Johann. In: *VL²*. Vol. 1, col. 599–600.

42 LEIPOLD (see note 22), p. 245. See also WILLY BOEHM (Ed.): *Friedrich Reiser's Reformation des K. Sigmund: mit Benutzung der ältesten Handschriften nebst einer kritischen Einleitung und einem erklärenden Commentar*. Leipzig 1876, pp. 6–11.

redacted as to render his sources unrecognizable. Further, as he had done with the three aforementioned texts, he prefaced *Küchenmeisterei* with his usual introductory tropes assuring buyers of the book's utility and quality (*e.g.*, »nüczlich zu wissen«, »nüczliche materi«, »nüczliche…vnderweisung«, »nüczliche ler«, or simply »nüczlich«).

Bämler's Access to *Küchenmeisterei*'s Sources

It is unlikely that any one individual would have had the requisite expert knowledge of culinary recipes, winemaking, distillation of spirits, and regimens for mothers of newborns as well as for individuals suffering from various physical problems, including the plague, to write *Küchenmeisterei* based solely on his own knowledge. Instead, creating *Küchenmeisterei* required access to texts containing not merely culinary recipes but also information on a relatively wide range of topics, and/or access to individuals who collectively possessed such knowledge. Unfortunately, except for the reference to the pseudo-Albertus text *Secreta mulierum*, which appears in the book's closing lines, *Küchenmeisterei* yields few clues to precisely what sources the author may have relied on, but it is not unique in this regard. In her study of Bämler's publications, Inge Leipold points out that German-language texts of the 15th century were largely reworkings of earlier texts in the form of translations, prose renderings of texts originally composed in verse, or reconfigured summaries of much longer texts. In addition, she points out that the lack of clear delineation among the roles of author, translator, printer, and corrector increases the difficulty of determining authorship as it is understood today.[43]

Prefatory matter in numerous titles printed by Bämler and his contemporaries attests to Leipold's observations. In Bämler's ca. 1473 edition of *Andechs: Von dem Ursprung und Anfang des heiligen Bergs zu Andechs*, for example, we learn in the opening lines that the content was derived from information found on tablets or plaques mounted on the walls of the church. Additional content was gleaned from notes scattered among the pages of an old missal which were merely summarized or in some cases omitted entirely (»…das vnd anders man alles in alten tafeln in der kirchen hangend besunder auch in einem gar alten messbůch zersträt an vilen blettern geschriben vindet, das alles ist noch auff disem heiligen berg darab vnd darauss wir es zesamen gesamelt vnd hie nach geschriben habent vnd mit anderen worten begriffen nach dem kürczisten vnd es hat mügen gesein, auch von kürcz wesen haben wir auss gelassen vnnd über lauffen«) (ISTC ia00573950, GW 1639). Prefatory matter found in editions of Ortolf's *Arzneibuch*[44] and editions of Johann von Cube's *Gart der Gesundheit*[45] further illustrate Leipold's observations.

Although such summarizing and paraphrasing have rendered the original sources of *Küchenmeisterei* especially difficult to identify, Gloning has pointed out in his assessment of the recipes for wines and vinegars found in *Küchenmeisterei* Part Five that the recipe for *Alantwein*

[43] LEIPOLD (see note 22), p. 237.

[44] See ANTON KOBERG'S 17.3.1477 edition of Ortolf's *Arzneibuch*, in which the author stated in the foreword that he wished to create a German-language medical book based on all the medical books known to him which were written in Latin. (»Darumb will ich Ortolff von Bayerlandt doctor der ertzney ain artztpuch machen zedeutsch aus allen artztpüchern die ich in latein ye vernam.«) (ISTC io00110000, GW M28462).

[45] See PETER JOHANN VON CUBE'S *Gart der Gesundheit*, in which the prefatory matter describes how a medical doctor was engaged to gather the content for this landmark volume by relying on information found in the works of the most prominent of earlier physicians who are cited. (»Dennoch habe ich solichs löblichs werck lassen anfahen durch einen meyster in der artzney geleret, der nach myner begirde vß den bewerten meistern in der artzney Gallen, Avicenna, Serapione, Diasconde, Pandecta, Plateario vnd andern viel kreuter krafft vnd naturen in ein bůch zů samen hait bracht.«) (ISTC ig00097000, GW M09766).

closely approximates that found in Bämler's 1479 edition of *De vinis*, even though it lacks the lengthy description of the medicinal benefits of *Alantwein* which *De vinis* describes.[46] Albeit a significant difference between the two recipes, the instructions for making *Alantwein* provide further evidence of Bämler's possible role in creating *Küchenmeisterei*. Gloning also cites one of several recipes for vinegar found in *Küchenmeisterei* and describes the close similarities it, too, shares with the instructions found in *De vinis*, but here as well he emphasizes the differences between the two sets of instructions,[47] differences which would illustrate the author's manner of paraphrasing the recipes selected for *Küchenmeisterei*.

It is precisely the vinegar recipes in *Küchenmeisterei*, however, that reveal further parallels between *De vinis* and *Küchenmeisterei*. Part Five of *Küchenmeisterei* opens with 11 recipes for making vinegar. While similar in terms of ingredients and methods of preparation, none is a verbatim copy of those found in *De vinis*, but several of the recipes exhibit such strong similarities with those in *De vinis* as to suggest at least a common source. Evidence that their origin was indeed *De vinis* or that both texts shared a common source is further supported by the sequence of the first four of these recipes in *Küchenmeisterei* which is identical to their sequence in *De vinis*. In addition, vinegar recipes viii, xi, and xii in Part Five correspond closely to three other recipes in *De vinis* although their sequence in the two texts differs.

To find other source material sufficient to create an entirely new text for publication, Bämler would not have needed to look too far beyond his own printing office, nor would he have needed to look beyond his professional and social circles. His own editions of Hans Folz's *Von der Pestilenz, Ordnung der Gesundheit*, and *Von den ausgebrannten Wassern* contain content similar to that found in portions of *Küchenmeisterei*. These sources and any number of texts issued by competing presses would have afforded Bämler ample opportunity to glean and synthesize regimens and information of a medical or dietary nature in order to write what he considered a more comprehensive and potentially more marketable text than may have been otherwise available.

Where expert medical knowledge was required, Bämler's social circles and professional networks assured him access to any number of public health physicians (*Stadtphysici*), employed by city councils to serve the needs of their citizenry, and personal physicians (*Leibärzte*) who served members of the nobility and the church hierarchy. Both of these groups of physicians were present in Augsburg and other cities Bämler frequented in the 1470s and 1480s. Evidence of their knowledge, whether originating directly from them or gleaned from texts they had written, appears early in Part One of *Küchenmeisterei*. Recipe xvii, for example, references the dietary needs of women and higher mortality rates among women than men, observations which a cook in even the most prominent kitchen would not normally include in a collection of recipes. The knowledge that only a physician would possess is particularly apparent throughout large portions of Part Five where symptoms of specific digestive problems are outlined and recommendations for treating such

---

[46] GLONING (see note 10), pp. 105–107.

[47] GLONING (see note 10), p 107.

problems are provided. Here too, details for preparing some of the treatments are quite precise and clearly reflect a degree of medical knowledge which only a trained physician would have possessed. The Latin instructions in recipe xxviii in Part Five resemble a physician's prescription to be prepared by a druggist. These few examples and many more like them underscore Bämler's reliance on physicians or their texts as sources for certain content scattered throughout *Küchenmeisterei*.

Central to the question of sources used in creating *Küchenmeisterei* is the occurrence of Alsatian and Swabian lexical items found in a number of the culinary recipes. Wegener explained their use by simply stating that the first printed edition was based on a Swabian manuscript.[48] This explanation is not only plausible but it also supports Bämler's role in authoring *Küchenmeisterei*, as he resided in Augsburg which is located within the Swabian dialect region, an area where one would expect Alsatian terms to be similar and, therefore, recognizable if not in common use. In addition, it is known that Bämler had access to Alsatian texts, some of which may have included culinary recipes. If one shares the longstanding opinion that he received his training as a printer from Johann Mentelin in Strassburg[49] or that he resided in Strassburg when he rubricated various texts which Mentelin had printed,[50] he would have had ample opportunity to acquire one or more manuscripts containing Alsatian culinary recipes. Further, it is known that Bämler used the Alsatian manuscript Cod. Pal. Germ. 475, now preserved in Heidelberg, when printing his edition of Twinger's *Chronik von allen Kaisern und Königen seit Christi Geburt* (ISTC ik00038000, GW M48346). That manuscript dates from the mid-1400s and was taken to Augsburg not long thereafter by Jörg Rephon.[51]

Summary

The most salient points supporting Bämler's role in creating *Küchenmeisterei* are the similarities it shares with vernacular texts he printed prior to the appearance of the earliest extant editions of *Küchenmeisterei*. Like the incipits and forewords in many first editions which he printed, *Küchenmeisterei*'s foreword assures the reader that its content will prove useful and instructive to many people. Further, like his editions of *Menschenspiegel*, *Von den ausgebrannten Wassern* and *Chronik von allen Kaisern, Königen und Päpsten*, *Küchenmeisterei* is a derivative work in that its content is drawn from multiple sources which its author summarized and paraphrased. Its format, like so many of Bämler's vernacular texts, is pamphlet-like, a "little book" (*büchlin*), the term he used to describe many of his vernacular texts. Looking beyond the text proper, Bämler's access to manuscripts and printed sources as well as to medical experts combined with his knowledge of the burgeoning interest in vernacular texts and his entrepreneurial acumen as bookseller and author positioned him far better than other printer-publishers of vernacular texts to create *Küchenmeisterei*. The sheer number of first editions of German-language texts,

---

[48] WEGENER (see note 5), p. 9.

[49] SHEILA EDMUNDS: From Schoeffer to Vérard: Concerning the Scribes Who Became Printers. In: *Printing the Written Word: The Social History of Books, circa 1450–1520*. Ed. SANDRA HINDMAN. Ithaca and London 1991, pp. 21–40, here p. 34.

[50] KURT OHLY: Bämler, Johann. In: *VL*. Vol. 1 (1933), col. 159. Sheila Edmunds argues that Bämler was never in Strassburg and that he did not need to be there to rubricate the texts in question. See her New Light on Johannes Bämler. In: *Journal of the Printing Historical Society* (1993), pp. 29–53, here p. 34.

especially instructional texts, which he printed lends further justification for attributing the text's origins to him. Whether Bämler alone authored the text or whether he led a collaborative effort with one or more persons assisting with the identification, translation, editing, and organization of its content may be impossible to determine. The cumulative evidence supporting Bämler's role in creating *Küchenmeisterei* presented in this article, however, renders it difficult to conclude that he did not play a major role in creating *Küchenmeisterei* and in bringing about its publication.

---

51 JÜRGEN WOLF: Konrad Bollstatter und die Augsburger Geschichtsschreibung: Die letzte Schaffensperiode. In: *Zeitschrift für deutsches Altertum und deutsche Literatur*. 125 (1996). pp. 51-86, here p. 62-63.

Vinicius de Freitas Morais

Das Blut Christi und die blutenden Hostien in den Inkunabeln zum Sternberger Fall (1492):
Überlegungen zu ihren Bildern, den Normen ihrer antijüdischen Andachtstypen und zur Genese der Endfassung der Erzählereignisse

The alleged case of profanation of the Host in Sternberg is treated in a number of illustrated incunabula. These prints follow an official narrative which emerged from the trial against the Jews of Sternberg and the priest Peter Däne. The incunabla were produced only after the rendition of judgement against the local Jewish community. It is the aim of this article to contextualize the official narrative and the alleged events concerning the profanation of the Host and its miraculous bleeding. In order to appreciate the final version properly, it is crucial to show the genesis and development of this narrative from its beginning on August 29, 1492, until the end of the trial on October 22, 1492. This narrative change also illustrates the relation between the adaptations and the theological debate over the appearance of blood pouring out from miraculous Hosts as well as their relation to the realisation of the Blood of Christ. The six versions of incunabula show variations in their texts and woodcuts. The varying depictions illustrate different aspects of the devotion to the Bleeding Hosts and demonstrate the significance of pilgrimage devoted to the Passion of Christ. An additional iconographical analysis is meant to provide insight into how this miraculous Blood was represented and how it was interpreted by the incunabula's readership. There are several well-known treatments of these events. Among them are Hartman Schedels' Chronicle and the Latin version of the *Mons Stellarum*, which was written in Rostock by the former's fellow humanist Nikolaus Marschalk in 1512.

Verschiedene Inkunabeln zum Sternberger Hostienfrevelvorwurf von 1492 können nicht nur die Verbreitung der antijüdischen Legenden und ideelle Präsenz im deutschen Sprachraum nachweisen,[1] sondern auch verschiedene Aspekte der spätmittelalterlichen Frömmigkeit erklären. Ein wichtiger Aspekt der spätmittelalterlichen Soteriologie war die Wertschätzung des historischen und eucharistischen Blutes Christi. Die Legenden über den Ritualmord und Hostienschändungen waren eine spezielle Interpretation der Vergegenwärtigung der Kreuzigung Christi. Diese besaß ebenfalls eine intrinsische, eucharistische Bedeutung.

Die Unterschiede und Abweichungen zwischen den Inkunabel-Exemplaren[2] zeigen eine blutzentrische Frömmigkeit, die auf die Bluthostie von Sternberg hin ausgerichtet ist. Ihre Texte und Bilder liefern ausführliche Beschreibungen der Vergegenwärtigung der Marterung

---

[1] VOLKER HONEMANN: Die Sternberger Hostienschändung und ihre Quellen. In: *Literaturlandschaft. Schriften zur deutschsprachigen Literatur im Osten des Reiches.* Hrsg. von RUDOLF SUNTRUP. Frankfurt am Main 2008, S. 188–201.

[2] Es existieren sechs verschiedene Versionen, welche in diesen Aufsatz analysiert werden. Vgl. Anm. 48–53 dieses Aufsatzes.

Jesu in der Entweihung gestohlener Hostien. Diese Entweihungen stellen die Kreuzigung in der Gegenwart dar. In den Beschreibungen sollen den Christen das Leiden und Blut Christi durch neue Reliquien[3] zugänglich machen.

Die Vermittlung der antijüdischen Legenden in den Einblatt- und Kleindrucken fällt in die Hochphase des Antijudaismus im Westeuropa.[4] Die Hostienentweihungslegenden beziehen sich auf die Transsubstantiationslehre, die Messopfertheologie, die Soteriologie des Spätmittelalters und die Erinnerung an die Kreuzigung während der Messe als Preis für die Erlösung der Menschheit.[5] Nach dieser Vorstellung wurde Christus nicht nur in biblischer Zeit für die Sündenvergebung geopfert, sondern auch jedes Mal wenn die Hostie von dem Priester geweiht und erhöht wurde.[6]

Die Entstehung dieser Legenden und ihre eigenen Erzählstrukturen[7] stellen einen Wandel im mittelalterlichen Antijudaismus dar, welcher die Juden in verstärkter Weise als die Schänder des mystischen und gesellschaftlichen Körpers der Christenheit darstellte.[8] Der Begriff *Erzählstruktur* entspricht einer wiederholbaren Abfolge der Geschehnisse aus den antijüdischen Legenden, die auf verschiedene Weisen wiederholt wurden. Aus ihr wurde eine Endfassung der Erzählereignisse, beziehungsweise Beschreibung, der Ereignisse konzipiert, die eine ausführliche Erklärung zu einer Tat, wie der Hostienentweihung, liefern sollte.

Die Hostie war das wesentlichste Sakrament der Sündenvergebung, der ewigen Erlösung und der Heilung von Körper und Seele.[9] Für Christen stellt sich dementsprechend die Frage, wie nicht-Christen oder Dissidenten von der Macht des Heiligen Sakraments profitieren konnten. Wie wurde mit den geweihten Hostien beziehungsweise dem gegenwärtigen und unsichtbaren Leib Jesu in den falschen Händen umgegangen? Diese Fragen stehen in direktem Zusammenhang mit den antijüdischen Legenden vom den Hostienfrevel und ihre Bedeutung erklärt die erfolgreiche und rapide Verbreitung der judenfeindlichen Erzählungen in Europa.

Der wachsende Stellenwert der Transsubstantiationslehre beförderte auch die Erzählungen über Juden, die geweihte Hostien entweder von einem Christen (meist einer Frau) kauften oder diese aus Sakristeien entwendeten.[10] Um sich gegen die Entweihung zu verteidigen, blutet

---

3 CAROLINE WALKER BYNUM: A Matter of Matter. Two Cases of Blood Cult in the North of Germany in the Later Middle Ages. In: *Medieval paradigms. Essays in honor of Jeremy Duquesnay Adams*. Bd. 2. Hrsg. von STEPHANIE A. HAYES-HEALY. New York – Basingstoke 2005, S. 181–210. Die Publikation *Pilgrimage and Pogrom* darf nicht außer Acht gelassen werden. Der Autor Mitchell Merback diskutiert ausführlich die Entstehungen verschiedener Kultorte für Bluthostien innerhalb des deutschen Sprachraumes: MITCHELL B. MERBACK: *Pilgrimage and Pogrom. Violence, Memory, and Visual Culture at the Host-Miracle Shrines of Germany and Austria*. Chicago 2012.

4 Für die Entstehung und Verbreitung der Hostienfrevelerzählstruktur gilt das Buch von Miri Rubin als Standardwerk: MIRI RUBIN: *Gentile Tales. The Narrative Assault on Late Medieval Jews*. New Haven 1999.

5 Für eine ausführliche Diskussion aller erwähnten Themen vgl. CAROLINE WALKER BYNUM: *Wonderful Blood. Theology and Practice in Late Medieval Northern Germany and Beyond*. Philadelphia 2007.

6 Zur spätmittelalterlichen Soteriologie vgl. das 10. Kapitel *Sacrificial Theology* und das 11. Kapitel *The Aporia of Sacrifice* in BYNUM (s. Anm. 5), S. 210–244.

7 Hier soll *Erzählstruktur* nicht mit dem Strukturalismus der 1960er und 1970er Jahre in Verbindung gebracht werden, sondern als ein zusammenfassender Begriff für die Analyse der antijüdischen Legenden, deren Geschehnisfolge und Historizität gebraucht werden. Zum Strukturalismus vgl. FRANÇOIS WAHL: *Einführung in den Strukturalismus*. München 1992.

8 GAVIN LANGMUIR: Historiographic Crucifixion. In: *Toward a definition of Antisemitism*. Los Angeles 1996, S. 282–298.

9 CAROLINE WALKER BYNUM: Women mystics and eucharistic devotion in the thirteenth century. In: *Women's Studies. An interdisciplinary Journal*. 11/1–2 (1984), S. 179–214; ALEXANDRA REID-SCHWARTZ: Economies of Salvation Commerce and the Eucharist in The Profanation of the Host and the Croxton Play of the Sacrament. In: *Comitatus. A journal of Medieval and Renaissance Studies*. 25/1 (1994), S. 1–20.

10 Für eine tiefere Kontextualisierung des Beginns der Ausbreitung der Hostienfrevellegende: Vgl. RUBIN (s. Anm. 4), S. 33–48; JOANIE DEHULLU: L'Affaire des Billettes: une accusation de profanation d'hosties portée contre les juifs à Paris, 1290. In: *Bijdragen, tijdschrift voor filosofie en theologie*. 56/2 (1995), S. 135–139; FRIEDRICH LOTTER: Hostienfrevelvorwurf und Blutwunderfälschung bei den Judenverfolgungen von 1928 (»Rintfleisch«) und 1336–1338 (»Armleder«). In: *Fälschung im Mittelalter*, Bd. 5: Fingierte Briefe, Frömmigkeit und Fälschung, Realienfälschungen. Internationaler Kongreß der MGH, München 16–19. September, Hannover 1998 (MGH Schriften 33/5), S. 533–583; FRIEDRICH LOTTER: Die Judenverfolgung des »König Rintfleisch« in Franken um 1298. Die endgültige Wende in den christlich-jüdischen Beziehungen im Deutschen Reich des Mittelalters. In: *Zeitschrift für historische Forschung*. 15 (1988), S. 385–422.

dann das Heilige Sakrament und setzt damit ein Zeichen seiner Unzerstörbarkeit.[11] Das erschienene und sichtbare Blut verweist nicht auf die Transsubstantiation, sondern viel mehr auf die Juden als die fortwährenden Lästerer und Marterer des vergegenwärtigen Leibes Christi. Der jüdische Unglaube sei verantwortlich sowohl für die historische Kreuzigung, da die Juden in der biblischen Zeit Jesus nicht als den Messias angesehen hatten, als auch für die gegenwärtige Kreuzigung durch die Marterung des Heiligen Sakraments.[12]

Der erste dokumentierte Vorwurf einer Hostienentweihung war der Pariser Fall 1290, auch bekannt als *L'Affaire des Billettes*. Die zugrundeliegende antijüdische Erzählstruktur verbreitete sich in zwei Wellen in den deutschen Sprachraum, namentlich in den Rintfleisch- (1298) und den Armleder-Pogromen (1336–1338). In der Folge wurde die Legende des Hostienfrevels während des 14. und 15. Jahrhunderts mehrmals überall in Europa wiederholt.[13]

Die Transsubstantiationslehre wurde erst auf dem vierten Laterankonzil (1215) offiziell festgelegt. Sie besagt, dass Brot und Wein sich in der Feier der Eucharistie *substanziell* in das Blut und Leib Christi verwandeln. Obwohl die äußere und sichtbare Gestalt bzw. die Akzidenz[14] von Brot und Wein erhalten bleibt, wandelt sich deren Substanz vollständig in Blut und Leib Christi. Diese Wesensverwandlung ist für das physische Auge unsichtbar, da sie substanziell ist und die äußere Gestalt unberührt lässt.[15]

> Quod enim secundum naturam contingit in accidentibus, hoc secundum miraculum accidit in naturis. Est autem duplex conversio, substantialis videlicet et formalis. Nam sicut aliquando forma convertitur sine substantia, sic interdum substantia convertitur sine forma, nonunquam vtraq; cum altera. Substantia vero, quandoq; convertitur cum substantia. Quandoque convertitur in id quod erat, et non sit, vt panis in Eucharistiam, et tunc substantia convertitur sine forma.[16]

Gemäß der aristotelischen metaphysischen Theorie meint der Begriff *Substanz* ein nicht sinnlich wahrnehmbares Wesen. In diesem Sinne wäre »Substanz« das metaphysische Wesen eines Dinges im Unterschied zu dem Material, aus dem es tatsächlich besteht. Die individuellen Akzidentien können nicht ohne eine individuelle Substanz, die ihnen inhärent ist, existieren.[17] Akzidentien sind an ihre Substanz gebunden und können sich nicht von ihr lösen. In der Transsubstantiation verändert sich nur die Substanz, was der aristotelischen Theorie nicht widerspricht.

Die eucharistischen Wunder und Bluterscheinungen einer Hostienentweihung stellen ein Problem für die Transsubstantiationslehre dar, da sie implizieren, dass sich auch die Akzidentien und die Substanz von Brot und Wein der Eucharistie verwandeln könnten. Es kommt zu sichtbaren Bluterscheinungen aus einer konsekrierten Hostie heraus. Dieses erschienene Blut kommt der zeitgenössischen Interpretation gemäß aus dem substantiellen Leib Christi, welcher in der Substanz des Brotes liegt. Dieser Interpretation zufolge ist die wunderliche Erscheinung mit der Macht der Hostie und ihrer Unzerstörbarkeit verbunden. Nach der Erörterung dieses theologischen Problems ist es notwendig die Frage zu

---

11 Vgl. HARTMUT KÜHNE: ›Ich ging durchFeuer und Wasser...‹: Bemerkungen zur Wilnacker Heilig-Blut-Legende. In: *Theologie und Kultur. Geschichten einer Wechselbeziehung: Festschrift zum einhundertfünfzigjährigen Bestehen des Lehrstuhls für Christliche Archäologie und Kirchliche Kunst an der Humboldt-Universität zu Berlin*. Hrsg. von GERLINDE STROHMAIER-WIEDERANDERS. Halle 1999, S. 51–84. Für eine weitere wesentliche Referenz siehe das 6. Kapitel *A concern for Immutability*. In: CAROLINE WALKER BYNUMM: *Fragmentierung und Erlösung: Geschlecht und Körper im Glauben des Mittelalters*. Frankfurt am Main 1996; und das 3. Kapitel *Der Leib Christi im Spätmittelalter – Eine Erwiderung auf Leo Steinberg* (Ebd., S. 61–108).

12 Vgl. INNOZENZ III: *Innocentii Papae Hoc Nomine tertii, de sacro altaris mysterio, Libri Sex*. IV. Buch Kap. XX De Modo transsubstantiationis fol. 138r139v Lovanii, gedruckt von Hieronymum Wellaeum, 1566. Exemplar der BSB. Sig: P. lat. 842.

13 Vgl. LOTTER (s. Anm. 10). S. 385–422.

14 Akzidentien bestehen als die sichtbare Gestalt des Heiligen Sakraments. Am Gegenteil ist die Substanz die unsichtbare Gestalt der Eucharistie. Die Letzte wandelt sich in den Leib Christi.

15 PETER BROWE: *Die Eucharistie im Mittelalter: Liturgiehistorische Forschungen in kulturwissenschaftlicher Absicht*. Berlin 2015. Von Interesse ist hier insbesondere das Kapitel *Die scholastische Theorie der eucharistischen Verwandlungswunder* (Ebd., S. 251–263).

16 INNOZENZ III, (s. Anm. 12).

17 DOMINIKUS KRASCHL: Artefakte, Substanzen und Transsubstantiation. Ein Klärungsversuch. In: *Zeitschrift für katholische Theologie*. 134/2 (2012), S. [181]–[201], hier besonders S. 183.

stellen, wie das unsichtbare und substanzielle Blut Christi sichtbar werden kann.[18]

Die Frage, ob dieses wundersam erschienene Blut als eine sichtbare Vergegenwärtigung des Blutes Christi angesehen werden sollte, war in den gelehrten theologischen Debatten des Spätmittelalters sehr präsent. Zwischen dem 13. und 16. Jahrhundert wurde vor allem das Kernelement der Transsubstantiationslehre immer wieder vorgebracht, um Veränderungen des Heiligen Sakraments zu negieren. Demzufolge finde in der Weihung der Hostie keine äußere Verwandlung statt, sondern nur die Substanz von Brot und Wein werde zu Fleisch und Blut Christi. Im Sinne dieses Arguments zitierten die Erfurter Theologische Fakultät,[19] Jan Hus[20] und Nikolaus von Kues[21] oftmals die *Canones* des Transsubstantiationsdogmas aus dem 4. Laterankonzil und die Theorie Thomas von Aquin zu den eucharistischen Wundern.

Zur Beantwortung der oben gestellten Frage ist es wesentlich, einen Blick auf die Theorie des Thomas von Aquin zu werfen. Thomas zufolge gibt es zwei Arten von eucharistischen Wundern. Die erste Art des Wunders wird immer nur von einer Einzelperson wahrgenommen. In dieser Art von Erscheinung bleiben die Akzidentien des Brotes und Weines unverändert. Das Sinnbild der Veränderung oder eine wunderliche Erscheinung wird von Gott etwa durch eine Vision verdeutlicht, wie zum Beispiel die Vision Gregors des Großen nach der Hostienweihung (Gregorsmesse)[22].

In der zweiten Form findet eine sichtbare Veränderung statt. So auch in den Bluterscheinungen bei einer Hostienentweihung oder infolge der Zweifel gegenüber der realen Präsenz des Leibes. Obwohl diese Veränderung sichtbar ist, darf sie nicht als eine tatsächliche Gegenwart des Blutes Christi angesehen werden. Hier bezeichnet das Paradox der Multilokation Christi, dass Christus unmöglich zugleich leibhaftig im Himmel und an verschiedenen irdischen Orten sein kann.[23] Seine körperlichen Materien können nicht gleichzeitig an verschiedenen Orten sein.

Aus diesem Grund sollten solche sichtbaren Veränderungen in den Akzidentien der Hostie nicht als reale Gegenwart des wahren Blutes Christi interpretiert werden, sondern nur als wunderbare Bluterscheinungen in den sekundären Akzidentien der Eucharistie, die die Macht und Unzerstörbarkeit der Hostie unterstreichen. In diesem Sinne erklärt Thomas von Aquin, dass die Grundakzidentien der Hostie zwar nicht verändert würden, aber die sekundären Akzidentien des Brotes und Weines sich veränderten, das heißt ihre Formen, Farben, Gerüche und Geschmäcker nähmen das Aussehen von Fleisch, Blut oder einem Kind an.

---

18 Diese Frage wurde erst von Claudia Gärtner für die Analyse der Gregorsmesse gestellt: Vgl. CLAUDIA GÄRTNER: Die ›Gregorsmesse‹ als Bestätigung der Transsubstantiationslehre? In: *Das Bild der Erscheinung. Die Gregorsmesse im Mittelalter.* Hrsg. von ANDREAS GORMANS und THOMAS LENTES. Berlin 2007, S. 125–154, hier besonders S. 143.

19 Vgl. RUDOLF DAMERAU: *Das Gutachten der theologischen Fakultät Erfurt 1452 über ›Das heilige Blut von Wilsnak‹.* Marburg 1976.

20 JAN HUS, VÁCLAV FLAJŠHANS: *Spisy M. Jana Husi. 3, De sanguine Christi.* / Jan Hus; vydal Václav Flajšhans. Praha: Bursík: Vilímek, 1903. S. 26–37.

21 RUDOLF HAUBST: *Die Christologie des Nikolaus von Kues.* Bonn 1955, S. 295–303.

22 Die Vision der Gregorsmesse bildet ein übliches Thema der christlichen Kunst des 15. Jahrhunderts. In den letzten Jahren charakterisiert die Kunsthistoriographie solche Repräsentationen viel mehr als eine Verbildlichung der Erscheinung des Schmerzensmannes, welche eine Vision des Papstes während der Hostienweihung bilden, als eine dargestellte sichtbare Verwandlung der äußeren Gestalt des Heiligen Sakraments. Zur ausführlichen Erklärung zu einem Unterschied zwischen einer Vision, Erscheinung und ein eucharistisches Wunder bei dem Bildthema. Vgl. ESTHER MEIER: *Die Gregorsmesse: Funktionen eines spätmittelalterlichen Bildtypus.* Hier besonderes das Kapitel: Forschung und Begriffsgeschichte: von der »Erscheinung Gregorii« zur »Gregorsmesse«. S. 16-29.

23 BROWE (s. Anm. 15), S. 251–263.

Sternberger Hostienfrevel und die Wiederholung der Erzählstruktur des Hostienfrevels (1492)

Nach dieser Einführung wollen wir uns nun der Frage zuwenden, wie diese theologischen Probleme durch die Hostienentweihungslegende vermittelt wurden. Die Texte und Bilder verschiedener Inkunabeln zum Sternberger Hostienfrevel versetzen uns in die Lage, die theologischen Diskussionen über die Vergegenwärtigung des Blutes Christi in entweihten Hostien nachzuvollziehen. Dafür erörtern wir, wie im 15. Jahrhundert das Blut profanierter Hostien ausführlich von der Erfurter Theologischen Fakultät beschrieben wurde.

Der Sternberger Hostienfrevelfall war eines der ersten Ereignisse dieser Art, für die Druckmedien genutzt wurde, um Erzählungen über die historischen Ereignisse zu verbreiten. Einige Publikationen vermitteln Details des Sternberger Falles und seine Konsequenzen für die Judenverfolgung des 15. Jahrhunderts im deutschen Sprachraum.[24] »Als typisches Phänomen seiner Zeit war der Vorwurf für die Verbrennung von insgesamt 27 Menschen jüdischen Glaubens«[25] verantwortlich. Verschiedene Inkunabeln vermitteln eine Zusammenfassung der sogenannten *Urgicht*,[26] die am 29. August 1492 begann und erst am 24. Oktober 1492 endet.[27]

Dank der Analyse von Kristin Skottki wissen wir bereits, dass die hier erwähnten Inkunabeln möglicherweise im Laufe des Jahres 1493 entstanden. Da sie sich am Wortlaut der *Urgicht* orientieren, können sie nicht vor dem 24. Oktober 1492 gedruckt worden sein.[28] Skottki geht davon aus, dass der Hildesheimer Einblattdruck[29] das früheste Beispiel einer Publikation zum Sternberger Hostienfrevel sein muss, das bis heute erhalten ist. Alle weiteren gedruckten Bücher wurden erst später angefertigt. Dieser Einblattholzschnitt erwähnt, dass der Priester Peter Däne, einer der Hauptangeklagten des Prozesses, immer noch im Gefängnis saß. Folglich muss das Blatt zwischen dem 24. Oktober 1492 und dem 13. beziehungsweise 15. März 1493 gedruckt worden sein. Die Inkunabeln erwähnen weder die Strafe noch Peter Dänes Gefangenschaft.[30] Dies weist darauf hin, dass der Priester wahrscheinlich bereits tot war, als die Bücher gedruckt wurden. Es ist gleichfalls vorstellbar, dass die Wiegendrucke vor der Bestrafung Peter Dänes angefertigt wurden. Die heute noch erhaltenen dreizehn Exemplare[31] wurden in Lübeck, Bamberg, Köln,[32] Speyer[33] und Magdeburg gedruckt.

Vor einer textlichen und bildlichen Analyse der Inkunabeln ist es notwendig, den Sternberger Fall und die Entstehung einer Endfassung seiner Erzählereignisse, die durch die Bearbeitung der Aussagen der Angeklagten erfolgte, zu kontextualisieren. Der Aufbau dieser Erzählfolge basiert auf einer Beschreibung der *Urgicht*. Die Angeklagten mussten eine zuvor vorhandene Erzählstruktur des Hostienfrevels unter Folter wiederholen[34]. In Sternberg wurde das Narrativ allerdings nicht vollständig aus vergangenen Fällen übernommen. Einige Einzelheiten wurden aus dem Alltag der Gemeinde eingebaut. Dies bot den Einwohnern

---

[24] FRITZ BACKHAUS: Die Hostienschändungsprozesse von Sternberg (1492) und Berlin (1510) und die Ausweisung der Juden aus Mecklenburg und der Mark Brandenburg. In: *Jahrbuch für brandenburgische Landesgeschichte*. 39 (1988), S. 7–26.

[25] KRISTIN SKOTTKI: Sternberg 1492. Zur Genese eines Hostienfrevelprozesses. In: *Absichten, Pläne, Strategien: Erkundungen einer historischen Intentionalitätsforschung*. Hrsg von JAN-HENDRYK DE BOER und MARCEL BUBERT. Frankfurt am Main – New York 2018, S. 283–308, hier: S. 283.

[26] Die von Kristin Skottki aufgestellte Definition zur *Urgicht* lautet: »›Urgicht‹ (mittelhochdeutsch urgicht = Aussage, Bekenntnis) bezeichnet allgemein das endgültige, schriftlich festgehaltene Geständnis eines Delinquenten; im engeren Sinne bezeichnet es die Wiederholung beziehungsweise Bestätigung eines zunächst unter Folter (zeitgenössisch durch eine ›peinliche Befragung‹) hervorgebrachten Geständnis durch den Angeklagten.« (SKOTTKI (s. Anm. 25), S. 287).

[27] SKOTTKI (s. Anm. 25), S. 289.

[28] SKOTTKI (s. Anm. 25), S. 289.

[29] Vgl. GW M44011. Dieses Exemplar liegt in der Dombibliothek Hildesheim. Der Einblattdruck wurde nach dem Ende der Urgicht (24.10.1492) von Simon Koch in Magdeburg gedruckt.

[30] SKOTTKI (s. Anm. 25), S. 290.

[31] SKOTTKI (s. Anm. 25), S. 289. Für eine Beschreibung der heutigen Exemplare. Vgl. Anm. 41–45.

[32] Vgl. Anm. 44.

[33] GW M44005.

[34] Wie Ronnie Po-Chia Hsia argumentiert, mussten die Angeklagten des Trienter Ritualmordprozesses eine zuvor erfundene Erzählfolge unter Folter wiederholen. Vgl. RONNIE PO-CHIA HSIA. *Trent 1475: Stories of a Ritual Murder Trial*. New Haven 1992 S. 1–204. Hier besonders S. 43–44.

die Möglichkeit einer Rekonstruktion der Hostienfrevelerzählung, brachte den Vorwurf näher an sie heran und machte seine Bedeutung fassbar. So wurde ihnen sozusagen eine adaptierte Version für ihre eigene Wirklichkeit geboten.

Bevor ein Hostienfrevel- oder Ritualmordvorwurf in einer Gemeinschaft aufkam, waren deren Erzählstrukturen für die Bevölkerung nur durch eine mündliche oder textliche Tradition, die auf verschiedenen vergangenen Fällen basierte, zugänglich. Die angeblich *bösen* Juden der Gemeinde werden in der Rolle der Frevler des eucharistischen Körpers Christi dargestellt. Gleichzeitig erscheinen *schlechte* Christen als Akteure dieser Erzählfolge. Schließlich musste *jemand*, der in der Regel außerhalb der jüdischen Gemeinde stand, eine konsekrierte Hostie an die Ungläubigen verkauft haben.[35] Die Beschuldigung eines christlichen Nachbarn oder eines ortsansässigen Priesters diente als Erklärung, wie die Juden den Zugang zum Heiligen Sakrament erhalten hatten. Die narrative Struktur der Hostienentweihungslegende schafft eine heilsgeschichtlich präfigurierte Zeit,[36] welche in der Gegenwart eskaliert und einen Erwartungshorizont erzeugt: Die Gründung eines künftigen Pilgerortes als Triumph des Christentums über das Judentum[37].

Um die Entstehung der Endfassung der Erzählereignisse des Sternberger Hostienfrevelfalles nachvollziehen zu können, sei hier die chronologische Abfolge[38] der Ereignisse nachgezeichnet. Hiernach soll die Geschehnisfolge anhand der Historiographie und weiterer Quellen hernach ausführlich analysiert und diskutiert werden.

1. Die erste Version der Erzählung wurde in einem Vorwurf verbreitet, der im August 1492 in der Stadt Sternberg aufkam. Demzufolge sollten sich ein russischer und ein Sternberger Jude in Penzlin[39] mit einem Franziskanermönch getroffen haben, um einen Handel abzuschließen. Der Mönch, der auch Kaplan war, habe seine geistliche Kleidung gegen weltliche getauscht, um in den Besitz einer konsekrierten Hostie zu kommen. Diese große geweihte Schauhostie habe er dann den Juden gegeben. Zuvor hätten die Juden noch eine weitere kleine Hostie von einer christlichen Frau aus Teterow gekauft. Die Frevler hätten die beiden Hostien zu einer Christusfigur zusammengefügt und sie dann an Händen, Füßen und an der Seite mit Nadeln malträtiert.

    Als daraufhin das *wahrhaftige* Blut aus der Hostienfigur erschienen sei, seien die Juden aufgrund des eucharistischen Wunders erschrocken. Aus Furcht vor der Macht des Heiligen Sakraments hätten die Frevler beschlossen, die Wunderhostie an den Priester zu Sternberg zurückzugeben. Eine jüdische Frau soll beide Hostien in Tüchern gelegt und diesen mit den Worten: »Hir is dyn Got[40]« zurückgebracht haben. Aus Furcht habe der Priester die beiden Bluthostien auf dem Kirchhof vergraben. Letztendlich erklärte er gegenüber anderen Geistlichen, dass ihn ein Engel drei Mal im Schlaf besucht habe und ihm den Ort, an dem die Hostien vergraben waren, gezeigt habe. Ebenfalls verkündete der Priester, dass nur die Juden für die Hostienvergrabung verantwortlich gewesen sein könnten.

---

[35] Es gibt trotzdem ein paar Ausnahmen, in denen Juden selbst die Hostien aus der Sakristei geraubt haben sollen. Ein bekanntes Beispiel ist die Erzählung des Heiligengraber Falles (Vgl. DIRK SCHUMANN: Die Legendentafeln des Zisterzienserinnenklosters Heiligengrabe. In: *Von blutenden Hostien, frommen Pilgern und widerspenstigen Nonnen. Heiligengrabe zwischen Spätmittelalter und Reformation*. Hrsg. von FRIEDERIKE RUPPRECHT. Berlin 2005, S. 61–77, hier besonders S. 62).

[36] JOCHEN MECKE: Die Mimesis der Zeit im Prozess. In: *Das Ricœur-Experiment. Mimesis der Zeit in Literatur und Film*. Hrsg. von WOLFRAM AICHINGER und JÖRG TÜRSCHMANN. Tübingen 2009, S. 13–28. Hier besonderes S. 16; Vgl. PAUL RICŒUR: *Zeit und Erzählung, Bd. I Zeit und historische Erzählung*. München 1988.

[37] Für die Gründung neuer Kirchen anstelle vernichteter Synagogen: Vgl. J. M. MINTY: Judengasse to Christian Quarter. The Phenomenon of the Converted Synagogue in the Late Medieval and Early Modern Holy Roman Empire. In: *Popular religion in Germany, and Central Europe, 1400–1800*. Hrsg. von ROBERT W. SCRIBNER. London 1996, S. 58–86.

[38] Diese aufgebaute Geschehnisfolge basiert sich auf eine Auseinandersetzung folgender erwähnter Quellen und Aufsätze. Diese Stringenz diente einer Zusammenfassung der Etablierung der Endfassungsversion der Erzählung zur Sternberger Hostienfrevelbeschuldigung. Vgl. Anm. 1, 23, 40, 48, 49, 50, 50, 51, 52, 53, 56, 58.

[39] Penzlin befindet sich 100 km von Sternberg entfernt.

[40] Vgl. GEORG CHRISTIAN FRIEDRICH LISCH: Anhang zur Geschichte der Stadt Sternberg. Actenstücke zur Geschichte der Stadt Geschichte der Stadt Sternberg. Nr. 1: »Erstes Verhör der Juden über die Verspottung des Sacraments zu Sternberg (1492. Aug. 29). In: *Jahrbücher des Vereins für Mecklenburgische Geschichte und Altertumskunde*. 12 (1847), S. 257.

2. Die Vision des Priesters und das eucharistische Wunder sollten anschließend in einer Untersuchung überprüft werden. Bei der Ausgrabung der Hostien war eine Vielzahl von Adligen und Geistlichen aus der Region anwesend und die Hostien wurden in hölzernen Leuchter gefunden. Daraufhin wurden die Juden aus der lokalen Gemeinde und der Priester Peter Däne verdächtigt. Jedoch gelang den Hauptangeklagten, dem Juden Eleazar und dem Franziskanermönch die Flucht, noch bevor es zu einem Prozess kam.

3. Am 29. August 1492 wurde die erste *Urgicht* dokumentiert. Ihr Zweck war es, den Verkauf und Entweihung der Hostien aufzuklären und vor allem die genaue Rolle des Priesters Peter Däne bei der Tat aufzudecken.

4. Die Befragungen dauerten bis zum 22. Oktober 1492. Von Anfang an galt die Schuld des Priesters Peter Däne für den Hostienverkauf bereits als sicher. Schon zu Beginn des Prozesses gab er zu, dass er am 10. Juli tatsächlich zwei Hostien an die Juden für die Auslösung seines Kochtopfes verkauft hätte. Er beichtete ebenfalls, die Frau des Juden Eleazar hätte die Bluthostien am 21. August zusammen mit dem Kochtopf zurückgebracht.

5. Durch die Aussage von Eleazars Frau, die als erste Hauptzeugin des Hostienfrevels angesehen wurde, kamen weitere Details zu Tage. Zuerst sagte sie aus, dass ihr Mann vier geweihte Hostien erworben habe, von denen er zwei einem weiteren Juden mit Namen Jakob weitergegeben habe. Dann berichtete sie, dass die beiden Hostien mit Nadeln und Messern, deren genaue Zahl noch nicht berichtet wurde, geschändet worden seien. Bei ihrer letzten überlieferten Aussage gab sie an, dass die Hostienentweihung während der Hochzeit ihrer Tochter durchgeführt worden sei. Schließend beichtete sie, dass der besagte Jude Jakob über den Erwerb und die Entweihung der Hostie informiert war. Daraufhin wurde Jakob Hauptzeuge des Prozesses.

6. Während seiner Befragung gab Jakob an, dass die zweite Hostie tatsächlich von einem Mönch aus Penzlin gekauft worden sei. Hierbei wurde erstmals die Rolle des geflohenen Franziskanermönches angesprochen und dokumentiert. Da dieser zum Judentum habe konvertieren wollen, habe er bereits ein Jahr lang Kontakt zu den Juden gehabt. Zusammen mit den Juden Eleazar und Michael (Michol) habe er zwischen Ostern und Pfingsten eine konsekrierte Schauhostie an die Juden verkauft. Beide Hostien seien von drei Männern geschändet und mit Messern und Nadeln gestochen worden. Nach der Entweihung habe Eleazar sie in einen heißen Kochtopf geworfen. Als Grund für die Freveltat nannte Jakob, die Juden hätten mehr über die eucharistische Spezies erfahren wollen.

7. Bei der letzten Befragung Jakobs beschrieb er die Hostienentweihung ausführlich. Seine Aussagen dienten als Vorlage für die späteren bildlichen Darstellungen.

8. In der Folge der Befragungen von Jakob und der Frau Eleazars wurden weitere Juden der lokalen Gemeinde gezwungen, die bisher aufgebaute Version der Ereignisse zu bestätigen.

9. Am 22. Oktober 1492 endeten die Befragungen. Die dokumentierte *Urgicht* resultierte in einer Endfassung der Erzählung, die die Ereignisse erklären sollte. Diese letzte Version der Erzählereignisse besagt, dass die Juden zwischen Ostern und Pfingsten, in diesem Jahr dem 22. April und dem 10. Juni, die erste Hostie durch einen Mönch aus Penzlin bekommen hätten. Der Mitbeschuldigte Peter Däne gab am 10. Juli zu, eine zweite geweihte Hostie an die Juden verkauft zu haben. Beide Hostien wurden anschließend während der Hochzeit der Tochter Eleazars am 20. Juli mit drei Messern und Nadeln entweiht. Als die geweihten Brote im kochenden Wasser geworfen wurden, bluteten sie. Hernach brachte Eleazars Frau am 21. August die entweihten Hostien dem Priester zurück. Dieser entschloss sich, alles zu vergraben und das Wissen über den Vergrabungsort als Vision auszugeben.
10. Am 24. Oktober 1492 wurden 27 Menschen jüdischen Glaubens auf dem Judenberg nahe Sternberg umgebracht.
11. Der Franziskanermönch und der Jude Eleazar blieben flüchtig. Die Inkunabeln warnten ihr Publikum vor den beiden Hauptangeklagten, über die man vermutete, dass sie im Besitz von zwei weiteren geweihten Hostien waren und sich in einer jüdischen Gemeinde verstecken.
12. 246 Mecklenburgische Juden wurden über weitere gemeldete Hostienfrevel befragt. Danach wurden sie aus Mecklenburg vertrieben und die Herzöge haben ihre Vermögenswerter einkassiert.
13. Der Priester Peter Däne wurde am 13. oder 15. März 1493 in Rostock hingerichtet.

Der Priester Peter Däne berichtete am 21. August 1492 davon, dass Hostien auf dem ehemaligen Kirchhof, der an die Häuser der Juden in der Pastiner Strasse grenzte, vergraben seien.[41] Eine Woche später fand eine Wunderuntersuchung statt und einen hölzernen Leuchter mit den Bluthostien wurde ausgegraben. Bei der Freilegung waren die beiden Mecklenburger Herzöge Magnus II. und Balthasar von Mecklenburg, sowie der Markgraf Johann Cicero von Brandenburg, der Herzog von Pommern, Bogislaw X. und Herzog Heinrich I. zu Braunschweig und Lüneburg als Vertreter der weltlichen Macht anwesend. Die Vertreter der Geistlichkeit waren der Bischof von Ratzeburg, Johannes von Parkentin, der Bischof von Carmmin, Benedikt von Waldstein, der Bischof von Schwerin, Konrad Loste und der Erzbischof von Magdeburg, Ernst von Sachsen.[42] Schon allein die Präsenz der Adligen und des Hochklerus demonstriert die gesellschaftliche Bedeutung solcher Untersuchungen. Dies zeigt ein Interesse der Potentaten an einer territorialen und politischen Ordnung, für die offenbar die Vertreibung der Juden eine wichtige Voraussetzung war.

Eine ungeklärte Frage ist, wie der Priester Däne so schnell vom Ankläger zum Angeklagten der *Urgicht*[43] wurde. Ursache hierfür könnte die Art und Weise sein, wie der Vorwurf in Sternberg seinerzeit aufkam. In typischen Fällen meldeten Christen einen Hostienfrevel bei einem

---

[41] DAVID FRANCK: *Gründlicher und Ausführlicher Bericht Von denen durch die Jüden zu Sterneberg Anno 1492 zerstochenen und dahero Blutrünstigen Hostien*. Rostock 1721, S. 8; Vgl. SKOTTKI (s. Anm. 25), S. 285.

[42] KRISTIN SKOTTKI: Sternberg. In: *Pilgerspuren: Wege in den Himmel. Von Lüneburg an das Ende der Welt*. Lüneburg 2020, S. 325–326.

[43] Vgl. LISCH (s. Anm. 40) S. 256–257.

Priester. Häufig wurde dann ein Christ, der im Alltag mit Juden in Kontakt war, als verantwortlich für den Verkauf der Heiligen Hostien angesehen.[44] Im Sternberger Fall wurden, gemäß der letzten Version der Erzählung, die Schändung und Vergrabung zuerst von Peter Däne, also dem Priester selbst, gemeldet. Dabei nannte Peter Däne keinen bestimmten Hostienverkäufer. Da also keine schlechten Christen hierfür erwähnt wurden, war es eine logische Schlussfolgerung, ihn selbst als den Verkäufer anzusehen.

Dies zieht sich in die *Urgicht* der jüdischen Gemeinde hinein, die sich an der Erzählfolge der Hostienschändungslegende orientierte. Am Ende stand die letzte Version der Erzählereignisse, die in den Inkunabeln zu lesen ist. Diese erzählt, dass Peter Däne dem Juden Eleazar am 10. Juli 1492 zwei geweihte Hostien verkauft habe, eine große und eine kleine für einen ganzen Rheinischen Gulden[45] Auf der Hochzeit der Tochter Eleazars sei dann der Hostienfrevel begangen worden. Das Heilige und Gesegnete Sakrament sei mit Nadeln und mit drei Messern[46] mehrmals durchstochen worden. Nach der wundersamen Erscheinung des Blutes[47] sollen die Frevler sehr erschrocken sein, woraufhin die Frau Eleazars die Bluthostien zusammen mit einem Kochtopf Peter Däne zurückgab. Dieser entschied, die Wunderhostien zu vergraben und später der Gemeinde das Versteck zu melden. Diese Erzählfolge würde ebenfalls erklären, warum Priester Däne von Beginn an eine große Rolle für eine Rekonstruktion beziehungsweise Wiederholung der Erzählstruktur der Hostienschändung spielte. Einige Lücken der ersten Version der Erzählung entsprachen letztendlich dem damaligen Sternberger Kontext und dem untypischen Anfang des Vorwurfes. Sie wurden erst während des weiteren Verlaufes des Prozesses ausgefüllt.

Es existiere sechs verschiedene Inkunabel-Ausgaben zum Sternberger Hostienfrevel, von denen insgesamt 14 oder 15 Exemplare nachgewiesen sind. Die erhaltenen Inkunabeln zum Sternberger Hostienfrevel sind im Gesamtkatalog der Wiegendrucke in sechs verschiedene Ausgaben unterteilt. Diese sind: GW M44004,[48] GW M40005,[49] GW M44006,[50] GW M44007,[51] GW 44008[52] und GW 44009.[53] Die Ausgaben GW M44006, GW M44008 und GW 44009 wurden auf Niederdeutsch gedruckt. Die Inkunabel GW 44008 enthält einige Unterschiede in der Beschreibung des Hostienfrevels und der *Urgicht* gegenüber den anderen Drucken, stimmt aber mit der Erzählfolge der offiziellen und letzten

---

44 In einigen Fällen rauben schlechte Christen eine Hostie direkt aus einer Monstranz, so wie bei dem Knoblocher Hostienfrevel. Vgl. FRITZ BACKHAUS: Die Hostienschändungsprozesse von Sternberg (1492) und Berlin (1510) und die Ausweisung der Juden aus Mecklenburg und der Mark Brandenburg. In: *Jahrbuch für brandenburgischen Landesgeschichte*. 39 (1988), S. 7–26.

45 Vgl. LISCH (s. Anm. 40), S. 11.

46 Zuerst wurden nur Nadeln als Marterwerkzeuge erwähnt. Danach berichtete Eleazars Frau von Messern und zuletzt beichtete Jakob, dass drei Messer und Nadeln benutzt wurden, um die Hostien zu entweihen.

47 Für eine ausführliche Erklärung zu den Blutwunderuntersuchungen: Vgl. HARTMUT KÜHNE: Zur Konjunktur von Heilig-Blut-Wallfahrten im spätmittelalterlichen Mecklenburg. In: *Mecklenburg sacra*. 12 (2009), S. 76–115.

48 Es existiere zwei Exemplare. Eins liegt an der BSB Sig. Nr.: Inc. s. a. 1278. Eine weitere Kopie befindet sich an der Haag KglB. Sig. Nr.: KW 232 F 46. Dieses Buch wurde in Bamberg von Heinrich Petzensteiner und Johann Sensenschmidt gedruckt. ISTC is00790100.

49 Zwei Exemplare liegen in der UB Basel Sig. Nr. (UBH Ai II 22b:4) und in UB Frankfurt am Main Sig. Nr.: Inc. oct. 298. Die Ausgabe wurde in Basel von Jakob Wolff gedruckt. ISTC is00790200.

50 Das einzige Exemplar liegt in der Wissenschaftlichen Bibliothek der Stadt Trier. Sig. Nr. 254. Es wurde wahrscheinlich in Köln gedruckt. Christine Mittlmeier argumentiert, dass die Zuweisung zu Ludwig von Renchen, Köln vermutlich falsch ist (vgl. CHRISTINE MITTLMEIER: *Publizistik im Dienste: spätmittelalterliche und frühneuzeitliche Flugschriften und Flugblätter zu Hostienschändungen*. Frankfurt am Main 2000, S. 161; Siehe auch: JOACHIM SCHÜLING: *Der Drucker Ludwig von Renchen und seine Offizin: ein Beitrag zur Geschichte des Kölner Buchdrucks*. Wiesbaden 1992. (Buchwissenschaftliche Beiträge aus dem Deutschen Bucharchiv München 41), Druck Nr. 17. ISTC is00790220.

51 Zwei Kirchenbibliotheken in Brandenburg und Wittbrietzen und ein Ex. eventuell in einer Braunschweiger Privatsammlung. Ein weiteres Exemplar befindet sich in SB PK. Sig. Nr.: Inc. 1494/10. Diese Bücher wurden von Simon Koch in Magdeburg gedruckt. ISTC is00790150.

52 Es gibt zwei Faksimile-Versionen, obwohl kein originales Exemplar vorhanden ist. Die erste Version wurde in Wien 1889 gedruckt. *Sterneberch. Wan den bosen ioden volget hyr eyn gheschicht*. Wien, Antiquariat Gilhofer & Ranschburg, 1889. Eine spätere Version wurde 2009 in Arizona publiziert. Vgl. *Sterneberch. Wan den bosen ioden volget hyr eyn gheschicht* Hrsg. J. Owens Arizona, Thorn Books, 2009. ISTC is00790260. Die Besonderheiten dieses Buches erlauben eine kritische Nachfrage zu seiner Identifikation als Inkunabel.

53 Fünf Exemplare sind in öffentlichen Sammlungen vorhanden. In der SB PK, Sig. Nr.: Inc. 1496/2, StB Braunschweig, Sig. Nr.: Camman C 57 (4°), UB Hamburg, Sig. Nr.: AC IX, 96., B. des Ratsgymnasiums Osnabrück, UB Princeton, Sig. Nr. 2021-0004N exi. Diese Ausgabe wurde in Magdeburg von Simon Koch gedruckt. ISTC is00790250.

Erzählversion, wie sie auch in den anderen Wiegendrucken enthalten ist, überein. Jedes Exemplar ist mit einem Holzschnitt illustriert, der die Hostienschändung darstellt.

In allen vier Szenen [Abb. 1–6] sieht der Betrachter einen Tisch, auf dem das Heilige Sakrament entweiht wurde,[54] sowie drei Messer, die als die Marterungswerkzeuge dienten. Sie stellen eine Anspielung auf die Passionswerkzeuge dar. Um die Frage zu beantworten, wie diese bildliche Repräsentation konzipiert wurde, konzentrieren wir uns auf die beiden Verhörprotokolle des 29. August und 22. Oktober sowie die aus ihnen folgende letzte Version der Erzählung und Zusammenfassung der Urgicht, wie die Inkunabeln sie uns vermitteln. Somit soll verdeutlicht werden, welcher Teil der letzten Erzählversion schließlich für den Leser beziehungsweise Betrachter bildlich dargestellt wurde. Weiterhin stelle ich die Frage, ob die Bluterscheinung des Hostienfrevels als eine Vergegenwärtigung des Blutes Christi interpretiert werden konnte. Hierfür analysiere ich im Anschluss, wie dieses Blut in den Inkunabeln und Verhörprotokollen beschrieben wurde und wie der Humanist Hartmann Schedel in seiner berühmten Weltchronik über den Sternberger Fall berichtete.

Anfang und Ende des Verhörprotokolls und die Entstehung der Endfassung der Erzählereignisse der Inkunabeln zwischen dem 29. August 1492 und 24. Oktober 1492

Zwei Verhörprotokolle wurden 1847 in den Jahrbüchern des Vereins für Mecklenburgische Geschichte und Altertumskunde veröffentlicht. Dort finden wir eine Transkription der originalen Blätter.[55] Kristin Skottki stieß in ihrer ausführlichen Analyse des Sternberger Hostienfrevels auf einen Umstand, den sie als »Rekonstruktionsschwierigkeiten«[56] bezeichnet. Die Version Lischs,[57] wurde in ein erstes und zweites Verhör aufgeteilt. Diese fanden am 29. August und am 22. Oktober 1492 statt.[58] Der Hildesheimer Einblattdruck gilt als die älteste noch erhaltene Version des zweiten Verhörs. Eine weitere Transkription des zweiten Protokolls, die von einer alten Holztafel im Rathaus zu Sternberg stammt, ist in Michael Guntzmers Buch *Kurzer Bericht von denen zum Sterneberge*[59] zu finden.

[54] Die Tischplatte, auf der die Hostien angeblich entweiht wurden, ist bis heute in der Stadtkirche St. Maria und St. Nikolaus in Sternberg ausgestellt. Sie wird von Caroline Walker Bynum als eine Kontaktreliquie charakterisiert. Da dies jedoch die Berührung eines Heiligen voraussetzt und zudem keine Bedeutung für die Sternberger Wallfahrt hatte, kann dies ausgeschlossen werden. Vgl. CAROLINE WALKER BYNUM: Bleeding Hosts and their Contact Relics in Late Medieval Northern Germany. In: *The Medieval History Journal.* 7,2 (2004), S. 227–241; CHRISTINE MAGIN: »6.3.a Mutmaßliche Tischplatte des vermeintlichen Hostienfrevels aus der Heilig-Blut-Kapelle der Stadtkirche Sternberg« In: *Pilgerspure: Wege in den Himmel/ Von Lüneburg an das Ende der Welt.* Lüneburg 2020. S. 329. Als weitere Kontaktreliquien fand der Besucher einen Stein mit Fußabdrücken, den Kochtopf, die Nadeln und schließlich die Bildtafel im Rathaus. Alle diese Objekte sollen den Gläubigen die Marterung darstellen (vgl. HONEMANN, S. 195).

[55] Details zum originalen Dokument berichtet Lisch: »Nach dem öfter während des Schreibens corrigirten Original-Concept von einer bekannten gleichzeitigen Canzleihand auf einem halben Bogen Papier in großherzogl. Geh. u. Haupt-Archive zu Schwerin. Ohne Zweifel ist dies das Concept des in Gegenwart der Herzöge gehaltenen ersten Verhörsprotocolls. Das Blatt ist in Octav zusammengefaltet gewesen und daher die Schrift am Ende sehr abgescheuert. – Von der Hand des Canzlers Caspar von Schöneich aus den ersten Zeiten seiner Amtsführung steht auf der Rückseite die Registratur: ›Von dem heiligen Sacraments zum Sternberg‹ – Das Datum dieses Protocolls ist wahrscheinlich des 29. Aug. also der Tag der Enthauptung S. Johannis des Täufers, da der Tag ›Johannis baptistae im Sommer‹ genannt wird, zur Unterschreibung von Johannis b. T. Geburtsfest am 24. Junius«. LISCH (s. Anm. 40), S. 257–258.

[56] SKOTTKI, (s. Anm. 25) S. 301–304.

[547] Skottki geht davon aus, dass Lischs Version aus einem Dokument stammt, das eine Transkription der Abschrift einer Holztafel hatte. »Da Ihr Wortlaut mit der von Michael Gutzmer überlieferten Abschrift des Holztafel aus dem Sternberger Rathaus überstimmt.« Vgl. SKOTTKI (s. Anm. 25), S. 289. Dennoch stimmen Lischs und Gutzmers Versionen erst bei dem zweiten Verhörprotokoll vom 22.11.1492 überein (Vgl. Anm. 40). Das erste Protokoll vom 29.08. wurde nicht in Gutzmers Transkription erwähnt, das heißt es wurde nicht bei den Abschriften der Holztafel verfasst. Eine Erklärung ergibt sich aus dem Umstand, dass in der Holztafel – wie bei den Inkunabeln – erst die letzte und offizielle Geschichte der Ereignisse vermittelt wurde. Daher wurde die anfängliche Version der Erzählung des ersten Verhörprotokolls nicht erwähnt. Ein Aspekt, den ich zur Erklärung der Entstehung der offiziellen Erzählversion später ausführlich analysieren werde. In einem großen Stadtbrand verbrannte im Jahre 1659 die Holztafel (Vgl. SKOTTKI (s. Anm. 25), S. 288). Für die Transkiption der Holztafel aus dem Jahr 1628 vgl. MICHAEL GUNTZMER: *Kurzer Bericht von denen zum Sterneberge für der Stadt aufm Juden-Berge verbrannten Juden: aus dem publicirten Historien, aus der verbrannten Juden eigenen hierbey angehängten peinlichen Bekändtnüssen und aus der mündlichen Relation alter lebendiger Leute zusammengebracht.* Güstrow: Johann Jäger 1628. S. 10–12.

[58] LISCH (s. Anm. 40), S. 256–260.

[59] MICHAEL GUNTZMER (s. Anm. 57), S. 10–12.

Die hier diskutierte Vermutung würde einen Teil der Widersprüche zwischen dem ersten erwähnten Hostienhandel des Penzliner Mönchs mit dem Juden Eleazar und der späteren Rolle des Priesters Peter Däne als Hostienverkäufer erklären. Weiterhin erkannte Skottki die wesentliche und fragwürdige Rolle des Priesters Peter Däne als wahrscheinlichen Urheber des Vorwurfs.⁶⁰ Dies ist eine Rolle, die erst in den Inkunabeln deutlicher identifizierbar ist.⁶¹ Dieser Punkt kann uns einige weitere Erklärungen zum Sternberger Fall liefern.

Der Hostienfrevelvorwurf war eine verbreitete und berühmte Erzählung im Westeuropa des ausgehenden 15. Jahrhunderts. Dementsprechend waren die Angeklagten fähig seine Erzählstruktur während des Prozesses nachzuahmen. Sie mussten unter Folter die Erzählfolge solcher Entweihung wiederholen und bestätigen. Dieses Narrativ wurde trotzdem nicht vollständig aus vorangegangenen Fällen übernommen, sondern durch einige Details des Alltages der Gemeinde ausgebaut und adaptiert.

Die Inkunabeln wurden nicht vor dem 24. Oktober gedruckt, da alle Ausgaben die Strafe der Juden erwähnen. Dies ist wichtig, um ihre letzte Version der Erzählung der Ereignisse zu verstehen. Das Protokollverhör zeigt, wie sich die erste Version der Beschreibung der Ereignisse zum Hostienfrevel zu Sternberg zwischen dem 29. August und dem 22. Oktober 1492 verändert hatte. Im ersten Teil des Protokolls wurden untypischerweise keine Namen der Akteure genannt, dennoch sind einige Elemente der endgültigen Version der Erzählung zu erkennen.

Nun ist es notwendig die Endfassung der Erzählereignisse kritisch zu hinterfragen. Sie war nicht nur ein Versuch, die vorgezeichnete Erzählstruktur des Hostienfrevelvorwurfs zu einer fassbaren Erzählfolge in der Gegenwart aufzubauen, sondern sollte auch eine letzte bzw. offizielle Version etablieren, die als Erklärung des Blutwunders dienen und spätere Erinnerungsorte rechtfertigen konnte. Kristin Skottki erkannte, dass die Texte der Inkunabeln mit den Aussagen der *Urgicht* offensichtlich in Zusammenhang stehen. Vor allem die letzte Fassung der angeblichen Ereignisse zu Sternberg ist mit dem zweiten Verhörprotokoll vom 22. Oktober 1492 grundsätzlich vergleichbar.

Die Version Lischs der Urgicht lautet: »Anno domini M.CCCCXCII amme daghe Seuery vnde Seueryny (Oct. 22) heben ápenbar de quadeen, bosen yoden sundèrghen vorvolghers der hylighen crystenheyt durch ere bôsheyt.« In GW M44009 liest man: »Item am tag Seuerini ym tzweundneuntzigsten iare der myndern tzal haben offenbar dy verstocken vnd bösen Juden sunderlich vervolger der heyligen Christenheyt«.⁶² Siehe auch im GW 40008: »Int iaer vnses herẽ Dusentveerhunderttwevndnegentich, an deme dage sunnte Seueri vnde Seuerun hebben de bosen quaden vñ snoden yoden sunderges de hilligen cristenheyt dorch ere bosheyt.«⁶³

---

60 Hier betrachte ich die Rolle des Priesters Peter Däne als wesentlich für die Analyse der Beschreibung des Prozesses und seines Anfanges. Vor allem wurde Däne bereits im ersten Verhörprotokoll vom 29.08.1492 erwähnt. Auch wenn er nicht allein der Auslöser war, hatte er einen wesentlichen Anteil an der ersten Verbreitung in der Stadt Sternberg. Dies erklärt, weshalb er von Anfang an als Schuldiger des Hostienverkaufes galt (Vgl. SKOTTKI (s. Anm. 25), S. 285). Bezüglich der Entstehung des Korneuburger Falles (1302) hält die Historiographie es für wahrscheinlich, dass auch hier der Urheber des Vorwurfs ein Priester war. Bischof Wernhard von Passau (1285–1313) und der Magistrat Ambrosius von Heiligenkreuz organisierten eine Kommission und Befragung zu diesem Fall. Die Befragung zur Überprüfung des eucharistischen Wunders umfasste 21 Zeugen. Der vor Ort ansässige Priester Friedrich spielte eine große Rolle für die Verbreitung der Beschuldigung gegen den Juden Zerkelin. Ein Bäcker behauptete, durch eine Vision erfahren zu haben, wo die auf drei Teile zerteilte Bluthostie liege. Die wiedergefundene Hostie wurde angeblich von dem Priester Friedrich zusammen mit etwa 200 Menschen in die Kirche zurückgebracht und als Reliquie verehrt. Nach sechs Jahren schrieb Ambrosius von Heiligenkreuz einen Traktat zu seiner eigenen Rechtfertigung. Zusammen mit dem Bischof von Passau urteilte Ambrosius, dass der Priester, der der erste Zeuge der damaligen Kommission gewesen war, auch der Verfasser des Hostienfrevelvorwurfs gewesen sein musste. Ambrosius schrieb, dass ein Priester zum Bischof von Passau gekommen sei und sich als Autor des Vorfalls zu erkennen gegeben habe. Er habe selbst eine nicht geweihte Oblate mit dem Blut eines Ziegenbocks befleckt und in das Haus des Juden geworfen, um den Vorwurf auszulösen (Vgl. BIRGIT WIEDEL und EVELINE BRUGGER (Hrsg.): Regesten zur Geschichte der Juden in Österreich im Mittelalter Bd. 1: Von den Anfängen bis 1338. Innsbruck 2009, S.123–124; WINFRED STELZER: Am Beispiel Korneuburg. Der angebliche Hostienfrevel österreichischer Juden von 1305 und seine Quellen. In: *Österreich im Mittelalter. Bausteine*, S. 323–324). Zu einer späteren Quelle für die die Erzählung des Korneuburger Falles: Vgl. ANONYM: *»Ausführlich- und eigentlicher Bericht der ... Histori, welche sich bald nach Anfang des dreyzehenden christlichen Saeculi ... zu Corneuburg in eines Judens Behausung ... mit dem – Sacrament des Altars hat zugetragen«* gedruckt bey Gregor Kurzböck/ Univ. Buchdr. in den Bognergassen, Wien 1746. Privatbesitz des Autors. Ein weiteres Exemplar ist in der ÖNB vorhanden. Sig. Nr.: 306.295-A Alt-Rara.

61 GW M40007, fol. 2r–3r.
62 GW M44007, fol. 3r.
63 GW M40008, fol. 1r.

Sprachlich ist das zweite Exemplar Lischs Version näher als das erste. Den beiden Wiegendrucken ist das wesentliche Datum, der Severinstag am 22. Oktober, gemeinsam. Nach dem ersten Verhörprotokoll bildet sich aus der Erzählung in der letzten Version eine zusammengefasste Ereignisfolge heraus, in der die Namen der Akteure erwähnt sind. Erst danach wurde diese spätere Version Erzählung durch die Inkunabeln vermittelt.

Die Historiographie verließ sich oftmals auf diese letzte Version der Erzählung. Als Grundlage für weitere kritische Fragen nahm sie bis heute diese offizielle und letzte Zusammenfassung als Beginn der Vorwurfsverbreitung an, ohne zu berücksichtigen, ob die Erzählfolge sich während des Prozesses verändert hätte. Der erste Versuch, gegen diese historiographische Tendenz anzugehen, war sicherlich der Aufsatz von Kristin Skottki. Auch hier soll versucht werden, dem Ursprung der Erzählungen über den Sternberger Hostienfrevel auf andere Weise auf den Grund zu gehen.

Es ist eine Tatsache, dass es sich beim ersten Teil der *Urgicht* in der Version Lischs um den Anfang des Prozesses handelt. Bei der Version Lischs handelt es sich um eine im 19. Jahrhundert angefertigte Transkription der originalen Quelle.[64] Diese ungewöhnliche Version besagt, dass ein Jude aus Russland zusammen mit anderen Juden nach Penzlin gegangen sei. Dort hätten sie sich mit einem Mönch des grauen Ordens, also einem Franziskaner, getroffen. Der Ordensmann sei in weltlicher Verkleidung einer Hostie habhaft geworden und habe die große konsekrierte Schauhostie bei diesem Treffen verkauft. Bereits zuvor hätten dieselben Juden eine kleine Hostie von einer christlichen Frau aus Teterow gekauft. Diese Grundlagen des Heiligen Sakraments hätten die Juden in der Mitte geteilt und eine kleine gebackene Figur Christi mit Händen, Körper und Füßen für die geplante Schändung geschaffen.[65]

Weiter heißt es, dass die Frevler gleich danach beide konsekrierten Hostien in die Stadt Sternberg gebracht hätten, um diese bei einer Hochzeitsfester oder dem Laubhüttenfest[66] zu martern. So hätten sie dann auch das Heilige Sakrament in ihren Händen und in ihren Füssen mit Nadeln[67] verwundet, bis »dat blot wärliken[68]« daraus floss. Aus der Schauhostie wurde an der Seite ein Stück herausgeschnitten und sie wurde mit Nadeln gestochen bis das wahrhaftige Blut aus der Seitenwunde der eucharistischen Spezies hervortrat: »warafftig blot dar vth der syden der ostien, so die mit natelen gesteken wart, warafftich blot gesprungen is«[69].

Es wird weiter berichtet, dass die Juden nach dem eucharistischen Wunder misstrauisch und ängstlich geworden seien. In Todesangst habe sich schließlich eine jüdische Frau entschlossen, beide Hostien in ein Tuch zu legen und sie so dem lokalen Priester zu Sternberg zu übergeben. Bei der Übergabe habe sie zu ihm gesagt »Hir is dyn got«[70]. Selbst in Furcht habe der Geistliche die Bluthostien im Kirchhof vergraben. Derselbige Priester berichtete den anderen Klerikern von einer Vision, in der ein Geist[71] ihm in Zeichen angedeutet habe, wo die profanierten Hostien lagen. So wurden die Ereignisse allen Einwohnern der

---

64 Vgl. LISCH (s. Anm. 40), S. 256–257. Die originale Quelle ist im Landeshauptarchiv Schwerin vorhanden: Landeshauptarchiv Schwerin: Bestand 2.12-3/4-2 Sig. 11105 Hostie (Abendmahlsbrot).

65 Dies baut eine engere Verbindung mit dem Bild der fünf Wunden Christi auf. Eine weitere Diskussion des Themas folgt. Vgl. Anm. 101, 102, 103 und 104. Skottki erwähnt ebenfalls diese Assoziation. Vgl. SKOTTKI (s. Anm. 22), S. 301.

66 Vgl. SKOTTKI (s. Anm. 25), S. 302.

67 Scheinbar wurde dann das Messer erst später beim zweiten Verhörprotokoll als Marterungswerkzeug des Hostienfrevels erwähnt. LISCH (s. Anm. 38), S. 269–260.

68 LISCH (s. Anm. 40), S. 257.

69 LISCH (s. Anm. 40), S. 257.

70 LISCH (s. Anm. 40), S. 257.

71 Im ersten Verhörprotokoll wurde der genaue Ort durch einen Geist mitgeteilt. Erst in den folgenden Verhörprotokollen trat der Engel an diese Stelle.

Das Blut Christi und die blutenden Hostien

Stadt bekannt. Schließend behauptete Peter Däne, dass eine solche Tat nur von Juden ausgeführt worden sein könnte. Damit stimmte er mit der in den Inkunabeln dargestellten finalen Version überein: »vñ haben dem vorgemeltem her Peter gesagt woe doch das heilige Sacrament an di stat kũmen sei. Do antwort er vñ sprach nach dem das die zwu hostien also blutig zu stochẽ gefunden worden sint muß võ nymãt dan võ den iuden dahin kõmen sein.«[72]

Eine alternative Interpretation dieser Erzählung, in der Priester Däne nicht Urheber dieses Vorwurfs ist, ist schwer vorstellbar. Es ist wahrscheinlich, dass er die Hostien selbst im Kirchhof vergraben hat. Um eine vollständige Geschichte zu erzählen, meldete er, dass die Hostien durch die lokalen Juden und einen russischen Juden[73] einem franziskanischen Mönch aus Penzlin und einer einfachen Christin aus Teterow abgekauft worden seien. Das Heilige Sakrament wurde dann mit dem Plan nach Sternberg gebracht, bei einer jüdischen Zeremonie einen Hostienfrevel zu begehen. Der Penzliner Mönch und der Hauptfrevler Eleazar flohen. Von dieser Flucht ist in einer späteren Version am Ende des Inkunabeltextes zu lesen. Die »einfache« Frau aus Teterow wurde unterdessen im zweiten Verhörprotokoll vom 22. Oktober 1492, und in der offiziellen und letzten Erklärung der Ereignisse, nicht mehr erwähnt:[74] »Item syt der zeyt hat sich sein gnade bevleissigt vnd der vbeltettigen Jüden noch. vi. vberkomẽ die auch des feureß sterben solten. vnd vil der schuldigen Juden mitsambt dem verleugneten Munich sein nach der marck vñ furter nach Nüremberg vnd Venedig yn willen zu flyhen.«[75]

Der Priester Peter Däne schuf die Schulderzählung einer Hostienentweihung, die zunächst auf einer Vision beruhte. Dann wurde ein Mönch aus Penzlin und der Jude Eleazar hinzugefügt, ohne dass diese zunächst namentlich erwähnt zu werden. Die Tatsache, dass der Mönch als flüchtiger Hostienverkäufer erst in der späteren Version der Erzählung erwähnt wurde, lässt den Priester Peter von Anfang verdächtig erscheinen. Wie erfuhr Peter Däne vor allen anderen von dem genauen Ort, an dem die Hostien vergraben lagen? Die von ihm gemeldete Vision galt auch zeitgenössisch nicht als ausreichende Erklärung, sondern eher als eine entlarvte Lüge, mit der er sich vor der Todesstrafe hatte retten wollen. Bereits am Ende des ersten Verhörprotokolls vom 29. August 1492 können wir lesen: »Item na vermeldinge dessuluen presters hefft die vorgegeuen, wo em bynnen der nacht eyn geyst to gekamen is vnde van der orsake wegen des sacramentes eyn warteyken gegeuen[76]«.

Die unglaubwürdige Vision und die Abwesenheit des Franziskaners und des Juden Eleazars,[77] also der beiden Hauptangeklagten, erklären, warum der Vorwurf gegen den Priester, die Hostien vergraben zu haben, sich schnell zum Vorwurf des Hostienverkaufs wandelte. Um diese Auslegung der Ereignisse offiziell festzulegen, musste die Version durch die Aussage der Angeklagten wiederholt werden. Somit wird der erste und unvollständige Vorwurf, der in dem ersten Verhörprotokoll vom 29. August 1492 zu finden ist, besser erklärt.

Die Befragungen, orientierten sich, nachdem die reine Geistervision verworfen war, rasch an der Frage, wer die Hostie an Eleazar verkauft

---

72 GW M44004, fol. 2r. Exemplar der BSB. Sig: Inc. Sa. 1278.

73 LISCH (s. Anm. 40), S. 256.

74 LISCH (s. Anm. 40), S. 258-260.

75 GW M44005, fol. 4v.

76 LISCH (s. Anm. 40), S. 257

77 Beide Akteure wurden nicht mehr in der Zusammenfassung der *Urgicht* erwähnt.

hatte. Erst danach zielten sie auf eine ausführliche Beschreibung des Frevels. Schon bevor die Aussagen der Angeklagten in den Inkunabeln präsentiert werden konnten, lesen wir, wie Eleazars Frau berichtet haben soll, wer ihrem Mann die konsekrierten Hostien verkauft hatte: »*Uppe dusse wort vñ vornemen der ouersten iß Eleazarß wyff geuenklich geset worden welcke ein sunderlike vorgiftige slange yegē der Cristenheyt gewest iß vñ gevraget vme de gescheste Alßo hest se gemeldet den her Peter oben vñ vp ohn bekant dat he on de twe hostien vorkoft het.*«[78]

Diese Vermutung würde gleichfalls erklären, warum es zwei Versionen der letzten und offiziellen Erzählung der Ereignisse zu geben scheint.[79] In der ersten Version verkaufte der Priester Peter Däne zwei geweihte Hostien zu Zwecke der Auslösung seines Kochtopfes.[80] Dafür habe er die Hostien auf dem Allerheiligenaltar geweiht. Ebendiese geweihten Hostien verwendete nach der ersten Version der Jude Eleazar auf einem Schweißtuch am 10. Juli für einen Hostienfrevel.

Die Hostien wurden mit drei Messern und Nadeln[81] entweiht. Sobald jedoch das Blut, welches in dieser neuen Version nicht mehr das wahrhaftige Blut der ersten Version war, herausgeflossen sei, hätten die Juden Angst bekommen und Eleazars Frau habe sie schließlich Peter Däne zurückgegeben. Dieser habe die Hostie aus Furcht auf dem Kirchhof vergraben und meldete den anderen Geistlichen seine Geschichte, die er mit einer Vision erklärte. In der zweiten Version hatte Eleazar, sowie die Juden Michael und Jakob, die später ebenfalls Angeklagte wurden, beinahe ein Jahr lang Kontakt mit einem Penzliner Mönch, der vorgehabt habe, zum Judentum zu konvertieren. Dafür verkaufte dieser zwischen Ostern, am 22. April, und Pfingsten, am 10. Juni, eine in zwei Teile zerteilte konsekrierte Schauhostie an die Juden.

Dennoch kann diese von Kristin Skottki aufgestellte Einteilung der Endfassung der Erzählung der Ereignisse in zwei Versionen allein die Rolle des geflohenen Mönchs und der christlichen Frau nicht erklären. Die spätere Erklärung der Rolle des Mönches im zweiten Verhörprotokoll sollte nicht als eine alternative letzte Version der Ereignisse interpretiert werden. Der geflohene Mönch taucht erst wieder in der Aussage Jakobs auf, als dieser zu einem Hauptangeklagten des Prozesses wurde. Wichtig ist, dass der Mönch gleichzeitig mit dem Käufer der Hostie, dem Juden Eleazar, floh. Daher wurde Eleazars Frau mehrmals zu Beginn des Prozesses erwähnt und wurde zunächst, als die erste Hauptzeugin der ganzen Tat angesehen. Doch gab sie an, dass ein gewisser Jude namens Jakob ebenfalls über die Schändung Bescheid wusste. Dieser Moment gilt als wesentlicher Wendepunkt des Verlaufes der Befragung, welcher auf den Inkunabeln identifizierbar ist: »*Item furder bekant daß verflucht weyb/ daß Eleazar tzwo hostien hat mit ym hynweg genommen/ eyn grosse vnd ein klyne/ Alß daß Jacob wol bewust sey.*«[82]

Erst danach tauchte der Mönch in Jakobs Aussage wieder in der Rolle des Hostienkäufers auf. Daher sollte sie nicht als zweite Version der Erzählung angesehen werden, sondern nur als späterer Erklärungsversuch für die Rolle des geflohenen Mönches. Zu Anfang scheint der Mönch ein wesentliches Element der Erzählung gewesen zu sein, weshalb

---

78 GW M44009, fol. 2v–3r.

79 Kristin Skottki geht davon aus, dass die letzte Beschreibung der Ereignisse in zwei Versionen aufgeteilt werden kann. Vgl. SKOTTKI (s. Anm. 25), S. 285–286; HONEMANN (s. Anm. 1), S. 188.

80 Weitere Details wie z. B. die Geliebte Peter Dänes, die an Trinksucht leiden und die die Besitzerin des Kochtopfs gewesen sein soll, ist nicht in der ersten Urgichtversion oder deren Zusammenfassung in den Inkunabeln zu finden. Sie wurde erst in späteren Werken aufgenommen. Bei der ersten offiziellen Geschichte der Ereignisse wurde lediglich die Auslösung eines Kochtopfs erwähnt. NIKOLAUS MARSCHALK: *Res a iudaeis perfidissimis in monte Stellarum gesta: ad illustres príncipes Hinricum: et Albertum germanos: duces Megapolenses inclytos: ab egregio viro Nicolao: Marscalco: Thurio: LL: et Canon doctore nuper verissime scripta: obiterque miracula inde facta: et perfidia iudaeorum máxima Rostock*, 1512 UB Rostock Sig. MK-12246.7 fol. 3r.; HONEMANN (s. Anm. 1), S. 188.

81 Zuerst wurden Nadeln als Marterwerkzeuge der Sternberger Hostienentweihung genannt. Im zweiten Verhörprotokoll wurden gemäß Jakobs Aussage drei Messer hinzugefügt.

82 GW M44007, fol. 3v.–4r.

er als Akteur im zweiten Protokoll wiedererwähnt wurde. Unterdessen wurde die einfache christliche Frau aus Teterow weiterhin nicht mehr genannt.

Wahrscheinlich übernahm Peter Däne zu Beginn des Prozesses die Rolle der Frau, die die zweite konsekrierte Hostie an die Juden verkaufte. Es ist bedeutsam, dass es von Anfang bis zum Ende des Prozesses wichtig war, zwei Hostienverkäufer zu erwähnen. Die Frau wurde dabei wahrscheinlich nicht vergessen, sondern durch Peter Däne, einen passenderen Händler, ersetzt. Schließlich wusste dieser bereits am Anfang, wo sich die beschädigten Hostien befanden. Diese Lücke in der ersten und unvollständigen Version des ersten Protokolls wurde durch die Aussage Jakobs erklärend gefüllt. Diese spätere Ergänzung erscheint einem heutigen Leser wie eine Unterbrechung der in den Inkunabeln vermittelten letzten bzw. offiziellen Erzählung. Dennoch stellt dieser Teil der *Urgicht* eine präzisere Erklärung zur Rolle des geflohenen Mönches bei dem Hostienverkauf dar.

Der ausführlichste Bericht über den Hostienverkauf des Mönchs aus Penzlin an die Juden wurde von Jakob unter Folter erzwungen. Hier gab er an, er habe von Anfang an gewusst, dass Eleazar durch einen Vertrag mit dem Mönch die konsekrierte Hostie in zwei Partikeln für einen Gulden gekauft hatte und er, Jakob, sei selbst dabei gewesen, als der Mönch die Hostien nach Sternberg brachte:

»Item furter hat bekannt ein Jud genant Jacob daz Eleazar vom Sternberg macht ein vertrag mit eynẽ Munch yn der Stat Penzlein der yn der Capellen zu Pentzlein was daz er ymc solt das Sacrament vbergeben yn beywesen Jacobs vnd Michol Juden vnd so gelobt Eleazar dem Munich ein guldẽ. vñ vff die zeit als der Munich das Sacrament solt zum Sternberg bringen do rayd Jacob Jüd dohyn vñ der Munich kam dar zum Sternberg vnd pracht zwoe Parth die entpfienge Eleazar Jacob vnd Michol.«[83]

Kurz darauf änderte sich Jakobs Erzählung noch einmal und er sagte aus, dass Eleazar, Michael und er selbst den Vertrag bereits ein Jahr zuvor mit dem Mönch aus Penzlin geschlossen hatten. Dieser Vereinbarung zufolge habe der Geistliche das Heilige Sakrament nach Sternberg bringen und den Juden übergeben sollen. Der Mönch habe nicht nur das Geld für das Allerheiligste bekommen, sondern auch zum Judentum konvertieren wollen. Schließlich sei der Mönch mit einer Mark in zwei Rheinischen Gulden bezahlt worden. Diese subtilen Änderungen zeigen uns, die wesentliche Absicht der Befragung nämlich eine lückenlose Aufdeckung der Ereignisse. Es sollte ausführlich erklärt werden, was mit den verkauften und entweihten Hostien geschehen war. Dafür wurden die Juden vermutlich bis zu ihrer Erschöpfung gefoltert, bis sie die letzten Einzelheiten wie gewünscht berichteten. Bei jedem Verhör erweiterten sich die Details zu den Ereignissen:

Item furter bekannt Jacob daz Michol wol in Jar mit dem Munich gehandelt het daz der munich wolt ein Jüd werden. das ist geschehen daz Jacob Eleazar vnd Michol die Jüden tzusammen waren tzu Pentzlein vmb Liccht meßda gab sich der Munich zu yrer sammelung vñ Eß vff Michols hoden. ...

[83] GW M44005, fol. 3r.

do gelobt der selbig Munich den Juden daß zr ewig wolt ein Jud beleiben daruff gaben sie dẽ munich eyn marck welcher marck uj zwen Reynisch gulden thun vß yrer opffer buchsen zu hilff an seyner zerung.[84]

Zu Beginn des Prozesses schien die Aussage von Eleazars Frau die wesentlichsten Anhaltspunkte für die Rekonstruktion der Ereignisse zu liefern. Nachdem sie Jakob als weiteren Hauptakteur erwähnt hatte, verblasste ihre Rolle im Prozess. Dieser Wandel der Urgichtbeschreibung kann uns ebenfalls erklären, warum Jakobs Beichte Grundlage der bildlichen Darstellung der Hostienentweihung in den Inkunabeln wurde. Sein vermeintliches Geständnis war das erste, welches den Wünschen des Prozesses nach einer ausführlichen Beschreibung des Hostienfrevels genügte.[85]

Letztlich sollen gemäß der letzten Version und von den Inkunabeln vermittelten Erzählung zwei Hostienverkäufe stattgefunden haben. Der erste als Resultat einjähriger Verhandlungen zwischen dem Penzliner Mönch und Eleazar in der Zeit zwischen Ostern, am 22. April, und Pfingsten, am 10. Juni. Der zweite innerhalb der folgenden Wochen bis zum 10. Juli. Bei diesem soll Peter Däne dem Juden Eleazar die Hostien verkauft haben. Am 20. Juli sollte die Hostien entweiht und erst danach, am 21. August, dem Priester von Eleazars Frau zurückgegeben worden sein. Noch am gleichen Tag habe Priester Peter die Bluthostien vergraben. Die zwei verbleibenden Hostien sollen schließlich von Eleazar mitgenommen worden sein.

Die Untersuchung der Ereignisse fand zeitnah in den folgenden Tagen nach der Ausgrabung und Entdeckung der Bluthostien statt. Am 29. August begann der Prozess und endete am 22. Oktober. An den darauffolgenden zwei Tagen wurden 27 Menschen der örtlichen jüdischen Gemeinde auf dem Judenberg[86] umgebracht. Peter Däne wurde gefangen gesetzt, bis er am 13. oder 15. März 1493 in Rostock hingerichtet wurde.[87] Aus einigen weiteren Spuren in den Texten geht hervor, dass die letzte Version der Erzählung weitere Elemente der ersten Version adaptieren musste. Bei diesen Veränderungen handelt es sich um angepasste Beschreibungen des Blutes, das aus den entweihten Hostien erschienen war.

Das wahrhaftige Blut Jesu oder ein einfach erschienenes Blut?

Die Vergegenwärtigung des Blutes und Leibes Christi geschieht immer dann, wenn die Hostie von einem Priester geweiht wird. Die Weihung beinhaltet eine substanzielle Verwandlung der Akzidentien von Brot und Wein während der Messe, welche unsichtbar bleiben muss. Wie bereits erwähnt, argumentierte schon Thomas von Aquin, dass eine Veränderung der Hostienakzidenz nicht als eine sichtbare Vergegenwärtigung des Blutes Christi, sondern als eine einfache Veränderung in den sekundären Akzidentien des Brotes interpretiert werden sollte. Diese konstituiert sich als erschienene Materie auf der sichtbaren Gestalt der eucharistischen Spezies. Ein wesentlicher Aspekt der Debatte zu diesem

---

[84] GW M44005, fol. 3r–3v.

[85] Vgl. SKOTTKI (s. Anm. 25), S. 298.

[86] Vgl. SKOTTKI (s. Anm. 25), S. 286.

[87] Das genaue Datum wurde bei der Transkription Lischs des zweiten Verhörprotokolls erwähnt. Vgl. LISCH (s. Anm. 40), S. 260.

Unterschied wird im Gutachten der theologischen Fakultät Erfurt zum Wilsnacker Blut (1452) ausführlich zu diskutiert:

> **Trotzdem ist die der Wahrheit entsprechende Aussage nicht möglich, dass die rote Farbe dieses Blutes Christi mit der Gottheit hypostatisch geeint sei. Christus hat nämlich unter einer derartigen Erscheinungsweise die eucharistische Spezies nicht eingesetzt, in gleicher Weise hat es die Universalkirche nicht übernommen in dieser Art. Man darf also nicht glauben, dass dieses Blut in Wilsnack das natürliche Blut Christi sei.**[88]

Hier scheint es zuerst wesentlich für die gelehrten Theologen zu sein, dieses erschienene Blut eucharistischer Wunder von dem historischen Blut Christi zu unterscheiden. Eine oft gestellte Frage in den theologischen Diskussionen zum historischen Blut Christi ist, ob aus der Passion Christi noch Blut auf der Welt verblieben war. Die Christologie des Spätmittelalters hatte in diesem Thema niemals Konsens erreicht. Trotzdem verteidigten die Erfurter Theologen, dass das historische Blut Christi bis zur Himmelfahrt immer mit Christus vereint war. Verschiedene Kontaktreliquien wie zum Beispiel die Vorhaut des Herrn, die es nur einmal geben dürfte, sind an mehreren Orten vorhanden. Dies verstößt gegen die Wahrnehmung und Authentizität der verbliebenen Spuren Christi auf der Welt.[89] Die Argumentation geht weiter:

> **Das Blut sei in diese veränderte Materie eines Blutes gewandelt und ihm so die blutige Farbe entzogen worden. Die Wahrheit darin kenne ja der Schöpfer der gesamten Kreatur, während sich der Glauben des Frommen an das halten möge, was ihm mehr an Glaubenssicherheit bietet. Mag nun der Tatbestand so oder anders sein, so darf man trotzdem nicht glauben, dass das sogenannte Blut in Wilsnack das uns hinterlassene, natürliche Blut Christi sei. Wir haben oft gelesen, dass an den verdorbenen Hostien auch um die gewandelten Hostien herum etwas von dem wunderbaren Blute Christi gefunden sei.**[90]

Schließlich resümieren die Erfurter Theologen, das in Wilsnack erschienene Blut solle nicht als wundersame Erscheinung angesehen werden, da dies der Förderung einer wahren Frömmigkeit nicht dienlich erscheint. Vermutlich hatte die theologische Diskussion der Gelehrten zu den Bluterscheinungen einige oder eine leichte Wirkung auf die Entstehung des Kultes zu den Bluthostien von Sternberg gehabt haben soll. Dieser Einfluss lässt sich noch an Details der schriftlichen Überlieferung erkennen.

Aus beiden Verhörprotokollen können wir entnehmen, wie sich die Beschreibung des erschienenen Blutes änderte. Der feine Unterschied zeigt eine Adaptation der ersten Erzählung, welche den Argumenten der gelehrten theologischen Diskussion nicht entsprach. Im ersten Verhörprotokoll wird Folgendes berichtet: »Item die ander hostie hebben sie an henden vnde vothen besneden in gestallt vnde figuren, so vor ogen is vnde man apenbarlik sehn mach, warafftig blot dar vth gefallen vnde ock vth der syden der ostien, so die mit natelen gesteken wart, warafftlich blot gesprungen is.«[91]

Die Juden sollen die mit konsekrierten Hostien aufgebaute Jesusfigur in ihre Füße, Hände und Herzseite gestochen haben, woraufhin das wahrhaftige Blut daraus geflossen sein soll. Diese offensichtliche

---

[88] DAMERAU (s. Anm. 19), S. 32.

[89] DAMERAU (s. Anm. 19), S. 33. Als weitere Referenz zum Thema. Vgl. ERNST BREEST: Das Wunderblut von Wilsnack (1383–1552). Quellenmäßige Darstellung seiner Geschichte, in: *Märkische Forschungen*. 16 (1881), 131–302.

[90] DAMERAU (s. Anm. 19), S. 33.

[91] LISCH (s. Anm. 40), S. 257.

Parallele zwischen dem Hostienfrevel und der Passion Christi ist nicht in der letzten Erzählung der Inkunabeln zu lesen. In erstem Protokoll vom 29. August ist dagegen die Rede davon, dass die Juden aus zwei Hostien eine Jesusfigur gestaltet hätten, damit sie nicht nur die Kreuzigung Christi wiederholen konnten, sondern auch das Blutvergießen Jesu durch seine fünf Wunden.[92]

Die Frömmigkeit gegenüber den fünf Wunden war im Spätmittelalter populär und zahlreiche bildliche Darstellungen zum Thema sind in der Graphik des 15. Jahrhunderts zu finden.[93] Dennoch kann keine spätmittelalterliche Darstellung zur Hostienentweihung eine direkte Verbindung zwischen der Marterung der Hostien und den fünf Wunden vermittelten.[94] Darüber hinaus müssen wir uns fragen, warum in dem zweiten Protokoll, in dem das erschienene Blut der entweihten Hostie beschrieben wird, das Adjektiv *wahrhaftige* nicht mehr zu finden ist. Das erschienene Blut wird nach dem zweiten Verhörprotokoll, beziehungsweise in den Inkunabeln mit Ausnahme des Buches *Van den bosen Ioden*[95] ohne Adjektive beschrieben: »Alze Eleazars dochter byslep, bynnen deme Sternebarghe vnder ener louynghen erer v myt natelen ghesteken hebben, dar dat blot vth ghelopen ys.«[96]

Beide Änderungen zeigen uns jedoch, dass die letzte Version der Erzählung des Hostienfrevels sich zu einer gelehrten theologischen Debatte über das Paradox der sichtbaren Vergegenwärtigung des Blutes Christi in einem eucharistischen Wunder entwickelte. Das Adjektiv *wahrhaftig* bezeichnet eine offensichtlichere Verknüpfung mit einer Erscheinung des Blutes Christi, welche nicht der Transsubstantiationslehre entsprach. Wahrscheinlich um weitere kritische Hinterfragungen der gelehrten Theologen zur Wunderhostien von Sternberg zu vermeiden, beschlossen die lokalen Geistlichen und Adligen, die die wichtigsten Akteure bei der Entstehung des Kultes zu Sternberg waren, kleine Adaptationen zur Beschreibung des erschienenen Blutes in die letzte Version der Erzählung entfließen zu lassen. Daher wurde die Assoziation mit den fünf Wunden Christi und einer sichtbaren Vergegenwärtigung des Blutes Jesu nicht schon in den Inkunabeln und im zweiten Verhörprotokoll formell erwähnt.

Die Authentizität der GW M44008: eine Inkunabel-Fälschung aus dem 18./19. Jahrhundert?

Die Inkunabel GW M44008 gilt als eine Ausnahme unter diesen Adaptationen, denn dort wird das erschienene Blut nicht nur als wahrhaftiges Blut, sondern sogar als *gebenedeites*[97] Blut beschrieben. Dies suggeriert dem Leser gleichermaßen eine öffentliche Verbindung zwischen der Hostienentweihung und der Vergegenwärtigung des Blutes Christi: »Vorder heft Jacob bekāt dat Eleazar vnde Mochel. Dat sacramēt. Alss dat de monnik to dē Sternbarge brachte. Nemē vñ eyn yowelk vā en hebbē dat bynnē Eleazars huße vp eyner tafelē dar vp eyne dwele gespreydet was mit mestē gestekē so dat dat gebenediede blot dar vth gevlotē is.«[98]

---

92 Eine Diskussion zu dem Thema folgt, vgl. Anm. 129, 130 und 131.

93 Es gibt einige Beispiele in einem Ausstellungskatalog des Germanischen Nationalmuseums zur Druckgraphik des 15. Jahrhunderts Vgl. PETER PARSHALL, RAINER SCHOCH (Hrsg): *Die Anfänge der europäischen Druckgraphik. Holzschnitt des 15. Jahrhunderts und ihr Gebrauch*. Nürnberg 2005, Kat-Nr.: 47, 49, 72, 73, 74, 77, 78, 79. S, 181, 185–187, 242–249, 255–262.

94 Lediglich zwei spätere Darstellungen aus dem 17. und 18. Jahrhundert, die den Fall zu Röttingen darstellen, gelten als einzige Beispiele, die die fünf Wunden Christi zusammen mit einem Hostienfrevel repräsentieren. Beide Gemälde liegen heute im Depot des M am Dom in Würzburg. Zu der Darstellung aus dem 18. Jahrhunderts vgl. KARLHEINZ MÜLLER: *Die Würzburger Judengemeinde im Mittelalter: von den Anfängen um 1100 bis zum Tod Julius Echters (1617)*. Würzburg 2004, S. 103–104.

95 GW M44004, fol. 2v.

96 Vgl. LISCH (s. Anm. 40), Nr. 2: Letztes Bekenntniß oder Urgicht der Juden über die Verspottung des Sacraments zu Sternberg (1492. Oct. 22.) In: *Jahrbücher des Vereins für Mecklenburgische Geschichte und Altertumskunde*. 12 (1847), S. 259.

97 GW M44008, fol. 2r.

98 GW M44008, fol. 3r–3v.

Im Gegensatz zu allen anderen Inkunabeln aus denen hervorgeht, dass das Blut aus der eucharistischen Spezies geflossen sei, schreibt der Autor in der Inkunabel *Vā den bosen ioden volget hyr eyn gheschicht* (GW M44008), dass das »gebenediede[99]« Blut aus dem Heiligen Sakrament geflossen sei[100]. Adjektiv *gebenedeite* ändert die Interpretationsweise des aus der Wunderhostie erschienenen Blutes. Das Wort *gebenedeit* ist die germanisierte Form des lateinischen Partizips *benedictus – gesegnet*. Dieses weist eine Assoziation mit dem *Ave Maria* Gebet auf: *Gegrüßet seist du, Maria, voll der Gnade, der Herr ist mit dir. Du bist gebenedeit unter den Frauen, und gebenedeit ist die Frucht deines Leibes ....* Ein Blutgebet eines Walldürner Wallfahrtbuches[101] für die Pilger aus Mainz und Aschaffenburg aus dem 18. Jahrhundert lautet: »Gegrüszt seyst du, o gütigster Jesu, du bist voller Gnaden; die Barmherzigkeit ist mit dir: du bist gebenedyt unter allen Menschenkindern: und gebenedeiet seye dein heiligs vergossenes Blut.«[102] Dieses Gebet wurde als Heiligblutrosenkranz mit sieben Gesätzen anstelle des *Ave Maria* gebetet.

Der Autor des Buches GW 44008 setzt eine interessante Parallele zwischen der gebenedeiten Frucht des Leibes Mariens und dem Blut der entweihten Hostie, indem er dieses erschienene Blut als *gebenedeit* qualifizierte. Dies ist eine Beschreibung, welche in allen anderen Texten nicht verwendet wurde und keine offensichtliche Assoziation mit der Frucht des Leibes beinhalten. Das gebenedeite Blut floss aus dem Heiligen Sakrament, nicht als einfaches akzidentielles Blut, sondern als gebenedeites Blut Christi. Am Beispiel des Walldürner Blutgebets scheint diese Assoziation zwischen der Frucht des Leibes Mariä und dem vergossenem Blut Jesu, erstmal üblich für die Bluthostienverehrung des 18. Jahrhunderts gewesen zu sein. Einige Vermutungen können auf dieser abweichenden Beschreibung des erschienenen Blutes im Wiegendruck GW M44008 aufgebaut werden. Hier stellt sich die Frage, warum das Adjektiv *gebenedeit* nur in dieser Inkunabel in Bezug auf das Blut verwendet wurde. In den anderen Wiegendrucken wurden die konsekrierten Hostien zwar als *gebenedeit* bezeichnet, das wunderbare Blut wurde jedoch kein einziges Mal mit diesem Adjektiv qualifiziert[103].

Dieser Punkt führt uns zu Überlegungen über die Authentizität des Lübecker Exemplars GW M44008. Hierbei stellen sich die Fragen, warum dieses Buch nur in Form eines Faksimiles vorhanden ist und ob dieses Faksimile als Fälschung gelten kann. Die heutigen Spuren können uns nicht sicher beweisen wann das Faksimile entstand lässt sich nicht genau bestimmen, doch legen die Parallelen mit dem Walldürner Blutgebet nahe, dass es vermutlich erst im 18. oder 19. Jahrhundert geschaffen wurde.[104]

Die unterschiedlichen Arten und Weisen die Bluterscheinung zu qualifizieren, lassen eine alternative Interpretation vermuten, dass die Etablierung einer neuen Pilgerfahrt zu einer als Reliquie verehrten Bluthostie zusätzlich einer theologischen Debatte und Adaptation bedurfte. Diese erfolgte hier im Buch (GW M44008) aus einem nicht mehr zu rekonstruierenden Grunde nicht. Die Befassung mit einer solchen theologischen Debatte war für die Etablierung einer neuen Reliquie,

---

99 GW M44008, fol. 2r.

100 GW M44004, fol. 2v.

101 Für eine tiefergehende Kontextualisierung der Entstehung und Verehrung der Bluthostie zu Walldürn vgl. WOLFGANG BRÜCKNER: *Die Verehrung des Heiligen Blutes in Walldürn: Volkskundlich-soziologische Untersuchungen zum Strukturwandel barocken Wallfahrtens*. Aschaffenburg 1958.

102 Für das originale Zitat vgl. JOHANNES HEUSER: *Heilig-Blut in Kult und Brauchtum des deutschen Kulturraumes: ein Beitrag zur religiösen Volkskunde*. Dissertation der Uni Bonn 1948, S. 91.

103 GW M44008, fol. 3r–3v.

104 Die Darstellung der Hostienfrevelszene der GW M44008 weicht vollständig von allen anderen Aufgaben. Dies kann auch als weiteres Indiz einer Fälschung betrachten werden. Vgl. [Abb. 6].

Abb. 1 Die Juden entweihen die konsekrierte Hostie GW M44005, Holzschnitt, Jakob Wolff, Basel nach 24.10.1492

Abb. 2/3 Die Juden entweihen die konsekrierte Hostie, GW M44007, Holzschnitt, Simon Koch, Magdeburg, nach 24.10.1492 (oben). GW M44009, Holzschnitt, Simon Koch, Magdeburg (unten)

beispielsweise nach einen Hostienfrevelvorwurf, wichtig. Dementsprechend versuchten die Autoren die Beschreibungen eucharistischer Wunder anzupassen, damit keine Hinterfragungen die Wunderhostien und die neuen entstandenen Pilgerfahrten in Zweifel ziehen konnten.

Schließend kann diese niederdeutsche Version gleichfalls als der früheste Druck der letzten Version der Erzählung interpretiert werden, da sie, im Gegensatz zu den anderen Inkunabeln, nicht den vollständigen Verlauf der Anhörungen und Verhandlungen der Befragung beschreibt. Auch die Konsequenzen des Prozesses für weitere 246 Mecklenburger Juden werden nicht erwähnt. Dies würde letztendlich erklären, warum sie nicht vollständig in die Debatte der Gelehrten einfloss. Diese kleine und wichtige Adaptation wurde erst später in die anderen Wiegendrucke, die vermutlich kurz danach entstanden, aufgenommen. Die Abwesenheit von Exemplaren aus dem 15. Jahrhunderts lass uns trotzdem vermuten, dass die erste Interpretation wahrscheinlicher ist.

Die graphischen Darstellungen des Sternberger Hostienfrevels und die Abweichungen ihrer Titel

Jede Inkunabelausgabe ist anders überschrieben. Die Bezeichnungen der Wiegendrucke GW M44004 und GW M44009 lauten *Von der Mishandelung des heiligen Sacraments von den Juden zu Sterēberg* und *Van den Mysehandelinge des hiligen Sacraments der bösen Ioden to dē Sterneberge*. Sie gleichen sich stark bis auf die Beschreibung der Juden als *böse* in dem letztgenannten Druck. Für die Autoren und Drucker beider Versionen war es wichtig, die Misshandlung des Heiligen Sakraments, die Juden als deren Urheber und den Ort des Geschehens hervorzuheben.

Die Bücher GW M44005 und GW M44007 wurden mit den Titeln *Die geschicht der Juden tzum Sternberg ym lande zū Mecklenburg die sye begangen mit dem heiligsten Sacrament* und *Die geschicht der Juden tzum Sternberg ym landt tzu Mecklenburg* gedruckt. Der zweite Titel ist der kürzeste der sechs Werke. Er erwähnt, dass die Erzählung über die Juden sich in Sternberg, einem Ort, der im damaligen Herzogtum Mecklenburg lag, ereignet habe. Es werden darin jedoch weder die Ausdrücke *heiligstes Sakrament* noch *die Misshandlung der Juden gegen die Hostien* verwendet.

Die fragwürdige Inkunabel (GW M44008) trägt den Titel: *Sterneberch/ Vā den bosen Ioden volget hyr eyn gheschicht/ Dar to vā den sulvē eyn merklik ghedycht*. Wieder werden die Juden mit dem Adjektiv *böse* beschrieben. In diesem Titel wird, wie in den Büchern GW M44005 und GW M44007, der Ort des angeblichen Frevels und das Wort *Geschichte* verwendet. Der letzte Satz »Dar to vā den sulvē eyn merklik ghedycht« gilt als eine Besonderheit des Wiegendrucks GW M44008 im Vergleich mit den anderen Exemplaren. Die Lübecker Inkunabel ist die Einzige, die ein zweisprachiges Gedicht am Ende des Buches enthält. Dieses wechselt vom Niederdeutschen ins Lateinische. Es gilt als eine Ode an die Wunderhostien und als Fluch gegen alle Juden, nicht nur die angeblichen Frevler. Diese bildlichen Unterschiede der GW M44008 können gleichfalls auf eine spätere Entstehung des Werkes hinweisen.

Das Blut Christi und die blutenden Hostien 107

Das letzte Beispiel ist die Inkunabel GW M44006, welche einen vergleichsweise langen Titel hat und als kleine Zusammenfassung der Erzählung interpretiert werden kann. Der Titel lautet: *Allen Christen mynschen sy/ tzo wyssen dat in den land van Mecklenberch in der stat Sternenberch eyn groyß myrakel gesey et sa vā den verblynden Juden an dem allerhallyschsten hoechwerdychsten Sacrament dat sy myt messer doer stochen baen dat bloet der vysz gevlossen is als dese figuyr vysy wyser*. In dieser kurzen Beschreibung werden die wesentlichen Elemente der Erzählung bereits vermittelt. Darüber hinaus schreibt der Autor, dass die folgende Geschichte in einem Holzschnitt dargestellt wurde. Im Gegensatz zu den Titeln der Bücher GW M44008 und GW M44009 werden die Juden als *verblindet* statt *böse* bezeichnet. Weitere Besonderheiten finden wir in den Erwähnungen der Wörter *Christen, Menschen, wissen, Mirakel, hochwürdig, Messer, stechen, Blut, fließen* und *Figur*. Alle diese Wörter wurden in den anderen Titeln nicht verwendet. Vermutlich diente dieser lange Text als zusammenfassende Einführung in die folgende Erzählung, sodass der Leser sofort in der Lage war, den Holzschnitt zu interpretieren.

Bei der Analyse sehen wir die Wörter *Sternberg* und *Juden* in allen erwähnten Texten. Vor allem scheint für die Autoren wichtig gewesen zu sein, zumindest den Ort der Hostienentweihung und die vermeintlichen Täter bei der Betitelung der Inkunabeln zu erwähnen. Alle anderen Worte sind austauschbar und nicht in allen Titeln präsent. Trotz dieser feinen Unterschiede der Titel ist der Leser immer sofort in der Lage zu erkennen, welches Thema die Erzählung behandelt. Außerdem zeigen sie, dass einige Elemente der Erzählung regional unterschiedlich wiedergegeben wurden.

Das ebenso wichtige Wort *Sakrament* ist in den Inkunabeln GW M44007 und GW M44008 nicht zu finden, obgleich es sich um einen Hauptbegriff der letzten Version der Erzählung handelt. Es ist nicht abschließend zu erklären, warum die Drucker den Wiegendrucken unterschiedliche Titel gaben. Neben den Abweichungen, die augenscheinlich auf örtlichen Besonderheiten beruhen, kann angenommen werden, dass bestimmte Drucker ihre einige Version des Buches fertigen wollten, um sich von anderen abzusetzen.

Unter den sechs Versionen der Inkunabeln zur Sternberger Hostentweihung finden wir vier verschiedene graphische Darstellungen. Alle basieren auf der vierten Aussage des Juden Jakob zur Hostienentweihung, welche in der Inkunabel GW M44008 nicht wiedergegeben wird:

> Item furder bekannt Jacob/ daß Eleazar der erst waß/ daß bewilliget/ daß man daß heyligsten Sacrament allso stechen solde/ vnd do sie das tetten/ daß waß bej abent bej licht/ vnd Eleazar nam daß Sacrament awß der tzwehel doruff es gestochen waß/ vnd warff daß vn einen hulzen Topf/ der oben vber latern oder lewchten gewest waß nach lants gewonheit/ vnnd wandt die tzwehel dorumb vnd gab daß seinem weyb/ vnd auch yr dreyer messer behielt daß weyb/ vnnd yn dem lewchttopf lag ein dock/ dorynne der Munich daß hochwirdigest Sacrament bracht tzum Sternnberg/ yn einer hultzen gedreyeten buchssen vnd do der Munich hort/ daß daß also geschohen waß/ daß gefiel ym wol.[105]

Abb. 4 Die Juden entweihen die konsekrierte Hostie GW M44004, Holzschnitt, Bamberg, nach 24.10.1492

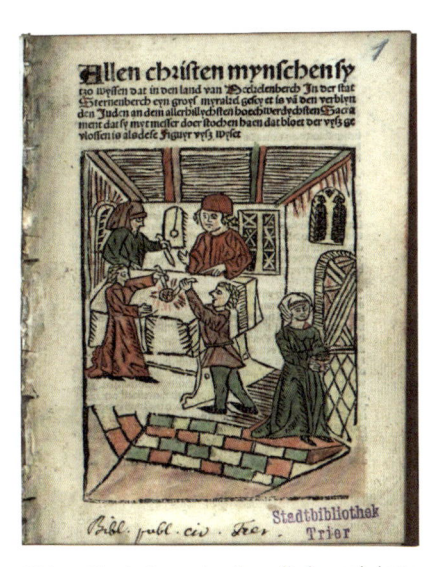

Abb. 5 Die Juden entweihen die konsekrierte Hostie, GW M44006, Holzschnitt, Köln, nach 24.10.1492

---

105 Vgl. GW M44007, fol. 4v–5r.

Abb. 6 Die Juden entweihen die konsekrierten Hostien, GW M44008, Holzschnitt, Lübeck, Matthäus Brandis, nach 24.10.1492 In: *Sterneberch. Wan den bosen ioden volget hyr eyn gheschicht*. Wien, Antiquariat Gilhofer & Ranschburg, 1889

106 Ich bedanke mich bei Kristin Skottki und Silvan Wagner, die mich im Rahmen eines Oberseminars auf die Darstellung des Priesters Peter Däne hingewiesen haben. Laut der letzten Version der Erzählungen hatte der geflüchtete Mönch seine Mönchskleidung ausgezogen und als Hilfspriest verkleidet, um in den Besitz einer konsekrierten Hostie zu kommen.

107 Eine Ausnahme ist das Bild von GW M44008 [Abb. 6].

108 Ein übliches Motiv der spätmittelalterlichen Darstellung der Juden. Vgl. DANIÈLE SANSY: Marquer la différence : l'imposition de la rouelle aux XIII e et XIV e siècles, in: *Médiévales* 41 (2001), S. 15–36.

Die Ausgaben GW M44005, GW M44007 und GW M44009 weisen vergleichbare Darstellungen auf Abb. 1, 2 und 3. Das Gefäß in den Händen von Elezars Frau und ihre Gesichtszüge sind in M44007 [Abb. 2] und M44009 [Abb. 3] im Vergleich mit der [Abb. 1] leicht abweichend. Diese allgemeine Szene stellt drei Männer um einen Tisch dar. Bei dem Mann auf der linken Seite des Tisches könnte es sich entweder um den Priester Peter Däne oder um den geflüchteten Mönch handeln. Durch seine Position, seine Kleidung (insbesondere sein Birett) und die segnende Handgeste wird für den Betrachter eine Hostienkonsekration und der folgende Verkauf des Heiligen Sakraments an die Juden angedeutet[106]. Da die Erzählung von zwei Hostienverkaufen berichtet könnte es sich gleichfalls um beide Personen handeln. Die vierte Aussage des Juden Jakob konzentriert sich auf den Mönch aus Penzlin, doch halte ich für wahrscheinlicher, dass hier Peter Däne dargestellt sei, da er der zentrale Akteur des Textes ist. Die verkaufte Hostie liegt rechts auf dem Tisch. Es sind zwar drei Messer erkennbar, doch kommen nur zwei bei der Entweihung zum Einsatz. Das Dritte liegt lediglich auf dem Tisch, was andeuten dürfte, dass der Priester Däne nicht an der Hostienentweihung teilnimmt, sondern eine Hostienkonsekration ausführt.

In seiner dritten Aussage erwähnte Jakob die weiteren beiden Hauptfrevler Eleazar und Michol, die ebenfalls in dieser Szene zu sehen sind. Eine Reihe von Linien, die aus dem Heiligen Sakrament kommen, bezeichnen das Blut der Wunderhostie, welches in allen anderen Inkunabeln nur als *Blut* beschrieben wird[107], dar. Die Profanierung der eucharistischen Spezies findet in Eleazars Haus statt, und die Wände, drei Fenster und eine Tür auf der linken Seite deuten auf einen Innenraum hin. Links im Bild wird die Frau Eleazars mit einem urnenähnlichen Gefäß in den die Bluthostie hineingelegt wurde, dargestellt. Dieses Bilddetail zeigt den Moment, in dem Eleazars Frau die Hostie dem Priester Peter Däne zurückbringt. Im Grunde genommen stellt die Szene drei verschiedene Momente der Sternberger Erzählung dar: die Konsekration und Profanierung des Heiligen Sakraments und die Zurückgabe des konsekrierten Partikels an Peter Däne, der selbst die wiedergefundene Bluthostie geweiht hatte. Dieser implizite Zyklus stellt eine Zusammenfassung der Ereignisse der Misshandlung der Wunderhostie dar.

Die einfachen gestochenen Linien gehören ebenfalls zum Stil der Szene in GW M44004 [Abb. 4]. Diese ist stilistisch ähnlich gehalten wie die zuvor beschriebene Szene. Die Schnitttechnik dieses zweiten Bildes ist allerdings noch einfacher als die der anderen Holzschnitte [Abb. 1]. Ein auffallendes Merkmal sind die ringförmigen Abzeichen[108] die auf der Kleidung der drei Juden zu sehen sind. Dieses typische jüdische Zeichen wird nicht auf der Kleidung des Peter Däne dargestellt, der hier in der gleichen Position wie in [Abb. 1] zu sehen ist. Ein weiterer Unterschied ist das dritte Messer, das nun nicht mehr auf dem Tisch liegt, sondern vom Priester Däne gehalten wird, der andermal alleine auf der anderen Seite des Tischs steht.

Der Holzschnitt des Exemplars GW M44006 [Abb. 5] scheint wie ein Spiegelbild des Bildes in GW M44004 [Abb. 4]. Auch dort werden alle drei Messer von den Frevlern in den Händen gehalten. Ein unterscheidender Aspekt, der dritte Hauptfrevler (Michol) dieses Mal dargestellt ist. Insgesamt basiert jedoch auch diese Inkunabel auf der dritten Aussage Jakobs. Diese erlaubt nicht, den vierten dargestellten Mann zu benennen.

Was [Abb. 5] besonders auszeichnet ist ihre Kolorierung. Diese schmückt nicht nur die Kleidung der Dargestellten und unterstreicht die Raumdarstellung, sondern lässt vor allem die blutenden Hostien deutlicher als in den anderen Drucken erscheinen.[109] Kleine rote Linien entlang der Hostien und den drei verwendeten Messer Zeugen vor der blutigen und zugleich wundersamen Tat. Durch die rote Kolorierung fokussiert die Darstellung auf die Entweihung der Hostien.

Auch der Kochtopf, in Händen von Eleazars Frau, welcher benutzt wurde, um die profanierten Hostien zu dem Priester zurückzubringen, ist mit kleinen roten Linien eingefärbt, um die Erzählfolge zu unterstreichen. Die roten gefärbten Gesichter der Frevler können als Anzeichen für deren Wut aufgefasst werden. So galt gemäß der Vier-Säfte-Lehre die Farbe Rot als Zeichen der Choleriker.[110] In diesem Zusammenhang bildet diese Farbe ein Antonym zwischen dem cholerischen Blut der Juden und dem erlösenden Blut der beschädigten Hostie. Das erste bringt den Zweifel, den Unglauben und die Verdammnis, das zweite erwirkt die Frömmigkeit, die Wahrnehmung der Passion Christi und die ewige Erlösung.

Der Holzschnitt des Buches GW M44008 [Abb. 6] unterscheidet sich in fast allen Aspekten von den anderen drei Bildern. Darauf sind elf Juden in der Szene des Hostienfrevels dargestellt, obgleich der Text selbst zwölf Juden erwähnt: Eleazar und seine Frau, Jakob, Mochel (Michael) und seine Frau, Martus (Maxl) von Robel, Aaron von Brandenborch und Mannik sein Sohn, Iosken (Joslen) von Malchin, Masse (Moses) und Abraham.[111] Auf dem Tisch liegen zwei geweihte Hostien, eine kleine und eine Große. Die erste wurde mit einem Messer durchstochen während die Schauhostie von zwei Juden gleichzeitig profaniert wurde. Die Frevler, die die Marterungswerkzeuge verwenden, sind Michael, Jakob und Eleazar. Die weiteren acht auf dem Bild dargestellten Juden können nicht identifiziert werden.

Weitere Motive, die nicht außer Acht gelassen werden dürfen, sind die Leinentücher, die unter den Hostien liegen. Die Erzählung berichtet, dass Peter Däne die Hostien beim Verkauf mit Tüchern bedeckt habe.[112] Dies ruft eine Assoziation mit dem Bildthema der Veronika hervor. So wie Christus vor seiner Kreuzigung sein Abbild auf dem Tuch hinterließ, ließen auch die Hostien Abdrücke zurück.[113] Auch hier wird sinnbildlich auf die Wiederholung der historischen Kreuzigung angespielt, von der man glaubte, dass sie den mittelalterlichen Juden zur Verspottung des christlichen Glaubens diente.

Außerdem findet der Betrachter auf dem Tisch einen Teller mit einem Stück Lamm – ein weiteres Symbol, das das jüdische Pessach in einen Vergleich mit dem christlichen Osterfest setzt. Die Juden werden hier nicht nur als die Gottesmörder charakterisiert, ihre Riten stammen

---

[109] Zur vollständigen Erklärung über den theologischen und devotionalen Zusammenhang zwischen der roten Farbe und dem Blut Christi. Vgl. MICHEL PASTOUREAU: Ceci est mon sang : le christianisme médiéval et la couleur rouge. In: *Le Pressoir mystique: Actes du colloque de Recloses*. Paris 1990. DANIÈLE ALEXANDRE-BIDON [Hrsg.] S. 49–50. Siehe auch MICHEL PASTOUREAU: *Rouge : Histoire d'une couleur*, Paris 2016. S. 64–68.

[110] PASTOUREAU (s. Anm. 109) S. 48.

[111] Vgl. GW 44008, fol. 3v.

[112] »am tag der syben Brüder consecryrt vñ gebenedeyt / vnd dye deß andern tagß dem verflüchten vnd blinten Eleazar Jüden vberantwordt yn einem seydē tuch daß er abgeschniten hat vor dem altar der heyligen drey könig« Vgl. GW M44007, fol. 3r. Siehe auch: »heft her Peter dene tho deme Sternberge in der kerken vppe deme altare aller hilgen an deme dage der seuen broder ij ostien ghebenedyet vnde consacreret vñ des anderen daghes deme vorbenomeden Eleazar in eynem syden doke den he vā deme altare der hilgen dyrer konninge af das muss heißen ›af ghesneden‹, hadde ouer gheant wordet hebbe«. Vgl. GW M44008, fol. 1v.

[113] Die Vera Icon wäre als die wahre Imago Jesu verstanden, da diese Reliquie die Abdrücke des Gesichts Christi enthält. Vgl. »Die Maske und die Person Christi«. In: HANS BELTING, *Das echte Bild: Bildfragen als Glaubensfragen*. München 2005, S. 45–85. Siehe auch JANICE BENNETT: *Sacred Blood, Sacred Image: The Sudarium of Oviedo: New Evidence for the Authenticity of the Shroud of Turin*. San Francisco 2001, S. 1–223. Diese implizite Assoziation zwischen dem Tuch, mit dem die profanierte Hostie transportiert wird, und dem *Sudarium* ist im Korneuburger Hostienfrevelfall (1302) deutlicher zu erkennen, vgl. Anm. 60.

Abb. 7 Detail. Geschichte der Juden von Passau mit dem Sacrament, GW M29568, Holzschnitt, Kaspar Hochfeder, Nürnberg um. 1497. In: ACHIM RIETHER: *Einblattholzschnitt des 15. Jahrhunderts Bestand der Staatlichen graphischen Sammlung München*. München: Deutscher Kunstverlag GmbH, 2019.

114 Nur im Holzschnitt von GW M44008 ist die Darstellung von Eleazars Frau nicht deutlich.

115 Mit der Ausnahme von [Abb. 5], die anhand ihrer Kolorierung (rote Färbung der entweihten Hostie) eine deutlichere bildliche Sichtbarkeit zur Bluterscheinung bildet.

116 GW M29568, GW M29569. Der Einblattdruck M29568 wurde 1477 angefertigt. Das Blatt GW M29569 wurde wahrscheinlich um 1500 von Johann Froschauer in Augsburg gedruckt. Für eine detaillierte Analyse des Passauer Hostienfrevelfalls und seines Einblattdrucks vgl. MORITZ STERN: Der Passauer Judenprozeß 1478. In: *Jeschurun* 15. (1928), S. 541–560.

117 Die deutsche Fassung wurde von Georg Alt (1450–1510) aus dem Lateinischen übersetzt. Die deutsche Fassung wurde von Georg Alt (1450–1510) aus dem Lateinischen übersetzt. Vgl. EMIL JULIUS HUGO STEFFENHAGEN: Alt, Georg. In: *Allgemeine Deutsche Biographie* 1 (1875), S. 355.

118 GW M40796. hartmann schedel *Register des Buchs der Croniken und geschichten mit figuren und pildnussen von anbeginn der welt bis auf dise unnsere Zeit*. Nürnberg, Koberger, 1493. fol. 257v.

auch aus den Gesetzen des Alten Testaments und erscheinen als veraltet und nicht wirksam. Da die jüdische Lehre den Opfertod Jesu zur Vergebung der Sünden nicht anerkennt, hatten die Juden nach damaliger Meinung keine Hoffnung auf den Himmel. Das Lamm auf dem Teller soll hier erneut den Opfertod Christi symbolisieren, da es als ein entscheidendes soteriologisches Bildelement aufzufassen ist. Auffällig ist, dass in diesem letzten Bild die Bluterscheinung im Unterschied zu den anderen Holzschnitten durch kein Element dargestellt wird.

Trotz dieser augenscheinlich feinen Unterschiede zwischen den Bilddarstellungen stehen der Tisch, die drei Frevler und die Frau Eleazars als wesentliche bildliche Motive fest.[114] Diese Details, die aus der vierten Aussage Jakobs stammen, wurden von den Holzschneidern ausgewählt, um die Schlüsselszene der Entweihung des Heiligen Sakraments im ersten Folium der Wiegendrucke darzustellen. Nun stellt sich die Frage nach der Interpretation des Blutes durch Leser und Betrachter.

Ein wesentlicher Unterschied zwischen den graphischen Darstellungen und den Texten ist die Gewichtung der Darstellung des Blutes[115]. Die Bilder legen einen geringeren Wert auf die Veranschaulichung des erschienenen Blutes. In allen Szenen scheint den Holzschneidern vornehmlich daran gelegen, dem Betrachter die Hostienentweihung bzw. die »böse« Tat der Juden gegen den christlichen Glauben darzustellen. Erst bei der Lektüre sollte das Publikum dann näher über das erschienene Blut nachdenken und reflektieren, ob es sich bei dieser wundersamen Erscheinung um eine tatsächliche Vergegenwärtigung des historischen Blutes Christi handelte.

Es bleibt die Frage: Wer hat diese Erzählungen zum Sternberger Fall gelesen? Es fällt schwer, ein bestimmtes Publikum für diese Inkunabeln auszumachen. Auch ist es nicht einfach zu erkennen, wie das erschienene Blut interpretiert wurde, da es in den Inkunabeln in der Regel nur mithilfe sechs einfacher Linien dargestellt wird. Auf anderen Drucken, wie der vierten Szene des berühmten Einblattdrucks *Ein grawsamlich geschicht geschehen zu passaw von den juden als hernach volgt*[116] [Abb. 7] wurde das erschienene Blut um einiges deutlicher dargestellt. In dieser Szene finden wir vier Juden, von denen zwei den ringförmigen Abzeichen auf ihrer Kleidung tragen. Der Jude auf der linken Seite entweiht eine Hostie, die auf der Ecke des Tisches liegt. Das erschienene Blut fließt hier in Strömen und versickert im Boden. Das Blutvergießen der Hostie wird in der Passauer Darstellung viel deutlicher zum Ausdruck gebracht als in den Szenen der hier erwähnten Inkunabeln.

Ein berühmtes Beispiel einer Interpretation der Ereignisse zu Sternberg und der Erzählungen darüber ist der folgende Text des Blattes CCLVII verso der *Schedelschen Weltchronik*. Hartmann Schedel hatte vermutlich Zugang zu dem Druck GW M44004, der in Bamberg von Johann Sensenschmidt angefertigt wurde. Der Nürnberger Humanist schreibt[117]:

> Eleazar ein iud vñ sein mituerwandten durch einē briester Petrus genant das allerheilligst sacrament des fronleichnams Cristi in einer größern vnd klainern hostia zu inen gebracht. vnd dieselben hostien durchstochen also

Das Blut Christi und die blutenden Hostien **111**

Abb. 8 Juden wurden im Scheiterhaufen verbrannt GW M40796 In HARTMANN SCHEDEL: *Register des Buchs der Croniken und geschichten mit figuren und pildnussen von anbeginn der welt bis auf dise unnsere Zeit.* Nürnberg, Koberger, 1493, Holzschnitt: Michael Wolgemut und Hans Pleydenwurff Fol. CCLVII V. In STEPHAN FÜSSEL: *Das Buch der Chroniken*. Köln, Taschen Verlag, 2018

Abb. 9 Hostienentweihung zu Sternberg In NIKOLAUS MARSCHALK: *Mons Stellarum*. Rostock, Holzschnitt Ludwig Dietz 15. Exemplar der UB Rostock

119 SCHEDEL (s. Anm. 104), fol. 257v.
120 SCHEDEL (s. Anm. 104), fol. 257v.
121 SCHEDEL (s. Anm. 117) fol. 257v.
122 SCHEDEL (s. Anm. 104), fol. 257v.
123 SCHEDEL (s. Anm. 104), fol. 257v.
124 Vgl. RUBIN (s. Anm. 4), S. 173.
125 Vgl. MARSCHALK (s. Anm. 80).
126 HONEMANN (s. Anm. 1), S. 204.

> das dz plüt alßpald herauß floße vnd ein leineins weiß tuch dauon plütfarb ward. Als nw die iuden ab solchem wunderzaichen erschracken do trügen sie es wider zu dē benanten briester Petro.[118]

In diesem Absatz wurde das erschienene Blut durch keinerlei Adjektive qualifiziert, weshalb eine explizite Erwähnung einer Vergegenwärtigung des Blutes Christi hier nicht vorhanden ist. Doch liest man, dass »ein leineins weiß tuch dauon plütfarb ward[119]«. Wieder findet sich mit dem Veronika-Bildmotiv eine Anspielung auf die in den Narrativen allseits gegenwärtige Wiederholung der Passion Christi. Hartmann Schedel schreibt weiterhin:

> vnd als aber die ding an die durchleuchtigen hertzogen Balthazarn vnd Magnus gebruedere gelangt. sich der ding erkündigten vnd die narbē der wūden vnd stich sahen do hießen sie nach den iuden greiffen vnd dieselben als schmeher der götlichen maiestat cristi vnd vnßers glawbens verprennen. darumb sol aller zweyfel des vnglawbēs abgestelt sein vn nymants zweyfeln das die ersten creatur auß willen götlichs gewalts in gegwēertigkeit der hohsten maiestat in die natur des leibs vnßers herren geen mugen.[120]

Als die Herzöge Balthazar und Magnus von den wiedergefundenen Bluthostien erfuhren und die Narben des Heiligen Sakraments sahen, wurde die Juden angegriffen. Interessanterweise wird hier »narbē der wūden[121]« berichtet. Diese tauchen in der offiziellen Erzählung der Inkunabeln nicht auf, sollen aber wohl den Fokus auf das Blutvergießen des Heiligen Sakraments lenken. Weiterhin werden die Juden als die »schmeher der goetlichen maiestat cristi vnd vnßers glawbens[122]« charakterisiert. Da die »gegwēertigkeit der hohsten maiestat in die natur des leibs vnßers herren[123]« jedoch nicht angezweifelt werden durfte, wurden Ungläubige angegriffen und bestraft.

Neben dem Text steht ein ebenfalls berühmter Holzschnitt, der 26 Juden auf dem Scheiterhaufen zeigt [Abb. 8]. Das Bild wird unter anderem zur Darstellung der Strafe gegen die Mecklenburger Juden zu Sternberg benutzt. Generell soll es die allgemein erwünschte Bestrafung aller Frevler zeigen. Diese Darstellung wurde mehrfach verwendet, um die Folgen der bösen Taten der Juden zu illustrieren. Den Lesern wurde gleichfalls suggeriert, dass die Juden tatsächlich die Schänder des christlichen Glaubens seien.[124] Diese Charakterisierung gilt als die höchste Entfaltung des spätmittelalterlichen Antijudaismus des ausgehenden 15. Jahrhunderts, welcher oft zu regionalen Vertreibungen der Juden im deutschen Sprachraum führte.

Als letztes Beispiel einer graphischen Darstellung zum Sternberger Fall sei noch der Holzschnitt des *Mons Stellarum* [Abb. 9] erwähnt.[125] Dieses Werk wurde von dem Humanisten Nikolaus Marschalk im Jahr 1510 in deutscher und 1512 in lateinischer Sprache verfasst. Marschalk war Doktor beider Rechte und Rat der mecklenburgischen Herzöge.[126] Das Exemplar zählt zwar nicht als Inkunabel, da es erst im Jahr 1512 im Rostock von Ludwig Dietz gedruckt wurde, beinhaltet aber ein wichtiges Bild, das die Geschehnisfolge der Tat darstellt. Der Holzschnitt ist in vier Abbildungen aufgeteilt. Auf der oberen linken Seite findet man eine Monstranz, in der eine verehrte Bluthostie ausgestellt wird. Auf

Abb. 10 Detail. Geschichte der Juden von Passau mit dem Sacrament, GW M29568, Holzschnitt, Kaspar Hochfeder, Nürnberg um 1497

127 Für eine ausführliche Erklärung zur Entstehung der Kapelle zur Bluthostie und die Gründung der St. Salvator Kirche zu Passau vgl. ANTON MEYER: Die Gründung von St. Salvator in Passau – Geschichte und Legende. In: *Zeitschrift für Bayerische Landesgeschichte*. 18 (1955), S. 256–278.

128 Für eine ausführlichere Erklärung zu Gier als Todsünde und ihre soziale mittelalterliche Bedeutung vgl. CARLA CASAGRANDE und SILVANA VECCHIO: *Histoire des péchés capitaux au Moyen Âge*. Paris 2009, S. 153–191.

129 GW M44007, fol. 4v.

130 BYNUM (s. Anm. 54), S. 177–178.

131 PETER DINZELBACHER: Das Blut Christi in der Religiosität des Mittelalters. In: *900 Jahre Heilig-Blut-Verehrung in Weingarten 1094–1994 Festschrift zum Heilig-Blut-Jubiläum am 12. März 1994*. Hrsg. von NOBERT KRUSE und ULRICH HAND RUDOLF. Ostfildern 1994, Bd. 1, S. [415]–[434], hier besonders S. 421; UTA REINHOLD: Das Fritzlarer Vesperbild. In: *Frühe rheinische Vesperbilder und ihr Umkreis: neue Ergebnisse zur Technologie: Ergebnisse der Tagung an der FH Köln (27.–28.10.2006)*. Hrsg. von ULRIKE BERGMANN. München 2006, S. 34–38; WALTER PASSARGE: *Das deutsche Vesperbild im Mittelalter*. Köln 1924, S. 99. BYNUM (s. Anm. 5), S. 177–178.

132 PASSARGE (s. Anm. 131), S. 99.

der Hostie selbst ist die Kreuzigung Jesu mit Maria und Johannes unter dem Kreuz dargestellt. Eine ähnliche Bildkonzeption findet sich für die Darstellung der Kapelle der Bluthostie zu Passau in GW M29568 [Abb. 10.][127] In dieser zwölften Szene eines Flugblattes, findet der Betrachter einen Altar mit einem Kreuz zusammen mit den Statuen von Maria und Johannes. Darüber befinden sich Exvotos (Votivgaben), die Zeichen der Entstehung eines Wallfahrtsortes zu einer anderen Wunderhostie im deutschen Sprachraum sind. Vor der Kapelle sind drei Gläubige dargestellt. Diese erhoffen sich durch die Macht des Heiligen Sakraments, das unzerstörbar nicht nur eine Entweihung überstand und triumphierte, weitere Wunder.

Der zweite Bildteil des *Mons Stellarum* [Abb. 9] enthält den Hostienverkauf zwischen Eleazar und Peter Däne. Die Szene zeigt den Kochtopf und damit ein Motiv, das in den früheren bildlichen Beispielen nicht erscheint. Eleazar steht in der Tür als Peter Däne ihm den Kochtopf mit aushändigt. Der Kochtopf symbolisiert den Hostienverkauf und damit die Geldgier des Priesters Peter Däne, der das Heilige Sakrament an den Juden verkaufte.[128] Geld gilt als übliches Motiv in der Darstellung eines Hostienverkaufes und wird auch in anderen Bildserien verwendet. Darüber hinaus wird auf die 30 Silberlinge angespielt, die Judas für den Verrat Jesu erhielt. Dies wird explizit durch einen Geldbeutel, den ein Jude in der zweiten Szene des GW M29568 in seiner linken Hand hält [Abb. 11.]

Die dritte Bildszene des *Mons Stellarum* [Abb. 9] stellt den Moment der Hostienentweihung selbst dar. Hier wird das Heilige Sakrament jedoch nicht mit Messern, sondern mit Nadeln durch die drei Juden Eleazar, Jakob und Michol malträtiert.[129] Ein weiterer Mann hält eine Nadel mit seiner rechten Hand, verwendet sie aber nicht zur Entweihung der Hostie. Sieben Juden werden in diesem Teil des Holzschnittes dargestellt, ohne mit Namen genannt zu werden. Im Unterschied zu seinem Text, in dem das erschienene Blut mit keinem Adjektiv qualifiziert wird, scheint das Bluten der Hostie im Bild des *Mons Stellarum* deutlicher als in anderen graphischen Darstellungen abgebildet zu sein. Das wundersame Blut wurde als Tropfen[130] anstelle der Linien dargestellt, ein bildliches Detail, das dem Betrachter die Zentralität des Wunders deutlich machen sollte.

Als oftmals verwendetes Motiv des Blutvergießens Jesu haben die Tropfen verschiedene Bedeutungen für die christliche Ikonographie und deren Devotionen. Caroline Walker Bynum zufolge wurden Tropfen von einigen Historikern[131] als Weintrauben mit eucharistischer Bedeutung interpretiert.[132] Hawel argumentiert, dass sich Trauben und Blut auf die fünf Wunden Jesu beziehen. Hier lässt sich eine Parallele zum Sinnbild Christus in der Kelter herleiten. Auch darin liegt eine Assoziation mit dem erlösenden Blut Jesu. In diesem Sinn deuten die Tropfen aus den gepressten Weintrauben und aus der mystischen Kelter das kontinuierliche Blutvergießen an, das in der Passion Christi anfing und mit der Eucharistie während der Messe in der Gegenwart für die Sündenvergebung immer noch fließt.

Abb. 11 Detail. Geschichte der Juden von Passau mit dem Sacrament, GW M29568, Holzschnitt, Kaspar Hochfeder, Nürnberg um 1497

133 ALOIS THOMAS: *Die Darstellung Christi in der Kelter: eine theologische kulturhistorische Studie, Zugleich ein Beitrag zur Geschichte und Volkskunde des Weinbaus*. Düsseldorf 1981, S. 50.

134 Predigt an den Weihnachtsfesten von den syrischen Schriftsteller und Heiligen Ephräm (†373). Vgl. (s. Anm. 133), S. 57–58.

135 Für eine kunsthistorische Diskussion zum Begriff »Schmerzensmann« bzw. »Imago Pietatis« Vgl. GRAŻYNA JURKOWLANIEC, The Rise and Early Development of the Man of Sorrows in Central and Nothern Europe In: *New Perspectives on the Man of Sorrows*. Hrsg. von CHATHERINE S. PUGLISI, WILLIAM R. BATCHAM. Kalamazoo 2013, S. 48–50.

136 PETER HAWEL. *Die Pietà: eine Blüte der Kunst*. Würzburg. Echter Verlag 1985, S. 64–66.

137 »Bei der Bescheidung und sechs Mal bei der Passion« Vgl. HEUSER (s. Anm. 102), S. 90.

138 Die Verknüpfungen zwischen den siebenfachen Blutvergießen Christi, dem Rosenkranz und den Bluttropfen des Herren wurde auch von Johannes Heuser in der Blutverehrung zu Weingarten identifiziert (Vgl. HEUSER (s. Anm. 102), S. 90).

Sinnbildlich sind diese Tropfen aus Trauben ein weiteres Bildthema, das den mystischen Saft aus der Weinkelter mit dem historischen Blut des gekreuzigten Gottessohnes in einen Vergleich setzt:[133] »Laßt uns den Hirten preisen, der das Opfer der Versöhnung darbrachte und selbst zum Opferlamm wurde ... Laßt uns die Trauben, die ausgepreßt sie wurden und mit ihrem Safte den Kelch unseres Heiles füllt.«[134] Unter dem mystischem Saft wurde die Mischung aus den gepressten Weintrauben und dem Blut Jesu in der Weinkelter verstanden. Diese bezieht sich auf die Ankündigung des Opfers des Herrn im Alten Testament, der Passion selbst und ihrer Wiederholung während der heiligen Messe.

Weiterhin begründet diese mystische Verquickung von gepressten Weintrauben und Blut Christi, ein Sinnbild zur aristotelischen Dualität zwischen Substanz und Akzidenz, die die Transsubstantiationslehre sinnbildlich erklärt. Der »mystischer Saft« der Weinkelter fließt in den Kelch der Weinweihung. Aus diesem Kelch wurde das eucharistische Blut während der Messe getrunken. Das Weinkelter-Motiv führte dem Betrachter die Art und Weise vor Augen, wie die Wesensverwandlung bei einer Weinkonsekration stattfinden sollte. Das Sichtbare sind die gepressten Trauben. Was jedoch unsichtbar bleibt ist das Opferblut Christi, welches durch die Akzidenz des Weins konsumiert wird. Nach der Wandlung wird die Weinsubstanz zum Blut Christi. In diesem Sinne sind die Darstellungen der Weinkelter ein Versuch die Sichtbarkeit des unsichtbaren eucharistischen Blutes zu visualisieren. Der Schmerzensmann[135] der Kelter presst die Trauben mit seinen Füssen, sodass den Wein konsekriert werden kann. Seine schmerzhafte Aufgabe zusammen mit seinem Blutvergießen bildet die unsichtbare Wandlung der Konsekration.

Die Rosetten in zahlreichen Beispielen von Vesperbild beziehen sich auf die Wunden Christi und gelten als ein Zeichen für seine Geduld während seiner Passion. Die Rosen sind ein Teil verschiedener Symbole, welche die Gläubigen zur Meditation über Leiden und Schmerzen Jesu einladen.[136] Die Bluttropfen der Passion bilden die fünf Blütenblätter der mystischen Rose Mariens, welche wiederum eine Verknüpfung mit der Frucht ihres Leibes herstellt. Die fünf Wunden Christi sind mit den fünf Blütenblättern vergleichbar und symbolisieren zusammen die Opfergabe Jesu in der Vergangenheit und der Gegenwart.

Wie oben diskutiert, wurde das erschienene Blut im Buch GW M44008 als *gebenedeit* beschrieben. Dieses Adjektiv stellt eine Parallele mit der Frucht des Leibes Mariens und der Opfergabe Jesu dar. Es ist lohnend, darüber nachzudenken, ob die Tropfen des *Mons Stellarum* tatsächlich einen Zusammenhang zwischen den fünf Wunden, den siebenfachen Blutvergießen Christi,[137] der Weinkelter, der mystischen Rose Mariens,[138] der Frucht ihres Leibes und den entweihten Hostien suggerieren sollen. Schließlich wurde diese verknüpfende Interpretation zum Opferblut Jesu bereits für das Vesperbild und weitere christliche Bildthemen verwendet. Ein Christ, der das Buch las, hätte sich bei der Betrachtung der Bluttropfen durchaus an die Tropfen des Vesperbildes erinnert. Darüber hinaus erfolgt in der Darstellung der Szene ein Vergleich

Abb. 12 Detail. Geschichte der Juden von Passau mit dem Sacrament, GW M29568, Holzschnitt, Kaspar Hochfeder, Nürnberg um 1497

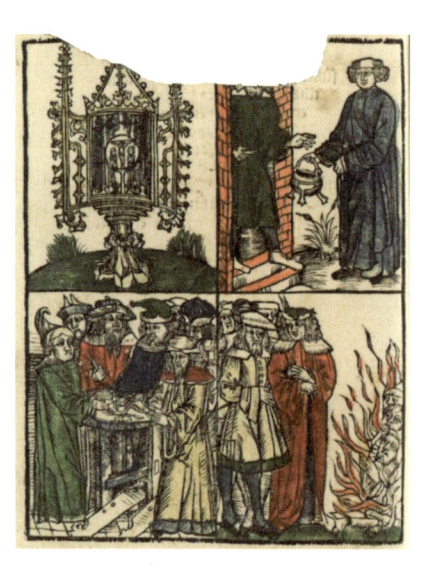

Abb. 13 Hostienentweihung zu Sternberg In: NIKOLAUS MARSCHALK: *Mons Stellarum*. Rostock, Holzschnitt Ludwig Dietz 15. Exemplar der UB Erfurt. Sig. Druck 8. O

139 Vgl. HONEMANN (s. Anm. 1), S. 209.

140 Eine erfundene Darstellbarkeit, welche jeweils das Paradox der Repräsentation des Unsichtbaren begründet.

141 Honemann argumentiert, dass die Darstellung des Scheiterhaufens im *Mons Stellarum* [Abb. 9] vergleichbar mit dem Holzschnitt der Schedelschen Weltchronik [Abb. 8] ist. Dieser diente wahrscheinlich als Inspiration für die spätere Anfertigung eines Schnitts für das Rostocker Buch im Jahr 1512, vgl. HONEMANN (s. Anm. 1), S. 204.

zwischen dem Leiden Christi in biblischer Zeit und seiner Wiederholung während einer Hostienentweihung.

Auf diese Weise konnte der Gläubige tatsächlich nicht die Transsubstantiationslehre visualisieren, da eine unsichtbare Wesensverwandlung nicht dargestellt werden kann, sondern viel mehr sich das Leiden Christi und seine Vergegenwärtigung in der jüdischen Entweihung deutlicher vorstellen. Oftmals wurde in der Historiographie argumentiert, diese Erzählungsstruktur deute auf einen gewissen gesellschaftlichen Zweifel an der Realpräzens des Heiligen Sakraments hin. Doch möchte ich mit diesen bildlichen Beispielen aufzeigen, dass diese Bilder in Verbindung mit den Texten eine Einladung zur ausführlichen Meditation über das Leiden Jesu bieten sollten.[139] Die Christen sollten erkennen, dass Jesus bisher für die Menschheit gelitten hatte und dass dies durch die jüdische Bosheit in der Gegenwart weiterhin ermöglicht werde. Die Tropfen können ein weiteres Symbol sein, das eine komplexe Assoziation zwischen den antijüdischen Legenden und der spätmittelalterlichen, auf das Blut Jesu orientierten, Soteriologie begründet.

Das theologische Paradox der Darstellung der Bluterscheinungen bei Wunderhostien diente einem Wunsch der Sichtbarkeit der Vergegenwärtigung des Blutes Christi. Die Bilder eucharistischer Erscheinungen galten als ein begrifflicher Widerspruch zur Eucharistielehre und ihrer Dualität zwischen Substanz und Akzidenz. Andererseits begründen sie eine Darstellungsform der Sichtbarkeit des Unsichtbaren (die Wesensverwandlung der Eucharistie), die dem Sujet von Jesus in der Weinkelter ähnlich ist, in dem die Transsubstantiation durch die quälende Aufgabe des blutigen Schmerzensmannes verbildlicht. Beim Hostienfrevel leidet das Heilige Sakrament ebenfalls, was die Gläubigen als ein Zeichen der eucharistischen Macht verstehen konnten. Die Bluterscheinung bei einer Hostienentweihung deutet nicht auf eine vereinfachte Erklärung oder Abbildung der Transsubstantiationslehre, sondern viel auf eine intendierte Darstellbarkeit[140] ihrer unsichtbaren Wesensverwandlung hin.

In der letzten Szene dieser Serie wurde die Strafe gegen die Angeklagten am 24. Oktober 1492 dargestellt. Hier finden wir acht Juden, von denen drei bereits auf dem Scheiterhaufen verbrannt wurden, während die anderen fünf Männer noch auf ihren Tod warten. Ähnlich wie in der *Schedelschen Weltchronik* [Abb. 8] und im *Flugblatt zum Passauer Hostienfrevel* [Abb. 12] wurde die Strafe als Folge künftiger Missetaten gegen die Eucharistie vor Augen geführt.[141] *Mons Stellarum* wurde erst zwanzig Jahre nach Ende des Prozesses gedruckt. Dieses Buch demonstriert uns, dass die offizielle Erzählung mit weiteren Elementen beziehungsweise einer ausführlicheren Beschreibung der Ereignisse angereichert wurde.[142] So kann erklärt werden, warum es wesentlich war, andere Inhalte der offiziellen Erzählung als nur die Hostienentweihung selbst darzustellen.

Der teilweise beschädigte Holzschnitt des Exemplars »Mons Stellarum« der UB Erfurt wurde mit vier verschiedenen Farben (gelb, rot, grün, oder Blau) koloriert [Abb. 13]. In dieser Szene werden die Kleidungen der Akteure, die Monstranz, der Boden, die Tischecke und die

Flammen der letzten Szene eingefärbt. Im Unterschied zur [Abb. 5] wurde die auf dem Tisch beschädigte Hostie nicht mit roter Farbe versehen. Dies deutet darauf hin, dass die verwendete Kolorierung nur dem visuellen Aspekt des Bildes diente und keine theologischen oder devotionalen Bedeutungen hatte. Die kolorierten Kleider unterstreichen die Individualität der dargestellten Juden, das rot der Flammen mag hier auf die schmerzhafte Bestrafung der Frevler vorausweisen.

Zwanzig Jahre später kam eine Vielzahl von Besuchern zur Pilgerfahrt nach Sternberg.[143] Bereits Ende 1494 errichtete man eine eigene Heiligblut-Kapelle für die Wunderhostien.[144] Die Erzählfolge wurde durch immer weitere Details angereichert und ausgeschmückt, was ein weiterer Grund dafür sein könnte, dass eine neue bildliche Darstellung mit weiteren Motiven angefertigt wurde. Die Bilder, die Texte und die Reliquie der Bluthostie dienten der Entstehung und dem Weiterleben der Sternberger Pilgerfahrt. Weitere Objekte wurden zu Kontaktreliquien erklärt, doch alle nachträglich aufgebauten Erzählungen, Bilder und Dokumente dienten, von politischen und wirtschaftlichen Absichten abgesehen, wohl als Einladung zur Meditation über die Vergegenwärtigung des Blutes und Leides Jesu.

Nach der offiziellen Vertreibung der Juden aus dem Königreich Kastilien im Jahr 1492 folgte der Höhepunkt des europäischen Antijudaismus. Der Wunsch einer christlichen Gesellschaft ohne Juden war nicht auf die iberische Halbinsel begrenzt. Die Geschichte um den Hostienfrevel zu Sternberg und deren spätere Visualisierung in verschiedenen Inkunabeln gelten als weiteres Indiz der Festigung eines äußerst ausgeprägten Antijudaismus des 15. Jahrhunderts, der sich durch die weite Verbreitung der antijüdischen Erzählstruktur der Hostienentweihung verstärkte.

Am Ende des Textes der Inkunabeln zum Sternberger Fall steht stets eine Warnung an alle Städte, die eine jüdische Gemeinde hatten: Die geflüchteten Täter des Sternberger Hostienfrevels, Eleazar und der Mönch, könnten sich zusammen mit anderen örtlichen Juden in Besitz von zwei konsekrierten Hostien befinden und irgendwo versteckt halten.[145] Die ausgelöste Verfolgung von 246 unschuldigen Juden aus Mecklenburg verdeutlicht die Auswirkungen der Erzählung für die örtliche Judenverfolgung.[146] Nachdem Hartmann Schedel in seiner Weltchronik über den Sternberger Fall berichtet hatte, folgten andere bekannt gewordene Erwähnungen der Tat wie die in den Schweizer Chroniken von Peter Etterlin und Diebold Schlling, die ebenfalls ein Bild zur Sternberger Hostienentweihung enthalten.[147] Durch die Festlegung auf eine offizielle Erzählung konnte sich das Wissen um den Sternberger Fall an anderen Orten verbreiten. Daraus folgte eine Rechtfertigung der Wallfahrtsorte und deren Reliquien sowie eine Warnung an alle Christen vor den Juden, die wahrscheinlich weitere Frevel in der Zukunft verüben würden.

Eine ausgeprägte Stigmatisierung verursacht durch den Zusammenstoß von religiösen Symbolen und Riten der jüdischen und christlichen Lehre diente der eucharistischen Frömmigkeit und dem ihr inhärenten Wunsch einer Vergegenwärtigung des Leidens und Blutes

142 Es existiert auch eine deutsche Version, die 1510 gedruckt wurde. Weiterhin entstanden 1522 neue lateinische Exemplare (Vgl. HONEMANN (s. Anm. 1), S. 204–205).

143 Für weitere Details zur Entstehung der Sternberger Pilgerfahrt vgl. SKOTTKI (s. Anm. 42), S. 326–327.

144 Vgl. HONEMANN (s. Anm. 1), S. 190. Die Sternberger Pilgerfahrt zog auch adelige Besucher wie die dänische Königsfamilie und eine spanische Prinzessin an (Vgl. ebd., S. 191).

145 Vgl. SKOTTKI (s. Anm. 42), S. 331; GW M44007, fol. 5v.: »Aber etwo vil de schuldigen Jüden mit sampt dem verlaugneten munich sein nach der marck vnnd furder nach Nurmberg vnd Venedig yn willen tzu flyhen/ alß etlich vff sy bekant der halb wol not thut vffehung tzu habenn der geweichten hostien halben der sye tzwo hinwegk gebracht haben/ da mit got dem almechtigē nit furder lesterung yn landen vnd steten do Jüden wonē beschehe.«

146 Vgl. SKOTTKI (s. Anm. 42), S. 331.

147 Der Sternberger Fall wurde zwischen 1492 und 1501 in der Chronik erwähnt (Vgl. *Eidgenössische Chronik des Luzerners Diebold Schilling* (Luzerner Schilling) Luzern: Korporation Luzern, S. 293f. Pergament, Depositum in der ZB und HSB Luzern, verfügbar auf www.e-codices.unifr.ch); HONEMANN (s. Anm. 1), S. 204.

Christi. Die Juden wurden als die Multiplikatoren des erschienenen Blutes Jesu in der Gegenwart charakterisiert. Doch dienten ihre Taten nicht der Erfüllung ihrer Wünsche, sondern dem Sieg des Christentums durch die Festigung des Glaubens an die Sündenvergebung und Erlangung des ewigen Heils. Als das kastilische Königreich über die Juden und Muslime triumphierte, um eine Gesellschaft ohne Ungläubige zu etablieren, wurden auch dort dieselben antijüdischen Legenden benutzt wie im deutschen Sprachraum des 15. Jahrhunderts. Neue Reliquien erschienen, die Blutverehrung setzte sich fort und immer wieder wurden jüdische Gemeinden vernichtet. Dennoch blieb das Ziel des Aufbaus einer christlichen Gesellschaft ohne die Juden weiterhin ein Ziel, das glücklicherweise niemals wahr wurde.[148]

---

[148] Für die Korrektur des Aufsatzes möchte ich mich bei Kristin Skottki, Paul Schweitzer-Martin, Falk Eisermann, Maximilian Nalbach und Bernd Peter Lother bedanken.

Randall Herz

O Vos Sacerdotes Dei
A New Broadside from Anton Koberger's Nuremberg Press

With notes on the content, audience, and transmission, including an analysis of the typographical relation to the Latin edition of the *Liber chronicarum* and its family of types

A new and unrecorded broadside from the press of the Nuremberg printer Anton Koberger has been discovered at the Universitätsbibliothek Erlangen-Nuremberg.[1] In contrast to other ephemera published by the printer, the broadside contains a unique sermon-like text addressed to priests, calling for spiritual purity in the mass celebration. Printed with the same type used for the 1493 Latin edition of the *Liber chronicarum*, it is also of special typographical interest. It joins a group of just three other works ever printed with type 16:110G. This paper will discuss the content, sources, and target audience of the broadside and will explore the origin and family relation of the type to a group of types in use in the same period in printing shops in Nuremberg, Basel, and Strasbourg.

Surviving 15th century broadsides show a great diversity of content and purpose. They were used to make public royal proclamations and issue town ordinances, to announce marksmen's festivals and publish printer's lists, to print almanacs, Aderlass calendars, medical tracts and even songs. Church and monastic communities made similar use of the medium to issue their own ecclesiastical writings, including Papal bulls and briefs, letters of indulgence, prayers, among many others. Over 2,500 editions of broadsides are currently recorded in ISTC and GW, issued on presses throughout Europe.[2] The actual number of broadsides printed was presumably much higher, but many were lost or destroyed once they had fulfilled their original purpose. It is thus of some interest that a new and previously unknown broadside has come to light at the Universitätsbibliothek Erlangen-Nürnberg. It survives in not one, but in two copies attached at the end of shelfmark H62/INC 1581 a. Its sermon-like character and theme make it unique among the church broadsides. The target audience was the community of cloistered priests and its theme spiritual purity in the Eucharistic celebration.

The discovery also offers an opportunity to look at a special typographical aspect relating to one of the incunabula period's most popular illustrated works. The *Liber chronicarum*, containing more than 1,800 woodcuts, was commissioned by the Sebald Schreyer-Michael Wolgemut

---

[1] UB Erlangen-Nürnberg, an H62/INC 1581 b (since 1951, before that date Inc. 1202).

[2] This count is based on GW and ISTC.

Fig. 1 *O Vos Sacerdotes Dei* … Nuremberg: Anton Koberger, about 1493–98. Broadside. UB Erlangen-Nürnberg, in H62/INC 1581 b (copy 1)

3 Liber chronicarum. Nuremberg: Anton Koberger für Sebald Schreyer und Sebastian Kammermeister 12.07.1493 2° (ISTC is00307000. GW M40784).

4 Apocalypsis cum figuris. Nuremberg: [Anton Koberger for] Albrecht Dürer 1498 2° (ISTC ij00226000. GW M12930). Reissued with several new woodcuts in 1511. Nuremberg: Albrecht Dürer 1511 (VD 16 B 5248).

5 MAXIMILIAN I, KING OF THE ROMANS: Der Landfriede (Ausschreiben). Worms 07.08.1495 [Nuremberg: Anton Koberger, after 07.08.1495] Bdsde (ISTC im00391560. VE 15 M-47. GW Ratsschulbibl. Nickel (Zwickau) 713). My thanks to Dr. Lutz Mahnke (Ratsschulb Zwickau) who kindly provided an image of the broadside.

6 CHRISTOPH RESKE: *Die Produktion der Schedelschen Weltchronik in Nürnberg*. Wiesbaden 2000 (Mainzer Studien zur Buchwissenschaft. 10), p. 61 (German) and also p. 181 (English version).

7 GRATIANUS: *Decretum*. Basel: Michael Wenssler 05.09.1482 2° (ISTC ig00371000. GW 11363).

8 It is listed in Pfeiffer's catalogue Ms 2350 under numerus currens 261 and in the Standort-Katalog 2° Ms 2555 [1], fol. 87r (under Ec I 32 – 261 Decretum); the old L was located at the Ritterakademie, B-Saal, Hauptstraße 16. The L relocated to the Altes Schloss in 1825 and to the present librarian building in 1912.

9 They are briefly mentioned today in the copy specific notes for the *Decretum* in the L's OPAC and in INKA http://www.inka.uni-tuebingen.de/cgi-bin/inkunabel?sinkanum=56000593 [22.01.2023].

10 In translation: Oh, how holy must he be, who would preside over the host (the Lamb of the Lord).

11 See Appendix 1 for the complete text of the broadside.

consortium, and printed in 1493 by Anton Koberger in a Latin and German edition. For the Latin edition,[3] a rotunda letterform was chosen which all but disappeared from use thereafter. It was used once again in 1498 and 1511 in Albrecht Dürer's Latin issues of *Apocalypsis cum figuris*,[4] and a sprinkling of uppercase letters appears interspersed among the main type in a broadside from the year 1495.[5] We can now add the Erlangen broadside to this small list of printed works. Given the costs and time for producing a type, it remains a mystery why the rotunda was so seldomly used. It has been suggested that the type was designed and specially cast for use in the Nuremberg chronicle and for that reason was never intended for further use.[6] My paper will explore this question and, focusing on the origin of the type, will examine its relationship to a family of types used by printers in Nuremberg, Basel, and Strasbourg, with special attention given to Georg Stuchs and his type 7:108G.

The discovery of the broadside

The two copies of the broadside were discovered in a 1492 edition of Gratian's *Decretum*[7] where they are attached to the verso side of the final folio leaf of the volume. The copies also have a fold line in the middle, indicating they were once folded in half and kept loosely in the same book by an early reader before then. That reader was a member of the Benedictine rule who made copious notes throughout the volume. He also made notes on one of the copies, establishing the relationship between copy and owner and also providing insights into his interest in the text of the broadside.

The copy of the *Decretum* was among the 354 incunabula transferred from the residence library of the Margraves of Ansbach-Brandenburg in Ansbach to the University Library at Erlangen in December of 1805, in advance of the former margraviate's incorporation into the Kingdom of Bavaria. Early catalogues from 1805 and 1811 document its arrival in Erlangen and record the shelf location at the old library site in the *Ritterakademie*.[8] There is no mention of the copies in the historical catalogues from this period, however, and indeed they have remained unrecorded until now. They will be described in this article for the first time.[9]

The content and argument of the broadside

The tract addresses the issue of spiritual purity and the priest's role as celebrant of the Eucharistic sacrifice – the central rite of the Roman Catholic mass. The theme is announced in the opening lines of the broadside: "O quam sanctus debet esse, qui volt agno preesse."[10] In stern language and using the words of Christ and the saints, the tract admonishes the priest to be ever aware of the holiness of his office, warning him of negligence and superbia.[11]

Vos sacerdotes dei. vos tangunt sermones mei. Magnum dignitatis agnum dei tractatis. Hieremias ore pphetauit. Johannes digito monstrauit. Maria in ventre portauit. Hij tres anteq̃ nati sunt sanctificati. O q̃ sanctus debet esse. qui agno debet preesse. Non ore pphetare: sed sumere τ manducare. Non digito monstrare: sed tractare. Non tm̄ in ventre. sed semp debet portare in mente. Ve autem bis τ iterum ve qui sordida τ polluta conscientia tractant corpus christi sicut carnes agni qui venduntur in macellis. Quos alloquit̃ beatus Ambrosius in psona christi dicens. O peccator tu indigne sacerdos. noli me amplius affligere peccando. Plus enim me ledit vulnus peccati tui q̃ vulnus lateris mei. τ subiungit. Magis em̄ delinquunt qui iam regnantem in celo contemnunt peccando. scilicet indigne tractantes τ sumentes corpus christi. q̃ qui crucifixerunt eum ambulantem in terris. Non quasi crucifixores: sed quasi tanti sacramenti indigni confectores τ presumptuosi perceptores. Quia illi semel dominu̅ crucifixerunt. isti quantu̅ in eis est quotidie eum crucifigu̅t. scilicet contra deum viuentes τ indigne sumentes ac sacrificantes. Quibus attendendus est illud beati Gregorij. Cu̅ ingratus ad intercedendu̅ mittit̃. irati animus ad deteriora puocatur. De qua libus etia̅ sic ait beatus Augustinus. Malle potius pilati. iude. herodis sustinere pena̅. q̃ sacerdotis indigne communicantis τ conficientis. Animaduertite igit̃ o vos sacerdotes in qua̅ta puritate τ timore dei accedere debetis ad illud sacrificium ad quod christus accessurus p angustia sudauit sanguinem. Attenta aũt tanta dignitate τ tamexpauescenda maiestate huius sacrificij. ad quod etia̅ digne sumendu̅ vix sufficiunt mille anni lacrimarum τ durissime penitentie. non ideo se quisq̃ debet abstrahere a pceptione ipsius immunis saltem a peccato mortali. Sed pfides in omnipotentis dei misericordia fiducialiter accedere. Nam bn̄ venerabilem Bedam sacerdos qui est sine peccato mortali τ in bono pposito. si no̅ celebrat cu̅ habet copia̅ celebrandi. quatu̅ in ipo est. priuat scta̅m trinitate̅ gloria; angelos in celesti hierusalem leticia. homines laborantes in terris beneficio et gratia: animas in purgatorio patrocinio et venia. Itaq̃ digne celebrare volenti octo sequentia sunt attendenda. videlicet

Intentionis discussio. Ne	{ Propter vanam gloriam Propter verecundiam Propter timorem Propter auariciam Ex consuetudine	} Celebret	
Generalis co̅tritio super	{ Omissis q̃ facere potuit Co̅missis q̃ face n̅ debuit	} corde ore τ ope	
Pura confessio	{ Notabilium Communium Ignoratorum	} Criminum	
Quid intendat consequi principaliter	{ Augmentum dilectionis Insepabilitate̅ vnionis Acceleratione̅ visionis	} dei	
Quid intendat facere	{ Deum p latriam colere Morte christi rememorari Totam ecclesia̅ adiuuare	} semp	
In canone habeat illa	{ Diligentia̅ ad co̅ficiendu̅ Reuerentia̅ ad tangedu̅ Deuotione̅ ad sumendu̅	} corpus xp̃i	
Attedere debeat que ibi fiat	{ Magna in signis Maiora i verbis Maxima i intetoe̅	} Misse	
Et hoc propter continentia̅	{ Tam excellentis corporis Excellentioris anime Excelle̅tissime diuinitatis	} christi	

Cum autem vt quidam ait. Turpius eijcitur q̃ non admittitur hospes Cauendum est cuiq̃ sic su̅pto venerabilissimo hospite ne redeat ad vomitum. et iterum volutet se in volutabro peccati. rursusq̃ crucifigat sibi filium dei. Et conquerat̃ domin̅ de eiusmodi illud Hieremi. xj. Quid est q̃ dilect̃ me̅us i domo mea facit scelera multa: Et illud de renouantibus dolorem suum dicens Zacharie xiij. His plagatus sum in domo eorum qui diligebant me. Sed pseruare studeat se in puritate τ mundicia cordis vt deu̅ videre possit in syon. Beati deniq̃ mu̅do corde quoniam ipsi deum videbu̅t. Amen.

Summary

The text of the broadside begins with a direct address to the priestly target audience: "O vos sacerdotes dei, vos tangunt sermones mei".[12] This, the first of eight Leonine verses, introduces the theme of priestly purity in the Eucharistic celebration: How holy must he be who presides over the Lamb of God, who may touch and eat of it. Then unlike John the Baptist, who was able only to point to Christ in recognition, or Mary, who carried the Savior in her womb, a priest must carry the Lamb of God constantly in his thoughts.[13] The tone then suddenly changes to a sharp condemnation of those priests who, of an impure state of mind ("sordida et polluta conscientia"), handle the Body of Christ "like lamb meat sold at market" ("sicut carnes agni qui venduntur in macellis").

Four saints are then invoked who each in turn addresses priestly motives at the altar, admonishing the priest to be worthy of his office, to keep Christ's sacrifice constantly in his thoughts and be always aware of his special role in the Christian cosmos. Acting as Christ's messenger, Saint Ambrosius relates Christ's complaint about the unworthy priest. Saint Gregory warns of God's anger towards the ungrateful priest who is sent as his intermediary. Saint Augustin would rather endure the punishment given to Pontius Pilate and Herod Antipas than be a priest who is unworthy of his sacramental duties.

The priestly reader is then asked to reflect on the degree of purity required when celebrating the Eucharistic sacrifice and to consider the majesty of Christ's sacrifice. Though a priest may not feel himself free of sin, he may enter confidently into God's mercy. According to Saint Bede, if a priest, who is free of mortal sin and in good intention, does not celebrate when he has so much to celebrate in Christ's abundance, that priest deprives the Holy Trinity of the glory, the angels of their joy, toiling mankind of benefit and favor and the souls in purgatory of patronage and grace. Extolling the priest's place and role in the Christian universe in this way, the main section of text ends.

An exercise to deepen the priest's spirituality follows, prefaced by this instruction: "Itaque digne celebrare volenti octo sequentia sunt attendenda".[14] It consists of eight meditations, each one building on the previous one, to enhance and strengthen the spirituality of the priest as celebrant of the mass.

The short conclusion returns to the severe tone of the first section. The unworthy priest is likened to a guest who, once invited into the home of the host, wallows in sin. The priestly audience hears Christ's complaint about the members of his household who abuse and betray this trust. Verses from the Old Testament underline the severity of transgression by the unworthy priest. The tract then ends on a hopeful note, promising the reward of heaven to the priests who remain pure of heart.

With its focus on priestly purity, the sermon/tract belongs to a larger body of literature on priesthood, which was a dominant theme in

---

[12] In translation: Oh, you priests of the Lord, my words are meant for you.

[13] The verses were attributed in the late Middle Ages to Saint Bernard of Clairvaux (see below).

[14] In translation: Therefore, if you wish to celebrate the mass with dignity, you must heed the following eight things.

15th century theological discourse.¹⁵ At the same time it also reflects reform efforts which were taking place at the end of the 15th century and aimed at raising the standards of the mass celebration. The specific circumstances which gave rise to the text are unknown. Was it written in conjunction with a reform within one of the monastic communities, i.e. the Benedictine order? Who was its author – was he a preacher at a local monastery or perhaps a provincial in a chapter of an order? While these questions are likely to remain unanswered, the tract, with its call to spiritual reform, was clearly meant to reach a broader monastic audience through its publication.

Sources and dependencies

Remarkable in its form and sharp tone, the text is also notable for its extensive use of borrowings from popular religious treatises and sayings of church authorities. The author was obviously well-versed in the literature on the mass. Among his sources were apocryphal texts attributed to several saints, a popular work called *Stella clericorum*¹⁶ and sententia by the Church Fathers as well as quotations from the Bible. The text can be seen as a prime example of medieval compilation, relying heavily on source materials. Yet its originality, if we may apply that criterium here as well, lies in the compiler's adept arrangement of those materials.

Typical of a sermon, the author uses an effective if also, when viewed from a modern standpoint, difficult psychological strategy. He begins in a tone of severity and reprimand, creating doubt and guilt, calling on priests to reflect on the grandeur of Christ's sacrifice and enter into his mercy. Following the process of introspection and cleansing, he ends positively, citing Saint Bede and the special role of the priest as intermediary between heaven and earth. By incorporating quotations into his text, he creates a sense of immediacy and directness as if Christ and the saints were speaking in person to the reader. In sum, the author employs a strategy of exclusion and reward, chastising priestly impurity on the one hand while promising the reward of heaven on the other. With its tone and rhetoric, the text cannot have failed in its call for inward examination, and it includes to this end a spiritual exercise in the section that follows. The tract ends with a renewed warning against negligence and priestly hubris.

What were the sources used by the author? The opening Leonine verses, with their artful internal and end rhyming, were attributed in the 15th century to Bernard of Clairvaux O Cist (†1153).¹⁷ Given their first appearance at the end of the 14th century, well after the saint's death, the verses are considered apocryphal.¹⁸

Two passages on priestly chastity and purity were taken from the anonymous popular tract *Stella clericorum*.¹⁹ In the tract the first passage, beginning "O peccator tu indigne sacerdos [...]", is spoken by Saint Augustin in a dialogue among several saints. In the broadside it is spoken by Saint Ambrosius to the priestly audience, a significant adaption

---

15 See ADOLPH FRANZ: *Die Messe im Deutschen Mittelalter. Beiträge zur Geschichte der Liturgie und des religiösen Volkslebens*. Freiburg i. Br. 1902.

16 Stella clericorum. Edited by ERIC H. REITER. Toronto 1997 (Pontifical Inst. of Mediaeval Studies).

17 *O vos sacerdotes dei, vos tangent sermons mei ... sed semper debet portare in mente*.

18 See HANS WALTHER: *Initia carminum ac versuum Medii Aevi posterioris Latinoris. Alphabetisches Verzeichnis der Versanfänge mittellateinischer Dichtungen*. Göttingen 1959 (Carmina Medii Aevi posterioris Latina. 1), no 13074.

19 Stella clericorum (see note 16), p. 32, ll. 28–31, and p. 35, ll. 43–51; see Appendix 2. A search using available online resources yielded over 150 manuscripts containing *Stella clericorum* in just the German speaking regions. The tract was also printed in many major European cities including Paris, Cologne, Deventer, and London from around 1475 on. See Manuscripta Mediaevalia for Germany; see ISTC for editions printed before 1500 in Germany.

(Appendix 2). If one of the many manuscripts which transmit *Stella clericorum* should also contain the broadside's variant, its place of origin may also help to identify where the broadside was written. Between the passages from *Stella clericorum* the author inserts a slightly adapted saying from Pope Gregory's *Liber regulae pastoralis*:[20] "Cum ingratus ad intercedendum mittitur, irati animus ad deteriora provocatur".[21] The section ends, as previously noted, with the apocryphal saying attributed to Saint Bede.[22]

The table of *octo consideranda*, the centerpiece of the tract, was a hugely popular text. It is transmitted in more than 150 manuscripts and in several redactions between c. 1385 and the year 1505. According to medieval tradition, the table was made by the Franciscan monk Saint Bonaventure (†1274), but it is more likely a product of a 14th century imitator.[23] In the form in which it appears in the broadside,[24] the table closely resembles a popular 15th century version of the text, but also differs from it in an important detail. In the popular version, the first spiritual exercise cites four false motives for wishing to say mass. The broadside includes a fifth: the vice of *avaricium*.[25] In this it joins a group of just five manuscripts which contain the variant (Appendix 3). The author of the broadside may have been familiar with one of them and must also have viewed avarice as a serious problem among the clergy.

Like the other sections, the short conclusion is compiled from various sources. It opens with a popular saying from Ovid's *Tristia* (Lamentations): "As some have said: *Turpius ejicitur quam non admittitur hospes* [...]"[26] It cites verses from the Old Testament Books of Jeremiah and Zechariah to underline Christ's indignation and anger at the abuse of the Lord's house by the sinful priest.[27] It ends with a verse from the Sermon on the Mount ("Beati [...] mundo corde quoniam ipse deum videbunt, Mt. 5:8"), assuring the priest that he who is pure of heart will see the Heavenly Father in Zion.

Such a generous borrowing from texts and tracts on the mass by the author would have been possible only in a well-stocked library such as would be found at a larger monastery or parish church. If that library has survived intact through the centuries, the books used by the author and any notes he may have made in them might still be present there today.

Parallel transmission

While writing this article, two other transmissions of the text came to light and will be briefly treated here. The first was found unexpectedly in a mass book for the Meissen diocese. This *Missale Misnense*, commissioned by Bishop Johann VI von Saalhausen (r. 1487–1518),[28] was published in late 1495 by the Leipzig printer Conrad Kachelofen.[29] The text is the last of five preliminary texts which precede the calendar of months and the texts of the mass at the beginning of the mass book.[30] It has the heading "Ite(m) nota alias pr(ae)paratio(n)es vtilissimas ad celebrandum".

---

20 GREGORIUS MAGNUS: Liber regulae pastoralis. Pars prima, cap. 10: Qualis quisque ad regimen venire debeat.

21 Roughly translated: When an ungrateful man is sent to intercede, an angry soul is provoked to meaner things.

22 Transmitted in at least sixteen manuscripts from southern Germany and Austria.

23 BALDINUS DISTELBRINK: Bonaventurae scripta. Authentica dubia vel spuria critice recensita. Rome 1975 (Subsidia scientifica franciscalia. 5), pp. 200–201 no 225 (Tabula de consideranda a Missa celebraturis).

24 Based on a survey of a transmission in over 100 manuscripts, I was able to distinguish 5 main redactions.

25 *Intentione discussion: Ne {propter vanam gloriam / propter verecundiam / propter timorem / propter consuetudine} Celebret.*

26 In translation: "An enemy is earlier kept out than thrust out." OVIDIUS NASUS, PUBLIUS: *Tristia*, Liber 5, section 6, vers 13; see P. OVIDI NASONIS TRISTIA (Ed.): John Barrie Hall. Stuttgart/Leipzig 1995 (Bibliotheca scriptorum Graecorum et Romanorum Teubneriana).

27 Book of Jeremiah 11:15: Quid est que dilectus meus in domo mea facit scelera multa; Zechariah 13:6: His plagatus sum in domo eorum qui diligebant me.

28 For an account of the bishop's life and deeds see JULIUS LEOPOLD PASIG: Johannes VI. Bischof von Meißen. Ein Beitrag zur Sächsischen Kirchen- und Landesgeschichte, insbesondere zur Geschichte des Hochstifts Meißen. Leipzig 1867, esp. pp. 104–106.

29 Missale Misnense (Meissen): Freiberg in Sachsen: Conrad Kachelofen, 9 Nov. 1495 2° (ISTC im00673400. GW M24538).

30 All of these texts are found in the first quire: fol. 1r: blank; fol. 1va: Dominicis diebus benediction salis et aquae; fol. 2ra (signiert Kreuz (✠) ij): Benedictio vini pro amore Johannis; fol. 2vb-4ra: Informaciones seu cautele obseruante pars verbo volenti diunina celebrare; fol. 4ra–5vb: Incipiunt catelae seruante quod agendum ...; fol. 5vb–6va: O Vos sacerdotes dei. I would like to thank Amanda Kistrup Vallys (Royal Danish L) and Dr. Kamil Boldan (Prague NL) for providing images of the preliminary pages of the Missale Meissen for study purposes.

To see if other mass books contained the tract *O vos sacerdotes*, a survey was made of editions published in the German speaking regions in the period 1495–1499. Among 19 consulted missals, the text was not found in any edition except the Meissen missal, underscoring just how unusual it was for it to be included in such a work. However, viewed together with the other preliminary texts, a reason for this becomes clear. *O vos sacerdotes* follows two long *cautelae*, i.e. instructions for priests performing the mass. They form a trio of texts and seem to be early evidence of Bishop Johann's efforts aimed at raising the standards of religious life in his diocese, an endeavor which found full expression in the *Statuta synodalia Episcopatus Misnensis* of 1504, which includes a list of regulations for priests and clergy members.[31] In addition, Bishop Johann was aware of the advantages of the printed press in its ability to provide uniform copies of liturgical texts. During his reign he commissioned a number of printed editions of works for the diocese, among which were horae, diurnals and additional missals.[32]

Although the texts of the broadside and the missal are all but identical, a few differences are worth mentioning. First, the format: The Meissen missal is set uniformly in two columns, including the tract and the table of *octo consideranda*.[33] The *considerando*, however, are now numbered 1 to 8, a helpful aid as the column format is all but congenial for performing the spiritual exercise. Second, there are minor omissions of text and changes in word order in the other sections, including also minor textual additions not present in the broadside.[34] Thirdly, the overall sparing use of punctuation is noticeable in comparison to the broadside. Small as such details may be, they suggest that the broadside and the missal, while clearly based on a common source text, were prepared and printed independently of each other.

The other transmission of the tract appears in a commonplace book (*Kollektaneenbuch*) compiled between 1502 and 1508, the tract dated 1505. The copyist was a Carmelite monk named Conradus Rudner, who served as the subprior in his Nuremberg priory from 1500–02 and again from 1519–1525, the year the priory was dissolved. As the textual variants follow the broadside, Rudner was almost certainly using a copy of the broadside present in the priory library.[35] He copied the text in full, occasionally revising the text.[36] However, he provides no information about the context or purpose of the tract. Yet its inclusion in a commonplace book a decade after its publication provides another instance of the broadside's reception among the Holy Orders, in this case the mendicant Carmelite order.

---

[31] *Statuta synodalia Episcopatus Misnensis*. Leipzig: Melchior Lotter the Elder after 18.03.1504 4° (VD 16 M-2263).

[32] See ISTC for a complete selection. The Leipzig printer Kachelofen printed the following books for Bishop Johann VI: Horae: Orationale secundum ecclesiam Misnensem (Meissen), about 1495 8° (ISTC ih00348050). Diurnale Misnense (Meissen), 1497 16° (ISTC id00285300. GW 0854610N).

[33] Octo consideranda, Bl. 6rb–6va.

[34] It omits the Lord's name "dei" on two occasions: "timore [dei]" and "in omnipotentis [dei]" and reverses the word order on two occasions: "qui *eum crucifixerunt* ambulantem in terries" and "Quia illi *dominum semel* crucifixerunt". Where the broadside reads "Nam secundum venerabilem Bedam sacerdos qui est ...", the preface adds an addressee: "Nam secundum venerabilem Bedam ad Bonauenturam ...". The preface adds "ac pluribus alijs bonis" to the end of the text before the table ("Animas in purgatorio patrocinio et *venia. ac pluribus alijs bonis*").

[35] The position of *auariciam* in Rudner's copy of the text follows Nuremberg and Meissen.

[36] GNM, Hs. 101221, fol. 149r–150r. See HARDO HILG: *Die lateinischen mittelalterlichen Handschriften. Teil 2. Hs 22922–198390*. Wiesbaden 1986, pp. 103–112, esp. 107.

Table 1 Comparison of Types used in the Broadside and the Liber chronicarum

Transmission and author

The publication of the tract as well as Rudner's commonplace book copy may indicate a wider dissemination than the surviving copies themselves are evidence of. One can fairly speculate that the broadside might also have circulated among other religious orders, even though this is not secured through evidence.

Given the strong regional ties in the early days of printing, the author may have been a member of one of the religious houses in Nuremberg, where the broadside was printed, or in the surrounding region. If the broadside was meant for circulation among the sister chapter houses of a particular order, the discovery of copies of it in a book from the Benedictine Abbey at Neresheim may point to that order as the primary target audience and to a member of the order as the author of the text.

The transmission of the tract all but ended with the Meissen mass book. A few echoes recur in the Catholic literature on the mass years later. In 1559, Johannes Leisentritt, then the newly appointed Dean at the Collegiate Church St. Peter in Bautzen,[37] quoted several passages from the tract in his *Libellus De Salutari Preparatione ad Sacrosanctae Missae celebrationem*, published in the same year he was appointed to the position.[38] The Meissen version was almost certainly his source. Some 150 years later, the first section of the tract was included in a collection of spiritual exercises for priests published in 1738 in the Hungarian city of Eger.[39] In place of the Pseudo-Bonaventure table and the conclusion, a popular parallel transmission called *Speculum Sacerdotum* was substituted.[40] At present, no other transmissions of the text are known.

Part two. The identification of the type

As stated above, the type used for the broadside was also the one used to print the Latin edition of the *Liber chronicarum*. The following examples and Table 1 will serve as illustration.

Among the uppercase letters, a key distinguishing feature in both works is the unique form of N. It is slightly smaller in height than any of the other uppercase letters and lacks the diagonal double bar in the bowl of the letter which the other letters have. According to BMC, the letter derives properly from Koberger's type 15:91G. Further, both works possess a second form of uppercase letter C. It has what appears to be a stub in its round, suggesting the C may have been made from uppercase letter E. Also, the Z in both works has a two-part diagonal stem with a thin upper border. The three letters not only show that both works were printed with the same type, they will later also serve as criteria to distinguish the font from very similar ones in use in the same period.

Among the lowercase letters, two forms of letter d occur in both works: one, a round 'd' (rotunda), and the other a form with a straight ascender ending in a serif. The same forms of the letter 'v', 'y' and 'z', as

---

[37] He would become General Commissioner of the Catholic areas of Lusatia in 1561 and Papal Administrator for the diocese of Meissen in 1567. On Leisentritt see KONRAD AMELN: Leisentritt, Johannes. In: NDB 14 (1985), p. 156 (available on https://www.deutsche-biographie.de, [23.01.2023]).

[38] JOHANN LEISENTRITT: *Libellus de Salutari Preparatione ad Sacrosanctae Missae celebrationem, ex Orthodoxae & Apostolicae Ecclesiae Doctorum scriptis, diligenter congestus, recognitus et Auctus.* [s.l.] 1559, fol. 30r-v. (VD 16 ZV 23493).

[39] Enchiridion seu dies seraphici ardoris in consueta spiritualis quotidianae pietatis exercitia & preces exortus. Eger: Johannes Augustine Orwansky 1738, pp. 76–79.

[40] For a discussion of the *Speculum Sacerdotum* see MATTHEW CHAMPION: Senses at the Altar in Late Medieval Northern Europe. In: *Quaestiones medii aevi novae* 22 (2017), pp. 127–148.

well as a unique diagonal double-hyphen occur in both works. Both also have the same forms of special characters, i.e. ligatures, letters with diacritical macrons, and several forms of Eszett (ß). Finally, when applying the Proctor-Haebler classification criteria, we find that in both works 20 lines measure to 110 mm and that both possess the same M-form (M89). These observations apply to Dürer's *Apocalypsis cum figuris* as well, which was printed with Koberger's type 16:110G.

For all its distinctive features, however, type 16:110G is not unique. As we will see in the following sections, it belongs to a larger family of type possessing common letterforms. We turn now to the larger problem of the origin of the type.

The origin of Koberger's type 16:110G

As we have seen, the period of use of Koberger's type 16:110G was almost entirely limited to the period 1493 and marked by two bookend publications in Latin: Schedel's *Liber chronicarum* (1493) and Dürer's *Apocalysis cum figuris* (1498). Given the resources and costs involved in creating a new type, why was it so rarely used?

In his definitive study on the production of the *Nuremberg Chronicle* (2000),[41] Christoph Reske discussed the origin of the types used to print the Latin and German editions. With the help of a newly discovered proofsheet for the German edition of the chronicle, Reske was able to show Koberger's attempt to modify an in-house Schwabacher typeletter for use as the text type.[42] In similar fashion, Reske believed that the rotunda employed in the Latin edition, Koberger's 16:110G, although representing a new type, was modelled on existing ones already in use in Koberger's printing shop.[43] Accordingly, the lowercase letters were modelled on type 9:165, the uppercase letters on type 12:64.[44] Indeed, many of the letters are very similar, and given Koberger's attempt to modify an existing type for the German edition, the theory has on its face much plausibility.[45]

Yet there is another way to explain the origin of type. In this we follow observations made by A.W. Pollard in BMC catalogue II (1912/II) where he noted a close similarity between Koberger's type 16:110G and the types used by his Nuremberg colleagues Georg Stuchs and Caspar Hochfeder as well as by the Basel printer Johann Amerbach.[46] We also build on research by Oliver Duntze (2005) and Riccardo Olocco (2017, 2019) concerning the sale and trading of fonts in the 15th century.[47] In the following, the focus will be on the printers Johann Amerbach[48] and Georg Stuchs.[49] We start with Stuchs, who, in the colophon of a book from 1488, noted that he had learned the *ars imprimandi* from Anton Koberger.[50]

Stuchs's rotunda type 7:108G is remarkably close in appearance to Koberger's 16:110. It was one of his main types. It was first used on the title page of a work dated to 1483,[51] then in a breviary commissioned in 1484 for the Hungarian diocese of Esztergom, and from then on was

---

[41] RESKE (see note 6), pp. 61 (German) and 181 (in English translation).

[42] RESKE (see note 6), pp. 61–62 and 180–181.

[43] "Interessant ist hier die Komposition der neuen großen Rotunda anhand eigener Bestände." RESKE (see note 6), pp. 61 and 181.

[44] RESKE (see note 6), pp. 61 and 181.

[45] The surviving contract between the consortium and Koberger sheds no light on the matter. It only stipulates that the types selected for the Latin and German editions must be pleasing to the consortium.

[46] Pollard: "110b [P. 16], large text type, indistinguishable from Stuchs 108a and Hochfeder 107a [P. 8], and from Amerbach [P. 6] in N, which properly belongs to 91 [P. 15]..." See Catalogue of Books Printed in the XVth Century Now in the BM, Part II: Germany, London 1912, p. 410.

[47] See OLIVER DUNTZE: Methodisches Ärgernis oder wissenschaftliche Chance? Beobachtungen zum Schriftenhandel der Inkunabelzeit. In: *Wolfenbütteler Notizen zur Buchgeschichte* 31 (2006) 2, pp. 119–136. See also RICCARDO OLOCCO: *A new method of analysing type: the case of 15th-century Venetian romans*. Reading 2019; see also his study The archival evidence of type-making in 15th-century Italy. In: *La Bibliofilia* 19 (2017), pp. 33–80.

[48] See FERDINAND GELDER: Amerbach-Studien. In: AGB 23 (1982), col. 661–692; RESKE, p. 66; see also Index typographorum editorumque Basiliensium (available on https://ub2.unibas.ch, [23.01.2023]).

[49] See WALTER BAUMANN: Die Druckerei Stuchs in Nürnberg. In: *GJ* 29 (1954), pp. 122–132.

[50] See colophon to Nicolaus de Ausmo: Supplementum Summae Pisanellae: "... Incola Nure(m)b(er)ge Ant(onius) koburge(m) vt illa(m) Imp(ri)me(n)t Jeorgo stuchs dedit er(is) ope(ram) Edi(tur) h(un)c sultzbach docuit..." Nuremberg: Georg Stuchs für Anton Koberger, 20 June 1488 (GW M26238. ISTC in00066000).

[51] Historia de passione Jesu Christi. [Nuremberg: Georg Stuchs 1483] 2° (GW M27590. ISTC ih00283770).

in use up until the year 1506. It appears in no fewer than 30 books and ephemera in that period. It was most often used in liturgical works such as breviaries and missals, often in combination with a smaller rotunda to produce striking typographical contrasts (in at least seventeen works). It was used in others as the main text type, and in still others for titles, head-lines, etc. Although slightly smaller over 20 lines, the face of the letter (as opposed to the body of the letter) is in size and design identical to Koberger's type 16:110G.[52] This applies to nearly all their characters – with several notable exceptions.

The key exception was referenced by Pollard in his notes in BMC. This is uppercase letter N, referred to already in section 2 of this study.[53] Stuchs's N, like the design of the other uppercase letters, has a decorative diagonal double bar in the bowl of the letter. Koberger's N lacks the bar and is also slightly smaller than the other uppercase letters in his type 16:110G. It derives from his type 15:91G.

Three forms of the uppercase letter C link the printers' types to each other. Together with a perfectly shaped letter C, two variants have the remains of a stub in the bowl of the letter, as if the punch for an uppercase letter E had been modified to make a letter C. These forms appear in both printers' books.

A lowercase letter is notable for its absence from Stuchs's typeletter after 1487. This is the variant form of 'd' with a straight ascender. Prior to 1487, it is used alongside round 'd', but in his books after this year only the rotunda form is used. Both forms are found in Koberger's type 16:110G and, significantly, in Johann Amerbach's type 6:108G, the sister type to Stuchs's 108G, which was in use parallel to Stuchs's type in the same period. Was it a way for the printers to distinguish their type material from each other? Whatever the reason, it provides an interesting case of contrasting typographical practice. In Koberger's *Liber chronicarum*, in the new broadside and in Amerbach's editions, round 'd' is used in the initial position of a word, whereas the second form only occurs in median and final positions. In Stuchs's books the rotunda 'd' appears in all positions of the word.

Turning to the Basel printer Johann Amerbach, the similarity of his rotunda type 6:108G to Stuchs's 7:108G immediately catches the eye, then they are identical.[54] What has been said about the similarity of characters used by Koberger and Stuchs also applies to the Basler printer's 6:108G. Amerbach's use of the type was very different, however. While Stuchs used the type in his liturgical books in combination with a smaller type to create stunning typographical contrasts, also using red to highlight passages, it was used by Amerbach solely as a display type and never in red. Only once was it ever used for the main text in a book, i.e. in the Latin grammar *Doctrinale*, his first book ever in which the type was employed.[55] Thereafter it appears exclusively on title pages and in head-lines. And, in contrast to the period of use in Stuchs's books, which extended to 1506, Amerbach stopped using the type in 1492.[56] This is of special note and will be discussed further below.

Stuchs 1492

Koberger 1493

Koberger 1493

Stuchs 1492

---

[52] The uppercase letters measure to 4,5mm, the lowercase letters to 3mm.

[53] See p. 125. In the interests of being thorough, the N was also compared to uppercase N in Stuchs's type 8:110G. Their forms are different.

[54] See also type 2*:92 used by the Printer of the Sermones Meffrath (Berthold Ruppel) in 1485; it is identical to Amerbach's type 3:92*, in use from 1479–86; also see below note 66.

[55] ALEXANDER DE VILLA DEI: Doctrinale (Partes I–IV). Basel: [Johann Amerbach] 1486 2°. (GW 995. ISTC ia00429000).

[56] THOMAS BRICOT: Textus abbreviatus in cursum totius logices Aristotelis. Basel: [Johann Amerbach, 14]92 8°. (GW 5530. ISTC ib01200000).

In the absence of archival materials such as bills and letters, it remains in the realm of speculation as to how the printers acquired the type: Was it commissioned by Stuchs or perhaps the anonymous Printer of the *Legenda aurea* who first used a similar type in his books in Strasbourg? Was it a goldsmith working freelance who made the punches and struck the matrices for the printers, or better for Georg Stuchs, the first in this family branch to use it? And the question whether the printers were selling or trading type material among themselves also remains unanswered. The type, however, is identical in all features and must have been made from the same matrices (see Table 2).

Although the Haebler classification of M-forms differs – M-88 for Stuchs and Amerbach, M-89 for Koberger –,[57] the forms of M are indistinguishable from each other, and the type itself is all but identical.

Koberger (M-89) aus
GW M40784, Registrum

Stuchs (M-88) aus
GW 5381, fol. AAiijv

Amerbach (M-88) aus
GW 3886, fol. bb5v

Regarding the difference in size of their type, an explanation is readily at hand. To review, the body (i.e. point size) of Koberger's type measures 110 mm while that of Stuchs and Amerbach measures 108 mm. Although a 2 cm difference seems negligible, it tells us that Koberger could not have been using either of the printers' type material. It is best explained if we assume Koberger acquired the matrices and had his own set of type cast to print the Latin edition of the *Liber chronicarum*. Here we reference Koberger's variant uppercase letter N once again. Did the printer deliberately substitute the letterform as a way of distinguishing his type from their types? It seems a logical, though tentative conclusion in lieu of archival evidence.

To briefly sum up: Koberger's type 16:110G was not a new type which was designed expressly for the production of the Latin edition of the *Liber chronicarum*. It is indistinguishable from a formal rotunda already in use in the printing houses of Stuchs and Amerbach and was most likely cast from the same matrices as their type 108G. Given the close business ties which existed between printers in Nuremberg and Basel, it should not surprise us that printers also engaged in the trading and selling of fonts. The use of identical types is documented for Koberger and Amerbach from as early as 1484 on and continued well into the 1490s and beyond.[58]

The first state of the rotunda used by Stuchs (7:108) and Amerbach (6:108G)

In the previous section, we saw that the rotunda used by the printers Koberger, Stuchs and Amerbach, apart from certain characters, is identical. In this section we will examine the original state of the rotunda in books printed by Stuchs and Amerbach during the period 1483 to 1487.

---

57 See TW: Koberger's M (16:110G = ma02060) is classified as M89 and Stuchs's M (7:108G = ma06692) is classified as M88. Yet the M form of the printers is all but identical.

58 BMC/II: Nuremberg, Anton Koberger, p. 410, see notes to types 120, 64a, 63, 74. See also Duntze, Methodisches Ärgernis, p. 122 and note 20, pp. 128–130.

If the tentative dating to 1483 is correct, the 108G rotunda made its first appearance on the title page of an octavo pamphlet published by Georg Stuchs, entitled *Officium de passione Christi*.⁵⁹ It was used again in the following year for one of his first major commissioned works – a breviary for the Hungarian diocese of Esztergom. In this handsome folio edition of 418 leaves, the entire stock of characters is displayed to striking effect in combination with his smaller rotunda 8:108G for the first time.

Two years later, the type also appeared in a Basel edition of Alexander de Villa Dei's *Doctrinale* (GW 995),⁶⁰ published by Johann Amerbach. Apart from a tailed ę and one form of a divis (hyphen), the type used to print the *Doctrinale* text is indistinguishable from Stuchs's type 7:108G. Though Amerbach may have possessed a complete set of type, his editorial practice, on display in the *Doctrinale* and thereafter, shows that many contractions, letters, ligatures, etc. were rarely used in his books or not at all.

The following table presents an overview of the main changes from the original to the second state of 108G. The key letters for each printer are shown side by side in both states. The new forms (second state) make their appearance in each printer's book at around the same time, at the latest by summer 1487.⁶¹

1st state 1483–87		2nd state after 1487		Differences in state
Stuchs	Amer	Stuchs	Amer	
A	A	A	A	Long upper serif ends parallel to the base of the letter; shortened in later state
C	C	C	C	Body of C is formed of a single contour; later state has a two-part body
Z	Z	Z	(?)	Thin border in diagonal stem placed at right; border at left in later state
ð	ð	ð	ð	Form is the same for both printers
d	d	—	d	Present in 1st state for both printers; later only in Amerbach with larger serif
e	e ę	e	e	Lowercase letter e with a tail occurs only in Amerbach's Basel edition of 1486
ʒ	ʒ	ʒ qʒ	debʒ	Long tail in 1st state; a slightly squatter form in later state, tail shorter
ðioc|	—	rĵ	—	The '-is' abbreviation appears only in Stuchs's books

Summary: In the second state, new forms have been substituted for uppercase letters A, C, and Z. A new form of lowercase letter d has also been introduced, recognisable by an ascender ending with a larger serif at the top. In books published by Amerbach (and Koberger), it is used together with the rotunda form of d, but in books published by Stuchs only the rotunda d appears from 1487 on. On the other hand, a special character

59 GW M27990. ISTC iho0283770.

60 See note 55; see also TW-SBB-PK https://tw.staatsbibliothek-berlin.de/ma02377, [23.01.2023].

61 Breviarium Numburgense. Nuremberg: Georg Stuchs 14.07.1487 2° (GW 5412. ISTC ib01172700); AUGUSTINUS: Explanatio psalmorum. Basel: Johann Amerbach [and Johann Petri de Langendorff, not after 08.09.] 1489 2° (GW 2909. ISTC ia01272000).

used by Stuchs provides a direct link to Koberger: the unique form of the 'is'-abbreviation present in Stuchs's type (in both the early and second states). It is found in both the *Liber chronicarum* of July 1493 and the broadside, but never appears in books printed by Amerbach. Despite these interdependencies, Koberger's type 16:108G is immediately recognisable and distinguishable from the types used by his Nuremberg and Basel colleagues by his uppercase letter N, which properly belongs to Koberger's type 15:91G.

The Strasbourg branch and the family of rotunda type

The rotunda letter was not exclusively a Basel and Franconian type – it also had a Strasbourg relation. This relation was older and made its first appearance in books printed by the Printer of the *Legenda aurea* (publ. 1479–83)[62] and in those issued on the press of the Strasbourg printer Martin Flach the Elder (publ. 1487–1500).[63] Similar to the Nuremberg printers, the type material used by Flach, cast on a slightly largely body, is identical to the type used by the Printer of the *Legenda aurea*. It also provides a further case of two typefaces which are identical despite a difference in body width: for his books printed after 1482, the Printer of the *Legenda aurea* had his rotunda letter recast from the original body of 108 mm down to a smaller body of 97 mm. The typeface remained unchanged, but there was now less space between individual lines.

Despite the striking family resemblance between the two branches, the Strasbourg branch can be told apart from its Basel-Franconian relation by letters that in comparison possess slightly different features:

LA	Fl	Frc	Basel	
𝕬	𝕬	𝕬	𝕬	Upper terminal extends further to the left
ð	ð	ð	ð	Flat upper rim of bowl, shorter finial
ō	ō	ȝ	ȝ	Flat upper rim of bowl, small-detached apostrophe
d d	d	d	d	Serif at top filed off in one state
ē	ē	ē	ē	Steeply angled crossbar at lower edge of bowl
fe	fe	fe	fe	Rectangular-shaped terminal at top of letter f
r	r	r r	r	Thicker hairline joining the stem and ear of letter
v	v	v	v	Slight left-hand tilt in the body of letter, oversized
ȝ	ȝ	ȝ	ȝ	Compact upper story, slightly longer descender

[62] First in use as 2:108G (M-89) in the years 1479–81, then cast on a smaller body as 2*:97G in the years 1482–83. See TW-SBB-PK (available on https://tw.staatsbibliothek-berlin.de, [23.01.2023]).

[63] Martin Flach the Elder, type 3:110G (M89).

The wider family of Basel printers

In the following, we shall look at two Basel printers who also used the same rotunda in their editions. While their type is very similar, it can also be easily distinguished by the variant forms of letters and characters appearing in their material. The first printer to be discussed is the Basel printer Jacob Wolff, whose name appears in the Latinized form Jacobus de Pforzheim in colophons, but who is referred to as Meister Jakob in the Basel municipal records.[64]

Wolff became a citizen of Basel and a member of the Saffran guild in late January 1482. In this year he also entered into a partnership with Johann Amerbach but had left it by 1489 to set up his own printing shop. Among the works of the early years of this press was a breviary commissioned for the Dominican friars in Basel.[65] Wolff employed the rotunda type there for the first time.

Wolff's rotunda 7:107G is all but identical to Amerbach's type 6:108G. Despite the height of the body of the letters differing by a millimeter, the typeface of the letters measures the same. Given the printers' former partnership and friendship, it is fair to speculate that Wolff acquired the type and matrices directly from Amerbach.[66] The latter never used the rotunda again after 1482. Wolff used it from that year on until 1511.[67]

Despite their similarity, Wolff's 7:107G rotunda can be readily distinguished from Amerbach's 8:108G. Several uppercase letters derive properly, as noted by BMC, from another type.[68] In table 3, selected upper- and lowercase letters from their fonts are shown in comparison. The letters are taken from Wolff's breviary for the Dominican priory in Basel (1492) and Amerbach's type 1:108G:[69]

Amerbach	Wolff	Furter	Amerbach	Wolff	Furter
𝔄	𝔄	𝔄			
ⅅ	ⅅ	ⅅ			
𝔅	𝔅	𝔅			
𝔫	𝔫	—			
𝔵	x	x			
—	y	y	—	Ymon	Yſmahelite
—	z	z	—		

[64] See BMC III (1913), pp. 775–779. For a short biography of Wolff see RESKE (see note 48), p. 67; see also Index Typographorum editorumque Basiliensium (available on https://ub2.unibas.ch, [23.01.2023]).

[65] GW 5224. GW's assignment of 7:107G to his breviary for Chur (GW 5332) is mistaken.

[66] The sale of type and matrices among printers is well documented from the 1480s on. One case concerns Amerbach and the Strasbourg printer Peter Attendorn, who was just beginning his career. In a letter of 1482, Adolf Rusch, himself a printer and paper trader, forwarded this young printer's query to Amerbach. Attendorn wanted to acquire sufficient type for a press, adding he was prepared to offer a fair price. See ALFRED HARTMANN (Ed.): *Die Amerbachkorrespondenz*. Vol. 1: Die Briefe aus der Zeit Johann Amerbachs 1481–1513, p. 3 Brief 2. See ISTC for a list of Attendorn's books. For other examples of types passing from one printer to another see Arnoldus de Colonia in Leipzig (1493–95), whose types 81 and 110 were acquired by Wolfgang Stöckel and used from 1496–1501; for further examples see also the Venetian printers Leonardus Aurl (1472–73, 1:116R) and Adam von Ammergau (1471–72, 2:116G), Johannes de Colonia/Johannes Manthen (1474–80: 4:99G, 5:200G, 18:109Gr) and Vindelinus de Spira (1471–73, 2:99G, 3:200G, 7:110Gr).

[67] Used in at least 12 editions, among them three breviaries. See BMC III (1913), pp. 775–779; see also the online TW table of his books (available on https://tw.staatsbibliothek-berlin.de, [23.01.2023]).

[68] BMC III (1913), p. 775.

[69] Breviarium Fratrum Praedicatorum, published by the Dominicans at the Basel priory (GW 5224), Basel: Jacob Wolff for Jacob von Kilchen 1492 2°. Online copy: UB Basel, UBH AN VII 53 (available online at https://www.e-rara.ch/id/2679550, [23.01.2023]).

Table 2 Comparison of selected letters from the rotunda used by Amerbach, Wolff, and Furter. Continued from previous page.

Amerbach	Wolff	Furter	Amerbach	Wolff	Furter
ð	ð	ð			
e	e	e			
ʒ	ʒ	ʒ	debʒ	tetruʒ	
⸋	⸋	⸋		diuitatʒ	singularʒ

Michael Furter, the other printer to use the rotunda, began his career as a bookbinder and book seller before setting up a printing office in 1488.[70] He began using the rotunda in 1495, casting his own set of type from matrices which Wolff had used. Its typeface measures 106mm over twenty lines, contrasting to Wolff's typeface of 108mm over twenty lines. The rotunda was used initially in small quarto editions for the main text, but later appeared primarily as a display type, i.e. for titles, head-lines, and headings. The characters in table 3 are taken from one of the early quarto editions using the type, the *Ars minor* of Aelius Donatus (GW 8926), published c. 1496.[71]

The wider family of Franconian printers

As in Basel, the rotunda also enjoyed a certain popularity among Franconian printers. Beginning in 1493, parallel to the publication of the *Liber chronicarum*, the type first appeared in books printed by Caspar Hochfeder (from 1493),[72] then in books printed by Ambrosius Huber (c. 1497),[73] the anonymous Printer of the *Doctrinale* (GW 1129, c. 1495/1500),[74] and the Bamberg printer Johann Pfeyl (1495–1501).[75] In 1511, Albrecht Dürer also issued a revised Latin edition of his illustrated *Apocalysis cum figuris*,[76] using the same type as in the editio princeps.

The impression that the type was widely used would be mistaken, however. Only Hochfeder and Pfeyl used it with any frequency. In the four-part grammar issued by the anonymous Printer of the *Doctrinale* (GW 1129), it appears only in the head-lines. And among the books assigned to two of the printers in this group, Ambrosius Huber and Caspar Hochfeder, two small prints stand out by virtue of an unusually shaped uppercase letter C, the body of which tilts to the right.[77] It appears alongside the single form C from the pre-1487 state of the type. A variant form of the 'is'-abbreviation also appears in both books. These characters seem to derive from Stuchs's type 3:68G.[78]

[70] BMC III (1913), pp. 780–89; see also the list of Furter's books in the TW online table of his books (available on https://tw.staatsbibliothek-berlin.de, [23.01.2023]).

[71] GW 8926, digital copy available at https://www.e-rara.ch/bau_1/content/zoom/5284449,[23.01.2023] (UB Basel, shelfmark UBH DC V 13:3).

[72] Type 7:107G in use from 1493 on. Hochfeder's folio issue of Breviarium Erfordense (1497, GW 5357) uses it in combination with the smaller type 11:107G to produce contrasts much in the same way as Stuchs does. BMC notes that type measures to 110G on the title pages in the years 1497–98. Hochfeder relocated to Metz in 1499 and continued to use the type to 1500. See EMIL VAN DER VEKENE: Kaspar Hochfeder: ein europäischer Drucker des 15. und 16. Jahrhunderts. Eine druckgeschichtliche Untersuchung. Baden-Baden 1974 (Bibliotheca bibliographica Aureliana. 52).

[73] Type 3:110G, appearing in GW M37026 in which it is used for head-lines. Capital A with a short terminal like the later Stuchsian A, but an unusually shaped uppercase letter C with a two-part body with a right-hand tilt; a second C has a single outline like the earlier form in use with Stuchs/Amerbach. In GW 11136, which is assigned to Caspar Hochfeder, the same two uppercase letter C forms appear.

[74] Type 1:110G used in a three-part *Doctrinale* dating to 1495/1500 for the head-lines.

[75] Type 13:110G, used in the period 1495–1501.

[76] VD 16 B 5248. Copy consulted: BSB, Rar. 49#Beibd.2.

[77] Remigius: Dominus quae pars. [Nuremberg: Caspar Hochfeder ca. 1496] (GW 11136); and Jacobus Randersacker: Practica Cracoviensis ad annum 1498 [Nuremberg: Ambrosius Huber ca. 1497] (GW M37026).

[78] See TW-SBB-PK www.tw.staatsbibliothek-berlin.de, [23.01.2023].

Conclusion

Rather than viewing Koberger's 16:110G as a unique type developed for the printing of the *Liber chronicarum*, one can assign it to a larger family of types in use in Franconia and Basel with a parallel branch in Strasbourg. Its typeface, as distinguished from the height of the body letterform, is identical to the second state of Stuchs's 7:108G and Amerbach's 6:108G. The three were likely cast from the same matrices. This assumes a commercial trading of matrices, and possibly of punches, among the printers, for which there is some historical evidence.

In the absence of historical sources such as sales invoices or letters, it is impossible to know exactly how Koberger acquired the matrices. The timeline initially suggests that his source was the Basel printer Amerbach. The signing of the contract between Koberger and the Schreyer-Wolgemut consortium took place on 16 March 1492 and, notably, the Basel printer stopped using type 6:108G in the same year. Yet several factors make this appear unlikely. First, the contract states that the choice of type had yet to be agreed upon (a letter was to be chosen which was pleasing to the consortium).[79] If indeed the types had not yet been chosen, time would be spent looking for suitable ones, for consulting with the consortium, for negotiating the purchase and, in the case of the Latin type, having the matrices sent to Nuremberg. Additional time would also be needed to produce the amount of type required for printing. As printing of the chronicle very likely began as early as May of 1492,[80] it seems unlikely that there was time enough for these steps to have taken place. Further, as the type was already used in a breviary printed by Jacob Wolff in 1492, by this juncture the type and the matrices may no longer have been in Amerbach's possession to sell to Koberger.

Given the proximity of Stuchs's printing shop to Koberger's – it was in Bergstraße near Albrecht-Dürer-Platz on the Sebaldus side of Nuremberg and thus within walking distance of Koberger's printing shop at Egidienplatz[81] – none of the problems highlighted above would have played a role. A loan or purchase of the matrices could have been quickly negotiated, and their transfer to Egidienplatz easily arranged, where casting the type could have begun without delay. Although Johann Neudöffer makes no mention of this group in his description of Koberger's printing office on Egidienplatz, it would seem strange if type-casters were not among the workers Koberger had in his employment.[82]

Even though only the rotunda form of lowercase letter 'd' is used in Stuchs's books after 1488, this does not exclude the possibility that he had the matrices for both forms. It may have been a matter of choice not to use a letter foreign in design to the rotunda, or, as in the case of Koberger's substitution of the uppercase N, not using the second form of 'd' may have been a way to distinguish his books from those of the Basel printer Amerbach. In any case, the presence of the 'is'-abbreviation and the absence of Koberger's variant uppercase letter N point directly to Koberger. They do not appear in any of Amerbach's editions in the period of his use of the type (1486–1492).

---

[79] See RESKE (see note 6), pp. 61–62 and 68.

[80] RESKE (see note 6), p. 69.

[81] Stuchs's printing office was in the upper section of Bergstraße near the corner where Obere Krämersgasse enters the street. See PETER FLEISCHMANN (Ed.): *Die Reichssteuerregister von 1497 der Reichsstadt Nürnberg*. Nürnberg 1993 (Quellen und Forschungen zur fränkischen Familiengeschichte. 4), pp. 288, no *166, and Tafel 2 precinct M7.

[82] See Des Johann Neudörf, Schreib- und Rechenmeister zu Nürnberg, Nachrichten von Künstlern und Werkleuten daselbst aus dem Jahre 1547 nebst der Fortsetzung des Andreas Gulden. Ed. GEORG WOLFGANG KARL LOCHNER. Wien 1873 (Quellenschriften für Kunstgeschichte und Kunsttechnik des Mittelalters und der Renaissance. 10), pp. 173–177.

The question whether it was Stuchs or Amerbach, or a goldsmith working freelance, who supplied Koberger with the matrices for the type, may never be known. The similarity of type used by the three printers, whatever the origin, is unmistakable. With the matrices in his possession, Koberger had at his printing office on Egidienplatz all the resources and personnel he needed. The type-casters, whether employed in-house or externally, could work quickly to produce the type in the amount needed.

It will ultimately remain a matter of speculation as to why type 16:110G was chosen for the Latin issue of the *Liber chronicarum* over others already in use in Koberger's printing house. The contract for the chronicle stipulated solely that a type pleasing to the consortium was to be used. Perhaps the consortium made use of its prerogative in the question of the choice of type or perhaps other factors relating to technical considerations played a role. Whatever the reason, our sense of awe at a masterpiece of early printing is in no small part inspired by the formal rotunda with which it was printed.

Part VIII. Codicological description

Description of the broadside

Anonymous: O Vos Sacerdotes Dei
[Nuremberg: Anton Koberger, 1493/1498], Bdsde.
1 leaf, printed on one side. Printed area: c. 312 × c. 205/6 mm. 56 lines.
Type: 16:110G. Space left for initial.

Line 1: [ ]⁵ Uos facerdotes dei, vos tangent fermones mei ... line 24f.:
... Jtaq(ue) digne celebrare volen‖ti octo fequentia funt attendenda.
videlicet.
Line 28 col. a: Jntentionis difcuffio. Ne [l. 26 col. b]: Propter vanam gloriam [l. 27 col. b]: Propter verecundiam ... Celebret
Line 55f. col. a: Et hoc propter continentiaz [line 54 col. b]: Tam excellentis corp(or)is ... [line 55 col. b]: Excelle(n)tiffime diuinitatis crifti

Line 27f. col. c: Cum autem vt quidam ‖ ait ... Line 50–52: Beati Denique mu(n)‖do corde quoniam ipfi ‖ deum videbu(n)t. Amen.

Watermark: Letter P – free standing, Gothic form, with brisure: flower with four leaves – Bow end is behind the shaft – Rounded shaft end – Shaft does not have a crossbar (not in Piccard watermark collection)
Dimensions: ‖ 29 mm (chain lines), width: 17 mm, height: 65/8 mm
The watermark is in the text area, and its features in the lower area are not fully recognisable; the height is approximated.

Dimensions of copies (exact measurements not possible due to water damage at edges):

Copy 1 (without marginalia): 391 × 284 mm
Copy 2 (with marginalia): 404 × 285/292 mm

Both copies attached to the last folio of:
Gratianus: Decretum cum apparatu
Basel: Michael Wenssler, 5 Sept. 1482 2°
ISTC ig00371000. GW 11363. BSB-Ink G-263. HC *7896.
Erlangen, Universitätsbibliothek, H62/INC 1581 b

Provenances: [Neresheim, Benedictine abbey (Baden-Württemberg)]. – [Heidenheim, Benedictine Abbey (dissolved in 1537), Middle Franconia; 1582 transfer of library holdings to Ansbach] – Ansbach, Schlossbibliothek of the Margraves of Ansbach-Brandenburg. – Erlangen, Universitätsbibliothek, transfer from Ansbach in December 1805 (historical shelfmarks: 260 (changed from 261; see notation in red chalk on 1st flying leaf; shelf location at Ritterakademie: Ec.I.32 (Standort-Katalog, I, 1811, books in folio format).

Decoration: Copy 1: Initial not carried out but rubricated (colour-stroked letters); copy 2: Initial O added in red by hand; red strokes on capitals, and additionally red brackets added in the table of *octo consideranda*.

The copies, like the volume of the *Decretum* in which they are found, show stains and former mould from past water damage in the top and lower margins.[83] There is no documentation concerning when the water damage occurred, but by then the copies of the broadside had already been in their present location for some time. Matching worm holes appear in the copies and in the final gathering, suggesting that the copies may have been attached as early as the 18th or beginning of the 19th centuries. As a part of the conservation measure, the copies were detached, dried, and reattached, but in the reverse order and with a slight mismatch in alignment of the worm holes. Missing today are the pastedowns which once lined the inside of the upper and lower boards.

Marginalia in the bottom margin of the first copy: *Sacerdotib(us) semp(er) est orand(um) Jdeo ipis a m(u)l(ie)rib(us) semp(er) est cavend(um) di 31 Si laic(us)* ‖ Vid Semp(er) orat qui ab horiscanonic(is) no(n) dicsistat.

Literature: Erlangen, Standortkatalog (Karteikatalog) of 1968 (Cat. H60/AN 22700 E69-2), noting change of shelfmark from Inc. 1202 to 1582 b. – Kyriß: Verzeichnis, Bd. I, 1951, workshop 72: k.a. aus Neresheim, p. 60 (under Inc. 1202), Tafelbd. 1, 1956, p. 26 and pp. 178f., Taf. 145, 146 – Heiland, manuscript catalogue, loose slips of paper (1907/25). – Standort-Katalog 2°, 1811, MS 2555 [1], fol. 87r (under Ec.I.32 = 261 Decretum). – Pfeiffer, Ms 2350, Catalogus incunabulorum, 1805, nr. 260 (originally 261). – Heidenheim, Benedictine Abbey, mention in an inventory of 1582.

83 The lower edge of the entire book has signs of previous water damage.

Appendices and tables

Appendix 1: Text of Erlangen UB, H62/INC 1581 b. The variants in the Missale Misnense are listed underneath as M.

1	[O] Uos sacerdotes dei. vos tangunt sermones mei.[84] Magnum dignitatis agnum dei tractatis.
2	Hieremias ore prophetauit. Johannes digito monstrauit. Maria in ventre portauit. Hij tres
3	antequam nati: sunt sanctificati. O quam sanctus debet esse. qui agno debet preesse. Non
4	ore prophetare: sed sumere et manducare. Non digito monstrare: sed tractare. Non tantum
5	in ventre. sed semper debet portare in mente.

ll. 1–5: [O] Uos sacerdotes dei ... in mente: Attributed to Bernard of Clairveau O Cist. See Walter, Initia carminum, no 10374.

6	Ue autem his et iterum ve qui sordida et polluta conscientia tractant corpus christi sicut
7	carnes agni qui venduntur[85] in macellis. Quos alloquitur beatus Ambrosius in persona christi
8	dicens. O peccator tu indigne sacerdos. noli me amplius affligere peccando. Plus enim me
9	ledit vulnus peccati tui quam vulnus lateris mei. et subiungit. Magis enim delinquunt qui iam
10	regnantem in celo contemnunt peccando. scilicet indigne tractantes et sumentes corpus
11	christi. quam qui[86] crucifixerunt eum ambulantem in terris. Non quasi crucifixores: sed quasi
12	tanti sacramenti indigni confectores et presumptuosi perceptores. Quia[87] illi semel dominum
13	crucifixerunt isti quantum in eis est quotidie eum crucifigunt. scilicet contra deum viuentes et
14	indigne sumentes ac sacrificantes. Quibus attendendum est illud beati Gregorij. Cum ingratus
15	ad intercedendum mittitur. irati animus ad deteriora prouocatur. De qualibus etiam sic ait
16	beatus Augustinus. Mallem potius pilati. iude. herodis sustinere penam. quam sacerdotis
17	indigne communicantis et conficientis. Animaduertite igitur o vos sacerdotes in quanta
18	puritate et timore dei[88] accedere debetis ad illud sacrificium ad quod christus accessurus per
19	angustia sudauit sanguinem. Attenta autem tanta dignitate et tam expauescenda maiestate
20	huius sacrificij ad quod etiam digne sumendum vix sufficiunt mille anni lacrimarum et
21	durissime penitentie. non ideo se quisquem debet abstrahere a perceptione ipsius immunis
22	saltem a peccato mortali. Sed confidens in omnipotentis dei[89] misericordia fiducialiter
23	accedere. Nam secundam venerabilem Bedam sacerdos[90] qui est sine peccato mortali et in
24	bono proposito. si non celebrat cum habet copiam celebrandi quantum in ipo est. priuat
25	sanctam trinitatem gloria angelos in celesti hierusalem leticia homines laborantes in terris
26	beneficio et gratia: animas in purgatorio patrocinio et venia[91].

[84] Title in Missale Misnense (afterwards M): Jtem nota alias praeparationes vtilissimas ad celebrandus.

[85] Venduntur] venditur M.

[86] qui crucifixerunt eum] qui eum crucifixerunt M.

[87] Quia illi semel dominum] quia illi dominum semel M.

[88] dei] missing M.

[89] dei] missing M.

[90] secundam venerabilem Bedam sacerdos] secundum venerabilem Bedam ad sanctum Bonauenturam sacerdos M.

[91] et venia] et venia ac pluribus alijs bonis M.

ll. 8–12 O peccator tu indigne sacerdos ... perceptores: From Stella clericorum; here with a variant attribution to Ambrosius and not, as usual, to Augustinus, cf. Reiter (ed.), section 11,43–51.

ll. 15 Cum ingratus ... prouocatur] an adapted quote from Pope Gregory's Liber regulae pastoralis, Pars prima, cap. 10: Cuncti enim liquido novimus, quia cum is qui displicet ad intercedendum mittitur, irati animus ad deteriora provocateur. See also Gratianus Decretales XLIX and Thomas Aquinas: "Multa cauendum est ne Deus ea offendatur, quia cum is qui displicet ad intercedendum mittitur, irati animus ad deteriora prouocatur", D. Thomae Aquinatis ...Opuscula omnia, cap. XIX, Quod magna didgentia adhabenda est circa custodian linguae, Venice 1587, p. 443 col. b.

ll. 17–19 Animaduertite ... sanguinam] Also from Stella clericorum, cf. Reiter (ed.), section 10,28–31.

ll. 23–26 Nam secundum venerabilem Bedam ... patrocinio et venia] Popular saying attributed to Saint Bede.

27	Itaque digne celebrare volenti octo sequentia sunt attendenda. videlicet[92]		
28	[Spiritual exercise]:		
29		{Propter vanam gloriam}	
30		{Propter verecundiam}	
31	Intentionis discussio.[93] Ne	{Propter timorem}	Celebret
32		{Propter auariciam}	
33		{Ex consuetudine}	
34	Generalis contritio super	{Omissis[94] qui facere potuit}	corde ore et opera
35		{Commissis qui facem non debuit}	
36		{Notabilium}	
37	Pura confessio	{Communium}	Criminum
38		{Ignoratorum}	
39		{Augmentum dilectionis}	
40	Quid intendat consequi	{Inseparabilitatem vnionis}	dei
41	Principaliter[95]	{Accelerationem visionis}	
42		{Deum per latriam colere}	
43	Quid intendat facere[96]	{Mortem christi rememorari}	semper
44		{Totam ecclesiam adjuuare}	
45		{Diligentiam ad conficiendum}	
46	In canone habeat illa[97]	{Reuerentiam ad tangendum}	corpus xpi.
47		{Deuotionem ad sumendum}	

[92] videlicet] missing M.

[93] In the exercise each meditation in M is numbered Primum, Secundum, Tercium est, Quartium est... etc. The table format is also converted into sentences using connectors such as ne aut ... aut... aut...

[94] Omissis] obmissis M.

[95] Inserted after principaliter: Et sunt tria scilicet M.

[96] Inserted after facere: Et sunt tria scilicet M.

[97] Rephrased in M: Sextum est in canone ab corpus cristi conficiendum habeat diligenciam ab tangendum reuerenciam et ad sumendum deuocionem.

48	{Tam excellentis corporis}	
49 Et hoc propter continentiam[98]	{Excellentioris anime}	christi
50	{Excellentissime diuinitatis}	

ll. 28–50 Intentionis discussion ... diuinitatis christi] Tabula de consideranda a Missa celebraturis, attributed to Saint Bonaventure; see Distelbrink: Bonaventurae scripta, no 225.

ll. 31f. ne {Propter auariciam} celebret] Mention of this vice occurs only in five of the more than 100 manuscripts in which the Tabula is transmitted; see above, p. 122.

51	[Conclusion]: Cum autem vt quidam ait.[99] Turpius eijcitur quam non admittitur hospes
52	Cauendum est cuiquam sic sumpto venerabilissimo hospite ne redeat ad vomitum. et iterum
53	volutet se in volutabro peccati. rursus que crucifigat sibi filium dei.[100] Et conquerat
54	dominus[101] de eiusmodi illud Hieremi. xj Quid est que dilectus meus in domo mea facit
55	scelera multa: Et illud de renouantibus dolorem suum dicens Zacharie xiij.[102] His plagatus
56	sum in domo eorum qui diligebant me. Sed[103] conseruare studeat se[104] in puritate et
57	mundicia cordis vt deum videre possit[105] in syon. Beati denique mundo corde quoniam ipsi
58	deum videbunt. Amen.[106]

ll. 28–50 Turpius ejitur ... hospes] A common saying in learned Latin, deriving from Ovid's *Tristia*, Liber 5, section 6, vers 13, see P. Ovidi Nasonis Tristia, edited John Barrie Hall.
ll. 54f. Quid est que ... scelera multa] AT, Book of Jeremiah 11:15.
II. 55f. Hi plagatus ... diligebant me] AT, Book of Zechariah 13:6.
II. 57f. Beati ... mundo cordo ... deum videbunt] NT, Mt 5:8.

Appendix 2

A comparison of the passages from *Stella clericorum* with the corresponding passages in the broadside. My source in the following is Caspar Hochfeder's edition of 1493/96:[107]

6v ll. 4–7: *Aug*[ustin]. *Animaduertite o vos sacerdotes in quanta puritate et tremore debetis accedere ad istud sacrificium ad quod christus accessurus sanguinem sudauit pre angustia*

7v ll. 6–15: *Aug*[ustin]. *O tu indigne sacerdos noli plus me affligere peccando : plus enim me vulnus peccati tui ledit quam vulnus lateris mei. Jdem. Magis delinquunt qui iam regnantem in celis contemnunt peccando .scilicet. indigne corpus xpi tractantes et sumentes quam qui crucifixerunt eum ambulantem in terris. Non quasi crucifigentes : sed quasi tanti sacramenti indigni confectores*

---

98 Et hoc propter continentiam] Rephrased as Quare fiant. Et fiunt propter tria scilicet propter continenciam *M*.

99 Ait] missing *M*.

100 Die] die prolut (?) *M*.

101 Et conquerat dominus de eiusmodi ...] et dominus de eiusmodi ... conqueritur dicens *M*.

102 Et illud de renouantibus dolorem suum dicens Zacharie xiij] rephrased as Et zacharie xiij. De renouantibus dolorem suum ditus *M*.

103 Sed] Jdeo *M*.

104 se] quisque *M*.

105 vt deum videre possit] vt deum possit videre *M*.

106 Amen] missing *M*.

107 Cited after the edition: Stella clericorum. [Nuremberg: Caspar Hochfeder between 1493–1496] 4°. GW M43917. ISTC is00775800. All abbreviations dissolved.

et presumptuosi perceptores. Quia illi semel deum crucifixerunt in terres isti quantum in eis est indigne tractantes et sumentes quottidie crucifigunt.

The passages appear in the opposite order in the broadside. In the second passage it is Ambrosius and not Augustin who speaks:

1r ll. 7–13: *Quos alloquitur beatus Ambrosius in persona christi dicens. O peccator tu indigne sacerdos.noli me amplius affligere peccando. Plus enim me ledit vulnus peccati tui quam vulnus lateris mei.et subiungit. Magis enim delinquunt qui iam regnantem in celo contemnunt peccando.scilicet indigne tractantes et sumentes corpus christi.quam qui crucifixerunt eum ambulantem in terries non quasi crucifixores.sed quasi tanti sacramenti indigni confectores et presumptuosi perceptores. Quia illi semel dominum crucifixerunt isti quantum in eis est quotidie eum crucifigunt.scilicet contra deum viuentes et indigne sumentes ac sacrificantes.*

1r ll. 16–18: *Animaduertite igitur o vos sacerdotes in quanta puritate et timore dei accedere debetis ad illud sacrificium ad quod christus accessurus prae angustia sudauit sanguinem*

Appendix 3

Table of manuscripts in which the vice of avarice is included among the false motives for saying mass (first exercise of the *octo consideranda*):
- Melk, Benedictine Abbey, Cod. 1776 (412, H27), fol. 80r (1431–1451)
- Innsbrück, ULBT, Cod. 207, fol. 167va (affiliation unknown; 1442)
- St. Gallen, Benedictine Abbey, Cod. Sang. 814, S. 249 (1464–68)
- Munich, Bayerische Staatsbibliothek, Clm 28431, fol. 26v (Buxheim O Cart; 1481–1501)
- Salzburg, Erzabtei St. Peter, Benedictine Abbey, a III 33, fol. 20r–20v (21r), and fol. 240r–240v (second half of 15th c.)

Harald Berger

Wer könnte der Verfasser der logischen Werke in den Drucken Basel 1487 sowie Hagenau 1495 und 1503 sein?

1 M. GERMANN: Kesler (Kessler), Nicolaus. In: LGB². Bd. IV, S. 203.

2 I. BEZZEL: Gran (Granius), Heinrich. In: LGB². Bd. III, S. 230–231.

3 Nachdruck Frankfurt 1967 unter dem falschen Titel: MARSILIUS VON INGHEN: *Commentum in primum et quartum tractatum Petri Hispani.*

4 Dieser Nachdruck wurde auch in der Forschung schon öfters verwendet, siehe z. B.: ALFONSO MAIERÙ: *Terminologia logica della tarda scolastica.* Roma 1972. (Lessico intellettuale europeo. 8), ab S. 234. MARSILIUS OF INGHEN: *Treatises on the Properties of Terms.* Hrsg. von EGBERT P. BOS. Dordrecht, Boston, Lancaster 1983. (Synthese Historical Library. 22), S. 32 Nr. XXXIII, 37, 209. ALAIN DE LIBERA: *Expositio* et *probatio per causas veritatis* chez Albert de Saxe et Marsile d'Inghen. In: *Preuve et raisons à l'Université de Paris. Logique, ontologie et théologie au XIVᵉ siècle.* Hrsg. von ZENON KALUZA und PAUL VIGNAUX. Paris 1984. (Études de Philosophie Médiévale. Hors Série), S. 127–147, ab S. 136. E. J. ASHWORTH: *Studies in Post-Medieval Semantics.* London 1985. (Variorum Reprints. CS227), s. Index, s. v. »Commentum«. STEPHEN READ: Thomas of Cleves and Collective Supposition. In: *Vivarium.* 29 (1991), S. 50–84. ELIZABETH KARGER: Some 15th and Early 16th Century Logicians on the Quantification of Categorical Sentences. In: *Topoi.* 16 (1997), S. 65–76. EGBERT P. BOS: Die Rezeption der *Suppositiones* des Marsilius von Inghen bei Johannes Dorp (Paris) und in einem anonymen Prager *Sophistria*-Traktat (um 1400). In: *Philosophie und Theologie des ausgehenden Mittelalters. Marsilius von Inghen und das Denken seiner Zeit.* Hrsg. von MAARTEN J. F. M. HOENEN und PAUL J. J. M. BAKKER. Leiden, Boston, Köln 2000, S. 213–238, hier S. 214, 215, 225. E. P. BOS: *Logica modernorum in Prague about 1400.* Leiden und Boston 2004. (Studien und Texte zur Geistesgeschichte des Mittelalters. 82), S. 15–16, 17, 38, 449–450. E. JENNIFER ASHWORTH: Descent and Ascent from Ockham to Domingo de Soto: An Answer to Paul Spade. In: *Vivarium.* 51 (2013), S. 385–410. HARALD BERGER: Which Hugo? This One! Hugo de Hervorst. In: *Vivarium.* 58 (2020), S. 89–110, hier S. 93–94, 98, 106–107.

Who could be the author of the logical works in the printed books Basel 1487 and Hagenau 1495 and 1503? An anonymous logical work consisting of commentaries on the first and fourth treatises of Peter of Spain and on the so-called *parva logicalia* of Marsilius of Inghen was printed not fewer than three times, viz. 1487 in Basel, 1495 and 1503 in Hagenau; the second edition was reprinted in 1967. In this study it is argued, first, that the work stems from the University of Vienna or at least is authored by a Viennese Master of Arts. Second, that the author comes from Salzburg. Third, that he seems to be named Wolfgang. Three members of the late medieval University of Vienna named Wolfgang of Salzburg meet the chronological criterion of having graduated not after 1487 (the date of the first edition), viz. Kydrer, Glimpf, and Dankenfelder. It is argued that Wolfgang Kydrer of Salzburg is most likely the author of that work. He was quite a remarkable scholar, being a scribe and owner of manuscripts as well as a writer and translator. Born in 1419 or 1420, he died in 1487 as a monk of the Benedictine cloister of Tegernsee in Bavaria, to which he donated 15 books, now among the Codices Latini Monacenses from Tegernsee in the BSB at Munich. In addition, a new feature of the genre of *parva logicalia* is presented, namely that Peter of Spain's first and fourth treatises were now counted among them.

Am 20. Juni 1487 beendete Nikolaus Kessler[1] in Basel einen Druck, der gemäß der „Titelseite" fol. a1r Folgendes enthält: *Commentum novum in primum et quartum tractatus Petri Hispani cum commento parvorum logicalium Marsilij* (GW, M32301). Dieses Werk wurde zwei weitere Male von Heinrich Gran[2] in Hagenau gedruckt, beendet am 3. März 1495 (GW, M32303)[3] bzw. am 30. Dezember 1503 (VD 16, J 645). Hier lauten die „Titel" *Commentum emendatum et correctum in primum et quartum tractatus Petri Hyspani et super tractatibus Marsilij de suppositionibus, ampliationibus, appellationibus et consequentiis* (1495) bzw. *Commentarium secundum modernorum doctrinam in tractatus logices Petri Hispani primum et quartum. Item commentarium in tractatus parvorum logicalium Marsilij, scilicet suppositionum, ampliationum, restrictionum, appellationum, consequentiarum, exponibilium. Itenque de descensu, de positione propositionum in esse, de statu, de alienatione* (1503). Im Folgenden werden diese Drucke der Reihe nach mit »A«, »B« und »C« bezeichnet. ABC sind als Digitalisate über den GW und das VD 16 auch im Internet zugänglich, der einfacheren Handhabung wegen verwende ich im Folgenden den Nachdruck von B[4].

Im Einzelnen enthält das Werk[5]:

Commentum in primum tractatum Petri Hispani (B, fol. a2r–i4r).
Inc. prol.: Circa initium parvorum logicalium quaeritur primo, utrum logica sit scientia. Priusquam magistri Petri Hispani textum aggrediar, de certis notandis movendisque dubiis videre restat.
Inc. comm.: »Dialectica est ars artium, scientia scientiarum ad omnium methodorum principia viam habens«. Pro illius litterae declaratione est notandum quod illa diffinitio, ut ponitur in verbis et de rigore, non est bona, quia non exprimit convertibiliter id quod per diffinitum significatur.
Expl.: et ergo qualitas, quantitas, oppositio et conversio attendendae sunt in eis sicut in aliis de inesse.

Commentum in quartum tractatum Petri Hispani (B, fol. i4r–m7r).
Inc. prol.: Circa initium quarti tractatus Petri Hispani quaeritur primo, quid sit subiectum in quarto tractatu Petri Hispani. Et an sit unus tractatus ab aliis tractatibus logicae distinctus. Pro illa quaestione est notandum quod subiectum praesentis tractatus est hoc totum »syllogismus captus pro praemissis et conclusione simul«, sive complexe sive incomplexe capiatur.
Inc. comm.: »Propositio est oratio affirmativa vel negativa alicuius de aliquo vel alicuius ab aliquo«. Pro isto textu est notandum quod ipse non est diffinitio, neque bona neque mala, ex quo in ea (!) ponitur diffinitum et diffinitio.
Expl.: Ex illis patet quo modo syllogismi imperfecti debeant reduci ad perfectos tam conversive quam per impossibile. Et tantum de huius quarti tractatus Petri Hispani materia. (Es folgt ein quadratisches Schema mit Kombinationen der syllogistisch relevanten Buchstaben »a« (universal affirmativ), »e« (universal negativ), »i« (partikulär affirmativ), »o« (partikulär negativ): aa, ii, ai, ia, usw.)

Regulae syllogismorum (Nr. 1-26, B, fol. m7v–n4v).
Inc.: Quia non aequale ingenium est omnibus, sed plerique propter ingenii obscuritatem et difficultatem quae vigere solent saepius in maximis erroribus se capi sinunt.
Expl.: Dumtaxat autem ex superabundantia et ad auxilium (A: et auxilio) incipientium adinventae.

Regulae suppositionum Marsilij (Nr. 1-19, B, fol. n4v–n6v)[6].
Inc.: Sequuntur regulae suppositionum Marsilij quarum decemnovem sunt in ordine. Prima regula: Terminus discretus in quacumque propositione positus stans pro suo significato ultimo, si supponit, supponit discrete et personaliter.

[5] Die lateinischen Texte sind behutsam »klassifiziert«, hauptsächlich »ae« statt »e« und »-tio« statt »-cio«.

[6] Vgl. MARSILIUS OF INGHEN: *Treatises on the Properties of Terms*, S. 64–70.

Expl.: Dicitur copulatum propter terminum qui sequitur disiunctum de praedicamento ubi vel quando, ut »in Saltzburga vel Wyenna Pataviae vel Romae«. (A, fol. 04r, add.: Et est notandum quod omnes istae regulae intellectae ad sensum sunt universaliter verae.)

De suppositionibus (B, fol. n7r–q6v).
Inc. prol.: Circa tractatum Marsilij de suppositionibus movetur dubium istud, utrum tractatus Marsilij de suppositionibus sit ab aliis tractatibus logicae distinctus.
Inc. comm.: Utrum terminum supponere sit possibile. Notandum <quod> haec quaestio quam magister Hugo movet super tractatum Marsilij de suppositionibus est cathegorica indefinita affirmativa.
Expl.: Unde descensus copulatus est descensus cuius consequens est una propositio de copulato extremo, ut patebit statim infra. Et tantum de illa quaestione.

De descensu (B, fol. q7r–r2r).
Inc.: Circa materiam descensuum quaeritur, utrum descensus sit consequentia formalis. Notandum quod descensus est quaedam proprietas logicalis veritatis et falsitatis propositionum probativa.
Expl.: ad veritatem propositionis requireretur quod non requiritur ad veritatem antecedentis nec econverso. Et tantum de materia descensuum.

De suppositione relativorum (B, fol. r2r–r5v).
Inc.: Utrum relativum supponat eodem modo sicut suum antecedens. Notandum quod quaestio est propositio cathegorica indefinita affirmativa.
Expl.: Aliquis homo non est illud animal quod est homo. Et tantum de tractatu relativorum.

De ampliationibus (B, fol. r6r–s8v).
Inc.: Circa tractatum Marsilij de ampliationibus quaeritur, utrum aliquis terminus possit ampliari. Notandum quod titulus uno modo sic formatur, utrum aliquis terminus sit ampliativus, et est Magistri Hugonis.
Expl.: et secundum eos impossibile non est significabile, ut dicunt, ergo non propositio. Et tantum de ampliationibus.

De appellationibus (B, fol. s8v–t4r).
Inc.: Circa tractatum appellationum quaeritur, utrum quilibet terminus sit appellativus. Pro ista quaestione est notandum quod ipsa est cathegorica universalis affirmativa in materia contingenti.
Expl.: quia non sequitur »Ego cognosco chimaeram, ergo omnem chimaeram quae est cognosco«.

De positione (B, fol. t4r–t5v).
Inc.: De materia positionis propositionum in esse notandum quod refert dicere propositio in esse et propositio de inesse et propositio ponibilis in esse.
Expl.: tunc appellarent suam formam pro eodem tempore verbi. Et tantum de appellationibus.

De statu (B, fol. t5v–t7r).
Inc.: Circa tractatum status quaeritur, utrum diffinitio status sit bona. Notandum quod ille terminus status in proposito capitur pro termino secundae intentionis.
Expl.: ut ly homo in illis duabus »Homo qui potest esse fuit« et »Homo fuit«. Et tantum de statu.

De restrictionibus (B, fol. t7v–t8v).
Inc.: Utrum diffinitio restrictionis sit bona. Notandum pro quaestione quod materia restrictionum valet ad salvandas veritates et falsitates propositionum.
Expl.: Similiter ly albus in illa »Homo albus currit«. Et tantum de materia restrictionum.

De alienationibus (B, fol. t8v–u1v).
Inc.: Utrum diffinitio alienationis sit bona. Pro ista quaestione est notandum quod diffinitio de qua quaerit quaestio non ponitur a Marsilio.
Expl.: ut homo rudibilis vel asinus hominis qui est cognoscit venientem. Et tantum de materia alienationum.

De consequentiis, ps. I (B, fol. u2r–z6v).
Inc.: Circa primam partem consequentiarum quaeritur, utrum diffinitio consequentiae a posteriori sit bona. Notandum primo quod iste est specialis tractatus logicae in quo tractatur de consequentiis, quomodo una propositio ad aliam vel ex alia nata est sequi.
Expl.: Et plures regulas consequentiarum magister Marsilius ponit quae saltem (! satis?) faciles sunt et paucae utilitatis, quas pro praesenti praetermitto.

De consequentiis, ps. II (B, fol. z6v–D7v).
Inc.: Circa secundam partem consequentiarum quaeritur, utrum omnis consequentia sit bona ab exponentibus ad expositam et econverso. Pro quaestione est notandum quod ipsa potest esse una cathegorica vel hypotetica.
Expl.: Sic etiam tunc non sequitur formaliter »Omnes apostoli dei sunt in caelo, igitur maximus numerus apostolorum dei est in caelo« etc. Pro quibus ipsi sit laus et gloria in saecula saeculorum.

Es fällt auf, dass es schon ganz am Anfang heißt »Circa initium parvorum logicalium«, die beiden Traktate des Petrus Hispanus I und IV also offenbar zu den *parva logicalia* gezählt werden. Solche Zusammenstellungen, Petrus Hispanus I und IV und *parva logicalia*, finden sich auch handschriftlich öfters, z. B. auch in den Tegernseer Handschriften Clm 19672 und 19676 der BSB, siehe auch weiter unten.

Die zwölf *Tractatus* des Petrus Hispanus (um die/vor der Mitte des 13. Jahrhunderts)[7] sind eines der einflussreichsten Logiklehrbücher überhaupt, der erste handelt *de introductionibus*, der vierte *de syllogismis*.[8] Die *parva logicalia* sind eigenständige Beiträge der Scholastiker zur Logik, die über Aristoteles, Porphyrius und Boethius hinausgehen,[9] im Spätmittelalter waren besonders einflussreich die Traktate des Thomas Maulfeld (um die/vor der Mitte des 14. Jahrhunderts)[10] und des Marsilius von Inghen[11] (Pariser Professor und Rektor, Gründungsrektor der Universität Heidelberg, dort 1396 gestorben)[12]. Marsilius gehört mit Johannes Buridan (Pariser Professor und Rektor, gest. 1360 (?))[13] und Albert von Sachsen (Pariser Professor und Rektor, Gründungsrektor der Universität Wien, gestorben 1390 als Bischof von Halberstadt)[14] zu den Hauptvertretern des Pariser Nominalismus. Der Nominalismus wurde im Wegestreit des 15. Jahrhunderts *via moderna* im Gegensatz zur *via antiqua* genannt[15], worauf der Titel des Drucks von 1503 (C) Bezug nimmt[16].

Der Parva-logicalia-Kommentar ab den Suppositionen ist ein Metakommentar zu Hugo von Hervorst[17]: Marsilius von Inghen, ein *magister artium Parisiensis* von 1362, hat seine Traktate über die *parva logicalia* wohl noch in den 1360er Jahren verfasst. Sein jüngerer Kollege Hugo von Hervorst, ein *magister artium Parisiensis* von 1373, hat um 1375 *quaestiones cum sophismatibus* zu diesen Traktaten geschrieben. An der Universität Wien wurden ab dem späten 14. Jahrhundert bis ins frühe 16. Jahrhundert etliche Kommentare zum Kommentar Hugos verfasst, es sind gegenwärtig 17 solche Metakommentare bekannt[18], das hier besprochene Werk ist einer davon.

---

7 JOKE SPRUYT: Peter of Spain. In: *The Stanford Encyclopedia of Philosophy*. Winter 2019 Edition (verfügbar auf www.plato.stanford.edu, [17.08.2022]).

8 PETER OF SPAIN (PETRUS HISPANUS PORTUGALENSIS): *Tractatus called afterwards Summule logicales*. Hrsg. von L. M. DE RIJK. Assen 1972 (Philosophical Texts and Studies. 22), S. 1–16 bzw. 43–54.

9 MAARTEN J. F. M. HOENEN: Parva logicalia. Towards the History of a Puzzling Literary Genre. In: *Mots médiévaux offerts à Ruedi Imbach*. Hrsg. von I. ATUCHA, D. CALMA, C. KÖNIG-PRALONG und I. ZAVATTERO. Porto 2011. (Textes et Études du Moyen Âge. 57), S. 517–526.

10 SÖNKE LORENZ: Thomas Manlevelt. Zu Verbreitung und Wirkung seiner Parva logicalia. Ein Beitrag zur spätmittelalterlichen Wissenschafts- und Universitätsgeschichte Zentraleuropas. In: *Text und Kontext. Historische Hilfswissenschaften in ihrer Vielfalt*. Hrsg. von SÖNKE LORENZ und STEPHAN MOLITOR. Ostfildern 2011. (Tübinger Bausteine zur Landesgeschichte. 18), S. 381–465.

11 MARSILIUS OF INGHEN: *Treatises on the Properties of Terms*. GRAZIANA CIOLA: Marsilius of Inghen on the Definition of *consequentia*. In: *Vivarium*. 56 (2018), S. 272–291. Die Dissertation von GRAZIANA S. CIOLA: *Marsilius of Inghen and the Theories of Consequentiae with a provisional edition of Marsilius' treatise on* Consequentiae. Pisa, Scuola Normale Superiore, 2017, ist inzwischen im Internet zugänglich, URL = https://ricerca.sns.it/bitstream/11384/86142/1/Ciola-PhD-Lettere-final-version.pdf (11.12.2022).

12 MAARTEN HOENEN: Marsilius of Inghen. In: *The Stanford Encyclopedia of Philosophy*. Summer 2021 Edition (verfügbar auf www.plato.stanford.edu, [17.08.2022]). HEIKE HAWICKS und HARALD BERGER: *Marsilius von Inghen und die Niederrheinlande. Zum 625. Todestag des Gründungsrektors der Heidelberger Universität*. Heidelberg 2021. (Beiträge zur Geschichte der Kurpfalz und der Universität Heidelberg. 1).

13 BERND MICHAEL: *Johannes Buridan: Studien zu seinem Leben, seinen Werken und zur Rezeption seiner Theorien im Europa des späten Mittelalters*. Teil 1 und 2. Berlin 1985. JACK ZUPKO: John Buridan. In: *The Stanford Encyclopedia of Philosophy*. Fall 2018 Edition (verfügbar auf www.plato.stanford.edu, [17.08.2022]).

14 HARALD BERGER: Albert von Sachsen. In: *Die deutsche Literatur des Mittelalters. Verfasserlexikon*, 2. Aufl. Bd. XI, Sp. 39–56. JOËL BIARD: Albert of Saxony. In: *The Stanford Encyclopedia of Philosophy*. Spring 2019 Edition (verfügbar auf www.plato.stanford.edu, [17.08.2022]).

15 Siehe z. B. MAARTEN J. F. M. HOENEN: *Via antiqua* and *Via moderna* in the Fifteenth Century: Doctrinal, Institutional, and Church Political Factors in the Wegestreit. In: *The Medieval Heritage in Early Modern Metaphysics and Modal Theory, 1400–1700*. Hrsg. von RUSSELL L. FRIEDMAN und LAUGE O. NIELSEN. Dordrecht, Boston, London 2003. (The New Synthese Historical Library. 53), S. 9–36, mit der älteren Literatur.

16 Auch der Druck des vergleichbaren Werkes des JOHANNES DE WERDEA (siehe unten) hat einen solchen Bezug im Titel: *Exercitata parvorum logicalium secundum viam modernorum*. Reutlingen 1487 (GW, M15005).

17 BERGER: Which Hugo? This One! Hugo de Hervorst. HARALD BERGER: Neue Funde zu Hugo von Hervorst und den Wiener Hugo-Kommentaren. In: *Codices Manuscripti & Impressi*. 121/122 (2020), S. 1–10. HARALD BERGER: Der Niederrhein in der Universitäts- und Philosophiegeschichte des Spätmittelalters. In: HAWICKS und BERGER: *Marsilius von Inghen und die Niederrheinlande*, S. 87–111, hier S. 101–108.

18 Gemäß HARALD BERGER: Katalog der Wiener Hugo-Kommentare, noch unveröffentlicht.

Die Petrus-Hispanus-Kommentare sind Expositionen, d. h. eigentliche Textauslegungen im Unterschied zu Quästionen als freien Problemerörterungen, wobei die *litterae* (d. i. die zu kommentierenden Textstücke) auch hervorgehoben sind. Ausnahmen sind Quästionen bzw. Dubia jeweils am Anfang und am Ende der beiden Traktate (B, fol. a2r–a3r, i3r–i4r, i4r–v, m6r–m7r). Außerdem findet sich vor dem letzten Dubium eine Quästion zu den expositorischen Syllogismen (d. i. Syllogismen mit singulären Prämissen), die bei Petrus Hispanus gar nicht vorkommen: »Sequitur de syllogismis expositoriis. Circa quam materiam quaeritur, utrum syllogismus expositorius teneat in omni figura« (B, fol. m4v–m6r).

Die anschließenden Parva-logicalia-Kommentare erörtern hauptsächlich die Quästionen und Sophismen des Hugo von Hervorst[19] zu den Traktaten des Marsilius von Inghen, sind also Kommentare zum Kommentar Hugos („Metakommentare"). Hinzu kommen eine einleitende Quästion (B, fol. n7r–v) sowie einige zusätzliche Quästionen (B, fol. q5v–q6v, s7v–s8v) und Sophismen (B, fol. s4r–v, s4v–s5v). Außerdem werden einige kleinere Materien behandelt, die bei Hugo nicht vorkommen: *descensus*, *positio*, *status*, *restrictio*, *alienatio*. Das Sophisma »Tantum unum est« wird bei Hugo zweimal behandelt, nämlich als Nr. 7 in den *suppositiones* und als Nr. 2 in den *consequentiae*, ps. II, hier nur an letzterer Stelle. – Der Konsequenzien-Traktat des Marsilius hat übrigens zwei Teile, von denen der zweite von *propositiones exponibiles* handelt, d. i. von analysebedürftigen Sätzen, weshalb es im Titel des Drucks C heißt »consequentiarum (= ps. I), exponibilium (= ps. II)«.

Demgemäß werden Marsilius und Hugo sehr oft zitiert, diese sind für die Wiener Artisten überhaupt Autoritäten auf dem Gebiet der Logik; bei Marsilius werden gelegentlich auch »sequaces«, »Marsilici« und »Marsiliaci« genannt. Häufig zitiert wird auch Johannes Buridanus (Biridanus, siehe oben), der Nestor des Pariser Nominalismus und eine allgemeine philosophische Autorität des Spätmittelalters – ein Kölner Dokument von Ende 1425 spricht vom »saeculum Buridani«[20]. Fallweise werden auch andere Pariser Philosophen des 14. Jahrhunderts zitiert, wie Albert von Sachsen und Thomas von Kleve[21] (B, fol. q6v).

Alle Texte dieser Drucke sind anonym, ich werde im Folgenden einen Vorschlag zur Identifizierung des Verfassers entwickeln, der meines Erachtens nicht nur eine Möglichkeit aufzeigt, sondern hohe Wahrscheinlichkeit beanspruchen kann. Der Einfachheit halber gehe ich davon aus, dass alle Teile ein und denselben Verfasser haben, aber das muss natürlich nicht so sein. Das Werk macht jedoch insgesamt einen sehr einheitlichen Eindruck, und es gibt auch einige vergleichbare Werke, die tatsächlich ein und denselben Verfasser haben, z. B. die einschlägigen Bände von Johannes von Werdea und Ulrich Greimolt von Tübingen.

Schon allein die Tatsache, dass es sich beim Marsilius-Kommentar um einen Metakommentar zu Hugo von Hervorst handelt, spricht für die Universität Wien als Ursprungsort, da bislang solche Kommentare nur von Wiener Magistern bekannt sind. Es gibt in den Texten in Beispielsätzen aber auch explizite Belege für Wien (z. B. B, fol. a2v, m5r,

---

[19] Verzeichnis der Titel bei BERGER: Which Hugo? This One! Hugo de Hervorst, § 5, S. 107–110.

[20] FRANZ KARD. EHRLE: *Der Sentenzenkommentar Peters von Candia, des Pisaner Papstes Alexanders des V. Ein Beitrag zur Scheidung der Schulen in der Scholastik des vierzehnten Jahrhunderts und zur Geschichte des Wegestreites*. Münster in Westf. 1925. (Franziskanische Studien. Beiheft 9), Anhang, Nr. 1, S. 281–290, hier S. 284.

[21] STEPHEN READ: Thomas of Cleves and Collective Supposition. HARALD BERGER: On Thomas de Clivis Sen. and Some Other Late Medieval Arts Masters in Paris, Prague, and Vienna. In: *Bochumer Philosophisches Jahrbuch für Antike und Mittelalter*. 25 (2022), erscheint Anfang 2023.

n6v), auch die Donau kommt vor (B, fol. a2v und x1r). Darüber hinaus ist von einer »communis schola Wiennensis« die Rede (B, fol. q6v und r4r)[22], so dass man es als gegeben annehmen kann, dass der Verfasser ein Wiener Magister ist. Aber nicht nur Wien, sondern auch Salzburg kommt in Beispielsätzen vor (B, fol. m5r und n6v). Unser Wiener Magister hat also einen Salzburg-Bezug, stammt wohl aus Salzburg.

Ferner finden sich nicht nur Orts-, sondern auch Personennamen in Beispielsätzen. Ein für unsere Zwecke besonders wertvoller Beispielsatz ist »Wolfgangus est nequam« (A, fol. f7r; B, fol. f5r; C, fol. f1r). Ein Akademiker und Kleriker jener Zeit würde wohl nur sich selbst als »Taugenichts« bezeichnen, ob der Ausdruck nun biblisch konnotiert ist oder nicht. Die Hypothese lautet demnach also, dass der Anonymus mit einem Wiener Magister Wolfgang aus Salzburg zu identifizieren ist.

Da das Werk gemäß dem Datum des Erstdrucks nicht nach dem 20. Juni 1487 entstanden ist, muss auch die Graduierung des Verfassers vor diesem Datum liegen. Das „Wiener Artistenregister" 1416 bis 1555 weist drei Wolfgange aus Salzburg aus[23], die in Frage kommen, alle haben auch einen Familiennamen: Kydrer ab 1439[24], Glimpf ab 1453[25], Danknfelder ab 1472[26], wobei ich Dank(e)nfelder mit dem Wolfgang aus Salzburg ohne Familienamen ab 1475[27] identifiziere, was naheliegend ist, da von Dankenfelder nur die Determination 1472 und die Wahl zum Prüfer der Sächsischen Nation 1480 belegt sind, von Wolfgang von Salzburg hingegen die Inzeption 1475 und Lehrveranstaltungen von 1475–1480, darunter der zweite und dritte Traktat des Petrus Hispanus (1475) sowie *Obligatoria* und *Insolubilia* (das sind Sparten der scholastischen Logik). Die anderen Wolfgange von Salzburg sind zu spät gemäß dem genannten chronologischen Kriterium.

Obwohl eigentlich Dankenfelder am besten und am längsten (1472-1480) belegt ist (1475 wurde er auch in die Rechtswissenschaftliche Fakultät aufgenommen[28]), glaube ich aber, dass es sehr gute Gründe gibt, die vielmehr für Wolfgang Kydrer aus Salzburg sprechen: Dieser war nachweislich mit einigen Verfassern von Wiener Hugo-Kommentaren bekannt[29], namentlich mit Johannes Krafft von Gmunden[30], Nikolaus

---

22 Die erste dieser Stellen, B, fol. q6v, schreibt aber eine bestimmte Auffassung, die auf Thomas de Clivis (mag. art. Paris. von ca. 1365) zurückgeht, irrig auch dem Albert von Sachsen (mag. art. Paris. von 1351) zu: »Est alia opinio communis scholae Wiennensis, magistri Alberti et Thomae de Clivis et multorum aliorum logicorum praesertim modernorum qui dicunt quod quatuor sint species suppositionis communis, videlicet tres tactae et quartam ponunt suppositionem collectivam«. Albert hat aber vielmehr eine Dreiteilung vertreten, die hier als erste Auffassung dem Marsilius von Inghen und seinen Anhängern zugeschrieben wird, B, fol. q6r. Vgl. ALBERT VON SACHSEN: *Logik. Lateinisch – Deutsch*. Übersetzt, mit einer Einleitung und Anmerkungen hrsg. von HARALD BERGER. Hamburg 2010. (Philosophische Bibliothek. 611), Tr. II, Kap. 1, S. 248, Z. 5–8. – Die andere Stelle, B, fol. r4r, verbindet die allgemeine Wiener Schule mit Marsilius (von Inghen) und Hugo (von Hervorst).

23 Vorher ist an der U Wien kein Wolfgang aus Salzburg belegt: *Acta Facultatis artium Universitatis Vindobonensis 1385–1416*. Hrsg. von PAUL UIBLEIN. Graz, Wien, Köln 1968. (Publikationen des Instituts für Österreichische Geschichtsforschung. VI/2/1), S. 570 (Wolfgangus) und 595 (Salzburg).

24 *»Wiener Artistenregister« 1416 bis 1447 (AFA II)*, bearb. von THOMAS MAISEL und INGRID MATSCHINEGG. Wien 2007 (verfügbar unter www.phaidra.univie.ac.at, [01.08.2022]), S. 116, 133, 137 (Nr. 7109, 7764, 7911).

25 *»Wiener Artistenregister« 1447 bis 1471 (AFA III-1)*, bearb. von THOMAS MAISEL und INGRID MATSCHINEGG. Wien 2007 (verfügbar unter www.phaidra.univie.ac.at, [01.08.2022]), S. 49, 71, 77 (Nr. 11131, 12019, 12247).

26 *»Wiener Artistenregister« 1471 bis 1497 (AFA III-2)*, bearb. von THOMAS MAISEL und INGRID MATSCHINEGG. Wien 2007 (verfügbar unter www.phaidra.univie.ac.at, [01.08.2022]), S. 15 und 68 (Nr. 17052 und 19108).

27 *»Wiener Artistenregister« 1471 bis 1497 (AFA III-2)*, S. 29, 33, 42, 51, 64, 71 (Nr. 17611, 17799, 18133, 18490, 18987, 19246).

28 *Die Matrikel der Wiener Rechtswissenschaftlichen Fakultät. Matricula Facultatis Juristarum Studii Wiennensis*. Hrsg. von THOMAS MAISEL und JOHANNES SEIDL, Bd. 2. Wien, Köln, Weimar 2016. (Publikationen des Instituts für Österreichische Geschichtsforschung. VI/3/2), S. 37: Magister Wolfgangus Dankenfelder de Saltzeburga 36 d(enarii).

29 VIRGIL REDLICH: *Tegernsee und die deutsche Geistesgeschichte im 15. Jahrhundert*. München 1931. (Schriftenreihe zur bayerischen Landesgeschichte. 9), S. 42, Anm. 167. – REDLICH, S. 41–42 und Anm. 167, hätte auch Licht werfen können auf die Cedula bei BERGER: Neue Funde zu Hugo von Hervorst, S. 8–10 mit Abb.

30 Zu Johannes von Gmunden (†1442) als Teilnehmer an der Disputation von Ende 1440 siehe auch PAUL UIBLEIN: *Die Universität Wien im Mittelalter. Beiträge und Forschungen*. Hrsg. von KURT MÜHLBERGER und KARL KADLETZ. Wien 1999. (Schriftenreihe des Universitätsarchivs Universität Wien. 11), S. 386 (lies »Cur sol et luna apparent nobis in superficie recta« usw. statt »apparent non in«, vgl. Clm 19678, fol. 115v).

von Aalen, Jodok Gartner von Berching und Ulrich Greimolt von Weilheim bzw. Tübingen ³¹, später wie Kydrer auch ins Kloster Tegernsee eingetreten. Auch mit Johannes von Werdea (seit 1439/40 an der Universität Wien, mag. art. Wienn. von 1445) dürfte Kydrer schon von Wien her bekannt gewesen sein, Johannes (später Hieronymus von Mondsee OSB genannt) erwähnt ihn jedenfalls freundlich in einem Brief an Christian Tesenpacher in Tegernsee³². Und unter den 15 Büchern, die Kydrer bei seinem Eintritt ins Kloster Tegernsee 1462 mitbrachte, befand sich auch der jetzige Clm 19676 der BSB mit dem Hugo-Kommentar von Jodok Gartner von Berching. Ein anderer dieser Bände, Clm 19818, geschrieben von Kydrer selbst, enthält auf fol. 183r–264v Bruchstücke eines Hugo-Kommentars (die übrigens nicht mit ABC übereinstimmen)³³ zusammen mit weiteren einschlägigen Texten sowie mit außerordentlichen und ordentlichen Disputationen Kydrers³⁴, Wien 1440, die auch viele Titel aus Hugo entlehnen und auch oft auf diesen verweisen. Und auf fol. 213r findet sich im Abschnitt *De appellatione* der Selbstverweis »Quid autem sit accipi secundum determinatam rationem, habes satis in parvo libello«, was sich durchaus auf die handschriftliche Vorlage von ABC beziehen könnte, vgl. B, fol. t2v: »Et est sciendum quod terminum accipi secundum determinatam rationem intelligitur dupliciter« usw.; aber leider ist jener Verweis zu unbestimmt. Auch Beispiele mit der Donau und dem Wasser (B, fol. x1r) finden sich hier auf fol. 254v und 256v, und noch weitere Ähnlichkeiten mit ABC fallen auf.

Außerdem ist von Dankenfelder sonst nichts bekannt, von Kydrer hingegen sehr wohl, er wurde sogar ins *Verfasserlexikon* aufgenommen³⁵. All das zusammen hat meines Erachtens weit mehr Gewicht als z. B. die Petrus-Hispanus-Vorlesung Dankenfelders. Hier ein biographischer Abriss zu Kydrer:

Wolfgangus Chydrer³⁶ de Salczburga wurde zwischen April und Oktober 1437 (Rektorat des Mag. Nicolaus de Grecz) in die Universität Wien aufgenommen, und zwar in die Rheinische Nation.³⁷ Im Jahre 1439 determinierte er an der Artistenfakultät, im Jahre 1441 erfolgte die *inceptio* zum Magister artium. Daraus kann man erschließen, dass er wohl um das Jahr 1420 geboren wurde³⁸, jedenfalls nicht später. Bei der Vorlesungsverteilung am 1. September 1441 übernahm der frische Magister das erste Buch der *Elemente* des Euklid.³⁹ Danach ist er an der Universität Wien nicht mehr belegt⁴⁰, und zwar anscheinend aus folgendem Grund: Im Jahre 1440 bat der Abt von St. Peter OSB in Salzburg, Peter Klughammer, den in Wien weilenden Hieronymus Posser aus Salzburg⁴¹, ihm von dort einen »discretum baccalarium in artibus, virum

---

31 REDLICH: *Tegernsee*, S. 41.

32 LUDWIG GLÜCKERT: *Hieronymus von Mondsee (Magister Johannes de Werdea). Ein Beitrag zur Geschichte des Einflusses der Wiener Universität im 15. Jahrhundert*. München 1930, S. 162.

33 Gemäß der Datierung Wien 1440 wäre es möglich, dass das Teile einer Mitschrift der Lehrveranstaltung von Nikolaus von Aalen sind, von der es eine vollständige Mitschrift in der Handschrift Melk, StiftsB, Cod. 899, fol. 68ra–211ra, gibt, vgl. BERGER: Neue Funde zu Hugo von Hervorst, S. 4–5. Ich kann das gegenwärtig nicht überprüfen. Der genannte Block im Clm 19818 beginnt auf fol. 183r mit »Utrum omnis consequentia bona sit simpliciter necessaria (= HUGO, Consequentiae, ps. I, qu. 4). Nota quidam dicunt quod ly consequentia sit species specialissima non habens sub se aliquas species inferiores«. Auf den folgenden Blättern werden etliche Wiener Magister von (vor) 1439/40 genannt, darunter Berühmtheiten wie (Thomas Ebendorfer von) Haselbach, (Johannes) Slitpacher (von Weilheim) u. a., am häufigsten aber ein gewisser Stedler (d. i. vermutlich Johannes Stedler von Landshut, gest. 1436).

34 Solche auch im Clm 19678, fol. 150r–178r und 178v–183r.

35 Und mit seiner *ars moriendi* sogar auch ins *Historische Wörterbuch der Philosophie*: A. HÜGLI: Sterben lernen (lat. ars moriendi). In: Bd. X, Sp. 129–134, hier Sp. 133, Anm. 35.

36 Auch „Bolfgangus" sowie „Chiedrer", „Kidrer", „Kydrär" und „Kydrer".

37 *Die Matrikel der Universität Wien*, Bd. 1. Graz und Köln 1956. (Publikationen des Instituts für Österreichische Geschichtsforschung. VI/1/1), S. 197, Nr. 46. – Zu Kydrer siehe besonders PIRMIN LINDNER: Familia S. Quirini in Tegernsee, Teil I. In: *Oberbayerisches Archiv*. 50 (1897), S. 18–130, hier S. 102–104. REDLICH: *Tegernsee*, S. 41–45. DENNIS D. MARTIN: Kydrer (Kidrer), Wolfgang, von Salzburg. In: *Die deutsche Literatur des Mittelalters. Verfasserlexikon*, 2. Aufl. Bd. V, Sp. 474–477 (eine kleine Korrektur dazu in Bd. XI, Sp. 904).

38 So auch MARTIN: Kydrer, Sp. 474. – Diese Annahme wird bestätigt durch einen Beispielsatz Kydrers von 1440: »Ego vixi 20 annis« (Clm 19818, fol. 219v), wonach er 1419 oder 1420 geboren wurde.

39 *»Wiener Artistenregister« 1416 bis 1447 (AFA II)*, S. 116, 133, 137 (Nr. 7109, 7764, 7911).

40 Wichtige Informationen zu Kydrers Wiener Zeit aus Notizen von ihm selbst bei REDLICH: *Tegernsee*, S. 41–43.

41 In der von Kydrer selbst geschrieben Liste von Wiener Magistern, REDLICH: *Tegernsee*, S. 42, Anm. 167, kommt auch ein Hieronymus de Salzburg vor. – Siehe GEROLD HAYER: Posser, Hieronymus. In: *Die deutsche Literatur des Mittelalters. Verfasserlexikon*, 2. Aufl. Bd. VII, Sp. 791–795 (eine kleine Korrektur dazu in Bd. XI, Sp. 1261).

maturum, pacificum ac scientificum« zu vermitteln, da er dringend jemanden für die Schule von St. Peter brauche.⁴² Offenbar fiel die Wahl auf Kydrer, der dann von 1442–44 als *rector scolarium* von St. Peter belegt ist⁴³, 1445 folgte ihm ein Magister Johann in diesem Amt nach. Nach seiner Salzburger Zeit⁴⁴ wirkte Kydrer in Mattsee (Salzburg) und Frankenmarkt (Oberösterreich) als Seelsorger, bis er 1462 ins bayerische Kloster Tegernsee OSB eintrat. Dort ist er am 13. August 1487 gestorben (übrigens nur ein paar Wochen nach dem Erscheinen des Baseler Drucks, A), knapp 70 Jahre alt. Er hat 15 Bücher nach Tegernsee mitgebracht⁴⁵, darunter auch den Hugo-Kommentar von Jodok Gartner von Berching (BSB, Clm 19676), wie bereits erwähnt. Die Tegernseer Bibliothek besaß übrigens die Inkunabel Hagenau 1495 (B, BSB-Ink C-480)⁴⁶.

Kydrer war nicht nur Schreiber⁴⁷ und Besitzer von Handschriften, sondern auch Verfasser⁴⁸ und Übersetzer⁴⁹. Wenn die Hypothese stimmt, dass er auch der Verfasser der Werke in den Drucken ABC ist, dann müsste man wegen seiner knappen Zeit als Wiener Magister (1441/42) auch Salzburg (1442–44) als Entstehungsort in Betracht ziehen⁵⁰. An der Schule von St. Peter wurden sicher auch die *artes* und somit vor allem auch die Logik als Grunddisziplin gelehrt⁵¹. An der Wiener Artistenfakultät waren für das Bakkalaureat unter anderem die *Tractatus* des Petrus Hispanus und die *parva logicalia* vorgeschrieben⁵². Auffällig ist aber, dass bei Petrus Hispanus meistens die Traktate II (*de praedicabilibus*, entsprechend der *Isagoge* des Porphyr) und III (*de praedicamentis*, entsprechend den *Categoriae* des Aristoteles) explizit angeführt werden⁵³, hier aber die Traktate I (*de introductionibus*, entsprechend *De interpretatione* des Aristoteles) und IV (*de syllogismis*, entsprechend den *Analytica priora* des Aristoteles) enthalten sind, wie auch in

---

⁴² SABINE WEISS: Das Bildungswesen im spätmittelalterlichen Österreich. Ein Überblick. In: *Die österreichische Literatur. Ihr Profil von den Anfängen im Mittelalter bis ins 18. Jahrhundert (1050–1750)*. Hrsg. von HERBERT ZEMAN. Graz 1986, Teil 1, S. 209–259, hier S. 215, vgl. auch Anhang I, S. 255. Posser war auch selber Schulleiter von St. Peter, ebd., S. 255, wo Kydrer ja zur Schule gegangen sein könnte. – Ich danke Frau Eva Riedlsperger, die gegenwärtig ihre Masterarbeit über die Schule von St. Peter schreibt, für freundliche Informationen.

⁴³ REDLICH: *Tegernsee*, S. 43, und nach ihm MARTIN: Kydrer, Sp. 475, schreiben »Mitte der vierziger Jahre«, aber die genannten Jahre 1442–44 sind eindeutig belegt (*Rechnungsbuch St. Peter*, Arch. St. Peter, Hs. A 622, fol. 130r, 147r, 159r).

⁴⁴ Es gibt keinerlei Hinweise darauf, dass er von Salzburg an die Universität Wien zurückgekehrt sein könnte.

⁴⁵ REDLICH: *Tegernsee*, S. 44–45, vgl. auch *Mittelalterliche Bibliothekskataloge Deutschlands*, Bd. 4, Tl. 2, München 1979, S. 734–863 zu Tegernsee (von GÜNTER GLAUCHE), S. 740 zu Kydrer, S. 775 zu Predigten von ihm im Katalog von 1483. Siehe auch MIECISLAUS MARKOWSKI: *Buridanica quae in codicibus manu scriptis bibliothecarum Monacensium asservantur*. Wrocław, Warszawa, Kraków, Gdańsk, Łódź 1981, S. 143–145.

⁴⁶ Und zwar gemäß einem Eintrag auf dem Einbanddeckel hinten innen schon seit 1496, also zur Zeit des Bibliothekars Ambrosius Schwerzenbeck, der spätestens ab 1481 und bis um 1500 wirkte, gest. 1508, siehe REDLICH: *Tegernsee*, S. 76–84, vgl. auch S. 263, s. n.

⁴⁷ Vgl. z. B. REDLICH: *Tegernsee*, S. 192, s. n.

⁴⁸ Siehe LINDNER, REDLICH und MARTIN. Einen Ethik-Kommentar hat Kydrer allerdings nicht verfasst, sondern nur mitgeschrieben: CHRISTOPH FLÜELER: Ethica in Wien anno 1438. Die Kommentierung der Aristotelischen ›Ethik‹ an der Wiener Artistenfakultät. In: *Schriften im Umkreis mitteleuropäischer Universitäten um 1400. Lateinische und volkssprachige Texte aus Prag, Wien und Heidelberg: Unterschiede, Gemeinsamkeiten, Wechselbeziehungen*. Hrsg. von FRITZ PETER KNAPP, JÜRGEN MIETHKE und MANUELA NIESNER. Leiden und Boston 2004. (Education and Society in the Middle Ages and Renaissance. 20), S. 92–138, hier S. 113, 122, 126–127, Nr. 11 und 12. CHRISTOPH FLÜELER: Teaching Ethics at the University of Vienna: The Making of a Commentary at the Faculty of Arts (a Case Study). In: *Virtue Ethics in the Middle Ages. Commentaries on Aristotle's Nicomachean Ethics, 1200–1500*. Hrsg. von ISTVÁN P. BEJCZY. Leiden und Boston 2008. (Brill's Studies in Intellectual History. 160), S. 277–346, hier S. 280, 281, 285–288, 290–292, 294–295.

⁴⁹ Zu Kydrer als Übersetzer siehe z. B. auch KLAUS WOLF: *Hof – Universität – Laien. Literatur- und sprachgeschichtliche Untersuchungen zum deutschen Schrifttum der Wiener Schule des Spätmittelalters*. Wiesbaden 2006. (Wissensliteratur im Mittelalter. 45), S. 19, 134, 162, 163, vgl. Reg., S. 403.

⁵⁰ Falls er diese Kommentare nicht schon vor der Magistergraduierung verfasst hat, was durchaus möglich wäre, siehe oben zum Clm 19818. In Tegernsee scheint er nur mehr »im Rahmen des Theologischen« (REDLICH: *Tegernsee*, S. 44) gearbeitet zu haben, und in ABC sind mir auch keine Hinweise auf Tegernsee untergekommen.

⁵¹ WEISS: Das Bildungswesen, S. 214–216 und 243–253. Die Schule war hochstehend, in den 1460er Jahren wurde sogar die Umwandlung in eine Universität erwogen, ebd., S. 216.

⁵² ALPHONS LHOTSKY: *Die Wiener Artistenfakultät 1365–1497*. Wien 1965. (Österreichische Akademie der Wissenschaften. Philos.-hist. Kl. Sitzungsberichte. 247/2), S. 88–97. SÖNKE LORENZ: Libri ordinarie legendi. Eine Skizze zum Lehrplan der mitteleuropäischen Artistenfakultät um die Wende vom 14. zum 15. Jahrhundert. In: *Argumente und Zeugnisse*. Hrsg. von WOLFRAM HOGREBE. Frankfurt am Main, Bern, New York 1985. (Studia Philosophica et Historica. 5), S. 204–258.

⁵³ ULRIKE BODEMANN: Cedulae actuum. Zum Quellenwert studentischer Belegzettel des Spätmittelalters. Mit dem Abdruck von Belegzetteln aus dem 14. bis frühen 16. Jahrhundert. In: *Schulliteratur im späten Mittelalter*. Hrsg. von KLAUS GRUBMÜLLER. München 2000. (Münstersche Mittelalter-Schriften. 69), S. 435–499, hier S. 486–499, Nr. 2.7. Eine Ergänzung z. B. bei BERGER: Neue Funde zu Hugo von Hervorst, S. 8–10 mit Abb.

manchen Handschriften⁵⁴. Das ist ferner deshalb auffällig, weil auch die sog. *ars vetus* im Lehrplan explizit vorgeschrieben ist, die die *Isagoge* des Porphyr sowie die *Categoriae* und *De interpretatione* des Aristoteles umfasst, so dass die Prädikabilien und die Prädikamente gleich zweimal gelehrt wurden. Die Erklärung für jene scheinbare Ungereimtheit ist offenbar, dass solche Werke nicht Lehrveranstaltungen zu Petrus Hispanus *und* den *parva logicalia* abbilden, sondern eben nur solche zu den *parva logicalia*, zu denen auch die Traktate I und IV des Petrus Hispanus gezählt wurden (siehe dazu ebenfalls oben), was in der Fachliteratur bislang nicht beachtet wurde, soweit mir bekannt ist.

Fazit: Die Texte der Drucke ABC legen nahe, dass sie von einem Wiener Artisten-Magister des 15. Jahrhunderts namens Wolfgang aus Salzburg verfasst wurden. Hierfür kommen drei Männer in Betracht: Kydrer, Glimpf und Dankenfelder. Obwohl die Daten des *Wiener Artistenregisters* eigentlich am meisten für Dankenfelder sprechen würden und am wenigsten für Kydrer, wurde aufgrund externer Daten dafür argumentiert, dass höchstwahrscheinlich Wolfgang Kydrer aus Salzburg (†1487) der Verfasser dieses dreimal gedruckten Werks (ABC) ist. Demnach lägen mehr als 40 und weniger als 50 Jahre zwischen der Abfassung und dem Erstdruck des Werks; »novum« im Titel von A hieße dann einfach »demselben Jahrhundert angehörig«.

Dass das Werk 1487 in Basel gedruckt wurde, wird mit der dortigen Universität (gegr. 1459) zu tun haben, der Drucker Nikolaus Kessler war auch ein bacc. art. dieser Universität. In der UB Basel finden sich auch Handschriften vergleichbaren Inhalts⁵⁵. Einen triftigen Grund für die beiden weiteren Drucke in Hagenau vermag ich nicht recht zu sehen, es wird aber wohl auch (Schul- oder) Universitätsbedarf gewesen sein.

---

54 Z. B. SBB-PK, lat. qu. 410; UB Graz, Ms. 1039; Melk, StiftsB, Cod. 899; BSB, Clm 14888, 14896, 19672, 19676 (zu diesen siehe MARKOWSKI: *Buridanica*, S. 139–140, 143, 144, an letzterer Stelle wäre aber nachzutragen: Clm 19676, fol. 42r–59v: Quaestiones super IV tractatum Petri Hispani); u. a. m.

55 Für ein Beispiel siehe BERGER: Neue Funde zu Hugo von Hervorst, S. 5–6.

Abb. 1 „Regula Und Testament [...]"
von 1644 – gedruckt von einem Gesellen der
Offizin Paur. (TLMF, FB 99470)

Hansjörg Rabanser

Buchhändler, verlegende Buchbinder und druckende Gesellen des 17. und 18. Jahrhunderts in Innsbruck

The history of book printing in the county of Tyrol began comparatively late with the founding of the first printing offices in the mid-16th century. The workshops were concentrated in the most important towns, where a single printer usually dominated the professional field, before other, competing printers increasingly appeared in the course of the 17th century. At the same time, we can observe an increase in the number of domestic and foreign booksellers, bookbinders and journeyman letterpress printers, who printed and published themselves. The aim of this article is to trace precisely these individuals and in particular, for the first time, to examine in more detail those representatives who were active in Innsbruck in the 17th and 18th centuries and whose traces have so far been difficult or impossible to find. The basis for this are not only new sources, but also the distributed publications of the individual representatives, which are included in an enclosed list of printed works. Of course, the fragmentary nature of the sources does not allow for a complete biographical account, but it provides a first basis for additional in-depth research.

Quellenfunde und Fragmente

Die Geschichte des Buchdrucks in der Grafschaft Tirol beginnt relativ spät. Nach dem kurzen Bestand einer privat geführten Offizin in der Bergwerksstadt Schwaz oder auf dem nahen Schloss Sigmundslust bei Vomp (1521–27), kam es erst 1548 zur Begründung einer durch die Tiroler Regierung initiierten und finanzierten Druckerei in Innsbruck. In der Folge entwickelten sich in der Grafschaft Tirol sowie in den Bistümern/Hochstiften Brixen und Trient weitere Offizinen, etwa in Riva del Garda (1557–63), Brixen (ab 1564), Trient (ab 1584), Bozen (ab 1659) und Rovereto (ab 1673).[1] In den genannten Städten beherrschte meist ein einziger Drucker das Feld, ehe im Laufe des 17. Jahrhunderts vermehrt Zweit- und damit Konkurrenzdrucker auftraten. Zeitgleich lässt sich eine merkliche Zunahme von aus- und inländischen Buchhändlern sowie vertreibenden Buchbindern feststellen. Auf den Titelblättern der Publikationen treten neben den Nennungen der amtierenden Drucker ab sofort auch neue Namen in Erscheinung.

Der Beitrag möchte genau diesen Personen nachspüren und die druckenden bzw. verlegenden Gesellen, Buchbinder und -händler, die speziell im 17. und 18. Jahrhundert in Innsbruck tätig waren und bisher

[1] Literaturangaben zu den Druckereien in Riva, Trient, Rovereto, Brixen und Bozen finden sich in: HANSJÖRG RABANSER: Die Literatur- und Quellenlage zur »Puechdruckhereÿ« in Nordtirol. Ein Arbeits- und Erfahrungsbericht mit einer Zeittafel und einer Quellensammlung im Anhang. In: *Der frühe Buchdruck in der Region. Neue Kommunikationswege in Tirol und seinen Nachbarländern*. Hrsg. von ROLAND SILA. Innsbruck 2016. (Schlern-Schriften. 366), S. 71–142, hier S. 87–8 (Anm. 45–7).

[2] So etwa bei: HELLMUT BUCHROITHNER: *Die Entwicklung des graphischen Gewerbes in Innsbruck*. Dipl. phil. Innsbruck 1961, S. 7. ANTON DURSTMÜLLER: *500 Jahre Druck in Österreich. Die Entwicklungsgeschichte der graphischen Gewerbe von den Anfängen bis zur Gegenwart. Band I: 1482 bis 1848.* Wien 1981, S. 151–52. DIETMAR KECHT: Typographie und Buchhandel in Tirol. Ein Beitrag zur 23. Österreichischen Buchwoche VI. In: *Tiroler Nachrichten*. 25 (1970), Nr. 251, S. 6.

kaum oder gar nicht eingeordnet werden konnten², erstmals genauer behandeln. Die Basis dafür bilden in erster Linie die geschaffenen bzw. vertriebenen Publikationen (s. dazu das Druckwerkeverzeichnis im Anhang) sowie neue Quellenfunde. Die fragmentarische Überlieferung erlaubt natürlich keine lückenlosen biographischen Darstellungen, sodass in vielen Fällen Unklarheiten bleiben werden. Eine erste Basis, die durch mögliche Neufunde ergänzt werden kann, ist damit jedoch gelegt.

Kaspar Mayr (belegt: 1638–44)

In keiner Darstellung zur Tiroler Druckgeschichte wird der Name Kaspar Mayr aufscheinen und das, obwohl dieser im Jahr 1644 als Drucker eines Buches in Erscheinung trat. Das Werk mit dem Titel *Regula Und Testament sampt den Constitutionibus der Minderen Brueder deß heyligen Francisci Ordens die Capucciner genandt.* [Abb. 1] enthält die Ordensregeln und Satzungen des Franziskaner- und Kapuzinerordens sowie Informationen zu weiteren Ordensinternen Organisationsarbeiten (Wahl des Generals, Einkleidung der Novizen etc.). Das Titelkupfer zeigt den Hl. Franz von Assisi (1182–1226), dem Gott die Ordensregeln überreicht, während man im Hintergrund die Stadt Innsbruck (links) bzw. die Ansicht eines Sakralbaus auf einem Hügel (rechts) erkennen kann. Die Signatur »Io. Bap. Iezl fecit« weist als Schöpfer der Illustration den angesehenen Innsbrucker Kupferstecher Johann Baptist Jezl (1610–66) aus.³ Ein weiterer Kupferstich (Seite 19) zeigt die Strahlenkranzmadonna mit Kind (»S. MARIÆ«); zusätzliche Vignetten ergänzen das Werk (auf den Seiten 1–2, 17–19, 21 und 90).

Der Druckervermerk – »Getruckt zu Ynßprugg, durch Casparum Mayr. Anno 1644.«⁴ – lässt aufhorchen, denn zu diesem Zeitpunkt waren in der Stadt nur zwei Buchdrucker tätig: Tonangebend war die Hofbuchdruckerei, welche offiziell der einzigen Tiroler Hofbuchdruckerin Maria Cleofa Paur (†1648) unterstand, die sich aber bereits durch ihren Sohn Hieronymus Paur (1609–69) unterstützen ließ, der 1645 die Werkstatt übernahm. Die damit konkurrierende Offizin wurde seit 1639 von dem aus Augsburg nach Tirol eingewanderten Michael Wagner (†1669) betrieben.⁵ Wie konnte ein gewisser Kaspar Mayr also mit einem Druckwerk in Erscheinung treten?

Um Licht in die Sache zu bringen, heißt es, einschlägige Quellenbestände zu sichten, um sich dem Erwähnten annähern zu können. Aber bereits der Blick in die Tauf-, Trau- und Sterbebücher ist ernüchternd, denn der recht häufig zu findende Name Kaspar Mayr erschwert die Suche deutlich, vor allem, da meist keine ergänzenden Angaben (wie Berufsbezeichnungen) gegeben sind.⁶ Es sind allerdings Zufallsfunde, die Mayr letztendlich doch noch fassbar machen, so etwa ein Eintrag im Raitbuch, dem landesfürstlichen Rechnungsbuch, des Jahres 1638: »*Casparn Maÿr* Puechtruckhern in der Hof Mallereÿ, beÿ *Daniel Paur*, erhält wegen der neulich doppelt gedruckten Zolltafeln: 6 fl.«⁷ In diesem Jahr befand sich Kaspar Mayr also in der Offizin des Hofbuchdruckers

---

3 Johann Baptist Jezl: *10.1.1610 in Hall; Ehe mit Ursula Zeller aus Rosenheim (†2.2.1667 in Innsbruck); elf Kinder; †18.9.1666 in Innsbruck. – Zur Künstlerfamilie Jezl vgl.: HANS HOCHENEGG: *Die Tiroler Kupferstecher. Graphische Kunst in Tirol vom 16. bis zur Mitte des 19. Jahrhunderts*. Innsbruck 1963. (Schlern-Schriften. 227), S. 43–53 hier S. 44–8 (J. B. Jezl).

4 Die Untersuchung erfolgte anhand des Exemplars unter: Tiroler LandesM Ferdinandeum, FB 99470.

5 HANSJÖRG RABANSER: Maria Cleofa Paur – die erste offizielle »Hofbuechtruckerin« in Innsbruck. In: *GJ* 94 (2019), S. 193–210, hier S. 207. DERS.: Der Innsbrucker Buchdrucker Michael Wagner (†1669) – der »Vater« des Universitätsverlags Wagner. In: *Tiroler Heimat*. 85 (2021), S. 11–45.

6 Ein Beispiel, hier mit klärender Berufsbezeichnung: Der Hofbüchsenmacher Kaspar Mayr aus Kaltern, ehelichte am 14.11.1650 in der Innsbrucker Stadtpfarrkirche Katharina Schindlechner, die Tochter des Paul Schindlechner, Schmied im Zeughaus. Vgl.: Arch. der Dompfarre St. Jakob/Innsbruck, Traubuch V (1634–60), fol. 106v.

7 Tiroler LandesArch., Kammerkopialbuch (KKB) Raitbuch 1638 (I), Bd. 170, fol. 205r. – Die aus den Quellen stammendenZitate berücksichtigen die Groß- und Kleinschreibung und die Zeichensetzung des Originals. Endungen (-en/-er) und Doppelkonsonanten (m/n) werden aufgelöst; Ergänzungen von Abkürzungen und Erklärungen durch den Verfasser sind in eckigen Klammern zu finden. Schreibungen im lateinischen Alphabet (vor allem bei Namen, Spezialbegriffen etc.) werden kursiv gesetzt.

Daniel Paur (zwischen 1572/77–1639), wo er offenbar eine gewisse Sonderstellung innehatte oder den Prinzipal durch die Übernahme von diversen Druckaufträgen unterstützte. Es war nämlich nicht der Hofbuchdrucker, der für die Zolltafeln mit sechs Gulden entlohnt wurde, sondern Mayr, der hier als Buchdrucker bezeichnet wird. Dass diese Benennung hinterfragt werden darf, zeigt der Umstand, dass in der Quelle von der »Hof Mallereÿ« und nicht korrekterweise von der Hofbuchdruckerei die Rede ist. Diese Ungereimtheit geht vermutlich auf einen Denk- bzw. Schreibfehler des Kanzlisten zurück.

In der Offizin des Daniel Paur absolvierte in den ersten Jahrzehnten des 17. Jahrhunderts ein gewisser Hans Gäch (†1639) seine Lehrlingszeit, der in der Folge eine Gesellenwanderung unternahm und 1626 in die Heimat zurückkehrte, um in Innsbruck eine eigene Druckerei zu eröffnen, die er bis zu seinem Tod 1639 betrieb.[8] Außerdem ehelicht Gäch die Innsbrucker Bürgerstochter Maria Jäger (1605–41) mit der er sechs Kinder hatte. Die Suche nach Kaspar Mayr führt direkt in das Eheleben – oder eigentlich: außereheliche Leben – Gächs: Am 10. Dezember 1638 wurde der Innsbrucker Stadtrichter Erasmus Friz (†1680)[9] mit der Nachforschung beauftragt, ob Gäch mit seiner Schwägerin »incestum« begangen habe.[10] Tatsächlich vermerkt das Taufbuch der Stadtpfarrkirche St. Jakob unter dem 19. November 1638 die Geburt von Gächs viertem Sohn Johannes. Allerdings fällt dabei auf, dass bei diesem nicht die herkömmlichen Paten hinzugezogen wurden, sondern der Druckergeselle Kaspar Mayr die Patenschaft übernahm, wie der Eintrag darlegt: »Gfatter Caspar Maÿr Puechtruckher gesell«.[11] Der Grund hierfür ist einfach: Nicht Gächs Gattin Maria Jäger war die Mutter des Kindes, sondern eine gewisse Sara Kien aus Telfs.[12]

Die Textstelle deutet nicht zwingend darauf hin, dass Kaspar Mayr seinen Dienst bei Paur quittiert hatte und in die Werkstatt Gächs übergewechselt war, um dort eine Stelle als Geselle einzunehmen. Vielmehr darf angenommen werden, dass sich Beide seit ihrer Gesellen- und/oder Lehrlingszeit bei Daniel Paur kannten[13] und nach Gächs Rückkehr nach Innsbruck wieder in Kontakt getreten waren. Mayrs Druck von 1644 liefert sogar den Beweis, dass er in der Paur'schen Offizin verblieben ist und dort tätig war.

Hofbuchdrucker Daniel Paur starb am 7. Februar 1639[14], womit das weitere Schicksal der Offizin ungewiss war, da dessen Sohn Hieronymus im Vorjahr die Stelle als fürstbischöflicher Drucker in Brixen angetreten hatte und dort gebunden war. Um die Werkstatt für diesen zu sichern, bewarb sich die Witwe Maria Cleofa Paur mit Erfolg um die Hofbuchdruckerstelle. Doch das Geschäfts- und Werkstattleben sowie der Kampf um Privilegien und Rechte zehrten an den Kräften der betagten Witwe, die immer häufiger auf die Hilfe ihres Sohnes zurückgriff, von dem sie mit Druckarbeiten von Brixen aus unterstützt wurde. Wenngleich in Werken des Jahres 1644 bereits Hieronymus' Name in den Druckervermerken aufscheint, so war doch noch Maria Cleofa Paur bis zum Jahresende 1645 als offizielle Hofbuchdruckerin tätig. Erst im Herbst 1645 reichte sie bei der Regierung ein Schreiben ein, in dem sie

---

8 Zu Gäch vgl.: HANSJÖRG RABANSER: Hans Gäch – ein Höttinger bzw. Innsbrucker Buchdrucker (1626–1639). Biographische Skizze mit dem Versuch eines Druckwerkeverzeichnisses. In: *Leipziger Jahrbuch zur Buchgeschichte*. 25 (2017), S. 35–86.

9 Der Handelsmann Erasmus Friz (†1680) stellte 1638, 1641, 1643, 1648 und 1651 den Stadtrichter sowie 1655, 1667 und 1671 den Bürgermeister. 1642 hatte er das Amt des Elemosinarii (Almosenamtskassier) inne, zwischen 1644 und 1646 wiederum jenes des Oberbaumeisters. Vgl.: WILFRIED BEIMROHR: *Die Geschichte der Verwaltung der Stadt Innsbruck im 17. Jahrhundert*. Innsbruck 1995. (Veröffentlichungen des Innsbrucker Stadtarchivs. Neue Folge 22), S. 74, 91–2, 258, 385, 404.

10 Tiroler LandesArch., Regierungskopialbuch (RKB) Causa Domini 1637–41, Bd. 27, fol. 267r.

11 Arch. der Dompfarre St. Jakob/Innsbruck, Taufbuch VI (1617–39), fol. 621v.

12 Zum illegitimen Kind Gächs vgl.: RABANSER (s. Anm. 8), S. 35–86, hier S. 52–4.

13 Einer Quelle vom Juli 1625 zufolge befanden sich nachweislich zwei Gesellen in der Paur'schen Offizin. Vgl.: Tiroler LandesArch., KKB Raitbuch 1625, Bd. 161, fol. 412v–413r.

14 Arch. der Dompfarre St. Jakob/Innsbruck, Sterbebuch IV (1617–39), fol. 406v (1639).

Abb. 2 Eine Vignette mit dem zentral platzierten Wappen der Familie Paur. (TLMF, FB 99470, S. 21)

darlegte, dass sie der »seit absterben Ires Manns, Daniel Paur geführten HofPuechdruckhereÿ nit mehr vorstehen khünde«. Sie bat deshalb, die Offizin ihrem Sohn Hieronymus – »(durch welchen sÿ selbige etlich Jar hero, als der Kunst genuegsamb erfahrnen verrichten lassen.)« – zuzusprechen. Von Seiten der Regierung bestanden diesbezüglich keinerlei Bedenken.[15] Das bekannte Druckoeuvre der nur über sechs Jahre amtierenden Hofbuchdruckerin ist bescheiden, weshalb anzunehmen ist, dass sie in erster Linie bemüht war, die nötigen Arbeiten für die landesfürstlichen Behörden auszuführen, doch nicht aktiv nach Aufträgen und neuen Absatzmärkten Ausschau hielt. Unter solch einer Führung war es einem langgedienten Gesellen, wie Kaspar Mayr wohl möglich, ein eigenes Druckwerk umzusetzen. Vermutlich war Maria Cleofa Paur sogar dankbar, dass dieser einen Auftrag übernahm und gewährte ihm deshalb die prominente Stelle im Druckervermerk. Betrachtet man diesen genauer und vergleicht ihn mit anderweitigen Kolophonen, lässt ein Wort stutzig werden: Anstelle des deutlich häufiger verwendeten »Getruckt [...] bey [...]«[16] benutzte Mayr die Formulierung »Getruckt [...] durch [...]«, womit offenbar verdeutlicht werden sollte, dass er die Arbeit geschaffen hatte, allerdings kein eigenständiger Drucker war.

Ein Vergleich der Drucktypen zeigt, dass Mayr die Arbeitsmaterialien der Paur'schen Offizin benutzt hatte. Am augenscheinlichsten zeigt sich dies an einer Vignette, welche sich am Ende des Vorwortes findet (S. 19), aus floralen Elementen, ineinander geschlungenen Voluten und Grotesken besteht und an zentraler bzw. prominenter Stelle – wenn auch klein und nur auf den zweiten Blick zu erkennen – das Wappen der Familie Paur zeigt [Abb. 2]. Dieses weist ein Pflugeisen auf rotem Grund auf und war dem Drucker Hans Paur (†1602) sowie dessen Brüdern Georg und Konrad am 22. September 1581 verliehen worden.[17] Dieselbe Vignette findet sich auch – um ein zeitnahes Beispiel herauszugreifen – am Titelblatt der ersten gedruckten Innsbrucker Feuerordnung, die 1642 unter der Ägide von Maria Cleofa Paur entstanden war.[18]

Dass ein fähiger oder langgedienter Druckergeselle eigenständig ein Druckwerk anfertigte, weil er für den Meister einspringen und diesem aushelfen musste, dürfte des Öfteren der Fall gewesen sein. Ein Beispiel dafür mag die folgende Anekdote darstellen: Am 17. September 1611 wandte sich der Arzt Hippolyt Guarinoni (1571–1654) an die Tiroler Regierung und informierte diese, dass er angesichts der grassierenden Fleckfieberepidemie in aller Eile eine Instruktion mit grundlegenden medizinisch-hygienischen Maßnahmen zusammengestellt habe. Da er diese wegen der Seuchensperren nur unter erschwerten Bedingungen in Druck geben könne – Guarinoni hatte bis dahin unter anderem Ingolstadt als Druckerort bevorzugt –, bat er die Regierung »dem *Danieli* Bawr Buchtrukher zu Ynsprugg, der zeit zu Brixen wohnhafften gnedigen bevelch zu geben, damit er solliches, durch seine zu Ynsprug habenden Truckher gesellen mit Ehisten fertigen, und ich durch die wacht, in die Statt zu der Trukerei zu weillen gelassen werde.«[19] Anstelle von Daniel Paur, der vermutlich durch einen Auftrag des Fürstbischofs in Brixen gebunden war, sollte die Arbeit ein Geselle vor Ort in Innsbruck

---

[15] Tiroler LandesArch., RKB Von der Fürstlichen Durchlaucht 1644–45, Bd. 37, fol. 887v–888r.

[16] Nur in den Druckwerken von Ruprecht Höller (tätig: 1550/51 und 1554–73) findet sich des Öfteren die Formulierung »Gedruckht [...] durch«. Vgl. das Druckwerkeverzeichnis in: HANSJÖRG RABANSER: Ruprecht Höller – der erste Innsbrucker Hofbuchdrucker (1550/51 und 1554–1573). In: *Leipziger Jahrbuch zur Buchgeschichte*. 29 (2021), S. 9–43, hier S. 33–43.

[17] Zum Wappen vgl.: Tiroler LandesM Ferdinandeum, Fischnaler'sche Wappenkartei.

[18] *New reformierte Ynßpruggische Fewr Ordnung*. Innsbruck 1642.

[19] Tiroler LandesArch., Geheimer Rat (Hofregistratur), Selekt Leopoldinum, Littera D/T, Nr. 130 (2. Teil), Karton 116 (o. Nr.; Schreiben Guarinonis vom 17.9.1611).

vornehmen. Möglicherweise dürfte es sich mit der Publikation, die Kaspar Mayr 1644 geschaffen hatte, ähnlich verhalten haben.

Im selben Jahr wie Daniel Paur starb am 17. Mai 1639 auch Hans Gäch und bereits am 13. August ehelichte dessen Witwe Maria den in der Offizin tätigen Gesellen Michael Wagner aus Augsburg. Die Ehe war nicht von langer Dauer, denn Maria verschied bereits am 24. März 1641 im Alter von 36 Jahren.[20] Mit der Heirat hatte Wagner allerdings die Gäch'sche Druckerei übernommen und am 11. Oktober 1639 aus der Hand der Landesfürstin Claudia de' Medici (1604–48) den Freibrief bzw. die Gewerbekonzession erhalten.[21] Wagner wird die von Gäch begründete Konkurrenz zur Hofbuchdruckerei mehr oder weniger fortführen und dabei 1666 einen Nachdruck jenes Werkes herstellen, das Kaspar Mayr 1644 geschaffen hatte; es unterscheidet sich von diesem lediglich im Umfang und in einigen Details.[22]

Wolfgang Moritz Endter (1653–1723)

Die berühmte, weit verzweigte Nürnberger Drucker- und Verleger-Dynastie Endter nahm vom 16. bis zum 18. Jahrhundert im Buchdruck- und Buchhandels-Sektor eine bedeutende Stellung ein und ist bereits seit 1659 in Wien als Niederleger nachzuweisen.[23] Einer ihrer Vertreter – Wolfgang Moritz Endter (1653–1723)[24] – wurde am 1. März 1653 als Sohn des Buchdruckers Wolfgang Endter d. J. (1622–55) und der Helene Clara Schacher geboren. Ursprünglich als Buchdrucker und -händler tätig, verkauft er 1699 seine Offizin und wurde im Folgejahr als Buchdrucker aus dem Nürnberger Ämterbuch gestrichen. Er konzentrierte sich fortan auf den Buchhandel und betrieb vorwiegend Niederlagen in Regensburg, München und Wien; außerdem hatte er eine Papiermühle inne. Wolfgang Moritz Endter ging zwei Ehen ein, nämlich 1674 mit Anna Juliana Betz von Lichtenhof (1652–94) und 1695 mit Susanna Maria Auer (1658–1716). Seit 1714 in den Quellen als kränklich bezeichnet, verschied er am 28. Februar 1723 in Nürnberg (Pfarre St. Sebald).

Im Jahr 1709 trat Endter auch in Innsbruck mit der Verlegung eines Buches in Erscheinung [Abb. 3]. Der Drucker- bzw. eigentlich Verlegervermerk lautet: »Inspruck, Verlegts Wolfgang Moritz Endter. An[no]. 1709.« Es handelte sich dabei um eine Darstellung des Lebens und Wirkens der Nonne Johanna Maria vom Kreuz (1603–73), die als Bernardina Floriani in Rovereto geboren wurde, dort 1630 ein Klarissenkloster begründete und als dessen Äbtissin fungierte. Seit 1638 konnten bei ihr die Wundmale Christi festgestellt werden, was ihr den Ruf einer Seherin einbrachte, weshalb rasch nach ihrem Tod erste Versuche einer Selig- bzw. Heiligsprechung unternommen wurden, die jedoch nie zustande kam. Denselben Zweck sollte auch die vorliegende Publikation erfüllen, welche durch den Franziskanerpater Franz von Cles ursprünglich in italienischer Sprache verlegt worden war. Die Übersetzung ins Deutsche bewerkstelligte Wilhelm Pock aus dem Prämonstratenser Chorherrenstift Wilten in Innsbruck, der das Buch Karl Philipp von der Pfalz

---

20 Arch. der Dompfarre St. Jakob/Innsbruck, Sterbebuch V (1622–64), fol. 164r.

21 Zur Gewerbekonzession für Wagner: Tiroler LandesArch., Kunstsachen I, Nr. 1677.

22 Titel: *Regula Und Testament, Sambt den Constitutionibus der Mindern Brüder deß heiligen Francisci Ordens, die Cappuciner genannt.* Druckervermerk: *Gedruckt zu Ynsprugg bei Michael Wagner, Im Jahr 1666.* Umfang: [1] Bl., 114 S., [12] Bl.; der Kupferstich der Madonna mit Kind fehlt.

23 CHRISTOPH JENSEN: *Die Druck- und Verlagsproduktion der Offizin Wolfgang Endter und seiner Erben (1619–72): Ein Beitrag zur Geschichte des Nürnberger Buchdrucks im 17. Jahrhundert mit einer Bibliographie der Drucke von Wolfgang Endter dem Älteren, Johann Andreas und Wolf dem Jüngeren sowie Christoph und Paul Endter.* Stuttgart 2021. (Bibliothek des Buchwesens. 30). RUDOLF SCHMIDT: *Deutsche Buchhändler. Deutsche Buchdrucker. Beiträge zu einer Firmengeschichte des deutschen Buchgewerbes.* Nachdruck der Ausgabe Berlin 1902–08. Hildesheim–New York 1979, S. 213–15. REINHARD WITTMANN: *Geschichte des deutschen Buchhandels.* München. 3. Aufl. 2011, S. 93, 95.

24 Zu Wolfgang Moritz Endter vgl.: NORBERT BACHLEITNER, FRANZ M. EYBL und ERNST FISCHER: *Geschichte des Buchhandels in Österreich.* Wiesbaden 2000. (Geschichte des Buchhandels. VI), S. 70. MICHAEL DIEFENBACHER und WILTRUD FISCHER-PACHE (Hg.): *Das Nürnberger Buchgewerbe. Buch- und Zeitungsdrucker, Verleger und Druckhändler vom 16. bis zum 18. Jahrhundert.* Nürnberg 2003. (Quellen und Forschungen zur Geschichte und Kultur der Stadt Nürnberg. 31), S. 271–83. JENSEN (s. Anm. 23), S. 386 (Stammbaum); DAVID L. PAISEY: *Deutsche Buchdrucker, Buchhändler und Verleger 1701–1750.* Wiesbaden 1988. (Beiträge zum Buch- und Bibliothekswesen. 26), S. 53. RESKE, S. 804–05.

Abb. 3 Das von Wolfgang Moritz Endter verlegte Werk „Wunder- und Tugend-Blum [...]" widmet sich der Nonne Johanna Maria vom Kreuz in Rovereto. (TLMF, FB 1876)

(1661–1742), dem kaiserlichen Statthalter über die Grafschaft Tirol sowie die Vorlande (1705–17), widmete. Warum Pock keine lokale Offizin mit dem Druck betraut, sondern auf Endter zurückgegriffen hatte, ist nicht bekannt; möglicherweise waren Empfehlungen oder Beziehungen dafür ausschlaggebend gewesen.

Dieses einzige Werk Endters mit dem Verweis auf Innsbruck sowie das Fehlen weiterer Nennungen in Quellen[25] lässt den Schluss zu, dass er sich offenbar nicht weiter darum bemühte, in der Stadt am Inn Fuß zu fassen. Ob dabei der Mangel an Absatzmöglichkeiten entscheidend war oder aber die Gegenwehr der ansässigen Drucker und Buchhändler, mag dahingestellt bleiben. Endters Zentrale war und blieb Nürnberg, wie der Vermerk in einem Kalender aus dem Jahr 1720 zeigt, den der Buchhändler Franz Egid Schmid (von dem in Kürze die Rede sein wird) vertrieb: »Innsprugg, Zu finden bey Frantz Egydius Schmiedt. Verlegts Wolfgang Moritz Endter, Buchhåndler in Nůrnberg. An[no]. 1720«.[26]

Franz Egid Schmid (1681–1743)

Franz Egid (oder Aegid, Ägid) Schmid wurde am 22. August 1681 in der Pfarrkirche Unsere Liebe Frau in Eichstätt (heute Dompfarrei) getauft[27]

---

25 Beispiel: Im Einwohnerverzeichnis der Stadt Innsbruck zu den Jahren 1689–1768 findet sich kein Eintrag zu Endter. Vgl.: Tiroler LandesM Ferdinandeum, FB 3689.

26 Etwa zu finden unter: Tiroler LandesM Ferdinandeum, W 5886.

27 Er war der Sohn von Anna und dem Buchbinder Michael Schmid; als Pate fungierte Egidius Pettmesser. Vgl.: Diözesan Arch. Eichstätt, Pfarrmatrikel, Eichstätt ULF 9, S. 33. Für die Übermittlung der Daten dankt der Verfasser dem Eichstätter Diözesanarchivar Dr. Bruno Lengenfelder. – Zu Schmid vgl.: PAISEY (s. Anm. 24), S. 228.

und war als Buchführer bzw. -händler tätig. Als solcher wurde »Frannz Egidi Schmidt von Aichstett aus der Pfalz gebirtig« am 13. März 1719 gegen die Zahlung von 60 Gulden in die Innsbrucker Bürgerschaft aufgenommen.[28] In einem Druckervermerk von 1723 bezeichnete er sich explizit als »Burgern und Buchhåndlern.«[29] Zuvor hatte er Maria Clara Sader, die Tochter von Joseph Sader aus Innsbruck, geheiratet, denn die Ehe (oder aber ernsthafte Eheabsicht) war eine Grundvoraussetzung zum Erwerb des Bürgerrechts.[30] Dem Paar wurden zwei Söhne geboren, die jedoch beide im Kindesalter starben: Franz Borgia Joseph (1720–21) und Franz Xaver Nikolaus (1721–25).[31]

Die Tätigkeit Schmids als Buchhändler führte erwartungsgemäß zu Konflikten mit dem ansässigen Drucker, der seinen Verkauf beeinträchtigt sah. Ein solcher Streit ist im Zeitraum Dezember 1720 bis Dezember 1721 zwischen Schmid und Hofbuchdrucker Michael Anton Wagner (1696–1766) belegt, wobei es vor allem um den Vertrieb von Kalendern ging. Bereits 1684 hatte die Familie Wagner ein kaiserliches Privileg erworben, »nit allein allerhandt Taffl, *Libell*, und Paurn Calender: sondern auch die *Ordinari* und *Extra* Zeitungen auf 10 Meihl [ca. 75 km; Anm.] weegs alda umb Insprugg herumb alleinig zu Truckhen, und zuverkhauffen befuegt« zu sein und sie konnte im Jahr 1700 die Verlängerung desselben erwirken.[32] Dementsprechend empfindlich reagierte Michael Anton Wagner im Herbst 1720, als er feststellen musste, dass das Privileg durch die Kalenderverkäufe des »verbürgerten Puechhandler Franz Ægidi Schmidt und andere Laädler« untergraben wurde. Der Fall gelangte bis in die Kanzleien der Tiroler Regierung, die sich am 14. Dezember 1720 an den Innsbrucker Stadtmagistrat wandte und diesem befahl, die betreffenden Händler innerhalb der nächsten drei Tage entsprechend ermahnen zu lassen.[33] Damit war die »strittigkheit« aber noch nicht aus dem Weg geräumt, denn im Dezember 1721 legte Wagner der Regierung das kaiserliche Kalenderprivileg »*in authentica*« vor und pochte zum wiederholten mal auf dessen Einhaltung. Franz Egid Schmid konterte allerdings, dass dieses nur für Kalender der Wagner'schen Offizin gelte, nicht jedoch »auf frembde Calender« abziele; auch sei er als Bürger befugt, solche in seinem Repertoire zu führen. Die letztendliche Entscheidung der Regierung betonte nochmals die Respektierung des Kalenderprivilegs, sprach Schmid aber den Verkauf von ausländischen Kalendern zu, etwa den »starckh in Schwung gehenden Augspurger Bauren Calender«, um auch ihm diesbezüglich »Einen Kleinen gewin« zu gönnen.[34]

Ein weiterer Konflikt zwischen Schmid und Wagner ergab sich aus dem Vorschlag des Rektors bzw. der Professorenschaft der Universität Innsbruck vom 24. September 1719 bzw. 11. April 1720, Schmid als »einen *academi*schen Neben-Puechtruckhern mit gewissen bedingnussen« anzustellen. Die Universität wollte damit ohne Zweifel an die Ära von Benedikt Karl Reisacher (1643–1700) anknüpfen, der von 1673–1700 als erster Universitätsbuchdrucker in Innsbruck tätig gewesen war.[35] Die kaiserliche Entscheidung vom 28. Dezember 1720 nahm allerdings davon Abstand, womit Wagners Position als alleiniger Drucker in der Stadt gewahrt blieb.

---

[28] StArch. Innsbruck, Bürgerbuch, fol. 306v. Entgegen der Angaben gehörte Eichstätt zum Fränkischen Reichskreis, allerdings befand sich einige Kilometer weiter südlich (bei Ingolstadt) bereits das pfalzbayerische Gebiet. – Schmid scheint auch in den Beschreibungen der Innsbrucker Bürgerschaft der Jahre 1720–24 auf. Vgl.: StArch. Innsbruck, Bürgerverzeichnisse: 1708–10 / 1712–24, fol. 113v, 122v, 130v, 138v, 147r.

[29] Vgl.: Tiroler LandesM Ferdinandeum, W 3505/3.

[30] Die Heirat fand nicht in der Stadtpfarre St. Jakob in Innsbruck statt; das dortige Traubuch weist zumindest keinen Eintrag auf.

[31] Arch. der Dompfarre St. Jakob/Innsbruck, Taufbuch XVII (1711–24), fol. 42r (1720), 69r (1721). Ebd.: Sterbebuch VIII (1711–44), fol. 99v (1721), 132v (1725).

[32] StArch. Innsbruck, Akten 1300–1800, Nr. 597, Schreiben vom 2.10.1700. Außerdem: INGRID MOSER: *»Neuer Schreibkalender auf das gemeine Jahr...«. Historische und strukturelle Wandlungen Tiroler Kalender von 1700–1820 im sozialen Kontext*. Dipl. phil. Innsbruck 1987, S. 20–21. – Das Privileg befand sich 1702 nachweislich im Wagner'schen Familienbesitz. Vgl.: FamilienArch. Winkler Innsbruck, Bestand Akten, Akt Wagner A, Inventar zum Vermögen des Jakob Christoph Wagner, 1702, fol. 5v.

[33] StArch. Innsbruck, Akten 1300–1800, Nr. 597: Schreiben vom 14.12.1720. – Eine weitere Quelle hierzu fand sich im Tiroler LandesArch. unter der Signatur ›Kunstsachen II, Nr. 592‹ in einem Konvolut mit Schreiben, Protokollen und Gutachten verschiedener Instanzen zum Zeitraum Dezember 1720 bis November 1722. Das betreffende Schriftstück konnte vom Verfasser 2014 noch eingesehen werden, gilt seit Jahresbeginn 2018 allerdings als Fehlbestand.

[34] StArch. Innsbruck, Akten 1300–1800, Nr. 597: Schreiben vom 15.12.1721.

[35] HANSJÖRG RABANSER: Benedikt Karl Reisacher. Der erste Innsbrucker Universitätsbuchdrucker und seine Nachfolger. In: *GJ* 96 (2021), S. 206–33.

Abb. 4 Das hochverehrte Maria Hilf-Bild von Lucas Cranach d. Ä. war mehrfach Gegenstand von Druckwerken. 1725 gab auch Franz Egid Schmid eine Publikation dazu heraus. (TLMF, W 13943)

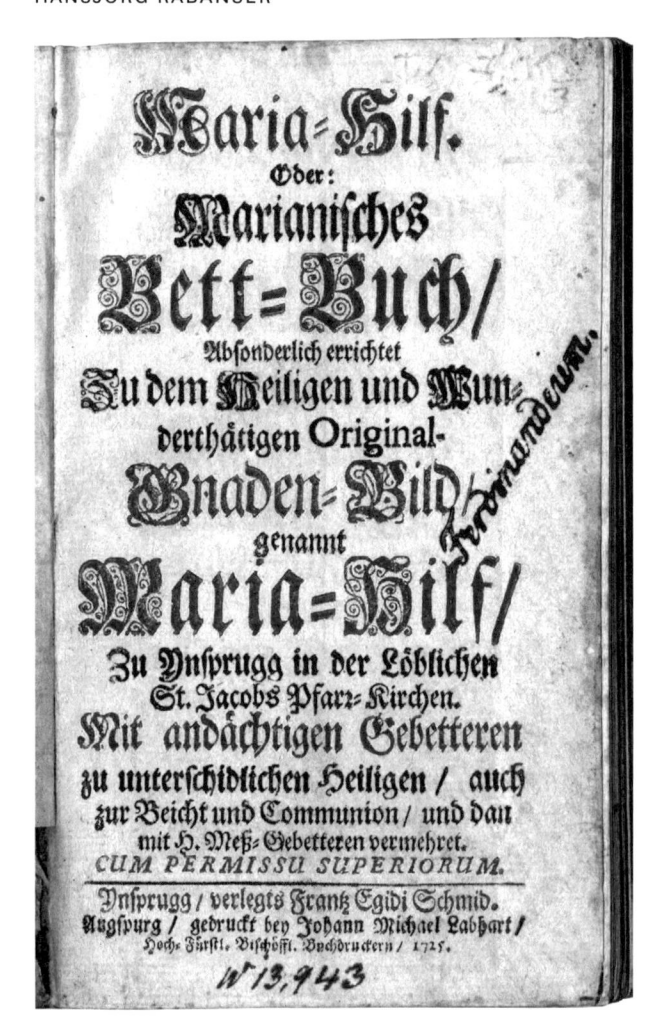

Franz Egid Schmid starb am 18. Juni 1743 in Innsbruck. Der Eintrag im Totenbuch der Stadtpfarre St. Jakob lautet: »Den 18. H[err]. Franz Egidi Schmid Bůrger und Buechhandler 4 gl[ocken].«[36]

Obwohl Schmid über 20 Jahre in Innsbruck verbracht hat und dort tätig gewesen war, ist sein Wirken anhand von Büchern mit seiner Nennung nur im Zeitraum von 1720 bis 1729 belegbar. Beginnend mit einem Kalender im Jahr 1720, der (wie bereits erwähnt) von Wolfgang Moritz Endter in Nürnberg verlegt worden war, über vorwiegend erbauliche Publikationen aus den Jahren 1723 und 1725 bis hin zum letzten, im Jahr 1729 verlegten Werk von Joseph Steiner, Pfarrorganist an der Stadtpfarrkirche St. Jakob. Dessen grammatikalisches Lehrbuch *Pentalogion [...]* war laut Vermerk »Zu finden bey Auctore, wie auch bey Frantz Egidi Schmid, Buch-Håndlern allda.« Der Blick in die Druckwerke zeigt, dass Schmid sich auch mehrmals einer italienischen Namensversion bediente, wie »Francisco Egidio Schmid«.[37] Außerdem stellte nicht nur Endter in Nürnberg seine Bezugsquelle dar; ein Buch aus dem Jahr 1725 zum berühmten Maria-Hilf-Bild im Innsbrucker Dom von Lucas Cranach d. Ä. (1472–1553) bezog Schmid bei Johann Michael Labhart (†1744), dem fürstbischöflichen Buchdrucker in Augsburg [Abb. 4].[38] Nach 1729 fehlen jegliche Belege aus der Hand des Buchhändlers Schmid.

[36] Arch. der Dompfarre St. Jakob/Innsbruck, Sterbebuch VIII (1711–44), fol. 39v (1743).

[37] Vgl. dazu: Tiroler LandesM Ferdinandeum, W 3505/3.

[38] Vgl. dazu: Tiroler LandesM Ferdinandeum, W 13943. – Zu Labhart vgl.: HANS-JÖRG KÜNAST: Dokumentation: Augsburger Buchdrucker und Verleger. In: *Augsburger Buchdruck und Verlagswesen. Von den Anfängen bis zur Gegenwart.* Hrsg. von HELMUT GIER und JOHANNES JANOTA. Wiesbaden 1997, S. 1205–1340 hier S. 1261. DERS.: Labhart Buchdruckerfamilie. In: *Augsburger Stadtlexikon.* Hrsg. von GÜNTHER GRÜNSTEUDEL, GÜNTER HÄGELE und RUDOLF FRANKENBERGER. Augsburg. 2. Aufl. 1998, S. 592.

Simon Holzer (†1741) und Georg Simon Holzer (1707–55)

Zwischen 1724 und 1747 gelangten Druckwerke auf den Buchmarkt, als deren Verleger die Innsbrucker Buchbinder Simon und Georg Simon Holzer – Vater und Sohn – namhaft gemacht werden können. Die lokale Quellenlage zu diesen ist im Vergleich zu den anderen behandelten Vertretern ausgesprochen gut, allerdings sorgt(e) die Namensgleichheit für manche Verwechslungen und Unklarheiten, die in der folgenden Darstellung entwirrt werden sollen.

In den *Matricula philosophica* der im Jahr 1669 gegründeten Universität Innsbruck liegen Notizen zu einem gewissen Simon Holzer aus Terenten (»Terantensis, Tyrolensis«) vor, der in den Matrikeln zu den Jahren 1695/96 als Logicus und 1696/97 als Physicus angeführt ist. Aufgrund der Herkunftsbezeichnung könnte es sich um den späteren Buchbinder Simon Holzer handeln, dem in der Folge das Interesse gelten soll.[39]

Im Einwohnerverzeichnis der Stadt Innsbruck zu den Jahren 1689 bis 1768 findet sich unter dem 18. September 1706 der folgende Eintrag: »*Simon Holzer* seiner Hanndtierung ain Buechbindter von Terendten G[eric]hts Schenëgg gebirtig, so die Johann Saurische Witib erheÿratet, Ist fir ainen Inwohner aufgenomben und belëgt worden. *Per Finffzëchen Marckh*. Solle Ihne umb ain Flindten sëchen.«[40] Die Beschaffung des Gewehrs resultierte aus der Wehrpflicht der Inwohner, die bewaffnete Kontrollgänge zu leisten und somit für die Sicherheit der Stadt einzustehen hatten.[41]

Wie die beiden Textstellen zeigen, stammte Simon Holzer aus Terenten (Gericht Schöneck) im Pustertal (Südtirol). Über seine Ausbildung zum Buchbinder ist wenig bekannt, doch verrät eine Quelle, dass er am 18. April 1700 in Salzburg seinen Lehrbrief erworben hat. Allerdings zog es Holzer wieder in die Grafschaft Tirol zurück, wo er am 10. Oktober 1700 vor den Buchbindern Jakob Kolb, Christian Stangl, Johann Will, Johann Lutz und Johann Georg Laiminger erschien und um die Aufnahme als Meister bat. Im Einschreibbuch des Innsbrucker Buchbinderhandwerks heißt es dazu: »Ist Erschinen Simon Holzer von Terenten im G[eric]ht Schenegg im Pussterthall, so weil Johann Saur Bůrger und Puechpindters sel[ig] witib alhier, zuerheÿrath vorhabens, produciert seinen Lehrnbrief von Salzburg de dato 18ten· Apprill A° etc. 1700. seines rödlich erlernten Puechpindter Handwerchs und bitet umb aufnemb[ung] für ainen Maister, Warüber Er Holzer bei Erheÿrather Maissters witib und unbedencklich befundenen Lehrnbrief, für ainen Maisster des Puechpindter Handwerchs aufgenomen worden, wellicher als ain Inlender dem Handwerch von zwaÿmahligen Fürkhomen 2 fl 24 k bezalt, dann ~~fu~~ wegen nicht vellig Erströckhter drei LehrnJar ~~für~~ zu ainem drunckh ied[e] aine Viertl wein, und für d[as] Maisstermahl und Maissterstuckh, zusamen Zechen Gulden, ~~Guetmachen~~ worbei Er und sein khonfftige Ehewiertin gegenwertig zusein, Guetmachen und Entrichten solle« [Abb. 5].[42]

---

39 UniversitätsArch. Innsbruck, Matricula Philosophica ab anno 1673 usque ad 1727, fol. 76v, 78v. Außerdem: FRANZ HUTER (Hg.): *Die Matrikel der Universität Innsbruck. Erster Band: Matricula philosophica. Erster Teil: 1671 bis 1700*. Innsbruck 1952, S. 53. – Zu Simon Holzer vgl.: REINHOLD FALKENSTEINER: *Beiträge zur Wirtschaftsgeschichte Innsbrucks im 18. Jahrhundert*. Innsbruck 1981. (Veröffentlichungen des Innsbrucker Stadtarchivs. Neue Folge 11), S. 58, 194. HUBERT FELDERER: *Die Geschichte der Verwaltung der Stadt Innsbruck von 1700 bis 1784*. Innsbruck 1996. (Veröffentlichungen des Innsbrucker Stadtarchivs. Neue Folge 23), S. 77, 84, 90, 125, 287. PAISEY (s. Anm. 24), S. 115.

40 Tiroler LandesM Ferdinandeum, FB 3689, fol. 44r.

41 BEIMROHR (s. Anm. 9), S. 160–61.

42 Tiroler LandesM Ferdinandeum, FB 32041, fol. 9r–10r. – Es handelt sich dabei um das *EinSchreibBuech Der geßsambten Maister des BuechPůndter Hanndtwerckhs, alhie zu Ÿnnsprugg [...]*.

Ein Schreib-Buech

Der gesambten Maister des Buechbinder handtwerchs, alhie zu Ynnsprugg.

So vnnter dem Schirm

Des WolEdl Vesten Wohlweisen Herrn Jacob Kolben Inneren Raths Verwohnten, vnnd Statt Schreibern alda, Als von Einem löblichen wolweisen Statt Rath hierzue wohl verordneten Comissari A°. 1689 Auf gericht worden.

Abb. 5 Das kunstvoll gestaltete Titelblatt des Einschreibbuches der Innsbrucker Buchbinder. (TLMF, FB 32041)

Unter demselben Tag wurde außerdem beschlossen, dass »derJenige so Maisster werden will und ain Maissters witib oder Maisters~~witib~~ tochter Erheÿratt, dem Handwerck für iedermahlig haltendtes Handtwerch da Er ain Inlender. 1 f 12 k da Er aber ein Auslender 1 f 30 k und für d[as] Maistermahl und Maissterstuckh 12 fl geben und bezahlen: ~~solle~~, sover Er aber khein Maissers witib oder tochter Erheÿrathen würde, sodann die beleg[ung] bei dem Handtwerch stehen solle«.[43] Holzer war mit seinem Ansuchen erfolgreich, denn bereits am 16. Dezember 1700 wird er im Einschreibbuch offiziell als Buchbinder angeführt.[44]

Dass Holzer in Innsbruck Fuß fassen konnte, wurde ihm durch den Umstand erleichtert, dass er auf eine vakant gewordene Buchbinderwerkstatt zurückgreifen konnte, indem er die Witwe des Buchbinders Johann Saur ehelichte, wie die zitierte Textstelle bereits aufzeigte. Noch als Buchbindergeselle ging Holzer am 26. Oktober 1700 in der Stadtpfarrkirche St. Jakob die Ehe mit Katharina Saur ein; als Zeugen fungierten der Maler Georg Gantner und der Bildhauer Konstantin Reiser († um 1703).[45] Das Eheleben war mit vier Kindern gesegnet: Maria Anna (*7. Februar 1703), Joseph Anton (*20. Juli 1705), Georg Simon (*7. April 1707) und Katharina Barbara († 18. März 1713).[46] Katharina Saur wird bei den Taufeinträgen in den Matrikeln stets mit ihrem Mädchennamen Guggenberger angegeben.

Vom Buchbinder war Simon Holzer offenbar zum Hofbuchbinder aufgestiegen, denn im Innsbrucker Ratsprotokoll vom 28. Mai 1717 wird er als »Inwohner und HoffPuechbindter« betitelt[47] und bezeichnete sich in einigen seiner verlegten Werke als »O[ber]: O[esterreichischer]: Regierungs-Buchbinder«.[48] Für gesellschaftliches Ansehen sorgte des Weiteren die Aufnahme Holzers in den Innsbrucker Bürgerstand am 8. Januar 1730, die er gegen die Erlegung von 75 Gulden erwirken konnte, sowie seine Tätigkeit als Gerichtsbeisitzer (ab 24. Januar 1733) und Gemeinredner der Stadt Innsbruck (1738).[49]

Als Meister war es ihm möglich, Lehrjungen bei sich zu beschäftigen, wobei er unter anderem auch Verwandte unterstützte. So nahm er am 11. Juni 1715 »seinen Vettern Sebastian Holzer gebirtig von Terenten auß Puster Thal« für drei Jahre als Lehrjungen auf; die Lossprechung desselben erfolgte am 20. Februar 1718.[50] Sebastian Holzer wird sich schließlich in der nahen Stadt Hall als Buchbinder sesshaft machen und dort das Bürgerrecht erwerben.[51]

Simon Holzer übte zwar in erster Linie das Buchbinderhandwerk aus, doch er betätigte sich auch als Buchhändler (»Buchbinder und Handler«[52]), nachweislich zwischen 1724 und 1741. Er konzentrierte sich dabei fast ausschließlich auf geistliche Werke, die (meist anonym verfasst) von mehreren Tiroler Druckern immer wieder neu aufgelegt und

---

[43] Tiroler LandesM Ferdinandeum, FB 32041, fol. 10v–11r.

[44] Tiroler LandesM Ferdinandeum, FB 32041, fol. 11r.

[45] »Simon Holzer Buchbindtergesöll und Frauen Catharina Saurin«. Vgl.: Arch. der Dompfarre St. Jakob/Innsbruck, Traubuch VII (1672–1710), S. 28 (1700).

[46] Zu den Kindern vgl.: Arch. der Dompfarre St. Jakob/Innsbruck, Taufbuch XVI (1698–1710), fol. 143v (1703), 57r (1705), S. 13 (1707); Sterbebuch VIII (1711–44), fol. 23r.

[47] An diesem Tag erschien Simon Holzer gemeinsam mit Johannes Peter vor dem Stadtrat und erbat für Zweiten die Aufnahme als Inwohner bzw. als Buchbinder. Peter beabsichtigte nämlich den Erwerb der »Teniflischen Werchstatt« und die Heirat von Holzers »Stiefftuechter«. Der Stadtrat beratschlagte darüber und entschied, dass Peter die Werkstatt der armen Witwe Denifle erwerben und sie heiraten solle, um in der Folge als Buchbinder zu wirken und in die Riege der Inwohner aufgenommen zu werden. Vgl.: StArch. Innsbruck, Ratsprotokoll 1716–19, fol. 58v.

[48] Tiroler LandesM Ferdinandeum, FB 136484–136485 oder Dip. 88/1. – Die Bezeichnung *oberösterreichisch* bezieht sich nicht auf das Bundesland Oberösterreich, sondern auf das oberösterreichische Regiment (Regierung) und die oberösterreichische Kammer (Finanzbehörde) der Grafschaft Tirol und der Vorlande.

[49] StArch. Innsbruck, Bürgerbuch, fol. 313v (Bürgerstand), 315v (Gerichtsbeisitz). Zum Gemeinredner vgl.: FELDERER (s. Anm. 39), S. 125.

[50] Tiroler LandesM Ferdinandeum, FB 32041, fol. 23r (Aufnahme), 26r (Lossprechung). – Sebastian Holzer wurde am 12.1.1700 als Sohn des Martin Holzer und der Ursula Unteregger in Terenten geboren. Vgl.: Pfarre Terenten, Tauf-, Heirats-, Sterbe- und Illegitimibuch 1694–1749, fol. 13r.

[51] Um die Verwirrung der Namensgleichheiten vollständig zu machen: So wie Sebastian Holzer protegiert und nach Innsbruck geholt worden war, so nimmt sich auch Sebastian eines (vermutlichen) Verwandten an, »mit Namen Simon Holzer gebirtig von Terenten gericht scheneg«. Dieser Lehrjunge wurde am 18.11.1725 nach fünfjähriger Lehrzeit freigesprochen und erhielt am 17.3.1737 vom Handwerk einen Lehrbrief für Raab in Ungarn ausgestellt. Vgl.: Tiroler LandesM Ferdinandeum, FB 32041, fol. 30v–31r (Aufnahme und Lehrbrief), 34r (Lossprechung).

[52] Tiroler LandesM Ferdinandeum, FB 3562.

Abb. 6 Anton Roschmanns Beschreibung des Landes Tirol erschien 1740 bei Simon Holzer. (TLMF, W 1282)

vertrieben wurden, oder von lokalen Autoren stammten, wie den Kapuzinern Johann Franz von Gianetti und Cäsar Maria Schguanin oder Adalbert Tschaveller (1676–1749), einem Prämonstratenser Chorherr und Archivar im Stift Wilten. Die Ausnahme dieses erbaulichen Oeuvres bildet einzig und allein die Beschreibung der Grafschaft Tirol des vielseitigen Gelehrten Anton Roschmann (1694–1760)[53], die Holzer 1740 in zwei verschiedenen Versionen verlegte [Abb. 6].[54] Welcher (lokale?) Drucker die Herstellung dieser Werke besorgte, ist nicht bekannt. Holzer vertrieb allerdings auch Augsburger Drucke, so etwa von Joseph Gruber (um 1670–nach 1740)[55] oder dem fürstbischöflichen Drucker Johann Michael Labhart.

Seine letzten verlegten Werke datieren in die Jahre 1740/41, als möglicherweise bereits Holzers Sohn die Werkstatt innehatte, doch noch mit dem bewährten Namen seines Vaters firmierte. Simon Holzer verschied am 11. Oktober 1741 als Buchbinder und Bürger des Äußeren Rats in Innsbruck.[56]

Die Nachfolge in der Buchbinderwerkstatt trat Georg Simon Holzer (1707–55) an. Bereits am 11. Juni 1715 hatte Simon »seinen Sohn Georg Simon Holzer den besagten Handtwerch vorgestölt und fir Einen volkumen gesöllen gemacht, in beÿsein auch einer Ehrbarn gesollschafft«.[57] Ob Georg Simon in der väterlichen Werkstatt lernte und tätig war, bei einem Kollegen unterkam oder eine Gesellenreise unternahm, lässt sich

[53] Zu Anton Roschmann vgl.: FLORIAN M. MÜLLER und FLORIAN SCHAFFENRATH (Hg.): *Anton Roschmann (1694–1760). Aspekte zu Leben und Wirken des Tiroler Polyhistors*. Innsbruck 2010.

[54] Tiroler LandesM Ferdinandeum, Dip. 631/7 bzw. W 1282 und FB 4084.

[55] Zu Gruber vgl.: RESKE, S. 57.

[56] Arch. der Dompfarre St. Jakob/Innsbruck, Sterbebuch VIII (1711–44), fol. 29r.

[57] Tiroler LandesM Ferdinandeum, FB 32041, fol. 22v.

nicht eruieren. Belegt ist allerdings seine Heirat mit Anna Maria Öttlmayr (oder Attlmayr) am 7. Juni 1735 in Innsbruck[58], die ihm in den folgenden Jahren zahlreiche Kinder gebar (darunter zweimal Zwillinge): Maria Anna (*13. November 1736), Maria Agnes Notburga (*3. April 1738), Maria Katharina (*30. November 1739), die Zwillinge Franz Xaver Georg und Simon Kilian (*29. Januar 1741), Joseph Georg (*8. Februar 1742), Petrus de Alcantara Cajetan (*31. August 1743), Maria Agnes (*12. September 1744), Maria Barbara (*3. Dezember 1745), Alois Georg (*5. Juni 1747), Georg Jakob (*11. Juli 1748), die Zwillinge Georg und Maria Theresia (*2. Juni 1749) und Joseph (*29. Februar 1752).[59] Bei der Geburt dieses Kindes starb Anna Maria Öttlmayr.[60] Für die Eingliederung in die städtische Gesellschaft war vor allem die Aufnahme Holzers in den Bürgerstand wichtig; diese erfolgte nur wenige Tage nach der Heirat am 14. Juni 1735. Außerdem fungierte er seit dem 16. Januar 1745 bis zu seinem Tod als Gerichtsbeisitzer; dieses Amt wurde am 30. Januar 1756 schließlich von Joseph Anton Schwaighofer übernommen. 1748 war Holzer außerdem als Gemeinredner der Stadt Innsbruck tätig.[61]

Im Zuge einer Lehrlingsaufnahme am 22. Februar 1739 wird Holzer als »JungMaister«[62] bezeichnet, was den Schluss zulässt, dass er die Buchbinderwerkstatt seines wohl altersbedingt ausgeschiedenen oder nicht mehr arbeitsfähigen Vaters übernommen hatte oder vielmehr diesen entsprechend unterstützte. Die Übergabe war aber vermutlich schon 1737 erfolgt, wie einige Aufnahmen von Lehrjungen beweisen, die bereits unter Georg Simon tätig waren.[63] In den folgenden Jahren sind immer wieder Zahlungen an Holzer für diverse Bindearbeiten belegt, so auch von der Tiroler Regierung.[64] Im Gegensatz zu seinem Vater war Georg Simon als Buchhändler und Verleger deutlich weniger aktiv, denn bis dato sind nur drei Werke mit seinem Namen (»GEORGII SIMONIS HOLZER« bzw. »Verlag Georg Holzers«) greifbar, die in die Jahre 1746, 1747 und 1749 datieren.

Georg Simon Holzer starb am 18. Juli 1755 als Buchbinder und Bürger des Äußeren Rats der Stadt Innsbruck.[65]

Johann Jakob Cremer

Interessanterweise scheint der Nürnberger Buchdrucker und -händler Johann Jakob Cremer in Nachschlagewerken bzw. der einschlägigen Literatur zum Nürnberger Druckergewerbe selten auf und wird in Publikationen nur mit spärlichen Informationen versehen. Deshalb ist einzig und allein bekannt, dass er in Nürnberg zwischen 1720 und 1754 als Drucker und Händler tätig war.[66]

Im Jahr 1740 ist Cremer mit einem Druckwerk in Innsbruck nachweisbar, denn er schuf die *Anatomia* [Abb. 7] von Hieronymus Leopold Bacchettoni (1691–1749), dem ersten Professor der Chirurgie in Innsbruck. Die Publikation besticht durch mehrere Kupferstichtafeln des Nürnberger Stechers Wolfgang Nicolaus Reiff (1705–77)[67] nach Entwürfen des aus Frankfurt am Main nach Innsbruck zugewanderten

---

[58] Arch. der Dompfarre St. Jakob/Innsbruck, Traubuch VIII (1711–44), fol. 150r.

[59] Arch. der Dompfarre St. Jakob/Innsbruck, Taufbuch XVIII (1725–37), fol. 242v (1736). Ebd., Taufbuch XIX (1737–44), fol. 33v (1738), 69v (1739), 95r (1741), 118v (1742), 158v (1743), 184r (1744). Ebd., Taufbuch XX (1745–51), fol. 32r (1745), 65r (1747), 88v–89v (1748), 113v (1749). Ebd., Taufbuch XXI (1752–63), fol. 4v (1752). – Die Tochter Maria Anna ehelicht am 21.5.1759 den Maurermeister Johann Michael Umhaus. Vgl.: Ebd., Traubuch IX (1744–63), fol. 40v–41r (1759).

[60] Arch. der Dompfarre St. Jakob/Innsbruck, Sterbebuch IX (1744–63), fol. 3v.

[61] StArch. Innsbruck, Bürgerbuch, fol. 317r (Bürgerstand), 327r (Gerichtsbeisitz), 332r (Gerichtsbeisitz an Schwaighofer). Außerdem: FELDERER (s. Anm. 39), S. 84, 125.

[62] Tiroler LandesM Ferdinandeum, FB 32041, fol. 48v.

[63] Georg Simon Holzer nahm am 19.5.1737 und 2.3.1738 einen Lehrjungen auf. Vgl.: Tiroler LandesM Ferdinandeum, FB 32041, fol. 46r, 47r.

[64] Tiroler LandesArch, KKB Entbieten und Befehl 1742, Bd. 1320, fol. 300r/v, 388r/v.

[65] Arch. der Dompfarre St. Jakob/Innsbruck, Sterbebuch IX (1744–63), fol. 25r. – Im Einschreibbuch der Buchbinder wird er erstmals am 12.10.1755 als »H[err] Holzer seligen« angeführt. Vgl.: Tiroler LandesM Ferdinandeum, FB 32041, fol. 57r.

[66] Zu Cremer vgl.: PAISEY (s. Anm. 24), S. 38.

[67] Zu Reiff vgl.: MANFRED H. GIEB (Hg.): *Nürnberger Künstlerlexikon. Bildende Künstler, Kunsthandwerker, Gelehrte, Sammler, Kulturschaffende und Mäzene vom 12. bis zur Mitte des 20. Jahrhunderts*. München 2007, S. 1211.

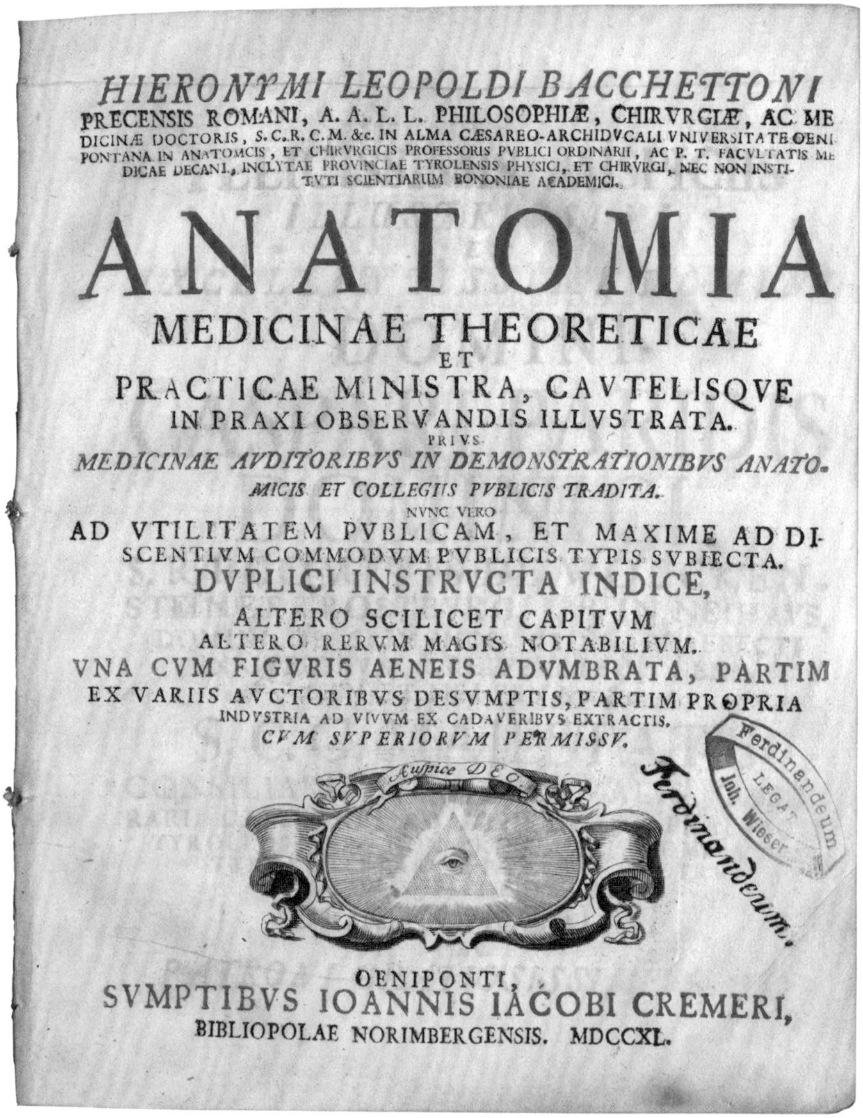
HIERONYMI LEOPOLDI BACCHETTONI
PRECENSIS ROMANI, A. A. L. L. PHILOSOPHIÆ, CHIRVRGIÆ, AC ME DICINÆ DOCTORIS, S. C. R. C. M. &c. IN ALMA CÆSAREO-ARCHIDVCALI VNIVERSITATE OENI PONTANA IN ANATOMICIS, ET CHIRVRGICIS PROFESSORIS PVBLICI ORDINARII, AC P. T. FACVLTATIS ME DICAE DECANI, INCLYTAE PROVINCIAE TYROLENSIS PHYSICI, ET CHIRVRGI, NEC NON INSTI TVTI SCIENTIARUM BONONIAE ACADEMICI.
ANATOMIA
MEDICINAE THEORETICAE
ET
PRACTICAE MINISTRA, CAVTELISQVE
IN PRAXI OBSERVANDIS ILLVSTRATA.
PRIVS
MEDICINAE AVDITORIBVS IN DEMONSTRATIONIBVS ANATOMICIS ET COLLEGIIS PVBLICIS TRADITA.
NVNC VERO
AD VTILITATEM PVBLICAM, ET MAXIME AD DISCENTIVM COMMODVM PVBLICIS TYPIS SVBIECTA.
DVPLICI INSTRVCTA INDICE,
ALTERO SCILICET CAPITVM
ALTERO RERVM MAGIS NOTABILIVM.
VNA CVM FIGVRIS AENEIS ADVMBRATA, PARTIM
EX VARIIS AVCTORIBVS DESVMPTIS, PARTIM PROPRIA
INDVSTRIA AD VIVVM EX CADAVERIBVS EXTRACTIS.
CVM SVPERIORVM PERMISSV.

OENIPONTI,
SVMPTIBVS IOANNIS IACOBI CREMERI,
BIBLIOPOLAE NORIMBERGENSIS. MDCCXL.

Abb. 7 Die von Johann Jakob Cremer verlegte „Anatomia“ des Chirurgen Hieronymus Leopold Bacchettoni ist mit repräsentativen Kupferstichtafeln ausgestattet. (TLMF, FB 1750)

Malers Franz Josef Textor (Weber; †1741).[68] Den Druck besorgte vermutlich der Hof- und Universitätsbuchdrucker Michael Anton Wagner, bei dem Bacchettoni mehrere seiner in der Folge verfassten Publikationen herstellen ließ. Außer diesem einzigen verlegten Werk Cremers gibt es keine weiteren Belege zu diesem in Innsbruck bzw. Tirol.

Allerdings existiert eine Klageschrift von 1742, mittels der sich der Fürstbischof von Brixen und der Dekan der Theologischen Fakultät in Innsbruck an die Tiroler Zentralbehörden wandten: Die Buchhändler Johann Jakob Cramer [!], Johann Adam Faber und Georg Christoph Weber – alle aus Nürnberg stammend – besaßen Konzessionen, um zweimal jährlich im Mai und November ihre Waren auf dem Haller Markt zu vertreiben. Im Anschluss daran war ihnen erlaubt, ihr Sortiment zwei Wochen lang auch in Innsbruck anzubieten, wozu sie Lokalitäten anmieteten. Allerdings hatten sie der Zensur wissentlich verbotene Bücher entzogen und auf den Märkten feilgeboten, ja gar die Visitatoren angeblich ungebührlich behandelt und mit »*respect*losen zugezochenen Reden«[69] bedacht. Hinter dem Zwist steckte der Umstand, dass die

68 DURSTMÜLLER (s. Anm. 2), S. 151–52. ERICH EGG und GERT AMMANN (Hg.): *Barock in Innsbruck*. Ausstellungskatalog Tiroler LandesM Ferdinandeum. Innsbruck 1980, S. 53 (Kat.-Nr. 160), 141. HANS HOCHENEGG: Vierhundert Jahre Buchdruck in Innsbruck. In: *Biblos. Österreichische Zeitschrift für Buch- und Bibliothekswesen, Dokumentation, Bibliographie und Bibliophilie*. 5 (1956) Heft 3 (Sonderheft Tirol), S. 110–23, hier S. 120. FRANZ HUTER: *Hieronymus Leopold Bacchettoni. Professor der Anatomie und Chirurgie an der Universität Innsbruck. Ein Beitrag zur Verselbständigung der Chirurgie als Lehrfach an den Universitäten nördlich der Alpen*. Innsbruck 1985. (Schlern-Schriften. 275), S. 39–48.

69 Tiroler LandesArch., RKB Ex Regime 1742 (1. Teil), Bd. 7, fol. 340v.

beanstandeten Drucke die Zensurstellen in anderen Städten ohne Probleme passiert hatten und die drei kämpferischen Händler dieses Argument gegen die Beanstandungen ins Feld führten. Die Regierung entschied den Fall jedoch zugunsten der kirchlichen Zensoren.[70] Ob der erwähnte Johann Jakob Cramer mit Cremer ident ist, ist allerdings ungewiss.[71]

Schlussbemerkung

Das Wirken einiger bis dato nicht oder kaum bekannter druckender Gesellen bzw. vertreibender und verlegender Buchhändler und Buchbinder in Innsbruck, die des Weiteren nur durch eine geringe Anzahl an Druckwerken in Erscheinung traten, standen im Mittelpunkt dieses Beitrags. Ihr Kreis muss jedoch durch den Namen eines weiteren Buchhändlers ergänzt werden, der sich in der zweiten Hälfte des 18. Jahrhunderts in Graz, Linz und auch in Innsbruck etablierte und dort eine rege Tätigkeit entwickelte: Joseph Wolff aus Augsburg.[72] Dieser hatte am 3. Dezember 1746 um das Privileg einer Buchhandlung angesucht und darum gebeten, »in einen offenen Gewölben durch einen aignen hierzue bestellten Bedienten all Gattungen der erlaubten Büecheren zu verkhauffen«. Dabei bekräftigte er ausdrücklich, keine Druckerei einrichten und somit dem Hofbuchdrucker Wagner keine Konkurrenz machen zu wollen. Nichtsdestotrotz legte Wagner am 15. März 1747 Beschwerde gegen das Ansuchen ein, jedoch ohne Erfolg: Wolff erhielt die auf drei Jahre beschränkte Bewilligung am 18. März und war mit seinem Buchladen ab 1748 in Innsbruck vertreten.[73] Er gilt als der erste Sortimentsbuchhändler in der Stadt. Allerdings wurde seine Buchhandelslizenz im Jahr 1766 nicht mehr verlängert, sodass er gezwungen war, Innsbruck zu verlassen und die Buchhandlung am Innrain Nr. 6 mit allen Marktrechten in Tirol am 4. Mai 1772 für 80.000 Gulden an Felizian Vischer (Fischer) abzugeben. Von diesem ging das Geschäftslokal 1796 wiederum an dessen Neffen Felician Rauch (1767–1832) über, der ab 1818/19 die bedeutende Buchdruckerei Rauch begründete.[74] Da das von Wolff in Innsbruck vertriebene Oeuvre recht umfangreich ist und seine Tätigkeit in Tirol eine eigene Darstellung verdient, wurde von einer Behandlung desselben an dieser Stelle abgesehen.

Unter der Regentschaft von Maria Theresia (1717–80) und Joseph II. (1741–90) setzte ohnehin ein Wandel im Buchdruckerhandwerk und Niederlagswesen ein: 1772 wurde eine eigene Ordnung erlassen, welche Buchdruck, -handel und -binderei strikt in eigene Sparten unterteilt und stärker an die Ausbildung knüpfte. Zwei Jahre später wurde zur Förderung von inländischen Großhändlern das Niederlagswesen beendet und am 5. April 1788 erfolgte schließlich die vollständige Freigabe des Buchdruck- und Buchhandelsgewerbes.

---

70 Tiroler LandesArch., RKB Ex Regime 1742 (1. Teil), Bd. 7, fol. 340v–344v. DiözesanArch. Brixen, Konsistorial-/OrdinariatsArch. (K.A./OA), Konsistorialprotokolle (KP) 68, S. 365–66 (26.5.1742). Außerdem: ANDREAS FALKNER: *Die Befugnisse der Theologischen Fakultät Innsbruck in der kirchlichen Bücherzensur während der Jahre 1740–1773. Ein Beitrag zur Geschichte der Theologischen Fakultät Innsbruck.* In: *Tiroler Heimat.* 33 (1969), S. 5–32, hier S. 8–9 (mit z.T. veralteten bzw. falschen Quellenangaben). MOSER (s. Anm. 32), S. 22.

71 Es ist unklar, ob es hier korrekterweise Cremer heißen müsste, denn es existierte in Nürnberg auch eine Buchhändler- und Verlegerfamilie Kramer. Vgl.: PAISEY (s. Anm. 24), S. 38.

72 Zu Josef Wolff (zu dem interessanterweise in der Literatur keine Lebensdaten überliefert sind) und dessen Vater vgl.: KECHT (s. Anm. 2), Nr. 251, S. 6 und Nr. 253, S. 5. THEKLA KOLLMANN: *Konkurrenz auf dem Innsbrucker Buchmarkt im Spiegel von Buchanzeigen in der periodischen Presse des 18. Jahrhunderts.* Bachelorarbeit. Innsbruck 2022, S. 24–6; KÜNAST, Dokumentation (s. Anm. 38), S. 1205–1340, hier S. 1270, 1283–84. DERS.: Wolffsche Verlagsbuchhandlung. In: *Augsburger Stadtlexikon* (s. Anm. 38), S. 937. PAISEY (s. Anm. 24), S. 291.

73 StArch. Innsbruck, Innsbrucker Ratsprotokolle 1746–50, fol. 26r/v, 27r/v (15.3.1747). Ebd., Innsbrucker Ratskopei 1744–48, fol. 177r–179r (17.3.1747). Tiroler Landesm Ferdinandeum, FB 1222, fol. 998r. Außerdem: ECKART VON SCHUMACHER: *Verlags-Katalog der Wagner'schen Universitäts-Buchhandlung in Innsbruck. Oster-Messe 1904. Nebst einer Geschichte der Firma. 1554–1904.* Innsbruck 1904, S. XXXIII–IV (Beilage X).

74 Tiroler LandesArch., KKB Geschäft von Hof 1766, Bd. 13, fol. 289v, 435r–436v. Außerdem: ANTON DÖRRER: *Das Innsbrucker Verlagshaus Felizian Rauch und seine Vorgänger 1673 bis 1929. Ein Beitrag zur Geschichte der Tiroler Drucke.* Linz 1929, S. 7. SCHUMACHER (s. Anm. 73), S. XXXIV–V (Beilage XI).

Druckwerkeverzeichnis

In der folgenden Aufstellung wurden in erster Linie Nordtiroler Bibliotheksbestände berücksichtigt, vorwiegend jene der Bibliothek des Tiroler Landesmuseum Ferdinandeum (TLMF), der Universitäts- und Landesbibliothek Tirol (ULBT) und der Theologischen Fakultätsbibliothek in Innsbruck. Weitere Druckwerke ergab die Suche anhand digitaler Datenbanken (VD 17, BSB, ÖNB etc.).

Einige elementare Informationen zum Druckwerkeverzeichnis: Die Wiedergabe der Titel und Druckervermerke erfolgt unter Berücksichtigung der Groß- und Kleinschreibung bzw. der Anführung in Großbuchstaben. Beim Umfang wird die Anzahl der Seiten und/oder Blätter genannt. Die je nach Sammlung unterschiedlichen Angaben zum Format der Werke wurden vereinheitlicht und orientieren sich an den Preußischen Instruktionen (8° bis 25 cm, 4° bis 35 cm). Bei der Auflistung der einzelnen Aufbewahrungsorte und Signaturen der Drucke wird besonderes Augenmerk auf die Originale in den genannten Tiroler Bibliotheken gelegt. Werke, die über die Datenbank VD17 zu finden waren, werden mit der entsprechenden Nummer und den nachgeordneten Aufbewahrungsorten angeführt.

Kaspar Mayr

1644
Regula Und Testament sampt den Constitutionibus der Minderen Brueder deß heyligen Francisci Ordens die Capucciner genandt.
Umfang: [1] Bl., 21, 142 S.
Format: 8°
Druckervermerk: *Getruckt zu Ynßprugg, durch Casparum Mayr. Anno 1644.*
VD17: 824:738027H – Universitätsbibliothek Eichstätt: 041/1 AÖ 691 (ehemals Kapuzinerkloster Neuötting bzw. Kapuzinerkloster München) – Bayerische Staatsbibliothek München: 154/S nv/Nd (b) 49 – TLMF, FB 99470

Wolfgang Moritz Endter

1709
Neue Wunder- und Tugend-Blum in dem Tyrolischen Gebürg aus dem Florianischen Geschlechts-Garten entsprossen. Das ist: Kurtzer Begriff des Lebens der Gottseligen JOHANNÆ MARIÆ Von Creutz zu Rovereid, aus dem Seraphischen Orden des Heiligen Francisci. Anfänglich beschrieben in Welscher Sprach Von dem WolEhrwürdigen und Hochgelehrten Pater Francisco de Clës, aus dem Seraphischen Orden der Reformirten Franciscaner, der Löbl. Provinz des Heil. Vigilii, In das Teutsche übersetzet von WILHELMO POCKH, einem

Priester der Regulirten Chor-Herren des Gottes Haus Wilthau in Tyrol, des Heiligen Norberti oder Præmonstratenser-Ordens.
Umfang: [7] Bl., 136 S.
Format: 8°
Druckervermerk: *Inspruck, Verlegts Wolfgang Moritz Endter. An. 1709.*
TLMF, Dip. 94/8 und FB 1876

Franz Egid Schmid

1720
Heiliger Jahrs-Calender, Das ist: Betrachtungen Uber Das Leben und Lehr unsers HErrn JESU CHRISTI, Auf alle Tag des Jahrs. Erstlich in Italiänischer Sprach auf und ausgesetzt Von R. P. FABIO AMBROSIO SPINOLA, der Societät JESU, Anjetzo in unser Hoch-Teutsche Sprach allen so wohl Predigern, als TEutschen Meditanten zu sonderbarem Nutz von einem andern Priester erwähnter Societät übersetzt. Der Erste Theil. Anzufangen von dem Ersten Sonntag des Advents, biß auf den Tag der Allerheiligsten Dreyfaltigkeit. Neben einem Zusatz von Betrachtungen für die 9. Wochen vor Weyhnachten, von den 9. Monaten, welche Jesus im Leib Mariä der Jungfrauen hat zugebracht. Cum Facultate Superiorum.
Umfang: [8] Bl., 101 S., [1] Bl.
Format: Gr.-8°
Druckervermerk: *Innsprugg, Zu finden bey Frantz Egydius Schmiedt. Verlegts Wolfgang Moritz Endter, Buchhändler in Nürnberg. An. 1720.*
TLMF, W 5886

1720
Anmerckungen, So vor Erweckung Einer rechten Reu und Leyd, Wohl zu Gemüth zu führen: Und von P. Ludovico Sanct. Victores, der Gesellschafft JEsu Priestern, in seinen Missionen gebrauchet worden. Neben unterschidlichen Ubungen der Reu und Leyd. Auf alle Täg deß Monats außgetheilt. Auß dem Welschen in das Teutsche versetzet. Und bey allen Missionen auch vor und nach sehr nutzlich zu gebrauchen.
Umfang: 59 S.
Format: 8°
Druckervermerk: *Insprugg, verlegt und zu finden bey Francisco Egidio Schmid. 1720.*
TLMF, FB 3219/3

1723
Anmerckungen, Vor Erweckung Einer wahren Reu und Leyd, Wohl zu Gemüth zu führen: So von P. Ludovico Sanct Victores, der Gesellschaft JEsu Priestern, in seinen Missionen gebrauchet worden. Neben unterschiedlichen Ubungen der Reu und Leyd. Auf Alle Täg der Wochen, außgetheilt. Aus dem Welschen in das

Teutsche versetzt. Und bey allen Missionen auch Recollectionen sehr nutzlich zu gebrauchen.
Umfang: [1] Bl., 82 S.
Format: 8°
Druckervermerk: *Insprugg, verlegt und zu finden bey Francisco Egidio Schmid, Burgern und Buchhändlern. 1723.*
TLMF, W 3505/3

1725

Maria-Hilf. Oder Marianisches Bett-Buch, Absonderlich errichtet Zu dem Heiligen und Wunderthätigen Original-Gnaden-Bild, genannt Maria-Hilf, Zu Ynsprugg in der Löblichen St. Jacobs Pfarr-Kirchen. Mit andächtigen Gebetteren zu unterschidlichen Heiligen, auch zu Beicht und Communion, und dan mit H. Meß-Gebetteren vermehret. CUM PERMISSU SUPERIORUM.
Umfang: [7] Bl., 292 S., [4] Bl.
Format: 8°
Druckervermerk: *Ynsprugg, verlegts Frantz Egidi Schmid, Augspurg, gedruckt bey Johann Michael Labhart, Hoch-Fürstl. Bischöffl. Buchdruckern, 1725.*
TLMF, W 13943

1725

Sichere Archen Wider Die anlauffende Wässer der Betrübnussen. Das ist: Sichere Gewissens-Reglen, Deren sich Alle ängstige, zweifelhafftige, und scrupulose Gemüther ohne einigen Scrupl gebrauchen können. Allen Scrupulanten zum Trost gemacht.
Umfang: 48 S.
Format: 8°
Druckervermerk: *Ynnsprugg, In Verlag bey Frantz Egidi Schmid, Buch-Händlern, 1725.*
TLMF, W 14241/3

1725

Anton Andreas Rudolphi (1682–1761) [Rektor der Universität Innsbruck im Studienjahr 1718/19]: *CENTURIA CONTROVERSARUM QUÆSTIONUM EX UTROQUE JURE SELECTARUM QUONDAM SUB NOMINE CENTURIÆ PALLADIS TOGATÆ &c. PRÆSIDE, & AUTHORE JOANNE UDALRICO RUDOLPHI, U.J.D. ac in Alma Leopoldina Cæsareo-Austriaca Universitate Œnipontana Codicis, & Juris Publici Professore Ordinario, ac tunc temporis RECTORE MAGNIFICO, Piæ Memoriæ. In Lucem edita, ac publica Disputationis submissa. Nunc verò AB EJusDEM AUTHORIS FILIO Prælibata CENTURIÆ pro tunc Defendente ANTONIO ANDREA RUDOLPI, U.J.D. ac in præsata Alma Cæsareo-Archi-Ducali Universitate Œnipontana Digestorum, & Juris Feudalis Professore Publico, nec non Excelsi Regiminis Superioris Austriæ Advocato Variis hinc inde Argumentis, maximè verò solutione Rationum Votis inibi contentis Contrariarum aucta, ac in aliam nonnihil Methodum modernæ in concipiendis Confiliis juridicis Praxi magis accomodatam redacta, atque ad*

desiderium non paucorum denuò prælo submissa. Quibus denique accessit forma, ac Character nonnihil major, nec non in fine Index pro celeriore Materiarum inibi contentarum inventione paulò fusior.
Umfang: [12] Bl., 607 S., [12] Bl.
Format: Gr.-8°
Druckervermerk: *ŒNIPONTI, Sumptibus FRANCISCI ÆGIDII SCHMID, Bibliopolæ, 1725.*
Theologische Fakultätsbibliothek Innsbruck, Sicherheitsspeicher, 151106 – TLMF, FB 1296[75]

1729

Joseph Steiner [Pfarrorganist an der Stadtpfarrkirche St. Jakob in Innsbruck]: *PENTALOGION, Das ist Gründliche Abhandlung: Oder Lehr-Kunst Der fünff Haubt-Schul-Wörteren, Welche benambst Substantivum, Adjectivum, Relativum, Verbum, Adverbium. Durch sonderlichen Fleiß, und vil-Jährige absonderliche Ubung Der studirenden Jugend, Meistens aber Denen Anfängeren zum nothwendigen Unterricht, Gehülff und Nutzen, Nebst einer Haubtsächlich-Die Rudiment- und Grammatisten betreffende Zugab deutlich außgemacht, mit neuen Fundamenten verfaßt, und auf eignen Kosten verlegt v. Joseph Steiner, der Zeit Pfarr-Organisten bey S. Jacob zu Ynnsprugg, 1729. Mit Ihro Röm. Käys. Majest. und der Hohen O. O. Weesen allda sonderbaren Privilegio und Approbation.*
Umfang: 284 S., [2] Bl.
Format: 8°
Druckervermerk: *Zu finden bey Auctore, wie auch bey Frantz Egidi Schmid, Buch-Händlern allda.*
Universitätsbibliothek Freiburg im Breisgau: D 4275 – TLMF, FB 177 und FB 203/2

Simon und Georg Simon Holzer

1724

Johann Franz von Gianetti: *Wohlmeynender Seelen-Eyffer, Erzeiget in verfaßten Sittlichen Predigen, Für alle Sonntäg deß Jahrs, Ehedessen Dem Christlichen Volck auf verschiedenen Cantzlen mit lebhaffter Stimm vorgetragen, Nun aber zur Seelen-Heyl der gesambten Welt durch offentlichen Druck vor Augen gestellt, und mit doppleten Register wohl versehen von P. JORDANO ANNA NIENSI Capuciner-Ordens, der Tyrolischen Provintz Priesteren und Predigeren, vormahligen Lectore der Philosophischen und Theologischen Wissenschafft. Mit Verwilligung und Benehmhaltung der Oberen, Wie auch Mit Röm. Kayserl. Cathol. Maiestät sonderbahrer Freyheit und Privilegio.*
Umfang: [10] Bl., 582 S., [7] Bl.
Format: 4°
Druckervermerk: *Insprugg, In Verlag bey Simon Holtzer O: O: Regierungs-Buchbinder. Augspurg gedruckt bey Joseph Gruber, Catholischen Buchdrucker, Anno M.DCC.XXIV.*
TLMF, FB 136484 – ULBT, Sondersammlungen, Depot A (22410)

---

[75] Die Bände 2 (1753) und 3 (1758) erschienen nicht bei Schmid. Zu diesen vgl. etwa: Tiroler LandesM Ferdinandeum, FB 1297–1298.

1724

Johann Franz von Gianetti: *Hell-klingender Ehren-Schall, Preiß-würdigister Heiligkeit, Erstlich zu Lob Deren im Himmels-Saal Glorreich-becrönten und Sig-prangenden Uberwünderen, So dan denen noch Auf Erden Streittenden Kämpferen Zu tapfferer Nach-Folg angestimmet. Das ist: Fest-Tägliche Predigen, Nit allein Auf alle gewöhnliche Feyr-Täg, Sondern auch Auf besondere, ausser-ordentliche Fest verschidener Heiligen, und Täg deß Jahrs, Mit doppelten Register eingerichtet. Von P. JORDANO ANNANIENSI, Capuciner Ordens, der Tyrolischen Provintz Priesteren und Predigeren, wie auch vormahligen Lectore der Philosophischen, und Theologischen Wissenschafft. Mit Bewilligung und Benehmhaltung der Oberen Auch sonderbarer Gnad und Freyheit Ihro Römischen Käyserl: Catholischen Majestät.*
Umfang: [11] Bl., 694 S., [10] Bl.
Format: 4°
Druckervermerk: *INNSPRUGG, In Verlag Simon Holtzer, O. O. Regierungs Buchbinder. Augspurg gedruckt bey Johann Michael Labhart, Hoch-Fürstl: Bischöffl: Buchdrucker. ANNO M.DCCXXIV.*
TLMF, FB 136485

1727

Manuale Clericorum Sæcularium, Sive TRACTATUS BENEFICIARIUS De Dominio Clericorum in redditus Beneficiales, & Materiam de Beneficijs Ecclesiasticis. Ad mentem Sanctorum Patrum, Sacrorum Canonum, & Conciliorum. AUTHORE P. CÆSARIO MARIA SHGUANIN Ord. Servor. B.V.M. Provinciæ GErmanicæ Definitore Actuali, ac in Conventu Oenipontano ad S. Josephum SS. Theologiæ Lectore Ordinario. Cum Facultate Superiorum.
Umfang: [8] Bl., 271 S., [6] Bl.
Format: Gr.-8°
Druckervermerk: *OENIPONTI, Apud SIMONEM HOLZER BIBLIOP. ANNO DOMINI M.DCC.XXVII..*
TLMF, FB 3052 – ULBT, Sondersammlungen, Depot A (41423)

1730

Kräfftige Ubung Fromm zu leben und seelig zu sterben. In Form und Weiß 10.tägiger Geistlichen Gemüths-Versam[m]lung. Höchst nutzbar Denen Ordens-Leuthen, Priestern, auch allen Christglaubigen insgemein. Erster Hand. In Frantzösischer Sprach an das Liecht gegeben Von R. P. Bernardino de Picquignij, Ord. Capucinorum S. Francisci olim Definit. & Lect. Jubil. Provinc. Paris. Anjetzo Umb gemeinen Nutzen willen nach der 4ten Edition von einem erwehnten Ordens-Priesteren Tyrolischer Provintz treulich in das Teutsche übersetzet. Cum Permissu Superiorum, & Privilegio Cæsareo.
Umfang: [7] Bl., 526 S.
Format: 8°
Druckervermerk: *Ynsprugg, In Verlag, und zu finden bey Simon Holtzer, Bibliop. 1730.*
TLMF, FB 10651

1732
AVE MARIA. DENA ICHNOGRAPHIA SEU DECEM PRÆCIPUA REGULARIS DISCIPLINÆ PRINCIPIA, EX SS. Patribus potissimùm, ac spiritualis vitæ Magistris collecta, PER QUEMDAM SACERDOTEM S. ORDINIS SERVORUM BEATÆ MARIÆ VIRGINIS Luci publicæ exposita. M.DCC.XXXII. CUM SUPERIORUM FACULTATE.
Umfang: [12] Bl., 343 S., [1] Bl.
Format: 8°
Druckervermerk: *OENIPONTI, Extant apud Dominum Simonem Holzer Bibliopegum ibidem.*
TLMF, FB 109910

1734
R. D. Adalbert Tschaveller: *Ur-alter Gnaden-Thron Von neuem aufgerichtet, zu Lob und Ehr der allzeit Wunderthätigen Jungfrauen, und Mutter GOTTES MARIÆ Unter denen 4. Saulen Zu Wilthau. Sonsten zwar in vier, allhier aber in zwey Theil zusammen getragen und beschriben Von R. D. Adalberto Tschaveller Canonico Præmonstratensi zu Wilthau. Anderer Theil. Cum Licentia Superiorum.*
Umfang: [7] Bl., 303 S.
Format: 8°
Druckervermerk: *INNSPRUGG, In Verlag Simon Holtzer, Buchbinder und Handler, Anno 1734.*
Theologische Fakultätsbibliothek Innsbruck, Sicherheitsspeicher, FW 1238 – TLMF, FB 3562

1737
Trost im Elend, Das ist: Historische Beschreibung und sonderbahre Verehrung Deß Uhralten wunderthätigen Gnaden-Bilds Unsers Lieben Herrn im Elend zu Mattray, Auß denen vormahls gedruckten alt-teutschen Reimen-Taflen (auch anderen sicheren Nachrichten) zusammen gezogen, und zu grösserer Bequemlichkeit deß andächtigen Volcks, Insonderheit aber allgemeinen Trost deren Elend-betrangten, allda Hülff-suchenden Wallfartheren, In Form eines kleinen Bett-Büchleins eingerichtet, und in Druck gegeben.
Umfang: [3] Bl., 56 S.
Format: 8°
Druckervermerk: *Insprugg, in Verlag Simon Holtzer, O. Oe. Regierungs-Buchbinder, 1737.*
TLMF, Dip. 88/1 – ULBT, Sondersammlungen, Depot A (25411)

1740
Anton Roschmann: *Kurtze Beschreibung Der Fürstlichen Graffschafft Tyrol, Verfertiget Von Antonio Roschmann, J.U.L. der Römisch-Kayserlich- und Königlich-Catholischen Majestät Ober-Oesterreichischem Universitäts-Notario.*
Umfang: 24 S.
Format: Gr.-8°
Druckervermerk: *Inspruck [Yhnsprugg*], In Verlag Simon Holtzers, Burgers und Buchhändlers daselbst, 1740.*

TLMF, Dip. 631/7 – TLMF, W 1282* – TLMF, FB 4084* – ULBT, Sondersammlungen, Depot A (24441)

1741

Heilige Station-Andacht, In kurtzen Reimen verfasset, Und nebst einem Zubereitungs-Bericht, Auch vollkommener Reu und Leyd Zu Allgemeinem, forderist aber derer gemeineren, Nutzen zum Druck beförderet. Durch Eine Christ-liebende, ihres und frembden Heyls beflissene Seel. Cum permissu Superiorum.
Umfang: 24 S., [13] Bl.
Format: 8°
Druckervermerk: *Ynsprugg, zu finden bey Simon Holzer Buchbinder, Anno 1741.*
TLMF, FB 3220/2

1746

DEVOTÆ MEDITATIONES piissimís Sacræ Scripturæ Textibús exornatæ ad dolorosam & amorosam Visitationem Viæ Crucis pro lucrandis Indulgentiis inservientes. Ab aliquo eximio, ignoto tamen, hujus sacratissimæ Devotionis CULTORE compositæ.
Umfang: 32 S.
Format: 8°
Druckervermerk: *OENIPONTI, Sumptibus GEORGII SIMONIS HOLZER 1746.*
TLMF, W 4456

1747

DEVOTÆ MEDITATIONES piissimís Sacræ Scripturæ Textibús exornatæ ad dolorosam & amorosam Visitationem Viæ Crucis pro lucrandis Indulgentiis inservientes. Ab aliquo eximio, ignoto tamen, hujus sacratissimæ Devotionis CULTORE compositæ.
Umfang: 32 S.
Format: 8°
Druckervermerk: *OENIPONTI, Sumptibus GEORGII SIMONIS HOLZER 1747.*
TLMF, W 4223/3

1749

Geistliches Hauß-Büchl, Aus welchem jedermann Etwas guts lehrnen kann. Zusammen getragen Von einem Hochwürdigen Seel-Sorger, etc.
CUM LICENTIA SUPERIORUM.
Umfang: 169 S.
Format: 8°
Druckervermerk: *Ynsprugg, In Verlag Georg Holzers, Burgers, und Buchhändlers, Anno 1749.*
TLMF, FB 3264/1[76]

---

[76] Dasselbe Werk wurde 1749 im Umfang von 158 Seiten vom Buchbinder Franz Xaver Gotter in Rattenberg (Unterinntal) verlegt. Eine Ausgabe ist zu finden unter: Tiroler LandesM Ferdinandeum, FB 3264/2.

Johann Jakob Cremer

1740
Hieronymus Leopold Bacchettoni: *ANATOMIA MEDICINAE THEORETICAE ET PRACTICAE MINISTRA, CAVTELISQVE IN PRAXI OBSERVANDIS ILLVSTRATA. PRIVS MEDICINAE AVDITORIBVS IN DEMONSTRATIONIBVS ANATOMICIS ET COLLEGIIS PVBLICIS TRADITA. NVNC VERO AD VTILITATEM PUBLICAM, ET MAXIME AD DISCENTIVM COMMODVM PVBLICIS TYPIS SVBIECTA. DVPLICI INSTRVCTA INDICE, ALTERO SCILICET CAPITVM ALTERO RERVM MAGIS NOTABILIVM. VNA CVM FIGVRIS ANEIS ADVMBRATA, PARTIM EX VARIIS AVCTORIBVS DESVMPTIS, PARTIM PROPRIA INDVSTRIA AD VIVVM EX CADAVERIBVS EXTRACTIS. CUM SVPERIORVM PERMISSV.*
Umfang: [16] Bl., 320 S., [12] Bl. mit gefalteten Bildtafeln
Format: 4°
Druckervermerk: *OENIPONTI, SVMPTIBUS IOANNIS IACOBI CREMERI, BIBLIOPOLAE NORIMBERGENSIS. MDCCXL.*
TLMF, FB 1750–1751 – ULBT, Sondersammlungen, Depot A (30505)

Marvin J. Heller

Hebrew printing in Novy Oleksiniec: A Rose in the desert: a Brief, Barely Remembered Hebrew Press [1]

A Hebrew press was active for a short period of time in Novy Oleksiniec, a village in the Tarnopol district, Ukraine. A majority of Novy Oleksiniec's small population was Jewish, among them several prominent rabbis. Its primary Hebrew press, active from 1767 through 1776, was motivated by the need to expand the output of Hebrew books, as the only other regional press active at the time was that in Zolkiew. The Novy Oleksiniec press issued a relatively small number of varied works, several described in this article in some detail, others in passing only. The first published work, R. Yom Tov Lipmann Heller's *Berit Melah* (1760) was published by an unidentified press, the only work from that print shop. The second, better known Hebrew press, that of R. Tsevi Hirsh ben Aryeh Leib Margolis, is credited with eighteen titles in the brief period it was active; four titles of the press's publications issued in 1767, its opening year. The titles printed in Novy Oleksiniec are small works, varied in content. They include biblical commentary, Talmudic novellae, ethical works, and even some books with kabbalistic content. Several are the only editions of those titles. The press's output, albeit limited and of short duration, is diverse and rich in content.

> I am but a rose of Sharon, A rose of the valleys. Like the rose among thorns, so is my faithful beloved among the maidens.
> (Song of Songs: 2:1–2)

> But earthlier happy is the rose distill'd,
> Than that which withering on the virgin thorn
> Grows, lives and dies in single blessedness.
> (A Midsummer Night's Dream: Act I Scene I Lines 76–78)

A Hebrew press flourished, briefly, in Novy Oleksiniec, a village in Kremenets (Krzemieniec), near Brody, today in the Tarnopol district, Ukraine, 226 miles W of Kyiv.[2] Then, like the rose, which blossoms, "grows, lives and dies in single blessedness" the press ceased to be active, withering, but leaving as its inheritance a number of rare publications.

The Oleksiniec estate was, at the end of the 18th century, part of the domain of Prince Józef Klemens Czartoryski (1740–1810), grandmaster of the Grand Duchy of Lithuania, of Pogoń Litewska, prince in Korets and Oleksińce. He was, from 1767, a knight of the Order of the White

---

[1] I would, once again, like to express my appreciation to and thank Eli Genauer for his helpful comments.

[2] Among the other forms of its name are Novyy Oleksinets [Rus], Nowy Oleksiniec [Pol], Aleksnitz [Yid], Oleksinets Novy, Olekiniec-Nowy, Novyy Aleksinets, Nove-Oleksyneć, Novyolekcenez (JewishGen Communities Database available on: www.jewishgen.org, [20.1.2023]).

Fig. 1 Order of the White Eagle (his coat of arms)

Eagle (his coat of arms at the left). Prince Józef Klemens Czartoryski was the last male descendant of the Korecki line. [Fig. 1] Prince Józef Klemens Czartoryski's daughter, Celestyna (1790–1850), married Gabriel Rzyszczewski of the Pobóg coat of arms (1780–1857) in 1812, later a general and marshal of the nobility of the Krzemieniec district, who received the Oleksiniec key as a dowry.³

Novy Oleksiniec and its suburb, Oleksiniec Stary, were noted for their leather products. A majority of its small population was Jewish, consisting of 203 registered Jewish taxpayers in 1765. The rabbis associated with Oleksiniec include R. Mordecai ha-Kohen Rappoport, who was also an apothecary, son of R. Shabbetai, author of *Imrei No'am* (Oleksiniec, 1767), and R. Jacob Joseph ha-Levi Horovitz of Brody, installed in 1790.⁴

Ch. Friedberg suggests, concerning the Hebrew press that flourished briefly in Novy Oleksiniec, that a motivation in opening the press there was to expand the output of Hebrew books and address the need for such works, there being one press only active at the time, that in Zolkiew.⁵ This article will address the Novy Oleksiniec press and its publications, albeit a relatively small number, describing several in some detail, most others in passing only, in chronological order.

I

Hebrew printing in Oleksiniec began with the publication of R. Yom Tov Lipmann ben Nathan ha-Levi Heller's (Tosefot Yom Tov, 1579–1654) *Berit Melah* in 1760 on the laws of salting and rinsing meat. First printed in Prague (c. 1552), this edition, an octavo in format, in Judeo-German (Yiddish), was the fifth edition of that work. It is the only work known to have been published by this, the first unidentified press in Oleksiniec.⁶

II

This unidentified press was followed, to use Ch. Friedberg's term, by a redeemer (גואל), R. Tsevi Hirsh ben Aryeh Leib Margolis (Margoliot), a kinsman of R. Israel Schor-Margaliot (*Minhah Hadasha*). Tsevi Hirsh established the press with the assistance of Abraham ben Avi Ezri Zelig, an expert and experienced craftsman of Gelona, who also helped train others in the printers' craft.⁷ Eighteen titles are credited to the press, two of them uncertain, in the brief period that it was active, from 1767 through 1776, perchance "grow[ing], liv[ing] and dy[ing] in single blessedness." Four titles are recorded among the press's publications in its first year, 1767, namely, R. Joseph Yoska ben Israel's *Ohel Yosef*; R. Elijah ben Aaron Segal's *Ben Aaron*; R. Menahem Azariah da Fano's *Asarah Ma'amarot*; and R. Israel Saruk's *Tikkunei Shabbat*.⁸

Printing of these works began with *Tikkunei Shabbat*, a relatively small work (18 cm. [50] ff.), printed in the year "the secret counsel of the Lord

---

3 (available on https://pl-m-wikipedia-org. translate.goog/wiki/Stary_Oleksiniec?_x_tr_sl=pl&_x_tr_tl=en&_x_tr_hl=en&_x_tr_pto=sc , [20.1.2023]).

4 Novy Oleksiniec. In: *Encyclopaedia Judaica*. Vol. 15, p. 324; CH. B. FRIEDBERG: *History of Hebrew Typography in Poland from its beginning in the year 1534...* Second Edition Enlarged, improved and revised from the sources. Tel Aviv 1950, pp. 72–73 [Hebrew].

5 CH.B. FRIEDBERG: *History of Hebrew Typography* (see note 4). Friedberg cites a like reason for the establishing of the Hebrew press in Turka at about the same time. Concerning Hebrew printing in Turka see MARVIN J. HELLER: Hebrew printing in Turka. Home to a Barely Remembered Hebrew Press. In: *GJ* 95 (2020), pp. 137–151.

6 BERNHARD FRIEDBERG: *Bet Eked Sefarim...*, n.d., bet 1516 [Hebrew]; YESHAYAHU VINOGRAD: *Thesaurus of the Hebrew Book. Listing of Books Printed in Hebrew Letters Since the Beginning of Printing circa 1469 through 1863* II. Jerusalem 1993–95, p. 30 [Hebrew].

7 FRIEDBERG: *History of Hebrew Typography in Poland*, p. 72 [Hebrew]. Parenthetically, Tsevi Hirsh ben Aryeh Leib Margolis' (d. 1786) son-in-law, Samuel ben Issachar Ber Segal Shemu'el Madpis (Samuel Madpis, Samuel the printer) would become a Hebrew printer of repute in his own right, being active in several locations in Poland-Russia, including establishing the first press in Berdichev in 1807, that with the approbation of R. Levi Isaac (Levi Yitzhak) ben Meir of Berdichev (1740–1810, Kedushat Levi). ZEEV GRIES: Shemu'el ben Yisakhar Ber Segal. In: *YIVO Encyclopedia of Jews in Eastern Europe*. New Haven & London, 2008. Vol. 2, p. 707.

8 VINOGRAD: *Thesaurus of the Hebrew Book* (note 6). Vinograd records R. Menahem Azariah da Fano's (1548–1620) kabbalistic *Asarah Ma'amarot* as a separate entry noting that it is included in *Tikkunei Shabbat*. It appears, however, that there is only a passing reference to that work in *Tikkunei Shabbat*.

Fig. 2a-b 1767, *Tikkunei Shabbat*. Courtesy of the NL of Israel

is with those who fear Him. להודיעם וּבְרִיתוֹ יְרֵאָיו ה' סוֹד (527 = 1767) "to them He makes known His covenant." (Psalms 25:14). It is comprised, as the title suggests, of subjects related to Shabbat. The title-page text includes a paragraph in Polish followed by a paragraph in Hebrew, both acknowledging Prince Józef Klemens Czartoryski. Included in *Tikkunei Shabbat* are Sabbath customs, beginning with erev Shabbat, zemirot (hymns), tractate *Avot*, and Shir ha-Shirim (Song of Songs), all with commentary, much from the compiler, author, R. Israel Saruk (Sarug, 16thcent.–1602). Among the *zemirot* are three hymns composed by the Ari (R. Isaac Luria, Ari ha-Kodesh, 1534–1572), published here for the first time, these with Saruk's commentary.[9]

R. Saruk, an Egyptian Kabbalist, was a student in Safed of R. Isaac Luria and R. Hayyim Vital (1542–1620), the Ari's foremost disciple. Saruk was an exponent and disseminator of Lurianic Kabbalah. In 1593, he left Eretz Israel to spread kabbalistic teachings, first going to Holland, was for a time in Salonika, and then in Poland. It is not clear whether he died in Europe or returned to Eretz Israel, passing away there. Among the kabbalists influenced by Saruk are R. Menahem Azariah Fano, R. Isaac Fano, R. Aaron Berechiah ben Moses of Modena, and R. Solomon Luria (Maharshal).[10]

Tikkunei Shabbat has been a popular and much reprinted work. This edition is the twenty-second printing of that work. It has, including a Ladino edition (Livorno, 1853) and editions with additional commentaries, been published forty-four times.[11]

---

[9] GERSHOM SCHOLEM: Sarug (Saruk), Israel. *Encyclopaedia Judaica*. Vol. 18, pp. 3–64.

[10] MORDECHAI MARGALIOTH (Ed.): *Encyclopedia of Great Men in Israel 3*. Tel Aviv 1986, cols. 995–96 [Hebrew]; SHIMON VANUNU: *Encyclopedia Arzei ha-Levanon. Encyclopedia le-Toldot Geonei ve-Hakhmei Yahadut Sefarad ve-ha-Mizrah 3*. Jerusalem 2006, p. 1386 [Hebrew].

[11] CH. FRIEDBERG: *Bet Eked Sefarim*, tav, no. 1881.

Fig. 3 1767–69, *Ben Aaron*. Courtesy of the NL of Israel

Fig. 4 1767 *Ohel Yosef*. Courtesy of Hebrewbooks.org

Margolis' second publication was *Ohel Yosef* (below) by R. Joseph Yoska ben Israel, *av bet din* in Pidkamin, novellae on several tractates of the Talmud. The lengthy text of the title-page gives Joseph Yoska distinguished rabbinic genealogy and informs that work *Ohel Yosef* was begun in the year "seek good for his people rapidly with great haste דורש טוב לעמו מהרה חושה (527 = 1767)". The colophon dates completion to the first third of the month of Tishrei 1768. Printed in folio format (2°: 40 ff.), this is the only edition of *Ohel Yosef*, R. Joseph Yoska's only published work. Other works by Joseph Yoska remain in manuscript, such as novellae on tractate *Hullin*.[12]

At this time Tsevi Hirsh ben Aryeh Leib Margolis began work on R. Elijah ben Aaron Segal of Satonav's *Ben Aaron*, a super-commentary on Rashi. This is the only edition of *Ben Aaron*, published as an octavo (8°: [2], 38 ff). The title-page dates *Ben Aaron* with the verse "Fortunate [is the one] whom the Almighty of Jacob is his help אשרי שאל יעקב בעזרו (527 = 1767)" (Psalms 146:5). The colophon dates completion of *Ben Aaron* to Wednesday, 23 Sivan [5]529 (June 28, 1769).

In contrast to *Tikkunei Shabbat*, the title-page of *Ben Aaron* has no Polish text. The Hebrew text, however, does include the de rigueur reference to Prince Józef Klemens Czartoryski. The title-page is followed by two approbations, from R. Abraham David ben Moses of Satonav dated Rosh Hodesh Kislev, 1769, and from R. Mordecai ha-Kohen Rappoport of Oleksiniec, dated 15 Sivan, 1765; Elijah ben Aaron's apologia; errata; and then the text, in two columns in rabbinic letters.

It is generally accepted that the front matter in early printed books was printed after the text, one reason that front matter has separate foliation, as its length was unclear when the text was being set. While Hebrew books were printed in the same manner as non-Hebrew works, front matter apparently may, in some instances, have been set prior to the text, evident from the earlier dating of the title-page and the later date of the colophon in the above examples.

---

12 NL of Israel, System no. 990000437600205171.

Fig. 5a 1768, *Takanata de-Moshe*. Courtesy of Otzar Hahochma

Fig. 5b *Zedeh le-Derekh ha-Rehokah*. Courtesy of the L of Agudas Chassidei Chabad Ohel Yosef Yitzhak

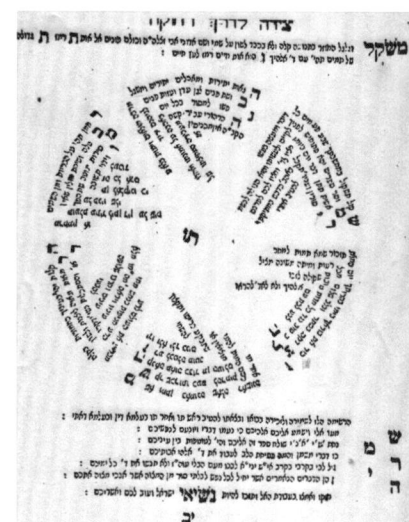

III

The following year, 1768, saw the publication of four titles, R. Mordecai Kanaha Rappoport's *Imrei No'am*, an ethical and medical work; two works by R. Aaron ben Nathan Neta Halprin of Trembovla, *Mahanah Aron*, novellae on *Berakhot* and *Seder Mo'ed*, and *Makelo shel Aharon*, discourses on the weekly parasha; and R. Shemarya ben Moses Berliner's *Takanata de-Moshe*, a multi-part ethical work.

Of the four works published in 1768 the two we will look more closely at are R. Shemarya ben Moses Berliner's *Takanata de-Moshe* and R. Aaron ben Nathan Neta Halprin of Trembovla's *Makelo shel Aharon*. The former, as noted above, is a multi-part work. It was published as an octavo (8°: [60] ff.). R. Shemarya ben Moses Berliner, *av bet din* Halametz, is given as the author and R. Zevi Ashkenazi (Chacham Zevi) as the co-author. The title-page describes the work as part one of *Takanata de-Moshe* but it appears that no other parts were ever printed. [Fig. 6b] It continues, describing the other parts comprising *Takanata de-Moshe*, that is, *Sefer Shevil ha-Nesher* by R. Zvi Ashkenazi, *Takanata le-Takanat, Pithei Teshuvah* part two, *Mishkel Tov Le-Hayyim*, and *Zedeh le-Derekh ha-Rehokah*. Shemarya Berliner's father R. Moshe Berliner, is noted, as well as the names of the various authors with their rabbinic positions and appropriate honorifics. The title-page dates completion of *Takanata de-Moshe* to the day that it says "it was good" (Genesis 1:9-12) twice (Tuesday) and He is upright הוא וישר" (528 = 1768).

The title-page is followed by six approbations among them from R. Hayyim ha-Kohen Rappoport, *av bet din*, Lvov; R. Aryeh Leib [Gunzberg], *Sha'agas Aryeh*; and R. Mordecai Kanaha Rappoport of Oleksiniec. These are followed by Berliner's introduction and then the text of *Takanata de-Moshe*, and the other works, generally comprised of concise entries, for example, on the weekly Torah portions, Talmudic novellae, and ethical teachings, frequently referencing midrashim. This is the only edition of *Takanata de-Moshe*.

Fig. 6a 1768, *Mahanah Aron*. Courtesy of the NL of Israel

Fig. 6b 1768, *Makelo shel Aharon*. Courtesy of the NL of Israel

Our second 1768 title is R. Aaron ben Nathan Neta Halprin of Trembovla's *Makelo shel Aharon*. Haplrin resident in Trembovla, built a bet midrash with an extensive library at his own expense, as Trembovla was not a learned place.[13] Halprin (1700-1770) was, on his paternal side, as he informs on the title-page of *Mahanah Aron*, a direct descendant of R. Mordecai Jaffe (*Levushim*. c. 1535–1612), and his grandmother was the daughter of R. Isaac, *av bet din* in Satanov. Among the other distinguished antecedents that Halprin mentions are, on his maternal side, the gaon R. Wolf, *av bet din* of Alik, son-in-law of the Maharshal.

Makelo shel Aharon is, as noted above, discourses on the weekly parasha. It is a small work, an octavo (8°: [25 ff.). Here too the title-page begins by referring to the author with honorifics, mentioning *Mahanah Aron* and that it is desirable novellae. Józef Klemens Czartoryski, is referred to as Duke, and the publisher. The title-page is dated "inscribe Aaron's name on the staff ואת שם אהרן **כתוב על** מטתו (528 = 1768)" (cf. Numbers 17:18).[14]

Makelo shel Aharon has two approbations, from R. Solomon Isaac *av bet din* of Tarnapol and Podolia and from R, Jacob, *av bet din* of Trembovla, and an unusually brief introduction which states,

> Because I have seen a desire among talmidim who have accustomed themselves to seek with depth by candle and to wander through the entire Talmud, seeking something in the Talmud relating to this week's Torah parsha and to relieve their thirst, I have prepared this small work to make it easy for those who look into it, for they will find in it leniencies and stringencies, and one who is sagacious will hearken and add insights and find reasons from Shabbat to Shabbat.

The text follows in two columns in rabbinic type. Entries are relatively concise. *Makelo shel Aharon* has been reprinted twice (Piotrków, 1908, Brooklyn, 1992/93) and in facsimile (2007).

---

[13] BIDSPIRIT: "Makelo shel Aharon". Auction No. 24 A special auction of Judaica details and rare and important Hasidic books from a private collection (available on www.il.bidspirit.com, [20.1.2023]).

[14] The verse actually reads "ואת שם אהרן תכתב על מטה." I would suggest the variances are due to a compositor's error, except that there are two unrelated variances at different places in the verse, leaving the reason for the changes to further speculation.

Fig. 7a-b 1772, Mishnayot *Seder Zera'im*, titled *Be'er Hayyim*. Courtesy of the NL of Israel

Two additional titles are credited to the press in the following year, 1769, R. Aaron ben Judah ha-Levi, maggid of Oleksinets' ethical *Zot Torat ha-Adam*, the first edition of this versified ethical work, reprinted six times; and R. Hanokh Zundel of Lublin's kabbalistic commentary on the *Zohar*, *Kokevai Nogah*, recorded by the *Thesaurus* as the only edition of this work and as questionable. A three-year hiatus in the presses' activities occurred after publishing these titles.

IV

The reason for the hiatus was that at this time the Jewish communities of Podolia and the Ukraine were devastated and despoiled by pogroms. Heinrich Graetz describes the situation, writing that Catherine the Great of Russia (1729–1796) plunged the land into fratricidal war. Under her the Russians "let loose against Poland the Zaporogian Cossacks – the savage Haidamaks – who inflicted death, by every known method, upon the Polish nobles, the clergy, and the Jews. The Haidamaks hung up together a nobleman, a Jew, a monk, and a dog, with the mocking inscription, 'All are equal,' Most inhuman cruelties were inflicted upon captives and the defenseless…. The Ukraine, Podolia, in general the southern provinces of Poland, were turned into deserts".[15]

15 HEINRICH GRAETZ: *History of the Jews*. Philadelphia 1956, v 388.

Gustav Pearlson is even more descriptive. In his work on the persecution of the Jews over several centuries, he described the Haidamaks as:

> organized bands of mutinous serfs and brigands whose sole motives were loot, murder, thuggery and the destruction of Jews and Poles…. Led by an assassin named Gonta hecatombs were slaughtered throughout the province of Kiev. The Jews seeking refuge in the synagogue, his followers blew open the door by firing a cannon and speared them, riding along the streets with the children impaled on their lances, flinging them from high walls and hanging them together with dogs. When the streets were impassable on account of the corpses of the butchered, they were carted outside the gates and flung as carrion to the pigs and dogs.[16]

V

Printing resumed in 1772 after a slow return to a more pacific environment. Two titles were published that year, R. Hayyim ben Zechariah (Ashkenazi) of Harobshov's commentary on Mishnayot *Seder Zera'im*, titled *Be'er Hayyim* and R. Aryeh Judah Leib ben Mordecai of Brody's *Zemir Aritsim ve-Haverot Tsurim*, a collection of anti-Hassidic polemics.[17]

Be'er Hayyim is a small work, published in octavo format (8°: [4], 17, [55] ff). In addition to Hayyim ben Zechariah, R. Jacob ben Mordecai is recorded as a co-author. The title-page is dated "How I love Your Torah! All day long it is my conversation מה אבתי תורתך כל היום היא שיחתי (532 = 1772)" (Psalms 119:97). It describes *Be'er Hayyim* as being a compilation of other commentaries with the addition of the author's own insights. It also states that it was published previously in Amsterdam in 1731 but has disappeared נעלם from the market, until the brother of the author, R. Mordecai (Ashkenazi) added material of his own and named the work *Be'er Hayyim*. That remark notwithstanding, this appears to be the only known edition of Hayyim ben Zechariah's commentary and the only work accredited to him.

Also published that year was R. Aryeh Judah Leib ben Mordecai of Brody's *Zemir Aritsim ve-Haverot Tsurim*, a rare collection of anti-Hassidic polemics.[18] *Zemir Aritsim ve-Haverot Tsurim* is a response to the spread and success of the Hassidic movement. The spread of Hassidism resulted in a strong negative reaction from its opponents, the Lithuanian, anti-Hassidic (Mitnagdim), followers of the Vilna Gaon (R. Elijah ben Solomon Zalman, Gr"a, 1720–97), representing the more traditional and rabbinic organization of the community. The Hassidic movement was compared to followers of Shabbetai Zevi and excommunicated by the established rabbinic leadership in Vilna in 1772.

Zemir Aritsim ve-Haverot Tsurim is the first published anti-Hassidic work.[19] A small book, it measures 18–20 cm and is comprised of [16] ff. The title is comprised of *Zemir Aritsim* "The singing of the tyrants" (Isaiah 25:5) and *ve-Haverot Tsurim* "flint knives" (Joshua 5:2). The text of the title-page begins with the theme, "To sing of tyrants and to know all the thorns … that surround the rose …" *Zemir Aritsim ve-Haverot*

---

16 GUSTAV PEARLSON: *Twelve Centuries of Jewish Persecution: A brief outline of the sufferings of the Hebrew race in Christian lands, together with some account of the different laws and specific restrictions under which they have, at various times, been placed*. Hull 1898, here reprint 1927, p. 276.

17 Parenthetically, there was a contemporary Aryeh Judah Leib, this the "Mokhi'aḥ" of Polonnoye (d. 1770) who was a popular Hasidic preacher in Poland and among "the first of the early Ḥasidim to accept the charismatic leadership of R. Israel ben. Eliezer Ba'al Shem Tov, the founder of modern Ḥasidism" (Aryeh Judah Leib (The "Mokhi'aḥ")) of Polonnoye, *EJ* 2: 538.

18 A copy of *Zemir Aritsim ve-Haverot Tsurim* was put up for auction by Kestenbaum & Company, *Fine Judaica: Printed Books, Manuscripts, Autograph Letters & Graphic Art* (June 22, 2017), Auction 73, Thursday, June 22nd, 2017; Lot 81. It was described as the "exceedingly rare first edition of the first anti-Chassidic polemical tract and informs that only two complete copies are known and that it is important for the earliest record of Chassidic lifestyle." The auction catalogue informs that there are only two extant complete copies of *Zemir Aritsim ve-Haverot Tsurim*. One copy is in the NL of Israel, the other in the Bodleian L, Oxford. The estimated price of the auction copy, of which leaves 13, 15–16 are in facsimile, was $40,000–$60,000. It appears that this copy of *Zemir Aritsim ve-Haverot Tsurim* was not sold. In Bidspirit Auction 113, Apr 8, 2019, Lot 136, a copy of *Zemir Aritsim ve-Haverot Tsurim* was on auction, the estimate was $40,000–$50,000, start price $18,000. Here too the copy was not sold.

19 Another *Zemir Aritsim*, this by R. Davis ben Benzion Ezekiel maggid of Makow, was published in Warsaw (1798) and republished in Königsberg (1860). It too is also a strongly anti-Hassidic polemic, although reportedly very different from our *Zemir Aritsim* (Bidspirit, Auction 113).

Fig. 8 1772, *Zemir Aritsim ve-Haverot Tsurim*. Courtesy of the NL of Israel

20 Kestenbaum & Company, Auction 73.

21 HAIM LIBERMAN: *Ohel Rahel III*. Brooklyn 1980–84, p. 34 [Hebrew].

22 NISSAN MINDEL: *Rabbi Schneur Zalman of Liadi*. New York 1969, p. 236.

23 The event is described in an article by MORDECAI L. WILENSKY in *Tarbiz* (1.7.1958). Vol. (ד) כז, pp. 550–555 [Hebrew] and summarized in English (available on www.merhav.nli.org, [20.1.2023]).

24 MINDEL, p. 281.

25 BIDSPIRIT, Auction 113.

26 ELI LEDERHENDLER: *The Road to Modern Jewish Politics: Political Tradition and Political Reconstruction in the Jewish community of Tsarist Russia*. New York, Oxford 1989, pp. 42–43.

Tsurim is divided into seven sections, the first part of which seeks to enumerate the "evil deeds" of the nascent "cult."²⁰ Included in *Zemir Aritsim ve-Haverot Tsurim* is the is *herem* signed by the Vilna Gaon and two Vilna Batei Din with 18 signatures.

Zemir Aritsim ve-Haverot Tsurim caused considerable difficulty for Hassidim, forcing many to relocate, unable to remain in their previous residences.²¹ These difficulties are referred to in a letter written by R. Schneur Zalman of Liadi (Alter Rebbe, 1745–1812), after the disputes in Shklov in 1772, that community being among the earliest opponents in Eastern Europe of Hasidism. The Alter Rebbe writes "the pamphlet *Zemir Aritzim* was published there (Brody) that summer. It resulted in great distress for the Zaddikim of Wohlynia, and they could not stay at home, and flocked at that time in Rovno to our great teacher, his soul rest in Eden, to deliberate and seek counsel…. I know all this well, and it is common knowledge. Thus, all the troubles which were visited upon us in the year 5559 (1799) were by order of a Beth Din who relied completely upon the personal signature of the Gaon of Wilno in 5532 (1772), as was made public there."²²

One response to *Zemir Aritsim ve-Haverot Tsurim* was its public burning by Hasidim in Grodno in 1772. This was done under the inspiration of Rabbi Ḥayyim Ḥaiqel the Admor of the Hasidim in that location.²³ It is also reported that this was not an isolated incident but rather that *Zemir Aritsim* quickly "sold out, but the buyers were Chasidim who destroyed them."²⁴ Similarly, "the Hasidic community destroyed every copy that they could, even paying high prices to acquire copies so that they might destroy them.²⁵

Mitnagdic response to the burning of *Zemir Aritsim* is noted by Eli Lederhendler, who attributes it to the weakness of their position and the absence of state sanctioned support. In a letter the Vilna kahal (communal organization) notes that "nothing could be done to avenge the 'blasphemous' act in Grodno. 'They [the Hassidim] are unscrupulous criminals, with wily tongues that they put to use in the courts of governors and rulers, so that we risk, God forbid, all of our communities being placed under restraint.'"²⁶

VI

Three distinct titles were published in 1774, R. Bahya (Bahye) ben Joseph ibn Paquda's popular and much reprinted ethical work *Hovot ha-Levavot*; R. Isaac Eizek ben Israel Schorr's *Minhat Hadashah* on *Even ha-Ezer* and *Hoshen Mishpat*, both parts in one volume; and R. Shabbetai ben Meir ha-Kohen's (Shakh), work on the number and reasons of the taryag *mitzvot*, *Po'el Zedek*.

R. Shabbetai ben Meir ha-Kohen's (Shakh), was appointed *dayyan* on the Vilna *bet din* of R. Moses Lima (*Helkat Mehokek*) at an early age, due to his great erudition. A prolific author, Shakh's most famous work is *Siftei Kohen*, a commentary and halakhic novellae on *Shulhan Arukh*

Fig. 9a–b 1774, *Po'el Zedek*. Courtesy of the NL of Israel

Yoreh De'ah and *Hoshen Mishpat*, the former part begun when he was only eighteen and published when he was twenty-four, both now regularly published with the *Shulhan Arukh*, and also the subject of numerous commentaries.

Po'el Zedek, printed in the year "I run in the way of Your commandments, for You will broaden my heart לבי תרחיב כי ארוץ מצותיך דרך" (Psalms 119:32), is a small work, octavo in format 8°: 20 ff.). It is an enumeration of the *taryag* (613) *mitzvot* to be said weekly, divided by day and arranged by *parshiot* (weekly Torah readings). A popular work, *Po'el Zedek* has, some editions with annotations, gone through twenty-five printings through 1948. First printed in Jessnitz (1720), this is the seventh edition.[27]

Three additional works are attributed to Margolis' press in the following years. In 1775 he published R. Israel ben Jacob's *Einei Israel*, novellae; in 1776, R. Aaron Zelig ben Judah's *Bet Aharon*, on the minor prophets of the Bible with the *Kizzur Alsheikh*; and, in 1778, R. Abraham ben Mordecai Azulai's *Hesed le-Avraham*, a kabalistic work, although the press's publication of this title is questionable.

VII

After these last works Tsevi Hirsh ben Aryeh Leib Margolis ceased to print in Novy Oleksiniec. Friedberg suggests that it became clear to Margolis, a diligent worker and merchant, that the Hassidic population was steadily increasing, was attractive to the local population that followed its path, and was interested in literature appropriate to that movement. However, in a small locale such as Oleksiniec, it was not possible to address that market, and so he ceased to print there.[28] Margolis

---

[27] FRIEDBERG: *Bet Eked Sefaim*, p. 71.

[28] FRIEDBERG: *History of Hebrew Typography in Poland*, p. 73.

subsequently printed, very briefly in Koretz, and then more extensively in Shklov.

The titles printed in Novy Oleksiniec are small works, varied in content. They include biblical commentary, Talmudic novellae, ethical works, and even some books with kabbalistic content. Several are the only editions of those titles. The presses output, albeit limited and of short duration, is diverse and rich in content. We can conclude then as we began, seemingly appropriate for this Margolis press.

> I am but a rose of Sharon, A rose of the valleys. Like the rose among thorns, so is my faithful beloved among the maidens.
> (Song of Songs: 2:1–2)

> But earthlier happy is the rose distill'd,
> Than that which withering on the virgin thorn
> Grows, lives and dies in single blessedness.
> (A Midsummer Night's Dream: Act I Scene I Lines 76–78)

Muriel Collart, Daniel Droixhe et Alice Piette

« Je suis à la troisième édition de *Bélisaire* ».
Une contrefaçon du *Bélisaire* de Marmontel par le Liégeois Jean-François Bassompierre (1767)

À la mémoire de Robert L. Dawson (1943–2007)

Nous remercions très vivement pour sa collaboration David Adams, Professeur Émérite, Manchester University, Department of French.

As it is well-known, Liège was one of the most important printing centres for pirated editions of best-sellers in the Enlightenment. In Liège in 1767, Jean-François Marmontel met Jean-François Bassompierre, the main counterfeiter in the city, as he accompanied Madame Filleul, who was in poor health en route from the spa town of Aachen to Paris. He relates in his memoirs that Bassompierre reminded him that he printed his works, which sold in large numbers throughout Germany; that he had already printed four large editions of his Contes moraux, and that he was printing the third edition of Bélisaire. Bassompierre argued that the privileges granted in France 'do not extend here' and the prince-bishopdom was a free country where 'everything which is good' is published. To identify one of these editions of Bélisaire, we used three types of sources: copies reproduced on the internet from national or university libraries, those sold by booksellers, and those coming from private collections. The typefaces of the books are compared. The frontispieces and the plates of two types of editions allow us to attribute them to Bassompierre as they are signed by the printer's son, Dieudonné François Bassompierre. We ask why one of these plates, which shows Antonine, Bélisaire's wife, naked, is covered with black ink in the copy in the New York Public Library. The attribution to Bassompierre is also based on three types of ornaments collected in his official or counterfeited editions: woodcuts (see the database Môriåne on https://www.swedhs.org/); composite head- and tail-pieces made up of typographical 'flowers'; ornamental capitals. The place occupied by the Bassompierre editions in the general table of counterfeited reproductions of Bélisaire is considered. We finally ask why the printer disguises the origin of his Bélisaire while he publishes at the same time with his address Marmontel's Nouveaux contes moraux. A question remains open, due to the fact that some French counterfeiters borrowed Bassompierre's address from him, complicating a book-market that will be discussed in other studies by the Groupe liégeois d'histoire du livre (Société wallonne d'étude du dix-huitième siècle).

Robert Granderoute a donné en 1994, à la Société des Textes Français Modernes, une édition du *Bélisaire* de Jean-François Marmontel. Il y consacre le chapitre IX de l'*Introduction* aux anciennes éditions de l'ouvrage. Il écrit : « Selon le *Catalogue hebdomadaire* du 7 février 1767,

Bélisaire (340 p.) paraît à Paris chez Merlin sous deux formats, in-8° avec figures (au prix de 5 livres) et in-12 avec ou sans figures (aux prix de 3 et 2 livres respectivement ».[1] Il rapporte comment les lettres de Marmontel à Voltaire et Scheffer des 8 et 27 mars 1767 font état de la polémique suscitée par le *Bélisaire* et mentionnent une suspension de la seconde édition. « Mais, en fait, très tôt » poursuit-il, « le livre a dû être l'objet de diverses émissions et aussi de nombreuses contrefaçons. Il en résulte que la description des *Bélisaire* datés de Paris, Merlin, 1767, in-8° ou in-12, et comprenant 340 pages n'est pas aisée. Maints exemplaires que nous possédons aujourd'hui révèlent entre eux des différences qui laissent soupçonner une floraison de tirages ou de réimpressions ». Il établit une description bibliographique des différentes éditions de 340 pages, qui forment une liste de six éditions. Il propose d'identifier l'édition originale avec celle portant à la Bibliothèque Nationale de France la cote Rés. Y 3666 (n° 1). On va y revenir.

Granderoute enregistre par ailleurs trois éditions portant l'adresse parisienne de Merlin qui n'ont pas 340 pages. L'une d'entre elles, en 249 pages, porte le sous-titre « Nouvelle Edition, revue et corrigée » et se signale par une « vignette (deux petits amours) » (n° 2). Elle est conservée à la Yale University Library. Elle correspond manifestement à une édition qui se présente sous deux formes et qui est due au Liégeois Jean-François Bassompierre l'aîné (1709–1776). L'histoire de cette édition s'inscrit dans les *Mémoires* de Marmontel.

1. La rencontre de Marmontel et de Bassompierre à Liège en 1767

On a souvent fait état de la visite que Bassompierre rendit à Marmontel, alors que celui-ci s'arrêtait à Liège sur le chemin qui le ramenait de l'Allemagne à Paris. Si l'épisode a été parfois daté de 1780, il prend place bien des années auparavant.[2] En août 1767, Marmontel se trouve à Aix-la-Chapelle en compagnie de Madame Filleul, qui, en mauvaise santé, espère se rétablir quelque peu dans la célèbre station balnéaire allemande. Madame Filleul est accompagnée de sa fille, de la marquise de Marigny et de la comtesse de Séran, dont on espère qu'elle pourrait remplacer Madame de Pompadour auprès de Louis XV. Marmontel correspond d'Aix-la Chapelle avec Voltaire en août.[3] La *Liste des seigneurs et dames qui sont venus aux eaux minérales de Spa, l'an 1767* mentionne la présence à Spa de la comtesse de Séran et de la marquise de Marigny – mais sans référence à Marmontel.[4] Celui-ci apparaît dans les listes spadoises le 9 septembre, installé à l'hôtel de la Cour de Mannheim. Il passera « trois jours à Spa », écrit-il. Il revient à Aix-la-Chapelle d'où il écrit à Catherine II le 12 septembre.[5] L'état de Madame Filleul s'était dégradé, et il fallait revenir à Paris, mais « à petites journées ». Le groupe est rentré dans la capitale française le 27 septembre, de sorte que la rencontre à Liège avec Bassompierre peut être située vers la mi-septembre 1767.

Marmontel raconte : « À Liège, où nous avions couché, je vis entrer chez moi le matin un bourgeois d'assez bonne mine, et qui me dit :

---

[1] JEAN-FRANÇOIS MARMONTEL : *Bélisaire*, édition établie, présentée et annotée par ROBERT GRANDEROUTE. Paris 1994, pp. LIX sv.

[2] Pour la datation fautive en 1780 : A. J. MATHIEU : Marmontel à Spa, Liège et Aix-la-Chapelle. In : *Les cahiers ardennais*. 20 (1950), pp. 20–22, 61–64.

[3] JEAN-FRANÇOIS MARMONTEL : *Correspondance*, texte établi, annoté et présenté par JOHN RENWICK. Clermont-Ferrand 1974, I, pp. 127–28, 138 ; VOLTAIRE : *Correspondance*, édition THÉODORE BESTERMAN. Paris 1985, n° 10283.

[4] MURIEL COLLART ET DANIEL DROIXHE : *Spa, carrefour de l'Europe des Lumières. Les hôtes de la cité thermale au XVIIIe siècle.* Paris 2013.

[5] MARMONTEL : *Correspondance*, p. 146.

Fig. 1 Vue de la rue Neuvice vers 1900. THÉODORE GOBERT: *Liège à travers les âges*. Bruxelles 1977, t. VIII, illustration 2155. L'immeuble occupé par Jean-François Bassompierre – à l'époque du *Bélisaire*? – est le plus élevé à l'entrée de la rue, qu'on aperçoit à droite

'Monsieur, j'ai appris hier soir que vous étiez ici. Je vous ai de grandes obligations, je viens vous en remercier. Mon nom est Bassompierre. Je suis imprimeur-libraire dans cette ville ; j'imprime vos ouvrages, dont j'ai un grand débit dans toute l'Allemagne. J'ai déjà fait quatre éditions copieuses de vos *Contes moraux* ; je suis à la troisième édition de *Bélisaire* ».[6] Marmontel s'indignera en vain qu'un contrefacteur vienne lui voler le fruit de son travail : à quoi Bassompierre lui répond que « Liège est un pays de franchise » où s'imprime librement « tout ce qu'il y a de bon », car les privilèges octroyés en France « ne s'étendent point jusqu'ici ». Ceux-ci permettront à l'écrivain d'être « encore assez riche ». Bassompierre invitera l'écrivain à venir déjeuner et à voir « une des belles imprimeries de l'Europe ». Les demoiselles Bassompierre firent fête à Marmontel sans le décider à s'établir à Liège, où tout ce qu'il écrira « la veille sera imprimé le lendemain »…

« Bassompierre pour me dédommager de ses larcins me fit présent de la petite édition de Molière que vous lisez : elle me coûte dix mille écus ». On a établi que cette édition correspond à celle donnée, en huit tomes in-12, sous la fausse adresse parisienne de « la veuve David, Quai des Augustins, Au S. Esprit », à la date de 1768.[7] L'ouvrage sortait donc des presses et portait la date qui suivait l'année d'impression, comme il était souvent pratiqué pour accentuer sa nouveauté.

2. La contrefaçon Bassompierre

Pour identifier l'une des éditions du *Bélisaire* données par Bassompierre, on s'est servi de trois types de sources : a) les éditions reproduites par Google d'après de grandes bibliothèques, les unes nationales, les autres relevant d'institutions universitaires bien connues ; b) des ouvrages mis en vente par des librairies spécialisées ; c) des exemplaires provenant de collections privées. L'édition de 249 pages mentionnée ci-dessus s'est présentée sous deux formes, selon que le même corps de texte n'est pas encadré ou qu'il est totalement encadré (la description de Granderoute ne permet pas d'envisager ce point). Un exemplaire de l'édition non-encadrée est conservé à la New York Public Library ; l'édition ou l'émission sera désignée par le type 1a (illustration 2). Un exemplaire de l'édition/émission encadrée se trouve dans une collection privée (D. Droixhe et A. Piette). Elle sera désignée par le type 1b (illustration 3). Considérer ces deux formes comme des éditions différentes eût compliqué inutilement la classification générale des éditions « Merlin » de 1767.

Le corps de texte des types 1a et 1b peut être défini comme suit : [V]–xij *Préface* – [1]–201 *Bélisaire* – [202] Titre demi-page : *Avis* – [203]–249 *Fragments de Philosophie morale* – [203]–228 *De la gloire* – 228–238 *Des grands* – 238–249 *De la grandeur* – 2 pages non numérotées *Approbation* et *Privilège du Roi*.[8]

Cet ensemble est complété de divers opuscules qui se présentent de la même manière selon qu'ils sont non-encadrés ou encadrés, offrent une nouvelle pagination mais relèvent d'une même édition puisque leurs

[6] JEAN-FRANÇOIS MARMONTEL : *Mémoires*, édition établie, présentée et annotée par JEAN-PIERRE GUICCIARDI et GILLES THIERRIAT. Paris 1999, p. 297.

[7] DANIEL DROIXHE : « Elle me coûte dix mille écus ». La contrefaçon des œuvres de Molière offerte par l'imprimeur Bassompierre à Marmontel. In : *Revue française d'histoire du livre*. 114–115 (2002), pp. 125–63 (disponible sur www.hdl.handle.net, [20.1.2023]).

[8] On adopte ici en partie le mode de description appliqué par Granderoute à l'édition originale, pour faciliter la comparaison.

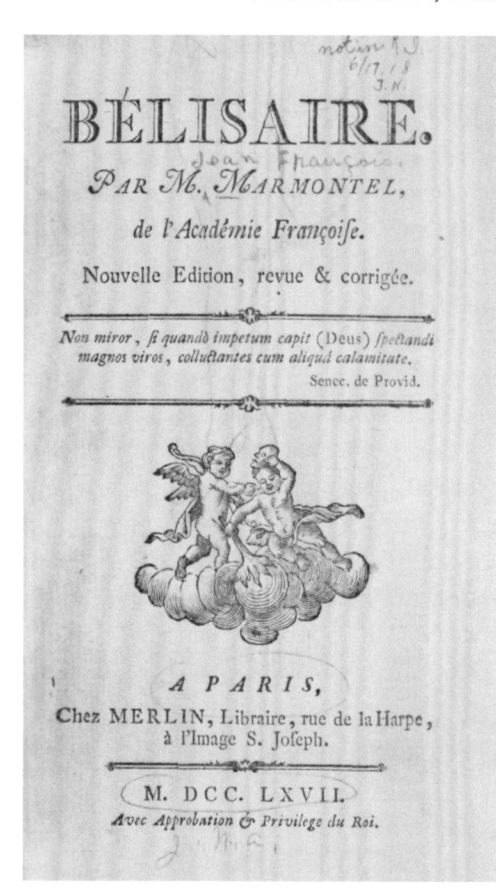

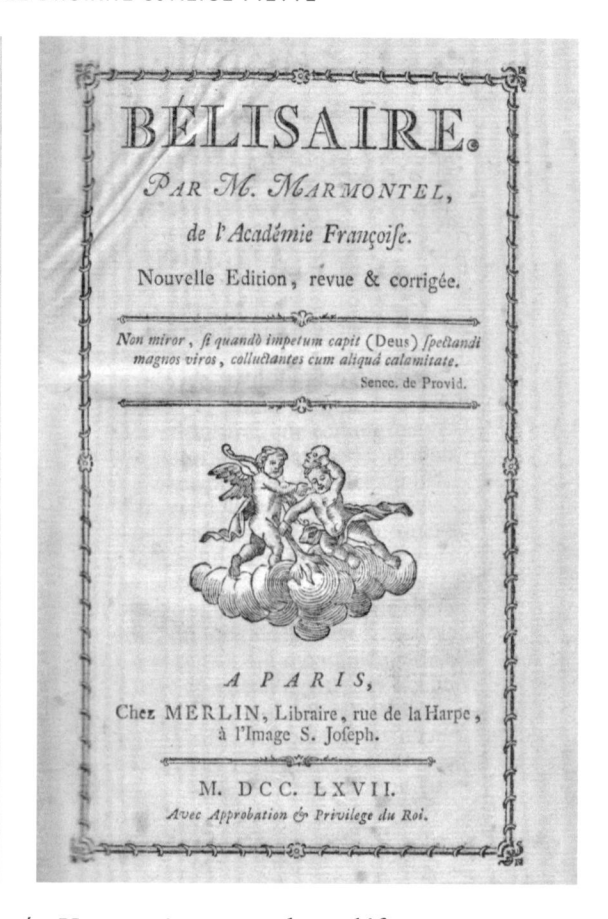

Fig. 2 Type 1a. The New York Public Library. Astor. Lenox and Tilden Foundations. 425361 R-1918-L

Fig. 3 Type 1b. Oupeye, collection Daniel Droixhe et Alice Piette

signatures sont continués. Un premier opuscule se définit comme suit : [1] *Pieces relatives à Bélisaire* – [2] p. blanche – [3]–19 / Aij–Bij *Anecdote sur Bélisaire* – 20–22 / Bij v°–Biij v° *Extrait d'une Lettre écrite de Geneve a M***. Sur la Liste imprimée des Propositions que la Sorbonne a extraites du Bélisaire pour les condamner* – [23–24] /Biv r°–Biv r° p. blanches. Un second opuscule s'intitule *Les XXXVII vérités opposées aux XXXIII impiétés de Bélisaire. Par un Bachelier ubiquiste*. Il se définit comme suit : [1] /Bv r° Page de titre, avec l'adresse « A Paris, Chez C. F. Simon, Imprimeur de l'Arche-/ vêché & de la Sacrée Faculté », 1767 – [2] / BV v° p. blanche – [iij]–xj /BVj–Cij r° *Avis* – [4]–32 / Cij v°–Dviij p. paires *Impiétés de Bélisaire. Indiculus propositionum excerptarum ex Libro cui titulus, Belisaire, A Paris, chez Merlin, 1767* – [5]–33/ Civ r°–Eij r° p. impaires *Vérités opposées aux erreurs de Bélisaire*. Suivent : [34] / Eij v° *Billet de Mr. De V., adressé à Mr. D.* – [1]–40 / Eiij r°–Gvj v° *Réponse de M. Marmontel, à une lettre de Mr. L'Abbé Riballier, syndic de la Faculté de Théologie de Paris* – 41–43/ Gvij r°–Gviii r° *Lettre de Mr. De V. à Mr. Marmontel* – [44] –52/ Giij v°–52 / Hiij v° *Exposé des Motifs qui m'-empêchent de souscrire à l'Intolérance civile* – [53]–54 / Fij r°–Fiij v° *Lettre de M. de Voltaire à Mr. Le Prince de Gallitzin*.

Granderoute confirme la distribution des textes dans l'exemplaire de Yale considéré en indiquant brièvement que suivent, après le *Bélisaire* et les *Fragmens* – en fait orthographiés *Fragments* dans 1a et 1b – les *Pièces* et les *XXXVII vérités*.

3. L'identification par les figures

Le premier élément permettant d'attribuer les types 1a et 1b à un atelier liégeois réside dans les quatre figures ou gravures qu'ils comportent. Elles sont constituées du frontispice et de planches illustrant des scènes des chapitres 6, 7 et 16. Elles comportent d'une part l'inscription « Gravelot Inv. » et s'inspirent donc des dessins du célèbre dessinateur, qui ont servi à illustrer la plupart des éditions de *Bélisaire* au XVIIIe siècle. Les figures des types 1a et 1b comportent par ailleurs l'inscription « D.F.B. Sculp. ». Ces initiales, mentionnées mais non identifiées par Granderoute, désignent à coup sûr le graveur liégeois Dieudonné François Bassompierre, fils de l'imprimeur, qui était établi comme celui-ci « en Neuvice ». « La rue Neuvice, voie favorite des orfèvres, l'était aussi jadis des imprimeurs et des libraires, qui relevaient du même métier ».[9]

Le fondateur de l'entreprise, Jean-André-François Bassompierre, né en 1709 avait épousé en 1726 – à dix-sept ans – Anne Rosy (1703–1762) dont il eut de nombreux enfants.[10] On retiendra Maria Aegidia Bassompierre (1728–1766), sa fille aînée, qui épousa Judocus c'est-à-dire Josse Vanden Berghen, imprimeur bruxellois. À la mort de Maria Aegidia, sa sœur Anne-Catherine (1736–1783) épousa Josse Vanden Berghen, qui vécut jusqu'en 1780 : on cultivait, à l'imprimerie liégeoise, le sens de la continuité commerciale.[11] On a rappelé à la suite de Philippe Minard qu'Anne-Catherine avait, d'autorité, pris le relais de la direction de la Maison Bassompierre à la mort du fondateur, en 1776 – et en faisant la nique à son frère aîné Jean-François (1732–1802), qui offre davantage l'image d'un aimable jeune homme courant le guilledou plutôt que celle d'un entrepreneur à la mesure de son père.[12] On doit se borner ici à mentionner une troisième Jean-François Bassompierre, trop souvent confondu avec les deux précédents.[13]

Les figures de 1a et 1b, placées en regard de la p. indiquée dans la gravure, se définissent comme suit : Frontispice, « Ecce spectaculum dignum, ad quod respiciat / intentus operi suo Deus : ecce par Deo dignum, / Vir sortis cum malâ fortunâ compositus. / Senec » ; « ch. VI. page 42 », « les Monstres ! voila sa recompense » ; « ch. VII. pag. 50 », « Qu'il approche, et que je l'embrasse » ; « ch. XVI. p. 188 », « Tremblez, Lâches ! son Innocence et sa Vertu me sont connues » (illustrations 4–7).

La gravure correspondant à la p. 42, dans l'exemplaire de la New York Public Library représentant le type 1a, offre un caractère particulier (illustration 8). Elle est en partie couverte d'encre noire : résultat d'une maladresse ou effet d'une projection intentionnelle ? Les taches couvrent notamment le personnage dénudé d'Antonine, l'épouse de Bélisaire. Celle-ci, découvrant qu'il est aveugle, « s'arrachoit les cheveux et se déchiroit le visage » et, « ouvrant ses bras tremblants », « couroit vers son époux, le pressoit dans son sein, l'inondoit de ses larmes ». Le jet d'encre traduirait-il l'émotion d'un lecteur ou d'une lectrice enfiévrés par le passage, ou le souci de masquer une image de nudité ? L'exemplaire porte en

---

9 THÉODORE GOBERT : *Liège à travers les âges. Les rues de Liège. Nouvelle* édition *du texte original de 1924–1929*. Bruxelles 1977, t. VIII, pp. 379 et 386 ; DANIEL DROIXHE : Maisons de la rue Neuvice occupées, dans la seconde moitié du XVIIIe siècle, par les imprimeurs Bassompierre, père et fils (nos 45 et 55). In : *Le siècle des Lumières dans la principauté de Liège. Musée de l'Art wallon et de l'Évolution culturelle de la Wallonie*. Liège 1980, notice 246, pp. 130–131 ; MURIEL COLLART, DANIEL DROIXHE et ALICE PIETTE : *Une visite aux maisons Bassompierre en Neuvice* à Liège. Document audio-visuel 2019 (inédit).

10 GUY PHILIPPART DE FOY : *Jean François Bassompierre (1677-1719)* (disponible sur www.gw.geneanet.org, [20.1.2023]).

11 GUY PHILIPPART DE FOY écrit qu'Anne-Catherine Bassompierre « épousa après 1761 Josse Vanden Berghen ». Ce devait être en 1766 ou après, puisque sa sœur Maria Aegidia vécut qu'à cette date.

12 PHILIPPE MINARD : *Typographes de Lumières, suivi des Anecdotes typographiques de Nicolas Contat*. Seyssel, 1989, p. 27 ; DANIEL DROIXHE : *Une histoire des Lumières au pays de Liège. Livre, idées, société*. Liège, 2007, pp. 91, 93, 109, 160, 212, 241.

13 MURIEL COLLART : La production voltairienne de Bassompierre & Nouffer de Genève (1776-1777). Un cas exemplaire d'heuristique éditoriale. In : *Revue Voltaire*. 21 (2022), pp. 371–392.

Figs. 4-7 Type 1b

14 DANIEL DROIXHE : De quelques critères en bibliographie matérielle. Contrefaçons de Stanislas Ier, Helvétius, Raynal et Caraccioli conservées en Espagne. In : *La memoria de los libros. Estudios sobre la historia del escrito y de la lectura en Europa y América*. édit PEDRO MANUEL CÁTEDRA GARCIA, MARIA LUISA LÓPEZ-VIDRIERO ABELLIO ET MARIA ISABEL DE PÁIZ HERNÁNDEZ. Salamanca, 2004 (disponible sur www.hdl.handle.net, [20.1.2023]).

15 DANIEL DROIXHE, ALICE PIETTE, MURIEL COLLART : Nouveau Môriâne (disponible sur www.swedhs.org/moriane/index.html, [20.1.2023]).

page de garde le nom de « Clara Rowlands » – sans doute la première propriétaire – et la date du 8 août 1770 (illustration 9). La signature désignerait-elle une des visiteuses de Spa, à l'époque du « Grand Tour » ? Il n'a pas été possible de l'établir.

La signature de Dieudonné Bassompierre a été repérée dans d'autres éditions de l'imprimeur liégeois. Elle figure par exemple en 1776 dans une édition revendiquée par son fils : les *Lettres intéressantes du pape Clément XIV* de l'insipide Louis-Antoine Caraccioli, dont l'ouvrage fut néanmoins un succès de librairie (illustrations 10–11). Pour rappel, les éditions de Caraccioli ont fait l'objet d'éditions qui portent l'adresse de Bassompierre mais qui lui peuvent être véritablement attribuées ou qui portent la fausse adresse du Parisien Nyon.[14]

4. L'identification par les ornements

Les types 1a et 1b comportent sept ornements typographiques. Ils se distribuent en : trois ornements gravées sur bois, formant une vignette de titre et deux bandeaux ; deux ornements composés, forment une vignette et un bandeau ; deux lettrines gravées sur bois.

Parmi les ornements gravés sur bois, celui décorant la p. de titre ne figure pas dans la base « Môriâne » de la Société wallonne d'étude du dix-huitième siècle (illustration 15).[15] Par contre, le bandeau sans cadre qui ouvre le texte du *Bélisaire* s'y trouve répertorié sous le n° 197. Mesurant 6,4 cm. de large, il a été enregistré dans différents types d'impressions de Bassompierre : des éditions portant les adresses conjointes de Bassompierre et de Vanden Berghen en 1773 (Griffet, *Sermons*) et en 1775 (Gayot de Pitaval, *Causes célèbres*), mais aussi la contrefaçon du célèbre *Spectacle de la nature* de l'abbé Pluche en 1771, sous l'adresse parisienne des Frères Estienne (illustrations 12–13).

L'illustration 14 fournit une autre preuve de la fabrication des types 1a et 1b par Bassompierre. La lettrine de la *Préface* est identique à celle qui figure à la p. [1] du *Bélisaire* (illustrations 14–15).

Figs. 8–10 Type 1a (gauche); Page de garde de 1a (centre); Liège, Bibliothèque de l'Université, 211586-A (droite)

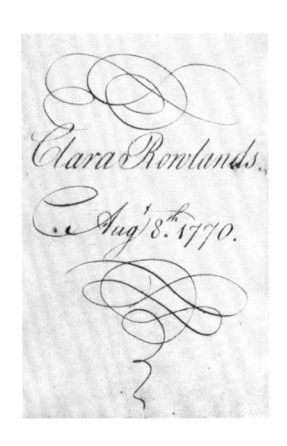

Fig. 11 N° précédent, frontispice

Un autre bandeau gravé est commun à la contrefaçon Bassompierre et aux éditions déclarées de l'imprimeur liégeois. Il figure notamment dans une édition avérée des *Lettres récréatives et morales* de Caraccioli portant l'adresse de Bassompierre père et fils (illustrations 17–18). On a noté ailleurs qu'un exemplaire de l'ouvrage, conservé à l'Université de Liège, mêle des volumes portant les adresses de Bassompierre et de Nyon : ceci confirme la concurrence et l'échange de fausses adresses dénoncées plus haut.

Un autre élément de l'illustration 18 confirme l'identification : la lettrine « L » est identique à celle qui ouvre le chapitre premier des *Progrès des Allemands, dans les sciences, les lettres et les arts* du baron de Bielfeld, qui porte l'adresse de J.-Fr. Bassompierre Fils en 1768 (voir illustration 19).

On n'a pas trouvé, dans les éditions Bassompierre contemporaines, d'ornements composés similaires à ceux employés dans sa contrefaçon de *Bélisaire*.

5. La place de la contrefaçon Bassompierre dans les éditions « Merlin » de *Bélisaire*.

On a vu comment, à l'origine, le *Bélisaire* était proposé dans un format in-8° avec figures et dans un format in-12 à des prix différents selon que l'édition comportait ou non les figures. Granderoute détaille ces « figures » et inscrit celles-ci parmi les critères qui, avec « la disposition typographique de l'épigraphe, la vignette de la page de titre le colophon », doivent être pris en compte pour distinguer les éditions. En ce qui concerne les figures, leur « position inversée » constitue un de ces critères : « dans le frontispice, il arrive en effet que le socle et la colonne

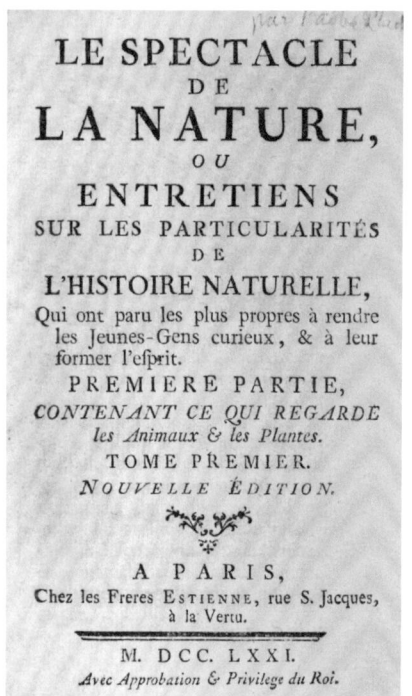

Figs. 12–14 Gent, Bibliotheek Universiteit, ex-libris v. M. P. Armellini (gauche); Pluche, Le spectacle de la nature, p. [iii] (centre); Types 1a et 1b, p. [1] (droite)

Fig. 15 Types 1a et 1b, p. de titre (ci-dessus)

Fig. 16 Types 1a et 1b, p. [1]

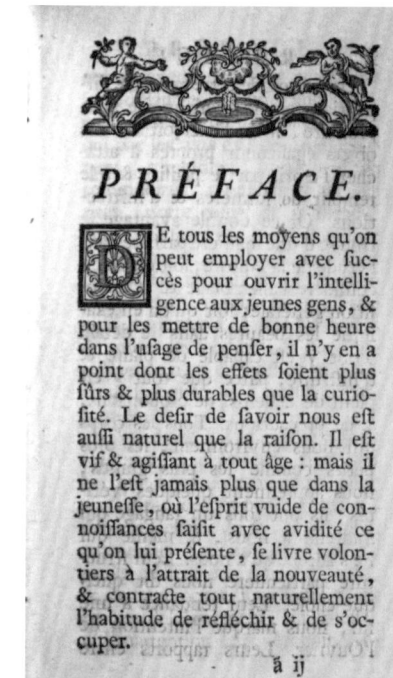

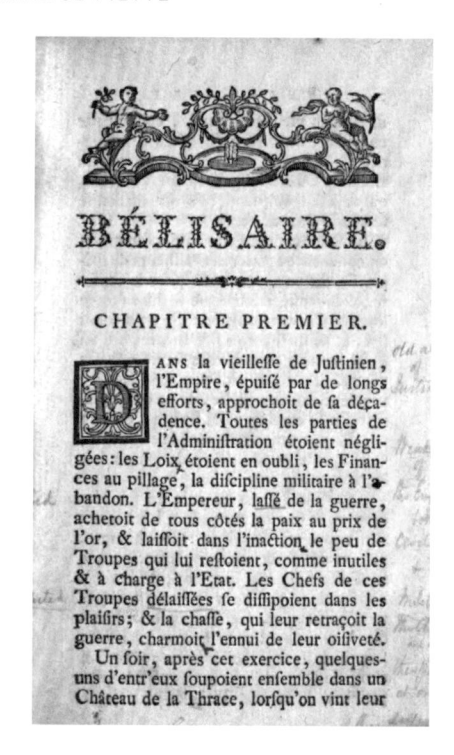

soient à droite de sorte que Bélisaire s'appuie sur son guide de la main droite et sur son bâton de la main gauche » et la « même inversion peut se produire dans les autres figures ».

Les types 1a et 1b des contrefaçons Bassompierre sont caractérisés par cette position inversée, en miroir, comme le montrent les illustrations 4 à 7, si l'on compare par exemple leur frontispice à celui de l'exemplaire conservé à la BNF sous la cote Y2-9566, où la gravure est du même type que celle décorant l'édition supposée originale (illustrations 20–21). Granderoute observe en effet, à propos de l'exemplaire de Yale : « Frontispice (face à la p. 9) : colonne à droite »; « Autres illustrations avec légendes et signatures (baldaquin à droite, portique à gauche, palais à droite) ». Dans les types 1a et 1b, le frontispice est à sa place, en regard de la p. de titre.

«Il faut aussi», ajoute Granderoute, « tenir compte de la place des figures (elles ne sont pas toujours situées en regard des pages 57, 69 et 255) » et « de la présence ou de l'absence de légendes ». On a vu que les figures, dans la contrefaçon liégeoise, sont légendées, comportent une indication de placement et que celui-ci est conforme : ces dispositions témoignent du soin apporté à la fabrication de l'édition, comme le montre également la qualité de la gravure réalisée par Dieudonné Bassompierre.

Granderoute mentionne un autre critère de distinction et de classement des éditions « Merlin » de 1767 : il concerne l'*Addition à la Note de la P. 237.* « Rédigée au temps des premières conférences tenues avec les représentants de l'Église », celle-ci parut « d'abord en feuille volante, soit au début de l'ouvrage soit à la fin » et elle « témoigne d'une émission postérieure à l'édition originale ». « Encore plus tardive doit être considérée l'émission/édition qui incorpore l'*Addition* à sa place dans le livre. Cependant ce critère reste insuffisant pour déterminer si l'on a affaire à des

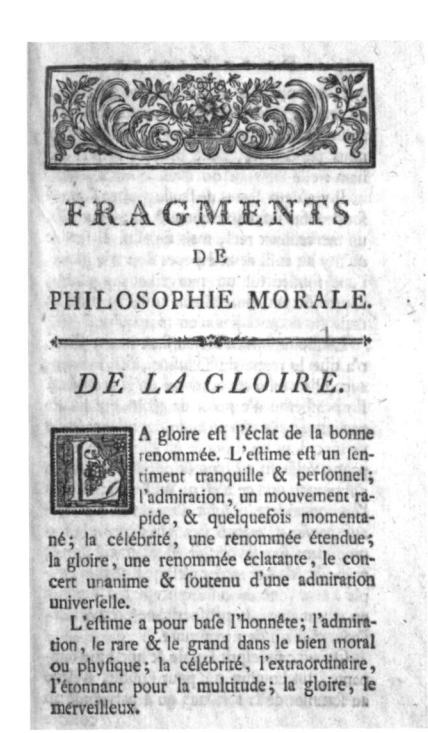

Figs. 17–19 Types 1a et 1b, p. [203] (gauche); Louis-Antoine Caraccioli, Lettres récréatives et morales, sur les mœurs du temps, Paris, Bassompierre, Père, Libraire, à Liege [et] Van den Berghen, Libraire, à Bruxelles, 1767, t. I, p. [1] (centre); Jacob Friedrich von Bielfeld, Progrès des Allemands, A Leyde, et se vend à Leipsick, en Foire, Chez J. F. Bassompierre, Fils, Libraire à Liege, 1768, p. [1] (droite)

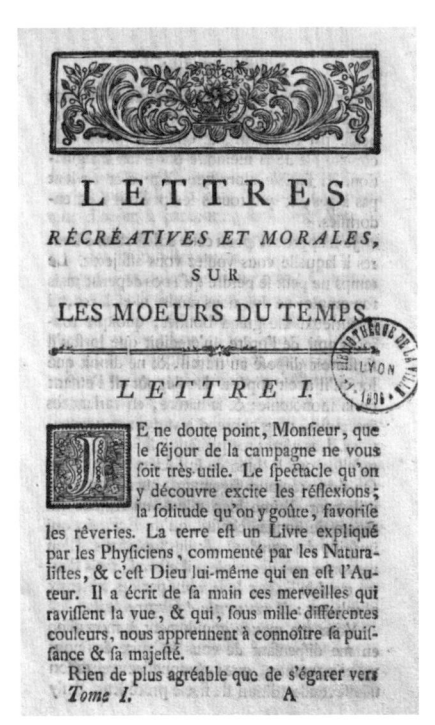

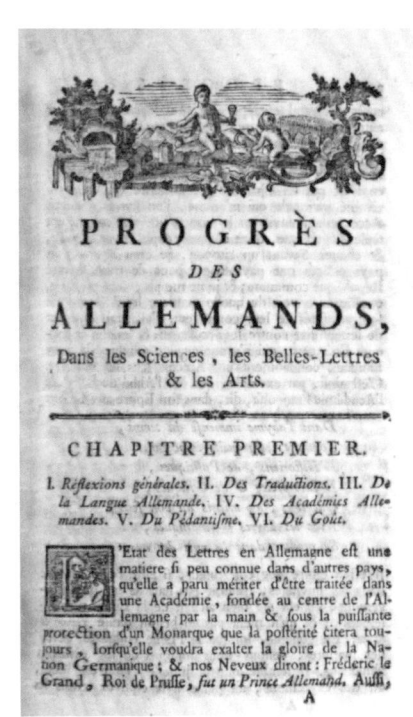

exemplaires réellement sortis de chez Merlin ou à des contrefaçons ». Granderoute observe à propos de l'édition liégeoise en 249 p. : « Addition à la note du chapitre XV intégrée ». Ceci, joint à la mention « Nouvelle édition » au titre, paraît confirmer le caractère tardif de l'édition.

La contrefaçon Bassompierre ne comporte pas le colophon indiquant, dans les éditions « Merlin » de 1767 en 340 p., que l'ouvrage été imprimé par Pierre-Alexandre Le Prieur. Reçu libraire en 1747 et imprimeur en 1749, il devint la même année imprimeur-libraire du Roi. Il avait racheté à Jean-Baptiste Delespine une imprimerie dont il se démit en 1773. Il était établi rue Saint-Jacques. Bassompierre, à la différence d'autres contrefacteurs de l'édition « Merlin », n'emprunte pas le nom de l'imprimeur : signe d'une correction ou d'une élégance confraternelle qui n'était pas coutumière chez le Liégeois.

Dans le classement des éditions de Merlin de 1767, la contrefaçon liégeoise est la seule qui, parmi celles qui n'ont pas 340 p., représente l'édition en 249 p., à côté de celles en 352 (1) et 238 p. (3). Elle se signale donc comme peu volumineuse, et donc économique. On l'inscrirait aisément parmi les contrefaçons Bassompierre qui réduisent les coûts de production en raccourcissant l'impression. Les éditions de 340 p. offrent un cas intéressant de classement par l'ornementation composée. Granderoute s'y montre sensible par l'attention qu'il accorde aux vignettes qui décorent certaines pages de titre. On croit devoir saisir l'occasion pour avancer quelques observations de morphologie ornementale.

Granderoute décrit très précisément la vignette qui caractérise au titre l'édition originale, que l'on désignera par le type 2 et dont il est opportun de reproduire à présent la p. de titre dans un plus grand format (illustration 22)

Figs. 20-21 Type 1b, contrefaçon Bassompierre ; Frontispice de l'édition de Merlin, 1767 in-12 de 340 pages, conservée à la Bibliothèque Nationale de France, Y2-9566

Il décrit la vignette comme suit : « un rectangle entouré de petits ornements décoratifs qui dessinent un cercle et formé de 5 carrés en haut et en bas, de 4 sur chacun des deux côtés, ces carrés contenant eux-mêmes des carrés noirs avec un point blanc au centre. À l'intérieur du resctangle, 3 croix en haut et en bas, 2 sur chaque côté, aux quatre coins des x ; à l'intérieur de l'espace ainsi délimité par les croix, 4 × en pointillé en haut et en bas ».

Les cotes du catalogue de la BNF ont été modifiées depuis 1994, de sorte que l'exemplaire désigné par Granderoute comme représentant l'édition originale, alors coté Rés. Y 3666, se présente aujourd'hui – pour autant qu'on puisse juger – sous la cote RES-Y2-3666. Cet exemplaire figure dans une liste qui renvoie à un exemplaire coté NUMM-9692151 numérisé sur Gallica. La page de titre de celui-ci ne correspond malheureusement à celle fournie par Granderoute. On désignera cette autre édition par le type 3 (illustration 23).

Ce type 3 correspond également à l'exemplaire de la BNF aujourd'hui coté Y2-9566, représentant une édition que Granderoute désigne par le n° V. Les références de cette édition sont : « 12° sig. A-aiv A-Avj – P-Pij ». L'épigraphe se présente en effet sous la forme [...] *si quandò* [...] *colluc-/tantes*. La figure du chap. 7 « porte les deux signatures ou celle de Gravelot seulement, selon les exemplaires » ; elle porte ici les deux signatures. Dans le type 3, l'*Addition à la Note de la Page 237* est « insérée soit au début

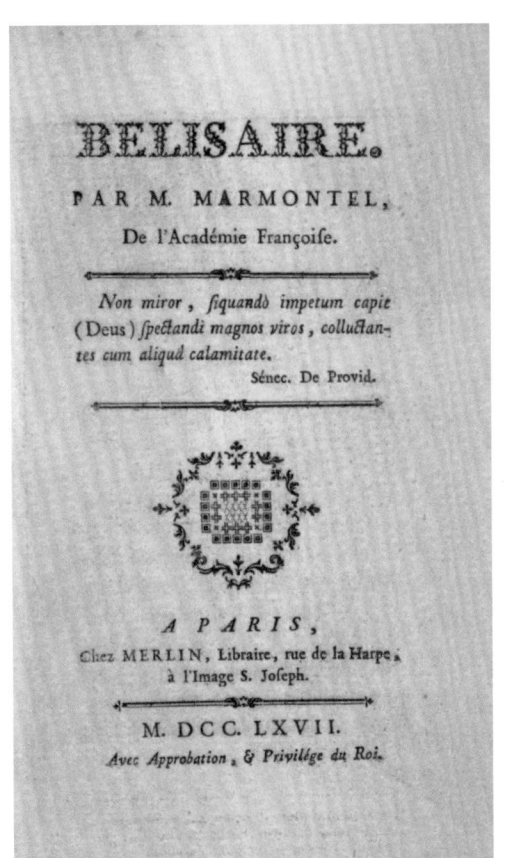

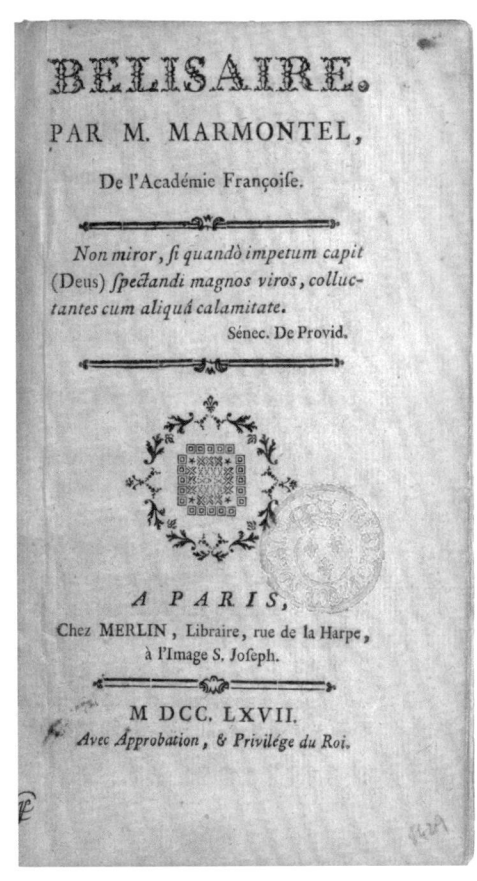

Figs. 22-23 Type 2. Edition supposée originale par Granderoute. Oxford, Taylor Institution Library ; Type 3. Page de titre de l'exemplaire NUMM-9692151

16 ROBERT L. DAWSON : *Additions to the Bibliographies of French Prose Fiction 1618–1806*. Oxford 1985, p. 256, n° 179.

soit à la fin du volume ». Elle se trouve à la fin du volume. Comme l'indique Granderoute, le colophon est ici : « De l'Imprimerie de P. ALEX, LE PRIEUR », etc., alors que le type 2 a : « De l'Imprimerie de P. ALEX. LE PRIEUR ». L'édition comporte les erreurs de pagination soigneusement relevées par l'historien : 319 pour 219, 321 pour 221, etc. L'édition est signalée par Robert L. Dawson.[16] Granderoute considère le type 3 comme une contrefaçon.

Les types 2 et 3 ont au titre des vignettes composées qui offrent une concordance générale assez marquée (illustration 24).

Granderoute décrit comme suit la vignette du type 3. « un carré entouré d'ornements décoratifs qui dessinent un cercle et formé de 5 carrés, chacun d'eux contenant lui-même un carré blanc ; à l'intérieur de l'espace ainsi délimité, 3 × sur chaque côté avec des étoiles dans les coins ; au centre, trois rangées de x en pointillé, 4 en haut, 4 en bas et 2 transversaux au milieu ». On soulignerait volontiers la correspondance structurelle qui unit les deux compositions : des caractères en croix avec un double tracé, disposés en signes « + » ou en « x », délimitent un noyau composé de manière identique au moyen des « x en pointillé » signalés par Granderoute.

Celui-ci est attentif aux variations que présentent les vignettes composées des pages de titre des éditions « Machuel » de 1767 de 340 pages. Il mentionne une autre édition in-12 désignée par le n° III et signalée par Dawson (n° 178). La vignette est décrite comme suit : « un rectangle entouré de petits ornements décoratifs qui dessinent un cercle et [est] formé par 5 carrés en haut et en bas, 4 sur les côtés, chaque carré ayant à l'intérieur un carré noir ; à l'intérieur de l'espace ainsi délimité, 5 × en haut et en bas, 4 × sur les côtés ; au centre deux rangées de 4 × en pointillé ». Il ne fait guère de doute qu'il s'agit de l'édition dont un exemplaire est conservé à la Bibliothèque Nationale de la République Tchèque sous la cote 12 k 788 (illustration 25).

Granderoute ne se prononce pas quant à la nature de cette édition. Le cas est-il à envisager par rapport à une autre édition conservée à la Bibliothèque Nationale de la République Tchèque (illustration 26) ? Celle-ci offre d'emblée des caractères qui font soupçonner une réalisation hâtive, une fabrication d'urgence imposée par le grand succès et le rapide débit de l'ouvrage. Le défaut de symétrie de la vignette de titre et l'absence d'un caractère, à droite, montrent une négligence que confirme le déplacement du caractère en-dessous du carré. Les figures, inversées, ne comportent ni indications de dessinateur et de graveur, ni indications relatives à l'endroit où elles doivent être insérées, de sorte qu'elles sont introduites de manière tout à fait désordonnée. Ainsi, la gravure reproduite à l'illustration 26 figure en tête du chapitre V alors qu'elle a trait, comme l'indiquent les gravures des autres types, au chapitre VI. Le relieur n'a évidemment pas compris où il devait placer les figures, qui apparaissent assez grossières, pour autant qu'on puisse en juger, y compris par rapport aux gravures liégeoises correspondantes.

6. Conclusion

On ne discutera pas ici de la nature des *Pièces relatives à Bélisaire* qui suivent le roman de Marmontel et les *Fragments de Philosophie morale*. Elles ont été suffisamment décrites plus haut. Le fait qu'elles soient également encadrées dans le type 1b, comme l'édition du *Bélisaire*, devrait suffire à identifier l'édition de ces *Pièces*, y compris dans la version correspondante du type 1a, comme contrefaçons.

La question que posent les anciennes éditions de *Bélisaire* dépasse celle que présente l'identification des contrefaçons orgueilleusement revendiquées par Bassompierre lors de sa rencontre avec l'écrivain. Une contradiction générale serait à expliquer, sur un plan strictement local : pourquoi se vante-t-il d'éditer en cette même année 1767 les *Nouveaux contes moraux* du même auteur, qu'il publie ouvertement à son adresse et à celle de son gendre Vanden Berghen, alors qu'il dissimule l'édition du *Bélisaire* en copiant très fidèlement l'adresse de Merlin au titre (illustration 26) ? S'il s'agit de profiter commercialement d'une attractive adresse parisienne censée recommander l'ouvrage au chaland, pourquoi user du brigandage dans un cas et s'en priver dans un autre ? On ne peut davantage alléguer une différence du moment d'impression, une évolution culturelle qui rendrait les *Contes* plus tolérables pour les autorités liégeoises de censure, sous le règne plus « libéral » de François-Charles de Velbruck. Rien n'établit actuellement que l'édition des *Contes* qui porte en 1780 la seule adresse « A Liege », enregistrée comme liégeoise par

Figs. 24a-b Type 2 Vignette de la page de titre ; Type 3 Vignette de la page de titre

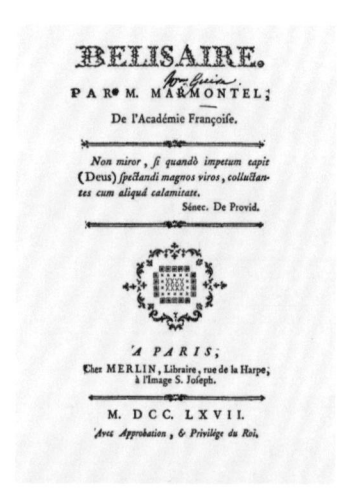

Fig. 25a Type 4. Prague, Bibliothèque Nationale de la République Tchèque, 12 k 788

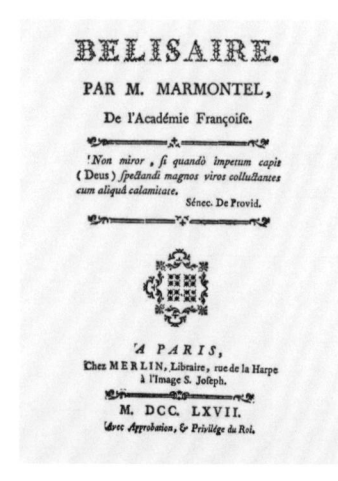

Fig. 25b Illustration 25. Type 5. Bibliothèque Nationale de la République Tchèque, K 6202

« Je suis à la troisième édition de *Bélisaire* » 197

x. de Theux, soit véritablement liégeoise (illustration 27). De Theux en donne les trois volumes comme joints « à la collection Cazin » : « elle contient la réduction de la suite des figures de Cochin et Marillier pour l'édition in-8 ».[17]

Si l'ornementation typographique sur bois suffit à résoudre assez facilement le problème d'identification, on attendrait de l'ornementation composée une confirmation qui engage l'enquête – et le débat – sur un terrain morphologique, comme il a été dit. L'interrogation relative à la valeur d'identification que comportent les formes ornementales n'a pas été suffisamment discutée. Jusqu'à quel point faut-il qu'une concordance soit établie entre plusieurs ornements composés pour que la présomption ou la certitude d'une origine commune puisse être soutenue ?

La correspondance doit-elle être totale, absolue, à l'instar de celle qui est fréquemment exigée à propos des ornements gravés sur bois ? Indépendamment du fait que des ornements sur bois qui paraissent similaires peuvent tout simplement provenir d'une même matrice en métal (comme il arrive souvent dans les éditions de Suisse romande considérées par Silvio Corsini), on a pu mettre en évidence l'extrême habileté des anciens graveurs à reproduire le plus exactement possible un modèle. Giles Barber l'avait souligné concernant les contrefaçons anglaises de *Candide* de 1759. Ces éditions comportent des copies d'une fidélité « surprenante » si on les compare aux originaux figurant dans les éditions Cramer. Le « réimprimeur (anglais) », écrit Barber, a consacré beaucoup de temps et d'argent « à donner, non seulement à sa page de titre mais aussi à son livre en général, une allure typographique qui rappellerait d'assez près celle de l'édition qu'il copiait ». L'emploi d'éléments typographiques eût été, en théorie, bien « plus facile, plus universel et plus anonyme ».[18] Ce caractère d'anonymat peut néanmoins être discuté.

La reproduction d'ornements composés permettrait-elle un même niveau de qualité, au prix d'empêcher des identifications de provenance de telle ou telle édition ? La réponse dépend dans une certaine mesure de la complexité des agrégats de caractères. Sur un plan plus général, une relative correspondance des modèles, quand ceux-ci comportent davantage de caractères et sont donc plus complexes, autorise-t-elle la supposition d'un rapport de provenance ? Peut-on croire qu'une certaine concordance structurelle de forme indique un mode de fabrication ? Est-il utile d'établir, en fonction des ateliers, des personnels et des périodes d'activité, des « styles » d'ornementation typographique éclairant la production de certains éditeurs ou donnant même lieu à des conjectures sur les conditions d'impression de certains ouvrages ?

Les éditions du *Bélisaire* portant l'adresse de Merlin et comportant en 1767 340 pages offre à cet égard un terrain d'enquête assez intéressant. Si l'on en croit R. Granderoute, le type 3 constituerait une contrefaçon de l'édition originale due à Merlin, et la vignette de page de titre copierait donc celle du type 2 – ce qui représente déjà, dans les termes de Barber, un travail long et coûteux. Il faut croire qu'il en valait la peine. L'imitation est-elle également à l'œuvre dans les vignettes plus grandes et plus complexes qui sont reproduites ci-dessous (illustration 28) ? On

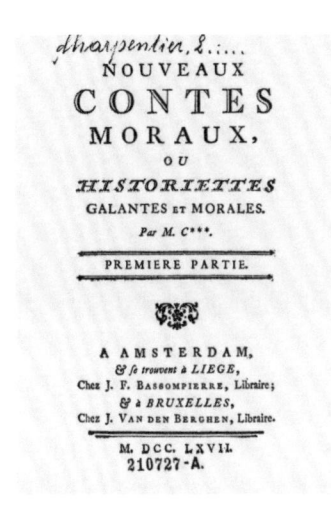

Fig. 26 Vienne, Bibliothèque Nationale d'Autriche

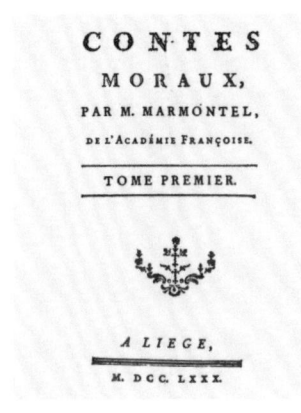

Fig. 27 Oupeye, collection Daniel Droixhe et Alice Piette.

[17] XAVIER DE THEUX DE MONTJARDIN : *Bibliographie liégeoise. Deuxième édition, augmentée.* Nieuwkoop 1973, col. 669.

[18] Cité dans DANIEL DROIXHE : À la recherche du *Candide* liégeois. In : *Australian Journal of French Studies*. 37/2 (2000), pp. 127–164 (disponible sur on www.hdl.handle.net, [20.1.2023]).

Fig. 28a Type 2, p. 20. Édition originale

Fig. 28b Type 4, p. 20. Prague, Bibliothèque Nationale de la République Tchèque, 12 k 788

voudra bien remarquer l'inversion des caractères qui se trouvent en-dessous du carré central, provoquant une rupture de symétrie, ainsi que le retournement du caractère qui constitue l'angle inférieur droit du carré.

De telles variations sont-elles imputables à l'ouvrier qui a composé le type 4, chargé de suivre « au plus près » le modèle, ou au responsable de la composition de l'original, habitué à reproduire mécaniquement le même type d'ornement ? L'interrogation sur la question pourrait être étendue en fonction d'autres informations sur la fabrication de ces éditions (et aussi à partir d'autres enquêtes plus précises sur les éditions de *Bélisaire*).[19] La question qui se pose dès lors pourrait être : comment la morphologie ornementale croise-t-elle la généalogie éditoriale dans le domaine des artefacts, comme le croisement s'est opéré dans l'histoire des sciences ? Comme la paléontologie, la textologie ne met-elle pas en jeu des relations entre des séries d'objets de comparaison et l'étude de leur origine et de leurs changements dans le temps, par des reconstructions progressives ? Est-ce trop demander à la recherche sur les textes que de réclamer, plus souvent qu'il n'est fait, ce fastidieux travail de reconstruction, ne serait-ce que pour véritablement éclairer leur diffusion, leur consommation et leurs effets sur l'histoire des idées ?

19 On n'ignore pas que Claudette Fortuny fait état d'une « contrefaçon lyonnaise de la première édition 'Paris, Merlin 1767' reproduisant l'approbation délivrée à Paris le 20 novembre 1766, et le privilège accordé à Joseph Merlin », « documentée dans la base Maguelonne » (CLAUDETTE FORTUNY : Les éditions lyonnaises de l'*Histoire des deux Indes* de l'abbé Raynal. In : *Histoire et civilisation du livre*. 2 (2006), pp. 169–188, ici p. 174). La base Maguelonne fournit la reproduction de la p. de titre de l'édition en question, qui est datée de 1765 ; mais la référence fournit l'indication « 1767 ? » – http://maguelone.enssib.fr/AddTome.php?NoticeTome=147&NoticeEdition=62&OpusEdition=mar-bel-67&AdresseEdition=A%20Paris,%20chez%20Merlin [20.1.2023]. L'édition est attribuée à la famille Vialon (avec lien vers celle-ci). La reproduction proposée ne permet malheureusement pas d'identifier avec certitude l'édition : l'édition de R. Granderoute n'est pas référencée. Pour une autre approche des ornements typographiques, à propos d'une contrefaçon liégeoise postérieure du *Bélisaire*, voir DANIEL DROIXHE : L'édition lyonnaise de la fausse édition Bassompierre du 'Bélisaire' de Marmontel (1777). In : *Histoire et civilisation du livre*. 13 (2017), p. 143–151 (disponible sur www.hdl.handle.net, [20.1.2023]).

Jade Samara Piaia and Priscila Lena Farias

Movable metal type trade between Germany and Brazil at the turn of the 19th to the 20th century

This article focuses on the effects that the tradition of book printing and the German letterpress printing processes had on São Paulo print culture through the German immigrants Heinrich and Theodor Hennies. These two men, who settled in São Paulo, maintained a letterpress print shop for generations, importing machines and graphic supplies, such as ink and paper, but mainly lead types, ornaments and vignettes used in a variety of printed artifacts. By doing so, they actively contributed to the circulation of typographic trends, not only among Brazilians and German immigrants but also among other immigrant communities. The relationship between the typefaces used by the Hennies Brothers Letterpress Printing Shop and those produced by major German type foundries active at the turn of the 19th to the 20th century is investigated in the following, evidencing a strong connection and a quick spread of German type taste in Brazil.

It is well known that movable type cast in Germany at the turn of the 19th to the 20th century reached overseas borders. German immigrants who arrived in South American ports brought with them their peculiar approach to printing with movable type traditions. Brazil has a short typographic history, more related to printing than to type manufacture, starting with the first letterpress printing shop established in Rio de Janeiro in 1808. Printing with movable type in São Paulo started only in 1827[1]. Germans, by contrast, have been trendsetters in typography since the days of Gutenberg. Type foundries such as Bauer, Berthold, Ludwig und Meyer, Schelter & Giesecke, Stempel and Klingspor employed important type designers in the 20th century[2]. There was, however, until now, no systematic survey on the typefaces produced by German type foundries that actually reached Brazil at the turn of the 19th to the 20th century.

The Hennies Brothers Letterpress Printing Shop

Typographia Hennies Irmãos – or Hennies Brothers Letterpress Printing Shop – was a printing shop established in São Paulo by German immigrants in 1891. The brothers Heinrich and Theodor Hennies were proud of bringing materials and technical knowledge of printing to São Paulo[3]. Their contribution was particularly important given Germany's long typographical tradition and the influence that German printers and founders had on local printing culture. The company was active for

[1] PRISCILA LENA FARIAS; DANIELA KUTSCHAT HANNS; ISABELLA ARAGÃO; CATHERINE R DIXON: Designing the early history of typography in Brazil, starting from printing in São Paulo. In: ICDHS 10th+1, Barcelona. Back to the Future. The Future in the Past. Conference Proceedings Book. Barcelona 2018, p. 493–498.

[2] CEES DE JONG; ALSTON W. PURVIS; JAN THOLENAAR: Type. A Visual History of Typefaces and Graphic Styles. Vol. 1. Köln 2009.

[3] They advertised their services in various newspapers, including those published in German, such as the newspaper Echo Paulistaner 3 (1894), No. 6, p. 4. Source: São Paulo State Public Archive (APESP).

a century, producing printed artifacts aimed at the most varied sectors of society and immigrant communities living in São Paulo.

The company, as announced over the years, offered letterpress, lithographic and stereographic printing, blank books, book binding and paper ruling services. It also sold graphic equipment and supplies (paper, ink and other articles for letterpress and lithographic printers), most of them imported (possibly from Germany). They also announced, in the beginning of the 20th century, being able to manufacture embossed fantasy cards.

In the light of this, the leading hypothesis that guided the investigation reported here was that a considerable part of the Hennies Brothers' typographic repertoire, and in particular the typefaces acquired up to the mid-1930s,[4] would be of German origin. Aiming at an accurate understanding of the foundry types that circulated in São Paulo at the turn of the 19th to the 20th century, the research undertook efforts to bring to light the Hennies Brothers letterpress printing shop typographic repertoire, and to identify its origins.

Research started with the collection of visual data[5] involving books, reports, pamphlets and periodicals – newspapers, magazines and annual reports – published by the Hennies Brothers letterpress printing shop. These artifacts were aimed not as much as at a Brazilian audience, but mainly at immigrant communities and speakers of German, Italian, French, Latvian, and Arabic, as well as Portuguese emigres living in and around São Paulo. From these artifacts,[6] it was possible to extract a representative sample of the typefaces used by the Hennies Brothers over a hundred years of printing activities.

This long period of activity, along with the large number of printed matter published, provides an interesting case to understand how commercial relationships between European type foundries and Latin American printers took place at the turn of the 19th to the 20th century.

Typographic repertoire

By *typographic repertoire* we understand the collection of typesetting materials available to a particular printer or a specific group of printers, including typefaces, ornaments and vignettes. What were the first typefaces that circulated in São Paulo? The original research initiative, of which the investigation reported here is part, aims at a better understanding of São Paulo city identity from a systematic examination of the visual characteristics of the printed artifacts that circulated within it, leading to a comprehensive typographic repertoire of São Paulo letterpress printers. Typefaces used by printers operating in the city between 1827 and 1927 – the first 100 years of printing with movable type in São Paulo – have been researched and cataloged in a digital platform, Tipografia Paulistana[7]. Since 2017, with the help of this platform, typographic repertoires used by São Paulo city letterpress printing shops have been recreated by extracting images of typographic elements from printed

4 This hypothesis was based on the testimonies of the last owner, Mr. Waldemar Hennies. JADE SAMARA PIAIA: *Sr. Waldemar Hennies em 20/11/2018, domingo à tarde. Interview*. Campinas / São Paulo 2018. Unpublished transcript. JADE SAMARA PIAIA: *Sr. Waldemar Hennies em 20/02/2020, sábado à tarde. Interview*. Campinas / São Paulo 2020. Unpublished transcript. In the same testimonies Mr. Waldemar Hennies stated that around and after 1940 they would purchase typefaces from Funtimod, a type foundry established in São Paulo, with branches in other Brazilian capitals, and also run by German emigres.
ISABELLA ARAGÃO: *Tipos móveis de metal da Funtimod: contribuições para a história tipográfica brasileira*. Tese de Doutorado. São Paulo 2016.

5 Over 560 artifacts printed by the Hennies, found in collections in Brazil – in São Paulo and Rio de Janeiro – and abroad, including Portugal, Latvia and Germany, were identified and cataloged.

6 Physically consulted, photographed or digitized.

7 This platform shows the location of these printers and their graphic suppliers, as well as information on the people involved with these companies. FARIAS et al (see note 1). This includes information like the addresses of printers and suppliers, and notes on the people who worked there. The platform can be consulted here: www.fau.usp.br/tipografiapaulistana

artifacts, and organizing those images in typefaces, separating different body sizes. The main source for the Hennies Brothers typographic repertoire[8] was the type specimen book *Specimen de Typos e Vinhetas, etc*[9], which was then supplemented with type samples gathered from other printed artifacts. The typographic repertoire includes samples of typefaces used in titles and subtitles of books and periodicals, advertisements published in almanacs, magazines and newspapers, capturing the graphic style of the publications[10].

Investigating typefaces and type foundries

Visual comparison, putting type samples side by side to type specimens, was enough to establish notable and obvious differences, but some typefaces proved to be very similar in almost all visual characteristics, differing only in a few aspects. A more detailed comparison using samples of characters from the Hennies Brothers' repertoire, reproduced on reticled photolite[11] and then superimposed on pages of German foundries type specimens,[12] revealed subtle differences in faces that seemed

---

[8] The Hennies Brothers typographic repertoire hosted in Tipografia Paulistana platform can be consulted here: www.fau.usp.br/tipografiapaulistana/empresa/93.

[9] HENNIES & CIA (Ed.): *Specimen de tipos, vinhetas, etc.* São Paulo: Tipografia, Encadernação, Pautação, Hennies & Cia. Collection: Hennies Family.

[10] Samples of words or phrases composed with movable type were extracted from the printed matter dating from the first twenty years of the Hennies Brothers' activity, 1891–1911. These have been also organized into a database hosted on the AirTable platform, called *Typeface Hennies Brothers, 1891–1911* url: airtable.com/shrQoy6P-ZJ2MRg3Nq. An important reference for methodological procedures was Dan Reynolds' PhD thesis. DAN REYNOLDS: *Schriftkünstler. A historiographic examination of the relationship between handcraft and art regarding the design and making of printers' type in Germany between 1871 and 1914*. PhD Thesis. Braunschweig 2019. One of the goals for organizing visual data on AirTable was to share information with other researchers who could help in identifying typefaces, point to type specimens where those typefaces could be found, and to archives and libraries that would hold such specimens, among other possibilities. Type samples were treated following specific protocols, described in PRISCILA LENA FARIAS: Tipografia Paulistana: a research protocol. In: *4th. Lab Visual Research Journey: methodological procedures*. Ed. by: GUSTAVO FUDABA CURCIO, JADE SAMARA PIAIA and ANAMARIA AMARAL REZENDE. São Paulo 2022, pp. 48–54.

[11] During the research developed in Brazil, typefaces collected from artifacts printed by the Hennies Brothers were digitally compared by overlaying them to images extracted from type specimens, using Adobe Photoshop. Similar procedures have been adopted by Olocco, see RICCARDO OLOCCO: *A new method of analysing printed type: the case of 15th-century Venetian romans*. Reading 2019. RICCARDO OLOCCO: Venice in the early 1470s: the inception of Roman type and some odd alternatives. In: *Gotico-Antiqua, Proto-Roman, Hybrid. 15th century types between Gothic and Roman*. Nancy / Frankfurt am Main 2021, pp. 43–76 and ARAGÃO (see note 4). The Hennies Brothers repertoire was compared with samples from a H. Berthold type specimen belonging to the Hennies family private collection. H. BERTHOLD. MESSINGLINIENFABRIK UND SCHRIFTGIESSEREI A.G. SCHRIFTEN UND ORNAMENTE: *Messing-Universalblatt und Vignetten. Spezial-Kataloge: Über messing-erzeugnisse, sowie russische, griechische und orientalische schriften stehen interessenten zu diensten*. Berlin. Collection: Hennies Family. The analysis revealed a strong connection between the Hennies Brothers repertoire and that of H. Berthold type foundry: 29 typefaces used by the Hennies Brothers were also present in the H. Berthold specimen consulted, see JADE SAMARA PIAIA and PRISCILA LENA FARIAS: Identificando a origem de fontes tipográficas a partir de um catálogo de tipos: o repertório do Specimen de Tipos da Tipografia Hennies Irmãos / Identifying the origin of typefaces from a typographic catalogue: the repertoire of the Hennies Brothers letterpress printing shop Type Specimen. In: *Estudos em Design* 29 (2021), n. 2, pp. 6–26. DOI: 10.35522/eed.v29i2.1207. For the research developed in Germany, the methodological procedures were adapted and a compilation of visual references of typefaces from the Hennies Brothers' repertoire was prepared. Samples were organized by typeface and size, and then printed on 27 A4 size transparent single sheets of photolite, with 55% of black (dots reticle), containing 132 typefaces in different sizes. This material allowed for an immediate comparison between samples from the Hennies Brothers' typographic repertoire and typefaces featured on type specimens books issued by German type foundries, speeding up archival research.

[12] The research was conducted in the Gutenberg Museum Library in Mainz, the Deutsches Buch- und Schriftmuseum at the Deutsche Nationalbibliothek in Leipzig, the Museum für Druckkunst in Leipzig, the Deutsches Technikmuseum in Berlin and the Klingspor Museum in Offenbach am Main. All documents regarding the German type foundries were examined. These documents were mainly type specimen books, catalogs, and boxes with typefaces booklets and leaflets that record the products marketed by these companies.

Fig. 1 Detail of some unsuccessful comparisons. Photos by Jade Piaia.

identical to the naked eye [figure 1]. Comparison criteria were established as there was a need to interpret those visual differences.

Some visual differences, such as those in size, subtle differences in thickness and absence of serif parts were defined as contestable. Other differences, such as the presence and shape of connections and terminals, the position of bars, rotation and contrast were defined as incontestable. Design differences were recognized as a way of slightly differentiating a set of characters produced by a particular foundry from others, a recurrent practice in the 19th and early 20th century. This could occur as a consequence of copying type designs with a pantograph, a tool that relies on manual control, making it possible to follow up an existing drawing or making modifications on it. Copying whole sets of type through electroplating was another technique that could be employed by someone in possession of a set of lead types. Differences in single characters may be a consequence of missing originals to be copied while subtle differences in the whole set may still be a consequence of enlargement or reduction from originals in different sizes. Therefore, copying processes can reflect differences such as those observed, in width or height, in design connections, terminals, bars position, rotation and contrast in line thickness of characters, as some examples in figure 1 show. Observing criteria for contestable and incontestable visual differences was fundamental in the process of identifying typefaces[13], narrowing down the huge range of possibilities and determining which foundries supplied types to the Hennies Brothers.

Once results were interpreted, it was possible to establish a list of type foundries that supplied types to the Hennies Brothers: H. Berthold, Berlin; J. G. Schelter & Giesecke, Leipzig; D. Stempel A.G., Frankfurt am Main; Schriftgiesserei Emil Gursch, Berlin; Schriftguß A.G. vorm. Brüder Butter, Dresden; Genzsch & Heyse and E.J. Genzsch GmbH, Hamburg and Munich; Haas'sche Gießerei, Basel, Switzerland; Wilhelm Wöllmer, Berlin; Ludwig & Mayer, Frankfurt am Main; Julius Klinkhardt, Leipzig; and J.H. Rust & Co., Vienna, Austria. The connection between the Hennies Brothers and the first five type foundries was clearly established: they were either the only producers of some of the typefaces found in the Hennies' repertoire, had exclusive typefaces with original design protected by law, produced typefaces identified by the exact same name by Hennies in their specimen, or were the producers of a large group of typefaces identified as part of the printers' repertoire. H. Berthold should be highlighted in this context, once 45% of the typefaces identified in the Hennies Brothers' repertoire were produced by this type foundry. Evidence gathered is enough to establish that the foundries listed above provided type to the Hennies, but it is not possible to state that they were the only connections of the Hennies in Germany or German speaking countries[14].

Other type foundries that may have provided typefaces to the Hennies are A.G. / Aktiengesellschaft für Schriftgießerei und Maschinenbau, Offenbach am Main; Ferd. Theinhardt, Berlin; Bauer & Co., Stuttgart and Düsseldorf; Emil Berger, Leipzig; and Gustav Reinhold, Berlin[15]. As

---

13 The results were organized in a spreadsheet with samples of 134 typefaces of which 113 were prioritized for research. 76 of those were identified as belonging to the repertoire of some German type foundry, a positive result that covers 67% of the corpus.

14 The list includes one type foundry from Vienna, Austria, and another one from Basel, Switzerland.

15 The last four type foundries listed were incorporated into H. Berthold, according to FRIEDRICH BAUER, HANS REICHARDT: *Chronik der Schriftgießereien in Deutschland und den deutschsprachigen Nachbarländern*. Frankfurt am Main 2011. URL: www.klingspor-museum.de/Chronik-Schriftgiessereien.html. Ferd. Theinhardt was acquired in 1908, pp. 25–7; Bauer & Co. in 1897, p. 27; Emil Berger was acquired by Gustav Reinhold in 1890 and then Gustav Reinhold's foundry was incorporated into H. Berthold in 1893, p 26.

Fig. 2 (Above left) Propaganda, 1892, J.G. Schelter & Giesecke, Leipzig. In: P. MELLO: *Lampejos*. Facesheet (detail), 1896. Source: Paulista Museum, Itu, São Paulo University (MP-USP).

Fig. 3 (Above right) Zierschrift Asträa, 1894, J.G. Schelter & Giesecke, Leipzig. In: *Revista do Grêmio dos Guarda Livros*, 1896, n. 5, p. 1 (detail). Source: National Library, Hemeroteca Digital Brasileira (BN-HDB).

the research has shown, a large number of typefaces circulated in Germany and elsewhere, in the turn of the 19th to 20th century, as part of the repertoire of numerous type foundries, pointing to multiple possible suppliers.

The identification of type foundries based in Germany or in other European countries that supplied types to the Hennies Brothers was then combined with temporal references: date of launch of the typefaces and the first use of the same typefaces in artifacts issued by those printers in Brazil. Distance or proximity between dates of launch and use were interpreted as in terms of the capacity and will of the Hennies Brothers to keep up-to-date with European trends. The case study of four display typefaces can exemplify how fast European trends reached Latin America.

The typeface Propaganda [figure 2] was launched by J. G. Schelter & Giesecke in 1892[16] – and designed in house. It was incorporated in the Hennies Brothers typographic repertoire and used in almost all artifacts printed from 1896. The scriptural and high-impact features of Propaganda found their way to titles and subtitles of books, newspapers and advertisements. Zierschrift Asträa [figure 3], launched in 1894[17] by J. G. Schelter & Giesecke – also designed in house –, was incorporated in the Hennies Brothers typographic repertoire two years later[18]. It is fair to assume that it was bought along, in the same shipment, as Propaganda. The ornamental lettering design provided by Zierschrift Asträa, quickly became a trend in advertisements published in periodicals, attracting attention to the advertiser's name.

Halbfette Künstler-Schrift and Magere Künstler-Schrift [figure 4] designed by F. Schweimanns, for D. Stempel A.G. and launched, respectively, in 1901 and 1902[19], were the Hennies Brothers' typeface choice for composing titles and advertisements in German language publications from 1906 at least until the 1940s. Künstler-Schrift was an original product of D. Stempel A.G., protected by law. As a representative of German early twentieth-century hybrid typefaces[20], it is an alternative design to German blackletter. The design mixes antiqua and fraktur typeface features, reflecting a new style with Jugendstil brush-drawn visual organic design flavor. Künstler-Schrift is somehow similar to other typefaces from the same period, such as Eckmann-Schrift by Otto Eckmann (1900) and Behrens-Schrift by Peter Behrens (c. 1902), both designed for Rudhard type foundry, later incorporated by Klingspor in Offenbach am Main.

---

16 EMIL WETZIG: *Handbuch der Schriftarten*. Leipzig 1926. URL: www.klingspor-museum.de/Handbuch-der-Schriftarten.html, p. 233.

17 WETZIG (see note 16), p. 171.

18 *Revista do Grêmio dos Guarda Livros*, 1(1896) n. 5.

19 WETZIG (see note 16), p. 68.

20 CHRISTOPHER BURKE: German hybrid typefaces 1900–14. In:*Gotico-Antiqua, Proto-Roman, Hybrid. 15th century types between Gothic and Roman*. Nancy / Frankfurt am Main 2021, pp. 161–74.

Fig. 4 (Above left) The typefaces Halbfette Künstler-Schrift, 1901, and Magere Künstler-Schrift, 1902, D. Stempel A.G., Frankfurt am Main. In: A. KUHLMANN: *Brasilianische Skizzen*, 1906 (cover detail). Source: Martius Staden Institute (IMS).

Fig. 5 (Above right) The typeface Schäffer Versalien, 1927, Schriftguss A.G. vorm. Brüder Butter, Dresden. In: A. ELLIS JUNIOR: *Pedras lascadas*, 1928 (cover detail). Source: Institute of Brazilian Studies, São Paulo University (IEB-USP).

The fastest connection between the launching of a typeface in Germany and its incorporation in the Hennies Brothers' repertoire is exemplified by Schäffer Versalien [figure 5]. This typeface, designed by Karl Hermann Schaefer[21] and launched in 1927, is a stripped modular typeface for two color printing. The composition can be adjusted to different widths by adding modular stripped spaces between the letters. The typeface design has modular geometric finishes and thick lines, appropriate for titles. It is described by the type foundry Schriftguss A.G. vorm. Brüder Butter as an original product and the company has K.H. Schaefer's design protected by law. The Schriftguss A.G. vorm. Brüder Butter produced an exclusive type specimen for this typeface (in booklet format) with different demonstrative compositions. The Hennies Brothers applied Schäffer Versalien to create a visual impact, as a block with green and yellow, in the cover of *Pedras Lascadas*, a book printed in 1928.

The shipment of metal type addressed to the Hennies was reported by Brazilian newspapers[22]. At the turn of the 19th to the 20th century orders must have been sent by mail to type foundries, who would then produce and ship to Brazil. The connection between the port of Santos and the city of São Paulo was made by freight trains. For this reason, it is possible to conclude that the Hennies Brothers were up to date with European, and especially with German, visual trends in typography.

21 HANS REICHARDT; OTMAR HOEFER (Ed.): Karl Hermann Schaefer. In: *Archiv der internationalen Schriftdesigner / International Type Designer Archive*. URL: www.klingspor-museum.de/KlingsporKuenstler/Schriftdesigner/Schaefer/KHSchaefer.pdf.

22 There are records of arrivals of boxes addressed to Hennies, which came from the port of Hamburg in 1910. O Estado de S. Paulo: São Paulo, N.11509, 17/06/1910, p. 9, and O Estado de S. Paulo: São Paulo, N.11600, 16/09/1910, p. 9. URL: https://acervo.estadao.com.br.

Final considerations

Aimed at contributing to broadening the understanding of movable metal type trade and trends between Germany and Brazil in the turn to the 19th to the 20th century, the research reported here brought to light the case of the Hennies Brothers letterpress printing shop, and the connection between those printers, established in São Paulo, and type foundries established in Germany and other German speaking countries. At a time when the printing industry in São Paulo was consolidating, during the city's first centenary of printing with moveable type, the contribution of immigrants was fundamental, in terms of graphic techniques and technologies, influencing the visual characteristics of local publications. As the results of research have shown, typographic novelties were quickly arriving in South American ports, updating Brazilian print culture and aligning it with German typographic trends. The Hennies Brothers contributed to spreading in Brazil a certain German type taste, with special appreciation for types produced by H. Berthold. Those printers were connected to Europe novelties and constantly updating their repertoire. This research opens perspectives for future research involving graphic supplies trade between Brazil and Germany, and between Latin America and European countries in general, aiming at a better understanding of graphic traditions, print culture and early graphic design exchanges.

Acknowledgements

Thanks go to Dan Reynolds and Stephen Coles for their suggestions regarding typeface names, possible type founders, and other relevant information. This research was supported by FAPESP postdoc grants no. 2019/07566-6 and 2021/10507-1, as well as a CNPq Productivity in Research grant no. 304361/2019-4.

Falk Eisermann

Neue Publikationen zur Inkunabelforschung: das Jahr 2022. Mit Nachträgen zu den Jahren 2020 und 2021

The article provides a hand-list of scholarly articles and books published in 2022 that are related to incunabula, including supplements to the list for 2020 and 2021. It forms the third installment of a continuing bibliography (see GJ 96 [2021], pp. 269–96).

Auch im Inkunabeljahr 2022, dessen wissenschaftlicher Ertrag hiermit dokumentiert wird, erlebten wir erneut einen Strom von Publikationen zu den beiden Jubilaren des Vorjahres, Sebastian Brant und Dante Alighieri, wobei hier noch diverse schon 2020/21 erschienene Titel nachzutragen sind. Während Brant und Dante überwiegend von deutschen bzw. italienischen Forscher:innen bearbeitet wurden, zeigt das Gesamtbild erneut eine breite internationale und interdisziplinäre Teilhabe an der Erforschung der Wiegendrucke. Unter den mehr als 300 verschiedenen Titeln findet sich auch ein gleichbleibend hoher, jedoch noch ausbaufähiger Anteil von Open Access-Publikationen. Erfreulicherweise sind wieder mehrere substantielle Dissertationen erschienen bzw. fertiggestellt worden (DÍAZ-BURILLO, SCHWEITZER-MARTIN, SCHWITTER, VACALEBRE), auch philologische Monographien und Editionen fehlen nicht (z. B. BERTELSMEIER-KIERST, 'Melusine'; *William Touris OFM*, hrsg. MACDONALD/MCDONALD). Die europaweiten Erschließungsarbeiten haben sich in zahlreichen gedruckten Katalogen niedergeschlagen, etwa in zwei neuen Bänden der produktiven italienischen Reihe ‚Incunaboli' (BELLAVIA u. a.; ERRANI u. a.). Aus der italienischen Inkunabelforschung kam des weiteren ein origineller Beitrag zum Thema Katalogpublikation mit Hilfe von Crowdfunding (INSERRA). Aus deutscher Sicht hervorzuheben sind der lang erwartete, kapitale Band zu den Wiegendrucken des Koblenzer Görres-Gymnasiums (*Inkunabeln ...* von MECKELNBORG/HANISCH) sowie das Verzeichnis der Inkunabeln der Anhaltischen Landesbücherei Dessau (NICKEL/KREISSLER). Bemerkenswert bleibt nach wie vor der hohe Ausstoß von Aufsätzen und Monographien aus Spanien, gekrönt von dem Jubiläumskatalog zur Ausstellung *Incunabula: 550 años de la imprenta en España* (REYES GÓMEZ). In einem anderen Beitrag liest man vom erstaunlichen Fund einer ‚Restauflage' von rund 450 gedruckten Ablassbrief-Formularen im Archiv der Kathedrale von Lérida (RIUS I BOU und REYES GÓMEZ).

In die Liste eingerückt sind auch Kuriositäten wie der Kriminalroman *Tod in der Schöfferstadt* (SELZER), der gewiss in den Mainzer und Frankfurter Buchhandlungen reißenden Absatz findet, sowie „die in kräftigen Sechshebern poetisch daherschreitende (Kurz-)Geschichte" *Ypsilon träumt* (CARL). Ein eher seltsames Zeugnis der Gutenberg-Rezeption präsentiert der Beitrag von HAIR.

Bei der Recherche fiel immer wieder der uneigentliche, übertragene und beim Bibliographieren eher störende Gebrauch der Begriffe „Inkunabel"/"incunabula" auf – bekannt aus Kunsthändlerphrasen wie „Inkunabel der Lithographie". Ein aktuelles Beispiel lieferte im vergangenen Jahr in dieser Hinsicht MATTHEW HALEY, Managing Director des Auktionshauses Bonhams. Seinen Beitrag 'The New Incunabula' (*Book Collector* 71,1 [2022], S. 90–93) nimmt man gespannt zur Hand, um sodann festzustellen, dass er über das neuerdings angesagte Sammeln von *born digital*-Artefakten bzw. NFTs ('non-fungible tokens') handelt; genannt werden z.B. der erste Tweet des Twitter-Gründers Jack Dorsey und der Original-Quellcode des World Wide Web, den der Internet-Erfinder Tim Berners-Lee für 5,4 Millionen Dollar bei Sotheby's versteigern ließ. HALEY dazu: "If NFTs are the new incunabula, then Berners-Lee's internet code was the Gutenberg Bible" (S. 92). Mit Genugtuung stellt der Inkunabelkundige fest, dass auch derlei als revolutionäre Innovationen gefeierte, indes nun zu merkantil verwertbaren Artefakten gewordene digitale Sammlerstücke offenbar nur unter Heranziehung von Vergleichen mit der Welt des frühesten Buchdrucks in ihrer relativen Wertigkeit angemessen zu beschreiben sind.

In die vorliegende Liste geschafft hat es HALEYs Titel aber nicht. Wie bisher werden auch kostenpflichtige Online-Publikationen, Antiquariats- und Auktionskataloge, Blogbeiträge, vereinzelte Exponatbeschreibungen in Ausstellungskatalogen, Gelegenheitsschriften, Miszellen, Reprints und Rezensionen ebenso wie nur beiläufige Erwähnungen inkunabelrelevanter Sachverhalte in thematisch anders gewichteten Publikationen nur ausnahmsweise aufgenommen. Nicht alle Titel konnten selbst eingesehen und ausgewertet werden, manche Titelaufnahmen beruhen lediglich auf Informationen aus Online-Ressourcen oder anderen bibliographischen Quellen.

Wo dies wünschenswert oder notwendig erschien, sind die Titel mit kurzen inhaltlichen Hinweisen versehen. Dabei sind als Referenz zumeist die Werkkatalog-Namen des GW, die GW-Kürzel für Inkunabelsammlungen oder die GW-Nummern angegeben, auf die sich die jeweiligen Beiträge beziehen.

ABAD, JULIÁN MARTÍN: Los fondos de carácter bibliofílico en las colecciones de incunables en España. In: *La palabra escrita e impresa. Libros, bibliotecas, coleccionistas y lectores en el mundo hispano y novohispano. In memoriam Víctor Infantes & Giuseppe Mazzocchi*. Hrsg. v. JUAN-CARLOS CONDE und CLIVE GRIFFIN. (Spanish Series. Hispanic Seminary of Medieval Studies. 172.). New York, Oxford 2020, S. 195–221.

Abriendo historias: perspectivas de estudio sobre el grabado del siglo XV. Hrsg. v. HELENA CARVAJAL GONZÁLEZ. Zaragoza 2022. Aus dem Inhalt:
- HELENA CARVAJAL GONZÁLEZ: El repertorio iconográfico del grabado medieval hispano: objetivos y retos (S. 9–24)
- JOSÉ LUIS GONZALO SÁNCHEZ-MOLERO: Xilografía y xilominiatura en la Europa medieval (S. 25–81)
- FERMÍN DE LOS REYES GÓMEZ: La imprenta incunable y el grabado en España (S. 83–101)
- MANUEL JOSÉ PEDRAZA GRACIA: La imagen en la imprenta incunable y postincunable zaragozana: aproximación a las características tecnicas de su incorporación al impreso (S. 103–21)
- MARÍA SANZ JULIÁN: El Repertorio de los tiempos de Andrés de Li: las ediciones zaragozanas y sus antecedentes alemanes (S. 135–49; zu GW M18082 und M18084)
- Matrices xilográficas al servicio de la estampa suelte (Mallorca, siglos XV y XVI) (S. 151–73)

AHERN, JOHN: The Naples *L'homme armé* Masses: A New Connection. In: *Journal of the Alamire Foundation* 14 (2022), S. 32–53. DOI: 10.1484/J.JAF.5.128983. Zur Provenienz des Exemplars London BL C.3.d.2 = IC.19694 von GW M34342.

ALEXANDROWICZ, PIOTR: The History and Normative Significance of *summaria* in the *Liber extra*. In: *Tijdschrift voor Rechtsgeschiedenis* 90 (2022), S. 148–76. U. a. zu GW 11479.

allmächtig und unfassbar. Geld in der Literatur des Mittelalters. Hrsg. v. NATHANAEL BUSCH und ROBERT FAJEN. Stuttgart 2021. (Relectiones. 9.). Darin u. a.: Hans Folz: Jüdischer Wucher. Edition: HANNS FISCHER. Übersetzung und Kommentar: NATHANAEL BUSCH (zu GW 10149–10151, ‚Die Rechnung Ruprecht Kolpergers'; S. 238–47, 352). Kaiser Karls Recht. Edition, Übersetzung und Kommentar: NATHANAEL BUSCH (zu GW M22696 und M22697; S. 248–57, 353).

ANDERSEN, ELIZABETH; WIECHMANN, MAI-BRITT: Birgittaverehrung in (Nord-)Deutschland. Von der Pilgerin zum Pilgerziel. In: *Pilgern zu Wasser und zu Lande*. Hrsg. v. HARTMUT KÜHNE und CHRISTIAN POPP. (Jakobus-Studien. 24.). Tübingen 2022, S. 265–302. Zum GW-Werkkatalog ‚Birgitta'.

ANDERSEN, PETER HVILSHØJ: Der Erstdruck des Narrenschiffs (Basel 1494) zwischen mittelalterlicher und neuzeitlicher Interpunktionspraxis. In: *Textkohärenz und Gesamtsatzstrukturen in der Geschichte der deutschen und französischen Sprache vom 8. bis zum 18. Jahrhundert. Akten zum Internationalen Kongress an der Universität Paris-Sorbonne vom 15. bis 17. November 2018*. Hrsg. v. DELPHINE PASQUES und CLAUDIA WICH-REIF. (Berliner sprachwissenschaftliche Studien. 35.). Berlin 2020, S. 359–78. Zu GW 5041.

BACKES, MARIA: hye merck waß zyt vnd monat im ior ein ieglicher visch am besten sig. Eine linguistische Analyse des Trierer Fischblattes (Einblattdruck, um 1493). In: *Kurtrierisches Jahrbuch* 60 (2020), S. 47–72. Zu GW 0567920N.

BALDACCHINI, LORENZO: La stampa e la "riproducibilità tecnica". In: *Il Cardinal Bessarione Abate a Casteldurante e Federico da Montefeltro*. Hrsg. v. MARCO MENATO und FELICIANA PAOLI. Urbino 2022, S. 67–75.

BAÑOS, PEDRO MARTÍN: *Nueva caracola del bibliófilo nebrisense. Repertorio bibliográfico de la obra impresa y manuscrita de Antonio de Nebrija (siglos XV–XVI)*. (Antonio de Nebrija V Centenario [1522–2022]. 1.). Salamanca 2022. Zum GW-Werkkatalog ‚Antonius Nebrissensis, Aelius'.

BARALE, ELISABETTA: Les devinettes des *Adevineaux amoureux:* hypothèses généalogiques et stratégies éditoriales. In: *Neophilologus* 106 (2022), S. 363–79. DOI: 10.1007/s11061-022-09725-w. Zum GW-Werkkatalog ‚Adevinaux' (GW 222, 223).

BARBERO, ALESSANDRO: *Inventare i libri. L'avventura di Filippo e Lucantonio Giunti, pionieri dell'editoria moderna*. Florenz 2022.

BARBIERI, EDOARDO: Rare edizioni del Santo Sepolcro di Gerusalemme. In: *La Bibliofilía* 123 (2021), S. 73–86. Zu den GW-Werkkatalogen ‚Peregrinationes' und ‚Processionale'. Mit englischsprachigem Abstract.

BEDWELL, LAURA K.: What *Should* a Knight Do for Ladies? Knightly and Scholarly Ethics and the Different Versions of the *Morte Darthur*. In: *Arthuriana* 32,2 (2022), S. 3–27. Zum GW-Werkkatalog ‚Malory, Thomas' (GW M20157 und M20161).

BELLAVIA, ALBERTO u. a.: *Incunaboli ad Agrigento 1. Biblioteca Lucchesiana e Biblioteca del Seminario Arcivescovile*. (Incunaboli. 7.). Rom 2022. Zu den Sammlungen Agrigento BLucchesi und Agrigento Sem.

BERTELSMEIER-KIERST, CHRISTA: *Thüring von Ringoltingen: ‚Melusine'. Der frühe Bucherfolg im Spiegel der Netzwerke städtischer und höfischer Eliten*. (Zeitschrift für deutsches Altertum und deutsche Literatur. Beihefte. 39.). Stuttgart 2022.

BERTELSMEIER-KIERST, CHRISTA: Die St. Petersburger Handschrift des ‚Ehebüchleins' Albrechts von Eyb. Wechselbeziehungen zwischen Handschrift und Druck im Inkunabelzeitalter. In: *Deutsche Kultur in russischen Buch- und Handschriftenbeständen. Beiträge zur Tagung des deutsch-russischen Arbeitskreises vom 16./17. April 2018 an der Lomonossow-Universität Moskau*. Hrsg. v. NATALIJA GANINA u. a. (Akademie gemeinnütziger Wissenschaften zu Erfurt. Sonderschriften. 52. = Deutsch-russische Forschungen zur Buchgeschichte. 5.). Erfurt 2022, S. 195–210. Zu GW 9520–9528.

BERTOLONI MELI, DOMENICO: Images & Color: The Strasbourg Printer Johann Schott (1477–1548) and his Circle. In: *Early Science and Medicine* 27 (2022), S. 527–71.

BIAGI MAINO, DONATELLA: *Arte e carità. Il complesso storico e museale dei Frati Minori Cappuccini di Bologna*. Bologna 2022. Zur Sammlung Bologna Kapuz (mit Katalog der Inkunabeln).

Biblija Gutenberga. Knigi Novogo vremeni. Katalog vystavki (The Gutenberg Bible. Early Modern Books. Exhibition Catalogue). Mitarb. TAT'JANA A. DOLGODROVA, G. V. DOROFEEVA und und SVETLANA V. MURAŠKINA. Ausstellungskatalog Staatliches Museum Hermitage, St. Petersburg, 8. Dezember 2021–13. März 2022. St. Petersburg 2021.

La biblioteca di Leonardo. Hrsg. v. CARLO VECCE. Florenz 2021.

BOHNERT, CÉLINE: La figure d'Adonis dans l'*Ovide moralisé* (XIVe siècle), la *Methamorphose* (1484) et le *Grand Olympe des histoires poëtiques* (1532). In: *Réécritures et adaptations de l'Ovide moralisé (XIVe–XVIIe siècle)*. Hrsg. v. CATHERINE GAULLIER-BOUGASSAS und MARYLÈNE POSSAMAI-PÉREZ. (Recherches sur le Réception de l'Antiquité. 3.). Turnhout 2022, S. 235–50. U. a. zu GW M28937.

BOLDAN, KAMIL: Lamentatio Nigropontis: An Unknown Print of Sixtus Riessinger, a Prototypographer of Naples. In: *Acta Musei nationalis Pragae. Historia litterarum* 67,1/2 (2022), S. 5–12. Zu GW M2711250.

BROMBERG, SARAH E.: The Position of Jewish Art and Exegesis in an Illustrated Christian Biblical Commentary: Ezekiel's Vision of the Tetramorph in Fourteenth-and Fifteenth-Century Manuscripts and Printed Copies of Nicholas of Lyra's *Postilla litteralis*. In: *Manuscript Studies* 7 (2022), S. 293–334.

BUSCA, MAURIZIO: 'La noix à casser': la place de l'allégorie dans les préfaces des traductions des *Métamorphoses* (1484–1697). In: *Réécritures et adaptations de l'Ovide moralisé (XIVe–XVIIe siècle)*. Hrsg. v. CATHERINE GAULLIER-BOUGASSAS UND MARYLÈNE POSSAMAI-PÉREZ. (Recherches sur le Réception de l'Antiquité. 3.). Turnhout 2022, S. 283–297.

CAPARRINI, MARIALUISA: A scuola di tedesco nel tardo Medioevo. Edizione critica di due testi didattici del XV secolo. (Ettwas von bůchstaben e Augsburger Fibel – Hannover, Kestner Museum, E(rnst) n. 128) . (Bibliotheca Germanica. 50.). Alessandria 2022. Zum Trägerband des Exemplars Hannover KestnerM von GW 5694.

CARELLO, FEDERICA: L'edizione Valdezoco. Una lettura del codice Vat. lat. 3195 attraverso l'incunabolo patavino. In: *Laureatus in Urbe II*. Hrsg. v. SILVIA ARGURIO und VALENTINA ROVERE. Rom 2020, S. 109–20. Zu GW M31636.

CARL, SIEGFRIED: *Ypsilon träumt. Eine frühneuzeitliche Kurzgeschichte als utopische Vers-Erzählung (aus einer Inkunabel von 1480)*. Norderstedt 2022. „Im ersten Moment erscheint ‚Ypsilon träumt' wie die faksimilierte wissenschaftliche Edition eines Frühdrucks des späten 15. Jahrhunderts, mit einer frühneuzeitlichen Verserzählung aus dem Umfeld Mechthilds von der Pfalz. Erst auf den zweiten Blick zeigt sich die in kräftigen Sechshebern poetisch daherschreitende (Kurz-)Geschichte (...) – als augenzwinkernde Analyse und Gegenüberstellung der Medienrevolutionen einerseits rund um die Erfindung des Buchdrucks vor 500 Jahren und andererseits rund um die Entwicklung von IT, Internet & Co. im ausgehenden 20. Jahrhundert" (Werbetext).

CARREÑO VELÁZQUEZ, ELVIA: De la oscuridad a la luz: los *Scriptores astronomici veteres* de Aldo Manuzio (*From Darkness to Light: Aldus Manutius's 'Scriptores astronomici veteres'*). In: *Titivillus* 8 (2022), S. 27–49. Zu GW 9981.

CARVAJAL GONZÁLEZ, HELENA: Circulación y uso del grabado a fines de la Edad Media en los Reinos Hispanos. In: *Journal of Medieval Iberian Studies* 14 (2022), S. 321–49. Zu spanischen Holzschnitten.

CAVERO DE CARONDELET, CLOE: Wounds on Trial: Forensic Truth, Sanctity, and the Early Modern Visual Culture of Ritual Murder. In: *Sacred Images and Normativity: Contested Forms in Early Modern Art*. Hrsg. v. CHIARA FRANCESCHINI. (Sacrima. 1.). Turnhout 2021, S. 68–85. DOI: 10.1484/M.SACRIMA-EB.5.122580. U. a. zum GW-Werkkatalog ‚Simon'.

CERRITO, STEFANIA: La nymphe Aréthuse dans la *Bible des poëtes* d'Antoine Vérard (Paris, 1493). In: *Réécritures et adaptations de l'Ovide moralisé (XIVe–XVIIe siècle)*. Hrsg. v. CATHERINE GAULLIER-BOUGASSAS und MARYLÈNE POSSAMAI-PÉREZ. (Recherches sur le Réception de l'Antiquité. 3.). Turnhout 2022, S. 211–33. Zu GW M28946.

COCKX-INDESTEGE, ELLY; DELSAERDT, PIERRE: *Le goût de la bibliophilie nationale. La collection de livres rares et précieux des ducs d'Arenberg à Bruxelles, XIX–XXe siècles*. (Bibliologia. 61.). Turnhout 2022. Darin: Liste d'une Collection de Livres (Incunables et livres rares et précieux) appartenant à S.A.S. Monseigneur le Duc d'Arenberg (S. 321–778).

COLDIRON, A. E. B.: William Caxton, Multi-Mediator. In: *Forum for Modern Language Studies* 58 (2022), S. 488–96.

CONTÒ, AGOSTINO: Giovanni Rosso e i suoi fratelli : due nuovi documenti su una famiglia di stampatori a Venezia tra Quattro e Cinquecento. In: *La Bibliofilía* 123 (2021), S. 251–58. Zur Druckwerkstatt Venedig: Bernardinus de Vianis. Mit englischsprachigem Abstract.

COUN, THEO: De Middelnederlandse vertalingen van de *Historia trium regum* van Johannes von Hildesheim. In: *Leuvense Bijdragen* 103 (2021), S. 59–89. U. a. zu GW M14026.

Dante a Novara. Edizioni e personaggi della 'Commedia' tra Sesia e Ticino. Catalogo della Mostra nel 7. Centenario. Hrsg. v. VALENTINA ZANON. (Quaderni del Laboratorio di editoria. 30.). Mailand 2021. Zur Dante-Sammlung in Novara BCiv.

Dante a Porta Sole: Dai manoscritti a Dante pop. Catalogo de mostra bibliografica. Perugia, Biblioteca comunale Augusta, 16 decembre 2020–30 novembre 2021. Hrsg. v. MARGARETHA ALFI, FRANCESCA GRAUSO und PAOLO RENZI. Chiugiana di Corciano 2021 (S. 30–8 zu frühen Drucken der Commedia [bes. GW 7958], S. 39–102 Katalog der Exponate, u. a. drei Inkunabeln).

„…dass die Codices finanziell unproduktiv im Archiv des Stiftes liegen". Bücherverkäufe österreichischer Klöster in der Zwischenkriegszeit. Hrsg. v. CHRISTOPH EGGER und KATHARINA KASKA. (Veröffentlichungen des Instituts für Österreichische Geschichtsforschung. 77.). Wien 2022. Die meisten Beiträge nennen oder streifen auch das Thema Inkunabeln, besonders Inkunabelrelevantes. Aus dem Inhalt:

- ANNELIESE SCHALMEINER: „In den meisten Fällen sind es Handschriften und Inkunabeln, die abgestoßen werden." Die Rolle der Denkmalbehörde bei den Veräußerungen und der Ausfuhr von Handschriften und Büchern aus kirchlichem Besitz in der Zwischenkriegszeit (S. 57–70)
- IRENE RABL: Notverkäufe und versuchte Verkäufe von Kunstgegenständen, Handschriften, Inkunabeln und Büchern des Zisterzienserstiftes Lilienfeld in der Zwischenkriegszeit (S. 133–42)
- FRIEDRICH BUCHMAYR: Die Verkäufe von Inkunabeln aus der Stiftsbibliothek St. Florian (S. 143–60)

DAVERIO ROCCHI, GIOVANNA: *L'editio princeps di Senofonte a Milano.* Alessandria 2022. Zu GW M51849

DAY, MATTHEW: William Caxton and Vernacular Classicism. In: *English Studies* 103 (2022), S. 19–41

DELLA ROCCA DE CANDAL, GERI: Lost in Transition: A Significant Correction in Aldus Manutius's *Psalterion* (1496/98). In: *The Library* 7,23 (2022), S. 155–79. Zu GW M36248

DELLE LUCHE, JEAN-DOMINIQUE: *Des amitiés ciblées. Concours de tir et diplomatie urbaine dans le Saint-Empire, XVe–XVIe siècle.* (Studies in European Urban History [1100–1800]. 51.). Turnhout 2022, S. 100–7: L'imprimerie comme arme de communication (zum GW-Werkkatalog ‚Schützenbrief')

DÍAZ BURILLO, ROSA MARÍA: El *Bellvm Ciuile* de Lucano: tradición incunable y postincunable (1469–1520). (Textes et Études du Moyen Âge. 101.). Basel 2022. Zum GW-Werkkatalog ‚Lucanus, Marcus Annaeus'. Zuerst unter dem Titel: *La tradición incunable y postincunable del Bellum civile de Lucano (1469–1520)*. Diss. Universidad Nacional de Educación a Distancia Madrid (UNED) 2018.

DÍAZ BURILLO, ROSA MARIA: Las primeras ediciones venecianas de la *Farsalia* de Lucano (1471-1486): Identificación y pervivencia de una nueva forma textual en el periodo incunable. In: *Latomus. Revue d'études latines* 81 (2022), S. 352–81. Zum GW-Werkkatalog ‚Lucanus, Marcus Annaeus' (bes. GW M18852, M18854, M18856).

DLABAČOVÁ, ANNA: The Digital Incunable: Opening or Closing the Book through Digitization? In: *Txt* 8 (2022), S. 139–51. hdl.handle.net/1887/3465923. Zum Problem der Digitalisierung von Sammelbänden.

DLABAČOVÁ, ANNA: Gerard Leeu en de Leidse schoolmeester Engelbert Schut. In: *Madoc. Tijdschrift over de Middeleeuwen* 35 (2021), S. 96–104. hdl.handle.net/1887/3238951. Zu GW 12125 und M40938.

DLABAČOVÁ, ANNA: Een boek- en een wapenhandelaar: twee zeventiende-eeuwse bezitters van Gerard Leeus 'Die vier uterste' (1477). In: *Om het boek. Cultuurhistorische bespiegelingen over boeken en mensen*. Hrsg. v. WIM VAN ANROOIJ u. a. Hilversum 2020, S. 268–73. hdl.handle.net/1887/138835. Zu GW 7519.

DONDI, CRISTINA: Material Evidence in Incunabula (MEI) and Other Tools for Searching the Provenance of Early Printed Books. In: *How the Secularization of Religious Houses Transformed the Libraries of Europe, 16th–19th Centuries*. Hrsg. v. CRISTINA DONDI, DORIT RAINES und RICHARD SHARPE. (Bibliologia. 63.). Turnhout 2022, S. 529–47.

DONDI, CRISTINA; MALASPINA, MATILDE: L'ecosistema digitale del CERL per lo studio del libro antico a stampa: dal progetto 15cBOOKTRADE a oggi. In: *DigItalia* 17,1 (2022), S. 134–57. DOI: 10.36181/digitalia-00044. Zum Projekt 15cbooktrade.ox.ac.uk. Mit englischsprachigem Abstract.

DONDI, CRISTINA; PROSDOCIMI, LAVINIA; RAINES, DORIT: The Incunabula Collection of the Benedictine Library of S. Giorgio Maggiore in Venice. Formation, Use and Dispersal According to Documentary and Material Evidence (from MEI). In: *How the Secularization of Religious Houses Transformed the Libraries of Europe, 16th–19th Centuries*. Hrsg. v. CRISTINA DONDI, DORIT RAINES und RICHARD SHARPE. (Bibliologia. 63.). Turnhout 2022, S. 567–658.

DORNINGER, MARIA E.: Perceptions of the "Unknown"? Medieval and Early Modern Accounts of Pilgrimage to Jerusalem. In: *On the Way to the "Unknown"? The Ottoman Empire in Travelogues (c. 1450–1900)*. Hrsg. v. DORIS GRUBER und ARNO STROHMEYER. (Studies on Modern Orient. 36.). Berlin, Boston 2022, S. 207–23. DOI: 10.1515/9783110698046-011. U. a. zu den GW-Werkkatalogen ‚Breidenbach, Bernhard von' und ‚Tucher, Hans'. S. 218 Anm. 32: "Ninety-two **incunabulae** are known" (Hervorhebung F. E.).

DUBOIS, RAOUL: Calendar Poems: Variances in Vernacular Versified Calendars as Expressions of Individual Perceptions of Time. In: *KronoScope* 20 (2022), S. 30–49. U. a. zum GW-Werkkatalog ‚Cisioianus' (GW 7054–7056¹⁰N).

DŽUNKOVÁ, KATARÍNA: Nový zákon Pražskej biblie (1488): jazyk a štýl (*The Language and Style in the New Testament of the Prague Bible [1488]*). In: *Clavibus unitis* 10/2 (2021), S. 33–50. acecs.cz/media/cu_2021_10_02_dzunkova.pdf. Zu GW 4323. Mit englischsprachigem Abstract.

DŽUNKOVÁ, KATARÍNA: Ideové aspekty v prekladateľskom postupe štvrtej redakcie staročeskej Biblie (*The fourth redaction of the Old Czech translation of the Bible and its ideological aspects*). In: *Clavibus unitis* 9/2 (2020), S. 39–54. acecs.cz/media/cu_2020_09_02_dzunkova.pdf. Zu GW 4323. Mit englischsprachigem Abstract.

ELBING, BERNHARD: *Antike Astronomie, mittelalterliche Medizin und Astrologie. Fachhistorie des mittelniederdeutschen Lübecker ‚nyge kalender' von 1519*. Oldenburg 2022. Auch zu Kalendern und astronomischen Drucken der Inkunabelzeit.

ERDOZAIN CASTIELLA, PABLO: *El santoral del Missale Mixtum Pampilonense*. Berlin u. a. 2022. Zu GW M2459310.

Erlesen. 200 Jahre Bibliothek des Metropolitankapitels Bamberg. Katalog zur gleichnamigen Ausstellung im Diözesanmuseum Bamberg, 2. Juli–13. September 2022. Hrsg. v. BIRGIT KASTNER, MARIA KUNZELMANN und CAROLA MARIE SCHMIDT. (Veröffentlichungen des Diözesanmuseums Bamberg. 31.). Regensburg 2022. Zu Inkunabeln: Kat.-Nr. 4 (SUSANNE RISCHPLER) und 8 (BETTINA WAGNER) sowie BETTINA WAGNER: „Pucher an die keten zu hencken" – Kettenbücher im Mittelalter (S. 53–9).

ERRANI, PAOLA; PALMA, MARCO unter Mitarbeit von GABRIELLA LORENZI und CLAUDIA MALPELLI: *Incunaboli a San Marino*. (Incunaboli. 6.). Rom 2022. Zu den Sammlungen San Marino BS und BU (29 Ausgaben in 28 Nummern).

FATTORI, DANIELA: Un incunabolo sconosciuto ritrovato: la *Leggenda de S. Alessio* (Venezia, Matteo Capcase e Bernardino Benali, prima del 12 agosto 1491). In: *Bibliologia* 16 (2021), S. 27–38.

FERNÁNDEZ AGUINACO, VIRGINIA: Incunabula. In: *Crítica* 1077 (2022), S. 46–51. Zur Ausstellung *Incunabula: 550 años de la imprenta en España*, Madrid BN, 21. April–23. Juli 2022 (siehe unten s. v. REYES GÓMEZ).

FERNÁNDEZ ÁLVAREZ, MARÍA: Del manuscrito al impreso en el siglo XV. Análisis textual y dialectal de la traducción castellana de Salustio de Francisco Vidal de Noya. In: *Lexis* 46 (2022), S. 281–313. DOI: 10.18800/lexis.202201.008. U. a. zu GW M39628. Mit englischsprachigem Abstract.

The Fifteen Oes and Other Prayers: Edited from the Text Published by William Caxton (1491). Hrsg. v. ALEXANDRA BARRATT und SUSAN POWELL. (Middle English Texts. 61.). Heidelberg 2021. Zu GW 0438805N.

FILIES-FEISST, ULRIKE: Die Werke von Horaz: Inkunabelforschung im Stadtarchiv. In: *Villingen im Wandel der Zeit* 44 (2021), S. 8–12.

FLANNERY, MARY C.: Delimiting Chaucerian Obscenity in Caxton's Second Edition of *The Canterbury Tales*. In: *Review of English Studies* 73 (2022), S. 442–58. Zu GW 6586.

GAMBA, ELEONORA: *Cento immagini per cento canti. L'edizione illustrata della Commedia dantesca per i tipi di Bernardino Benali e Matteo Capcasa, Venezia 1491*. Bergamo 2021. Zu GW 7969.

GHIONE, MARCO; FOLLI, LAURA; FAZZO, SILVIA: La tradizione a stampa della *Metaphysica Nova* arabo-latina negli incunaboli e nelle cinquecentine. In: *Aristotelica* (2022) Nr 2, S. 96–117. DOI: 10.17454/ARISTO2.05.

GARWOLIŃSKI, TOMASZ; KAMIŃSKI, KRZYSZTOF: Księgozbiór biskupa warmińskiego Jana Dantyszka – woluminy zachowane w Bibliotece "Hosianum" w Olsztynie (*Die Büchersammlung des Bischofs von Ermland Johannes von Höfen – Bände, die in der Bibliothek Hosianum in Allenstein aufbewahrt werden*). In: *Komunikaty Mazursko-Warmińskie* 2 (312) (2021), S. 311–27. DOI: 10.51974/kmw-135541. Zur Sammlung Olsztyn Hosianum.

GIALDINI, ANNA: Bookbinders in the Early Modern Venetian Book Trade. In: *The Historical Journal* 65 (2022), S. 901–21. Berichtszeitraum: ca. 1450–1630.

GILLE LEVENSON, MATTHIAS: Jeu de données de segmentation et de reconnaissance optique de caractères – Kraken – Incunables sévillans 1494–1500. In: *Zenodo* (18. August 2022). zenodo.org/record/7006981. Zu GW 7222.

La Gloriosissimi Geminiani Vita di Giovanni Maria Parente. Edizione critica. Hrsg. v. ANNA SPIAZZI. (Biblioteca di carte romanze. 12.). Mailand 2021. Zu GW M29404.

GRIESE, SABINE: ,Verbundprojekte' des 15. Jahrhunderts. Ein exemplarischer Blick auf Formen des versammelnden Buchs um 1500. In: *Die Hausbibel des Seidenstickers Hans Plock (ca. 1490–1570). Wege der Erschließung*. Hrsg. v. ALBRECHT HENKYS und CLAUDINE MOULIN. Heidelberg 2022, S. 15–24.

GRIESE, SABINE: Lauber und Brant. Kanonisierungseffekte eines entstehenden Buchmarkts im 15. und frühen 16. Jahrhunderts. In: *Klassiker der Frühen Neuzeit*. Hrsg. v. REGINA TOEPFER unter Mitwirkung von NADINE LORDICK. (Spolia Berolinensia. 43.). Hildesheim 2022, S. 171–99.

GUILLEMINOT-CHRÉTIEN, GENEVIEVE: « Ces Messieur de la Bibliothèque » : l'abbé Desaunays, Joseph Van Praet et la chasse aux premières éditions de 1784 à 1793. In: *Bulletin du bibliophile*. Nr. 2 (2021), S. 259–304.

Von Gutenberg zum World Wide Web. Aspekte der Wirkungsgeschichte von Gutenbergs Erfindung – zur Neukonzeption des Mainzer Gutenberg-Museums. Hrsg. v. STEPHAN FÜSSEL. (Mainzer Studien zur Buchwissenschaft. 26.). Wiesbaden 2022.

Gutenberg-Jahrbuch 97 (2022). Inhalt (ohne Rahmentexte):

[Beiträge der Heidelberger Tagung „Norm und Abweichung im frühen Buchdruck – Standards and Variations in Fifteenth-Century Printing", 29. September–1. Oktober 2021]:

- PAUL SCHWEITZER-MARTIN, FALK EISERMANN und OLIVER DUNTZE: Norm und Abweichung im frühen Buchdruck – zur Einleitung (S. 13–5)
- JEFFREY F. HAMBURGER: Between Basel and Lyon: Bernhard Richel, Martin Huss, and a Possible Printer's Vade Mecum (The Morgan Library & Museum, MS M. 158) (S. 16–37; zum Ex. New York MorganL von GW M43016)
- MALCOLM WALSBY: The Creation of the Title Page in French Incunabula (S. 38–46)
- ELISABETH RUDOLPH: Versuch und Irrtum. Über die ‚Register der Irrung' in den Destillierbüchern Hieronymus Brunschwigs (S. 47–62; zu GW 5595 und VD16 B 8698)
- RICCARDO OLOCCO: The Spread of the Scotus Roman (1481) and Variations in its Character Set (S. 63–81; zu den Antiquatypen der Werkstatt Venedig: Octavianus Scotus). Digitale Appendix: tw.staatsbibliothek-berlin.de/pdf/Olocco_Scotus.pdf
- ANNA DLABAČOVÁ: The Fifteenth Century Book as a "Work in Progress". The Dynamics of Dissection and Compilation in the Workshop of Gerard Leeu (d. 1492) (S. 82–104)
- PAUL SCHWEITZER-MARTIN: Innovation und Kooperation in der Inkunabelproduktion: der Druckort Speyer (S. 105–17)
- CATARINA ZIMMERMANN-HOMEYER: Illustrated Almanacs. Imaging Strategies on Bloodletting Calendars of the Incunabula Period (S. 118–45)
- CATHERINE RIDEAU-KIKUCHI: Des contrats pour imprimer: une étude comparative (Italie du Nord, 1470–1500) (S. 146–67)

[Weitere Beiträge]:

- GÜNTER HÄGELE: Nachhaltigkeit und Recycling: Fragmente eines Ablassbriefes von 1461 für Neuhausen [Mainz: Drucker des Catholicon] in einer Handschrift der Zentral- und Hochschulbibliothek Luzern (S. 169–74; zu einer bislang unbekannten Variante von GW 78)
- SVEN BEHNKE u. a.: Die illuminierte Polydeukes-Ausgabe aus der Bibliothek des Willbald Pirckheimer (Aldus Manutius 1502). Ein Fund in der Landesbibliothek Oldenburg (S. 175–202)
- FALK EISERMANN: Neue Publikationen zur Inkunabelforschung: das Jahr 2021. Mit Nachträgen zum Jahr 2020 (S. 203–28)
- WOLFGANG SCHMITZ: [Nachruf:] Peter Amelung. Der Erforscher des schwäbischen Wiegendrucks und der italienischen Renaissance (S. 245–48)

HACKE, MARTINA: Studentenbriefe als Quelle zur Erforschung des mittelalterlichen Kreditwesens. Die Darlehen von Bruno und Basilius Amerbach im Paris zu Beginn des 16. Jahrhunderts. In: *Das Mittelalter* 27 (2022), S. 390–409. DOI: 10.17885/heiup.mial.2022.2.24664.

HACKE, MARTINA: Messagers de l'Université de Paris et circulation des livres juridiques imprimés (fin 15s.–début 16.s.). L'example de Jean Cabiller. In: *Medieval Europe in Motion. Bd. 3: The Circulation of Jurists, Legal Manuscripts and Artistic, Cultural and Legal Practices in Medieval Europe (13th–15th Centuries)*. Hrsg. v. MARIA ALESSANDRA BILOTTA. Palermo 2021, S. 287–96.

HAIR, ROSS: 1450–1950: The Gutenberg Galaxy According to Bob Brown. In: *Modernism/modernity* 29 (2022), S. 457–93.

HAMM, JOACHIM: Sebastian Brants ‚Narrenschiff'. Anmerkungen zur Genese eines ‚Klassikers'. In: *Klassiker der Frühen Neuzeit*. Hrsg. v. REGINA TOEPFER unter Mitwirkung von NADINE LORDICK. (Spolia Berolinensia. 43.). Hildesheim 2022, S. 201–35.

HAMMER, ANDREAS: Das Buch, die Schrift und der Druck. Die Bildprogramme der Prosa-Fassung der ‚Reise des hl. Brandan' in den Handschriften und Drucken. In: *St. Brandan in europäischer Perspektive – St. Brendamn in European Perspective. Textuelle und bildliche Transformationen – Textual and Pictorial Transformations*. Hrsg. v. JÖRN BOCKMANN und SEBASTIAN HOLTZHAUER. (Nova Mediaevalia. 24.). Göttingen 2022, S. 135–64.

HENKEL, NIKOLAUS: *Verweisen* aus der Sicht der Wissens- und Bildungsgeschichte. Sebastian Brants *Narrenschiff* und die *Stultifera navi*s. In: *Verweiskulturen des Mittelalters*. Hrsg. v. SABINE GRIESE und CLAUDINE MOULIN. (Wolfenbütteler Forschungen. 167.). Wiesbaden 2022, S. 47–85.

HENKEL, NIKOLAUS: Sammeln aus der Perspektive der Wissens- und Bildungsgeschichte. Recht, Theologie, Bibel und Literatur in Sebastian Brants Marginalien zur Stultifera navis (1497). In: *Sammeln als literarische Praxis im Mittelalter und in der Frühen Neuzeit. Konzepte, Praktiken, Poetizität. XXVI. Anglo-German Colloquium, Ascona 2019*. Hrsg. v. MARK CHINCA u. a. Tübingen 2022, S. 173–89. Zu GW 5054.

HENRYOT, FABIENNE: De *l'oratoire privé à la bibliothèque publique: L'autre histoire des livres d'heures*. (From Text to Written Heritage. 1.). Turnhout 2022. Kapitel 2: Imprimer les Heures: la naissance d'une catégorie éditoriale (S. 61–108; u. a. zum GW-Werkkatalog ‚Horae').

HENRYOT, FABIENNE: La circulation européenne des livres d'heures (1470–1571). In: *Produire et vendre des livres. Europe occidentale, fin XVe–fin XVIIe siècle*. (Faits de religion. 7.). Hrsg. v. PHILIPPE MARTIN. Lyon 2022, S. 111–28. U. a. zum GW-Werkkatalog ‚Horae'.

HOLL, ALFRED: *The Earliest Printed Arithmetic Book in Each of 35 European Languages.* (Strömstads Akademis Fria Skriftserie. 23.). Strömstad 2022. stromstadakademi.se/FSS/FSS-23.pdf.

HOOGVLIET, MARGRIET; RIVAUD, DAVID: Tours around 1500: Deep Mapping Scribes, Booksellers, and Printers. In: *Peregrinations: Journal of Medieval Art and Architecture* 7,4 (2021), S. 73–120. digital.kenyon.edu/perejournal/vol7/iss4/6.

HUDOKOVÁ, SOŇA: Komplexné reštaurovanie prvotlače Pražská bible z roku 1488. Bachelorarbeit Universität Pardubice 2022. dk.upce.cz//handle/10195/80467. Zu einem Exemplar Brno UKn von GW 4323.

Impressa Argentine. Exposition d'incunables strasbourgeois à la Bibliothèque de l'Académie Roumaine de Cluj, inaugurée le 21 novembre 2022, à l'occasion de la visite d'une délégation universitaire de Strasbourg. Hrsg. v. ADRIAN PAPAHAGI und CARMEN OANEA. Cluj 2022. centrulcodex.com/2022/11/16/impressa-argentine-exposition-dincunables/.

Gli incunaboli della Biblioteca francescana di Milano. Una storia di libri, luoghi e uomini dotti. Hrsg. v. GIOVANNA BERNINI. (Carte e libri. 2.). Mailand 2022. Zur Sammlung Milano Franzisk.

Gli incunaboli della Biblioteca Universitaria di Napoli. Catalogo. Hrsg. v. GIANCARLO PETRELLA. Premessa di ANDREA MAZZUCCHI, Presentazione di MARIA LUCIA SIRAGUSA e RAFFAELE DE MAGISTRIS. Rom 2022. Zur Sammlung Napoli BU.

Die Inkunabeln der Bibliothek der Stiftung Staatliches Görres-Gymnasium Koblenz. Bearb. v. CHRISTINA MECKELNBORG unter Mitarbeit von EVELYN HANISCH. Wiesbaden 2022. Zur Sammlung Koblenz Gy.

INSERRA, SIMONA: Per una ipotesi di sostenibilità dei progetti culturali in biblioteca: crowdfunding e incunaboli. In: *Caffè storico Rivista di Studi e Cultura della Valdinievole* 7 Nr 13 (2022), S. 75–84. Mit englischsprachigem Abstract.

JACKEL, CHRISTINA: *Die Bibliothek lesen. Funktion und Dynamik des deutschsprachigen mittelalterlichen Textbestands im Stift Kremsmünster.* (Philologica Germanica. 40.). Wien 2021 U. a. zu den Handschriften und Inkunabeln des Peter Groß von Trockau (S. 307–33).

JAŠOVÁ, KATARÍNA; BUKOVSKÝ, VLADIMÍR: Príbeh dvoch rovnakých, a predsa rozdielnych inkunábul. In: *Knižnica* 23,2 (2022), S. 40–51. snk.sk/images/Edicna_cinnost/Casopis_Kniznica/2022/2022_07_29_Katarina_Jasova.pdf. Zu den Exemplaren Banská Bystrica UKn und Martin NKn von GW M24135. Mit englischsprachigem Abstract.

JENSEN, KRISTIAN: Locher's and Grüninger's Edition of Horace from Strasbourg 1498. At the Crossroads between Printed and Manuscript

Book Production and Use. In: *Interfaces* 7 (2020), S. 37–63. DOI: 10.13130/interfaces-07-04. Zu GW 13468.

JESTAZ, JULIETTE: Le ventre de Paris du 15e au 18e siècle: remarques sur les éditions de « La despense qui se fait chascun jour dans la ville de Paris » et sa fortune. In: *L'echauguette. Carnet de la Bibliothèque historique de la Ville de Paris* (19. Juli 2021). bhvp.hypotheses.org/3354. Zu « Les rues et églises de Paris » (GW M29449–M29454).

JIMÉNEZ CALVENTE, TERESA: La comida y el vestido en el debate político y moral en siglo XV: Hernando de Talavera y su *Tractado provechoso* sobre el vestir y el comer. In: *eHumanista* 51 (2022), S. 97–115. ehumanista.ucsb.edu/sites/default/files/sitefiles/ehumanista/volume51/05_ehum51.g.JimenezCalvente.pdf. Zu GW 9793.

KARDYŚ, PIOTR: Inkunabuły „medyczne" z Biblioteki Wyższego Seminarium Duchownego w Kielcach (*'Medical' Incunabula from the Library of the Major Seminary in Kielce*). In: *Archiwa, Biblioteki i Muzea Kościelne* 118 (2022), S. 141–70. DOI: 10.31743/abmk.9353. Zu fünf Inkunabeln der Sammlung Kielce Sem. Mit englischsprachigem Abstract.

KARR SCHMIDT, SUZANNE: Flaps, Volvelles, and Vellum in Pre-Modern Movable Manuscript and Print. In: *Journal of Interactive Books* 1 (2022), S. 6–22. DOI: 10.57579/2022JIB001SKS. U. a. zu GW M19457 und M37455.

KASCHPERSKAJA, ALEXANDRA: Die St. Petersburger Handschrift des ‚Ehebüchleins' Albrechts von Eyb. Kodikologische Beschreibung und die Rolle in der Überlieferung. In: *Deutsche Kultur in russischen Buch- und Handschriftenbeständen. Beiträge zur Tagung des deutsch-russischen Arbeitskreises vom 16./17. April 2018 an der Lomonossow-Universität Moskau*. Hrsg. v. NATALIJA GANINA u. a. (Akademie gemeinnütziger Wissenschaften zu Erfurt. Sonderschriften. 52. = Deutsch-russische Forschungen zur Buchgeschichte. 5.). Erfurt 2022, S. 211–9. Zu GW 9520–9528. Siehe oben den Beitrag von BERTELSMEIER-KIERST in demselben Band.

KATO, TAKAKO: Lost, Burned and Recovered: Tracing the Provenance History of a Copy of Caxton's *Golden Legend* in the Rylands Library. In: *The Library* 7,23 (2022), S. 323–45. Zum 2. Exemplar Manchester RylandsL von GW 14048.

KEMPF, CHARLOTTE: Buchwissenschaft und Praxeologie – ein Bericht. In: *Medium Buch* 1 (2019 [erschienen 2020]): *Praxeologische Studien zur historischen Buchwissenschaft*. Hrsg. v. UTE SCHNEIDER, S. 5–14. DOI: 10.13173/WIF.1.5 (gesamter Band). Behandelt auch Inkunabeln.

KENNERLEY, SAM: *The Reception of John Chrysostom in Early Modern Europe. Translating and Reading a Greek Church Father from 1417 to 1624*. (Arbeiten zur Kirchengeschichte. 157.). Berlin, Boston 2023 [erschienen 2022]. Zum GW-Werkkatalog 'Johannes Chrysostomus'. Kapitel 5.1: Incunabula Editions of Chrysostom (S. 105–10).

KETSCHIK, NORA; KIRCHHOFF, MATTHIAS: Der ‚Lobspruch auf Nürnberg' Hans Rosenplüts (1447) in der Redaktion Sertessbalts (Ende 1480er Jahre). Edition und Übersetzung. In: *Mitteilungen des Vereins für Geschichte der Stadt Nürnberg* 107 (2020), S. 1–56. Zu GW M38981, M38982 und M38983.

KIPF, JOHANNES KLAUS; RUDOLPH, PIA: Weltgeschichte sammeln – am Beispiel einer deutschsprachigen illustrierten Sammelhandschrift des 15. Jahrhunderts. In: *Sammeln als literarische Praxis im Mittelalter und in der Frühen Neuzeit. Konzepte, Praktiken, Poetizität. XXVI. Anglo-German Colloquium, Ascona 2019.* Hrsg. v. MARK CHINCA u. a. Tübingen 2022, S. 75–98. Der besprochene Sammelband enthält auch ein Exemplar von GW M18412.

KRASS, ANDREAS: Schiffbruch mit Weinfass. Daseinsmetaphorik bei Oswald von Wolkenstein und Sebastian Brant. In: *Germanisch-Romanische Monatsschrift* 72 (2022), S. 7–25.

KREIM, ERWIN: *Johannes Gutenberg: Unternehmer des zweiten Jahrtausends*. Oppenheim 2022.

KREMER, RICHARD L.: Exploring a Late-Fifteenth-Century Astrologer's Toolbox: British Library Add MS 34603. In: *Alfonsine Astronomy: The Written Record*. Hrsg. v. RICHARD L. KREMER, MATTHIEU HUSSON und JOSÉ CHABÁS. (Alfonsine Astronomy: Studies and Sources. 1.). Turnhout 2022, S. 107–41. DOI: 10.1484/M.ALFA.5.124925. Zum GW-Werkkatalog ‚Schinnagel, Markus'. Die besprochene Hs. enthält u. a. diverse Druckabschriften. Der gesamte Sammelband DOI: 10.1484/M.ALFA-EB.5.124044.

LACASTA, JAVIER u. a.: Tracing the Origins of Incunabula through the Automatic Identifications of Fonts in Digitised Documents. In: *Multimedia Tools and Applications* 81 (2022), S. 40977–91. link.springer.com/article/10.1007/s11042-022-13108-3.

LANGHANKE, ROBERT: Reynke als Familienvater. Zur Inszenierung der Kernfamilie im Lübecker Fuchsepos von 1498. In: *Studien zur mittelniederdeutschen und frühneuhochdeutschen Sprache und Literatur*. Hrsg. v. SARAH IHDEN, KATHARINA DREESSEN und ROBERT LANGHANKE. (Kleine und regionale Sprachen. 6.). Hildesheim 2021, S. 147–87. Zu GW 12733.

LANSKA, DOUGLAS J.: The Medieval Cell Doctrine: Foundations, Development, Evolution, and Graphic Representations in Printed Books from 1490 to 1630. In: *Journal of the History of the Neurosciences* 31 (2022), S. 115–75. Gegenüber dem Eintrag in der Bibliographie in GJ 2022 (basierend auf Online-Preprint) hier aktualisiert.

LAZCANO GONZÁLEZ, RAFAEL: Catálogo de incunables de San Agustín y autores agustinos en las bibliotecas de España (1467–1500). In: *Archivo Agustiniano* 106 (2022), S. 129–202.

LEMESHKIN, ILYA VASIL'EVICH: The Czech First Printed Psalter of 1487 and the Psalter of F. Skorina (1517) 'Ad Gloriam Venerationemque Dei'. In: *Russkaya literatura* (2022) Nr 1, S. 153–61. DOI: 10.31860/0131-6095-2022-1-153-161. In russischer Sprache.
Zu GW M36275.

L'ENGLE, SUSAN: Medieval Canon Law Manuscripts and Early Printed Books. In: *The Cambridge History of Medieval Canon Law*. Hrsg. v. ANDERS WINROTH und JOHN C. WEI. New York 2022, S. 299–321.

LENZ, KLAUDIA CHARLOTTE; MILLER, MATTHIAS: *Zeiten & Seiten. 200 Jahre Bibliotheken im Berliner Zeughaus*. Berlin 2022. Zur Sammlung Berlin DtHistM. S. 173–92: Inkunabeln.

Leonardo Bruni: De duobus amantibus Guiscardo et Segismunda. Hrsg. u. Übers. v. ANTONI BIOSCA I BAS und JOSÉ SOLÍS DE LOS SANTOS. Valencia 2022. Faksimile und spanische Übersetzung von GW 5634. Darin u. a.: José Solís de los Santos: El texto incunable valenciano "de duobus amantibus Guiscardo et Sigismunda" (S. 125–54).

LEVELT, SJOERD: *The Middle Dutch 'Brut'. An Edition and Translation.* (Exeter Medieval Texts and Studies.). Liverpool 2021. U. a. zu GW M38760 (Werner Rolevinck: ‚Fasciculus temporum', mittelniederländisch. Utrecht: Jan Veldener, 14. Februar 1480).

LITTERIO, SILVIA: Dal *Filostrato* ai rispetti di ambiente laurenziano: la ricezione quattrocentesca della prima lettera di Troiolo a Criseida. In: *Intorno a Boccaccio / Boccaccio e dintorni. Atti del Seminario internazionale di studi (Certaldo Alta, Casa di Giovanni Boccaccio, 12-13 settembre 2019)*. Florenz 2020, S. 207–29. DOI: 10.36253/978-88-5518-236-2.
U. a. zu GW 4472–4474 10N.

LONGHI, ALBERTO: I marginalia dell'incunabolo marciano 507 della Miscellaneorum centuria prima di Angelo Poliziano. In: *History of Classical Scholarship* 4 (2022), S. 69–95. hcsjournal.org/ojs/index.php/hcs/article/view/76/61. Zum Ex. Venezia BNMarc von GW M34760.

LÓPEZ CASAS, MARÍA MERCÉ: El incunable sevillano de las *Coplas* de Fernán Pérez de Guzmán (92PG). In: *Magnificat. Cultura i literatura medievals* 9 (2022), S. 247–61. DOI: 10.7203/MCLM.9.24066.
Zu GW M30941. Mit englischsprachigem Abstract.

LÓPEZ VAREA, MARÍA EUGENIA: El enredijo de la imprenta incunable de Salamanca y Nebrija. In: *La época de Nebrija en Salamanca*. Salamanca 2022, S. 179–97.

LÓPEZ VAREA, MARÍA EUGENIA: De los impresores incunables anónimos "Printer Nebrissensis Introductiones latinae" y "Printer Nebrissensis Gramatica" a la imprenta de Alonso y Juan de Porras en la Salamanca del siglo XV (*From the Anonymous Printers of Incunabula Printer Nebrissensis Introductiones latinae and Printer Nebrissensis Gramatica to the Printing Press of Alonso and Juan de Porras in Fifteenth-Century Salamanca*). In: *Titivillus* 8 (2022), S. 51–71.

LÓPEZ VAREA, MARÍA EUGENIA: Un incunable salmantino con tipos de Monterrey: el *Missale Compostellanum* de 1495. In: *Desafíos en el entorno de la información y la documentación ante las problematicas*. Hrsg. v. GEORGINA ARACELI TORRES VARGAS. Bd. 1. Mexico City 2022, S. 191–204. academia.edu/90150779. Zu GW M24335.

LORCA CABEZUELO, CELIA: *El papel en los libros ilustrados del Fondo Antiguo de la Biblioteca de la Universidad de Sevilla: desde la época incunable hasta el siglo XVII*. Abschlussarbeit (Trabajo Fin de Grado Inédito) Universidad de Sevilla. Sevilla 2021. idus.us.es/handle/11441/131242.

MAGOFSKY, BENJAMIN: Der heilige Hieronymus im Gemäuer. Religiöse Handschriften, Inkunabeln und Bücher aus dem Bielefelder Franziskanerkloster in der Schulbibliothek des Ratsgymnasiums. In: *Zeitarbeit. Aus- und Weiterbildungszeitschrift für die Geschichtswissenschaften* 2 (2020), S. 44–64. majournals.bib.uni-mannheim.de/zeitarbeit/article/view/147/104. Zur Sammlung Bielefeld Gy.

MAHONEY, CATHERINE: The Siren and the Satyr as Spiritual Curatives in Jacob Meydenbach's *Hortus sanitatis*. In: *Australian and New Zealand Journal of Art* 22 (2022), S. 59–70. Zu GW 13548.

MANEA, LĂCRĂMIOARA: Carte străină veche și rară (sec. XV–XVI) din patrimoniul muzeului tulcean (*Old and rare foreign books [the 15th–16th centuries] in the collections of Tulcea Museum*). In: *Peuce (Serie Nouă) – Studii și cercetari de istorie și arheologie* 20 (2022), S. 289–318. Zur Sammlung Tulcea M.

MANGAS NAVARRO, NATALIA ANAÍS: *La 'Criança y virtuosa dotrina' de Pedro de Gracia Dei. Edición crítica*. (Colección Cancionero, romancero e imprenta. 5.). Alicante 2022. Zu GW 11348. Zuerst unter dem Titel *La 'Criança y virtuosa dotrina' de Pedro de Gracia Dei: estudio y edición crítica*. Diss. Alicante 2020 (academia.edu/49040874).

MARIANI CANOVA, GIORDANA; RIVALI, LUCA: Una (quasi) sconosciuta miscellanea quattrocentesca veneziana della Biblioteca Generale della Custodia di Terra Santa e le sue prestigiose miniature. In: *La Bibliofilía* 123 (2021), S. 259–84.

MARTÍN BAÑOS, PEDRO: Las primeras ediciones salmantinas de los diccionarios Nebrisenses: un enigma editorial. In: *Antonio de Lebrixa grammatico en su medio milenio*. Hrsg. v. JOSÉ J. GOMÉZ ASCENSIO und CARMEN QUIJADA VAN DEN BERGH. (Aquilafuente. 325.). Salamanca 2022, S. 35–65. eusal.es/eusal/catalog/book/978-84-1311-668-6 (gesamter Band). Zu GW 2217–2220.

MARTOS, JOSEP LLUÍS: Estudio de un pliego poético incunable perdido: edición y ejemplares de las Coplas de Hernán Vázquez de Tapia (97*VT). In: *Lemir. Revista de Literatura Española Medieval y del Renacimiento* 26 (2022), S. 421–38. parnaseo.uv.es/Lemir/Revista/Revista26/15_Martos_JL.pdf.

MARTOS, JOSEP LLUÍS: Las "Coplas" de Hernán Vázquez de Tapia a la muerte del príncipe don Juan. In: *Revistia de poética medieval* 36 (2022), S. 271–306. recyt.fecyt.es/index.php/revpm/article/view/96939/70330. Beide Beiträge zu der verlorenen Inkunabel GW M4946810. Mit englischsprachigem Abstract.

MARTOS SÁNCHEZ, JOSEP LLUÍS: Contenidos y génesis de un incunable perdido: Obra en prosa sobre la veríssima Inmaculada Conceptió de la Mare de Déu. In: *Isabel de Villena i l'espiritualitat europea tardomedieval*. Hrsg. v. ANNA ISABEL PEIRATS NAVARRO. Valencia 2022, S. 135–66.

MASSA, PABLO: *Viua el gran Re Don Fernando* (*Historia Baetica*, Carlo Verardi, Roma, 1493) o de la pragmática de la música impresa. In: *Revista de Cancioneros Impresos y Manuscritos* 12 (2023 [erschienen 2022]), S. 73–92. DOI: 10.14198/rcim.2023.12.03. Zu GW M49593.

MCCALL, TAYLOR: Anatomical Icon: Dissection Scenes in Manuscript and Print, circa 1350–1550. In: *KNOW. A Journal on the Formation of Knowledge* 6 (2022), S. 7–46.

MCDONALD, GRANTLEY: Before *Melopoiae*: Conrad Celtis, Laurentius Corvinus, Arnold Wöstefeld and the Use of Music in the Teaching and Performance of Horace's Metres around 1500. In: *Horace across the Media. Textual, Visual and Musical Receptions of Horace from the 15th to the 18th Century*. Hrsg. v. KARL A. E. ENENKEL und MARC LAUREYS. (Intersections. 82.). Leiden, Boston 2022, S. 335–98. brill.com/view/book/9789004373730/BP000015.xml.

MCQUILLEN, JOHN T.: New Insights on German Provenances of Blockbooks in America. In: *Jahrbuch für Buch- und Bibliotheksgeschichte* 7 (2022), S. 177–82.

Medieval Romance, Arthurian Literature. Essays in Honour of Elizabeth Archibald. Hrsg. v. A. S. G. EDWARDS. Cambridge 2021. Inkunabelrelevantes aus dem Inhalt:
- BARRY WINDEATT: The Body Language of Malory's 'Le Morte DArthur' (S. 143–57; zu GW M20157 und M20161).
- E. D. KENNEDY: Malory's 'Morte Darthur' and the Bible (S. 172–88; zu GW M20157 und M20161)
- AD PUTTER: Dutch, French and English in Caxton's 'Recuyell of the Historyes of Troye' (S. 205–26; zu GW M17449)

Meluzine. Die erste niederländische Fassung (1491). Hrsg. v. RITA SCHLUSEMANN. (Relectiones. 11.). Stuttgart 2022. Ausgabe und Übersetzung von GW 12665.

MERCUZOT, DELPHINE: Caxton and the Reception of the *Artes moriendi*. In: *Religious Practices and Everyday Life in the Long Fifteenth Century (1350–1570): Interpreting Changes and Changes of Interpretation*. Hrsg. v. IAN JOHNSON und ANA MARÍA S. A. RODRIGUES. (New Communities of Interpretation. 2.). Tournai 2021, S. 241–72.

MERINO JEREZ, LUIS: Shedding Light on the Textual Genesis of Jacobus Publicius' "Ars memorie" (MS London, BL, Add. 28805). In: *Daphnis* 50 (2022), S. 85–127. Zum GW-Werkkatalog 'Publicius, Jacobus'.

MEYER, CHRISTIAN: *Pietro d'Abano, 'Expositio problematum (XIX)'. Édition, introduction et notes critiques et explicatives.* Leuven 2022. U. a. zu GW M31865 und M31867, Textausgabe nach Edition von 1519.

Meyer, Johanna: Mittelniederdeutsche Frühdrucke digital. Ein Projektbericht. In: *Korrespondenzblatt des Vereins für niederdeutsche Sprachforschung* 129 (2022), S. 75–81. nbn-resolving.de/urn:nbn:de:hbz:6-02079541659. Vgl. dazu die Posterpräsentation: nbn-resolving.de/urn:nbn:de:hbz:6-02079549960.

MLYNARSKI-JUNG, NATALIE ANN: „se enwysten nicht, dat he was eyn deeff". Zur scheiternden Vigilanz im *Broder Rusche*. In: *Diabolische Vigilanz. Studien zur Inszenierung von Wachsamkeit in Teufelserzählungen des Spätmittelalters und der Frühen Neuzeit*. Hrsg. v. JÖRN BOCKMANN u. a. (Vigilanzkulturen. 2.). Berlin, Boston 2022, S. 45–64. DOI: 10.1515/9783110774382-004. Zu GW 12745.

MONTANARI, ANNA; STOPPINO, ELEONORA: *Libri cavellereschi in prosa e in versi: repertorio di incunaboli*. (Studi boiardeschi. 13. = Studi. 103.). Novara 2022.

MORLINO, LUCA: Alessandro Magno in tipografia: la tradizione a stampa di un volgarizzamento italiano dell'*Historia de Preliis* e la sua importanza storico-culturale. In: *Alessandro Magno nel veneto medievale e dintorni. Tradizione mediolatina e tradizione romanza*. Hrsg. v. GIANFELICE PERON. (Romanistica patavina. 18.). Padua 2021, S. 133–63.

MÜHLMANN, DANA: *Studien zur populären Passionsliteratur des 14. Jahrhunderts: Der deutschsprachige ‚Extendit manum'-Traktat (auch bekannt als Passionstraktat Heinrichs von St. Gallen)*. Diss. Mainz 2020. o. O. 2022. DOI: 10.25358/openscience-6881. Anhang: Zur Erschließung der Inkunabeln und Frühdrucke des EMT (S. 587–610). Zum GW-Werkkatalog 'Heinrich von St. Gallen' (GW 12171–12182).

MÜLLER, FLORIAN: Der Blick als Erfahrung? Fremdbeschreibung und Selbstbeschreibung als erzählende Wissensformen am Beispiel des Reiseberichts des Bernhard von Breydenbach. In: *Reiseerfahrungen im Mittelmeerraum in Mittelalter und Moderne*. Hrsg. v. MARGIT MERSCH. (Mare Nostrum. Studentische Beiträge zur Mediterranistik. 1.). Bochum 2021, S. 20–31. DOI: 10.46586/MaNo.2021.8999.

MUÑOZ, MARÍA: El lamento de Caterina Sforza. In: *Voces disidentes contra la misoginia: nuevas perspectivas desde la sociología, la literatura y el arte*. Hrsg. v. PABLO GARCÍA VALDÉS, RAISA GORGOJO-IGLESIAS und ENRIQUE MAYOR DE LA IGLESIA. Madrid 2022, S. 371–81. Zu ISTC ic00789600 (noch nicht im GW).

MURANO, GIOVANNA: Ser Piero Cennini, copista ed editore. In: *La Bibliofilía* 123 (2021), S. 209–36. U. a. zu GW M41873. Mit englischsprachigem Abstract.

NEUMANN, MARKO; VOESTE, ANJA: Textsegmentierung in Handschrift und Frühdruck. In: *Vergleichende Interpunktion – Comparative Punctuation*. Hrsg. v. PAUL RÖSSLER, PETER BESL und ANNA SALLER. (Linguistik – Impulse & Tendenzen. 96.) Berlin, Boston 2022, S. 137–61.

NICKEL, HOLGER; KREISSLER, MARTINE: *Die Inkunabeln der Anhaltischen Landesbücherei Dessau. Geschichte und Bestand*. (Veröffentlichungen des Stadtarchivs Dessau-Roßlau. 29.). Dessau-Roßlau 2022. Zur Sammlung Dessau LB (189 Nummern und 163 Nummern „z. Z. Moskva GosB" bzw. Verluste).

NIGHMAN, CHRIS L.: "Impresse et Diligenter Correcte": Johann Koelhoff the Elder's Transmission of Francesco Griffolini's Latin Translation of Chrysostom's Homilies on John. In: *Journal of the Early Book Society* 24 (2021), S. 263–88. Zu GW M13297.

NISKANEN, SAMU K.: Anselm's so-called *Commendatio operis ad Vrbanum papam II*: its Affiliation, Transmission, and a New Critical Edition. In: *Revue d'Histoire des Textes* 17 (2022), S. 341–66. Zu einem auktorialen Paratext in GW 2032.

NUOVO, ANGELA; COLETTO, ALDO: Gli incunaboli di Umberto Eco. In: *AIB studi* 62 Nr. 1 (2022), S. 9–25. aibstudi.aib.it/article/view/13386. Die Bibliothek von Umberto Eco (Gutenberg-Preisträger 2014) mit 36 Inkunabeln wurde 2021 vom italienischen Ministero della Cultura erworben und befindet sich in Milano BNBraid.

OLIVETTO, GEORGINA: *Celestina* y la "publicación" antes de la imprenta. In: *Juan Ruiz, arcipreste de Hita, y el "Libro de buen amor". Mujer, saber y heterodoxia: 'Libro de buen amor', 'La Celestina' y 'La Lozana andaluza'*. Homenaje a Folke Gernert. Hrsg. v. FRANCISCO TORO CEBALLOS. Alcalá la Real 2022, S. 323–30. academia.edu/72555874. Zu GW M38597 und M38600.

OOSTERHOFF, RICHARD J.: Decline of the Calculators in Paris c. 1500: Humanism and Print. In: *Quantifying Aristotle. The Impact, Spread, and Decline of the 'Calculatores' Tradition*. Hrsg. v. EDITH DUDLEY SYLLA und DANIEL A. DI LISCIA. (Medieval and Early Modern Philosophy and Science. 34.). Leiden, Boston 2022, S. 328–51. U. a zu GW 9638 (,Dialogi', Bl. 18aff. und M4bff.).

OOSTERHOFF, RICHARD J.: Dialogue of Ingenuous Students: Early Printed Textbooks at Paris. In: *Teaching Philosophy in Early Modern Europe: Text and Image*. Hrsg. v. SUSANNA BERGER und DANIEL GARBER. Cham 2021, S. 11–30.

OPLL, FERDINAND: Eine Besonderheit unter den frühen Stadtansichten von Wien. Die Miniatur in einer Inkunabel in der Stiftsbibliothek Klosterneuburg aus den 1480er Jahren und ihr historisches wie kunsthistorisches Umfeld. In: *Studien zur Wiener Geschichte. Jahrbuch des Vereins für Geschichte der Stadt Wien* 78 (2022), S. 117–71. academia.edu/84534625. Zum Ex. Klosterneuburg Aug von GW M30416.

PALMER, NIGEL F.: Das Blockbuch Peters des Großen. Die heute Moskauer ‚Biblia pauperum' und ihre Rolle in der Diskussion um die Entstehung des Buchdrucks. In: *Deutsche Kultur in russischen Buch- und Handschriftenbeständen. Beiträge zur Tagung des deutsch-russischen Arbeitskreises vom 16./17. April 2018 an der Lomonossow-Universität Moskau*. Hrsg. v. NATALIJA GANINA u. a. (Akademie gemeinnütziger Wissenschaften zu Erfurt. Sonderschriften. 52. = Deutsch-russische Forschungen zur Buchgeschichte. 5.). Erfurt 2022, S. 39–72.

PANZANELLI FRATONI, MARIA ALESSANDRA: A Library for the Crown: Charles Albert of Saxony and the Foundation of the Biblioteca Reale of Turin. In: *Images of Royalty in the Nineteenth and Twentieth Centuries. Tradition and Modernity in Italy, Portugal and Spain*. Hrsg. v. PIERANGELO GENTILE u. a. Turin 2022, S. 139–57. academia.edu/93331838.

PASALODOS REQUEJO, SERGIO: *Michele Savonarola: De balneis et termis Ytaliȩ. Edición crítica, traducción y estudio*. (Micrologus Library. 114.). Florenz 2022. Zuerst Diss. Valladolid 2020: educacion.gob.es/teseo/imprimirFicheroTesis.do?idFichero=gEAdJ0yVlGU%3. U. a. zu GW M40693, M40695 und M40697.

PASSERA, CLAUDIO: L'Editoria al servizio del principe: la città in festa negli incunaboli italiani per nozze. In: *Medioevo e Rinascimento* 34 (NS 31) (2020), S. 123–55. Zu den anlässlich italienischer Fürstenhochzeiten veröffentlichten Gelegenheitsdrucken (z.B. GW 9064, M25801, M41940, M44707).

PAYNE, M. T. W.: Richard Pynson's Property in St Clement Danes, 1491–1500. In: *The Library* 7,23 (2022), S. 96–101.

PERUJO MELGAR, JOAN M.: Les traduccions romàniques de la *Historia destructionis Troiae* de Guido delle Colonne com a eina per a l'establiment del text llatí original (*The Romance Translations of Guido delle Colonne's 'Historia destructionis Troiae' as a Tool to Establish the Original Text in Latin*). In: *Arxiu de textos catalans antics* 33 (2021), S. 83–107. DOI: raco.cat/index.php/ArxiuTextos/article/view/397562. U. a. zu GW 7244. Mit englischsprachigem Abstract.

PETRELLA, GIANCARLO: *"Questi non sono tempi per libri". Il patrimonio incunabolistico delle biblioteche ucraine. Con una nota breve di ERRI DE LUCA e una Premessa di RAIMUNDO DI MAIO*. (Accapo. 23.). Neapel 2022. academia.edu/82292965.

PETRELLA, GIANCARLO: Un'integrazione agli annali di Antonio Zarotto (Niccolò Perotti, *Rudimenta grammatices*, 1488) e uno sconosciuto esemplare di un presunto incunabolo parigino. In: *La Bibliofilía* 123 (2021), S. 65–72. Zu GW 1884 und M3119050.

PETRELLA, GIANCARLO: "I bibliomani fanno molto conto di questo volume". Prime schede per un censimento dell'*Hypnerotomachia Poliphili* (1499): Esemplari, provenienze, collezionisti. In: *Hvmanistica* 15 (NF 9) (2020), S. 267–318. Zu GW 7223.

PFÄNDTNER, KARL-GEORG: Sole survivors & rare editions : unikale, seltene und illuminierte Inkunabeln der Staats- und Stadtbibliothek Augsburg – die Jahresausstellung 2021 der Staats- und Stadtbibliothek Augsburg zeigte weltweit einzigartige Wiegendrucke. In: *Codices manuscripti & impressi* Heft 134/135 (2022), S. 51–7. Zur gleichnamigen Ausstellung in Augsburg SStB, 24. September–23. Dezember 2021.

PILARCZYK, KRZYSZTOF: *Bibliological and Religious Studies on the Hebrew Book. Collected Essays.* (Eastern and Central European Voices. 5.). Göttingen 2022. Kapitel 7: Hebrew Incunabula from the Saraval Collection in the University Library in Wroclaw (S. 201–24; zuerst 2011 in polnischer Sprache).

PISKAŁA, MAGDALENA: O długim trwaniu antologii na przykładzie „Speculum exemplorum" (*On the Longevity of Anthologies: The Case of 'Speculum exemplorum'*). In: *Prace Filologiczne. Literaturoznawstwo* 12 (15) (2022), S. 45–59. DOI: 10.32798/pflit.793. U. a. zum GW-Werkkatalog ‚Speculum exemplorum'. Mit englischsprachigem Abstract.

Poeticon astronomicon. Gaius J. Hyginus. (Albireos astronomische Bibliothek. 2.). Köln 2021. „Originalgetreues Faksimile der Inkunabel [GW 13678], gedruckt in einer Auflage von 540 Exemplaren auf 110 g Bütten, handgeschöpft (Silberburg). Die Nummern 1–20 erscheinen als Premium-Edition mit Original-Blättern aus der 2. Auflage, Venedig 1486" (Verlagstext; gemeint ist wohl GW 13679 von 1485).

PRANDI, ANNA: *Letture francescane. La Biblioteca dei Minori Osservanti di San Nicolò dei Carpi nell'anno 1600*. Sesto San Giovanni 2020.

PRECHTL, FABIAN: *Giovanni Boccaccios ‚De casibus virorum illustrium' in Deutschland. Studien zur Überlieferung und Rezeption eines frühhumanistischen Werkes im 15. und 16. Jahrhundert.* (Münchener Texte und Untersuchungen zur deutschen Literatur des Mittelalters. 152.). Wiesbaden 2022. U. a. zu GW 4430.

PRINCIPI, PATRIZIA: Sulla Roma di Cesare Borgia: un'edita nota manoscritta firmata "Roterodamus" nella raccolta *Scriptores astronomici veteres* della Biblioteca Universitaria Alessandrina di Roma. In: *Scritti di donne. 40 studiose per la Storia dell'Arte*. Hrsg. v. STEFANIA MACIOCE. Foligno 2022, S. 339–45. Zum Ex. Roma BAlessandr von GW 9981.

Publishing Sacrobosco's De sphaera in Early Modern Europe. Modes of Material and Scientific Exchange. Hrsg. v. MATTEO VALLERIANI und ANDREA OTTONE. Cham 2022. DOI: 10.1007/978-3-030-86600-6 (gesamter Band). Zum GW-Werkkatalog ‚Sacro Bosco, Johannes de'. Inkunabelrelevantes aus dem Inhalt:

- MATTEO VALLERIANI; ANDREA OTTONE: Printers, Publishers, and Sellers: Actors in the Process of Consolidation of Epistemic Communities in the Early Modern Academic World (S. 1–23). DOI: 10.1007/978-3-030-86600-6_1.
- RICHARD OOSTERHOFF: Printerly Ingenuity and Mathematical Books in the Early Estienne Workshop (S. 25–59, u. a. zu GW M14652, M14608 und M15065). DOI: 10.1007/978-3-030-86600-6_2.
- CATHERINE RIDEAU-KIKUCHI: Erhard Ratdolt's Edition of Sacrobosco's Tractatus de sphaera: A New Editorial Model in Venice? (S. 60–98; zu GW M14652 und M14654). DOI: doi.org/10.1007/978-3-030-86600-6_3.
- RICHARD L. KREMER: Printing Sacrobosco in Leipzig, 1488–ca. 1521: Local Markets and University Publishing (S. 409–57; 15 Ausgaben, davon acht Inkunabeln). DOI: 10.1007/978-3-030-86600-6_12.

Prvotisky olomoucké kapituly. Hrsg. v. MARKÉTA POSKOČILOVA u. a. Olmütz 2022. Zur Sammlung Olomouc Kap.

PUGLISI, CARMEN: Boezio e Aristotele in uno sconosciuto incunabolo della Biblioteca Regionale 'Giacomo Longo' di Messina. In: *La percezione del libro. Studi in ricordo di Marco Santoro.* Hrsg. v. VALENTINA SESTINI. (Libri e biblioteche. 8.). Messina 2021, S. 47–63.

QUAGLIONI, DIEGO: Dal manoscritto alla stampa. Agli inizi della tipografia giuridica bolognese. In: DIEGO QUAGLIONI: *Scritti.* Hrsg. v. LUCIA BIANCHIN u. a. 2 Bde (durchgehende Seitenzählung). Foligno 2022, S. 517–50 (Erstveröffentlichung 2002).

RANACHER, CHRISTIAN: Effizienz aus Ordnung. Die Organisation der Rosenkranzbruderschaften als Grundlage für eine innovative Form der Jenseitsvorsorge um 1500. In: *Narrare – producere – ordinare. Neue Zugänge zum Mittelalter.* Hrsg. v. VIENNA DOCTORAL ACADEMY – „MEDIEVAL ACADEMY". (agora. 1.). Wien 2021, S. 205–15. DOI: 10.23783/9783706910637 (gesamter Band). U.a. zu GW 10860, M43168 und M4316910.

READ, STEPHEN: 'Everything True Will Be False': Paul of Venice and a Medieval Yablo Paradox. In: *History and Philosophy of Logic* 43 (2022), S. 332–46. DOI: 10.1080/01445340.2022.2040797. U.a. zu GW M30365.

REGGI, GIANCARLO: Tradizione umanistica milanese delle *Ad familiares* di Cicerone: le due mani del codice di Lugano, fra conservatorismo e restauri testuali antecedenti il Poliziano. In: *Fogli* 43 (2022), S. 26–66. bibliotecafratilugano.ch/content/fogli/43/fogli_43-2022.pdf (gesamtes Heft).

REYES GÓMEZ, FERMÍN DE LOS: *Incunabula: la imprenta llega a España*. (Tesoros de la Biblioteca Nacional de España. 4.). Madrid 2022. Katalog zur Ausstellung *Incunabula: 550 años de la imprenta en España*, Madrid BN, 21. April–23. Juli 2022.

REYES GÓMEZ, FERMÍN DE LOS; VALERÓN RAMÍREZ, NÉSTOR: Una bula ¿incunable? de la catedral de Las Palmas (*A Fifteenth-Century (?) Indulgence for the Cathedral of Las Palmas*). In: *Titivillus* 8 (2022), S. 11–25.

RIDEAU-KIKUCHI, CATHERINE: La construction d'un marché d'imprimeurs. Mobilités et relations économiques dans l'Italie du Nord incunable. In: *Mélanges de l'École française de Rome* 134 (2022), S. 193–217. Mit englischsprachigem Abstract.

RIEGER, HANNAH: Füchsische Poetologie. Zur Spiegelfiktion im *Reynke de Vos* (1498). In: *Poetica* 50 (2020), S. 193–218. Zu GW 12733.

RIUS I BOU, ÁNGELS; REYES GÓMEZ, FERMÍN DE LOS: Las indulgencias para la catedral de Lérida, un ejemplo más para el estudio de la edición de bulas incunables y de bibliografía material. In: *Revista general de información y documentación* 32 (2022), S. 467–94. DOI: 10.5209/rgid.85289. Zu einem Fundkomplex von ca. 450 Ablaßbrief-Formularen, zumeist in Lérida Catedr (GW-Werkkatalog ‚Mila, Luis de', mehrere zuvor unbekannte Ausgaben). Mit englischsprachigem Abstract.

ROCCATI, G. MATTEO: Les débuts de la production incunable à Genève: Adam Steinschaber et ses contemporains (années 1478–1481). In: *All'incrocio di due mondi. Comunità, ambiente, culture, tradizioni delle valli alpine, dal versante padano a quello elvetico*. Hrsg. v. ENRICO BASSO. Cherasco 2021, S. 347–64.

RODRÍGUEZ-MESA, FRANCISCO JOSÉ: *El Perleone de Rustico Romano. Un cancionero de la Nápoles aragonesa. Estudio y edición crítica*. Granada 2021. Zum GW-Werkkatalog ‚Perleone, Giuliano' (GW M31055).

ROLAND, MEG: *Mirror of the World. Literatur, Maps, and Geographic Writing in Late Medieval and Early Modern England*. Abingdon, New York 2022. U. a. zu GW 3414, 10966, 10967, M20161, M20422 und M20423.

ROTH, CHRISTOPH: Variatio prodest. Heinrich Knoblochtzers Wiederaufnahme von Titeln seiner Straßburger Zeit in Heidelberg. In: *heiDOK* (Heidelberger Dokumentenserver), 18. Juli 2022. DOI: 10.11588/heidok.00031921.

RUGGIO, LUCA: Poliziano e la collazione degli *Scriptores rei rusticae*. Le note all'incunabolo parigino Rés. s. 439. In: *Politien, humaniste aux sources de la modernité*. Hrsg. v. ÉMILIE SÉRIS und PAOLO VITTI. (Rencontres. 519.). Paris 2021, S. 141–54.

SACCENTI, RICCARDO: Manuscripts and Printed Editions of Book IV of the *Summa fratris Alexandri*. In: *Archivum Franciscanum Historicum* 114 (2021), S. 3–46. U. a. zu GW 871 und 872.

SAGGINI, ROMILDA; RAMAGLI, PAOLO: *Libri antichi tra Savona e Albenga. Inventari cinquecenteschi e catalogazione dei fondi di due diocesi liguri.* Introd. EDOARDO BARBIERI. (Libri e biblioteche. 45.). Udine 2020. U. a. Kataloge der Sammlungen Albenga BCap und Sem sowie Savona Sem und Archivio storico diocesano.

SAHM, HEIKE; RECKER, ANABEL: Wiedererzählen im Norden. Beobachtungen zu Übertragungsstrategien mittelniederdeutscher Erzähltexte. In: *Niederdeutsches Jahrbuch. Jahrbuch des Vereins für niederdeutsche Sprachforschung* 144 (2021), S. 127–49.

SCAPECCHI, PIERO: Aldo e San Marco in un esemplare del Poliziano aldino conservato alla Bodleian Library. In: *La Bibliofilía* 123 (2021), S. 285–90. Zum 2. Exemplar Oxford Bodl von GW M34727. Mit englischsprachigem Abstract.

SCARPATETTI, BEAT VON: *Bücherliebe und Weltverachtung. Die Bibliothek des Volkspredigers Heynlin von Stein und ihr Geheimnis.* Basel 2022. Zum GW-Werkkatalog ‚Johannes de Lapide'.

SCHLECHTER, ARMIN: Speyerer Buchbesitz vor 1689. I. Ein Sammelband aus dem Besitz der Speyerer Kleriker Johann Jochgrim und Jakob Hartlieb. II. Ein Speyerer Schulpreisband aus dem Jahr 1617 mit Wappensupralibros von Philipp Christoph von Sötern. In: *Literatur in ihren kulturellen Räumen. Festschrift für Hermann Wiegand zum 70. Geburtstag 1. Januar 2021.* Hrsg. v. WILHELM KREUTZ und WILHELM KÜHLMANN. Heidelberg 2021, S. 299–318.

SCHWEITZER-MARTIN, PAUL: Material und Format liturgischer Inkunabeldrucke. Eine Fallstudie zur Offizin Johannes Sensenschmidts. In: *Wissen und Buchgestalt.* Hrsg. v. PHILIPP HEGEL und MICHAEL KREWET. (Episteme in Bewegung. 26.). Wiesbaden 2022, S. 301–21, Farbtafeln S. 396–400. DOI: 10.13173/9783447118095.301. (gesamter Band: 10.13173/9783447118095).

SCHWEITZER-MARTIN, PAUL: *Kooperation und Innovation im Speyerer Buchdruck des ausgehenden Mittelalters.* (Materiale Textkulturen. 37.). Berlin, Boston 2022. DOI: 10.1515/9783110796599.

SCHWITTER, THOMAS: *Erinnerung im Umbruch. Die Fortsetzung, Drucklegung und Ablösung der „Grandes chroniques de France" im 15. und frühen 16. Jahrhundert.* (Pariser Historische Studien. 124.). Heidelberg 2022. DOI: 10.17885/heiup.854. Zu GW 6676–6685.

Sebastian Brant, das ‚Narrenschiff' und der frühe Buchdruck in Basel. Zum 500. Todestag eines humanistischen Gelehrten. Hrsg. v. LYSANDER BÜCHLI, ALYSSA STEINER und TINA TERRAHE. Basel 2022. schwabe.ch/Sebastian-Brant-das-Narrenschiff-und-der-fruehe-Buchdruck-in-Basel-978-3-7965-4758-4. Inhalt (ohne Rahmentexte):
- THOMAS WILHELMI: Einige Ergänzungen zur Biographie Sebastian Brants (S. 29–38)

- JOACHIM KNAPE: Das Medienregulativ der Textverfassung. Ein Vortrag mit Blick auf Sebastian Brant (S. 39–64)
- MICHAEL RUPP: Maria, Sebastian und Ivo. Beobachtungen zu den religiösen Dichtungen Sebastian Brants im Druck (S. 65–90; zu GW 5025 und 1228630N)
- BENJAMIN HITZ: Risikokapital und Schuldenberge. Drucker und Papiermacher im spätmittelalterlichen Basel als Handwerker und Unternehmer (S. 91–115)
- PETER ANDERSEN: Sebastian Brants Bildnisse von 1494 bis heute. Eine Untersuchung von 57 Darstellungen unterschiedlicher Verlässlichkeit (S. 117–62)
- CHRISTA BERTELSMEIER-KIERST: ‚Pictura' und ‚poesis' in Brants ‚Narrenschiff' (1494) (S. 165–89)
- LYSANDER BÜCHLI: ‚On vrsach ist das nit gethan'. Zum rhetorischen Hintergrund von Sebastian Brants ‚Narrenschiff' (S. 191–228)
- LINUS MÖLLENBRINK: Welterfahrung und ‚Wirklichkeit'. Das Weltbild des ‚Narrenschiffs' zwischen Mittelalter und Neuzeit (S. 229–57)
- JOACHIM HAMM: ‚Narragonia latine facta'. Jakob Locher und die ‚Stultifera navis' (1497) (S. 261–91)
- BRIGITTE BURRICHTER: Sebastian Brant und Jakob Locher in den französischen ‚Narrenschiff'-Übertragungen (S. 293–311)
- THOMAS BAIER: Horazische Narren. Josse Bade und Sebastian Brants ‚Narrenschiff' (S. 313–39)
- ALYSSA STEINER: ‚Jn disen spiegel sollen schowen | All gschlecht der menschen mann vnd frowen'. Die europäischen ‚Narrenschiff'-Bearbeitungen und ihre intendierten Leserinnen und Leser (S. 341–65)

SELZER, G[ERTRAUDE] T.: *Tod in der Schöfferstadt. Ein Kriminalroman aus Südhessen*. Frankfurt (Main) 2022. „Mehr als ein halbes Jahrtausend … ist die zweibändige Bibel alt und über eine Million Euro wert, die Anne Schäfer für einen Kunden an ein Auktionshaus in Hamburg vermittelt. Für sie ist es eine Ehrensache, wurde die Bibel doch 1462 in Mainz von Peter Schöffer gedruckt, dem berühmtesten Sohn ihrer Heimatstadt, der Schöfferstadt Gernsheim. Doch die kostbaren Bände verschwinden, und es gibt Tote. Die Spur führt vom Auktionshaus in Hamburg über Münster in Westfalen bis nach Frankfurt, wo die Kommissare Paul Langer und Johannes Korp in Aktion treten – und des jungen Kriminalobermeister Jens Schmidtbauers große Stunde schlägt." (Werbetext).

SIGNORELLO, LUCREZIA: *L'affaire* Laire e le edizioni romane del XV secolo negli scritti scambiati tra Tommaso Verani e Giovanni Battista Audiffredi. In: *Bibliothecae.it* 11 (2022) 1, S. 182–221. DOI: 10.6092/issn.2283-9364/15076. Mit englischsprachigem Abstract. Behandelt Giovanni Battista Audiffredi: Catalogus historico-criticum Romanarum editionum saeculi XV. Rom 1783 (books.google.de/books?id=6URkc21u2iMC).

SIGNORELLO, LUCREZIA: *Ars artificialiter scribendi*. Le edizioni quattrocentesche dell'Archivio Generale Agostiniano. In: *Analecta Augustiniana* 85 (2022), S. 213–22. Zur Sammlung Roma ArchAug.

SIMIĆ, VLADIMIR: Between Venice and the Danube. Hieromonk Makarije and His Cyrillic Incunabula at the Turn of the Sixteenth Century. In: *The Land Between Two Seas. Art on the Move in the Mediterranean and the Black Sea 1300–1700*. Hrsg. v. ALINA PAYNE. (Mediterranean Art Histories. 5.). Leiden, Boston 2022, S. 252–70. DOI: 10.1163/9789004515468_014. Zur Werkstatt Cetinje: Makarije (GW M27441, M2744110, M36271 und M4747310).

SLAVÍKOVÁ, MARCELA: Johannes Honorius Cubitensis (c. 1465–1504). Biography, Editorial Notes, and Editions. In: *Bohemian Editors and Translators at the Turn of the 16th Century*. Hrsg. v. MARTA VACULÍNOVÁ u. a. (Europa Humanistica: Bohemia and Moravia. 3.). Turnhout 2021, S. 55–182.

SLAVÍKOVÁ, MARCELA: *Librum pulcherrimum et utilissimum edidit*: Editions of Horace by Johannes Honorius Cubitensis (c. 1465–1504). In: *Horace across the Media. Textual, Visual and Musical Receptions of Horace from the 15th to the 18th Century*. Hrsg v. KARL A. E. ENENKEL und MARC LAUREYS. (Intersections. 82.). Leiden, Boston 2022, S. 445–79. Beide Titel zum GW-Werkkatalog ‚Johannes Honorius de Cubito'.

SLAVÍKOVÁ, MARCELA: *Disticha culta lege*: Some Remarks on the Edition of Martial's *Xenia et Apophoreta* by Johannes Honorius Cubitensis (1488; 1498²; 1508³). In: *Influence et réception du poète Martial, de sa mort à nos jours*. Hrsg. v. ÉTIENNE WOLFF. Bordeaux 2022, S. 161–72. Zu GW M21297 und M21298.

SOLANA PUJALTE, JULIÁN: A *Sammelband* of Incunabula of British Provenance Held at the Diocesan Library of Córdoba Containing the Only Known Copy of *Elegantiae terminorum ex Laurentio Valla et aliis collectae*, Antwerp: Gerard Leeu, 7.XI.1487 (GW M35200). In. *Quaerendo* 52 (2022), S. 83–118.

SOLVI, DANIELE: Verso un'edizione critica dell'*Arbor vite crucifixe Iesu* di Ubertino da Casale (*Towards a Critical Edition of Ubertino of Casale's ‚Arbor vite crucifixe Iesu'*). In: *Specula* 4 (2022), S. 59–85. DOI: 10.46583/specula_2022.4.1080. Auch zum GW-Werkkatalog ‚Ubertinus de Casali' (GW M48799).

SOMMER, DOROTHEA u. a.: Forschungsorientierte Inkunabelerschließung und -digitalisierung in deutschen Bibliotheken: Bedarfe und Perspektiven – DFG-Rundgespräch am 22. und 23. Februar 2022. Bericht der Bayerischen Staatsbibliothek. In: *Zeitschrift für Bibliothekswesen und Bibliographie* 69 (2022), S. 338–50.

SORIANO ROBLES, LOURDES: Els viatges dels incunables del *Tirant* (1490 i 1497) fins a la Hispanic Society of America. In: *Magnificat. Cultura i literatura medievals* 9 (2022), S. 281–301.

DOI: 10.7203/MCLM.9.23758. Zu den Exemplaren New York HispanSoc von GW M47103 und M47105. Mit englischsprachigem Abstract.

STAMPFER, ELISABETH; WUNDERLE, ELISABETH; ZÖHL, CAROLINE: Gut zum Druck: Ein bebildertes Schmähgedicht zwischen neu entdeckten Streitschriften gegen Wigand Wirt. In: *Maniculae* 3 (2022), S. 29–35. maniculae.de/index.php/maniculae/article/view/33. Zur neu erworbenen Handschrift München SB, Clm 30336 (um 1507/1510), die u. a. eine Aufforderung zum Druck humanistischer Streitschriften enthält.

STEIN, ROBERT: Van Blaffert naar Flappaert. Over de mislukking van een administratief experiment in Gouda (1490–1500). In: *De Schatkamer. Regionaal Historisch Jaarboekje 2020 Midden-Holland*, o. S. scholarlypublications.universiteitleiden.nl/access/item%3A3188484/view. Zu GW 10971.

Subiaco 1465. Nascita di un progetto editoriale? Atti del convegno Subiaco 2–3 ottobre 2015, Abbazia di Santa Scolastica. Subiaco 2021. Inhalt:
- EDOARDO BARBIERI: L'attività tipografica in alcuni monasteri del XV secolo: da Subiaco a Ripoli (S. 3-16)
- AUGUSTO CIUFFETTI: I libri di Subiaco, il commercio della carta e la civiltà appenninica, secoli XIV–XVI (S. 17-33)
- CONCETTA BIANCA: Il cardinale Juan de Torquemada (S. 51–62)
- LUCHINA BRANCIANI: La produzione incunabola della prima tipografia italiana narrata nelle cronache sublacensi (S. 71–99)
- VALENTINO ROMANI: Intorno alle prime stampe sublacensi (S. 101–18)
- PIERO SCAPECCHI: Viaggi di tipografi e di libri (S. 119–24)
- MARTIN DAVIES: Gli incunaboli sublacensi: la testimonianza della miniatura (S. 125–41)
- MARIA ANTONIETTA ORLANDI: Sweynheym & Pannartz, proto-tipografi sublacensi, e il De oratore di Cicerone (S. 161–80)

SUWELACK, HEDWIG: *Der „Herzmahner" als spätmittelalterliche Gebetserzählung*. (Spätmittelalter, Humanismus, Reformation. 127.). Tübingen 2022. Zu GW M07711.

Die Synodalstatuten der Kölner Kirche im Spätmittelalter 1261–1513. Bearb. von HEINZ WOLTER. (Publikationen der Gesellschaft für Rheinische Geschichtskunde. 84.). Köln 2022. Bd. 1, S. 63-7: „Die frühen Drucke" (GW M43456, M43458, M43459).

TAGLIABRACCI, MICHELE: Catalogo degli incunaboli della Biblioteca Comunale di Urbania. In: *Il Cardinal Bessarione Abate a Casteldurante e Federico da Montefeltro*. Hrsg. v. MARCO MENATO und FELICIANA PAOLI. Urbino 2022, S. 81-6. Zur Sammlung Urbania BCom (46 Nummern).

TAYLOR, DANIELLE: Anything You Can Do: Gawain, Lancelot, and Failure in Malory's *Le Morte Darthur*. In: *Arthuriana* 32,1 (2022),

S. 35–54. Zum GW-Werkkatalog ‚Malory, Thomas' (GW M20157 und M20161).

THEISEN, MARIA unter Mitarbeit von IRINA VON MORZÉ: *Mitteleuropäische Schulen VII (ca. 1400–1500). Böhmen – Mähren – Schlesien – Ungarn*. Mit Beiträgen von ULRIKE JENNY u. a. (Österreichische Akademie der Wissenschaften. Phil.-hist. Klasse. Denkschriften. 540. = Veröffentlichungen zum Schrift- und Buchwesen des Mittelalters. I. 17: Die illuminierten Handschriften und Inkunabeln der Österreichischen Nationalbibliothek.). Wien 2022. DOI: 10.1553/9780EAW88612 (Textband); austriaca.at/8861-2inhalt? (Text- und Tafelband). Mit Beschreibungen von ca. 45 Inkunabeln.

TOPP, BENJAMIN: ‚*Venenum de manibus credulorum extorquere'. Giovanni Pico della Mirandola: Disputationes adversus astrologos I–IV. Edition, Übersetzung und Anmerkungen*. Osnabrück 2022. Zu GW M33284 und M33308.

The Unexpected Dante. Perspectives on the Divine Comedy. Hrsg. v. LUCIA ALMA WOLF. Lewisburg, Washington (D.C.) 2022. Zu frühen Dante-Drucken in Washington (D.C.) LC. Aus dem Inhalt:
- SYLVIA R. ALBRO: A Florentine First. Dante Alighieri's 'Divine Comedy' in Print, 1481 Edition: Observations and Discoveries (S. 60–75; zu GW 7966)
- LUCIA ALMA WOLF: Crossing Borders with the 'Divine Comedy'. A Catalog of Selected Works from the Library of Congress (S. 76–153, Inkunabeln S. 76–88)

UTTENWEILER, BERNHARD: Älteste bildliche Darstellung der Legende des hl. Landelin von Ettenheimmünster zusammen mit den Quellen auf einem Frühdruck des 15. Jahrhunderts. In: *Die Ortenau* 101 (2021), S. 297–300.

VACALEBRE, NATALE: *A Book for all Seasons: Reading Habits and Material Reception of Dante's "Divina Commedia" in Early Modern Italy*. Diss. University of Pennsylvania. Philadelphia 2022.

VACALEBRE, NATALE: Grandi speranze, tempi difficili. La *Commedia* di Foligno, le sue origine e i suoi primi lettori. In: *Dante, l'Umbria e i santi. Atti delle giornate di studio di Foligno e Assisi (13–16 aprile 2021)*. Hrsg. v. CRISTIANA BRUNELLI. Ravenna 2022, S. 141–50. Zu GW 7958.

VACALEBRE, NATALE: A Hell of a Poem! Censoring Dante's *Commedia* in Early Modern Spain. In: *Reformation, Religious Culture and Print in Early Modern Europe. Essays in Honour of Andrew Pettegree*. Hrsg. v. ARTHUR DER WEDUWEN und MALCOLM WALSBY. Bd. 1. (Library of the Written Word. 107/1.). Leiden, Boston 2022, S. 189–214. U. a. zum Ex. Toronto TrinityC von GW 7972.

VACALEBRE, NATALE: Divine Markets: Producing, Selling and Reading Dante's *Commedia* in the Early 1470s. In: *Bibliothecae.it* 11 (2022) 1, S. 112–55. DOI: 10.6092/issn.2283-9364/15074.Zu GW 7958–7960.

VACALEBRE, NATALE: Nel mezzo della fiera. Nuove ipotesi sulle origine dell'edizione folignate della *Commedia*. In: *La Bibliofilía* 123 (2021), S. 237–50. Zu GW 7958. Mit englischsprachigem Abstract.

VACULÍNOVÁ, MARTA: Paulus Niavis (c. 1453–1517). Biography, Editorial Notes, and Editions. In: *Bohemian Editors and Translators at the Turn of the 16th Century*. Hrsg. v. MARTA VACULÍNOVÁ u. a. (Europa Humanistica: Bohemia and Moravia. 3.). Turnhout 2021, S. 35–54.

VAGNON, EMMANUELLE: When Religious Geography Meets the Geography of Humanists. The *Tabulae modernae Terrae Sanctae* in the Copies of the 'Geography' of Ptolemy in the Fifteenth Century. In: *Geography and Religious Knowledge in the Medieval World*. Hrsg. v. CHRISTOPH MAUNTEL. (Das Mittelalter. Perspektiven historischer Forschung. Beihefte. 14.) . Berlin, Boston 2021, S. 223–46. U. a. zu GW 3870, M36374 und M36379.

VOLPATO, GIANCARLO: Incunaboli e cinquecentine ritrovati nella Biblioteca Capitolare di Verona. In: *La percezione del libro. Studi in ricordo di Marco Santoro*. Hrsg. v. VALENTINA SESTINI. (Libri e biblioteche. 8.). Messina 2021, S. 9–46. Zur Sammlung Verona BCap.

VOSKOBOYNIKOV, OLEG: Michael Scotus' *Physiognomy*: Notes on Text and Context. In: *The Body as a Mirror of the Soul. Physiognomy from Antiquity to the Renaissance*. Hrsg. v. LISA DEVRIESE. Leuven 2021, S. 109–36. Zum GW-Werkkatalog ‚Scotus, Michael'.

WAGNER, BETTINA: Ausgaben für Kettenbücher in den mittelalterlichen Sakristeirechnungen des Bamberger Doms. In: *Jahrbuch für Buch- und Bibliotheksgeschichte* 7 (2022), S. 45–52.

WAGNER, BETTINA: "Duplum Bibliothecae regiae Monacensis": The Munich Court Library and its Book Auctions in the Nineteenth Century. In: *How the Secularization of Religious Houses Transformed the Libraries of Europe, 16th–19th Centuries*. Hrsg. v. CRISTINA DONDI, DORIT RAINES und RICHARD SHARPE. (Bibliologia. 63.). Turnhout 2022, S. 389–415. Zuerst in: *Papers of the Bibliographical Society of America* 111 (2017), S. 345–77.

WARDHAUGH, BENJAMIN; BEELEY, PHILIP; NASIFOGLU, YELDA: *Euclid in Print, 1482–1703. A Catalogue of the Editions of the Elements and Other Euclidean Works*. London 2020. bibsoc.org.uk/content/euclid-print-1482-1703. U. a. zu GW 9428 und 9429.

WARREN, MAUREEN: Gillet and Germain Hardouyn's Print-Assisted Paintings. Prints as Underdrawings in Sixteenth-Century French Books of Hours. In: *The Reception of the Printed Image in the Fifteenth and Sixteenth Centuries: Multiplied and Modified*. Hrsg. v. GRAŻYNA JURKOWLANIEC und MAGDALENA HERMAN. New York, London 2020, S. 81–96.

WEY, JEAN-CLAUDE; NAAS, LAURENT: *Jean Geiler de Kaysersberg. Trésors iconographiques humanistes.* Barr 2021. U. a. zu GW 10587.

WHITE, ERIC MARSHALL: New Light on the Histories of Albrecht Pfister's Bamberg Picture Books of the 1460s. In: *Jahrbuch für Buch- und Bibliotheksgeschichte* 7 (2022), S. 7–44.

William Touris OFM: 'The Contemplacioun of Synnaris'. Late-Medieval Advice to a Prince. Hrsg. v. ALASDAIR MACDONALD und J. CRAIG MCDONALD (Studies in Medieval and Reformation Traditions. 232 = Texts and Sources. 12.). Leiden, Boston 2022. Ausgabe von GW 7445.

WOLF, JÜRGEN: Mittelalterliche Handschriften und Inkunabeln in der Fürstlich Waldeckschen Hofbibliothek (FWHB). In: *Geschichtsblätter für Waldeck* 110 (2022), S. 39–78. Zur Sammlung Arolsen HB.

ZÖHL, CAROLINE: Buchschmuck in Inkunabeln – Perspektiven einer kooperativen Exemplarerschließung. In: *Bibliothek und Wissenschaft* 55 (2022): Faszination (Buch-)Handschriften im Jahr 2022. Tradition und Zukunft ihrer Erschließung in Bibliothek und Wissenschaft. Hrsg. v. CLAUDIA FABIAN, S. 203–35.

Nachruf auf Eckehart SchumacherGebler

© Familie Schumacher-Gebler

Präsidium und Vorstand der Internationalen Gutenberg-Gesellschaft in Mainz e. V. trauern um ihren Gutenberg-Preisträger und ihr langjähriges Mitglied Eckehart SchumacherGebler, der am 17. Dezember 2022 im Alter von 88 Jahren verstorben ist.

Eckehart SchumacherGebler stammte aus einer Münchner Druckerfamilie und war ausgebildeter Drucker und Schriftsetzer. Nach seinem Studium an der Hochschule für Grafisches Gewerbe in München übernahm er Anfang der 1960er Jahre die elterliche Druckerei.

Seit dieser Zeit hat er sich auf vielfältige Weise um die Buchdruckkunst, ihren Erhalt und ihre Weitergabe, verdient gemacht, insbesondere durch seine Offizin Haag-Drugulin in Dresden, ein Studio für Typografie, sowie seinen Verlag. Im Jahr 1994 gründete er das Museum für Druckkunst in Leipzig, das als „arbeitendes Werkstattmuseum" die handwerklich-künstlerischen Drucktechniken vermittelt. Im Jahr darauf rief er zudem die „Leipziger Typotage" ins Leben, die sich jedes Jahr im Rahmen einer internationalen Tagung der Schriftgeschichte und der zeitgenössischen Typografie widmen. Seit 2013 war er Honorarprofessor für Druckkunst an der Hochschule der Bildenden Künste Saar.

Erst vor wenigen Monaten verliehen die Internationale Gutenberg-Gesellschaft und die Stadt Mainz SchumacherGebler den Gutenberg-Preis 2022 für seinen unermüdlichen Einsatz, die Technik des Buchdrucks und damit das Erbe Gutenbergs lebendig zu halten.

Seit über 20 Jahren unterstützte Eckehart SchumacherGebler die Ziele unserer Gesellschaft und wir verlieren mit ihm nicht nur eine bedeutende Persönlichkeit, sondern auch ein hoch geschätztes Mitglied. Unsere Anteilnahme gilt besonders der Familie und allen Angehörigen.

Im Namen von Präsidium und Vorstand der Internationalen Gutenberg-Gesellschaft in Mainz e. V.

Univ.-Prof. Dr. Stephan Füssel
Vizepräsident

Dr. Julia Bangert
Geschäftsführerin

Jahresbericht der internationalen Gutenberg-Gesellschaft für 2022

Die Gutenberg-Gesellschaft kann auf ein gutes und spannendes Jahr 2022 zurückblicken: Am 13. Oktober wurde unser Präsident und Oberbürgermeister Michael Ebling zum Innenminister des Landes Rheinland-Pfalz ernannt. Wir freuen uns sehr für ihn, bedauern aber gleichzeitig auch, ihn dadurch als Präsidenten der Gutenberg-Gesellschaft zu verlieren. Bis zur Neuwahl des Mainzer Oberbürgermeisters im Frühjahr 2023 übertrug der Vorstand dem Vizepräsidenten, Prof. Dr. Stephan Füssel, die mit dem Präsidentensitz verbundenen Aufgaben. Wir bedanken uns an dieser Stelle sehr herzlich bei Michael Ebling für sein Engagement und seinen unermüdlichen Einsatz für die Ziele der Gesellschaft in den letzten zehn Jahren.

Besonders gefreut hat uns die bereits jetzt sehr gute Zusammenarbeit mit dem neuen Direktor des Gutenberg-Museums Dr. Ulf Sölter. So konnten wir innerhalb kurzer Zeit einen neuen, typografisch stilsicher gestalteten gemeinsamen Messeauftritt mit dem Museum und der Gutenberg Stiftung bei der diesjährigen Frankfurter Buchmesse realisieren.

Wie jedes Jahr konnten sich die Mitglieder auch wieder über ihr Exemplar des neuen Gutenberg-Jahrbuchs freuen, das in gewohnter Qualität pünktlich zur Mainzer Johannisnacht erschien. Ein weiteres Präsent erhielten unsere Mitglieder zu Weihnachten: den neuen Band in der Reihe „Kleine Drucke". Der Kleine Druck Nr. 114 enthält die Antrittsrede der Mainzer Stadtschreiberin 2018 Anna Katharina Hahn unter dem Titel „Ich kann mir alles vorstellen". Von den „Lettertypen" wurde der neue Kleine Druck mit einer hochwertigen Fadenheftung ausgestattet und auf einem Original Heidelberger Cylinder Baujahr 1954 gedruckt.

Aus der Geschäftsstelle

Praktikantinnen

Im Jahr 2022 waren sieben Praktikantinnen – mehrheitlich Studierende des Mainzer Gutenberg-Instituts für Buchwissenschaft der JGU – für jeweils drei Monate als Unterstützung in der Geschäftsstelle tätig. Für ihre engagierte Arbeit, die sie unentgeltlich geleistet haben, dankt die Gutenberg-Gesellschaft im Namen ihrer Mitglieder und Organe: Sonja Knobling, Huyen Tran Tran Thi, Malin Reinhard, Florentine Sofie

Wörner, Ines Kristin Rapp, Judith Theiß und Tabea Möller. Ohne ihren Einsatz könnten viele Projekte nicht realisiert und der Geschäftsstellenbetrieb nicht so effektiv geführt werden.

Förderung

Gemäß ihrer Satzung und dem Vereinszweck entsprechend förderte die Internationale Gutenberg-Gesellschaft in Mainz e.V. auch 2022 wieder die Erforschung des Druck- und Buchwesens durch Publikationen, Vorträge und andere Formate. Darüber hinaus unterstützte sie das Gutenberg-Museum Mainz durch eine Zuwendung in Höhe von 10.000 Euro für die Ausstellung „Hotspot Gutenberg-Museum – hoher Besuch in Rheinland-Pfalz" sowie weiteren 7.500 Euro für die Katalogisierung der Bestände des Mainzer Minipressenarchivs (MMPA).

Entwicklung der Mitgliederzahlen

Im Jahr 2022 erfuhr die Gesellschaft bedauerlicherweise 28 Mitgliedschaftskündigungen und verlor durch Todesfälle sieben Mitglieder aus ihren Reihen. Im gleichen Zeitraum kamen 13 neue Mitglieder hinzu. Zum Jahresende 2022 betrug die Anzahl der persönlichen und institutionellen Mitgliedschaften aus dem In- und Ausland kumuliert 692, inklusive zwei Probemitgliedschaften.

Trauer um Persönlichkeiten der Gutenberg-Gesellschaft

Die Internationale Gutenberg-Gesellschaft in Mainz e.V. trauert um die 2022 verstorbenen Mitglieder Karl Heinz Köhler, Helmut Kölbel, Hermann Reifenberg, Alfred Swierk, Hermann Hans Schmidt, Pamela Stokes und Gregory Jackson Walters. Es verstarb außerdem der aktuelle Gutenberg-Preisträger Eckehart SchumacherGebler. Mit dem bekannten Drucker und Schriftsetzer verliert die Gutenberg-Gesellschaft auch ein langjähriges und engagiertes Mitglied. Wir verabschieden uns von ihm in großer Dankbarkeit und Hochachtung.

Wirtschaftlicher Lagebericht

Die Gutenberg-Gesellschaft konnte im Jahr 2022 Spenden in Höhe von € 956,63 verbuchen, dazu kam von der Stadt Mainz die Zuwendung in Höhe von € 13.504. Insgesamt wurden im Geschäftsjahr 2022 Einnahmen in der Größenordnung von € 189.699,43 erzielt, denen Ausgaben von € 127.132,80 gegenüberstehen. Daraus resultiert ein positives Jahresergebnis, das sich auf € 62.566,63 beläuft und in den Folgejahren zur Unterstützung des Gutenberg-Museums eingesetzt wird.

Mitgliederversammlung

Am Samstag, den 25. Juni 2022, fand die 121. Mitgliederversammlung der Internationalen Gutenberg-Gesellschaft in Mainz e.V. statt. Nach zwei Jahren online konnten wir uns zu diesem Anlass wieder vor Ort im Forstersaal des Kurfürstlichen Schlosses Mainz versammeln. Nach der Begrüßung durch Prof. Dr. Stephan Füssel als Vizepräsident der Gutenberg-Gesellschaft folgten satzungsgemäß die Berichte der Geschäftsführerin (Dr. Julia Bangert) und des Museumsdirektors (Dr. Ulf Sölter). Anschließend gab der Schatzmeister (Thorsten Mühl) einen Überblick über den Jahresbericht 2021. Der Bericht der Rechnungsprüfer (Bernd Rehling und Holger Scharmann) zum abgelaufenen Geschäftsjahr 2021 wurde von Bernd Rehling vorgetragen.

Der Vorstand und die Geschäftsführung wurden einstimmig entlastet und mit Volker Hans und Florian Ott zwei neue Rechnungsprüfer für das Jahr 2022 bestellt. Wir bedanken uns an dieser Stelle sehr herzlich bei Bernd Rehling und Holger Scharmann für ihr jahrelanges und zuverlässiges Engagement in diesem Amt. Auch der durch den Schatzmeister vorgestellte Haushaltsplan für 2022 wurde einstimmig angenommen. Zuletzt beschloss die Mitgliederversammlung auf Antrag von Prof. Dr. Füssel und Prof. Dr. Corinna Norrick-Rühl der niederländischen Buchhistorikerin und Gutenberg-Preisträgerin 1989 Prof. Dr. Lotte Hellinga-Querido anlässlich ihres 90. Geburtstages die Ehrenmitgliedschaft zu verleihen.

Nach einer kurzen Kaffeepause folgte die anschließende Festveranstaltung mit der Verleihung des Gutenberg-Preises. Zunächst stellten dabei der Herausgeber Prof. Dr. Füssel und der Gestalter Ralf de Jong das neue Gutenberg-Jahrbuch 2022 vor. Dieses Jahrbuch ist das letzte, das unter der Herausgeberschaft von Prof. Füssel erscheint, da ab dem kommenden Jahr Prof. Dr. Gerhard Lauer für die Heraugabe zuständig ist. Prof. Füssel wurde daher anschließend eine kleine Schrift mit einem Überblick über alle von ihm herausgegebenen Jahrbücher der letzten 30 Jahre zum Dank überreicht und wir bedanken uns auch an dieser Stelle noch einmal sehr herzlich für sein unermüdliches Einsatz für ein stets pünktlich erscheinendes und inhaltlich sowie gestalterisch sehr hochwertiges Jahrbuch. Es folgte die Verleihung des Gutenberg-Preises, der 2022 erstmalig an zwei Preisträger ging: Prof. Dr. Jeffrey F. Hamburger, Kenner spätmittelalterlicher Buchmalerei und des Übergangs in die Druck-Ära und Eckehart SchumacherGebler, Drucker und Professor für Druckkunst. Die Laudatio für SchumacherGebler hielt Susanne Zippel und die Laudatio für Prof. Dr. Hamburger übernahm Falk Eisermann (nachzulesen am Beginn dieses Jahrbuchs). Die gelungene und festliche Veranstaltung beschlossen wir in großer Runde bei der traditionellen Gutenberg-Tafel im Restaurant im Landtag Rheinland-Pfalz RheinTisch.

Veranstaltungen und Öffentlichkeitsarbeit

Jour Fixe

Im Jahr 2022 fand der Jour Fixe wieder in Kombination mit einer kleinen Weinprobe regelmäßig in der Kulturei Mainz statt. Den Anfang machte im März Dr. Eberhard J. Nikitsch mit seinem Vortrag „Inschriften und (k)ein Ende? – Zur Genese einer neuen Publikation über die historischen Inschriften des Landkreises Mayen-Koblenz." Im April entführte uns Dr. Michael Schulte in ein neues Fachgebiet, die pharmazeutische Chemie, und berichtete über „Jesuiten gegen Galenisten – bitterer Bücherstreit über die Nützlichkeit der Fieberrinde gegen Malaria im 17. Jahrhundert". Nach einer kleinen Pause im Mai fand der dritte Jour Fixe erst im Juni statt. Nicht nur terminlich zwei Tage vor der Mitgliederversammlung, sondern auch inhaltlich bot dieser Jour Fixe eine Auftaktveranstaltung zu unseren Feierlichkeiten rund um die Johannisnacht mit einem Vortrag von Prof. Dr. Stephan Füssel über „Das Gutenberg-Museum im Kurfürstlichen Schloss Mainz – die Geburtsstunde des Weltmuseums der Druckkunst". Im September war der Verein Deutsche Sprache e. V. beim Jour Fixe zu Gast und Rigo Neumann erläuterte in einem Gespräch mit unserer Geschäftsführerin Dr. Julia Bangert den „#Süttember – Herbst der Handschrift". Im Oktober erwartete die Gäste schließlich ein Vortrag mit Büchern zum Anfassen, Blättern und Diskutieren von Silvia Werfel mit ihren „Gedanken übers Buch – über eine Buchreihe, die Stiftung Buchkunst und manches mehr".

Diskussionsrunde „Longdrinks"

Das studentische Gesprächsforum „Longdrinks" fand 2022 wieder einmal im Quartal statt. Im Februar starteten wir mit einer Videokonferenz zum Thema „Buchkonsum und -rezeption heute – Wo und wie werden Bücher gekauft? Von wem bekommt man den nächsten heißen Büchertipp?". Im Mai trafen wir uns dann wieder vor Ort und diskutierten über „Lesemotive – Warum lesen Menschen Bücher? Welche unbewussten Bedürfnisse beeinflussen den Buchkauf?". Das Quartier Mayence in Mainz erwies sich als passendes Lokal für unsere Diskussionsrunde und so trafen wir uns auch im August dort mit der Frage „Johannes Gutenberg als Medienikone – Prägt das Werk Gutenbergs die Digitalisierung?" und ein weiteres Mal im November zum Thema „Leseförderung – Jedes Kind kann lesen!?".

XXVII. Mainzer Kolloquium

Die Gutenberg-Gesellschaft war Mitveranstalter des maßgeblich vom Mainzer Gutenberg-Institut für Buchwissenschaft der JGU am 28. Januar 2022 ausgerichteten 27. Mainzer Kolloquiums zum Thema „Buch, Identitäten und die Freiheit der Sprache. Zur Politik von Verlagen in Zeiten aufgeheizter Debatten". Das Mainzer Kolloquium fand auch in diesem Jahr digital statt und diskutierte aus verschiedenen Perspektiven die Politik des Büchermachens.

Führungen und besondere Veranstaltungen

Im April 2022 luden wir zusammen mit der Gutenberg Stiftung Mitglieder und GUTE FREUNDE des Freundeskreises Gutenberg zum Osterdrucken in Gutenbergs Werkstatt in der Lulu Mainz ein. Bei einer Führung durch die Sonderausstellung „Road to Nowhere – Druckgrafiken von Tobias Gellscheid" im Gutenberg-Museum Mainz erhielten wir dann im Mai die Gelegenheit den neuen Museumsdirektor Dr. Ulf Sölter und die Kuratorin Dr. Anett Göthe kennenzulernen. Zum Abschluss des Jahres 2022 luden die Gutenberg-Gesellschaft und die Gutenberg Stiftung im Dezember außerdem wieder zum inzwischen traditionellen vorweihnachtlichen „Glühwein und Drucken" im Druckladen des Gutenberg-Museums ein.

Infostände

Auch im Jahr 2022 präsentierten sich die Gutenberg-Gesellschaft und die Gutenberg Stiftung dauerhaft mit einem gemeinsamen Infobereich unter dem Namen „Gutenbergs Werkstatt" in der lulu Mainz mit einer Druckstation mit Handpresse und Frottage und viel Infomaterial zu unseren Institutionen. Im September waren die Gutenberg-Gesellschaft und die Gutenberg Stiftung am Tag des offenen Denkmals wieder mit einem Infostand und einer Druckstation auf der von der Initiative Zitadelle Mainz e.V. veranstalteten Historischen Festungsmeile in der Kulturei Mainz vertreten. Und auch am zweiten Adventswochenende im Dezember 2022 beteiligten wir uns unter dem Motto „Glüh und Gloria" wieder mit einem Infostand und einer Druckstation an der bunten Veranstaltungsreihe der Initiative Zitadelle Mainz e.V. und der Kulturei.

Messebesuche

Im Jahr 2022 präsentierte sich die Gutenberg-Gesellschaft zusammen mit der Gutenberg Stiftung und dem Gutenberg-Museum unter dem Motto „Gutenberg para todos y todos para Gutenberg" mit einem neuen gemeinsamen Messestand auf der Frankfurter Buchmesse (19.–23. Oktober). Der neue Stand, der das Museum und seine Förderinstitutionen zukünftig auf allen großen Messen präsentiert, wurde von dem Grafiker Stefan Matlik gestaltet und zusammen von der Gutenberg-Gesellschaft und der Gutenberg Stiftung finanziert. Auch auf der Mainzer Büchermesse im November waren die Gutenberg-Gesellschaft und die Gutenberg Stiftung mit einem gemeinsamen Infostand vertreten.

Öffentlichkeitsarbeit

Die Gutenberg-Gesellschaft war auch im Jahr 2022 sehr aktiv auf ihren Profilen in den sozialen Netzwerken und einmal pro Monat wurde ein Newsletter in Deutsch und Englisch verschickt. Der Newsletter wie auch die Beiträge zu Gutenberg- und Buchthemen in den sozialen Netzwerken Facebook, Instagram und Twitter sind wesentlich vom Engagement der Praktikantinnen und Praktikanten hinsichtlich der Mitgliederkommunikation getragen und geprägt.

Präsidium und Vorstand

Dem Vorstand der Gutenberg-Gesellschaft gehörten 2022 folgende Personen kraft Amtes an: Oberbürgermeister Michael Ebling (bis Oktober 2022), der Vorsitzende des Senatorenrates *Dr. Peter Hanser-Strecker*, die *Ministerin Katharina Binz*, der Präsident der Johannes Gutenberg-Universität *Univ.-Prof. Dr. Georg Krausch*, die für das Gutenberg-Museum zuständige Dezernentin der Stadt Mainz *Marianne Grosse*, der Direktor des Gutenberg-Museums *Dr. Ulf Sölter* und der Inhaber des Lehrstuhls für Buchwissenschaft bei der Johannes Gutenberg-Universität *Prof. Dr. Gerhard Lauer*.

Weitere gewählte Vorstandsmitglieder in 2022 waren: Univ.-Prof. Dr. Stephan Füssel, Prof. Dr. Dr. Andreas Barner, Prof. Johannes Bergerhausen, Markus Kohz, Julia Lumma, Karl Michael Meinecke, Frank Mittelbach, Thorsten Mühl, Prof. Dr. Corinna Norrick-Rühl, Prof. Dr. Dipl.-Ing. Christoph Reske, Dr. Simone Schelberg, Werner von Bergen und Karsten Zerfaß.

Dem Präsidium gehörten 2022 an: Präsident Oberbürgermeister Michael Ebling (bis Oktober 2022), Vizepräsident Prof. Dr. Stephan Füssel, Schatzmeister Thorsten Mühl, Schriftführerin Prof. Dr. Corinna Norrick-Rühl, Direktor des Gutenberg-Museums Dr. Ulf Sölter und Werner von Bergen.

Fördermitglieder und Sponsoren

Die Gutenberg-Gesellschaft dankt allen Mitgliedern für ihr vielfältiges Engagement, die ehrenamtlichen Tätigkeiten und für die finanzielle Unterstützung durch beispielsweise einen freiwillig erhöhten Beitrag oder die zahlreichen Spenden. Besondere Verbundenheit drückt die Gutenberg-Gesellschaft den Spendern und Fördermitgliedern aus, die ihre Arbeit 2022 mit größeren Beiträgen unterstützt haben:
- Bundesverband Druck und Medien e. V.
- Hubert Burda Media Holding Kommanditgesellschaft
- Ringier AG
- Verlagsgruppe Rhein Main GmbH & Co. KG

Dr. Julia Bangert
(Geschäftsführerin seit 17.10.2017)

Abkürzungsverzeichnis

Archive, Bibliotheken, Museen und Universitäten

Arch.	Archiv, archive, archivio, archivo
B	Biblioteca, Bibliothek, Bibliothèque, Bücherei
BC	Biblioteca centrale, Bibliothèque centrale
BL	The British Library London (früher British Museum Library)
BM	British Museum London
B mun.	Biblioteca, Bibliothèque municipale
BN	Biblioteca nacional, Biblioteca nazionale, Bibliothèque nationale
BNC	Biblioteca Nazionale Centrale
BR	Bibliothèque royale
BNF	Bibliothèque nationale de France
BSB	Bayerische Staatsbibliothek München
Coll.	College, Collège
DB	Die Deutsche Bibliothek (bis 2007) (Deutsche Bücherei Leipzig, Deutsche Bibliothek Frankfurt am Main)
DLA	Deutsches Literaturarchiv Marbach
DNB	Deutsche Nationalbibliothek (ab 2008)
DSB	Deutsche Staatsbibliothek Berlin (bis 1991)
FB	Fachbibliothek, Fachbücherei
FHSB	Fachhochschulbibliothek
FLB	Forschungs- u. Landesbibliothek
GHB	Gesamthochschulbibliothek
GNM	Germanisches Nationalmuseum Nürnberg
HAB	Herzog August Bibliothek Wolfenbüttel
HSB	Hochschulbibliothek
Kgl. B	Königliche Bibliothek
L	Library
LB	Landesbibliothek
LC	Library of Congress Washington
LuHSB	Landes- u. Hochschulbibliothek
LuStB	Landes- u. Stadtbibliothek
M	Museum, Museo
NB	Nationalbibliothek
NL	National Library
NSuUB	Niedersächsische Staats und Universitätsbibliothek Göttingen
ÖB	Öffentliche Bibliothek, Bücherei
ÖNB	Österreichische Nationalbibliothek Wien
PL	Public Library
sArch.	Staatsarchiv
SB	Staatsbibliothek

SB PK	Staatsbibliothek zu Berlin – Preußischer Kulturbesitz – (bis 1991)
SBB-PK	Staatsbibliothek zu Berlin – Preußischer Kulturbesitz – (seit 1992)
Staatl. B	Staatliche Bibliothek, Bücherei
stArch.	Stadtarchiv
StB	Stadtbibliothek
StM	Stadtmuseum
StuLB	Stadt- u. Landesbibliothek
StuUB	Stadt- u. Universitätsbibliothek
SuStB	Staats- u. Stadtbibliothek
SuUB	Staats- u. Universitätsbibliothek
TH	Technische Hochschule
THB	Bibliothek der Technischen Hochschule
TU	Technische Universität
TUB	Bibliothek der Technischen Universität
U	Universität, University usw.
UB	Universitätsbibliothek
UL	University Library
UuLB	Universitäts- u. Landesbibliothek
UuStB	Universitäts- u. Stadtbibliothek
Wiss. StB	Wissenschaftliche Stadtbibliothek
zArch.	Zentralarchiv
ZB	Zentralbibliothek, -bücherei

Häufig zitierten Bibliografien, Nachschlagewerken und Zeitschriften

Bei Inkunabelbibliografien richtet sich die Zitierweise im Allgemeinen nach dem Verzeichnis: Abkürzungen für angeführte Quellen. In: *Gesamtkatalog der Wiegendrucke*. Neuausgabe. Bd. 8. Stuttgart, Berlin, New York 1978, S. *14–*38.

ADAMS Herbert Mayow Adams: Catalogue of books printed on the continent of Europe, 1501–1600 in Cambridge libraries. Vols. 1. 2. Cambridge 1967.

ADB Allgemeine Deutsche Biographie. Hrsg. durch die Historische Commission bei der Königl. Akademie der Wissenschaften (München). Bde. 1–56. Leipzig 1875 bis 1912. (Repr. Berlin 1967–71.) Online-Version, URL: http://www.deutsche-biographie.de

AGB Archiv für Geschichte des Buchwesens. Hrsg. von der Historischen Kommission des Börsenvereins des Deutschen Buchhandels. Bd. 1. Frankfurt am Main 1956 ff.

Baudrier Henri Louis Baudrier: Bibliographie lyonnaise. Vols. 1–12. Lyon 1895–1921. [Nebst] Tables. Genève 1950 (Travaux d'humanisme et renaissance. 1). (Repr. Sér. 1–13. Paris 1964/65.)

Benzing Josef Benzing: Die Buchdrucker des 16. und 17. Jahrhunderts im deutschen Sprachgebiet. 2., verb. und erg. Aufl. Wiesbaden 1982 (Beiträge zum Buch- und Bibliothekswesen. 12).

BL The British Library. General Catalogue of printed books to 1975. Vols. 1–360; Suppl. 1–6. London, München, New York, Paris 1979–87; 1987/88. – ... 1976 to 1982. Vols. 1–50. London 1983. ... 1982 to 1985. Vols. 1–26. London 1986 [...]

BMC Catalogue of books printed in the 15th century now in the British Museum. P. 1–10 und P. 12. London 1908–71 und 1985. (Repr. P. 1–6, Facs. P. 1/3, 4/7. London 1963.)

Borchling/Claussen Conrad Borchling und Bruno Claussen: Niederdeutsche Bibliographie. Gesamtverzeichnis der niederdeutschen Drucke bis zum Jahre 1800. Bde. 1. 2. 3, Lfg. 1. Neumünster 1931–57

Brunet Jacques Charles Brunet: Manuel du libraire et de l'amateur de livres. 5. éd. T. 1–6 [Nebst] Suppl. T. 1. 2. Paris 1860–80. (Repr. Berlin 1921; New York 1923; Paris 1923 und 1928.)

BSB-Ink. Bayerische Staatsbibliothek München. Inkunabelkatalog. Wiesbaden 1988 ff. Online-Version, url: http://www.inkunabeln.digitale-sammlungen.de

C/HC Walter A. Copinger: Supplement to Hain's Repertorium bibliographicum. P. 1. 2, vols. 1. 2. [Nebst] Index. London 1895–1902. (Repr. Berlin 1926; Milano 1950.)

CA Marinus Frederick Andries Gerardus Campbell: Annales de la typographie néerlandaise au 15e siècle. [Nebst] Suppl. 1–4. Le Haye 1874–90.

Cat. Gen. Catalogue général des livres imprimés de la Bibliothèque nationale. T. 1. Paris 1897 ff.

CIBN Bibliothèque nationale. Catalogue des Incunables. Paris 1981–96.

Claudin Anatole Claudin: L'histoire de l'imprimerie en France au 15e et au 16e siècle. T. 1–4. Paris 1900–14. T. 5: Tables alphabétiques. Red. sous la dir. de L. Delisle par Paul Lacombe. Paris 1917. (Repr. Nendeln / Liechtenstein und Wiesbaden 1971 bis 1976.)

DBI Dizionario Biografico Degli Italiani. Hrsg. vom Istituto della Enciclopedia Italiana Giovanni Treccani. Bd. 1. Rom 1961 ff. Online, URL: www.treccani.it/biografie/

EBDB Datenverbund der Sammlungen von Einband-Durchreibungen der Württembergischen LB Stuttgart (Sammlung Kyriss), der HAB Wolfenbüttel (Sammlung Wolfenbüttel), der BSB München (Sammlung München), der SBB-PK (Sammlung Schunke und Sammlung Paul Schenke), der UuLB Darmstadt (Sammlung Darmstadt) und der UB Rostock (Sammlung Floerke). Online, URL: www.hist-einband.de

Einbl. Einblattdrucke des 15. Jahrhunderts. Ein bibliographisches Verzeichnis. Hrsg. von der Kommission für den Gesamtkatalog der Wiegendrucke. Halle / Saale 1914 (Sammlung bibliothekswissenschaftlicher Arbeiten. 35 / 36). (Repr. Nendeln / Liechtenstein und Wiesbaden 1968.)

Essling Victor Prince d'Essling Duc de Rivoli: Les livres à figures vénetiens de la fin du XVe siècle et du commencement du XVIe. 6 Vols. Florence, Paris 1907–14.

Geldner Ferdinand Geldner: Die deutschen Inkunabeldrucker: Ein Handbuch der deutschen Buchdrucker des 15. Jahrhunderts nach Druckorten. Bde. 1. 2. Stuttgart 1968–70.

GJ Gutenberg-Jahrbuch. Begründet von Aloys Ruppel. Jg. 1 ff. Mainz 1926 ff.

GK Gesamtkatalog der Preußischen Bibliotheken mit Nachweis des identischen Besitzers der Bayerischen Staatsbibliothek in München und der Nationalbibliothek in Wien. Hrsg. von der Preußischen Staatsbibliothek. Bde. 1–8 [Buchst. A.]. Berlin 1931–35. [Forts.:] Deutscher Gesamtkatalog. Hrsg. von der Preußischen Staatsbibliothek. Bde. 9–14 [bis Beethordnung]. Berlin 1936–39.

Goff Frederick Richmond Goff: Incunabula in American libraries. A third census of fifteenth-century books recorded in North American collections. 1. 2 (Suppl.). New York 1964–72.

Graesse Jean George Théodore Graesse: Trésor de livres rares et précieux ou nouveau dictionnaire bibliographique. T. 1–7. Dresde 1859–69. (Repr. Paris 1900/1; Berlin 1922; Milano 1950; New York 1950/51.)

GW Gesamtkatalog der Wiegendrucke. Hrsg. von der Kommission für den Gesamtkatalog der Wiegendrucke. Bde. 1–8, Lfg. 1. Leipzig 1925–40. – 2. Aufl. (Durchgesehener Neudruck der 1. Aufl.) Bde. 1–7. Stuttgart 1968. – Neuausgabe Bd. 8. Stuttgart 1978 ff. Online-Version, URL: http://www.gesamtkatalogderwiegendrucke.de

H Ludwig Hain: Repertorium bibliographicum, in quo libri omnes ab arte typographica inventa usque ad annum md. typis expressi … recensentur. Vol. 1, P. 1. 2; Vol. 2, P. 1. 2. Stuttgartiae & Lutetiae Par. 1826–38. (Repr. Frankfurt am Main 1920; Berlin 1925; Milano 1948 und 1964.) [Nebst] Register von Konrad Burger. Leipzig 1891 (Zentralblatt für Bibliothekswesen [ZfB]. Beih. 8).

Haebler Konrad Haebler: Typenrepertorium der Wiegendrucke. Halle an der Saale 1905. (Repr. Nendeln /Liechtenstein, Wiesbaden 1968.) Online-Version, URL: http://tw.staatsbibliothek-berlin.de/

Haebler/Schunke Konrad Haebler: Rollen- und Plattenstempel des 16. Jahrhunderts. Unter Mitwirkung von Ilse Schunke. Bde. 1. 2. Leipzig 1928/29 (Sammlung bibliothekswissenschaftlicher Arbeiten. 41. 42). (Repr. Wiesbaden 1968.)

HHBD Handbuch der historischen Buchbestände in Deutschland. Hrsg. von Bernhard Fabian et. al. 30 Bde. Hildesheim 1992–2000.

Helwig Hellmuth Helwig: Handbuch der Einbandkunde. Bde. 1–3. Hamburg 1953–55.

IBE Catálogo general de incunables en bibliotecas españolas. Coordinado y dirigido por Francisco García Craviotto. 2 Bde. Madrid 1989 ff.

IGI Indice generale degli incunaboli delle biblioteche d'Italia. Comp. da Teresa Maria Guarnaschelli. Vols. 1–6. Roma 1942–81 (Ministero dell'educazione nazionale. Indice et cataloghi. NS I, 1–6).

IISTC Illustrated Incunabula Short Title Catalogue on CD-ROM (IISTC). In association with the British Library. CD-ROM. 2nd ed. Reading 1998.

Isaac Franc Isaac: An index to the early printed books in the British Museum. P. 2: 1501 to 1520, Section 2 / 3: Italy, Switzerland and Eastern Europe. London 1938.

ISTC The British Library. Incunabula Short Title Catalogue. London 1980 ff. Online-Version: http://istc.bl.uk/

STC (Johnson/Scholderer) Alfred Forbes Johnson – Victor Scholderer: Short title catalogue of books printed in the German-speaking countries and German books printed in other countries from 1455 to 1600 now in the British Museum. London 1962.

STC (Johnson/Scholderer/Clarke) Alfred Forbes Johnson – Victor Scholderer – Derek Ashdown Clarke: Short-title catalogue of books printed in Italy and of Italian books printed in other countries from 1465 to 1600 now in the British Museum. London 1958 [1959].

Kyriß Ernst Kyriß: Verzierte gotische Einbände im alten deutschen Sprachgebiet. Text- [nebst] Tafel-Bde. 1–3. Stuttgart 1951–58.

LGB² Lexikon des gesamten Buchwesens. 2., völlig neubearb. und erw. Aufl. Hrsg. von Severin Corsten†, Stephan Füssel, Günther Pflug† und Friedrich-A. Schmidt-Künsemüller†. Bd. 1 ff. Stuttgart 1987 ff.

NDB Neue deutsche Biographie. Hrsg. von der Historischen Kommission bei der Bayerischen Akademie der Wissenschaften. Bd. 1 ff. Berlin 1953 ff. Online-Version, URL: http://www.deutsche-biographie.de

Nijhoff/Kronenberg Wouter Nijhoff en Maria Elizabeth Kronenberg: Niederlandsche Bibliographie van 1500 tot 1540. Deel 1–3, 3. [Nebst] Suppl. 1–3. 's-Gravenhage 1923–71.

NUC The National Union Catalog. A cumulative author list represented by Library of Congress printed cards and titles reported by other American libraries. Vol. 1 ff. Washington 1956 ff. ... 1952–55 imprints. Vols. 1–30, Ann Arbor / MI 1961; ... 1982. Vols. 1–21. Washington 1983.

Oates John Claud Trewinard Oates: Catalogue of the fifteenth-century printed books in the University Library Cambridge. Cambridge 1954.

PA Georg Wolfgang Panzer: Annales typographici ab artis inventae origine ad annum md. Vol. 1–11. Norimbergae 1793–1803. (Repr. Hildesheim 1963.)

PDA Georg Wolfgang Panzer: Annalen der älteren deutschen Literatur … welche von Erfindung der Buchdruckerkunst bis 1526 in deutscher Sprache gedruckt worden sind. Bde. 1. 2 [und] Zusätze. Nürnberg (& Leipzig) 1788–1802. (Repr. Hildesheim 1961/62.)

Pellechet/Polain Marie Pellechet: Catalogue général des incunables des bibliothèques publiques de France. T. 1. 2 et 3 cont. par Marie-Louis Polain. Paris 1897–1909. (Repr. Nendeln / Liechtenstein 1970.)

Polain Marie-Louis Polain: Catalogue des livres imprimés au 15e siècle des bibliothèques de Belgique, 1932–78. T. 1–4. [Nebst] Suppl. Bruxelles 1932–79.

RSTC (Pollard / Redgrave) Alfred William Pollard – Gilbert Richard Redgrave: A short-title catalogue of books printed in England, Scotland and Ireland and of English books printed abroad 1475–1640. (First print 1926, repr. 1946, 1948, 1950.) London 1950. – 2nd ed., revised and enlarged by W. A. Jackson and F. S. Ferguson, completed by Katharine F. Pantzer. Vol. 1: A–H. London 1986. Vol. 2: I–Z. London 1976.

Pr Robert Proctor: An index to the early printed books in the British Museum … to the year 1520. With notes of those in the Bodleian Library. P. 1. 2. Suppl. 1–4. London 1898–1903. (Repr. in 1 Bd.: London 1960.)

R/HCR Dietrich Reichling: Appendices ad Hainii-Copingeri Repertorium bibliographicum. Additiones et emendationes. Fasc. 1–6 [Nebst] Indices and Suppl. Monachii (Suppl.: Monasterii Guestph.) 1905–14. (Repr. Milano 1953.)

Renouard Philippe Renouard: Répertoire des imprimeurs parisiens jusqu'à la fin du seizième siècle. Paris 1898. (Repr. 1965.)

Reske Christoph Reske: Die Buchdrucker des 16. und 17. Jahrhunderts im deutschen Sprachgebiet. 2. überarb. und erw. Aufl. Wiesbaden 2015.

Ritter Incun. / 15e et 16e siècle. François Ritter: Répertoire bibliographique des livres imprimés en Alsace aux 15e et 16e siècles. Fasc. hors Sér. I–V (Partie prélim.): Les incunables. P. 1. 2, vols. 1–4. P. 3. 4. Strasbourg 1932–60.

Rouzet Anne Rouzet: Dictionnaire des imprimeurs, librairies et éditeurs de 15e et 16e siècles dans les limites géographiques de la Belgique actuelle. Nieuwkoop 1975 (Collection du Centre-national de l'archéologie et de l'histoire du livre. Publ. 3).

Sander Max Sander: Le livre à figures italien depuis 1467 jusqu'à 1530. Essai de sa bibliographie et de son histoire. Vols. 1–6. Milan 1942 (Repr. Nendeln/Liechtenstein 1969).

Schr Wilhelm Ludwig Schreiber: Manuel de l'amateur de la gravure sur bois et sur métal au 15e siècle. T. 1–8. Berlin (4–8: Leipzig) 1891–1910.

Schramm Albert Schramm: Der Bilderschmuck der Frühdrucke. Bds. 1–23. Leipzig 1920–43.

Schreiber HANDBUCH Wilhelm Ludwig Schreiber: Handbuch der Holz- und Metallschnitte des 15. Jahrhunderts. Stark vermehrte und bis zu den neuesten Funden ergänzte Umarbeitung des Manuel de l'amateur de la gravure sur bois et sur métal au 15e siècle. Bde. 1–8. Leipzig 1926–30. – 3. Aufl. (Vollst. Neudruck des Gesamtwerkes.) Bde. 1–10. Stuttgart 1969; Bd. ii [Abbildungsband zum Gesamtwerk]: Heinrich Theodor Musper: Der Einblattholzschnitt und die Blockbücher des 15. Jahrhunderts. Stuttgart 1976.

Stevenson Enrico Stevenson: Inventario dei libri stampati Palatino-Vaticani. Vols. 1, 1. 2; 2, 1. 2. Roma 1886 – 89.

Thomas STC Henry Thomas: Short-title Catalogue of books printed in France and of French books printed in other countries from 1470 to 1600 now in the British Museum. London 1924. (Repr. London 1966.)

VD 16 Verzeichnis der im deutschen Sprachbereich erschienenen Drucke des 16. Jahrhunderts. Hrsg. von der BSB in München in Verb. mit der HAB in Wolfenbüttel. Redaktion Irmgard Bezzel. I. Abt.: Autoren – Körperschaften – Anonyma. Bd. 1 (1993) – 22 (1995). – II. Abt.: Register der Herausgeber, Kommentatoren, Übersetzer und literarischen Beiträger. Bde. 23/4 (1997) – III. Abt.: Register der Druckorte, Drucker, Verleger und Erscheinungsjahre. Bd. 25 (2000). Stuttgart 1983–2000. Online-Version, URL: www.vd16.de

VD 17 Verzeichnis der im deutschen Sprachraum erschienenen Drucke des 17. Jahrhunderts. Online, URL: www.vd17.de

VE 15 Falk Eisermann: Verzeichnis der typographischen Einblattdrucke des 15. Jahrhunderts im Heiligen Römischen Reich Deutscher Nation. 3 Bde. Wiesbaden 2004.

VGT Veröffentlichungen der Gesellschaft für Typenkunde des 15. Jahrhunderts. Jg. 1–33 (2460 Tafeln). Halle an der Saale und Berlin & Leipzig 1907–39. (Repr. Osnabrück 1966.) Typenregister zu Tafel 1–2460 von Rudolf Juchhoff und E. von Kathen. Osnabrück 1966.

WEALE/BOHATTA W. H. Jacobus Weale – Hanns Bohatta: Catalogus Missalium ritus Latini ab anno MCCCCLXXIV impressorum. London & Leipzig 1928. (Repr. Stuttgart 1990.)

Weller Emil Weller: Repertorium typographicum. Die deutsche Literatur im ersten Viertel des 16. Jahrhunderts. [Nebst] Suppl. [1.] 2. Nördlingen 1864–85. (Repr. Hildesheim 1961.)

Wing STC Donald Wing: Short-title catalogue of books printed in England, Scotland, Ireland, Wales and British America and of English books printed in other countries 1641 to 1700. Vols. 1–3. New York 1945 – 51. – 2nd rev. and enlarged ed. Vol. 1. New York 1972.

Ehrentafel der Internationalen Gutenberg-Gesellschaft

Gutenberg-Preisträger

1968	GIOVANNI MARDERSTEIG †1977
1971	HENRI FRIEDLAENDER †1996
1974	HERMANN ZAPF †2015
1977	RUDOLF HELL †2002
1980	HELLMUT LEHMANN-HAUPT †1992
1983	GERRIT WILLEM OVINK †1984
1986	ADRIAN FRUTIGER †2015
1989	LOTTE HELLINGA London (GB)
1992	RICARDO J. VICENT MUSEROS †2019
1994	PAUL BRAINERD Seattle, WA (USA)
1996	JOHN G. DREYFUS †2002
1998	HENRI-JEAN MARTIN †2007
2000	JOSEPH M. JACOBSON Cambridge, MA (USA)
2002	OTTO ROHSE †2016
2004	ROBERT DARNTON Princeton, NJ (USA)
2006	HUBERT WOLF Münster
2008	MICHAEL KNOCHE Weimar
2010	MAHENDRA PATEL Ahmedabad (Indien)
2012	ELIZABETH L. EISENSTEIN †2016
2014	UMBERTO ECO †2016
2016	KLAUS-DIETER LEHMANN Berlin
2018	ALBERTO MANGUEL Buenos Aires (Argentinien)
2020	GERHARD STEIDL Göttingen
2022	JEFFREY F. HAMBURGER Cambridge, MA (USA) und ECKEHART SCHUMACHERGEBLER †2022

Ehrenmitglieder der Internationalen Gutenberg-Gesellschaft

HERMANN HANS SCHMIDT †2022
GUDRUN ZAPF-VON HESSE †2019

Träger des Ehrenringes der Internationalen Gutenberg Gesellschaft

HANS KLENK †1983
PROF. DR. ALOYS RUPPEL †1977
DR. LUDWIG STRECKER †1978

Senatorenrat der Internationalen Gutenberg-Gesellschaft

DR. PETER HANSER-STRECKER (Vorsitzender) Mainz
WOLFGANG A. HARTMANN Barcelona (E)
JOST HOCHULI St. Gallen (CH)
DIPL. KFM. DR. ERNST-ERICH MARHENCKE Molfsee
EMIL VAN DER VEKENE Niederanven (LUX)
RICARDO J. VICENT MUSEROS †2019

Ehrenvorstandsmitglied der Internationalen Gutenberg-Gesellschaft

DR. ANTON M. KEIM †2016

DRUCKKUNST MIT HERZ

Wie schon in den vergangenen 120 Jahren treibt die Gutenberg-Gesellschaft nicht nur die Gutenberg-Forschung voran, sondern ist auch ein wichtiger Partner für das Gutenberg-Museum auf seinem Weg in eine neue Zukunft. Wir freuen uns, als Förderer viele spannende Projekte mit zu unterstützen.

www.mainzer-stadtwerke.de

MAINZER STADTWERKE

VON ALLEN WELTEN, DIE DER MENSCH GESCHAFFEN HAT, IST DIE DER BÜCHER DIE GEWALTIGSTE.
Heinrich Heine

Wir drucken Bücher für die Ewigkeit.

memminger medien centrum

Fraunhoferstraße 19
87700 Memmingen
Tel. 0 83 31 / 92 77-0

info@mm-mediencentrum.de
www.mm-mediencentrum.de

Auf Wunsch Klimaneutral
ClimatePartner

Ideen nach vorne

peyer COVER

Impressum

Anschrift des Verlages
Harrassowitz Verlag
D-65174 Wiesbaden
Telefon (+49) 611.53 09 05
Telefax (+49) 611.53 09 99
verlag@harrassowitz.de
www.harrassowitz-verlag.de

Anschrift des Herausgebers
Gutenberg-Institut für Weltliteratur
und schriftorientierte Medien,
Abteilung Buchwissenschaft
Johannes Gutenberg-Universität
D-55099 Mainz
Telefon (+49) 61.31.3 92 25 80
Telefax (+49) 61.31.3 92 54 87
gerlauer@uni-mainz.de

Internationale Gutenberg-Gesellschaft
in Mainz e.V.
Liebfrauenplatz 5
D-55116 Mainz
Telefon (+49) 61.31.22 64 20
Telefax (+49) 61.31.23 35 30
info@gutenberg-gesellschaft.de

Gutenberg-Jahrbuch 2023, 98. Jahrgang. Die für den Buchhandel bestimmten Exemplare vertreibt der Harrassowitz Verlag, Wiesbaden.

ISSN 0072-9094
ISBN 978-3-447-12016-6

Herausgeber Prof. Dr. Philip Ajouri, Dr. Julia Bangert, Prof. Dr. Gerhard Lauer, JProf. Dr. Nikolaus Weichselbaumer
Korrektorat Julia Kammerzelt, Olga Lemmerich

Das Gutenberg-Jahrbuch veröffentlicht Beiträge in deutscher, englischer, französischer, italienischer, spanischer und lateinischer Sprache. Die Autorinnen und Autoren werden gebeten, ihre Manuskripte auf digitalen Datenträgern in druckreifer Form dem Herausgeber vorzulegen. Merkblätter über die Manuskriptsgestaltung können aufgefordert werden. Der Einsendetermin für die Manuskripte ist jeweils der 30. September des Vorjahres.

Nachdruck und Wiedergabe, auch in elektronischen Medien (auch auszugsweise), sowie fotomechanische Reproduktion einzelner Beiträge nur mit ausdrücklicher Genehmigung durch die Gutenberg-Gesellschaft.

Design Dr. Dan Reynolds, Krefeld
Schriften Signifier und National, beide entworfen von Kris Sowersby/Klim Type Foundry (NZ)
Druckerei Memminger MedienCentrum AG, Memmingen
Binderei Conzella, Aschheim
Einbandmaterial Doublesse von Peyer
Textpapier Fly 05 1,2-fach, 115 g/qm von Inapa
Vorsatzpapier Surbalin linea von Peyer

Wappen der Gutenberg-Gesellschaft auf dem Einband nach einem Entwurf von Jost Hochuli, St. Gallen.